PRESIDENTS AND PEONS

Presidents and Peons

RECOLLECTIONS OF A LABOR AMBASSADOR
IN LATIN AMERICA

by Serafino Romualdi

FUNK & WAGNALLS : NEW YORK

Dedicated to Miriam, Jim, and Jesse

Preface

THE MAIN PURPOSE of this book is to highlight the activities and achievements of the United States labor movement in combating the attempts of Communists and other totalitarian forces to gain control of organized labor in Latin America since 1946, the year I was appointed American Federation of Labor (AFL) representative for that area, a position in which I was continued after the merger in 1955 of the AFL and the Congress of Industrial Organizations. The book is not, however, an official or even authorized publication of the AFL–CIO, for I have written it on my own personal responsibility after retiring from active duty in the fall of 1965. It is a personal and firsthand account of the objectives and accomplishments over a twenty-year period of struggle: to help the wage earners of Latin America to raise their living standards by assisting in the organization of stable and strong unions; to strengthen the cause of freedom and representative democracy; to combat and defeat Communist and other totalitarian movements; and, above all, to assist in the development of a new type of Latin American labor leader who would reject the stale concept of class struggle in favor of constructive labor-management relations in a democratic, pluralistic society.

Latin American labor does not exist in a political vacuum. From the very beginning of my assignment I learned that a healthy free trade unionism could not develop apart from a dynamic, progressive, democratic, free society. The achievement and preservation of freedom became, therefore, the main objective of Latin American trade unionism in the postwar phase—an objective which required a great measure of cooperation with political parties devoted to the cause of freedom and social justice. Almost everywhere the two movements grew up intermingled, interlocked. Thus my extensive cooperation in many of the countries discussed in this book, with the outstanding political leaders of democratic, antitotalitarian belief.

As implied in the title of this book, the struggle for free trade unions in a free society has involved all the strata of the population, from the exalted presidents to the lowly peons. I would have liked to write about all of them, about all the Latin American and Caribbean countries I have visited and worked in during my long service. But then the book would have been too long, too impractical to publish, and the resulting fare would have been too heavy to read and digest. I wish, however, to assure my friends in Uruguay, Bolivia, Paraguay, Ecuador, Colombia, Panama, Nicaragua, and Mexico—the countries for which I have not written separate chapters and where I have had less dramatic personal involvement than elsewhere—that this omission does not imply that their problems and their contribution to the cause of trade union freedom are less deserving than those of other countries.

Since the book is mainly concerned with the events of the past, I have made only occasional side references to the issues of today and the recommended policies for tomorrow. But I do have some definite views and ideas, and perhaps something worthwhile to say, about the theory and practice of democracy, numerical as well as qualitative, in Latin America; the respective role of the military, the intellectuals, and the professional politicians; the Alliance for Progress and its great potential; the need to reshape the structure and the functions of the Organization of American States; the real meaning of the "Latin American revolution of rising expectations"; the contribution of U.S. capital with "social significance"; and the new responsibility of organized labor in the developing countries. But obviously this requires a separate full-fledged publication which I hope to be able to write in the future.

In order to write this book, I had to engage in extensive research and had to consult many documents and the voluminous correspondence accumulated over more than a quarter of a century. My friend Professor Robert J. Alexander of Rutgers University, one of the outstanding authorities on Latin American trade unionism and political movements, put at my disposal many of his reports and documents, a gesture which I wish to acknowledge with grateful appreciation. Elliot Marcus, director of Information Services for the American Institute for Free Labor Development (AIFLD) was also of great assistance in doing outside research and in assisting me in planning the structure of the book. But my greatest debt of gratitude goes to the personal secretaries I have had over the years at the AFL–CIO and the AIFLD—Mrs. Thurman Arnold, Jr., Mrs. Rosa Sabroso Stamp, Mrs. Asela Foster, Mrs. Julia Cosentino, Miss Helen Clarke, Miss Joan Pattinson, and Miss Eileen Mundy—for the care with which they saved and filed away my personal correspondence, every clipping, document, photograph, press release, and bit of paper connected with my work. Without their loyal cooperation and foresight (every one of them voiced the hope that some day I might write my memoirs) this book would have been almost impossible to assemble in the present form.

I have done the writing all by myself, in longhand or by two-finger pounding at the typewriter. My native language, and the only one I studied at school, is Italian. I do think most of the time in Spanish; English is, however, my operational language, at least here in the United States. So I chose this language to write the manuscript; but since I learned English only by sight and sound, frequent impurities in grammar and in the construction of the sentences have inevitably crept in. Milton Plumb, a newspaperman and writer of experience and renown, graciously consented to do the literary dry-cleaning, after which Mrs. Alexandria B. Burtnick did the long painstaking job of typing and retyping until the manuscript was ready for the publisher.

SERAFINO ROMUALDI

Bethesda, Maryland
May 1967

Contents

Foreword

THE EXTENT AND DEPTH of clashing forces seeking to control Latin America during and after World War II is virtually unknown in the United States. Happily, Serafino Romualdi, for twenty years representative of the American Federation of Labor, later of the AFL–CIO, now makes public his story of part of the great contest. Shot with romance, adventure, danger, and high politics, this volume is a first source of major history, written by a notable actor in it. No one who reads the fascinating chronicle will be tempted to succumb to those easy generalizations which confuse too many Americans when they think of their Latin American neighbors.

Through the influence of David Dubinsky and the International Ladies' Garment Workers' Union, Romualdi was assigned in 1946 as Latin American representative charged with the task of organizing an inter-American federation of free labor unions. The need was pressing. A group of Communist trades unions, headed by Lombardo Toledano of Mexico and backed by the Soviet Union's propaganda resources, had already undertaken such a mission. These had formed alliance with Fascist trade unions organized—notably under Perón in Argentina and Vargas in Brazil—in imitation of Mussolini's government-dominated Italian labor syndicates.

Romualdi had seen that before. In his Italian youth he had fought the rise of the Fascist movement, had nearly been killed by Mussolini's bully boys, and had taken refuge in the United States, where he immediately joined the staff of the International Ladies' Garment Workers' Union, serving there for a number of years. As World War II came on, he was assigned by Nelson Rockefeller—then Coordinator of Inter-American Affairs under President Franklin Roosevelt—to work on labor relations in Latin America. The combination of experience made him a logical choice for the representative of the American labor movement—"labor's ambassador"—in the area. His early struggles had given him thorough understanding of Fascist and Communist organization tactics, for he had already met both in Europe in Mussolini's time.

When protracted social struggles broke out in all the twenty Latin American countries as World War II closed, Romualdi found himself in the thick of them. The situations were complex. Social conditions in Latin America were not then in good shape (and are not now): homegrown revolutionary movements were plentiful, many of them fully justified, and dictators ruled, often with surprising brutality, in many countries. With its appetite whetted by its success in Europe, the Soviet Union, possibly on the recommendation of Oumansky, Ambassador to Washington and Mexico, undertook to exploit these situations. Communist revolutions were sought—less, perhaps, because of their social content than because Stalin considered the time ripe for foreign conquest by the cheap and satisfactory route of controlled revolutions.

High on the list of strategic objectives was control of the labor movement in each of the Latin American nations, and his propaganda apparatus was excellent. A new technique of imperialism—in this case propelled from Moscow—thus entered the Western Hemisphere. Democracy and the United States were their enemies. Local Communist leaders, its field representatives, were quite willing to make transient deals against democrats with dictators like Perón, Trujillo, and Batista. Communist-led trade unions preferred to support, infiltrate, and in time take over Fascist labor organizations rather than tolerate free labor unions. Romualdi here gives the documents and details. Recognizedly, the principal popular opponent of these attempts was the free United States–based trade-union movement Romualdi was chosen to represent.

Many American intellectuals either denied or minimized the fact of "cold war" in Latin America, for it was more agreeable to consider ferment there as mere regional reformist agitation against social injustice. It became—perhaps still is—downright unpopular in the United States to suggest that the Soviet Union through its diplomatic, propaganda, and psychological warfare machinery was taking powerful advantage of the situation. Romualdi's volume should go far toward setting that balance right. Home-grown social struggles certainly existed—they still do—but these ought not to have obscured the parallel fact that the Soviet Union was also seeking to create client-states in the region, as she finally succeeded in doing in Cuba in 1959. At bottom a three-cornered struggle for control was on, with a continent at stake. Confusion about the situation was easy, and one result was to deprive the American Federation of Labor (and Romualdi with it) of a good deal of the support it should have had from public opinion in the United States.

Basically, the American free trade-union movement supported and promptly became allied to the cause of socially oriented Latin American democracy. Where successful, as in Venezuela under President Rómulo Betancourt, in Costa Rica under President José Figueres, and in Colombia under President Lleras Camargo, it has proved the most authentic and effective method for Latin American reconstruction. "Inter-Americanism without imperialism" was the phrase Romualdi coined to express the movement. It is still one of the most popular slogans in the region. Latin American democratic leaders knew the overseas Communist empires were both imperialist and dangerous to real popular development. The issue was not "Communist conspiracy" so much as Soviet expansionism. Democracy, including the United States, was the "enemy" to be defeated—by force if necessary. It took the landing of thirty thousand Russian troops in Cuba and the Cuban missile crisis of 1962 to make clear to Washington the real nature of the game. Meantime, social reconstruction in the region had to go forward.

The blow-by-blow account of the long contest is passionately interesting if only as drama. It is even more significant as revealing what American diplomatic policy sometimes looks like from the point of view of the populations involved. Rómulo Betancourt, for example, was nearly hounded out of the hemisphere by the State Department lest his presence complicate relations with the dictators in Venezuela and Colombia. The problems of the outstanding authentic democracy in Central America— that of Costa Rica—were made greater by the intrigues of the Dominican despot Trujillo, of dictator Pérez Jiménez in Venezuela, and of the elder Somoza in Nicaragua, and were compounded by Washington's fear of offending them. The movement for socially oriented Latin American democracy was thus engaged on two fronts—against reactionary dictatorships on the one side and against Soviet-oriented Communists on the other, sometimes in alliance. There were periods when no one knew which forces were being supported by the Department of State. If the situation is rather better now than it was from 1946 to 1962, a substantial part of the credit must go to George Meany, David Dubinsky, Serafino Romualdi, and their trade-union colleagues. Partly from within the government and partly from outside, I had occasion to observe and where possible to help the work that they did. I can—and am glad to— bear personal witness to their achievements and particularly to Serafino Romualdi's steadfast faith and courage in a difficult, dangerous task.

Happily, Dr. Milton Eisenhower, toward the end of his brother's administration, and President John F. Kennedy, at once on his election, moved to adopt as American policy a straightforward support of socially oriented Latin American democracy—and with it the free trade-union movement. Matters have been going somewhat better since then, though the contest is far from over. It may (as President Kennedy once suggested) last for half a century.

Here, for the first time, the inside history of one phase of the vast struggle is presented to the public. Mr. Romualdi is to be thanked, not merely for the work he did, but for the factual account he now contributes. It deserves careful reading: this is what the battle really looked like. It should make the next phase of the Latin American epic more comprehensible in the United States. When, as I am sure it will be, the book is translated into Spanish and Portuguese, it will explain political and social threads whose influence has been increasingly decisive in the southern part of the Western Hemisphere.

ADOLF A. BERLE

Columbia University
May, 1967

I

Assignment to Latin America

CUBAN DICTATOR Fidel Castro and "Che" Guevara, the military strategist of the Cuban revolution, have both boasted that they would "make the Andes the Sierra Maestra of Latin America." [1] In even more direct language, they have made clear that a basic purpose of the present Cuban government—the first Communist state in the Americas—is to extend Communist rule over the Western Hemisphere.

Their boast has gone unrealized, despite the fact that the Castro dictatorship has been the base for one of the most extensive strategies of subversion that the world has ever known. Not only is Cuba today the center of world Communism's planned propaganda campaign to discredit the United States in the eyes of other nations, but it is the training ground and the seat of operations for Communist guerrillas carrying on continuing acts of armed terrorism against democratic governments in Latin America. Although the Communists have not been successful in capturing control of South America, no one familiar with what has been happening throughout Latin America and the Caribbean can seriously doubt that they have tried—and are trying—to achieve this goal.

Why has this intensive Communist effort, carried on now for over a decade since Castro's revolutionaries landed in Oriente Province in December 1956, failed? What force has prevented the spread of Communism throughout Latin America?

Certainly, the conditions of poverty, underdevelopment, exploding

1

population, concentrated wealth, feudal social patterns, and political turbulence which exist throughout the area created a situation favorable to the spread of Communist propaganda and strategy. Moreover, although the great social and economic reforms of the Alliance for Progress are now under way, they were late in starting, and had it not been for the added time democracy and freedom have gained because another opposing force stood in the way of Communist revolution, they might have been "too little and too late."

The startling truth is that democracy has survived in many parts of Latin America simply because Castro and his Communist supporters repeated an error which in the long run has been the downfall of most of the dictatorships of history—they underestimated the power, and the devotion to freedom, of the working masses. Castro and Guevara have failed to extend Communism out of Cuba because they have not been able to get the support of organized labor in the Americas. Although the Communist leaders did succeed in infiltrating and winning the support of the radical student groups, and drew much of their early support from this source, the overwhelming majority of organized workers, both in Cuba and in other nations of the Americas, refused to accept the Communist objectives and program.

Had not organized labor and the peasants of Latin America actually opposed the subversive program of the Communists, the political map of our hemisphere today would be quite different. Venezuela, emerging from years of brutal dictatorship, could not have survived the terrorist attacks launched from Cuba to become the proud symbol of democracy and social progress it is today. Likewise, without the support of organized workers in the Americas, democracy and representative government would quite likely by now be gone from Colombia, Guatemala, and Peru. Brazil, the largest nation to the south, also would probably be another Communist nation.

The successful defense of most of Latin America and the Caribbean against Communism and other forms of totalitarianism has been one of the most important battles of the cold war. It began, of course, many years before Fidel Castro applied the teachings of Niccolò Machiavelli to a modern revolution and, by appealing to the Cuban people's hatred of dictatorship and their love of democracy, enlisted their support only to betray their goals, which he falsely had professed in order to make Communist victory in Cuba possible. The Communists' efforts to seize the reins of political power in Latin America actually date back to the decade before the Second World War. Their failure throughout this period has been due, in the main, to the profound changes that organized labor in the United States and Latin America succeeded in bringing about through the activities of a group of dedicated democratic trade union leaders, inspired and supported by the American Federation of Labor (AFL) at first alone and later in cooperation with the Congress of Industrial Organizations (CIO).

This book tells for the first time the inside story of the vital role the free trade unions of the Americas have played in the struggle not only for "bread, peace and freedom," but to preserve our democratic society in the Western Hemisphere.

At the close of World War II the American Federation of Labor, in order to avoid isolation from the world labor movement, was faced with the necessity of engaging in independent international activities of its own. The old International Federation of Trade Unions (IFTU) with headquarters in London, which the AFL had joined a few years before the war, went out of existence. In its place there was organized, in November 1945, the World Federation of Trade Unions (WFTU), which included the trade unions of Russia and its Communist satellite countries. The AFL refused to join the WFTU, which it regarded from the outset as a Communist front organization. Most of the other national trade union centers, including the Congress of Industrial Organizations in the United States, had different views. They believed the Communist protestations of democratic faith and went along—to their subsequent regret—with the experiment in Communist coexistence.

The AFL decision to enter, independently, the international labor field, in an effort to check and eventually destroy the Communist influence in the trade union movement was a courageous and ambitious stand fully consistent with the Federation's antitotalitarian tradition, eloquently recorded both previously and later in its convention resolutions condemning Fascism, Nazism, and Communism. During the war, the AFL had recognized the Soviet Union as a military ally but never as an actual or potential bona-fide partner in the reconstruction of the world along the democratic lines enunciated in the Atlantic Charter.

The organization entrusted with the gigantic task of gaining for the AFL allies in its opposition to the WFTU, and support for its efforts to eventually bring about a reorganization of the world labor movement along democratic lines, was the AFL Free Trade Union Committee. Its chairman was AFL Vice-President Matthew Woll. Other members were President William Green, Secretary-Treasurer George Meany, and Vice-

President David Dubinsky, President of the International Ladies' Garment Workers' Union, in whose New York City headquarters the Free Trade Union Committee was located. Jay Lovestone was the Committee's Executive Secretary.[2]

While war-devastated Europe was obviously the region to which the Free Trade Union Committee gave first priority, its leaders were also aware of the growing world importance of Latin America—our own backyard. AFL relations with Latin America had flourished at the time of Samuel Gompers's presidency, when the Pan-American Confederation of Labour—known as COPA by its Spanish-language initials—was organized. These relations, however, were practically discontinued during the period after Gompers's death in 1924, when COPA fell into inactivity and then went out of existence.[3] During World War II, relations between the North American labor movement and the trade unions in Latin America were somewhat resumed through the exchange of trade union delegations,[4] mainly under the auspices of the Office of the Coordinator of Inter-American Affairs, and by the publication from the office of AFL Secretary-Treasurer George Meany of a bimonthly Spanish language clip sheet called the *Noticiario Obrero Norteamericano,* which achieved from the beginning wide airmail circulation in Latin American labor circles.[5]

Organized labor in Latin America, particularly in the southern half of the hemisphere, was strongly influenced in its beginnings—around the turn of this century—by anarcho-syndicalist theories and practices imported from Europe, especially from Italy and Spain. Strikes and violence were its hallmarks, and were used to extract concessions from employers. Collective bargaining, signed agreements, and even the rudimentary forms of a trade union structure were unknown. Political influence on the part of labor, as it is known today, was also nonexistent. Not only did anarcho-syndicalism, per se, shun political action, but the political parties, as constituted, were impervious to any pressure from the lower working classes.

In the period between the two world wars, the socialist parties—and those holding left-wing, populist concepts—began to take hold of the labor movement in Latin America, displacing the anarcho-syndicalist dominance and giving it a cohesiveness and some degree of respectability. While labor agitation under anarcho-syndicalism was considered mainly a criminal matter dealt with by the police, the emerging socialist-populist leadership stimulated prolabor interest in some responsible sectors of society. They brought into the trade union movement a number of intellectuals; students from middle-class and even "oligarchic" families; lawyers, doctors, and other professionals; and also political leaders who saw in the growth of labor a new potential among the electorate. On the other hand, labor itself needed and welcomed such outside help because it possessed technical and even leadership capabilities that the workers generally lacked. Even more important, in some countries these new forces were ousting the traditional ruling classes from the control of the governmental machinery. Labor sought an alliance with these new forces, hoping to get political protection and support for favorable legislation.

Communist influence in the Latin American trade union movement did not assume significant proportions until the late thirties, when the Communist International, chiefly as a result of the Hitler menace, extended to the trade unions the propaganda line of the "popular front," based on the concept of unity of all the forces opposed to Fascism and Nazism for the ultimate purpose of the "democratic" conquest of power. The campaign culminated in the organization, on September 8, 1938, in Mexico City, of the Latin American Workers' Confederation, better known by its Spanish-language initials CTAL. Once before, in 1929, the Communists had promoted the organization of a Latin American labor confederation with headquarters in Montevideo, Uruguay. Operating strictly along sectarian Communist lines, it failed to gain any appreciable support and in 1936, when the new popular front line was adopted by Moscow, it was disbanded.

The approach adopted by CTAL was different. Ostensibly, it was a united front of all democratic forces, in which the Communists were simply one of the participating groups. However, the Communists managed to retain for themselves from the very beginning the key organizational post which gave them de facto control of the organization.

The call for the constituent convention of CTAL was issued by the Workers' Confederation of Mexico (CTM), of which Vicente Lombardo Toledano was General Secretary. Lombardo, then forty-four years old, was an intellectual, born in a well-to-do family, who attended the university and was graduated with a law degree. However, labor politics and journalism were Lombardo Toledano's strong interests. By 1920 he had already become most influential in a group of young leaders who were determined to make organized labor the strongest pillar of the Mexican revolution, which by then was emerging from long years of internal strife and was beginning its era of consolidation.

In 1927 Lombardo Toledano became General Secretary of the National Federation of Mexican Teachers; in 1933 he organized the Mexican General Federation of Workers and Peasants, and in 1936 took part in the organization of the CTM. Until 1935 he had given no indication of being sympathetic to the Communist movement. In that year, however, he visited Russia. When he returned to Mexico, he began to support the "popular front" line of the Communist International, including active cooperation with the Communists—a policy to which he has remained faithful to this very day.

The call for the CTAL founding convention was answered by labor organizations of the most important Latin American countries, such as Argentina, Peru, Venezuela, Chile, and Uruguay. Many of the delegates were social democrats, liberals, and independents who had accepted in good faith the objectives of the "popular front" policy and believed that cooperation with the Communists, especially in view of what was by then considered a probable clash with Nazi Germany, was possible and desirable. There were also in attendance prominent labor leaders from the United States and Europe, among them Léon Jouhaux, head of the General Confederation of Labor of France; Ramón González Peña, leader of the Asturian miners who represented the Spanish General Labor Union (UGT) in exile; and John L. Lewis, the President of the Congress of Industrial Organizations of the United States. An invitation was also sent to the AFL, but its leadership refused to attend. AFL President William Green declared that "the record of the person who has issued the invitation indicates that the gathering would be another Communist propaganda scheme."

Lombardo Toledano was elected the CTAL's first and only President.[6] From the very beginning he and the CTAL followed closely the international policy of the Soviet government. Thus, after the Molotov-Ribbentrop Pact, which in August 1939 ushered in World War II, CTAL opposed the war efforts of the Allies as being "capitalistic and imperialistic"; but after the Nazis attacked Russia in June 1941, Lombardo Toledano lost no time in becoming a strong advocate of all-out efforts to help the Allies, which now included Russia. The war gave CTAL an unprecedented opportunity to consolidate its forces and to extend its sphere of influence. Lombardo Toledano made peace with all the dictators that were at war with the Nazis, such as Getulio Vargas in Brazil, "Tacho" Somoza in Nicaragua, and Leonidas Trujillo in the Dominican Republic. The Communists, on their part, did the same in their respective countries, whether the government was military, conservative, or reactionary. The price the Communists generally sought for their collaboration was an opportunity to gain control of organized labor.

Many voices of warning were raised during the war period against the danger of giving too much credit and support to the CTAL. However, such warnings, coming mainly from the AFL in the United States, were not heeded. As a result, Lombardo Toledano and his supporters gained prestige and more power. They influenced the labor policy of the Pan American Union, were received as fraternal delegates in the old CIO councils, were recognized as the legitimate spokesmen for Latin American labor even in our own State Department, and took a prominent role in the 1945 formation of the WFTU, of which Lombardo Toledano himself became a vice-president.

When I returned to the United States in the fall of 1943 after an assignment for the Coordinator of Inter-American Affairs in Latin America, I prepared a memorandum which I sent, under date of December 18, to Matthew Woll, chairman of the AFL Free Trade Union Committee. In it I gave a summary of my Latin American trade union observations and concluded by recommending a series of concrete steps "to lay the groundwork for the eventual organization of an inter-American labor body, democratically controlled, and composed of free, independent, bona fide unions." Excerpts from that memorandum, which may be regarded as the cornerstone upon which the inter-American labor structure was built in the ensuing twenty years, follow:

While the bulk of Latin American organized labor is federated with the CTAL (Confederación de Trabajadores de América Latina), which is under the leadership of Lombardo Toledano, well-known follower of the Communist Party line, it is not to be assumed that all of the CTAL's components agree with him. In fact, among many of them, notably in Argentina, Uruguay, Chile, Mexico, and Cuba, and among several independent unions, there is a genuine desire to come into closer contact with the American Federation of Labor, in spite of Toledano's antagonistic stand against it. This was confirmed to me by Brother Bernardo Ibáñez, President of the Chilean Federation of Labor, when he passed through Washington on his way to Montreal, on December 12. Dr. Juan Antonio Solari, former member of the Argentine Parliament, who has just visited the United States on the invitation of the New School for Social Research, expressed the same belief. And I can add that during my stay in South America (which extended from July 1941 to September 1943) I met several labor leaders, especially in Uruguay, who actually begged me to devise means to bring them in close contact with the AFL. . . .

Barring any idea of forming, right now, any new inter-American labor body, mainly because this would necessarily resolve into an anti-CTAL move and our friends in Latin America are not yet ready for it, it is felt, nevertheless, that the AFL could greatly enhance the disposition toward a better understanding and a closer relationship between laboring masses of the three Americas, by embarking on a program of education and publicity whose immediate objective could be, for instance, to make our achievement and labor policies known to our brothers of Latin America, and vice versa. From this exchange of information, to be eventually supplemented by exchange of visits, there would undoubtedly result a meeting of minds and a desire to act together for the common good of the working people of the continent, and for the eventual organization of an inter-American labor body, composed of free, independent, democratic unions.

Following other assignments in Italy and in South America, I terminated my wartime services at the end of September 1945 and returned to the ILGWU.[7] When I reported to ILGWU President David Dubinsky, he told me about plans the American Federation of Labor had to expand its international activities and asked me if I would consider accepting assignment as the AFL representative for Latin America. My activities there during the war had made me, Dubinsky argued, the right person for the job.

The prospect of actively participating in the proposed international program of the AFL in its Latin American front—a program which I had myself suggested two years before—was exciting and challenging. Without hesitation I authorized Dubinsky to inform President Green and his colleagues George Meany and Matthew Woll on the AFL Free Trade Union Committee that I was available for the assignment. My appointment as AFL representative for Latin America was announced by the Executive Council at its January 1946 meeting in Miami, Florida. It was agreed, however, that I would continue to work from the ILGWU headquarters in New York City, where the Free Trade Union Committee was located.[8] I rolled up my sleeves and went to work. Latin America had become my province, and it was to remain so for the next twenty exciting, truly rewarding years!

Notes

1. After landing in Cuba in December 1956, Castro's guerrilla forces successfully held out in, and launched their successful revolution from, the Sierra Maestra, a great mountain range in Oriente Province. The Andes are a group of mountains running the entire length of South America from Cape Horn to the Isthmus of Panama and the Caribbean Sea, and, hence, are symbolic of the whole of Latin America.

2. Jay Lovestone, who during the twenties gained international notoriety as leader of the Communist Party of America, broke with the Communists in 1929 and subsequently evolved into one of the most knowledgeable and effective anti-Communist fighters. During World War II he became associated with Matthew Woll and David Dubinsky, who appointed him director of the ILGWU International Department. A while after the merger of the AFL and the CIO, the Free Trade Union Committee was discontinued. Jay Lovestone was transferred to the AFL-CIO International Department, of which he became the Executive Director in 1964.

3. A detailed account of the life and achievements of COPA is given by Professor Philip Taft in his book *The AFL in the Time of Gompers*.

4. One such delegation, called the United Labor Delegation, visited Chile and other South American countries in the spring of 1943. It was composed of David McDonald, Secretary-Treasurer, United Steel Workers of America, CIO; Sam Philips, Brotherhood of Firemen and Enginemen, Independent; Edward Brown, President, International Brotherhood of Electrical Workers, AFL; and John Herling, Director, Labor Relations Division, Office of the Coordinator of Inter-American Affairs, who organized the mission and managed the tour.

5. In 1967, the *Noticiario Obrero Norteamericano* entered its twenty-fourth year of continuous publication.

6. CTAL held its last Convention in 1953 in Santiago, Chile. Soon after, it was dissolved to make room for another, all-inclusive, "nonaligned" Latin American labor federation, which, however, never materialized in spite of repeated attempts under different auspices.

7. The author joined the publications department of the International Ladies' Garment Workers' Union (ILGWU) in 1933. In 1944 he obtained leave of absence for the duration of the War. He is still a member in good standing of the Office and Distribution Employees' Union, Local 99, ILGWU.

8. This arrangement continued until March 1948, when the author became a full-time AFL employee operating from Washington national headquarters.

II

Anti-Fascist Flashback

AT THE END of the First World War Italy witnessed the emergence of a strong labor and socialist movement which presaged a profound change in the Italian social structure. The agrarian conservative forces, especially in the northern and central regions where farm labor had become strongly organized, bitterly resented this upsurge of labor power. They joined hands with industrial and commercial interests in the cities, where the workers had adopted a revolutionary posture and were clamoring for the conquest of total power. The specter of the "dictatorship of the proletariat" drove the conservative forces into a frantic search for a counterpower that could destroy the threat. They found it in the Fascist movement.

Founded by Benito Mussolini, a former socialist who converted to nationalism during the war, the Fascist movement lacked a well-defined policy. Its program was based on a vague mixture of syndicalism and nationalism, so loosely defined that it could appeal to every section of the society that had grievances or had experienced frustrations or disillusions during the long war, which left the country victorious but exhausted. Thus, some students were attracted to Fascism by the vision of a resurgent Italy striving to regain the prestige and glory of the ancient Roman Empire; war veterans who felt that Italy had been cheated at the 1919 Versailles Peace Conference swelled the ranks of the movement with a feeling of *revanche;* former officers who found it difficult to adjust themselves to the penury of civilian life joined the Fascist military apparatus which offered them the opportunity to again become officers and commanders; and the white-collar employees of class-conscious Italy, jealous of their little privileges threatened by the rising working class, joined in hopes that Fascism would come to their rescue. All these elements had a common denominator—opposition to the socialist-labor masses. The latter, on their part, confident of an early victory, remained isolated, defiant, rigid in their revolutionary posture.

To achieve their ultimate objective, the conquest of the state, the Fascists first had to destroy the organized working class and the Socialist Party, which constituted the major obstacle in their march to power. Organized along military lines, copied from the structure of the Roman legions, the Fascists adopted the use of violence as their standard tactic—intimidate, demoralize, terrorize, and destroy the opponents, and then force them to submit to the Fascist will. The workers' leaders who resisted were beaten, forced into exile, even murdered.

The traditional Italian parties, including the liberals, felt that the Fascists could be easily brought into line once they were through with their job of castigating and reducing to impotence the revolutionary labor and socialist masses. But many political personalities and leading intellectuals recognized in Fascism the characteristics of a totalitarian system just as dangerous as the threat of the proletarian dictatorship. The Popular Party, forerunner of the present Christian Democratic Party of Italy, founded by the Italian priest and philosopher Don Luigi Sturzo, was among the forces that saw in Fascism the danger of a future dictatorship. They hoped that the Socialists would abandon the intransigent, revolutionary policy which was feeding the counterrevolution, and would adopt the policy of parliamentary action, within the framework of the Italian constitutional tradition.

As a reaction to the excesses committed by the Fascists, and in obedience to my belief that the Socialist Party had in itself the elements that could eventually lead Italy along the path of necessary social and economic reforms, I joined the Party as a youth twenty years old in my native province of Perugia. When, in January 1921, the Party split into two wings—the Communists and the Socialists—I refused to follow the great majority of the youth section that went over to the Communists.

Two months later my province was overrun by Fascist squads from nearby Tuscany, and the known Socialist leaders had to flee for their lives. I was appointed "clandestine" provincial secretary. As such, I directed the Congressional campaign of that year. In spite of every kind of violence and no possibility whatsoever for meetings or distribution of campaign literature, we managed to elect, under the system of proportional representation, three congressmen out of the ten allotted to our province.

My role in the Party was soon discovered. A "punitive squad" was sent to my home town of Bastia Umbra.[1] However, the *squadristi* did not find me. I had gone into hiding at the bottom of a well, thanks to a family friend who warned me in advance. After the raid was over I rushed home, where my mother, sobbing with fear and indignation and with a baby in her arms, related to me the insults and the threats to which she had been subjected during the raid. The hoodlums, pistols and clubs in hand, had searched for me in vain in every room of the house. My mother pleaded with me to go away, and thus, with some food, a few clothes, and a handful of lire, I went out into the night, for my first exile, inside my own country.

I settled in the nearby province of Pesaro, where I spent almost a year as editor of the weekly newspaper *Il Progresso*. For a while it looked as if the central government in Rome was going to take some strong measure to reestablish law and order. But to succeed it needed the support in Parliament of the large contingent of Socialist congressmen, or at least their neutrality. This, however, was denied because the Socialists were still determined to remain loyal to their traditional uncompromising opposition to any bourgeois government, regardless of circumstances. On a Fascist motion of censure, aimed at defeating the government of Ivanoe Bonomi,[2] who had begun to crack down on the Fascist hoodlums, the Socialists voted with the Fascists. The motion of censure was carried and Bonomi was thus forced to resign.

The refusal of the Socialist Party in the years 1921–1922 to combine its parliamentary strength with the democratic parties of the center so as to make possible the formation of a coalition government that could successfully resist the encroachment of totalitarian Fascism, was undoubtedly one of the major contributing factors that paved the way for the Fascist victory. This attitude of the early twenties contrasts with the policy adopted in the early sixties, when, in order to strengthen the democratic state threatened by totalitarian Communism, the Italian Socialist Party first supported and then entered the democratic coalition government.

Following the resignation of the Bonomi cabinet in February 1922, the king appointed an old-line liberal, Luigi Facta, as Prime Minister. The Facta government from the beginning showed weakness and indecision.

The Fascists stepped up their destruction of Socialist and trade union centers: cooperatives were occupied, newspaper plants burned down, municipalities overthrown, private offices ransacked, and thousands upon thousands of labor leaders, especially in the small towns and the country-side, were brutally beaten or murdered. Every show of resistance was futile. Government forces were either on the side of the Fascists or simply looked the other way.

Soon the province of Pesaro was overrun by Fascist squads from Ferrara led by Italo Balbo.[3] In the summer of 1922 I was severely beaten and wounded in the town of Pergola, where I had gone with a member of Parliament to investigate Fascist crimes. A few weeks later I exposed a local Fascist boss in the vicinity of Pennabilli who had organized an armed assault against a group of defenseless peasants. Instead of being commended, I was arrested and sentenced to thirty days in jail by the magistrate of San Leo, a hill town near the Republic of San Marino—a sentence which I never served thanks to a subsequent general amnesty.

In October 1922 I was back in Rome, taking part in the Party congress where the moderate socialist forces split from the Revolutionary Socialists (Maximalists) and organized the Social Democratic Party. But even before the Party could organize its parliamentary group and participate in the formation of a new Government that could stand up to the Fascist menace, the March on Rome took place, followed by the king's appointment of Mussolini as Prime Minister. The new party, nevertheless, marked a turning point in the history of Italian socialism. It brought it back into the democratic fold and it became the home of all those who wanted a social revolution without sacrificing freedom. Among the new recruits there was a young economist from Turin, Giuseppe Saragat, who later became President of the Italian Republic.

Unable to go back to my home town or to find employment elsewhere, I decided to migrate to the United States. I arrived in New York in January 1923, the first known refugee from Fascism after the March on Rome. I was then barely twenty-two years old.

June 10, 1925, is an historic date in the annals of Italian democracy. On that day Giacomo Matteotti, leader of the Italian Social Democratic Party, was kidnaped and murdered by Fascist gunmen. The crime created such a commotion throughout Italy that the Fascist regime was almost toppled. Matteotti had fearlessly denounced, in Parliament and in the press, the crimes of the Fascist regime. Threats were made against him, but he refused to abandon his crusade. When threats were repeated in

Parliament from the Government benches, Matteotti realized that his days were numbered, and so confided to some of his close friends a few days before the assassin's dagger pierced his heart. Today's democratic Italy has honored Matteotti's memory by naming after him squares and streets in practically every town and village.

The democratic opposition issued a manifesto—signed, among others, by Giovanni Gronchi and Alcide De Gasperi, who in post-Fascist Italy became President of the Republic and Prime Minister, respectively— charging Mussolini with direct responsibility for the crimes of the Special Fascist Police popularly known as *Cheka*,[4] including Matteotti's assassination. I still have in my possession, in galley proof, the text of this historic document.

Matteotti's murder had deep repercussions in the United States. Various liberal, labor, and radical groups united in forming the Anti-Fascist League, grouped around Carlo Tresca, the editor of *Il Martello* (The Hammer). He was a hard-to-describe radical agitator, who liked to call himself a libertarian but was actually a kind of factotum of all the underdog causes. Max Eastman included him among the personalities described in his book *Heroes I Have Known*. Fiorello La Guardia was among Tresca's close friends; so was America Firster John T. Flynn. Norman Thomas and the world-famous defense attorney Clarence Darrow often lent their support to Tresca's various defense committees on behalf of this or that anti-Fascist victim of a frame-up who was threatened with deportation. In January 1943 Tresca was murdered in lower Fifth Avenue, in New York, by unknown assassins probably hired by Communist or Fascist agents.[5]

The main support for the Anti-Fascist League came from organized labor. The AFL, at its 1923 convention, less than one year after the March on Rome, adopted a resolution denouncing the antilabor character of the Fascist movement. The Italian language locals of the Amalgamated Clothing Workers of America (ACWA) and the International Ladies' Garment Workers' Union (ILGWU), centered in New York, Chicago, Philadelphia, Baltimore, and Boston, gave the League the numerical and financial basis for its activities. They also furnished the initial financial aid to launch the daily anti-Fascist Italian language newspaper *Il Nuovo Mondo*. Shortly after my arrival in the United States, I became a member of its editorial staff.[6]

In 1933, I joined the editorial staff of the International Ladies' Garment Workers' Union. This organization, under the pressure of the strong anti-Fascist leadership of its various Italian language locals, and the equally strong anti-Fascist sentiments of its Jewish leadership—President David Dubinsky and his predecessors Morris Sigman and Benjamin Schlesinger—had repeatedly gone on record condemning the antilabor policies of the Fascist regime. In the fall of 1934, it invited the internationally known Social Democratic leader Giuseppe Emanuele Modigliani,[7] then in exile in France, to come to the United States for a lecture tour. I was assigned to him as tour manager and translator. Modigliani's captivating personality and eloquence, which had made him the best speaker in Parliament before the advent of Fascism, contributed immensely to a broader understanding of the nature of Fascism in American labor circles. For me, it marked the beginning of a most rewarding association with a man of sterling character and firm democratic conviction who had a profound effect on the growth of my political thinking.

After Mussolini's Ethiopian and Spanish adventures [8] and his promulgation, in 1938, of the racial anti-Semitic laws, a number of leading Italian intellectuals came to the United States, joining those who had arrived earlier in this country in protest against the Fascist regime.[9] After the fall of France in the summer of 1940, another wave of Italian exiles came from Europe, including Count Carlo Sforza, the distinguished Italian author, diplomat, and Foreign Minister; Alberto Tarchiani, former editor of Milan's *Il Corriere della Sera*, who after the war became Italian ambassador to Washington; Don Luigi Sturzo, and many others. They joined with other Italian anti-Fascists already in the U.S. in forming the Mazzini Society, which became, until the downfall of Fascism, the most representative democratic Italian organization in the United States. Max Ascoli became its President. The Mazzini Society supported the war aims of the Allies and saw in their victory the means to restore dignity and freedom to the Italian people.

The vehicle which the Italian anti-Fascist intellectuals used to express their views and programs was the monthly bilingual magazine *Il Mondo*. It was founded by my brother-in-law, Giuseppe Lupis, who married my only sister Lucy, an ILGWU organizer and leading anti-Fascist militant. Himself a refugee from Fascism and a lifelong member of the Italian Socialist Party, Lupis later was elected Member of Parliament and became Italian Undersecretary of State for Foreign Affairs.

The objectives of the anti-Fascist democratic movement were fully synonymous with the objectives of the Western democracies, at war with Nazism-Fascism. Thus I joined as a charter member the Committee to Defend America by Aiding the Allies and set about to practice what I preached. Alberto Tarchiani, in agreement with Count Carlo Sforza and other leaders of the Mazzini Society, was endeavoring to organize an Italian Legion to fight alongside the Allied forces by recruiting among the Italian war prisoners in India and other countries. In May 1941 I was "enrolled" in the Canadian Army—the cover devised for the intended operation—and got ready to sail together with other volunteer recruiters. But at the last moment the British War Office vetoed the plan as contrary to the Geneva Convention on War Prisoners. I then was offered, and accepted, an assignment to go to South America as the representative of the Mazzini Society.

In 1941 the Fascists were strong and popular in the Italian communities of South America. The initial successes of Nazi Germany in the war against the Allies had encouraged them in believing that, in spite of Mussolini's initial military reverses, the final victory would be theirs. In Argentina, government officials were openly sympathetic to the Nazi-Fascist cause. In Brazil, President Getulio Vargas's Estado Novo (New State) was imitating Mussolini's corporate state. In these countries, scattered anti-Fascist groups were in existence, but their influence was minimal. Even in Uruguay, where public opinion was ideologically and traditionally opposed to totalitarianism, the anti-Fascists in the large Italian community were a minority.

There was in South America a Free Italy Association which was the counterpart of the Mazzini Society in the United States. My task was to help organize anti-Fascist groups in every South American country, co-ordinate their work and programs with the Mazzini Society, and help them in their efforts to enlighten the Italian communities on the disastrous consequences of an eventual victory of the Nazi-Fascist powers. We also wanted to convince the Allies that there were many good, influential Italians opposed to Mussolini and his war, and that the counsel of these Italians should be sought and carefully considered. And above all, we wanted to convince Allied statesmen, in whose ultimate victory we never doubted even in the darkest days of 1940, that anti-Fascist Italians deserved to be trusted.

During my stay in South America, which lasted six months, I traveled constantly throughout Argentina, Uruguay, and Brazil, helping to organize branches of the Free Italy Association, delivering lectures, making radio addresses, and giving press interviews. Uruguay was the country where I received the most enthusiastic and encouraging support. My first public address in Montevideo, on August 28 at the *Ateneo,* was held under the auspices of a sponsoring committee which comprised all the leading political personalities of the country, including Tomás Berreta and Luis Batlle Berres, who later became presidents of the Republic.

Organized labor in Argentina and Uruguay was very helpful to my work. Most of my meetings, especially in Argentina, were cosponsored by local labor unions, particularly those of workers on the railroads which were then under British ownership and management. At the end of our meetings, collections would invariably be taken to help buy Spitfires for the Royal Air Force. Most helpful were also the local groups of Spanish anti-Franco refugees who hoped that the victory of the Allies would hasten the downfall of their own hated pro-Nazi-Fascist dictator.

December 7, 1941, Pearl Harbor Day, found me in São Paulo, Brazil. The state of war between Italy and the United States followed almost immediately. I wanted to return home without delay in order to serve in whatever capacity possible the country that morally, politically, and sentimentally had become my own. It took me some time to devise a way to return, but finally, in February 1942, I was able to sail on the SS *Brazil,* the last American passenger boat to make the Buenos Aires–New York run before the war emergency brought a discontinuance of service.

While engaged in my anti-Fascist work in South America I started writing a series of reports on Nazi and Fascist activities. I sent them to the Mazzini Society's President Max Ascoli, who had in the meanwhile become a consultant to Nelson Rockefeller's Office of Inter-American Affairs. Those reports were processed and distributed to government agencies in Washington by the Bureau of Latin American Research.[10] Apparently they were well received because on the very day of my return I was invited to go to the capital, where I was asked to go back to South America, this time under direct U.S. government auspices.

The activities of Fascist elements in South America were of great concern to Washington officials responsible for conducting our war efforts, particularly to the Coordinator of Inter-American Affairs. The Bureau of Latin American Research, of which I became field representative, had up to that time confined its activities to the collection and dissemination of political and socioeconomic intelligence, mainly on the large Italian and German national minority groups. I was to undertake organizing work and propaganda.

At that time, the United States had not yet set up any of the agencies and bureaus that are now engaged in the collection and evaluation of intelligence and in operational planning. We were brand new in this whole field and practically everything had to be improvised. The role of the Coordinator of Inter-American Affairs therefore, was not only of paramount importance but was limited only by the ingenuity and resourcefulness of its director and his assistants.

On June 2, 1942, the Mazzini Society met in Washington for a solemn commemoration of the sixtieth anniversary of the death of Giuseppe Garibaldi, the great hero of the Italian Risorgimento and legendary warrior in the cause of freedom in Italy, France, Brazil, and Uruguay. The main speakers were Count Carlo Sforza, Max Ascoli, Luigi Antonini,[11] and Dean Acheson, then Assistant Secretary of State, who spoke on behalf of the United States government. Acheson repeated President Roosevelt's statement that the war was not directed against the Italian people but only against the Fascist Government that was oppressing Italy and had plunged her into the abyss of war, contrary to the will and the true historical interests of her people. Then Acheson added that the American government was asking for the cooperation of the Free Italians in the great war efforts that would lead to common victory.

In agreement with the leadership of the Mazzini Society, the Coordinator's Office assigned to me the task of organizing, as my first activity, a Congress of Free Italians, to be held as soon as possible in Montevideo, Uruguay, with the participation of Count Carlo Sforza. At the meeting, the Free Italians would proclaim their solidarity with the war aims of the United States and the Allied countries.

By the first week of July, I was already back in South America. An organization committee of the Congress was set up with active elements from the Free Italy Associations of Uruguay and Argentina. Branches were established in Chile, Brazil, Peru, Venezuela, Colombia, and Ecuador. All the Uruguayan political leaders, including those not of Italian extraction, joined the Conference Sponsoring Committee. The date was set for August 14–16, 1942.

When Count Sforza arrived in Uruguay he was received with honors similar to those reserved for a chief of state. The municipality of Montevideo proclaimed him official guest. The conference's inauguration took place the night of August 14, 1942, at the *Ateneo* of Montevideo and ended with a huge mass meeting, preceded by a street parade, at the *Sodre* theater. Tomás Berreta was chosen President of the Conference. As representative of the United States group I was elected the conference's Vice-President.[12] Sforza was solemnly proclaimed *Abanderado de los Italianos Libres* ("Standard-bearer of the Free Italians"). The conference proceedings were broadcast to all the countries of the Americas and to Italy, where they created a veritable sensation among clandestine listeners.

The addresses delivered by dozens of speakers and the resolutions adopted were not solely directed against the Fascist regime that was dragging Italy down the road to ruin; they also proclaimed, without reservation, the Free Italians' solidarity with the war efforts of the Americas. The resolution which I introduced on behalf of the Mazzini Society was reported by the United Press, datelined Montevideo, August 15. It read as follows:

> Our brothers, the Italian immigrants in the United States, are fighting not only for the political and territorial defense of their adopted country, but also for the political and territorial integrity of all the American republics. And they also fight, above all, for the preservation of the American way of life, which has made it possible for all the Italians who have come to this hemisphere to live, work, and prosper under a regime of freedom and equal opportunity.

Following the conference I organized the Committee for Democratic Education, of which Dr. Ricardo Rimini was Secretary-Treasurer and Manager. Its main activities consisted in a daily news program named *Il Giornale dell' Aria* ("The Newspaper of the Air") broadcast from a powerful radio station whose radius extended to all Uruguay, southern Brazil, Argentina, Chile, and Peru; press releases to all the leading media of the five countries; and lectures and meetings to promote the Free Italy cause.

Montevideo was the headquarters of the Inter-American Committee for the Political Defense of the Continent, created at the 1942 Foreign Ministers' meeting of Rio de Janeiro. It was headed by the Uruguayan Foreign Minister, Alberto Guani, with Dr. Carl Spaeth, of Stanford University, as the U.S. representative. I cooperated with Dr. Spaeth in combating the political activities of our enemies, the Fascists, who were still enjoying freedom of action in Argentina and Chile, the two countries that had not yet broken diplomatic relations with the Axis powers. I also succeeded in organizing, especially in Argentina and Brazil, a string of first-class volunteer political reporters and analysts. Some of them were newspapermen or former diplomats who simply wanted to help the Allied cause. They furnished me invaluable material which was greatly appreciated in Washington and by the Montevideo Political Defense Committee.

After the invasion of Italy by the Allied forces from North Africa and the downfall of the Fascist regime in July 1943, I felt a strong urge to transfer my activity to the Mediterranean theater of operations. I particularly wanted to go to Italy to help in the reorganization of the trade union movement. In September 1943, after having received permission to leave South America, I returned to Washington.

In the month of November I submitted to Professor Adolf A. Berle, then Assistant Secretary of State, a lengthy memorandum on postwar Italian labor problems. In it I pointed out that any attempt to reconstruct Italian society along democratic lines would need from the start the support and loyal cooperation of labor. However, twenty years of complete Fascist domination over every trade union activity had left the field quite bare of trained labor leaders. Thus the reconstruction of the labor movement had to be of necessity largely the work of a new leadership "whose type and tendency"—I emphasized to Berle—"was still a matter of conjecture." Undoubtedly, I wrote, the Communists would take advantage of the freedom to organize, already reestablished by the Allied Military Command, to seek control of the labor movement for their exclusive political interests and designs. I concluded by asserting that, in my opinion, "the democratic elements of the Italian working class need to be organized, advised, and, if necessary, led to take a more militant stand in all matters affecting organized labor and its role in the future."

The memorandum was well received. Berle became my sponsor for an assignment to Italy that would give me an opportunity to work with the trade union movement. Eventually he concluded that the war agency best suited for my intended work would be the Office of Strategic Services (OSS). I readily concurred, and in the spring of 1944 I left the Labor Relations Division of the Coordinator's Office [13] to undertake the new assignment. However, my two-year wartime association with Nelson A. Rockefeller, rather than coming to an end, was soon to be renewed and transformed into one in which I have ever since received his sincere encouragement and effective support for every one of the many labor, political, and educational activities in Latin America in which I later became engaged.

My OSS assignment was not of the cloak-and-dagger nature generally attributed to anyone who worked in that outfit. I was assigned as Special Agent with the assimilated rank of major to the Italian Division, SI (Special Intelligence) Mediterranean Theater of Operations. I was indeed so "special" that I operated completely in the open and my voluminous mail from the United States and Latin America was so addressed as to leave no doubt with whom I was working: "Hq. Det. 2667 Regiment,

OSS, APO 512 c/o Postmaster, N.Y." My chief in Washington was Earl Brennan, a former diplomat with years of service in Italy, who was recalled from his home in New Hampshire to organize from scratch the Italian section of OSS. It was largely composed of volunteer civilians and soldiers, drawn from American youngsters of Italian parentage who grew up in an anti-Fascist environment. The war in Italy had for them a special meaning—to serve their country of birth or adoption, and at the same time to help liberate the land of their fathers from the yoke of Nazism and Fascism.[14]

From the moment I arrived in Italy in July 1944 until I left at the end of April 1945, I worked under the immediate supervision of Vincent J. Scamporino, a Middletown, Connecticut, lawyer who was the field director of the Italian OSS division. I quickly came to admire his natural intelligence, resourcefulness, and sound political judgment. We hit it off right away.

My brother-in-law Giuseppe Lupis was still in the United States, but his brother Filippo was in Rome. I got from Filippo the use of his sister's vacant Rome apartment in Via di Trasone, where the Socialist leader Pietro Nenni had lived for a while during the Nazi occupation under the name of Pietro Emiliani. Giuseppe Saragat was living wth Filippo's family in Via Taro. There I was invited to take my noon and evening meals. The apartment was the meeting place of prominent Socialist and labor leaders, as it had been during the Nazi occupation. Many of the people whom I met there are now occupying the highest positions in Italian political life and government. The generous food supply Scamporino provided for me was a welcome addition to the meager fare available through ration coupons and occasional forays into the countryside.

Liberated from the Nazi yoke only a few weeks before, Rome was going through very hard times. Electricity was available for only a few hours a day and by rotation in certain sections of the city. Water mains were not yet fully repaired. Fuel was almost impossible to obtain and food was rationed and scarce. When winter came the situation became worse. In going through my correspondence of that period I found a letter, addressed to Luigi Antonini, in which I conveyed a request from Pietro Nenni, the spokesman for the Socialist Party in liberated Italy. I wrote:

. . . In addition, Nenni begs you to send packages of vitamins and food for the needy leaders of the Party. Also, he wants you to ask *The Nation* that instead of sending him money in payment for his article, they send him—if possible —a package of food and possibly two or three pairs of socks. These are the things that even a political leader in today's Italy wishes more than anything else.

An Anglo-American trade union mission composed of representatives of the AFL, the CIO, and the British Trades Union Congress (TUC) arrived in Italy at the end of August 1944. I was assigned to it as technical adviser to the AFL representative, Luigi Antonini.[15] We traveled all over liberated Italy, including Sicily. The labor movement was being re-organized on a coalition basis—Communists, Socialists, and Christian Democrats were to share the leadership more or less on an equal basis. However, the Socialists were weak in leadership and organizational abili-ties and in pre-Fascist times had not been too strong in insular and southern Italy, which was then the territory under Allied control. As a result, the Communists were gaining the upper hand.

I do not remember any prominent Socialist political or trade union leader in the summer of 1944 who was opposed to the policy of unity of action with the Communists in the government or in the labor move-ment. This policy was then defended by Pietro Nenni as well as by Giuseppe Saragat. Furthermore, it was the policy of the Allied Military Government. I remember having manifested many times, in conversa-tions with Pietro Nenni, for instance, my preoccupation and misgivings for the future consequences of this policy. Nenni never failed to reiterate his awareness of the danger by repeating an expression which has re-mained indelible in my memory: "I well know what they, the Com-munists, would do to me, if they ever gained total power: *Mi impicche-ranno*—'They will hang me.' "

Among the many arguments advanced in defense of the unity-of-action policy was the fact that the war was still going on, and that in the rest of Italy still occupied by the Nazis partisans of all political beliefs were fighting side by side in the mountains and the city underground. How-ever, efforts were being made, at least in some sectors, particularly the Italian OSS section, to strengthen the Socialist forces at the expense of the Communists. We were preparing for the day—which many of us re-garded as inevitable—when the Communists would have to be opposed. On their part, the Communists were preparing to do the same to the Socialists, the Liberals, the Christian Democrats, and all other non-Communist forces once the war was over and they would be free to go on with their own revolution.

A group of prominent Italian political and labor leaders still remained in Switzerland, awaiting permission to cross French territory in order to return to liberated Italy. This permission, however, was slow in coming. When it became obvious that perhaps it would still be a matter of months, the OSS Italian unit was asked to bring to Italy at least two of them—Giuseppe Emanuele Modigliani, the Socialist Party leader, and Ignazio Silone, the Socialist author of the best sellers *Fontamara* and *Bread and Wine*. They belonged to the anti-Communist faction inside the Socialist Party and it was thus felt that their presence in liberated Italy would be helpful in keeping the Party from moving to the extreme left.

Early in October, Vincent Scamporino assigned me to escort to Annecy, France, two planeloads of arms and ammunition for the *maquis* operating in the Franco-Italian Alpine region. My arrival at Annecy was to coincide with the arrival there by land from Annemasse on the Franco-Swiss border of Modigliani and Silone and their wives. The OSS detachment in Switzerland would take care of that.

I left the Capodichino military airfield on the outskirts of Naples the morning of October 12. The airplane's motors were warming up and its doors had already been closed. Suddenly, I felt a strange uneasiness, a powerful urge to change planes. I took courage and asked a sergeant to open the door and let me out.

Once out, I frantically motioned the pilot of the other plane, who finally saw me through his cabin window. With considerable gestures of protest—I could not hear him over the roar of the motors but I was probably being cussed out—he opened the door and let me in. Less than one hour later, when the two planes had just left the Anzio coast behind and were heading northwest over the Tyrrhenian Sea, my original plane caught fire and went down. Our plane circled the spot and we saw some members of the crew bailing out with their life vests on. After notifying the base we continued on our way. I still remember the expression of the pilot who came to me and, touching my head gently, said in awe: "You must have had word from the Almighty!"

The airfield near Annecy was just a level pasture and we had to shoo away a herd of cattle before we could land. The sky was gray. So close to the Alps, in mid-October, snowstorms are not uncommon. The pilot, sizing up the uncertain weather, announced the departure for home (Naples) for very early the following morning. He had no orders to bring back the expected civilians from Switzerland. The operation assigned to me had been planned outside normal channels and had to be carried out with speed and discretion. It was now up to me to convince the pilot to take aboard the four extra passengers and to delay the departure until their arrival. It was with considerable difficulty and cunning that I finally succeeded. When the party arrived at our airfield the following day, around noon, we were still there waiting with the airplane ready to take off. Modigliani and his wife Vera, and Silone and his wife Darina crowded around me. We embraced with tearful emotion, but then we were practically shoved on the plane by the impatient crew. It was really getting late.

When we arrived at the Capodichino airfield it was already dark. Modigliani, with his Biblical flowing beard, upon setting foot again on Italian soil, kneeled down and with tears in his eyes kissed the ground, exclaiming: *"Oh, terra divina!"* He and Vera had left Italy eighteen years before, at night, in a clandestine flight to Egypt. And now they were returning to their homeland, also at night, almost in the same fashion.

Lacking documents and travel orders, our guests were of course taken into custody by the airport military police; but I had the number of a special direct line, and soon was talking to Captain James Montante at OSS Caserta Headquarters. Montante (he is now a circuit judge in Michigan) could hardly believe his own ears when he heard my voice. He kept repeating: *"Questo è un vero miracolo—*'This is really a miracle!' "

What had happened was that the dispatch officer at the airport, who had registered me as a passenger in the plane that went down, did not know of the last-minute switch. Upon receiving the message of the plane loss, he notified Captain Montante that "presumably Romualdi was lost at sea." Earl Brennan was in turn notified in Washington. But now, suddenly, I was back alive again. After obtaining the release of our guests, we lost no time in arranging a real celebration. When we arrived at OSS headquarters in Caserta we were taken to the officers' mess for dinner. There we all rejoiced, old acquaintances and new, in typical Italian-American style—over succulent home-made *fettuccine* and goblets of red wine.

Early in November I left on a special mission to Siena and Florence, accompanied by Sergeant Samuel J. Prete, a lawyer from Detroit, Michigan, who drove the jeep. We had planned to return by slow stages by way of Casentino and Umbria, where I had relatives whom I had not seen for twenty-two years. I wanted also to go back to Bastia, my home town, a few miles south of Perugia.

My uncle Ettore was living in the town of Soci, in the province of Arezzo. Our reunion was a mixture of joy and tears. One of his sons, my first cousin, had never come home from the war, and another one had chosen the perils and hardships with the partisans. Prete went back to

Florence for the night, and I settled down with my relatives catching up on family news. I learned that in that area there was much misery, almost starvation. Polish troops of General Anders's division were occupying the town; but they either did not have enough food for themselves or were reluctant to share it with the native population as British and American soldiers were doing in nearby valleys. Fortunately my uncle, being the town baker, had been given the assignment of rationing out the flour provided by the government. "At least we will always have enough to bake bread for our family," said my Aunt Giusta, raising her eyes to Heaven in a gesture of thankfulness.

The following morning my aunt, visibly embarrassed, took me aside and apologetically confessed:

"Serafino, the only two eggs we had left in the house I fried yesterday for the sergeant, before he went back to Florence. I searched in vain this morning all over town for eggs to make *pasta,* but I could not find one at any price. I had to make *pasta* without eggs. It will not taste too good; but *pazienza!"*

I assured her that it really did not matter, that I had never been too particular; but then she added:

"I have looked, also, for some meat to make the sauce and the stew. But again, no luck. *Non c'è più niente!*—There is nothing left. So I sent your cousin Serafino (my namesake) to hunt rabbits, up the hill. He is not home yet. That's why the meal is being delayed."

Well, cousin Serafino finally returned with a rabbit and eventually we sat down to eat.

In the late afternoon Prete picked me up and we drove to Perugia and then moved on to Bastia. I stopped first at the cemetery, one mile outside town, where my mother, father, and three brothers were buried—all dead since I had left for America. When we left the cemetery it was getting dark, so I said to Prete:

"Let's turn around. It was night when I left Bastia, way back in 1922, alone, frightened, by a roundabout way. Now, I want to go back by daylight, tomorrow, in full view of everybody."

The following day we parked the jeep in front of Aunt Dinda's, the only relative I had left in town. Soon the word spread like wildfire: "Serafino is back; Serafino is back." They came up the long flight of steps of Dinda's house, all my *vecchi compagni*—"the old comrades," alone or with their families. Two, three, ten, twenty, fifty, until the small parlor was crowded, and they waited in the kitchen, in the bedrooms. Tears and embraces, expressions of rejoicing, and then the inevitable bits of sad news about this or that family, about the victims of the bombings, the houses destroyed. The nuns of the Benedictine cloister, in whose chapel I used to serve Mass as an altar boy, rang their church bell. Then the parish priest came, still alive after so many years, and the new Socialist mayor, just appointed by the local British military commander.

Later came, hesitant at first, the wives and the mothers of the Fascists who had been taken away and sent to jail or the detention camps. They came pleading for their loved ones. My officer's uniform must have created the false impression that I was someone in authority, that perhaps I had the power to punish or to absolve.

"Sor Serafino, I am the wife of Memmo. Do you remember? He warned you when the punitive squad came that accursed night. Please help him to come home."

"I am the wife of Tonino, the son of Peppetiello. He went to school with you. He always said nice things about you. He is now in the camp at Terni. Please, help me go to see him. We have children. . . ."

"I am the daughter of Michetto. They said that my father took part in beatings of anti-Fascists. But it is not true. There are witnesses here that can prove his innocence. . . ."

And it went on and on. Many old friends joined in the pleadings. Aunt Dinda, too. But my mind was wandering back, trying to penetrate the fog of the distant past to re-create events of decades ago: . . . the terrified agonized face of my mother, the night they came looking for me, the last time I saw her, her loveliness sculptured in my memory; . . . the beating of my brother Ottavio, years later, the same day our house was attacked, and my other brother Antonio going into hiding behind a pile of wood in a cellar and staying there in fear of his life for almost two days, until the pangs of hunger forced him out; . . . my father, almost blind, wandering for days in the countryside, sheltered by friends, from farmhouse to farmhouse, to escape the Fascist mob that was looking for his sons. And the day that my sister Lucy and I were branded "traitors to the Fatherland" in the provincial Fascist paper because in distant America we were serving the cause of freedom; . . . and my own sufferings, the burning of my flesh under the whiplashes of the Fascist bullies—all came back, vivid in my mind. Yet there was no bitterness inside me. Not a single irate word of reproach came out. For a score of years I had awaited the day of my triumphant return. It had finally come, but without vengeance. Presently I found myself murmuring in answer to the pleas:

"I shall see what I can do. . . . Rest assured, I'll try to do the best I can."

The visit to Italy of the Anglo-American trade union delegation had been concluded, toward the end of September, with a mass meeting in Rome during which the policy of labor unity was reaffirmed on the basis of a tripartite leadership at all levels—national, provincial, local— with solemn pledges of strict adherence to democratic procedures and independence from political control. To help attain this objective, the U.S. members of the joint delegation, particularly Luigi Antonini representing the AFL, pledged "moral support and, whenever necessary, financial support also." Meanwhile, this pledge had been endorsed by the AFL annual convention at New Orleans, Louisiana, which unanimously approved the report of the joint mission as submitted by Antonini.

With the permission of my OSS superiors I became the agent-representative of the Italian-American Labour Council (IALC) in its dealings with the Italian political movement (mainly the Socialist Party) and the General Italian Confederation of Labor (CGIL). My duty included the handling of funds which as a token of solidarity the IALC would send from time to time.

The CGIL held its first postwar convention in Naples during the first week of February 1945. That convention marked the triumph of a cleverly prepared and executed plan on the part of the Communists to eventually dominate, bit by bit, step by step, the reunited, all-inclusive Italian house of labor. Here is how it happened, as I read again, twenty years later, the notes that I sent to the IALC when the convention ended:

The Communists were in the majority (about 44 percent of the total voting strength) but they refrained from taking advantage of this situation. In fact, in their speeches and in their actions they leaned backward, afraid that by over-playing their hand labor unity might be jeopardized. I say they did everything in their power in order not to antagonize the others (especially the Christian Democrats) and to create a feeling of harmony. To give more weight to this Communist unitarian role, Di Vittorio's [16] speeches at the convention invariably advocated a labor policy based on moderation, patriotism, even class collaboration, repudiation of strikes in public services, exaltation of the Catholics' contribution to labor unity, etc. It was, in short, their "present line" applied to the maximum. Were they sincere? To me they were only playing a given role.

During the convention I met with many delegates from the central Italian regions that had been liberated after bloody fighting between the retreating Nazis and the advancing Allied troops. I learned that in practically every large city—Florence, for example—Communist partisans would swoop down from the hills ahead of the advancing Allies and occupy, first of all, post offices and banks, carrying away all the currency and valuables left behind. I learned, also, that before evacuating a city or large town the Nazi-Fascist police often managed to discover, through never explained means, the hiding places of many anti-Communist underground leaders, who were arrested and summarily executed. And I also learned that while the Communists were pleading poverty inside the CGIL councils, they actually had plenty of money at their disposal and were thus able to pay salaries, expenses, printing bills, transportation costs, and everything else needed to conduct a steady, efficient recruiting campaign, especially inside the labor unions.

Faced with this situation, it became imperative to earmark whatever help was available from the U.S. labor movement to the anti-Communist forces exclusively, especially to the Socialist Party (the Christian Democrats seemed to be quite able to take care of their own needs), rather than continue to channel this aid through the CGIL. In this I found Luigi Antonini fully in accord. Plans were made to strengthen and intensify the trade union activities of the Socialists. Special organizers were recruited and projects for training young leaders were drafted. However, it soon became obvious that all these measures would be mere palliatives, for the roots of all our labor difficulties were elsewhere—in the Allied Military Command itself.

As long as the Communists were recognized as a legitimate "democratic" movement, eligible for every kind of assistance including weapons and material for their underground formations (which they, incidentally, stashed away for the day of their revolution) —and as long as this policy was encouraged and even imposed on the provisional Italian government of which the Communists were an integral part—little could actually be done to effectively prevent the more aggressive, better-equipped, firmly disciplined, and fanatically inspired Communists from gaining control of organized labor. Only a reversal of the Military Government's policy vis-à-vis the future role of the Communists in Italy, particularly in the labor movement, could have galvanized the flagging spirit of the anti-Communist elements inside the Socialist Party and stiffened their latent determination to resist the siren song of "unity of all costs." Two more years had to pass before this self-evident truth regarding the antidemocratic, totalitarian character of the Communists could be openly recognized, proclaimed, and adopted as part of the policy of the Italian government and of its democratic supporters. I say "openly" recognized, because it would be unfair to the many Italian political leaders at the highest levels with whom I was then meeting frequently—Socialists, Republicans, Christian Democrats, Liberals—not to say that privately they were aware of the growing Communist danger facing the country. But they invariably commented, almost in a mood of despair: *"Abbiamo le mani legate—*'Our hands are tied.' "

The big Allied push through the Gothic Line on the Tuscan-Emilian Appennines, where the front had been stabilized during the winter, was approaching. Perhaps, if the Americans within the Allied Military Government could at least be persuaded to help by giving jeeps and supplies to non-Communist elements so that they could "get there fustest with the mostest," the initial control of the local labor councils (*Camere del Lavoro*) would fall into safe hands. But I found no takers. Even Charles Poletti, the American Military Governor who had moved up from Sicily to Naples to Rome, and was now getting ready for the final lap of his proconsular journey up to Milan, could not help. Not that he did not understand the soundness of my requests, but it was outside his province!

In these circumstances I came to the conclusion that it was useless for me to stay on in Italy. Having learned that Nelson A. Rockefeller, now Assistant Secretary of State for Inter-American Affairs, had asked Earl Brennan if I would be coming back from Italy soon, in which case he would like to use my services again, I asked to be sent back to the States. This was accomplished in a matter of few weeks, but just before I left Scamporino asked me to undertake one more mission—an interview with the Lieutenant General of the Italian Kingdom, Humbert of Savoy. Since the retirement and pending the abdication of his father Victor Emmanuel, Humbert was exercising all the prerogatives of the king. The mission was delicate and had possible political repercussions. Therefore, I obtained permission to take Pietro Nenni, Giuseppe Saragat, and Filippo Lupis into my confidence.

The interview, which Scamporino arranged through his contacts at the Royal Palace, was scheduled for the morning of April 9. A marchesa who was helping the OSS as interpreter-secretary instructed me on Court etiquette, from the form of address to the manner of wearing gloves. Before being admitted to the presence of His Highness, I was notified that ten minutes had been allotted to my interview. It lasted over one hour. We parted with an effusion of cordiality and, for my part, with the feeling that I had succeeded in conveying the thoughts that had been entrusted to me, along with a few of my own.

When in Rome I had to report quite often to OSS headquarters, located at *La Camilluccia,* the villa Mussolini had built for his mistress Claretta Petacci. There I was getting my mail, food supplies, gasoline for the civilian car at my disposal, travel orders, etc. So little cloak-and-dagger was the atmosphere surrounding *La Camilluccia* that one day, as the car slowed down to go through the gate, an old lady with a basket of flowers for sale stopped us to ask:

"Allì stanno le spie americane?—Are the American spies up there?"

The question floored me. But before I had time to recover, Giovanni the driver answered gallantly:

"Yes, get in. I'll take you up there."

"Giovanni, are you crazy?" I angrily interjected. "You must never say what you have just said."

"But, Sor Serafino," he replied meekly. *"Lo sa tutta Roma!*—All Rome knows that!"

Upon returning to Washington, at the end of April—the same week the war ended in Italy—I was transferred to the Bureau of Latin American Research. It was still operating under the Office of the Coordinator of Inter-American Affairs. Nelson Rockefeller was highly interested in knowing what repercussions the Allied policies in Italy were having among the large Italian communities in South America. Were they showing any sense of appreciation or were they resentful in any way? I was asked to go down and find out. The anti-Fascists showed a great sense of appreciation, but the Fascists, or those who had sympathized with Mussolini, were resentful and bitter.

This tour of duty, which took me back to Brazil, Uruguay, Argentina, Chile, and Peru, lasted until September 15. After that, my war service ended and, as related in the first chapter, I reported to David Dubinsky for reassignment in my trade union work. I thought my work in Latin America had ended with the war, but in fact, it had only begun.

I left behind many friends in the anti-Fascist movement in South America. It would be impossible to write about all who were outstanding for their courage, devotion, and spirit of sacrifice. I shall refer to just three of them, who epitomize that Italian libertarian romantic trait which so many writers have attempted to describe and so few people actually understand.

Gioacchino Dolci, a self-made mechanical engineer, chemist, and physicist—he is now with ENI's (Ente Nazionale Idrocarburi) Nuclear Research Center—grew up in Rome where he took part in the early active resistance to Fascist violence. Following a number of arrests, he was sentenced to prison in 1926, first on the island of Ustica and then on the island of Lipari, where Mussolini used to keep his most dangerous political adversaries. Dolci's term was relatively short. When he was freed at the end of 1928, he managed to cross the Yugoslav frontier and from there went into exile in France. Dolci, however, carried in his head a daring and almost fantastic plan to execute a lightning raid on the heavily guarded island and rescue some of the prisoners—right under the nose of Mussolini's militiamen.

With the active cooperation of Alberto Tarchiani, who was already in France, the plan was successfully executed on the night of July 27, 1929. In a sequence of exciting events, starting with his clandestine departure from France on a motor launch flying the British flag, hiding in North Africa on the little island of La Galitte before Tunis, and then swooping with split-second timing on the prearranged rendezvous, Dolci rescued from Lipari: the leader of the *Giustizia and Libertà* movement, Carlo Rosselli (assassinated years later in France together with his brother Nello by hired Fascist murderers); Emilio Lussu, the much decorated Italian World War I hero; and Fausto Nitti, a nephew of Francesco Saverio Nitti, a famous economist, author, and statesman who was Italy's Prime Minister in 1919–1920.

The sensational exploit, which was widely reported in the world press and so humiliated Mussolini that he swore vegeance to the death, was celebrated in a number of magazine articles and in a book by Nitti himself, entitled *Escape from the Fascist Hell*.

Gioacchino Dolci had hardly recovered from the stress and strain of the Lipari adventure when he conceived another caper—flying over Milan to scatter anti-Fascist leaflets. Dolci paired with Giovanni Bassanesi, another Italian anti-Fascist exile. They learned how to fly, and when master organizer Tarchiani finally provided them with a flying crate, they took off in the early morning of July 11, 1930, from a clandestine Swiss "airfield," flew over Milan, dropped the leaflets, and, out of gas, crash-landed in a Swiss valley. They managed to get off with minor concussions and a light sentence for having violated a half-dozen Swiss laws and regulations.

By this time Mussolini was boiling. A price was put on Dolci's head— dead or alive. But he went on with his work—maintaining contacts with the Italian underground to keep the flame of freedom aglow. Then a personal loss cast a pall on his generous heart. His lovely wife, Luigia Nitti, an artist-intellectual who had given him two children and the inspiration to find poetry and glory in the daily, unrelenting grind against tyranny, suddenly died. Gioacchino retreated into himself to mourn the loss and to live with his memories. Years later he went to Buenos Aires. There Dolci recovered his will to action and became his old self again.

I met Sigfrido Ciccotti once or twice in Italy, when we were both active at the beginning of the anti-Fascist struggle. He was the son of Francesco Ciccotti, a prince of Italian journalism, Socialist Member of Parliament from my own province of Perugia, founder of the daily *Il Paese* and challenger of Mussolini to a duel. Sigfrido was hardly eighteen years old when he received his first wound in a scuffle with Fascist thugs. In 1922, his ebullient character landed him in a hospital for the second time, for the same reason. In 1926 Sigfrido was arrested and confined to the island of Lampedusa, transferred in 1927 to the island of Ustica (together with Gioacchino Dolci), to the Ucciardone jail of Palermo in 1928, then to the penitentiary of Orvieto, and finally to the island of Ponza, where he stayed until the end of 1929, when his term expired. He went to France and after a few years moved to Argentina.

When I arrived in Buenos Aires at the end of July 1941, Sigfrido was waiting for me at the dock, heading the Free Italy Association reception committee. From that moment on we worked closely together as planners, organizers, speakers, writers—a close relationship that has continued to this very day.

Together Gioacchino and Sigfrido resumed in Buenos Aires their anti-Fascist activities. One day, when the chief of the Yugoslav Government in Exile, General Simovich, announced that Churchill had pledged to him that Trieste would be given to Yugoslavia, Sigfrido and Gioacchino led a demonstration in the streets of Buenos Aires, carrying placards stating: "With or without Churchill's permission, Trieste is and will remain Italian."

Anxious to do something dramatic and spectacular against the Fascist regime at war with the Allies, Gioacchino and Sigfrido planned a number of operations. But one day they came to see me, highly agitated and indignant, muttering epithets against "that man with the two missing fingers." *"Ci ha atrocemente insultati—*'He has insulted us in an atrocious manner,' " Sigfrido heatedly repeated in his typical, staccato fashion.

This is what had happened. The "man with the two missing fingers," a British subject, suggested to the pair a job that, as Gioacchino put it, "was repulsive to our Italian sensibility and would have been politically idiotic and self-defeating." Furthermore, he also hinted that some sort of compensation could, of course, be arranged. After a few seconds of chilling silence, enough to absorb the enormity of the proposition, Sigfrido shot back:

"We are not mercenaries. . . . We want to risk our lives to liberate our country . . . not to engage in gangsters' actions against cultural institutions that have no military significance. . . ."

"Well," I interjected, *"como finì?"*

"We told him to go to hell, turned around and walked away."

Following the September 8, 1943, armistice, the Badoglio Government announced that Italy was at war with Nazi Germany. Sigfrido and Gioacchino lost no time in rounding up Italian anti-Fascists of fighting age, anxious to go back to Italy to enlist. On September 10, a few days before I was to fly back to Washington, I saw them at the head of a group of a hundred and fifty or so Italians assembled in front of the Italian consulate, demanding to be repatriated so that they could join the war against the Nazis. I had helped to draft a travel plan, but the British vetoed everything as "not really necessary, quite premature, and too loaded with political complications." On the other hand, the U.S. Embassy sympathized fully with our efforts to repatriate the Italian volunteers.

I met Trento Tagliaferri for the first time in 1941, in Brazil. A self-styled libertarian of the old school, he was friend and biographer of the world-famous anarchist Enrico Malatesta. Though he was reticent about his past, I managed on different occasions, bit by bit, to extract from Tagliaferri the highlights of an extraordinary and colorful life.

"In 1912–1913," he told me, "I worked for the Milan daily *Il Corriere della Sera,* then I moved to *Il Secolo* and wound up at the *Avanti!,* then under the direction of Benito Mussolini. In 1914 I joined the Mazzini Legion, composed of Italian volunteers in France under the command of Peppino Garibaldi, grandson of the Hero of the Two Worlds." [17] We fought the German hordes at the Battle of the Argonne. Bruno first, and then Costante—Peppino's brothers—died at my side. Over a thousand young Italians lost their lives in that bloody battle to uphold the tradition of our *Risorgimento* . . . ! !"

"Weren't you once in Milan, a member of the *Arditi del Popolo?*"

"Yes, they were battalions of street fighters—republicans, anarchists, Socialists, and even Communists. We were a sort of political *minestrone* designed to give the Fascists indigestion. With the writers Mario Mariani and Leonida Repaci—the former an ex-captain of the Alpine troops and Repaci an ex-artillery officer—we organized the armed defense of the newspaper *Ordine Nuovo,* in Turin. But as you know, in the end all was in vain. After the Fascists ambushed and beat me rather badly, I managed to escape from Italy by hiding in the women's water closet of the Turin-Bordeaux express. From there I went to Peru."

"A propos of Peru; on many occasions labor leader Arturo Sabroso has mentioned your name with a deep feeling of appreciation and gratitude. What did you do there?"

"At the invitation of Victor Raul Haya de la Torre, the famous leader of APRA,[18] I delivered a lecture on the crimes of Fascism. Sabroso introduced me to the audience. When I left the theater, I realized that I was surrounded by a group of policemen in civilian clothes. I spotted them because they all look alike, all over the world. This was on a Saturday. The following Monday I was arrested and three days later expelled. Hundreds of Peruvians came to the port of Callao to bid me good-bye before the police put me aboard the Chilean *Mapocho* bound for Valparaiso. There I was immediately arrested, then released, arrested again, and then deported. I went to Buenos Aires, and finally to Montevideo, where I started breathing the air of a free country."

"I heard your name mentioned in Panama," I asked him on another occasion. "I understand you went there for a revolution, in 1930 . . ."

"My involvement in the revolution was purely coincidental. I went to Panama with a group of Frenchmen on a business venture. I had a letter of introduction from Eduardo Santos, then Colombian Minister of Foreign Affairs—the same Santos who later became President of the Republic. The first thing I learned from Santos's friends was that a revolution was in the making. It was aimed at overthrowing what they called an intolerable reactionary oligarchy. I pledged silence regarding the plot and later became an active participant, pleading the need to be kept in training for our own future anti-Mussolini revolution. The coup—the one in Panama, not in Italy—started at midnight January 1, 1931. It was successful and with only four killed. The new government offered me first money then the post of Panamanian Consul in Brazil—offers which I firmly declined. They did not understand that we crazy Italians love to risk our lives for the sake of an ideal. . . .

"By the way, while still in Panama, in 1931, I met the Peruvian chief of police who had served under dictator Leguía. This was the official who had insulted me and ordered my deportation from Peru. He too had been forced into exile. We met by chance at the Hotel Firenze. What a scene, what a scene! I was seized by a combination of rage and laughter. We actually became for a long while the talk of the town!"

Trento returned to France from Panama in 1932. There he was promptly arrested and was about to be deported to Italy in handcuffs when Pietro Nenni intervened. The leader of the Italian Socialist Party in Exile contacted his highly placed French friends and managed to save Tagliaferri just in time. Then came his migration to Brazil. Trento settled in Bahia, where he obtained backing for an amusement park that actually made him temporarily prosperous.

"And what did you do with the money?" I asked him one day.

"I used it for the cause," replied Trento with fire in his eyes. "It was my duty to help those in need. My house in Bahia became the general headquarters of the Italian anti-Fascists, coming in from every direction. Of course, soon I went bankrupt. . . ."

Tagliaferri was the Brazilian delegate to the Montevideo Free Italy Congress of August 1942. There I learned that at one time he had been secretary to Count Carlo Sforza and had translated the Count's articles written for the *Estado* of São Paulo and other Brazilian publications. When Sforza later became Foreign Minister, the Italian government employed Tagliaferri in its consulate in Rio until his retirement. It took him years to obtain a small pension, and that only after prominent Italian leaders, among them Pietro Nenni and Giuseppe Lupis, interceded on his behalf.

Early in 1966 Trento wrote to me:

"After passing the seventy-year mark I have taken up painting. Soon I will have a one-man exhibition of my works, entitled 'Visions of Italy.' I made the sketches in the course of my two visits there after an absence of almost forty years. I wanted so much to see again, before dying, my beautiful native land. And thanks to the generosity of our Peppino Lupis, the Undersecretary of State for Foreign Affairs, the dream came true, not once, but twice. What more can I desire now from my full life?"

Notes

1. The order for the punitive raid was issued by the Fascist Provincial Secretary, Giuseppe Bastianini, who later became a member of the Fascist Grand Council and Ambassador to Great Britain.

2. Bonomi remained in Italy during the entire period of the Fascist regime, took active part in the underground activities, and again became Prime Minister after the Allied occupation of Rome.

3. Italo Balbo, one of the triumvirs who organized and led the March on Rome, was for many years considered the number two man in the Fascist hierarchy. He was appointed Governor of Lybia, lost his life in an airplane accident.

4. The *Cheka*, so called after the Russian secret police, was later institutionalized and was given the name of OVRA (Volunteer Organization for Antifascist Repression).

5. Two versions of Carlo Tresca's murder persistently circulated for many years in New York's labor and liberal circles. One attributed the crime to professional killers hired by Fascist agents; the other attributed it to GPU (Russian Secret Service) agent Vittorio Vidali, alias Enea Sormenti, alias Commander Carlos Contreras, who achieved infamous notoriety during the Spanish Civil War as chief liquidator of the anti-Communist opposition inside the Loyalist forces. The latter version appeared in *Giustizia*, official Italian language organ of the ILGWU.

6. Outstanding labor leaders in anti-Fascist propaganda and activity, as well as in support of *Il Mondo*, were Luigi Antonini and August Bellanca, vice-presidents of the ILGWU and ACWA, respectively.

7. Giuseppe Emanuele Modigliani was the brother of painter Amadeo Modigliani.

8. Mussolini invaded Ethiopia on October 5, 1935. In 1936 he sent "volunteers" to Spain to help rebel General Francisco Franco defeat the Spanish Republic.

9. Best known in this group were the great conductor Arturo Toscanini; Harvard professor and historian Gaetano Salvemini; Professor Max Ascoli, who first taught at the New School for Social Research and later became founder, editor, and publisher of the magazine *The Reporter;* Professor Giuseppe Antonio Borgese, author and literary critic who joined the faculty of the University of Chicago; and Massimo Salvadori, Dwight Morrow Professor of History at Smith College, Northampton, Mass.

10. The Bureau of Latin American Research was a government-sponsored agency set up by the Office of the Coordinator of Inter-American Affairs. It was directed by Dr. Bruno Foa, economist and political analyst, who came to the United States in 1939 from England where he had taken refuge when the Fascist racial laws deprived him of his chair at the University of Messina.

11. Luigi Antonini spoke as President of the Italian-American Labor Council, an organization composed of trade unionists of Italian descent, which was organized in 1942 for the specific purpose of helping the war efforts of the United States and her Allies.

12. Other Conference officers were: Nicolas Cilla of Argentina, General Secretary; Dr. Riccardo Rimini of Uruguay, Treasurer; Juan Cappello of Chile, Vice-President. Sigfrido Ciccotti of Argentina and Trento Tagliaferri of Brazil were members of the Steering Committee. Torcuato Di Tella, a successful Argentine industrialist who had been among the founders of the Free Italy Association, raised most of the needed funds.

13. The staff of the Division, under its director John Herling, well-known labor journalist, author, and researcher, started the collection and classification of documents and data concerning the strength and the ideological orientation of the labor movement in Latin America, about which there was a great deal of confusion and misunderstanding. From this office both the AFL and the CIO received practical assistance in the development of sound inter-American relations. Another member of the staff was a young university graduate, Robert J. Alexander, who in later years developed into the most knowledgeable historian and analyst of the labor movement in Latin America.

14. Outstanding in this group of volunteers was a young private from Connecticut named Max Corvo, who became the promoter, planner, and organizer of special operations in the field, and ended his military service with the rank of major and many ribbons on his chest including the Legion of Merit and the War Cross. Also, Antonio Camboni from Chicago, son of a Sardinian poet and Socialist leader, who was one of the first to enroll, landed under cover of night in Sardinia, was captured and saved from execution as a saboteur by the timely armistice when the Italians surrendered to the Allies in September 1943. Finally, there were the Zamparo brothers from Brooklyn, who sneaked into Rome while the Nazis were still there and helped bring out to liberated Italy a number of prominent labor leaders.

15. Other members of the trade union mission were George Baldanzi for the CIO and William Lawther and Thomas O'Brien for the TUC. Walter Schevenels, General Secretary of the International Federation of Trade Unions (IFTU) accompanied the group. Also, as advisers from the Allied Military Command, Colonel Thomas Lane for the United States and Major Edward Scicluna for the British.

16. Giuseppe Di Vittorio was the Communist Secretary of CGIL. The other two were Achille Grandi for the Christian Democrats and Oreste Lizzadri for the Socialists.

17. Literary expression used to identify the Italian patriot Giuseppe Garibaldi.

18. *Alianza Popular Revolucionaria Americana* (American Revolutionary Popular Alliance) , later synonymous with the APRA political party of Peru, also founded by Haya de la Torre.

III

Looking for Friends and Allies

IN THE COURSE of my previous visits to Latin America I had established friendly relations with a number of democratic labor leaders, among them Bernardo Ibáñez, General Secretary of the Chilean Confederation of Labor (CTCh) and Arturo Sabroso, General Secretary of the Confederation of Labor of Peru (CTP). On their way back from the International Labor Organization's 1945 conference, held in Paris, Ibáñez and Sabroso visited me in New York. With them was also Albino Barra, CTCh Assistant Secretary. Although their organizations were affiliated with the CTAL and the newly created WFTU, they expressed a strong interest in the idea of reviving, under different conditions and name, the old association with the AFL that had existed at the time of COPA.

A meeting of the visiting Latin Americans with Matthew Woll, Chairman of the AFL Free Trade Union Committee, was quickly arranged. It took place December 5 in Woll's New York office. At the conclusion of the meeting it was agreed that Ibáñez, Sabroso, and Barra would form a sort of unofficial committee "to seek advice and exchange views with leaders of the AFL and labor people of other American countries." To put this into immediate effect, it was also agreed that on their way back to Chile, Ibáñez would stop in Venezuela and Brazil, and Barra would visit Mexico and Guatemala.

The press announcement of my appointment as AFL Latin American representative also contained a short description of the nature of my

assignment, with the implication that I was going to attempt the organization of a new inter-American labor group, as a rival to the CTAL. Lombardo Toledano and the Communists reacted like wounded tigers. An
example of their fury is the following news story which appeared on the
front page of the Communist daily *Hoy* of Havana, on February 13, 1946:

Mexico City, Feb. 8: (ALN) The decision of the AFL to send a mission to
Latin America has provoked caustic comment on the part of Lombardo Toledano, President of the CTAL. "The Latin American labor movement," declared
Toledano, "will have to proceed to the immediate expulsion of each and every
one of the agents of William Green (President of the AFL) and of the foreign
monopolists who may attempt to interfere in the domestic affairs of our countries. The majority of the Latin American countries have laws which prohibit
activities of foreigners that may lead to political repercussions. This would be the
case if the AFL attempts to organize a rival to the CTAL."

Referring to the appointment made by the Executive Council of the AFL of
Serafino Romualdi (a member of the ILGWU) to head an AFL mission, Toledano stated: "I do not know Romualdi personally but if he is acting under the
orders of William Green, his work in Latin America will necessarily be that of
an agent provocateur. We shall receive and treat him as such." And as to reports
that Romualdi would invite Latin American labor leaders to visit the United
States in order to see how the AFL operates, Lombardo said, "We already know
very well how the leaders of the AFL act."

Previously the leader of the CTAL stated that the plan for the organization of
a dual federation as announced by the AFL is equivalent to a declaration of war.
"Let me remind you," said Toledano, "that they have been the ones, and not
we, who have declared such war."

The first impact of the war declared by the Communists against those
who were willing to cooperate with the AFL was felt in Chile when,
during the latter part of February 1946, Bernardo Ibáñez, Albino Barra,
and other socialists were "expelled" from the Chilean Confederation of
Labor. The pretext was their refusal to support a Communist-led general
strike called for political purposes. However, Bernardo Ibáñez and his
friends in turn "expelled" the Communist faction and their allies with
the result that two confederations of labor emerged in Chile. The AFL
continued its relations with the Ibáñez-led group, which openly proclaimed its intention to promote the organization of a new, democratically led inter-American labor federation—now badly needed by them in
order to mobilize international, and especially North American, support
in their war against the Communists.

It was obvious that in order to successfully launch a new inter-American labor group, a fight to the finish against the CTAL was inevitable. However, a good number of anti-Communist unions were not yet ready for that. To oppose Lombardo Toledano's leadership, yes; but to break up the unity of the CTAL, no. The idea of maintaining the unity of that organization, which had been supported from its inception in 1938 by all the Latin American unions, was still very strong. Furthermore, the Congress of Industrial Organizations (CIO) in the United States, which was affiliated to the WFTU and had maintained close friendly relations with the CTAL, was pressuring its friends in Latin America not to break up the CTAL. Nevertheless, a good number of its leaders were gradually but clearly moving away from Lombardo Toledano.

This wavering, uncertain attitude vis-à-vis the CTAL was reflected in the deliberations of the Inter-American Congress of the Socialist and Democratic Parties which was held in Santiago, Chile, April 28–May 3, 1946. The Congress was attended by representatives of the Socialist parties of Chile, Argentina, Uruguay, Colombia, Ecuador, Cuba, and Panama, the Democratic Action Party of Venezuela and the Aprista Party of Peru.

Juan A. Acuña, labor editor of *El Sol* of Montevideo, who attended the Congress as one of the Uruguayan delegates, described the trade union implications of the Congress in a letter to me dated May 17, 1946:

In reference to labor unity on a continental scale, the Congress voted for the "strengthening of the CTAL" but it strongly condemned its leadership, particularly Lombardo Toledano, charging him with acts of treason to the true interests of the working class.

As you can foresee, this resolution puts before the CTAL and without evasive terms the issue of either getting rid of Toledano and the Communists or losing the Socialists. At any rate, its immediate result, so I do hope, will be to draw in the labor movement of every Latin American country a dividing line, ever more sharp and accentuate, between the Socialists and the Communists. It was time, indeed!

I dare say that, in my opinion, now the die is cast for the organization or reorganization within or without the CTAL of a true trade union, proletarian movement opposed to the Communists, for they repeatedly and eloquently demonstrated, until we should really feel tired, that no unity is possible with them because they are subordinated simply and exclusively to Stalinist Russia.

During the month of April 1946 the III Regional Conference of American States members of the International Labor organization (ILO) took place in Mexico City. The AFL delegation took advantage of this meeting to initiate consultations with worker delegates from Latin American countries for the purpose of "feeling them out" on the proposition of establishing "working relationships on a permanent organizational basis."

George Meany was the U.S. worker delegate, with A. T. Cadena, AFL organizer from Texas, and Michael Ross and Willard Townsend from the CIO as his advisers. Robert Watt, AFL International Representative, represented the Workers Group of the ILO Governing Body. I too was around, as a sort of observer, but Lombardo Toledano and his stooges in the ILO staff immediately barred me from attending the meetings of the Workers Group. However, George Meany promoted me on the spot to the rank of "personal assistant," thus obtaining for me the necessary pass to be admitted wherever he was going. Ross and Townsend, of course did not participate in any of our behind-the-scenes maneuvers to win converts to our project.

The delegates from Chile, Canada, Peru, and Venezuela immediately became part of our caucus. So did Father Benjamin Núñez of the Confederation of Labor "Rerum Novarum" of Costa Rica. But the delegates from Bolivia, Colombia, Costa Rica, Cuba, the Dominican Republic, Ecuador, Guatemala, and Panama—some of whom were known to us as anti-Communists—followed the CTAL line laid down by Lombardo Toledano who headed the Mexican delegation. They were still afraid of being branded "traitors" to the cause of unity.

The Argentine delegation was in a special situation of its own. At the ILO conference held in Paris the year before, the Argentine worker delegates' credentials had been rejected. Their credentials were also challenged at this Mexico City conference and by a majority vote they were barred from attending the meetings of the Workers Group. They tried to get close to the AFL people but they only succeeded in getting from George Meany a promise that their request for an American delegation to visit Argentina "to investigate the real trade union situation" would be considered by the AFL leadership.

In spite of the obvious fact that we did not have the votes, Lombardo Toledano's leadership as President of the Workers Group was nevertheless challenged. In a secret ballot six delegates voted against him—United States, Canada, Chile, Peru, Venezuela, and probably Ecuador. Eight delegations voted for him. Had all the countries sent their worker delegations Lombardo Toledano would undoubtedly have been defeated. He himself realized that. By the time the next American ILO conference assembled three years later, the CTAL influence had reached such a low point that they did not even bother to put up a candidate against the democratic forces, which had gained overwhelming control.

Although Lombardo Toledano was the General Secretary of the Mexican Confederation of Labor (CTM), the largest and most influential in the country, that organization was not under actual Communist control or even Communist oriented. But it was still unquestionably one hundred percent pro-CTAL and was, therefore, averse to any contact with the AFL. There were, however, other labor groups in Mexico with which we could work. Our stay in Mexico City, which extended to almost three weeks, gave us an opportunity to establish relations with the Confederación Regional Obrera Mexicana (CROM) led by Luis Morones—one of the architects of COPA; the Electrical Workers Union, headed by Senator José Rivera Rojas; the National Proletarian Confederation (CNP); the Confederation of Workers and Peasants (COCM); the General Confederation of Labor (CGT); and two other groups with jurisdiction in the textile industry. These were banded together in a National Labor Council, whose combined strength, however, was less than that of CTM. Still, it was important to have with us, from the very beginning, representatives of some legitimate Mexican trade unions as Mexico was enjoying considerable prestige throughout Latin America. To have allies in the very seat of CTAL was a factor of great psychological importance for us.

George Meany hosted a dinner for the worker ILO delegates who had gone along with us and for the leaders of the Mexican unions comprising the National Labor Council. Also present were representatives of the General Workers' Union (UGT) of Spain in Exile, who had effectively assisted us in establishing the Mexican contacts. The dinner was followed by addresses from the host and the leading guests. Their tone clearly indicated that another forward step toward the achievement of our goal had been made.

The Free Trade Union Committee had previously decided that if the Mexico approaches were encouraging, I should go on a tour of South America for the purpose of establishing new contacts and expanding those already existing. I left in the early part of June 1946 carrying with me, for good measure, letters of introduction from prominent influential friends, among them Nelson Rockefeller; Max Ascoli; Adolf A. Berle, former Assistant Secretary of State and Ambassador to Brazil; and Ecuadorian Ambassador to the United States and later President, Galo Plaza. Incidentally, one such letter from Berle, addressed to Ambassador George S. Messersmith in Buenos Aires, turned up years later in the Peronista press as "proof" of my being an agent of the State Department.

I visited, in this order, Venezuela, Brazil, Uruguay, Argentina, Chile, Bolivia, Peru, Ecuador, Colombia, and Mexico. The tour lasted twelve weeks. I was looking for friends and allies, and although in a couple of countries the initial results were disappointing, I returned home with the firm conviction that we were making definite progress.

My visits to Venezuela, Brazil, Peru, and Uruguay were highly satisfactory. In Venezuela I met for the first time Rómulo Betancourt, who was then Provisional President of the country; in Peru I came into contact, also for the first time, with Victor Raul Haya de la Torre. I realized then that without their support my task would have been almost impossible, for they exercised a decisive influence over the labor movements in their countries. However, they sided with me with deep conviction and vibrant enthusiasm, and thus became and have remained until now the strongest and most influential supporters of my mission in Latin America.

My visit to Chile was arranged mainly to confer with Bernardo Ibáñez and other leaders of his Confederation of Labor on the next concrete step to advance the plans agreed upon at Mexico City. The results of our conversation were included in a memorandum that I sent from Santiago to Matthew Woll and other AFL leaders. I reported that Bernardo Ibáñez was prepared to take the leadership in Latin America for the organization of an inter-American labor body opposed to the Communists and the CTAL. He wanted definite assurances, however, that the new organization would not lack the necessary financial support to combat the opposition, and to carry out its own program of concrete trade union activities. It was proposed that the AFL should call a meeting of Latin American labor delegates to the forthcoming ILO Conference in Montreal, scheduled for September 1946, where the issue of organizing a new inter-American confederation could be discussed, and that the Latin American ILO delegates be invited to attend the 65th AFL Convention, scheduled to be held in Chicago right after the Montreal ILO meeting.

When I arrived in La Paz, Bolivia, early in August 1946, the revolutionary atmosphere of the previous month—which had brought about the overthrow of the Nationalist Revolutionary Movement (MNR) regime and the hanging from a lamppost of President Gualberto Villaroel—was still in the air. Groups of armed civilians roamed the streets engaging in sporadic night shooting. Despite such handicaps I managed to establish contacts with some labor leaders belonging to the Left Revolutionary Party (PIR), but found them to be completely on the side of Lombardo Toledano, the CTAL, and the WFTU. I also met with other trade unionists who had supported the revolution but were not pro-Communist and were opposed to the CTAL. However, I had decided, in full agreement with our Ambassador and the Labor officer, to keep my presence in La Paz practically incognito, out of the newspapers, and above all, brief. So I left after a few days without any definite commitments but with the promise to return in the near future.

My visit to Ecuador was also inconclusive. There I met a group of very fine Socialist labor leaders, headed by a lawyer, Juan Isaac Lovato, who subsequently became Mayor of Quito and briefly Minister of Labor. They were sharing, with the Communists, the leadership of the Confederation of Labor of Ecuador (CTE) but claimed they would have liked to get rid of them. Yet, they were going about it in such a naive and indecisive way that I soon became convinced of the futility of their tactics. I reported to the Free Trade Union Committee at the conclusion of my Ecuadorian visit that Lovato and his friends pledged all their efforts to obtain the affiliation of their own CTE to the proposed inter-American labor organization, provided, however, such affiliation would not require the severance of their connections with the CTAL. This would lead, they said, to a split in the CTE ranks for which they did not wish to be responsible at the present time.

In the meantime the Socialists decided to maintain with the AFL a cordial relationship and regular correspondence—including eventual requests for technical assistance and trade union counsel. Lovato was selected as "confidential" correspondent. And so it remained, very "confidential," for many more years to come with the negative result that the CTE remained affiliated to the CTAL and the Socialists now have practically disappeared from its leadership.

In Colombia a split took place at the Colombian Confederation of Labor's (CTC) convention held in Medellín during the month of August, 1946. I wired the Chairman of the Free Trade Union Committee on August 19, 1946, that all of the non-Communist delegates walked out and held their own meeting—exasperated by "Communist dictation, fraud, multiplication of paper locals, political interference. . . ." I noted that the democratic labor leaders were claiming title to the CTC name and funds, that they clearly represented a majority of the bona-fide membership and apparently enjoyed the support of the Liberal Party. I also informed Woll that after meeting with these CTC leaders I pledged AFL assistance without going into specifics.

My last stop was in Mexico City, where on August 26 I met with the members of the National Labor Council whom I had not seen since April, at the time of the ILO Conference. I was informed that our Mexican friends had decided to send to the forthcoming Montreal ILO conference two or three representatives in order to establish contacts with representatives of democratic labor organizations of the United States, Canada, and Latin America, and to take the initiative in bringing about the formation of a preparatory committee—representing at least five to seven countries. This committee while in Montreal would meet for the purpose of (a) issuing an official call for an inter-American labor conference; (b) making up a list of organizations to be invited; (c) selecting the date and site of such a conference; (d) drafting the agenda, rules, and regulations and any other measures deemed necessary to insure its success.

Upon returning to the United States I prepared a series of recommendations which were submitted to the AFL International Relations Committee. At its meeting of September 13, 1946, the Committee authorized Robert Watt, AFL International Representative and U.S. workers' delegate to the Montreal ILO Conference, to extend an invitation to visit the Chicago AFL convention to about fifteen labor delegates from Latin America. The list of those to be invited was to be made in consultation with me and I was instructed to attend the Montreal conference as adviser to Robert Watt. The Committee also recommended that one session or part of a session of the Chicago AFL convention be set aside as "Pan-American Day" to be devoted exclusively to the reception of this Latin American labor delegation and that the text of the greetings that would be exchanged, together with the text of a resolution pledging AFL cooperation with Latin American labor and other related statements which the convention might approve, be printed in a special supplement of the AFL Spanish language clipsheet or in booklet form for distribution in all Latin American countries.

At the request of Albert Tarchiani, who had returned to Washington as Italian Ambassador, I took advantage of my 1946 tour of Latin America to prepare the ground for the official visit of Count Carlo Sforza. He had been assigned by Prime Minister Alcide De Gasperi to visit various Latin American countries with the view of reestablishing diplomatic relations broken during the war.

Sforza's itinerary followed mine by a few days, but our paths met at the last stop, Mexico City. It was there, while dining in the roof restaurant of the Hotel Majestic, that Sforza advanced the suggestion that I join the Italian diplomatic service. Later when a reshuffling of the Cabinet made him Foreign Minister, Sforza obtained my appointment to the rank of Consul General and Minister Plenipotentiary.

I gave careful consideration to all the pros and cons of accepting this post. Among the latter the loss of my American citizenship, the abandonment of my campaign against the Communist-dominated CTAL, and the desertion of my American friends and sponsors who had set so much store by my Latin American trade union plans were the key factors that induced me to decline the appointment. Count Carlo Sforza himself, in his official letter of acknowledgment, wrote to me: *"Mi rendo conto dei nobili sentimenti che ispirano la Sua decisione*—'I do understand the noble reasons that have motivated your decision.' "

David Dubinsky, the President of my alma mater, the ILGWU, from whom I sought advice and support in those days, said to me: "You'll be better off, Romualdi, to remain here. It is more important that you continue as the labor ambassador to all of Latin America."

The Montreal contacts during the ILO conference were highly encouraging and fruitful. We had several meetings, all concerned with planning the next step in the preparatory work for the organization of a new inter-American trade union group. The Latin American Labor representatives believed that it was still necessary to proceed with caution and that the initiative for other future meetings be left to the Latin Americans. With this in view, it was decided to organize a "Latin American Labor Information Committee," a sort of provisional agency to prepare a meeting to be held in Lima early in 1947. The agreement creating such a committee was signed by the representatives of the labor movements of eight Latin American countries.

The visit of the Latin American group to the Chicago AFL convention was a complete success. It took place at the afternoon session of October 11, the day before Columbus Day—observed throughout Latin America as the "Dia de la Raza." The Latin American delegates, whom Robert Watt and I had accompanied to Chicago from Montreal in a chartered pullman car, entered the Convention Hall of the Hotel Madison during the morning session. We were seated on the platform, where we became the object of attention and curiosity on the part of the delegates. Visitors from abroad are now a common sight at AFL-CIO conventions. They come from every part of the world, hundreds of them. The delegates are used to them and the pressure of business hardly permits more than a routine acknowledgment of their presence. Only the most important of them are called upon to address the convention. But in 1946, a group of visitors from Latin America was a novelty. Their presence and the enthusiasm with which they were received marked a truly historical event in the annals of the AFL.

President Green, before adjournment of the morning session, announced that the Latin American delegates would receive guest badges and would be called upon to address the convention at the start of the afternoon session. We entered the hall marching down the center aisle to the thunderous applause of the delegates, who continued to cheer until we reached the platform, where President Green presented each visitor with a guest badge.[1]

One speaker for each country was called upon to address the convention. Then I was called upon to speak—the first time before an AFL convention. Because I was busy the whole morning translating the visitors' addresses, I had to speak impromptu. The following passages still strike me as being significant:

I believe that this meeting is of historic significance. I wish that the newspapermen and the molders of opinion in the United States and many government officials, including those in high brackets who for the last several years have insistently repeated that organized labor in Latin America is dominated by a single totalitarian-minded individual, could be here and see the true representatives of democratic labor organizations in Latin America, who happen to be the overwhelming majority of all organized labor south of the Rio Grande.

. . . The best way to fight totalitarian infiltration in the American continent is not to confine ourselves to pious enunciations. We must give concrete evidence to our brothers in Latin America that we really mean to help them, not only through theoretical assertions of good will and solidarity but through a practical demonstration of our interest in their daily lives and in their struggle to attain a better future.

. . . There is no possibility for a successful defense of the American continent from the political and from the military point of view unless we achieve complete democratic unity among the workers. . . . It is not sufficient to sign an inter-American military pact. We must at the same time reach a close understanding for cooperation and unity in international policy with the workers of Latin America. . . . Those who control the port workers and other means of communications have a far stronger power than several military divisions.

The address that made the deepest impression on the Latin American visitors was the one that followed, by Secretary-Treasurer George Meany. It marked the first authoritative pronouncement of the AFL objectives in Latin America—from which it has never departed and which can still be regarded as the guideline of today's AFL-CIO Latin American policy. George Meany said:

When we look back into history we find that despots and dictators have always looked to the natural resources and riches of a land before they set out on their aims of conquest. Latin America represents one of the richest parts of the world's surface. Before the last war we had a demonstration of the dictator's interest in those countries. Hitler's Germany had infiltrated into many sections of Latin America.

. . . . Today we find another type of dictatorship looking with eager eyes upon Latin America. A tremendous wave of anti-American sentiment has been created in a few spots by representatives of another totalitarian regime. It is up to the American Federation of Labor to see to it that the workers of Latin America understand our philosophy, understand our desire to create a solid front among the working people of this Hemisphere and to see to it that these people do not listen to the mouthings of those who receive their orders from Moscow.

We hear a great deal of talk on the part of the Communist leaders in Latin America about Yankee imperialism. I think we should let these Latin American brothers who are here today know that we are keenly conscious of the sorry spectacle that some American capitalists have made of themselves in Latin America. We should let them know that we spend all our waking moments to keep American capital from exploiting American labor, and that we are just as much opposed to American capital exploiting Latin American labor as we are to American capital exploiting American labor.

We would like to see the development of Latin America pressed forward with the assistance of American capital, but any capital that goes to Latin America should go in the spirit that capital could be a blessing and should not under any circumstances be a curse.

The program was concluded with a lengthy address by Matthew Woll, Secretary of the Convention Committee on International Relations, who submitted a resolution which advocated "the establishment of a permanent inter-American trade union association of democratic, independent, and effective labor organizations." The motion to adopt the Committee's report was carried by unanimous vote.

The Latin American Trade union leaders who were at the Chicago AFL convention agreed that the work of preparing for the inter-American labor conference should be done mostly by the Latin Americans themselves. They set up a committee with headquarters in Buenos Aires headed by the representatives of the Argentine General Confederation of Workers (CGT) with Ibáñez and Sabroso acting as members. Everything looked auspicious, but subsequent events in Argentina threw the whole plan into disarray and caused a disappointing delay in our program to establish a new democratic organization of labor in the Americas.

Notes

1. The Latin American fraternal delegates so honored were:
Aniceto Alpuy, National Federation of Federal Employees; Assistant Secretary, General Confederation of Labor, Argentina.

Juan B. Ugazio, National Union of Municipal Employees; Treasurer, General Confederation of Labor, Argentina.

Renato Socci, National Federation of Maritime Workers, Brazil.

Bernardo Ibáñez, President, Confederation of Labor, Chile.

Miguel Ángel Guzmán, General Secretary, Garment Workers' Federation; Assistant Secretary, Confederation of Labor of Ecuador.

Cesar Enrique Coronel, Secretary, Confederation of Catholic Unions, Ecuador.

Agustín Carrillo, Confederation of Electrical Workers, Mexico.

Manuel Rivera Anaya, National Proletarian Confederation, and Mrs. Manuel Rivera Anaya, Mexico.

Roberto Cornejo Cruz, Confederation of Electrical Workers, Mexico.

Arturo Sabroso Montoya, Textile Workers' Union; General Secretary, Confederation of Labor, Peru.

José D'Elia, Federation of Commercial and Industrial Employees, Uruguay.

José Marcano, President, National Association of Commercial Employees, Venezuela.

Jesús Salvator Barreto, Secretary, Oil Workers Union "El Tigre," Venezuela.

Luis Tovar, President, Petroleum Workers' National Federation, Venezuela.

IV

The Break with Perón

THE ADVENT to power of the dictator Juan D. Perón ushered in an era during which most of the leaders of the labor movement in Argentina felt they had achieved a position of political influence after many years of neglect of the workers' interests by former government administrations. Lured by Perón's promises, they were ready to overlook the fact that he had a Fascist outlook, developed when he spent time in Italy as part of an Argentine military mission to Mussolini's "empire." During this service Perón had learned well the demagogic technique of building a base for political power upon support of the underprivileged masses.

Earlier, the process of constitutional government in Argentina had been interrupted for the first time in this century in the year 1930 when a military clique headed by General José F. Uriburu, aligned with politicians of the Conservative Party, overthrew the decaying and tired Radical Party administration of President Hipólito Irigoyen. This revolt marked the initial appearance of the military in the political life of Argentina— a problem which today still remains unresolved. Until the coup which brought Perón to power, there followed a succession of de facto and legal governments which were notorious for a complete lack of social responsibility.

While Perón unquestionably copied many of his methods from Mussolini, he introduced in the Western Hemisphere a new type of dictatorship that was based, not on the naked power of the *caudillo* emanating from his office alone, but rather on a power of leadership deriving its strength from false use of the aspirations of the masses. In Perón's case, this power came from the support given him by the workers in the streets, who freed him from prison and later, under his direction, organized a Labor Party which brought him to full power as President. His own Peronista Party was not formed until after he had assumed dictatorial powers. Just as a number of trade unionists (the anarcho-syndicalists and Socialists especially) had opposed Mussolini's methods in Italy, Perón was opposed in Argentina by the Social Democrats, the Radicals,[1] and the Conservatives.

Participating in the pro-German military coup of June 1943 against President Ramón S. Castillo, Colonel Perón was named Secretary of Labor and Social Welfare the following November and immediately launched a program to win labor support by granting many long-ignored demands of the workers and encouraging the growth of those unions willing to co-operate with him. Although some segments of the Argentine labor movement recognized Perón as a dangerous demagogue, the majority of its leaders, as well as most of the workers themselves, were strongly attracted by his promises that his regime would do away with the oligarchy and inaugurate a policy recognizing labor's rights. This was especially true of the agricultural workers, who at that time did not have even a minimum wage law to protect them although they were by far the most numerous group of workers in the country.

Emerging as the dominant personality of the military regime which had ousted Castillo's oligarchic Conservative Party from power, Perón steadily consolidated his control over the Argentine labor movement as Director of the Department of Labor, Secretary of Labor and Social Welfare with Cabinet status, Minister of War, and Vice-President. Using both the carrot and the stick, Perón increased wages, doubled the number of organized workers, pushed through labor and social security legislation, decreed a Christmas bonus, etc.

Alarmed by his growing influence, a group of Army officers under General Eduardo J. Avalos forced Perón's resignation on October 9, 1945, and briefly sent him to prison. However, his henchmen and labor supporters arranged street demonstrations and imposed a compulsory work stoppage that brought about his release from jail and lifted him to even greater power. From mid-October, Perón was in full control of the government, even though Edelmiro Farrel remained in office as nominal President.

Although his support by a substantial segment of Argentine workers could not be doubted, the antidemocratic and dictatorial nature of Perón's leadership had already become clear.

The international labor movement also was aroused by the fact that the Perón regime was considered pro-Nazi. As a matter of fact, Argentina did not break diplomatic relations with Germany and Japan until January 1944 and war was declared only in March 1945 when their defeat was practically assured. At the International Labor Organization conference held in Philadelphia in 1944 an attempt was made to deny a seat to the worker delegate from Argentina on the grounds that the CGT had fallen under government control. Later, the Argentine worker delegation was rejected by an almost unanimous vote at the ILO conference held in Paris October 15–November 5, 1945.

Consequently, I prepared an article for publication in the November 1945 issue of the AFL publication, *American Federationist,* which was strongly critical of "dictator" Perón, his Nazi-Fascist supporters, his "fake" General Confederation of Workers (CGT), and other aspects of his regime. The article concluded that "such a dictatorship cannot have and will never have the support of free, honest, intelligent, patriotic trade unionists who constitute the bulk of the Argentine laboring masses." *The Noticiario Obrero Norteamericano* reprinted my article in its January 1946 issue, and it was widely disseminated throughout Latin America in Spanish. In the same month, Angel Borlenghi, President of the Argentine Federation of Commercial Employees, upon learning of the AFL's interest in promoting the establishment of a new inter-American labor group as a rival to the Communist-controlled CTAL, wired AFL President William Green offering cooperation and support.

Perón was elected President of Argentina on February 24, 1946, with about 54 percent of the popular vote, thanks to the massive support of the urban industrial workers who had become incensed by the policies being followed by most employers. The latter had refused to comply with the provisions of the labor laws enacted by Perón, including his decree for payment of the Christmas bonus and other fringe benefits. A major factor in his victory was the new Partido Laborista, led by Luis Gay, head of the Telephone Workers' Federation, and backed by most of the leaders of the CGT.

Meanwhile, top officers of the Argentine CGT sent a long official communiqué to AFL President William Green protesting against my article and inviting the AFL to send a committee to survey the labor situation in Argentina. Following Perón's election, Argentine delegates at the ILO

Conference in Mexico City in April 1946 declared that the Argentine labor movement, especially the CGT, was democratic and independent of government domination. In an interview with AFL Secretary-Treasurer George Meany—already reported in the preceding chapter—they renewed the CGT invitation sent earlier to President Green, and the following month the AFL International Relations Committee voted to accept. Accordingly in June 1946 President Green wrote the CGT advising them that the AFL had accepted their invitation to send a committee to study labor conditions in Argentina and that this delegation, consisting of myself from the AFL and two other members, one from the Spanish labor movement in exile and the other from the Labor Confederation of Chile, would arrive in Buenos Aires in July. The CGT officials were assured by Green that "Romualdi will come to you with an absolutely open mind and that he will have no difficulty in revising his views in regard to your organization should the factual conclusions of his visit require him to do so."

The other members of the committee, Belarmino Tomás of the General Union of Workers of Spain (in exile) and Manuel Hormazabal representing the Chilean Confederation of Labor, met me in Buenos Aires in July 1946 and we established contacts with the CGT and the independent unions. We also met with Foreign Minister Bramuglia and Interior Minister Borlenghi. All of the meetings were very cordial and there was no mention of my *Federationist* article. Although reaffirming their solidarity with Perón's labor and social policy, the CGT leaders insisted that they had complete freedom of action vis-à-vis the government. A statement to this effect was published in the official organ of the Union Ferroviaria (Railway Union).

The committee also met with a number of democratic labor leaders who had gone into open opposition to the Perón regime, among them Joseph Domenech, for many years the Argentine spokesman at international labor meetings, and Francisco Pérez Leiros, head of the Municipal Workers' Union. We also met with Socialist Party leaders Juan Antonio Solari, Américo Ghioldi, and Nicolás Repetto. The latter warned the visitors, "I realize that the CGT looks to you like a tasty morsel, but you will never be able to digest it!" What prophetic words of wisdom events later proved them to be!

The AFL-sponsored delegation sent a report to President Green dated July 31, stating that it was very difficult to determine whether the close collaboration between the CGT and Perón stemmed from voluntary adhesion or governmental coercion. After noting that the application of the October 1945 decree (Personeria Gremial) placed the legally recognized unions in a preferred position in contrast to the independent unions, and reporting the pledge by the CGT to amend this decree, the three-man committee recommended that the CGT be recognized as the legitimate representative of the Argentine labor movement and that the credentials of its delegates be accepted at the forthcoming ILO conference in Montreal, scheduled for September 1946.

Meanwhile, in August, the Argentine Ambassador to the United States, Dr. Ivanissevich, wrote to President Green inviting representatives of American workers to go to Argentina "so that they may get a real picture of what is happening . . . in regard to labor conditions and rights." The Ambassador noted that there was a great deal of controversy in the United States about Argentine labor conditions, with some critics insisting that the unions there had no freedom. The letter declared that the Perón administration had been put into power by the free vote of millions of workers. The invitation was extended in the name of President Perón and was also sent to the CIO and Railway Labor Executives Association. The CIO rejected the invitation immediately, charging that Perón had converted Argentina into a "corporate state along Nazi lines."

In September 1946, President Green acknowledged the invitation to the AFL but postponed a decision, pending a translation and careful study of the committee's July 31 report on Argentine labor conditions. At the ILO conference in Montreal, CGT delegates were seated and invited, together with labor representatives of seven other Latin American countries, to attend the 65th AFL Convention in Chicago the following month.

In Chicago the CGT spokesman declared that his organization "follows as ever the straight line of those sound principles which guide the trade union activities of the most progressive labor organizations in the world."

Later in October, President Green informed the Argentine Embassy that the AFL accepted the invitation of the Argentine government and would name a delegation to visit that country, provided that a supplementary invitation was received from the organized labor movement of that country.

The Secretary General of the Argentine CGT responded and sent supplementary invitations to the AFL and the Railway Labor Executives Association (RLEA). In a press release issued December 23, President Green stated that the main purpose of the forthcoming AFL mission to Argentina was "to investigate labor, economic, and political conditions." His statement appeared in all leading U.S. newspapers and was distributed throughout Argentina by the Associated Press.

Before leaving Washington on January 15, the American labor delegation [2] agreed on the text of a statement to be released to the press upon its arrival in Buenos Aires. The delegation arrived on the nineteenth and issued its statement:

Our purpose in making this trip is to see for ourselves the actual trade union and economic conditions that exist in this country. . . . We intend to conduct our own survey. We intend to see and talk to anyone and everyone who can contribute to a better understanding on our part of the matters in which we are interested. . . . As free trade unionists, we believe that workers everywhere should be free to organize into unions of their own choice and to bargain collectively with their employers. We realize, however, that conditions in other countries do not coincide entirely with our own. In all good will, we intend, therefore, to see for ourselves what conditions obtain in Argentina and reach our conclusions in accordance with the facts. We are deeply grateful to our hosts for affording us this opportunity.

It must be kept in mind, in assessing the full purpose of the mission, that the AFL and Latin American anti-Communist labor groups wanted the CGT to join the proposed inter-American trade union organization. In fact, at the Montreal meeting of the ILO in September 1946 they had selected Argentina as the seat of the provisional committee responsible for preparing the organization of the new inter-American labor group.

We traveled on a plane furnished by the Argentine government and were accompanied throughout the journey by an official of the Argentine Embassy in Washington, Martín Luis Drago. At Rio de Janeiro a welcoming committee from Argentina headed by Supreme Court Justice R. Valenzuela boarded our plane. It was obvious that Perón was attaching considerable importance to our mission.

A few hours after our arrival, on Sunday, January 19, 1947, we were notified that President Perón would receive the delegation at seven the following morning. However, after discussing it with the chairman and other members of the delegation, I requested a postponement of the 7 A.M. reception for several reasons: some of the delegates were exhausted after a three-day trip and needed a full night of rest; we all felt that before seeing Perón we should pay a courtesy call on our Embassy, making clear the private nature of the mission. After much grumbling on the part of the reception committee, the meeting with Perón was postponed to 5 P.M.

Another unfortunate incident arose in connection with the choice of the hotel. In Washington I had notified the Argentine Embassy of our desire to stay at the City Hotel, located downtown within easy walking distance of the Government House (Casa Rosada), the Ministry of Labor, the U.S. Embassy, the Calle Florida shopping center, etc. Besides, it was "my hotel," where I had stayed regularly during previous visits to Buenos Aires and I was well known from the front desk to the dining room waiters. We were given assurances that this would be arranged, and to make it doubly sure I had written the hotel manager myself. But when we arrived the reception committee informed me that reservations had been made at the "more comfortable and spacious" Alvear Palace, which was distant from downtown Buenos Aires and would have made the free movements of the delegation more difficult. Of course, we won the argument but not without arousing some displeasure on the part of our hosts.

It soon became known to us through statements made by CGT members that, although the Confederation was a cosponsor of our trip with the Argentine government, the CGT had been completely ignored in the selection of the official reception committee—which had been appointed by the Department of Labor and Welfare—as well as in the preparation of the program covering our activities and entertainment for the first week. This program had already been arranged by the government and published in the local press. Furthermore, we noted that Perón was trying to give our presence political overtones. For example, immediately after our arrival we were given a reception at the Department of Labor and Welfare, and were invited to remove our coats because of the extreme heat and humidity. Photographers and cameramen swarmed around us, because the removal of one's coat in public in Argentina was already widely regarded as a symbolic gesture of support for Perón—the self-styled champion of the "descamisados," or shirtless ones. The progovernment press and newsreels featured the "shirtless" AFL mission and interpreted it as an indication of support for Perón.

On Monday morning, January 20, our delegation met to discuss Perón's published plans for our first week in Argentina. We decided not to accept it without modification, because it included too many official receptions and entertaiment tours. In addition, we resented the fact that the CGT had been bypassed in the preparation of the program.

Later that afternoon CGT Secretary General Luis F. Gay and members of his executive committee came to our hotel to accompany the delegation to Perón's reception. Since the CGT was a co-host, this procedure was absolutely correct. However, in the lobby of the hotel an official of the Department of Labor and Welfare informed Gay that the delegation would be accompanied to the presidential palace only by the official reception committee of Argentine workers appointed by the Department of Labor. Gay and his CGT colleagues had to step aside and were excluded from attending the ceremony.

The reception was marked by Perón's angry outbursts, especially against me, because I insisted that we had come to "investigate" and not to "fraternize," as he kept repeating. I stated that the purpose of the trip was clearly spelled out in the exchange of correspondence between President Green and Ambassador Ivanissevich. At one point, Perón screamed: "The airplane is ready to take you home."

"As you wish, Mr. President," I replied.

"I know what you are up to, Mr. Romualdi," he shouted, adding in Italian: *"A bravo intenditor poche parole,"* meaning, "A word to the wise is sufficient."

However, he calmed down and invited the group to sit around a conference table. We were joined by Eva Perón, Foreign Minister Atilio Bramuglia, Interior Minister Ángel Borlenghi and other government officials. I requested that we be permitted to map out our program of activities in consultation with both the CGT and the government. Perón rejected this argument, pointing out that the reception committee members and officials of the Department of Labor were also members and officials of CGT unions. However, after we let him know that our position on this matter was firm, Perón instructed his Secretary of Labor to withdraw from further active participation in our mission and told us to go ahead and make our own arrangements directly with the CGT.

Early that same morning limousines appeared at our hotel. There was one for each delegate and they had uniformed chauffeurs. It did not take me long to realize that they were either police agents or people under orders to report our every movement. I managed to get in touch with my friend Aldo Pechini, who was a member of the Italia Libre branch which I had helped to organize in the course of my wartime visits to Argentina. Pechini, who had worked with Argentine Congressman Juan Antonio Solari during the war investigating anti-Argentine (Nazi) activities, was then involved in the organization of an embryonic underground. Aldo quickly realized my plight and promised to help. When I returned to the City Hotel from the Casa Rosada, Pechini was waiting for me with the good news that chauffeurs had been "switched" and the one now assigned to me was a trusted Spanish Republican in exile. Every morning my new driver would submit false reports to Perón's agents on my whereabouts the previous night. Thus I was able to see a number of prominent people within the opposition without the police ever finding out.

On Monday evening the CGT gave the American delegation a warm reception that was an outstanding demonstration of trade union understanding and solidarity. The main speakers, chairman Felix Knight and Luis Gay, referred to the desirability of organizing an inter-American labor group. However, a disquieting aura enveloped the reception: Luis Gay told us that he had just come from a meeting with Perón and that the extent of the CGT participation in the planning of our program had not been resolved. We made an appointment with Gay for the following morning.

On Tuesday morning Gay and his executive committee did not show up and we never saw them again. Almost all of the pro-Perón press ignored the CGT reception of the night before in its morning editions. That afternoon a subcommittee of the delegation was summoned to the Ministry of Foreign Affairs and we knew that something had gone wrong. Foreign Minister Bramuglia was highly critical of my attitude during the presidential reception and made references to my 1945 article in the *American Federationist* on the Argentine labor situation. He added that the government was considering withdrawing its sponsorship of the mission in view of our "rejection" of its prepared program. If this were done, he added, we would be regarded as tourists. During this interview Bramuglia told the subcommittee that Gay would be removed as the head of the CGT, because he had been a party to the "maneuver" to disrupt the official program that had been mapped out by the Department of Labor. While we were still in conference with the Foreign Minister, pro-Government afternoon papers appeared carrying a reprint in full of my 1945 article headlined "with such a man Yankee-Argentine relations are impossible."

On Wednesday morning the press published reports that Gay, having incurred the displeasure of Perón, had resigned from all of his government posts, including the presidency of the Postal Savings Bank, the vice-presidency of the Telephone Company, membership on the Board of Directors of the Central Bank, and Secretary General of the CGT. Before the delegation left Argentina I was able to learn that Eva Perón had demanded that the CGT cancel its reception for us that was held on Monday evening, January 20. Earlier that day Gay had been summoned to the Casa Rosada and told to cancel the reception because we had dared to challenge her husband's "guided tour." Gay refused, most of the CGT leadership backed him, and the reception was held. Perón immediately padlocked the CGT headquarters, deposed the entire leadership, and set new elections for February 8. Gay and his executive committee "resigned" and acquiesced without protest—fearing for their lives.

Perón met with a subcommittee of the delegation on Wednesday January 22 and agreed that the original understanding on the basic objective of the mission would be honored, that he regarded the matter as closed and that he would meet with the entire delegation on the following day and publicly announce the "misunderstanding" had been cleared up.

I had originally planned to go to Montevideo on private business right after the end of the investigation. However, as the press campaign against me became more virulent I consulted with the other members of the delegation over the desirability of my going at once. An incident in the lobby of the City Hotel on the afternoon of the twenty-second precipitated my decision to leave immediately. The chief of police and armed agents stormed into the lobby causing panic among the wives of the delegates. He assured them in a loud voice that they had nothing to fear because they were looking "only for Romualdi." In the light of the impending meeting of the full delegation with Perón the following day to announce the restoration of harmony, I decided to go to Montevideo that night and avoid the possibility of hampering the rapprochement. The driver of my limousine and some friends helped me obtain a visa and passage on the overnight boat. I left unobserved and the announcement of my departure was released to the press by our delegation on the following morning. The announcement was carefully phrased to make the Peronistas believe that I had gone for good. Upon my arrival in Montevideo I refused to comment on the situation. Thus, the Argentine government was led to believe that it had succeeded in completely eliminating me from the scene.

On the twenty-third Perón met with the full delegation, except for me, and publicly stated that harmony had been restored between the American delegation and his Government, that we were free to consult with any person or organization in Argentina and obtain any information related to our objectives. However, the following day Perón warned at a mass meeting of workers in front of the Casa Rosada: "Cursed be he who at our side pretends to be a comrade but when the hour of decision arrives stabs us in the back." The pro-Government and Communist press headlined this warning and carried a statement by the "Defense Committee Against Treason" in which Luis Gay was formally accused of having entered into a conspiracy with Serafino Romualdi, secretary of the delegation, and with the then Assistant Secretary of State, Spruille Braden, "to deprive President Perón of the workers' support . . . to organize an inter-American Confederation of Labor as a tool of the imperialists . . . to sell the Argentine workers to American imperialism, . . ." etc.

I suddenly reappeared at the City Hotel on Monday, January 27, announced that I had rejoined the delegation, and immediately branded as totally and completely false the accusations of "conspiracy" leveled against me, Gay, and Braden.

On the night of January 28 the Central Committee of the CGT met in secret session to consider the "resignation" of Gay. The meeting was preceded by a street demonstration staged by "workers" demanding strong punishment for "traitor Gay." Gay himself was not present at the meeting and had dropped out of view without even a statement to the press. When it was announced that the resignation of Gay and his Executive Committee had been accepted by the Central Committee, and that a new General Secretary would be elected February 8—the scheduled date of our departure from Argentina—we decided that it would be futile to try to resume our contacts with the CGT. After all, our contacts with the CGT had been interrupted on the very day after our arrival and our first and only meeting with them took place January 20. Therefore, we reluctantly followed the program of the Department of Labor and during the remainder of our stay conferred with representatives of various unions, including the independent ones, visited a number of factories, and interviewed business, civic, and political leaders.

One of the more unpleasant episodes took place en route to the resort city of Mar del Plata. I was subjected to threats of physical violence by Raul Costa, a Perón henchman, known as "Costa el Tuerto," then an officer of the Food Workers' Union. Costa had been assigned as a member of the committee of Argentine workers to escort the delegation. Perón was trying to scare us into cutting short the visit. These threats and verbal attacks so disgusted us that at one point we declared that we would confer with the U.S. Ambassador regarding an immediate return home, unless our escorts stopped their inexcusable behavior.

Aurelio Hernández, who had led the attack against Gay at the earlier meeting of the Central Committee, was elected CGT General Secretary on February 8—the day of our scheduled departure but one day before we actually left Argentina because of bad weather. Almost a third of the Central Committee members who attended this meeting expressed their disagreement by abstaining from the voting. The fate of Luis Gay remained a mystery up to and including the moment of our departure. We vainly tried to contact him to offer at least an expression of regret for any problems inadvertently caused by our presence in Argentina. Every sort of rumor reached the delegation, including one to the effect that he had been arrested, held incommunicado, and then confined in a sort of protective custody. It was difficult for us to believe that such could be the fate of the leader of an organization of more than a half million workers solely because of alleged differences with the trade union plans of the President of the country. Before leaving on the ninth, we inquired as to Gay's fate and whereabouts from the leaders of the official reception committee and officials of the Department of Labor. To our consternation, they also said that they knew absolutely nothing about him. Years later I learned that Gay had gone into hiding and retired from both political and labor activities.

Our departure contrasted sharply with our arrival. The farewell dinner was cancelled and replaced by a hastily arranged testimonial honoring the gangster "Costa el Tuerto," which Evita herself attended. Costa, formerly the janitor in Eva Duarte's apartment building—before her marriage to Perón—had finally found "room at the top." Perón showed an unsurprising lack of interest in our departure—two minor clerks showed up at the airport to say goodbye.

Upon its return to the United States, the delegation made a thorough analysis of all its material and information, in the light of the fundamental objectives of the mission. A detailed report was submitted to the International Relations Committee of the AFL in early March. Following are the highlights of the conclusions of that report:

The General Confederation of Labor (CGT), especially as presently constituted, is completely dominated by the Perón Government. This is evident not only from the statements submitted to the delegation; the events that took place within that organization during our stay in Argentina have removed "any possible doubt." The CGT has now been converted from a trade union movement into a political arm of the Government. It cannot elect its officers independently of the Government; it cannot and does not determine its policies independently of the Government; it cannot carry on collective bargaining with the employers independently of political and economic direction of the Government; it cannot administer its own internal affairs.

Though there is little formal action by the Government to suppress civil liberties, a general atmosphere of fear and mutual suspicion definitely exists and it interferes with the exercise of ordinary civil liberties—particularly by workers' organizations unsympathetic to the Government or those which merely wish to remain aloof from political activities.

Because of the favorable economic situation now prevailing in Argentina, the Government has been able to carry out a large number of overdue economic reforms. However, these reforms have been used largely for political purposes.

Social legislation without freedom is entirely inadequate and may even serve as a cover for tyranny.

There still exist in Argentina independent trade unions composed of free workers who are fighting to preserve their organizational integrity and their independence from governmental domination. These organizations, while in most cases deprived of the legal status which is necessary for serving the interests of their members, are nevertheless doing so to the best of their ability.

Because of the diplomatic implications of the report, the AFL delegation deliberately had no contact whatsoever with the State Department upon their return to the United States, until after the report was released. The AFL International Relations Committee adopted the report and it was released to the press on March 9 with the following statement:

The accompanying report of the U.S. Labor Delegation to Argentina brings into sharp relief the grave threat to human liberties that is raised whenever and wherever labor's rights of free association and organization into trade unions are undermined or destroyed.

The delegation, representing the American Federation of Labor and the Railway Labor Executives Association, conducted its mission with complete objectivity, free from prejudice of any kind. Its report is factual and its conclusions are based on direct observation of actual conditions and events. Its impartiality and accuracy will be accepted by anyone who seeks to learn the truth about labor in Argentina.

This committee, to which the report of the delegation was submitted, is actively interested in promoting free trade unionism throughout the world. With this objective in mind and after a careful study of the report on Argentina, we make the following recommendations:

1. That no collaboration is possible with the Argentine Confederation of Labor as at present constituted, because it is not a free instrument of the workers but has become a political arm of the Government.

2. That the free labor movements of the world should do everything possible to encourage those independent trade unions in Argentina which are resisting dictatorial efforts of the Perón Government to place them under subjection and Government control.

Five thousand copies of the final report in Spanish were distributed throughout Latin America, including Argentina. On the eve of the publication of the report, anticipating strong AFL condemnation, President Perón told a mass meeting of labor leaders that the labor policies of his revolutionary regime could not be classed as intervention since "the Government is merely the continuation of the working classes in Government House." Noting that "the AFL wants to free our CGT" from official intervention and influence, he added that "they, who never thought of the workers of this land while they were being exploited and cheated, are just now beginning to remember them."

The AFL report caused an uproar in Argentina and it received a tremendous amount of space in the press. The independent *La Prensa* of Buenos Aires, one of the great newspapers of the world at that time, devoted seven columns to the AFL report. Reportedly incensed, Perón immediately cracked down by backing the unreasonable financial demands of his controlled labor union against *La Prensa*. At that time Perón had been urging the boycott of the "enemy press," the newspapers opposed to his regime. The CGT under its new head, Aurelio Hernández, denounced the report as "full of untruth," announced that it was preparing a document to refute the charges "point by point," and added that "the AFL is seeking to orientate and direct the labor movement in this country." The Perón-dominated General Confederation of Commercial Employees described the AFL report as "aggressive" and "imperialistic," adding that it had obviously been dictated by Spruille Braden, former U.S. Ambassador to Argentina and a bitter foe of Perón. The Peronista press echoed their leader's assertion that the workers and the government were synonymous because the Casa Rosada was a labor government. The official Communist *Ahora* labeled the report "calumnious, humiliating, and offensive for Argentine workers—an imperialistic plan to divide and conquer South American labor." On the other hand, the Socialist *La Vanguardia* called the report a true picture of the CGT, headlining its favorable comments: "They Asked for a Judge and He Passed Sentence."

An editorial in *The New York Times* stated that "this report sustains those who never trusted or respected the Perón Government. It has a moral, too, for our own extremists of the left and right who look to government to 'do things' for them." Another *Times* editorial, in commenting on Perón's crackdown against *La Prensa,* cited the AFL report as evidence that a dictatorial drive was present and "we hope that American advocates of a 'soft' policy toward Perón will take note of the situation." *The New Republic* summarized the highlights of the report, adding that "Perón's junket boomeranged."

On March 11, two days after the report was released to the press, Matthew Woll, Chairman of the AFL International Relations Committee, wrote similar letters to Ambassador Ivanissevich and Aurelio Hernández,

CGT Secretary General. After noting that the report was highly critical of the Argentine labor movement "as judged by the standards of a free, independent labor movement such as we have here in the United States," Woll added, "Nevertheless, I want to express the hope that in the near future new conditions may prevail again in your organization (CGT) so that it may be possible to resume the cordial relationship which existed in the past." Although we had slammed the door, we deliberately left it unbolted.

Notes

1. The Radical Party in Argentina, like the Radicals of France, is a centrist organization, not far different from the so-called "Tammany Democrats" in the United States.
2. Members of the delegation selected by the AFL and RLEA were: Felix H. Knight, AFL Vice-President, as chairman; Arnold S. Zander, President of the State, County and Municipal Employees, Vice-Chairman; Lee W. Minton, Vice-President of the Glass Blowers Association; Miguel Garriga, Vice-President, Hotel and Restaurant Employees International Union; William L. Munger, staff member, United Hatters, Cap and Millinery Workers' Union; and three representatives of the RLEA: J. L. Elliot, of the Railway Telegraphers; William J. Trost, of the Switchmen's Union; and George H. Pedersen, of the International Association of Machinists. I served as secretary of the delegation, representing the ILGWU. The Argentine government had also extended an invitation to a number of newspapermen. Among those who came with us were Philip Pearl, AFL Publicity Director; John Herling, labor columnist; Pierre Loving, International News Service; and Sylvia Salmi, photographer for *Time-Life-Fortune*. A few of the delegates were also accompanied by their wives.

V

Lima Conference

AFTER THE PUBLICATION of the AFL report on Argentina it became necessary to have another look at the trade union situation in Latin America before officially convoking the inter-American trade union conference. For one thing, the Argentine CGT, which was supposed to coordinate the preliminary work of the conference in cooperation with the Chileans and the Peruvians, could no longer be asked to undertake this task. The preparatory meeting which had been scheduled for Lima during the month of February was therefore cancelled and a tentative meeting was set for the latter part of April in Venezuela—with the intention of shifting to the labor organization of that country (CTV) the role that had been assigned originally to Argentina. However, this Venezuela meeting also did not materialize and it was not until the ILO's annual conference in June 1947 in Geneva that Latin American trade union representatives got together and decided to go ahead with their plans.

The meeting in Geneva was attended by representatives from Chile, Peru, Mexico, Uruguay, Venezuela, and Ecuador. The same delegates, plus representatives from Cuba, met with me in New York a few weeks later. It was unanimously agreed to hold the inter-American trade union conference in Lima during the last week of November—a date that was later postponed, for the last time, to the second week of January 1948.

Meanwhile, I had resumed making contacts, trying to firm up the commitments of those unions which had pledged participation and looking for additional supporters in other countries.

In Argentina, most of the democratic unions that had remained outside the Perón-controlled CGT banded together in a Labor Committee for Independent Trade Union Action (COASI), which immediately pledged its participation in the proposed conference.

The AFL had kept in touch with individual Cuban labor leaders, some of whom held office in local unions or national federations. The Cuban CTC was controlled by Communists and was considered one of the strongest bulwarks of the CTAL. However, early in 1947 I had conferences in Washington with two leaders of the Trade Union Committee of the Auténtico Popular Party, Eusebio Mujal and Francisco Aguirre. They assured me that, together with leaders of the so-called independent unions (CONI) and with the support of Minister of Labor Carlos Prío Socarrás (who later became President of the Republic), they would soon gain control of the CTC and would take part in the inter-American conference.

The Confederation of Labor of the Dominican Republic (CDT) was still a dues-paying member of the CTAL. As a matter of fact, Lombardo Toledano had even extolled Trujillo for his "progressive" policies—which permitted the Communists to operate in the open and other dissenting elements to organize an "opposition" labor party. All this soon turned out to be a tragic farce. However, the possibility of having a national labor organization quit the CTAL in order to join our proposed group had to be fully explored. So we took the CDT's assurances of "independence and democratic faith" at their face value and listed it as another prospective participant in the Lima conference.

In the spring of 1947 I went to Central America—my first trip to that part of our hemisphere. In Costa Rica the Confederation "Rerum Novarum" did not have to be convinced. Its leader, Father Benjamin Núñez, had attended the ILO meeting in Mexico City and pledged his cooperation. The "Rerum Novarum," organized in 1945 in opposition to the Communist-dominated confederation, was led by a group of young enthusiastic workers. Among them was a baby-faced, self-educated youth from the province of Guanacaste, Luis Alberto Monge, who was destined to play a leading role in the trade union and political life of the Americas.

At that time, there were no labor leaders in Honduras that we could approach for our purpose. The few leaders I was able to see in Guatemala were either afraid of the Communists or were noncommittal. Similar conditions prevailed in Nicaragua. Those three countries were set aside as first business for the new inter-American organization we were preparing to launch. In El Salvador, on the other hand, I found at least one group of trade unionists who, although not in control of any sizable organization, expressed the desire to help and promised to come to the conference.

On my way back from this Central American trip I stopped in Mexico where some unfavorable complications had arisen.

As I have already stated, the largest and most representative Mexican labor organization, the CTM, was the main support of CTAL, with Lombardo Toledano in the dual role of leader of both groups. A movement was on foot within the CTM to end his leadership, but it had not yet reached the surface and it did not look as if anything concrete would happen before our contemplated conference. As it turned out, it was while we were meeting in Lima, on January 8, 1948, that Lombardo Toledano was expelled from the CTM. Meanwhile, the Electrical Workers' Union of Senator Rojas had pulled away from us and Morones's CROM had assumed a dubious role whose objectives became clear only when, unfortunately, it was too late to head them off.

Luis Morones, having been such a leading figure in the old COPA, could not resign himself to play a secondary role in the planning and organization of the new inter-American labor group. When I returned to Mexico he avoided me, but I learned from our friends of the National Proletarian Confederation (CNP) that he had been strongly criticizing the AFL—even charging that Matthew Woll, who was supposed to be his old friend and pal, had "betrayed" him. Morones was also critical of our break with Perón. He was not the only Latin American labor leader who "regretted" our denunciation of the Argentine CGT. But how could we exclude Morones from the Lima conference on the sole ground of his disagreement with one aspect of AFL policy?

Problems also arose in Colombia. The Colombian CTC, of which Juan C. Lara was the General Secretary, had at its August 1946 Medellín convention expelled the Communist faction, which subsequently held a rump meeting of its own and tried to be recognized as the legitimate CTC. After an exhaustive investigation that lasted more than two months and called for the presentation of records, membership lists, financial receipts, etc., the Minister of Labor concluded that the anti-Communist group had a clear majority of 65 bona-fide delegates and recommended that it be recognized as the legal CTC of Colombia. Meanwhile, the funds of the CTC had been frozen and its headquarters padlocked.

In December 1946, while Lara was absent from Colombia, having been invited to the United States by the AFL Free Trade Union Committee, a sector of the non-Communist group—followers of Liberal Party leader Dr. Jorge Eliecer Gaitán—made a pact with the Communists and joined them in the formation of a CTC provisional committee. Upon the recommendation of the Minister of Labor, who belonged to the "gaitanistas," the government issued a decree on February 10, 1947, giving legal recognition to the new group. The top leaders of the anti-Communist CTC, Lara and Medina, apprised of the decree in advance, tried vainly to persuade conservative President Ospina Pérez to withhold the decision at least until after they had a chance to call a convention.

What was left of the anti-Communist CTC refused to accept the Liberal-Communist pact and announced a fight to the finish to be carried to the next CTC convention. Of course, Lara and his followers counted on, and promptly received, support from the AFL Free Trade Union Committee.

During May 1947 the CTC, led by the Communist-Liberal coalition, called a general strike of a political nature designed to force the resignation of the Ospina Government. However, the strike was a failure and resulted in loss of prestige and influence for the Communists, who had been the main force behind it. The government suspended the legal recognition of the CTC, but a court order issued in July restored it. That was the situation when I arrived in Colombia a month later on the first leg of a whirlwind South American tour to tie up the last remaining loose ends before the inter-American labor conference was convened.

I soon realized that unless the Liberal Party leadership instructed its trade union members to break with the Communists, any individual or small rebellion, such as the one proclaimed by the Lara-Medina group, would be doomed to failure. Furthermore, the Liberal Party leadership then in command expected discipline, and those who broke it would be blacklisted for top posts in the labor movement. The reader may wonder how a labor movement in a nontotalitarian state could be subject to such strict discipline from a political party. But that was then the situation in Colombia, Peru, Venezuela, and other countries on my itinerary. I had to see things as they were no matter how distasteful, if I wanted to accomplish my mission.

The leading Colombian newspaper El Tiempo, owned by former President Eduardo Santos, was voicing the sentiments of the Liberal Party faction opposed to cooperation with the Communists inside the CTC. It gave full coverage to my press interview and when the Communist-controlled CTC unleashed virulent attacks against me and the AFL, editor Enrique Santos, brother of Eduardo, strongly defended us. Following are excerpts from the August 15 editorial signed "Caliban," the pen name of Enrique Santos:

The CTC has published an alleged rebuttal to the statements of Mr. Romualdi, representative of the American Federation of Labor, in which it tries to present this distinguished citizen and the AFL as capitalist agents. This stupid assertion is not worthy of denial. The only thing the CTC has succeeded in accomplishing with its declaration is to bring into the open its Communist affiliation which it has vainly tried to cover up. . . .

The AFL has in its ranks the majority of American organized workers and has shown itself to be an efficient force in the defense of the working class. However, being zealous of the true interests of its members, it has closed the door to the Communists and to their destructive tactics. At present, in almost all the American trade unions there is in progress a purge of Communist elements who would otherwise have captured the key positions as they did here in Colombia.

While maintaining my contacts with the Lara-Medina group and encouraging them to continue their fight to oust the Communists, I found additional support among two other groups: the independent Federation of Employees of Bogotá and the newly organized (under Catholic Church sponsorship) Unión de Trabajadores de Colombia (UTC). The Federation of Employees was a white-collar organization that—consistent with the Latin American distinction between *empleados* and *obreros*—remained aloof from what we in the United States call the blue-collar unions. "Employees" considered themselves a class apart from and superior to manual workers. The Federation's Executive Board honored me with a reception at which it was agreed that they would be represented at the forthcoming inter-American conference.

The most important find of my visit to Bogotá was, however, the UTC. Hardly one year old, it had already gained the support of a group of dedicated, enthusiastic young workers, led then by Justiniano Espinosa, who later went to ILO headquarters in Geneva in charge of Latin American trade union relations. They were few, but promising. They even lacked legal recognition because Colombian labor law did not permit, at that time, more than one nationwide central labor organization. Against the advice of many, including the anti-Communist Liberals who were up in arms against the Church's attempt to invade the labor field through its sponsorship of UTC, I decided to offer the UTC friendship and moral support. The UTC leaders were extremely responsive and pledged outright to come to Lima for the inter-American conference. Today the UTC is unquestionably the dominant national labor organization of Colombia.

The next stop was Ecuador. The day before my arrival in Quito, the father of CTE President Gonzalo Maldonado Jarrín passed away. I made arrangements to attend the funeral—a gesture which was much appreciated by the Maldonado family and friends. I was not told, however, that after the church service the funeral cortege would proceed on foot to the cemetery, almost three miles away. Dr. Juan Isaac Lovato discreetly suggested that perhaps walking such a distance would be too much for me; but I spurned the suggestion and took my place among the trade union notables. Well, walking up hill, down hill, up hill again, and so on, at an altitude of over nine thousand feet soon became really too much for me— a middle-aged, somewhat overweight sea-level softy. My legs became shaky, my head swam. I collapsed and had to be carried back.

The CTE was still under the same cautious Socialist leadership I had met the year before. The Free Trade Union Committee had sent them some financial help, which "prudently," according to their own expression, was not deposited in the treasury of the Confederation but was disbursed independently by a committee of four men of "high character and responsibility" who gave me a very detailed account. The help that really gained prestige for the AFL was, however, the statement issued the previous year by President William Green protesting the contemplated move to dissolve the CTE as had been recommended by Congress to President José María Velasco Ibarra. It was freely admitted to me in Quito that the AFL statement had been the decisive factor in preventing President Ibarra from issuing the decree. But the danger had reappeared again and although the CTE was a CTAL affiliate, Lombardo Toledano had so far kept silent. Our friends wanted very much to have the AFL come to their rescue again. I wired Matthew Woll who promptly sent the following cable to President Ibarra:

Greatly disturbed by reports that very existence of the Confederation of Labor of Ecuador is threatened by resolution of National Assembly calling for its dissolution, seven and one-half million members of American Federation of Labor appeal to Your Excellency to prevent promulgation of such law which would be distinct violation of trade-union clauses of Act of Chapultepec enacted for specific purpose of guaranteeing freedom of labor organization in every country of our Hemisphere.

This and additional pressure resolved the problem again in favor of the CTE.

Bernardo Ibáñez came up from Chile to join me in Peru, where— together with Arturo Sabroso and other leaders of the CTP—we drafted the call for the inter-American conference to be issued under the joint signature of the Chilean CTCh and the Peruvian CTP, and approved the list of the organizations to be invited. We were not sure, however, of the participation of the Brazilians, whose initially copious correspondence had slowed down to a trickle. I was therefore asked to go home by way of Brazil, stopping off in Bolivia where the labor situation remained confused. The Peruvians, for reasons of prestige, wanted very much to have a delegation from Bolivia—their backdoor neighbor.

In La Paz I found that the Bolivian Labor Confederation was definitely and completely under Communist control. The tin miners, however, were independent and still led by elements of the outlawed MNR, such as Juan Lechín and Mario Torres. But they were unable to meet with me, and I had to deal with two minor trade union leaders, one a printer and the other a chauffeur—both strongly anti-Communist but also anti-MNR. We badly needed the Bolivian flag at Lima and these two carried it quite well. But when, in 1952, the MNR regained power, we clearly recognized the mistake we had made.

Today's jet travelers, accustomed to crossing the South American continent from Peru to Brazil in a few hours nonstop, cannot possibly imagine what it was to make the same flight twenty years ago in a two-motor propeller plane. First there was the trip from Lima to La Paz, with a stop at beautiful Arequipa. The Andean peaks were almost scraped by the bumpy but sturdy little planes, struggling to get up and over the crests. But once over the Bolivian plateau a passenger, with the oxygen hose in his mouth, could relax and enjoy a wondrous vista of endless Indian villages, Lake Titicaca and the Illimani peak looming ahead—like a mythological giant threatening to bar any further progress. Then came the descent from La Paz to Santa Cruz, thousands upon thousands of feet below, through frightening gorges close to the side of the mountains! But the little DC-3's always went through, and once out in the open, toward Santa Cruz, the passengers would quickly forget the upset stomachs caused by the air pockets.

What has happened, I wonder, to the little, cute, colonial hotel, outside Santa Cruz? Those who had to change to the PanAm plane for Corumbà, Campo Grande, and São Paulo were housed there overnight. I hope "progress" has not obliterated it. Santa Cruz, now a bustling city, would not be the same without that eighteenth-century jewel.

From Santa Cruz eastward, nothing but jungle—dense, green, forbidding. With the passenger seated next to me, I engaged in a sort of game guessing how many minutes would pass before seeing another clearing or another Indian hut alongside a river. Finally, we arrived at Campo Grande, on the southwestern edge of Mato Grosso; but what a surprise when we learned that for some reason which I can't recall there would be no plane for São Paulo for at least another two or three days. I became really excited. Three days in the wild west of Brazil—for that was exactly the reputation of that frontier town, little changed from the days of the *bandeirantes,* the early nineteenth-century pioneers who pushed west on horseback and covered wagon.

At the PanAm office I was told that I could get a room at the local hotel. At least, that was what they called it. It was a combination lodging-restaurant-saloon. My room was on the ground floor and could be reached only through the saloon. It was unlit, almost unfurnished save for a brass bed and a washbasin. As night came the saloon filled up with noisy "western" characters—boots, six-shooters and a week's growth of beard. Every time I have a chance now to view Kitty Russell's Long Branch Saloon on the Gunsmoke television show, I can't help remembering my own "western" experience in Campo Grande. Well, this city slicker had a rough night. I was not able to undress, to lay my head on what passed for a pillow, or to snatch even a few winks.

The next morning I went to the PanAm office. Pleading, threatening, cajoling, I finally got permission to move to the guest house reserved for the crew. Needless to say, I ate well, slept well, and read a lot. The lure of the wild west for this dude dissipated rapidly in the short experience of a single night.

The problem I found in Rio resulted from the Brazilian labor legislation which did not permit national trade union federations or confederations to affiliate to any international organization except by an act of Congress and only under specific recommendation of the President. Furthermore, the unions could not spend a cent for the expenses of delegates going abroad without the approval of the Minister of Labor. Obviously, there was no time to go through this procedure before the date set for the Lima conference. The only solution was to get the Minister of Labor's and the President's provisional permission pending action on the part of Congress. Helped by most of the Brazilian national trade union leaders who were genuinely anxious to join with us, I sought their agreement, but the Minister of Labor and the Presidential entourage wanted to know many, many things before committing themselves. Above all, they wanted to know the position of the American Embassy and the United States Government vis-à-vis this proposed Lima meeting. Although I could not speak for the State Department, I assured the Brazilians that my demarche was favored by Washington. In a few days I was promised that a large Brazilian delegation would attend the Lima conference. On September 4 I was received by President Gaspar Dutra, who himself made the announcement.

After that, I rushed home to New York to keep an important date—my marriage to Miriam Blecher Friedman, with whom I continue to share a wonderful and most happy life.

In the course of my address at the 1946 AFL Convention in Chicago, I made a strong criticism of the State Department that caused quite an uproar in Washington. My remarks were:

> Our work in trying to reach an understanding with our brothers in Latin America . . . extends to the wider field of democratic defense of the American continent and the defense of the American way of life.
>
> I hope that these objectives will be taken into consideration by those responsible for our foreign policy, and particularly by those responsible for the Latin American section of our policy. They have for too long a time remained silent and continue to remain so. If not openly allied, they are definitely supporting groups in Latin America who are enemies of the American way of life and who are followers of the Communist Party line."

Although in Washington itself and in the field some medium-level Foreign Service officers were sympathetic with our efforts to create an anti-Communist hemispheric labor organization, no official support had come from higher-ups, especially from the Department's International Labor Division. Perhaps this was due to their desire not to take sides between the AFL and the CIO. The latter group, as I have already noted, was a member of the WFTU and considered itself bound to the CTAL of Lombardo Toledano—the Communist front designed to control the Latin American labor movement. This State Department neutrality, while it did not adversely affect our work in such countries as Venezuela and Peru, where the official U.S. position was of no concern to the local labor movement, did handicap our plans in the many countries where the labor movement was dependent on the government, which was careful not to encourage anything that would displease the American Embassy. During those days the close relationship with the U.S. government created by the war had not yet started to wear out.

Following the publication of the AFL report on Argentina, Spruille Braden, then Assistant Secretary of State for Latin American Affairs, began to show a keen interest in the AFL plans for Latin America. On April 3, 1947, I accompanied Bernardo Ibáñez, who was passing through Washington en route to Europe, to Mr. Braden's office. He received us flanked by his assistant John Dreier (later appointed Ambassador) and Dan Horowitz, chief of the Department's International Labor Division. The results of our conversation were reported in a memorandum, dated April 15, which I drafted specifically for Woll, Meany, and Dubinsky. It read in part:

Bernardo Ibáñez expressed his views on the increasing dangers that Communist influence in Latin American labor unions represents to the security of the democratic institutions in the Western Hemisphere and specifically to the security of the United States. He made some pointed remarks on the situation in his own country, Chile, and criticized the attitude of those American diplomatic representatives who still regard Communists as democratic types and consequently view with suspicion if not open hostility attempts of antitotalitarian labor elements to oppose them.

Mr. Braden replied, openly and specifically, that the attitude of the State Department toward our efforts to combat Communist and other totalitarian influences in Latin American labor will from now on be not only sympathetic but cooperative. He informed us that the International Labor Division of the Department had undergone a radical change and that in the future it will be guided by different policies.

He went even further by pledging to me and to Ibáñez whatever assistance (compatible with the obvious limitations of nondirect government interference and diplomatic propriety) we may require in our work in preparation of the forthcoming inter-American labor conference.

Although I have had several occasions in the past to discuss with Mr. Braden the issues of Communism and totalitarianism in Latin America and the plans and hopes of the AFL in this respect, he never expressed himself so completely in agreement with our plans as he did in the April 3 conference. It is also significant, in my opinion, that he made those statements in the presence of those of his assistants who are directly concerned with social and labor developments in the Western Hemisphere.

A couple of months later Spruille Braden left the State Department. He was replaced by Ambassador Norman Armour, a senior career diplomat whom I had met in 1941–1942 when he was heading our Embassy in Buenos Aires. I wanted to be reassured that, as far as the AFL's Latin American policies were concerned, Armour's view would not differ from that of his predecessor. I requested an interview, which was granted for the morning of July 8. The results were most satisfactory.

When informed that I was planning to leave for a tour of South American countries early in August to complete the preparations for the inter-American trade union conference, Armour asked Dreier to communicate with the American embassies in the countries I planned to visit, instructing them to give me all possible assistance. Further details were worked out the following day at a meeting arranged at the Assistant Secretary's own suggestion.

Bernardo Ibáñez, Victor Raul Haya de la Torre, and other prominent sponsors of the Lima conference advised me that it would be appropriate and highly desirable for a few leading authorities on inter-American relations to openly express their views on the importance of this Lima conference in advance of its opening date. Accordingly, I sent a letter to a number of distinguished Americans, explaining to them:

For the first time, trade unions from Latin America will discuss their problems jointly with trade unions from the United States. Also, for the first time, an attempt will be made to put Latin American trade unionism on a nonpolitical basis; to give it a constructive purpose; to make it realize that it has a great opportunity in performing a cardinal role in the social and economic development of the less advanced nations in the Western Hemisphere. It is also our sincere hope to make the labor movement in Latin America, until recently dominated by the totalitarian forces of Communism or Fascism, a bulwark of socially conscious democracy, a link in the chain of Pan-American solidarity, a force to be relied upon in the strengthening of the American way of life.

Strong, favorable response came from Nelson A. Rockefeller, Adolf A. Berle, Spruille Braden, and others. Sumner Welles, replying from his Florida home, stated that he was "deeply interested in the objectives sought by the Conference now to open shortly in Lima." Much welcomed throughout Latin America was the following response from Norman Thomas, which was published in full in many of the leading newspapers of the region:

As I look toward a new year which has all too few signs of hope, I rejoice at the news of the forthcoming Inter-American Trade Union Conference which will open in Lima on January 10th.

It will be a tragedy which may contribute to a catastrophe if in this world the workers are given no choice except allegiance to regional and divided labor unions, or no unions, on the one hand; and, on the other, allegiance to a federation dominated by fifth column labor organizations of communist totalitarian states. Even in a democratic socialist world, there will be a place for inde-

pendent labor unions. They will be functionally necessary and they will constitute a protection against the omnipotent and omni-competent state. How much
more necessary are such independent unions in achieving the world we want!

It is perhaps the bitterest irony of our times that we should see a numerically
powerful federation of trade unions which is in its fundamentals, the creature of
a dictatorship and the apologist for slave labor.

Confronted with such a spectacle, angels might weep. Men have to act, and the
formation of an inter-American conference or federation of free trade unions is
the best single action that can immediately be taken. Such a federation could
give new meaning and value to Pan-Americanism and make Pan-Americanism
more than ever a force for a worldwide fraternity of workers.

Meanwhile, I received good news from Cuba and Venezuela. The
promise made to me earlier in the year by Mujal and Aguirre that the
Communists would be purged from the CTC was kept. A new and democratic Cuban trade union leadership was in command. Its first act, at the
May 1947 convention, was to break relations with the CTAL. Later, the
CTC sent Vicente Rubiera, leader of the telephone workers, as fraternal
delegate to the convention of the Confederation of Labor of Venezuela,
which met in Caracas, November 14–18. The CTV, too, decided to break
with Lombardo Toledano. On the other hand, the Communists and the
Peronistas intensified their attacks against the AFL, the Lima Conference,
and its chief organizers, adding "international adventurer" and "imperialist" to the long list of pejoratives they customarily attached to my
name.

George Meany had planned to head the U.S. delegation. He had already
prepared his policy address with the specific purpose of making it the
cornerstone of the new inter-American labor edifice. But at the last moment he was prevented from going by other urgent business. His place as
chairman of the delegation was taken by Philip Hannah, secretary of the
Ohio State Federation of Labor and former Assistant Secretary of Labor.[1]

The U.S. delegation assembled in Washington on January 5 for a final
briefing from the AFL leadership. The following day we left for Peru.

From a window of the mezzanine floor of the Hotel Bolívar, together
with Jules Dubois of *The Chicago Tribune,* Milton Bracker of *The New
York Times,* and Jerry Hannifin of *Time,* I was gazing at Lima's Plaza
San Martín. It was the afternoon of January 10, the day set for the inauguration of the Inter-American Conference. The Communists and their
fellow travelers were holding a demonstration to protest against the
conference and particularly against the presence of the North American

delegates. How many would they be? I was worried. We saw a band, a few flags, some posters—and heard a great deal of noise—but when the parade was over and the marchers assembled around the San Martín statue for the speeches we could count not more than three hundred participants. "A complete flop," Dubois exclaimed.

Soon a counterdemonstration developed. From every street leading into Plaza San Martín came hundreds of trade unionists belonging to the CTP. They converged on the center of the square where the Communist group was quickly cordoned off for their protection by mounted police. The counterdemonstrators started waving white handkerchiefs, the gesture of adherence to the democratic APRA party. Then the police charged, opened a path and led the besieged Communists away to safety. The first battle had been won!

Arturo Sabroso, president of the host CTP, was designated permanent chairman of the conference. Bernardo Ibáñez was selected keynote speaker on behalf of the organizing committee. The inauguration—a solemn ceremony without precedent in inter-American labor annals—took place in the Municipal Theater, which was packed to the rafters with workers and peasants, political leaders and diplomats, city officials and other notables. In addition to more than 5,000 people who had managed to squeeze into the theater, over 10,000 flocked outside listening to the proceedings, which were broadcast by short- and medium-wave radio and carried by amplifiers to the assembled crowd. Many distinguished guests, including the APRA founder and Jefe (chief) Victor Raul Haya de la Torre and U.S. and Latin American diplomats, witnessed the opening ceremonies.

The AFL delegation, "diplomacy wise"—as *Time* magazine reported [2]—remained backstage. The spotlight focused on Chile's Bernardo Ibáñez. In his opening address he cried: "We reject Lombardo Toledano and Stalin. We are building hemispheric union in spite of both of them. We may have to fight to organize but we are ready to fight."

Philip Hannah had been designated as one of the conference Vice-Presidents and as such he was scheduled to speak at the opening ceremony on behalf of the U.S. delegation. His turn came toward the end. His address was practically the one that George Meany had intended to deliver himself. Since Hannah could not speak Spanish, it was arranged that I would follow with the Spanish translation, section by section, as he was delivering it. I sensed that the building of a creditable, viable alliance between the workers of the United States and those of Latin America hinged on the success of that speech. We had to make it, therefore, at the very first try, that night. The audience was already gripped with enthusiasm. We had to bring it to an even higher pitch. Phil's delivery was masterful—as a good trouper he had rehearsed and rehearsed it until he had almost learned the entire speech by heart. Finally we came to the last sentences, which I repeated in Spanish with all the emphasis at my command:

We want a democratic inter-Americanism without imperialism. We want better living and working conditions for the workers—for all the workers—of the Western Hemisphere. We want the advancement of social justice and the protection of the rights of labor. We want democracy strengthened and extended. We want to see, in our own time, the Four Freedoms of the Atlantic Charter become a living reality. We want to see our America, the New World, become the unconquerable bulwark of human rights, social progress, and true Christian civilization.

Pandemonium rocked the theater—applause, cheering, stomping, waving, shouting of "Viva America, Viva AFL, Viva Hannah!" He was embraced, hugged, and kissed by everybody on the platform. Many even shed tears. A new chapter in inter-American relations had begun. The Pan-Americanism of the working people had become a reality.

At the beginning of the next day's session, held in the chamber of the Peruvian House of Representatives, the Credentials Committee reported that 156 delegates from 17 countries were attending the conference: 14 delegations with full powers; two fraternal delegations (Dominican Republic and Venezuela) ; and one observer, Ecuador.

The Committee for the Organization of a National Confederation of Labor in Uruguay, which represented the majority of organized workers in that country, sent a telegram pledging full support and immediate affiliation as soon as its organization work was completed. In addition, a warm telegram of greetings, which was interpreted as a promise of future affiliation, was received from Percy Bengough, president of the Canadian Trades and Labor Congress.

The Credentials Committee report was unanimously approved with the exception of the following recommendation on the Argentine delegate:

Alfredo Fidanza, representing the Workers' Committee for Independent Trade Union Action (COASI) . This organization comprises the minority of Argentine labor that has refused to submit to government control and is still valiantly struggling for survival. The COASI delegate has not been able to enter Peru for lack of a passport, which presumably he could not obtain in his own country. The Committee recommends to seat delegate Fidanza, considering him present by proxy given collectively to all the delegations present.

At this point, delegate Luis Morones (representing CROM of Mexico) objected. He wanted to know why the CGT of Argentina had not been invited, and why the Organizing Committee had permitted itself to be influenced by the AFL on Argentina. He claimed that the conference was being masterminded by Romualdi, "an agent of the State Department."

Protests came from different sectors of the chamber. Some delegates cried "Shame!" When calm was restored, Morones methodically repeated, in what was obviously a premeditated action, his accusations, adding:

"There are in this hall, delegates who have been bought by Serafino Romualdi."

"The names! the names!"—replied many, standing up, shouting.

I asked for the floor. Many of my American colleagues tried to get me to sit down, not to pay attention. . . . But I knew better. I immediately realized that unless that accusation was nailed down, right there, as a calumny, a barefaced lie, the Conference would lose its moral authority.

"Brother Chairman"—I said in a deliberate, calm manner—"I move that you appoint a Committee of Honor, right away. I put myself at the Committee's disposal. I assume that Brother Morones will do the same. If the Committee finds me guilty of having paid or bribed in any way, form, or manner, directly or indirectly, any of the delegates present here in this convention, I pledge to withdraw as a delegate and to retire from further trade union activity in Latin America."

The motion was carried. The session was suspended. When it resumed in the afternoon the Committee reported that Morones had refused to appear before it, that he had left the conference, and that his name had been stricken from the list of delegates. May I add, modesty aside, that I received a standing ovation and, in typical Latin American fashion, I was embraced by many.

The following days were devoted to the discussion of the reports of various committees beginning with the one on "Analysis of the Labor Movement in the Western Hemisphere." Bernardo Ibáñez of Chile was its rapporteur. He concluded by recommending the organization of an Inter-American Confederation of Labor (CIT—Confederación Interamericana de Trabajadores). The motion was supported by all the delegations present and was approved by acclamation. The CIT was born. The historic event took place on the night of January 12, 1948.

The convention adopted a number of resolutions, two of which were of international significance. The first called for the organization of a new International Federation of Trade Unions to supplant the existing Communist-dominated World Federation of Trade Unions, whose program was proclaimed "incompatible with the policies and the democratic program of the CIT." The second instructed the Executive Committee to invite the American Federation of Labor to join with the CIT in setting up a committee "to investigate, at some future date, the working conditions existing in the Canal Zone with a view to presenting a solution that would end, once and for all, existing discriminations."

At the final session on January 13 the following officers of the new organization were elected unanimously: President, Bernardo Ibáñez of Chile; Vice-Presidents, George Meany of the United States, Bert M. Jewell of the United States, Arturo Sabroso of Peru, Enrique Rangel of Mexico, Juan C. Lara of Colombia, Francisco Aguirre of Cuba, C. Cabral de Mello of Brazil, Luis A. Monge of Costa Rica, Leo E. Eleazer of Dutch Guiana, and one member to be designated by the Confederation of Labor of Venezuela when it affiliated formally; Assistant to the President and Secretary of Economic and Social Affairs, Isidoro Godoy of Chile; Secretary of Organization, Eusebio Mujal of Cuba; Administrative and Financial Secretary, Arturo Jáuregui Hurtado of Peru; and Secretary of International Relations, Serafino Romualdi of the United States.

The officers of the CIT were then introduced to the public—a multitude of more than twenty-five thousand workers assembled in the square facing the House of Representatives.

On Thursday, January 15, part of the American delegation joined in a visit to the industrial village of Vitarte, in the vicinity of Lima, the scene of a famous early Peruvian strike where several workers were killed by the police. The "Vitarte Martyrs" are honored annually by the CTP. After having spent some time inspecting a textile plant and talking to the workers, the delegation took part in an impromptu mass meeting in the village square, where the whole population had assembled. A group of workers, headed by an Indian woman, approached Philip Hannah and presented him with a bouquet of flowers, to express, as she said "our gratitude and joy for having been honored by a visit of North American trade union brothers."

Commented Sabroso: "Remember, this is the first time that visitors from the United States have received flowers from Peruvian workers! . . ."

The New York Times of January 26 carried a special dispatch from Buenos Aires, which I consider a fitting epilogue to our Lima battle. It speaks for itself:

BUENOS AIRES, Jan. 24 (Delayed) —Luis Morones, Mexican labor leader whose charges against the American Federation of Labor on the Argentine issue were unanimously rejected by the Lima Conference, received a hero's welcome here last night.

Following a two-hour audience with President Juan D. Perón, he was a guest of honor at an Argentine Labor Confederation rally at Luna Park—the Madison Square Garden of Buenos Aires.

The meeting was regarded in some quarters as completing the circumstantial case for those who are sure that President Perón's labor movement and Señor Morones schemed in advance to wreck the conference at Lima.

The Mexican leader had told how he had risen at the Lima meeting to oppose the anti-Argentine resolution and how he had accused Serafino Romualdi, Latin American representative of the AFL, of having "rigged the conference just as Romualdi had rigged the AFL condemnation of Argentine labor a year ago."

Señor Morones added that he had been branded a liar at Lima only because "I dared to impugn the reputation of a member of the United States delegation."

Notes

1. Other members of the AFL group besides the author were James M. Duffy, President of the National Brotherhood of Operative Potters, and Thomas J. Lloyd, substituting for Secretary Patrick Gorman of the Amalgamated Meat Cutters and Butcher Workmen of North America. Other U.S. representatives were Bert M. Jewell, for the Railway Labor Executives' Association, and Roy Brown, Vice-President of the International Association of Machinists.

2. *Time*, January 19, 1948.

VI

The Life of CIT

THE DELEGATES to the founding convention of the Confederación Interamericana de Trabajadores had hardly returned to their homes when Interior Minister General Manuel Odría issued a decree forbidding operation of the new organization on Peruvian territory. The government claimed that the CIT had meddled in domestic political matters. The move was clearly aimed at the APRA party, which had openly supported and enthusiastically embraced the CIT as its own offspring.

Consultation among the newly elected members of the CIT Executive Board led to the decision to transfer the organization's headquarters to Santiago, Chile. They were inaugurated on March 27, 1948, with a ceremony attended by representatives of Chilean and Peruvian labor organizations and by representatives of the Chilean government. Previously, President Gabriel González Videla had assured CIT President Bernardo Ibáñez that his government would extend to the inter-American labor organization all the facilities needed to function on Chilean territory.

Working at CIT's Santiago headquarters, in addition to President Bernardo Ibáñez, were Secretaries Isidoro Godoy Bravo and Arturo Jáuregui. The latter had moved from Peru in order to devote his full-time activities to the organization as its administrative secretary.

In March 1948 the first issue of *Informativo Obrero Interamericano*, the CIT publication in the Spanish language, was published. An English-language monthly, the *Inter-American Labor News*, was prepared in

81

Washington mostly for distribution in the United States, Canada, and the Caribbean area. Its first issue also appeared in March 1948.

Learning how North Americans and Latin Americans could coexist and work together inside the CIT was not a simple task. We wanted to make the new organization a live entity, capable of functioning every day, week, and month of the year. Different mentalities and, above all, varying conceptions of the role of organized labor in society and conflicting basic economic philosophies had to be reconciled. Latin American labor was still committed predominantly to statist solutions; North American labor was a firm believer in free enterprise.

The first clash over this all-important issue took place at the Lima conference itself. The Committee on Economic Program submitted a report calling for economic planning, proposing socialistic methods, and criticizing the "imperialistic manifestations of U.S. economic policy in Latin America." Bert M. Jewell, the U.S. member of the Committee, did not sign the report. I felt, however, that this mild manifestation of dissent was not enough. The U.S. delegation met and I was designated to move, at the plenary session, to refer the report to the incoming Executive Committee with instructions to modify it and make it acceptable to all CIT-affiliated organizations which did not believe in state socialism.

During the debate that followed the introduction of my motion, the North Americans made it very clear that they did not object to any member organization advocating, in its own country, the adoption of measures that might be contrary to the economic views of the U.S. labor movement, provided that no attempt was made to impose such views, via a majority vote, on trade unions of other countries. Bernardo Ibáñez supported our position by stating, "We are absolutely not going to use CIT as a political instrument . . . the way Lombardo Toledano and the Communists used CTAL." The motion was carried by unanimous vote with the specific understanding that the CIT, as a body, would refrain from advocating economic and social theories that might divide the membership; it would concentrate, instead, on practical measures to better the conditions of the workers of the Americas and to defend and strengthen democracy and freedom.

As CIT Secretary of International Relations, I felt that the time had come to ask the United Nations, the Pan American Union, and the International Labor Organization to recognize the CIT as a labor organization of international standing. This matter was discussed at the first meeting of the CIT Executive Committee, which took place in Lima immediately after the adjournment of the conference. President Bernardo Ibáñez was asked to submit to the forthcoming IX Conference of American States, scheduled to open March 30, 1948, in Bogotá, a memorandum on labor's proposed role in the reorganized inter-American system.

The CIT memorandum, which was circulated among the delegates during the first week of the Conference, requested that the organic pact of the inter-American system be amended to include "nongovernmental organizations, including responsible, democratic, solvent labor organizations." Such an amendment would enable the CIT—the only democratic inter-American labor organization—to enjoy consultative status and thus serve as spokesman for the workers of the hemisphere, representing their interests before the governments of the American republics. The CIT memorandum further developed this position, requesting provision for the tripartite representation of labor, management, and government in future inter-American conferences. Thus as early as 1948 the CIT presented the argument, which has now become so accepted, that the success of any program of economic cooperation must depend upon the full and equal participation of all the major sectors of society.

Another important item on the Bogotá agenda was a Declaration of Human Rights. In its memorandum, CIT stated that the proposed Declaration must also provide for the exercise and regulation of collective rights, such as the right to organize and strike, and the rights of petition, assembly, free speech, etc. Similarly, the CIT declared that the Declaration should concern itself with man's collective duties in the struggle for the protection of human freedom and dignity and for the defense of democracy. Finally, the memorandum called upon the nations of the hemisphere to sponsor a program for the development of social services, specifically citing such areas as social security, protection of working women and youth, and full employment.

The Bogotá meeting had been played up in advance in the press of the Western Hemisphere as a milestone in the life of the inter-American system: its structure was to be overhauled, a new charter was to be formulated. However, the basic agreement on inter-American economic cooperation, prepared by the Economic and Social Council (IA-ECOSOC) as a working document for the conference, completely ignored any role for organized labor within the reorganized system.

Since the CIT could not submit formal proposals it had to limit itself to the circulation of documents on an individual basis among the various delegations attending the Bogotá Conference. Our affiliated organizations were urged to request from their respective governments the inclusion of one or more labor advisers in their delegations. I contacted the State Department but was told that "lack of housing in Bogotá" prevented any addition to the membership of the appointed United States delegation. I entered a protest against the exclusion of a labor representative, pointing out that "inasmuch as the Bogotá Conference is mainly economic in character, the availability of the on-the-spot advice of representatives of organized labor would be greatly beneficial to the members of the United States delegation."

In another very important matter, however, my first efforts as CIT "Foreign Minister" were auspicious. The State Department informed me that, according to the draft of the Organic Pact, the Governing Board of the Pan American Union "would be authorized to enter into agreements with governmental and nongovernmental groups," but that it was "unlikely" that the Conference would "take any action in this respect other than to enter into such agreements, leaving it to the Board to execute this authority." Translated from "gobbledygook," this meant that the CIT could get consultative status, and that was what eventually happened despite backstage intrigue and obstructions by hostile totalitarian Latin American regimes.

Among the few popular leaders of Colombia, Jorge Eliecer Gaitán was the one who had won the most affection and understanding. A fairly young lawyer, only forty-seven years old, he had been one of the candidates in the presidential election of 1946 and was at that time one of the top leaders of the Liberal Party.

Although the Communists surrounded him with friendliness and flattery, Gaitán, after the pact his followers had made in 1946, maintained an independent and firm attitude toward them. On the eve of the inauguration of the IX Pan American Conference he publicly denounced and repudiated plans to sabotage the Conference as "acts against democracy and the unity of the Americas."

Bernardo Ibáñez had an appointment with Gaitán for Friday, April 9. "My intention," he wrote to me later, "was to discuss with him the problem of trade unionism in Colombia and to put him on guard against the treacherous conduct of the Communists in Chile and the Americas." But less than four hours before that meeting Gaitán was killed, the victim of an assassin's bullets. His murderer was beaten to death by the angry crowd and tremendous confusion reigned throughout the city.

According to the eyewitness account of CIT Vice-President Juan C. Lara, "the women ran and the men also; they cried and shouted menacingly, they asked vengeance and justice; all cried 'revolution,' 'to arms,' 'down with the Conservatives,' 'the Government assassinated Gaitán.' " [1]

Within minutes after Gaitán's death, the Communists had taken over all the radio stations in Bogotá, inciting the people to revolt and instructing them to plunder, burn, and destroy, specifically ordering the looting of all establishments where weapons might be obtained. Lara reported that "there were ears only for the calls for disorder and the fall of the Government, public disorder and civil war."

The mobs invaded the building where the Pan American Conference was taking place and destroyed the equipment there. Ibáñez wrote: "The incident that attracted my attention most was the fact that the rioters concentrated on the destruction of the offices of the Chilean and United States delegations. In my opinion this was due to their firm anti-Communist attitudes."

Reflecting on the events he had witnessed before fleeing Bogotá for Panama for fear of his own life, Ibáñez concluded unequivocally that the assassination of Gaitán and the surrounding events were clearly Russia-inspired. According to his own account, the techniques used to incite the people and the orders given over the radio, as well as the unusual activity of the Soviet Embassy, "all prove that this assassination was a cold-blooded and ferocious international act of incitement conducted by the Russians on the weak democracy of Colombia, against the interests of the people of the Americas."

A few weeks after the *Bogotazo*—the word coined to describe the Bogotá disorders—the Peruvian leader Victor Raul Haya de la Torre, who was a close friend of Gaitán, addressed a luncheon in Washington. According to *ADA World*, the official organ of Americans for Democratic Action, he stated that "Gaitán was the most democratic leader in Colombia and the Communists 'could make no progress against him.' " The night before his death, the APRA chief revealed, Gaitán agreed to talk with a representative of the Inter-American Confederation of Labor (CIT) about cooperation with the new anti-Communist labor group. Haya indicated that this revealed Gaitán's intention to break with the Communists. "Something's rotten in Denmark—or in Colombia," the APRA leader suggested.[2]

In June 1948 two events of importance to the CIT took place in San Francisco, California—the second meeting of its Executive Committee and the annual conference of the International Labor Organization.

Among those at the CIT meeting, in addition to the President and the members of the Secretariat, were seven Vice-Presidents, including

George Meany. The meeting noted the remarkable progress made in the few months since the Lima Conference and drafted a program of activities for the immediate future. With the admission to membership of the Federation of Labor of Haiti and the Confederation of Labor of Bolivia, the number of CIT affiliates had reached twenty, with two more national organizations (Venezuela and Uruguay) awaiting convention approval for their affiliation.

In his report, President Ibáñez reviewed the progress of the CIT, country by country, adding that "other elements which have opposed the CIT before and after the Lima Conference—such as the CGT of Argentina—seem now to be animated by a desire for cooperation." "We do appreciate," stated President Ibáñez, "this willingness to reach an amicable understanding with our organization and we are anxious to encourage it by adopting a similar attitude on our part."

I knew all about this new approach from the Argentine CGT. A few weeks before, as a matter of fact, a close friend of mine, the Argentine industrialist Torcuato Di Tella, saw me in New York and told me that, through José W. Agusti, editor of the daily *Noticias Graficas,* he had learned of President Perón's interest in discussing the terms of a possible *entente* with the AFL and the CIT. Di Tella volunteered to take back to Argentina whatever answer or comment I cared to make. I gave him a copy of Matthew Woll's letter to Ambassador Ivanissevich, accompanying the text of the AFL mission's report on Argentina, where our conditions for the resumption of relations with the CGT were clearly spelled out.

The CIT Executive Committee unanimously approved the text of a resolution on Colonies and Dependent Territories in the Western Hemisphere which (a) supported the transfer of those lands which by geographical and historical reasons belong to independent American nations but are still under the rule of extra-continental powers, and (b) advocated the right of the inhabitants of colonial countries or non-self-governing territories to reach, by democratic referenda which are the true expression of the will of the people, whatever decision they consider best suited to their national interests.

The Committee also adopted a resolution instructing the CIT to promote an early meeting between the National Farm Labor Union of the United States and Mexican unions of farm workers for joint action on Mexican migrant matters. This was the first step that eventually led to the organization of the Joint United States–Mexico Trade Union Committee, which is still in existence and has greatly contributed to the solution of the *bracero* and other border labor problems.

At the San Francisco ILO Conference the CIT scored two notable victories—the election of its President to the ILO Governing Body, replacing Lombardo Toledano, and the acquisition of consultative status.

The labor delegates from Latin America attending the conference were mostly members of CIT-affiliated organizations. Lombardo Toledano was not even named as the Mexican worker delegate. Anticipating defeat, Lombardo chose not to run for reelection to the ILO Governing Body. His logical successor was Bernardo Ibáñez, president of the young organization that in the short period of six months had already displaced the CTAL as the dominant inter-American trade union body. With Ibáñez were elected, as substitute members, Syndulfo de Azevedo Pequeño of Brazil and Angel Cofiño of Cuba, both members of organizations affiliated to the CIT.

The issue of extending to the CIT the same privileges of consultative status already approved in principle for the WFTU was hotly debated in several sessions of the ILO Governing Body. Finally, on June 19, 1948, it adopted, 31 to 1, a resolution by which, upon completion of certain specific requirements on the part of the applicants, recognition for consultative purposes was granted to the WFTU, the International Federation of Christian Trade Unions, and the CIT. The negative vote was cast by Alfred Roberts, the worker member of the Governing Body from Great Britain, who was opposed to giving any recognition and prestige to organizations outside the WFTU, of which the British TUC was a member.

A notable development took place outside the conference hall. Antitotalitarian delegates and representatives of the CIT got together and took steps to create a new worldwide body of free trade unions to rival the Communist-dominated WFTU. The nucleus of the new international organization would be the CIT and the newly formed Asian Federation of Labor. Liu Sun-sen of China, representing the Asian Federation of Labor, and myself, on behalf of the CIT, were appointed to constitute a joint secretariat. After the meeting I told the press that this secretariat "would take joint action toward calling, as soon as possible, an international conference to form a genuine international confederation of free trade unions."

We were indeed getting ambitious—first the Western Hemisphere, and then the whole free world!

On October 3, 1948, units of the Peruvian Navy revolted in the port of Callao. Although the event was strictly a military affair, it was blamed on the People's (APRA) Party and the Confederation of Labor of Peru

(CTP), both of which were subsequently outlawed. Their leaders were arrested, their headquarters closed, and their property confiscated by government decree. A few weeks later a military junta headed by General Manuel Odría took power. Those labor leaders and other democratic elements who were imprisoned were subjected to every sort of violence and persecution. Peru entered a long period of brutal military dictatorship described in a later chapter.

One of the two organizations that had fathered the CIT was gone, and one of its Vice-Presidents, Arturo Sabroso, was in jail. The situation called for a quick counteroffensive, for a worldwide appeal on behalf of trade union and human rights being violated in Peru. We decided to launch it in Cincinnati, Ohio, at the annual AFL Convention scheduled for the third week of November.

The President of the CIT came to Cincinnati. On Tuesday, November 16, 1948, he addressed the Convention, relating the Peruvian events, and ending with a moving appeal for solidarity with our Peruvian brothers. On Thursday, November 18, it was my turn to speak. There I urged for the first time—and unfortunately it was not to be the last—sanctions against governments that violated trade union and human rights.

Every Latin American government has solemnly subscribed to at least a dozen international covenants, requiring full respect of the freedom of trade union organization. Membership in the United Nations requires that; so does membership in the ILO, the Pan American Union, and many other international agencies.

Time has come to demand that these commitments be respected. Time has come to advance the suggestion that those governments guilty of violation of trade union freedom be treated as unworthy members of the family of democratic nations. The victims cry for protection. We can at best offer them moral assistance and limited material aid. But the governments of true democratic countries can do something more concrete. They can refuse, for instance, loans and other economic facilities to those countries where legitimate and legal trade union freedom is being persistently and willfully violated.

At the morning session of November 22, the 67th AFL Convention adopted a resolution protesting the repression by the Peruvian Government of democratic labor organizations and the arrest of hundreds of trade union leaders, as well as the abolition of constitutional guarantees and civil rights by the military dictatorship. The resolution urged that the imprisoned unionists be given a public trial in the civil courts. Finally, it reaffirmed AFL solidarity with the persecuted leaders, specifically Arturo Sabroso, and pledged full support for the recovery of their individual freedoms and the right to organize and strike.

Just as the Convention came to a close, news arrived that the democratic government of President Romulo Gallegos of Venezuela had been overthrown and that the military junta's first act was to arrest all the leaders of the Venezuelan Confederation of Labor. President Ibáñez agreed to bring the Venezuelan and Peruvian situations before the ILO immediately. Its Governing Body, of which Ibáñez was a member, was scheduled to meet the first week of December, 1948. Responding to Ibáñez's plea, the Workers Group of the ILO Governing Body unanimously approved a resolution condemning the practice of arresting individuals without formal charges or due process of law. Specifically, it called for the release of labor leaders jailed but not charged by the Governments of Peru and Venezuela, in accordance with the principles of freedom of trade union association subscribed to by the ILO. The resolution further requested that those individuals against whom charges had been filed be tried immediately in a public civil court.

The Peruvian military regime acknowledged the CIT complaints and issued a statement asserting that the labor leaders had been jailed because of their Aprista activities and participation in the Callao revolt. On December 28 the CIT angrily rejected the junta's statement, reaffirmed its original charges, and demanded that in order to prove to the world that it did not subscribe to an antilabor policy, the junta immediately release from prison the hundreds of trade union leaders. The CIT accused Odría of seeking to stifle democracy through the destruction of the CTP and denying fundamental individual rights by convicting its leaders, without the benefit of a public trial, of crimes they did not in fact commit.

On December 29, 1948, the AFL consultants before the United Nations —Matthew Woll and David Dubinsky—addressed to UN General Secretary Trygve Lie a complaint against the government of Peru for violating trade union rights. The complaint was received with little enthusiasm by even those members of the United Nations Economic and Social Council who might ordinarily have supported such a protest, because it was presented to the Council together with a series of WFTU complaints against governments known for their firm anti-Communist stance. Seeking to avoid the dismissal of all the complaints, as was recommended by the Peruvian representative, the AFL submitted additional documented evidence of the Peruvian Government's violation of trade union rights and persecution of trade unionists. We succeeded in winning the Council's support, at its session of February 7, 1949, for the recommendation that the entire matter be addressed to the ILO and the Commission on Human Rights.

Meanwhile, the situation was getting worse in Venezuela. Following the coup in November 1948, the ruling military junta began to take steps to dissolve the democratic CTV, hampering or prohibiting union activities, arresting the leaders or forcing them into hiding, and permitting the violation of collective contracts by employers and landowners. Acting upon the protest of CTV Secretary General Augusto Malavé Villalba, who had gone into exile in Havana, and similar statements from CIT President Bernardo Ibáñez and national labor organizations throughout the hemisphere, the worker members of the ILO Governing Body requested an ILO investigation of the Venezuelan trade union situation. On March 7, 1949, the Governing Body approved a proposal that this matter be examined at its next session.

The situation in Peru and Venezuela was causing the CIT serious concern. I was worried about the future of the free labor movement in those countries. As far as a moral victory was concerned, we had met all possible tests in both Peru and Venezuela. Despite vicious totalitarian repression, the workers in those countries had remained loyal to their democratic labor organizations. Leaders and rank and file members both refused to bend to the will of the military dictators. That was why the jails were crowded with trade unionists. In Venezuela, four months after the coup, ninety-two top labor leaders were in jail with no specific charges against them. In two elections which the Peruvian Government had set up in the textile and petroleum unions, the democratic candidates had won hands down, but the junta promptly annulled the results. These facts and others which I was assembling from various sources proved that the resistance of the democratic trade unionists remained unbroken.

But we also recognized that trade unions cannot effectively function underground. Contracts have to be negotiated, grievances have to be taken up, contacts with management and government itself have to be maintained, and scores of other activities have to be taken care of almost daily. As long as unions do not enjoy such freedoms, either because they cannot legally function or because their leaders are in jail, the members will remain unprotected and will be exposed to the constant temptation of going over to the other side in order to get bread for their families.

The military dictators of Venezuela had gone to great lengths in their plan to destroy free trade unionism. Having dissolved, without the slightest degree of judicial procedure, all the national and local unions (with the exception of the few controlled by the Communists), the government had called for new elections of officers within thirty days. It warned, however, that it would recognize only those new officers who met certain specifications laid down by the government itself.

Faced with this brazen attempt on the part of the government to dominate the labor movement of Venezuela, the Governing Body of the ILO had taken some steps which, it was hoped, would soon lead to a thorough investigation and world condemnation of the labor repression in Venezuela and other countries.

But the free labor movements of the world had to rally to the support of the persecuted trade unionists of Latin America if the steps taken by the ILO and other international organizations were to be more than an empty gesture. The American Federation of Labor had shown the way. Other labor movements, in the Western Hemisphere as well as in Europe, Asia, and Oceania, had to follow suit. International public opinion had to be informed, the collective conscience of civilized America aroused.

After several meetings with George Meany and the recently appointed AFL International Representative, George (Phil) Delaney, it was agreed that we would take our fight to the forthcoming IV ILO regional conference of American States, scheduled to meet in April 1949 in Montevideo, and demand an investigation and condemnation of the antilabor policies of the Governments of Peru and Venezuela. It was a tall order and had never been done before; but we decided to try it convinced that, regardless of the outcome, our efforts would encourage our brothers fighting in the underground and might even restrain the two juntas from further violations and persecutions.

Philip Hannah, who had done such a fine job at the Lima Conference, was appointed U.S. worker delegate to the Montevideo ILO Conference. I went along as his adviser. Phil Delaney attended the sessions as one of the two worker members of the ILO Governing Body. The other was veteran French trade unionist Léon Jouhaux.

That meeting was Phil Delaney's baptism in international gatherings. After Montevideo, he became the staunchest supporter in ILO councils of trade union rights and delivered many blows for freedom against totalitarianism in the Western Hemisphere. Following years of ILO service Delaney moved to the Labor Department, where he became Assistant to Secretary of Labor James P. Mitchell, and later to the State Department, as Special Assistant to the Secretary of State. Trade unionists in Latin America developed a deep affection for Phil Delaney. They also respected him for his frankness and integrity.

Meanwhile, CIT President Ibáñez was busy in Santiago obtaining the support of worker and government delegates for a condemnation of the two military regimes in Peru and Venezuela. Voting at ILO conference is conducted on the basis of two votes for each government delegation, and one separate vote for each labor and management delegate—a total of four votes for each country. Obviously, no motion or resolution introduced by a worker delegate has any chance of being adopted unless it is supported by a substantial number of government delegates.

Events at Montevideo were indicative of the stature gained by the CIT as the leading labor group in the Western Hemisphere. The change that had taken place since the ILO meeting in Mexico City three years earlier was best described in a May 1949 issue of *Time:*

When the last regional International Labor Organization (ILO) conference of American states was held in Mexico City three years ago, most workers' delegates were Communist or Communist-led. Vicente Lombardo Toledano, Mexico's Communist-line labor boss, ran the show.

Last week a new and very different regional ILO convened in Montevideo. In the three years since Mexico City, Latin American labor movements have pretty well repudiated Communist leaders. Of the 280 delegates and advisers at the meeting (from all countries except Peru, Venezuela, Honduras and Paraguay), Communists numbered so few that they even had trouble making much noise. Lombardo Toledano was absent.

This time the man who supplied the leadership was a plump little Italian-born U.S. labor leader named Serafino Romualdi. As the American Federation of Labor's walking delegate in Latin America, he had tirelessly gone up and down the continent lining up pro-democratic trade unionists. He knew intimately the leader of every ILO worker delegation, and though his role at the conference was only an adviser's, he was unquestionably the most influential man present. Even the Argentines, who had bustled in 37-strong, handing out *Peronista* tracts, wisely decided to string along with him.

With the Communists silenced and *Peronistas* taking it easy, Romualdi attacked hemispheric military dictatorships. He brought out letters, documents, underground newspapers and lists of prisoners as evidence that military regimes in both Peru and Venezuela had jailed workers and smashed unions. Under pressure of U.S. Government delegates, headed by Ambassador to Uruguay Ellis O. Briggs, he withheld a resolution of condemnation, but got through a statement demanding ILO investigations in Peru and Venezuela.

In order not to leave with the readers a false impression regarding the views of the U.S. government delegates (Ambassador Briggs and Assistant

Secretary of Labor Ralph Wright), I want to make it clear that they urged me to withhold a resolution of condemnation only after they had come to the conclusion that there were not enough favorable votes for it to pass. On the other hand, the statement demanding an ILO investigation in Peru and Venezuela represented substantially what the CIT was seeking, and it was approved (the Workers Group was unanimous) thanks largely to support received from the U.S. government delegates, who carried with them the votes of most other official delegations. However, most employers, including the U.S. delegate, voted against our resolution despite our plea and warning that freedom is indivisible; if labor loses it, management eventually will suffer the same fate.

The CIT Executive Committee met following the conclusion of the Montevideo ILO Conference for the purpose of selecting the date and the site of the next convention. It was set for September 7, 1949, in Havana.

When the Second CIT Convention convened, the Credentials Committee reported the presence of delegates from 37 affiliated organizations as well as representatives from 12 groups which had not yet joined formally but, nevertheless, shared the views and objectives of the CIT. Among the new affiliates since the Lima founding conference were the Trades and Labour Congress of Canada and national labor organizations from British Guiana, Haiti, Panama, and Uruguay.

President Ibáñez' report reflected an aura of general optimism and positive hopes for the future that prevailed at the conference. He spoke with pride of CIT achievements and the corresponding failure of both Communist and government-controlled groups to gain any appreciable support on a continental basis.

Among the most important resolutions passed by the convention was one dealing with the crisis of democracy. It condemned Communist activities in the labor field, as well as the antilabor policies of the military juntas of Peru and Venezuela and of the governments of Argentina, Nicaragua, and the Dominican Republic. The resolution also censured the recognition of de facto regimes established by military coups. Further, it called upon the UN, the ILO, and the OAS to examine the continuing violation of trade union rights in Latin America and to take steps to end these practices.

Another resolution urged democratic governments to deny economic, financial, and political aid to the Latin American dictatorships and to cut off the supply of arms to these governments. The CIT addressed a letter to Vincent Tewson, Secretary General of the British Trades Union

Congress, urging pressure upon the British government to stop arms shipments to the dictatorships. The CIT informed the TUC that the British government reportedly had recently sold military equipment to the Dominican Republic and Venezuela.

In the communication the CIT commended the U.S. government for its refusal to send arms to the dictatorships, a measure that had been taken largely as the result of the demands of democratic labor groups throughout the hemisphere. The letter suggested that similar pressure from the powerful TUC on the British government might prove effective.

Of paramount importance for the future of the CIT was the decision to recommend affiliation with the proposed new international organization of free trade unions. When the British Trade Union Congress, the CIO, the Dutch Labor Federation, and other democratic national labor groups left the Communist-dominated WFTU earlier in 1949, CIT President Ibáñez issued the following statement from Santiago:

> The CIT believes that the time has come now to take the first steps toward the organization of a new international labor body. We are prepared to cooperate with all bona-fide free trade unions in the preparation of preliminary measures leading to the achievement of this goal.

At a preparatory meeting for the new international organization in Geneva during June, concurrently with the annual ILO Conference, representatives of CIT members played a prominent role and pledged unreserved support.

The Havana Convention became in a sense the last for the CIT as an autonomous body. Everyone anticipated that soon the CIT would have to become the regional arm of the proposed new democratic international labor group. For this reason, the Convention decided to move CIT headquarters from Santiago to Havana, so as to be closer to most of the organizations that were expected to form part of the new regional body. Bernardo Ibáñez remained President; but the constitution was amended to make the General Secretary the chief executive officer, and Francisco Aguirre of Cuba was elected to this post.

The International Confederation of Free Trade Unions (ICFTU) was established in London in December 1949 in an atmosphere of enthusiasm and great expectations. CIT affiliates attended in large numbers and received wide recognition by being elected to important posts on Conference committees and in the top leadership of the new organization. In London it was also agreed that the ICFTU would stress regional decentralization, thus recognizing the pioneering work done by the CIT and the Asian Federation of Labor.

When CIT's Executive Committee met again in Havana in January 1950, its main task was to set the stage for the calling in the near future of a constituent convention of the ICFTU regional organization. The overwhelming majority of the Western Hemisphere national labor organizations affiliated to the ICFTU were also members of CIT and were anxious to keep the name and the structure of their organization intact. On the other hand, those who were outside the CIT, particularly the CIO, the Mexican CTM, and the Canadian CCL, wanted a new name and a new structure. Responding to the enthusiasm for democratic unity, the CIT leadership finally agreed to the change. CIT was abolished and transferred lock, stock and barrel, into what eventually became, from its Spanish language initials, the ORIT (*Organización Regional Interamericana de Trabajadores*—Inter-American Regional Organization of Workers).

"Same headquarters, same executive officers," those with doubts were reassured. "It would practically be the same thing!" However, as I point out in a later chapter, ORIT turned out to be quite a different thing and, for a number of years, quite a disappointment.

Notes

1. From personal accounts of CIT President Ibáñez and CIT Vice-President Lara. *Inter-American Labor News,* May 1948.

2. *ADA World,* May 10, 1948.

VII

The Zonians

DURING THE 1940's the labor situation in the Panama Canal Zone was an issue raised at every annual conference of the International Labor Organization, where the Panamanian delegation, usually through the worker delegate, attacked the practice of paying native employees lower wages than those paid United States citizens doing the same type of work. Racial segregation and discrimination in the Zone were also condemned.

During my travels in various Latin American countries prior to the calling of the Lima Conference which set up the CIT, I had been warned that an effective cooperation of other American labor unions with the trade union movement of the United States could not be established unless the AFL would take a strong public stand against the labor conditions prevailing in the Panama Canal Zone, and would urge its affiliated unions with locals in the Zone to end racial and nationality discriminations.

The division of Canal Zone workers into "gold" and "silver" rolls, which was established when the construction of the Canal started, had been discontinued but in its place there was established the classification of "local-scale" and "American-scale" employees—which was practically the same thing. The old policy of segregation and discrimination remained unchanged.

American scale workers—nicknamed the Zonians—most of whom were members of unions affiliated to the Canal Zone Metal Trades Department and Central Labor Union, were strongly in favor of continuation of the status quo. In this they were supported by practically the entire community of U.S. citizens in the Canal Zone. Living isolated in their enclave—a ten-mile wide segment of land across the Isthmus—with little or no contact with the people of Panama, handicapped by language difficulties, and dominated by the racial prejudices of the old settlers, they selfishly ignored the needs of the native Canal Zone employees and concentrated exclusively on getting benefits for themselves. Since their wages, working conditions, vacation and retirement benefits, educational and recreational facilities, housing, hospitalization, commissary privileges, and practically everything else depended upon legislation of the U.S. Congress, lobbying in Washington became extremely important to the Zonians. In these legislative efforts, the labor unions were concentrating on the enactment of legislation that would favor the Zonians, and them alone. Year after year, at the annual AFL conventions, their delegates would present about a dozen resolutions which the convention always unanimously endorsed, urging the passage of this or that bill—all designed to take care of grievances, aspirations, and demands of U.S. citizens employed in the Canal Zone. Never was a resolution introduced calling for increased benefits for native workers.

The AFL unions with locals in the Canal Zone, even those which had a reputation for being progressive-minded, rarely questioned the policies pursued by their Zone members. It was a sort of unwritten rule that any request coming from a Canal Zone local had to be automatically endorsed by its parent union in the States.

Matters pertaining to wages and working conditions were mostly handled in Washington by the AFL Metal Trades Department; those requiring passage of specific legislation were the province of the AFL legislative representative. At that time, from 1946 to 1948, there was no disposition in either of the two offices to change appreciably the status quo prevailing in the Panama Canal Zone.

In my reports to George Meany, I informed him that, judging from my conversations and contacts throughout Latin America, the Canal Zone issue would undoubtedly come up at the forthcoming inter-American trade union conference in Lima. Meany, who had originally planned to attend the meeting, assured me that the AFL delegation would take a position that would be welcomed by our fellow trade unionists from Latin America. The general idea was to support the request for a thorough investigation if it were made by the Latin American delegations.

As predicted, the issue of the discriminatory labor policies in the Canal Zone was raised at the Lima meeting. The U.S. delegation supported a resolution instructing the Executive Committee "to invite the American Federation of Labor to join with the Inter-American Confederation of Labor (CIT) in setting up a committee to investigate, at some future date, the working conditions existing in the Canal Zone with a view to presenting a solution that would end, once and for all, existing discriminations." This resolution was adopted unanimously.

The first meeting of the CIT Executive Committee, held in San Francisco, in July 1948, discussed and implemented the Lima resolution. Luis Alejandro Cuellar, President of the National Union of Labor Syndicates of Panama (UNSO); Juan C. Lara of the Confederation of Labor of Colombia; and Luis Alberto Monge of the Confederation of Labor "Rerum Novarum" of Costa Rica were appointed by the CIT to make the investigation. Later, Lara was replaced by Efrain Iregui of the Colombian Confederation of Employees. The AFL appointed Anthony E. Matz, President of the Brotherhood of Firemen and Oilers, who became the committee chairman, and myself as secretary-translator. Matz was nominated by the Metal Trades Department.

The announcement of the investigation to be conducted by the joint CIT-AFL committee was first published in the Panamanian labor newspaper *El Obrero*, edited by Cuellar himself. It was warmly approved by Latin American trade unionists, particularly Panamanian labor circles, who regarded it as the first concrete attempt of the AFL to help correct the discriminatory practices which they strongly condemned. Among the Zonians, however, it caused resentment and misgivings. If the committee had been composed exclusively of North Americans, the reaction probably would not have been so hostile. But the very idea of "Latinos" entering the Canal Zone to "investigate" was to the Zonians totally unacceptable. Rumors to this effect reached me in Washington and were confirmed in conversations I had with Bill Hushing, the AFL legislative representative, who was an old Canal Zone hand, and James Brownlow, then Secretary-Treasurer of the AFL Metal Trades Department.

To better understand the reasons for the opposition from the Zonians, one must examine the mentality which they had developed through decades of quasi self-government. They regarded themselves as sovereign in Canal Zone affairs, and rejected any interference from outside. As a matter of fact, even the State Department had become their bête noire, and was accused of "softness" and of being "too prone to give in" to the demands of the Panamanians. The Zonians' reasoning was very simple:

"We Americans built the Canal! We are running it and we are protecting it! Panama gave it to us in perpetuity; therefore it is nobody's business, especially not the Latinos', to stick their nose in our affairs." It reminds me of the same kind of reasoning that today guides the conduct of the white minorities in South Africa and Rhodesia.

The isolationism in which the Panama Canal American community was living, the absence of an intellectual climate that would stimulate discussion and understanding of the grave issues already facing the West and its newly established leader, the United States, made the Zonians impervious to the objectives of a joint AFL-CIT investigating committee. Living under welfare state conditions, they remained preoccupied with questions that dealt mainly with the preservation of well-paying jobs for themselves and their children. They were imbued with a sense of chauvinistic patriotism that made them excessively proud of their American citizenship; yet they had no real desire, especially those born in the Zone, to return to live permanently in the United States. Climatic differences, and especially a change in social status, were the main factors. Regardless of their economic opportunities in the U.S., they knew they could not afford the servants and the services to which they had become accustomed in the Canal Zone. Anything resembling, even remotely, a threat to their privileged status, was therefore bitterly resented and opposed.

During the weeks that followed the announcement of the impending investigation there was a great deal of communication and correspondence between the spokesmen of the Canal Zone unions and their confidants in the AFL Washington headquarters. Feelings were exacerbated by innuendos that nothing as distasteful as a joint AFL-CIT investigation could take place were it not for the "crazy ideas" of George Meany, who was blamed, *sotto voce*, as being the prime mover. On this they were absolutely correct. I too was then convinced, as I am still convinced, that the investigation resulted mainly from Meany's awareness of the increasing importance of the Panama Canal issue. He was viewing it not only in terms of the local issues involved, but also in the wider context of the role of Latin America in the security of the United States and the Free World already confronted by the massive attacks of the international Communist conspiracy. This awareness—shared by Meany's internationally minded colleagues in the AFL top leadership—demanded a decisive and dramatic end to the AFL's traditionally passive acquiescence in the discriminatory wage policy in the Panama Canal Zone and the increasingly anachronistic and damaging attitudes of the American citizens working there. The appointment of the joint investigating committee proposed by the Lima CIT Conference was precisely the spark that would eventually lead to the desired break. George Meany knew it, and with his customary determination and persistence he went on with his plans despite the opposition.

An episode, which best illustrates Meany's attitude in the whole affair, occurred early in December 1948 when Panama Canal governor Francis K. Newcomer returned to Washington and asked to confer with him on the purpose of the AFL-CIT mission. A meeting was scheduled at the Panama Canal Office. Meany requested me to go along. As we were waiting in the anteroom of the Governor's office, his secretary came out and asked Meany to go in alone, which he did; but after a few minutes, not more than two or three, he stormed out, slammed the door, and grabbing my arm, said in a loud angry voice:

"Let's go, Serafino. They do not want you in there; and so I came out!"

As we were walking back to the AFL headquarters, then located a few blocks from the Panama Canal office, Meany related to me that before the interview started, he asked the Governor if he could bring me in as his adviser because I was more familiar with the details of the situation and the events leading to the appointment of the investigating committee. The request was sidetracked with the suggestion, "Let's first talk this matter over ourselves." Meany insisted, and when his request was denied the second time he got up and left. Although this meeting with Governor Newcomer never got beyond the preliminaries, we assumed that perhaps he wanted to persuade Meany to call the whole thing off.

As soon as he returned to his office, Meany telephoned several people at the White House and Department of Defense. As I remember clearly, the wires really burned that afternoon. The following day Meany received assurances that "everything was an unfortunate misunderstanding," that the Governor had no objections to the investigating mission, and that all facilities would be put at our disposal. An official letter was later sent, assuring Chairman Anthony Matz and me that we would be welcomed in the Canal Zone and offering us all possible cooperation.

The five members of the Committee arrived on the Isthmus by steamer and plane on January 4, 1949. We held our first meeting at the Tivoli Hotel, where we were housed. The following day Chairman Matz gave a press interview during which, as reported in the *Panama American* afternoon edition of January 5, he stated that, "the investigators will visit as many places of employment in the Canal Zone as possible, to talk with employees, both white and colored." He added that "the Committee will seek evidence from all labor organizations on the Isthmus except the Communist-dominated local of the United Public Workers–CIO," explaining that "although the UPW was the recognized 'silver' workers' union the investigators will not approach it for evidence of alleged discrimination. Instead, the probers will talk personally with as many of the employees as possible."

At that time it was well known that the Canal Zone local of the UPW–CIO was under Communist domination. In fact, the CIO national leadership expelled the United Public Workers later the same year. The investigating committee wanted to take all necessary precautions to avoid being charged with "having listened to the lies of the Communists."

Upon our arrival, a spokesman for Governor Newcomer told the press that "the Canal will not interfere with the Committee's investigation. They can see whatever they want to see." At the same time, I informed the public that the five-man committee was appointed by the CIT and the AFL "because of complaints against Panama Canal discriminations made at international labor conferences during the last three years."

Panama Canal authorities from the Governor down, the military establishments in the Zone, the Metal Trades Department, and the Central Labor Union cooperated with us in every way possible. Their hospitality, in all its external manifestations, was correct but cool. The special host committee appointed by the Central Labor Union acceded to all our requests for information, arranged all the interviews we needed, and took us to all the places we wanted to see. But their heart was not in it. They simply could not conceal their disappointment and bitterness over our presence and made their feelings known to us—at times deliberately and at other times unconsciously.

Questions asked by the Latin American members of the Committee, especially Luis Alberto Monge of Costa Rica, were often ignored or answered only partially until I repeated them and made them my own. One particular member of the host committee persisted in mispronouncing Monge's name so as to make it sound "monkey"; he would then apologize, pronounce it correctly, and repeat the "mistake" again the next time. This went on day after day until we departed. The Panamanian workers employed in the Canal were always referred to in disparaging terms by our labor hosts, knowing well that this would humiliate Luis Alejandro Cuellar, the Panamanian member of the committee, who had a fair understanding of the English language.

In a seemingly innocent way I was repeatedly asked whether I was an American. Upon my explanation that I was a naturalized American citizen of Italian birth, the questioner would then comment: "Oh, you are an Italian!," clearly implying that they regarded only the native-born as true Americans and that I was an interloper like the Latino members of the committee. Anthony Matz also received his share of barbs, when it was found out that his father was born in Italy and that the family name was originally Mazza.

Once we were reprimanded for drinking water from a fountain reserved for colored people. Another time a member of the host committee tried to persuade us to include in our report a condemnation of the practice recently established at the Balboa, C.Z., Post Office, requiring white people to wait in line together with colored people. The Post Office was practically the only nonsegregated public place. It was there that I met George Westerman, the noted Panamanian labor expert and author, who was so helpful to us. As a Negro, he was not allowed to enter the Tivoli Hotel where we were staying, since segregation was then the accepted policy in the Canal Zone. The querulous tone of the brother trade unionist on the host committee who complained about being forced to wait in line with Negroes obviously indicated that he was a victim of the social and psychological malaise that was then widespread not only in the Canal Zone but also in many parts of the United States.

We were continuously exposed to the sound of the word "they." "They" were the local workers, the Negroes, the Panamanians.

"Look what we are doing for them. 'They' are better off than their own people in the Republic of Panama. Yet 'they' are never satisfied. 'They' want to be like us Americans!"

One Sunday morning, Matz and I were escorted by a member of the host committee, an electrician named Sullivan, and his wife, to an open-air Mass celebrated in a park by the Bishop of Panama and attended by the full complement of the Canal Zone chapter of the Knights of Columbus. The Mass was also attended by a good number of Negro communicants freely intermingling with white Americans. After the Mass we asked Sullivan, "How is it that these Americans, who sit next to Negroes at Mass, insist on segregation in housing, schools, playgrounds, hospitals, and so on?"

Sullivan's reply still rings in my ears; "Segregation is imposed by a tightly knit minority of fanatics who dominate the American community and threaten everyone who disagrees with them. We can't stand it anymore. We are suffocating here. Soon we'll go back home to Brooklyn, for good!"

Before leaving the Canal Zone, I was asked to make a rough draft of a report on the mission so that all the members of the committee could initial it. In this report we agreed not to include our unpleasant experiences with individual American trade unionists because we wanted to continue the dialogue with them that we felt had been initiated during our stay. As AFL Latin American representative, I felt that it was my duty to continue the contacts with the Canal Zone AFL organizations and I wanted therefore to avoid any unnecessary remarks that could hurt their feelings. Now, after more than eighteen years, I feel that the voluntary restraints of 1949 are no longer justified.

Following are the major findings of the report on labor conditions in the Canal Zone that Chairman Matz and I submitted to the AFL Executive Council on January 24, 1949:

Wage Policies and Scales. The working force employed by the Panama Canal and the Panama Railroad Company—the chief employers in the Zone—is composed of two classes known as the U.S.-rate employees (formerly "gold") and the local-rate employees (formerly "silver"). The U.S.-rate category includes the skilled trades and the executive, supervisory, and professional positions and the wage scale is based on rates prevailing in the United States, plus a 25 percent bonus for working out of the country.

The working force of local-rate employees is composed entirely of natives of the tropics, mostly Panamanians—laborers, helpers, and semiskilled. Their wages bear no relationship to the wages of corresponding classes of workers in the United States because they were established to insure living standards similar to those prevailing in the Republic of Panama and the Caribbean area.

The wage scale for local-rate employees begins at $0.26 per hour for grade 1 up to $1.40 per hour at the top of grade 15. However, almost all of the local-rate employees fall within the first 11 grades. U.S.-rate employees in craft positions, on the other hand, receive a minimum of $2 an hour.

At least 200 employees paid at local rates are performing work which would warrant their promotion to the higher U.S. rate, even within the provisions of the current setup. Furthermore, a large number of local-rate employees are doing work normally recognized as semiskilled but are being paid less than the U.S.-rate employees doing similar work. This is particularly true of masons, carpenters, and painters in the construction field.

U.S. agencies in the Zone, including AFL unions, state that local-rate employees receive wages and other benefits (such as housing, hospital and commissary facilities, etc.) which give them a purchasing power equal to and in most cases higher than that obtained for corresponding jobs in the Republic of Panama. However, an examination of the payroll of the leading construction firm in the Republic of Panama reveals that wages for common laborers and unskilled workers are about the same as those prevailing in the Canal Zone. But in the skilled and semiskilled jobs, this firm paid somewhat higher wages than those paid in the Zone to local-rate labor, in a few cases.

Because of the sharp wage differentials, underpaid local-rate labor is displacing semiskilled and skilled American craftsmen. The U.S. Governor of the Zone stated that as long as local help is available under competent U.S. supervision, he does not see any reason why American workers should be brought to the Zone at a total expense of $2,000 per family, round trip. An example of the sharp wage differentials and the low ratio of American employees to those in the local-rate force is seen in the Panama Canal Press—the official printer for the Zone administration. There are eight skilled Americans with wages ranging from $2.56 to $2.79 per hour. The 146 native workers, who are assigned to various duties from operating individual machines and presses down through janitor and helper categories, earn from $0.34 to $0.80 an hour.

During the Committee's investigation several solutions were suggested to end existing wage inequalities. Almost everyone, including Zone officials, acknowledged that local-rate employees—especially in grades 1 to 4—had substandard living conditions, and that the minimum scale must be increased. The leadership of the Metal Trades Council and Central Labor Union favored the adoption of a scale calling for equal wages for equal work—provided the duties are performed by people who are qualified by on-the-job training or apprenticeship. This policy, if strictly observed, would undoubtedly result in an effective protection of the skilled jobs for American citizens.

A suggestion made by a group of Panamanian workers and supported by the Latin American members of the Committee calls for:

(a) Immediate increase of the minimum wage for local-rate employees up to the legal minimum in the United States;

(b) All employees performing work below the categories of mechanical helper and semiskilled mechanic should receive a higher rate of pay— somewhere between the rates prevailing in the United States and in the Republic of Panama, for similar work;

(c) Immediate equalization of pay for those who are doing skilled

work or who are employed in a professional or supervisory position—
minus the 25 percent differential paid to U.S.-rate employees.

Old Age and Disability Benefits. Local-rate employees of the Panama
Canal and Panama Railroad Company who are physically unable to perform their duties are granted special disability payment in lieu of a
retirement system. Currently, this payment amounts to $1.00 per month
for each year of service up to a maximum of twenty-five years. It is
almost impossible to live in the Republic of Panama on $25 a month. It
must be noted that when a worker ceases to be employed by a U.S. agency
in the Zone for any reason, he must leave the Zone within thirty days
and therefore loses the rights to his housing facilities. The inequality of
this system and the need for an immediate increase in benefits was acknowledged by the Governor's office.

Housing. Generally housing for U.S. employees is far below standards
in the United States for wage earners of similar categories; it is deplorable
for local-rate employees. Houses for the latter are completely unfurnished
and "overcrowding, limited floor space, improper ventilation, are the
main feature of termite-eaten barracks. . . ."

Segregation. Although segregation of races is not accepted as a national
policy by the Government of Panama, it has been the established official
policy in the Zone since the Canal was constructed. Governor Newcomer
informed the committee that segregation will continue in the Zone as
long as white Americans refuse to live together in the same housing
project with colored people. Segregation is practiced in residential areas,
schools, and hospitals.

The Executive Council of the AFL issued a statement on our report
singling out the existing wage inequalities as the heart of the problem. In
line with the fundamental AFL principle of "equal wages for equal
work," the Council recommended:

(a) An immediate increase of the minimum wage for local-rate employees in the Zone up to the legal minimum in force in the United
States;

(b) A gradual increase of the base pay for all employees performing
work generally falling under the categories of mechanical helpers and
semiskilled mechanics, until it ultimately reaches the level prevailing in
the United States;

(c) An immediate increase of the base pay for those local-rate employees in skilled jobs, or supervisory and professional positions, up to
full equalization with the base pay of U.S. employees.

The Council also called for improved housing and the approval by Congress of a new law to increase the retirement and disability benefits for local-rate employees. In order to achieve the wage goals indicated above and improve the living standards of the native workers in the Zone, the Council fully endorsed the Committee's recommendation that AFL affiliate international unions extend the protection of trade unionism to *all* employees of the Zone who fall under their respective jurisdiction.

In the course of frequent subsequent trips through Panama I have had numerous opportunities to meet with the leaders of the AFL unions in the Canal Zone. Most of them overcame their initial coolness toward me and I even detected a feeling of respect for the work I was doing and for the policies I was defending. At any rate, it was possible for me to discuss with them the changing conditions of the world and the inevitable necessity of changing the conditions in the Canal Zone, too.

Meanwhile, Nasser's seizure of the Suez Canal and the failure of the British-French military intervention in 1956 gave fresh impetus to the extreme nationalists in Panama. They intensified their campaign for further concessions—in spite of the 1955 amendments to the Panama–U.S. Treaty, which gave the Panamanians considerable additional benefits and pledged implementation of the so-called "single-wage policy" in the Canal Zone.

An AFL-CIO delegation touring South America—composed of President Meany, Vice-Presidents David Dubinsky and O. A. Knight and myself—arrived in Panama during the last week of November 1956.[1] Local-rate employees were by now organized into Locals 900 and 907 of the American Federation of State, County, and Municipal Employees. The Communist leadership had been completely eliminated. The AFL–CIO group met with them on November 26. The highlight of the meeting, as recorded in a memorandum which I drafted, was that Locals 900 and 907 were in favor of establishing in the Canal Zone a single wage rate for each operation. They were, therefore, in favor of the Green Bill (introduced by Senator Theodore Green of Rhode Island) which called for the establishment of such a single wage rate on the basis of the scale prevailing in the United States.

The following day we met with the representatives of the Central Labor Union and Metal Trades Department. The discussion was friendly and fruitful. It was obvious that a lot of water had passed under the bridge since January 1949. Central Labor Union Vice-President Louis Damiani reported on various items relating to the implementation of the United States–Panama Treaty. He read from a prepared statement, the tone of which is clear in the opening paragraph:

Organized labor in the Canal Zone neither approves nor disapproves the recently ratified treaty between the United States and the Republic of Panama. We assume that our State Department is acting in good faith, and in the best interest of our country. We do, however, have a recommendation with reference to the pending legislation implementing this treaty, namely, the "Single Wage Policy."

Their recommendation was that in promulgating the "Single Wage Policy" the United States base rate be maintained, as provided in the Green Bill, rather than follow what they termed the State Department intention "to achieve this equality by reducing the existing rates enjoyed by the U.S. citizens, in their attempt to arrive at a uniform rate policy." The Canal Zone trade unionists' position was of course sound and in line with traditional trade union practices of not permitting a lowering of wage scales.

Panama Canal Governor W. E. Potter invited the visiting AFL-CIO delegation to attend the monthly meeting of the American community. David Dubinsky was selected to speak on behalf of the delegation. In his address, which stirred the audience and was repeatedly applauded, he forcefully explained why organized labor in the United States was duty bound, for moral and political reasons, to fight against any type of discrimination—in jobs, wages, schools, and in housing.

The American Embassy in Panama gave a reception in honor of President George Meany and the members of his party. It was attended by Panamanian President Arias and his top officials, the Panama Canal Governor and his aides, the ranking U.S. military in the Zone, the diplomatic corps, and many guests. There were also representatives of all the Zone AFL-CIO unions and of the labor movement of Panama. In the latter group, there were a number of *campesino* leaders led by Ubaldino Franco—the first time they had ever entered the U.S. embassy, or any embassy for that matter. They came in their tropical Sunday best: neat pants, clean shoes, white shirt, no coat, no tie. And they mingled freely, nobody objecting to the color of their skin or to waiting in line with them for drinks and food.

The last ten years have seen much progress made in the elimination of discrimination against native workers and a steady advance in their wage scales, which now are at the same level as those of U.S. citizen employees. The chief union organization in the Canal Zone today is the American Federation of State, County, and Municipal Employees, AFL-CIO, which numbers some 6,000 workers among the membership of its two local unions. The AFL-CIO Maritime Union and the Metal Trades Department also include smaller numbers of Zonian workers in their membership. By far the largest single trade union organization is the AFSCME Local 900, composed mainly of employees of the Panama Canal Company–Canal Zone government which operates the canal and provides additional services like sanitation, hospital services, police surveillance, and the like. Several different races and nationalities can be found among this local's 4,000 members.

Local 900 was first chartered by the CIO Government and Civic Employees Organizing Committee and was originally made up of employees of both the Panama Canal and the U.S. Armed Forces agencies stationed in the Zone area for defense purposes. Some years later, however, the Armed Forces workers decided that they would be better able to protect their interests if they formed their own separate local and in 1954 a GCEOC charter was issued to Local 907, Armed Forces Employees Union, which had been formed with the help of Local 900. A year later the GCEOC and the AFSCME were merged and the two Canal Zone locals became a part of the State, County, and Municipal Employees.

Over the years the AFSCME has worked to improve the lot of Canal Zone workers in general. It has managed to raise salaries well over 100 percent in the last ten years and has contributed to vast improvements in general working conditions. Today, salaries in the Canal Zone, on the average, rank third highest in the Western Hemisphere, following only those paid in the continental United States and Canada. The AFSCME has undertaken a continuous drive against job discrimination and has been able to open to Panamanians many positions which formerly were reserved for U.S. citizens. These include supervisory positions and others in the technical and professional fields.

The AFSCME today has behind it a record of lobbying successfully for the inclusion of the Canal Zone workers in all Congressional legislation favorably affecting U.S. Federal employees. Among its most recent victories, for example, was the inclusion of Canal Zone employees under the 1965 legislation which extended severance pay benefits to government employees for the first time. The 2.9 percent across-the-board Federal pay increase bill, signed by President Johnson July 18, 1966, brought this benefit to thousands of non-U.S. workers in the Canal Zone. Even more recently, working in cooperation with the Government Employees Council, the AFL-CIO Legislative Department, and the Panamanian Embassy in Washington, the AFSCME succeeded in getting an amendment to the 1966 minimum wage legislation which extended provisions of the 1938 Fair Labor Standards Act to cover Canal Zone workers, beginning February 1, 1967. Under the latter legislation, Canal Zone workers who come under the coverage of the Act for the first time will begin to receive $1 an hour minimum wages on that date, and 15 cents will be added annually to this wage floor until the same $1.60 hourly minimum as will prevail in the United States is reached. In addition, the Secretary of Labor, in cooperation with the Secretaries of State and Defense, is to undertake a study of wage rates and classifications in the Canal Zone and their relationship to effective and economical operation of the Panama Canal. The results of this study and recommendations are to be submitted to Congress by July 1, 1968.

Inclusion of the Canal Zone Workers in the Fair Labor Standards Act coverage reflects the great change which has taken place over the years both in the official attitude of the United States government and the unions as well toward labor policies in the Panama Canal Zone. Even today, there still remains strong opposition in some quarters to extending the Federal minimum wage rates to the Canal Zone. This opposition had its origins in the 1903 Caribbean wage scale established by the Isthmian Canal Commission providing for Canal Zone rates "equal or slightly in excess of the local native prevailing rates for similar work in the Republic of Panama." However, as a result of the years of work by the AFL-CIO trade union forces, those advocating such a policy no longer can prevail. The 1966 legislation has successfully ended this form of discrimination against more than 6,000 Canal Zone workers who were earning less than the U.S. minimum wage rate when it went into effect.

Notes

1. Other activities of this AFL-CIO delegation are described in Chapters XI, XVII, and XVIII.

VIII

How ORIT Was Born

THE AFL and the CIO were both charter members of the ICFTU and their leaders agreed to join hands in helping to set up a regional organization for the Western Hemisphere. However, it was imperative that the international staffs of the two national labor federations reach an understanding on the future *modus operandi* before a constituent conference was convened. After a series of preliminary informal meetings, staff representatives met in New York, on April 5, 1950, at the Hotel Astor. Martin Kyne and Dr. Ernest Schwarz represented the CIO, George P. Delaney and the author the AFL.

We agreed to support the establishment of a regional organization comprising North, Central, and South America, including British, Dutch, and French possessions. We also decided to recommend that a constituent conference be called by the ICFTU before the end of 1950 and that invitations should be extended to all organizations affiliated with the CIT, the CIO, its Canadian and Puerto Rican affiliates, other groups already affiliated with the ICFTU, and organizations that were not affiliated provided they had made application to join by the time the conference was officially announced.

The agreement stipulated, however, that this last group did not include organizations under direct or indirect control of the Communist Party or those that were anti-democratic, such as the Perón-dominated CGT of Argentina.

It was suggested that the general problems of organization be left largely to the decision of the regional conference itself. We did, however, propose the following points:

(a) That the CIO and the AFL furnish one Assistant Secretary each.

(b) That the chief officer of the organization should have recognized experience in the field of international labor, be able to speak English and Spanish, and devote to the organization his full time.

(c) That headquarters of the regional organization be in Havana, unless the majority of delegates from Latin America had another choice. In such an event, the CIO and the AFL would urge that the headquarters be as close as possible to the United States for reasons of convenience and economy.

The above agreement was subsequently approved informally by the Canadian, Cuban, and Chilean ICFTU-affiliated organizations and was accepted by the top officers of the ICFTU at the May 1950 meeting of its Executive Board. Mexico City was finally chosen as the site of the regional founding conference which was scheduled to be held during the first week of January 1951.

It was now up to CIT to round up the largest possible attendance at Mexico City. I was assigned to work with the Confederation of Labor of Colombia (CTC) and labor organizations from Central America. The CTC, following a realignment in the Liberal Party leadership after the *Bogotazo,* first assumed a position of independence vis-à-vis the CTAL of Lombardo Toledano and then moved cautiously toward an anti-Communist stand. But a sudden about-face was hard for leaders who had supported the CTAL policy and had gone on record attacking the CIT and the AFL. Furthermore, there was the problem of the UTC, the Catholic-inspired rival organization, which was already a member of the CIT and which the CTC still refused to recognize as a legitimate group. The splinter CTC group, under Juan C. Lara, which had been admitted to the CIT at the Lima Conference, had been quietly dropped and was no longer functioning.

It soon became obvious that CTC leaders on their own could not be counted on to affiliate with the ICFTU and participate in the Mexico City meeting. For one thing, the powerful Railway Workers' Federation was actively campaigning against it. I decided, therefore, to put the issue squarely before Dr. Carlos Lleras Restrepo, powerful leader of the reorganized Liberal Party and a man of great influence and prestige in CTC circles. I met him in New York City in the summer of 1950. After hearing my problem, Lleras expressed the view that the Liberal Party of Colombia had a moral and political obligation to extend to the international field its domestic stand against Communist domination of the labor movement. He made a number of practical suggestions and promised to act as soon as it was safe for him to return to Bogotá. He had gone to New York for a brief rest after bombs had been thrown at his home by opposition terrorists.

A few weeks after Lleras returned to Bogotá, Arturo Jáuregui, CIT Assistant Secretary, passed through New York on his way to Colombia. I gave him a letter of introduction to Dr. Lleras reminding him of his promise to help and stating that Jáuregui was authorized to discuss the concrete details of the CTC affiliation. While he was stopping in Cartagena, the police searched Jáuregui's hotel room and confiscated my letter of introduction to Lleras. In an attempt to embarrass the Liberal Party and the CTC, which were both in the opposition, the Conservative Government leaked the letter to the press. The Communists immediately got on the bandwagon with their customary cries of "imperialistic interference." Actually, the publication of the letter helped our cause, because Dr. Lleras openly confirmed the existence of our understanding, defended it, and urged the CTC members of the Liberal Party to quit stalling and to join the forces of free labor. The CTC eventually joined ORIT and has been one of the staunchest bulwarks of democratic labor in the Western Hemisphere. In 1966 Carlos Lleras was elected President of Colombia largely as a result of the support of democratic labor.

The trade union conference called by the International Confederation of Free Trade Unions (ICFTU) for the purpose of creating a regional organization for the Western Hemisphere, was held in Mexico City, January 8–12, 1951. The auditorium of the Fine Arts Palace was filled to capacity when at 11 o'clock on Monday, January 8, Sir Vincent Tewson, General Secretary of the British Trades Union Congress, opened the meeting as official representative of the Executive Board of the ICFTU. He welcomed Mexican President Miguel Alemán, who delivered a brief address, declaring the conference officially open. The keynote speech was delivered by J. H. Oldenbroek, General Secretary of the ICFTU.

There were 55 delegates in attendance, 23 substitutes, and 11 observers, representing 29 organizations from 21 countries. Six Brazilian national organizations, the Confederation of Labor of Bolivia and the General Confederation of Labor of Puerto Rico—all affiliated to the ICFTU but unable to attend—wired warm messages of greetings pledging cooperation and membership in the new regional organization. The United States was represented by the AFL, the CIO, and the United Mine Workers.[1]

On behalf of the entire United States delegation, George Meany addressed the opening session, asserting in forceful terms:

> As far as organized labor in the United States is concerned, we believe that every country in need of capital investment from abroad has the sovereign right to fix the conditions under which such investment is to be permitted and regulated. Likewise, we believe that every country has the right to adopt its own form of economic and social organization according to the will of its people freely expressed in a democratic way. That was the unanimous stand taken by organized labor in the United States when our country launched the Marshall Plan for the recovery of Europe; this is also the stand we have taken in connection with the Point IV Program, and other international measures authorized by our Congress.
>
> The only restriction we have ever advocated—and we shall continue to advocate to the limit of our resources—is that no economic help be given to those countries whose governments follow aggressive policies that threaten the peace of the world, or consistently violate human rights, suppress civic liberties and deny freedom of trade union organization. On this last point, we place special emphasis because recent history has clearly demonstrated that there cannot be genuine freedom in any country unless, in that country, Labor is free. *Freedom of Labor is the gauge by which one can measure the degree of freedom enjoyed by the people at large.*

Permanent officers of the Conference were then elected, as follows: President, Fidel Velázquez, General Secretary of the Confederation of Workers of Mexico (CTM) ; Vice-Presidents: George Meany and Jacob Potofsky of the United States, Oscar Murillo of Costa Rica, Henry Middleton of British Honduras, Arturo Sabroso of Peru, and Bernardo Ibáñez of Chile; Secretaries: Francisco Aguirre of Cuba and Pat Conroy of Canada. These nine were also to constitute the Steering Committee of the conference to which Sir Vincent Tewson and J. H. Oldenbroek were added as ex-officio members.

Tuesday, January 9, was mainly devoted to the work of the committees. The following day, Wednesday, something like a bolt out of the blue threw the delegates into confusion. The morning newspapers had carried a story that a delegation representing the CGT of Argentina had arrived in Mexico City and was prepared to join the conference.

At the start of the afternoon session, Chairman Velázquez was asked by a delegate from Uruguay to explain this report. "We are all considerably alarmed," he stated. Velázquez replied:

I too have read such a story, but without surprise because I am aware of the Mexican delegates' view on this particular matter. However, I do not know if the Argentines themselves will ask to be admitted, nor if the Mexican delegation will ask the conference to receive them. In any event, the conference will have plenty of opportunity to deliberate and to decide.

There followed a brief attempt to initiate a debate, but the chairman ruled that no discussion of the Argentine issue would be allowed as long as there was no written proposal addressed to the chair to admit them. However, that same night and the following day the delegates talked of nothing else but the attempt of the Argentines to get in. The Mexicans were obviously determined to introduce a proposal in favor of admitting the CGT, but all the other delegations were equally determined to prevent it. Why were the Mexicans so determined—everybody asked—in the face of the outspoken opposition of all the others?

A clue was offered by United States Ambassador to Mexico William O'Dwyer, when he invited George Meany and David McDonald to a private meeting at the Embassy residence. They later informed their colleagues of the American delegation that Ambassador O'Dwyer had expressed concern over the possible reaction of the Mexican government if the Argentines were rejected. The Ambassador hinted that Mexican labor's sponsorship of the CGT had been decided with the knowledge and consent—if not at the urging—of the Mexican government itself. This attitude of the Mexican government was in line with its established policy of refusing to interfere in any way, directly or indirectly, in the internal affairs of another country. A rebuke to the CGT, whose close ties with Perón were well known, was considered by the Mexican government as a direct affront to the head of the Argentine state. The two American trade unionists told their Ambassador, politely but firmly, to leave this purely internal labor matter in the hands of the trade unionists who they felt were quite capable of handling it.

When the plenary session was reconvened on Thursday, January 11, Chairman Velázquez announced his irrevocable decision to resign the presidency of the conference. This decision was the result, he explained, of disagreements with the other members of the Steering Committee, who, in his view, had constantly undermined his prerogatives and prestige as presiding officer. However, before making his resignation effective he wanted to dispose of the pending matter of the CGT of Argentina. As leader of the CTM and spokesman for the entire Mexican delegation, Velázquez then proposed that three fraternal delegates from the CGT, who apparently had been invited to attend the Conference by the Co-ordination and Reception Committee, be seated despite the opposition of the Steering Committee. In executive session the day before the Steering Committee had ruled that the other Committee had had no power to issue such an invitation.

It seemed to me and others that Fidel Velázquez sounded as if he was merely reiterating a policy when he declared:

> Our relations with the CGT of Argentina date not from five days nor from five years. The glorious CGT of Argentina, which for more than fifty years has conducted an independent life, with dignity and decorum, has had its independence interrupted as a result of the political situation now prevailing in that country which we have no right to judge. In this respect I want to say that the international conduct of the Mexican labor movement is no other than the one of the government of the Mexican Republic.

Luis Morones—the same Morones of the Lima CIT Conference—asked for the floor. George Meany objected on the ground that Morones was not on the list of delegates. Velázquez produced, however, an invitation addressed to Morones's organization, the CROM, signed by the three members of the Conference's Coordination and Reception Committee, including John Brophy, ICFTU representative. Later, a similar invitation addressed to the CGT of Argentina was also produced. At this point, led by Morones, the Argentine group almost managed to get into the hall. Only the timely intervention of the chairman prevented a clash with a group of delegates already surging toward the door to block their entrance.

How those invitations were sent in the first place was heatedly debated during that fateful Thursday morning session, but in such an emotional atmosphere the matter was not and could not be clarified satisfactorily. A study of the stenographic notes of that session, as well as interviews and investigations which I subsequently conducted, have enabled me to reconstruct the following sequence of events.

When the decision was reached to hold the constituent conference of the regional organization in Mexico City, the General Secretary of the ICFTU felt that the preparations would be best served by an ad hoc committee composed of a representative of the ICFTU (John Brophy, of the CIO), of the CIT (Augusto Malavé Villalba, of the Venezuelan CTV), and one each of the three Mexican host organizations, namely the

Mexican Confederation of Labor (CTM), the National Proletarian Confederation (CPN), and the National Confederation of Workers (CNT). John Brophy, who as representative of the ICFTU was the most important officer of the group and could even exercise veto power, while a capable trade union leader, did not know a word of Spanish and knew little of the complex labor movement in Mexico and even less about the organizations of labor in the whole of Latin America.

The ad hoc organization committee soon named itself "Coordination and Reception Committee of the Inter-American Labor Congress of the International Confederation of Free Trade Unions." Under this letterhead invitations were printed, with a blank space to be filled in with the name of the organization invited "to send a fraternal delegation to said Congress." Space was provided for the signatures on behalf of the ICFTU, the CTM, the CPN, and CNT.

According to John Brophy, he was asked to sign a number of blank invitations for prominent citizens to attend the inaugural session at which the President of the Republic was scheduled to speak. He claimed that fifty or one hundred blank invitations were signed by him with his understanding that they were to be used only for the inaugural session. However, the invitations he signed stated specifically "to send a fraternal delegation" to the Congress and not to the inaugural session only.

Pérez Ríos and Manuel García declared to the Congress that, as representatives of the CTM and the CPN respectively, they signed the invitation to the CROM and the Argentine CGT after they had been signed by Brophy and that they knew perfectly well to whom the invitations were addressed and for what purpose.

Augusto Malavé Villalba explained that representatives of the CTM suggested to the Conference Coordination and Reception Committee that it extend invitations to all Mexican independent trade union organizations, including CROM. The Committee agreed and thus the invitation to Morones's CROM was sent, declared Malavé, with Brophy's full knowledge. The invitation to the CGT of Argentina was, however, an entirely different matter. The Committee, emphasized Malavé, never approved the sending of such an invitation; however, he and Brophy were present at a meeting of the Mexican Bloque Obrero—a sort of alliance of all the Mexican trade union organizations—at which it was resolved to "ask the Congress to invite the Argentine CGT." The implication was clear that one blank invitation, already signed by Brophy, was used by unauthorized persons to fill in the name of "Confederación General del Trabajo—Argentina." Brophy might have attached little importance to inviting one more Mexican organization, the CROM; but he surely knew that the CGT of Argentina was on the "black list" of the ICFTU and particularly of his own organization, the CIO. It was therefore inconceivable that he could have signed an invitation with the name of the CGT already typed on it.

With respect to Morones's right to sit in as a fraternal delegate, Chairman Velázquez settled it by referring the matter to the Steering Committee, which promptly decided in the negative, with Velázquez casting the only affirmative vote. The Argentine matter, however, was before the conference in the form of a formal request to give the CGT fraternal status. The debate was thus resumed and it continued well into the afternoon.

The Mexican spokesmen (Alfonso Sánchez Madariaga, A. Bustillo Carrillo, Leon V. Paredes, and Velázquez himself) pointed out that the degree of governmental control of Brazilian unions affiliated to the ICFTU was no less than that exercised by Perón over the CGT. "Why, then, the discrimination?," they asked. The replies came strong and fast from Jacob Potofsky, who opposed the Argentine admission on behalf of the entire United States delegation; from Eusebio Mujal, spokesman for the Cuban delegation; and from Cándido Gregorio, representative of the COASI, the Argentine democratic anti-Peronista labor group. When the debate ended and the delegates voted, only the Mexicans voted affirmatively. Fidel Velázquez then stepped down as chairman and Vice-President Arturo Sabroso of Peru was elected to fill the vacancy. It being late afternoon, the session was recessed.

The plenary session was resumed that night with the report of the Constitution Committee, which provided that the organization would be called "Inter-American Regional Organization of Workers," its Spanish version being "Organización Regional Interamericana de Trabajadores (ORIT), and that its administration would be vested in the Regional Conference, to meet every three years; in the Regional Council, composed of 31 representatives designated by the affiliated organizations divided in geographical groupings, which would meet once a year; in the Executive Committee, composed of seven members plus the Secretary and the President, elected by the conference among the members of the Regional Council, to meet at least once every three months; and by the Regional Secretary, to be elected by the conference. The Constitution also provided for the election of a President, who would preside over the Regional Conference and the meetings of the Regional Council and Executive Committee.

In the discussion of the report, the delegates from the CTM expressed disagreement with the draft prepared by the Committee, which, they considered, did not give full autonomy to affiliated organizations. They, therefore, presented two amendments. One, consisting of a detailed declaration of principles to be added to the Preamble of the Constitution, was accepted with the understanding that the Executive Committee would decide what portion of it would be added to the Preamble of the Constitution and what would, instead, be published as a separate official document of the organization. The other amendment would have made Mexico City the constitutional seat of the Regional Organization.

It was getting close to midnight and nerves were frayed. The Mexican delegates had boxed themselves into a corner; it was obvious that they were building up a case to justify their eventual withdrawal from the conference. On the other hand, the ICFTU leadership and the rest of the delegations were determined to stand firm.

The discussion on the second Mexican amendment relating to the permanent seat of the regional organization became bitter. It had been informally agreed in advance that, at least until the next Convention, the headquarters would be in Cuba. The Cuban delegation resented the Mexican amendment and reacted to it angrily. At one point the debate almost degenerated into a brawl. Finally a vote was taken and the Mexicans again found themselves isolated. I was reliably informed, years later, that if the headquarters of the new organization had been set in Mexico City, they would have found it possible to forget the rest and make peace with the other delegations. But communication had broken down between the Mexicans and the Steering Committee, which was deciding the course of the Conference. It was at this point that Bernardo Ibáñez, president of the still existing CIT, interrupted Fidel Velázquez, an old friend of his, while he was again speaking on behalf of the Mexican group. Ibáñez asked permission to make a statement; Velázquez consented, and that was the gesture that saved the Conference.

The Chilean delivered an impassioned appeal that commanded immediate attention from all delegates. Ibáñez asserted that only the reactionaries and the Communists would rejoice if the Conference failed. He called for an end to arguments and an immediate return to the business for which the Conference had been called—the creation of the regional organization of the ICFTU.

When Ibáñez finished, all the delegates stood up and applauded. The motion to adopt the first item of the Report of the Constitution Committee was then approved by acclamation. Thus ORIT was born!

Discussion of the Constitution was resumed at Friday morning's session, after an address of greetings by Luis Alberto Monge on behalf of the International Labor Organization, with which the ICFTU maintained consultative relationship.

Before the final adoption of the Constitution, Salvador Carrillo, on behalf of the Mexican CTM delegation, announced that his organization was withdrawing from the Conference. Fidel Velázquez spoke immediately after him and pledged "continued cooperation of the CTM with all the sister organizations of the Western Hemisphere, in all struggles and actions aiming at the strengthening of democracy and the promotion of the welfare of the wage earners." On the other hand, the delegates of the CPN announced that they were remaining, having decided to join the ORIT.

On recommendation of a special nomination committee, the Conference unanimously selected the city of Havana, Cuba, for the headquarters of the regional organization, and elected Arturo Sabroso Montoya of Peru to the post of President and Francisco Aguirre of Cuba to the office of Regional Secretary. It also elected the following seven members of the Executive Committee and their substitutes (the latter are listed in parentheses) :

Bernardo Ibáñez of Chile (Luis Colotuzzo of Uruguay)
John L. Lewis of UMW (John Owens, same organization)
George Meany of AFL (Percy Bengough of TLC of Canada)
Henry Middleton of British Honduras (L.E. Eleazer of Dutch Guiana)
Eusebio Mujal of Cuba (Hipólito Márcano of Puerto Rico)
Jacob Potofsky of CIO (Pat Conroy of CCL of Canada)
Manuel Rivera of Mexico (Claudio González of Costa Rica)

The Conference was closed with appropriate addresses by President Arturo Sabroso, Regional Secretary Francisco Aguirre, Sir Vincent Tewson of the ICFTU Executive Board, and Jacob Potofsky who spoke on behalf of the entire United States delegation.

Following adjournment, the delegates marched in a body to the monument of the Heroes of Chapultepec where they laid a wreath as an expression of admiration and respect for the Mexican nation and to the ideals which inspired and guided the makers of its independence.

On Saturday, January 13, the ORIT Executive Board held its first meeting, during which it worked out a financial budget, laid down some basic rules for the effective functioning of the organization, and appointed me Assistant Secretary in charge of International Relations and Education, and Dr. Ernest Schwarz as Assistant Secretary in charge of Research and Social and Economic Affairs. We were authorized to discharge some of our duties, when feasible, from our respective AFL and CIO offices in the United States. It also appointed Arturo Jáuregui of Peru and Augusto Malavé Villalba of Venezuela as organizers to work under the direct supervision of the Regional Secretary.

After the adjournment of the Conference, the General Council of the Inter-American Confederation of Workers (CIT) met in special session at the Hotel Virreyes, under the chairmanship of President Bernardo Ibáñez. Acting upon authorization received from the Second Convention of the CIT, held in September 1949 in Havana, Cuba, where the formation of the ICFTU and its Regional Organization for the Western Hemisphere was advocated, the General Council voted to dissolve the Inter-American Confederation of Workers and recommended to its affiliated organizations unreserved cooperation with the ORIT.

In the period of two days, after looking failure in the face, the delegates had regained confidence, were again buoyant, and prepared to go home determined to make the ORIT a living reality, worthy of all the labor pains that had preceded its birth. We all were sad over the incidents involving the Mexicans and their withdrawal from the organization. Yet, many of us were somehow confident that after the dust had settled, a friendly relationship and cooperation between the Mexican CTM and the rest of the free labor movement of the Americas would again prevail. It turned out exactly that way, as reported in the March 1953 issue of the *Inter-American Labor Bulletin:*

President George Meany and Secretary-Treasurer William F. Schnitzler entertained at lunch Fidel Velázquez, Secretary General of the Mexican Confederation of Labor (CTM) and the members of the ORIT Secretariat at the Hotel Monte Carlo in Miami Beach, Florida, on February 13. The CTM, which is the largest Mexican trade union national organization with a membership of over one million, recently joined the ICFTU and the ORIT.

I acted as interpreter between Meany and Velázquez. When Fidel entered, he proffered his hand to George, saying:

"I have come to tell you that I am suffering from amnesia. I can't remember a thing!"

To which Meany replied, grasping Velázquez's hand:

"Brother Fidel, I am down with the same sickness!"

Notes

1. The AFL delegates were: Secretary-Treasurer George Meany; William L. McFetridge, President of the Building Service Employees International Union; W. C. Doherty, President of the International Association of Letter Carriers; Dave Beck, Executive

Vice-President of the International Brotherhood of Teamsters; and Serafino Romualdi, Latin American Representative.

Those from the CIO were: Jacob Potofsky, President, Amalgamated Clothing Workers of America; David McDonald, Secretary-Treasurer, United Steel Workers of America; O. A. Knight, President, Oil Workers' Union; Martin C. Kyne, Vice-President, Retail and Wholesale Clerks' Union; William Pollock, Vice-President, Textile Workers Union of America; Lewis J. Clark, Secretary-Treasurer, Packinghouse Workers' Union; L. S. Buckmaster, President, United Rubber Workers; and Ernest Schwarz, Executive Secretary, Latin American Committee.

The United Mine Workers (UMW), who were attending an inter-American conference for the first time, were represented by John Owens, Secretary-Treasurer, and Denny Lewis, President of District 50.

IX

Painful Growth to Maturity

THE ORIT officers and staff left the Mexico City Conference determined to make the new organization an effective force in the struggle to improve the lot of the working people in the hemisphere. In our initial enthusiasm, however, we failed to anticipate many of the obstacles that would present themselves as the infant organization took its first steps toward assuming what has now become a significant role in the life of the hemisphere. ORIT's growth was not an easy one. In the first decade of its life, ORIT's progress was impeded by serious problems from within—weakness of organization, administration, and staffing—and it was buffeted although not destroyed by external opposition and crises that had to be surmounted.

As free trade unionists, we were convinced that our efforts to reach the millions of Latin Americans suffering under the yoke of military dictatorships would be futile unless and until the democratic nations of the hemisphere, particularly the United States, were willing to demonstrate through their actions their friendship and alliance with the oppressed—not with the oppressors. It was our contention that, in a world where isolationism had become an impossibility, there could be no such thing as a national policy of true nonintervention and that it was the responsibility of free nations to assist the people of every nation to mold the democratic institutions necessary for economic and social progress.

The ORIT Executive Board, at its second meeting in Havana, March 27–28, 1951, concurred in my suggestion that we send to each of the OAS

122

Foreign Ministers, who were meeting at the same time in Washington to consider crucial measures for the defense of the hemisphere, a statement expressing ORIT's views on each item of the agenda of their meeting. The ORIT message from Havana, which came as a logical sequence to the CIT Memorandum to the 1948 Bogotá Conference of American States, included among its recommendations a proposal that measures be adopted for the economic integration of the hemisphere. The message also called on the governments to reaffirm the Bogotá resolution repudiating international Communism and all other forms of government that deny fundamental human rights, to grant amnesty to democratic political prisoners and exiles, to permit political and trade union freedoms, and to conduct regular elections in conformity with democratic procedures. Finally, the message urged reestablishment of the Committee for the Political Defense of the Continent—set up in World War II—with the added task of combating Soviet subversion as well as promoting democracy.

ORIT's message was heard but not heeded by all, particularly not by the dictatorships in Venezuela, Peru, Argentina, and the Dominican Republic. Labor leaders in these countries were often being persecuted, arrested, driven into exile, or even assassinated. Those who managed to go into exile looked to ORIT for help in maintaining a campaign against dictatorial oppression and keeping alive the sparks of free trade unionism. Complaints against violations of rights were lodged by ORIT with the ILO, the OAS, and the Human Rights Commission of the UN.

ORIT meanwhile sought to launch organizing drives in Central America and the Caribbean, where its strength was minimal. The responsibility for this program under the ORIT constitution rested exclusively in the hands of the Regional Secretary, Francisco Aguirre of Cuba. Big of heart and a sincere and effective spokesman for free labor, Aguirre nevertheless was involved in too many activities—his duties as a Congressman, his own Hotel and Restaurant Workers Union, the international department of the Cuban CTC, and other labor and personal matters. He was rarely at his ORIT office. Organizers complained of delayed answers to letters.

Aguirre and I have had a close personal friendship. Years later, when he was arrested and sentenced by one of Castro's kangaroo courts to a long prison term, I wept as if he were my brother. But my AFL and ORIT responsibilities compelled me to express in no uncertain terms my concern over the lack of a full-time regional secretary.

The ORIT leadership problem was discussed with officials of the AFL and CIO and, informally, with representatives of other ORIT affiliates.

The idea of moving ORIT's headquarters from Havana and replacing Aguirre found increasing support.

Aguirre confided to me his intention to step down and agreed to sound out as his possible successor Luis Alberto Monge, the young Costa Rican labor leader who had taken part in the organization of CIT and was serving as chief of the ILO's Latin American Trade Union Division in Geneva. Not content with being an international bureaucrat and eager to resume an active role in Costa Rica's labor movement, Monge was tentatively receptive to the idea of taking Aguirre's place. However, he conditioned his acceptance on a move of ORIT's headquarters, changes in ORIT's structure, and advance assurance of widespread support. In October 1952 he resigned his ILO post and returned home.

Meanwhile, through the good offices of the late Trifon Gómez, a prominent Spanish labor leader in exile who was the Latin American representative of the International Transport Workers' Federation, discreet contacts were established with Mexican CTM leader Fidel Velázquez. At the invitation of the ICFTU, Velázquez went to Brussels and was received by ICFTU representatives. He gave a favorable interview, reprinted in the September, 1952, issue of the ICFTU's *Free Labor World*, in which he clearly hinted that the CTM was going to rejoin the ICFTU through ORIT. His contacts were expanded to include representatives of the AFL, the CIO, and the Canadian affiliates. The CTM was ready to join ORIT and would welcome transfer of ORIT headquarters to Mexico City, if the next convention should so decide. It was anticipated, however, that the Cubans would fight to retain the headquarters in Havana.

At the request of the two ORIT assistant secretaries from the United States (Dr. Ernest Schwarz and myself) the ORIT Executive Board agreed to move up the scheduled 1954 convention and it was called for December 12–17, 1952, in Rio de Janeiro.

The U.S. delegation to the second ORIT congress consisted of William C. Doherty, George P. Delaney, and myself for the AFL; Emil Mazey, R. J. Thomas, George Burt, and Ernest Schwarz for the CIO; and John L. Lewis and his daughter Kathryn for the United Mine Workers.

To prepare resolutions and rest up for the strenuous convention, Doherty, Delaney, and I, accompanied by my wife Miriam, decided to take a slow cruise to Rio. We were pleasantly surprised to find John L. Lewis and his daughter also passengers. Previously, I had met Lewis only briefly before he had taken his Mine Workers out of the AFL with his laconic scribbled note: "Green, we disaffiliate 12-12-47, Lewis."

During the voyage, Lewis and I often strolled on the promenade deck discussing Latin America and ORIT. One night he invited me and my fellow delegates to an impromptu reception arranged by the Maritime Union's ship unit in his honor. There I heard John L. Lewis the agitator in action, castigating the "greed" of the shipowners and urging the sailors to "unite and fight to break the chains of servitude."

When he had been head of the CIO, John L. had been a strong supporter of the pro-Communist CTAL and its Mexican leader, Lombardo Toledano. It also was said that he had employed Communists as CIO organizers. Mrs. Sarah Limbach, once ILGWU director in the Pittsburgh area, told me one time that in answer to her query about the wisdom of using Communist organizers, John L. answered gruffly: "I am using them as hunting dogs. Who in the end gets the bird—the dog or the hunter?"

Later, at the Rio convention, Lewis took an amiable, almost meek stance vis-à-vis the Latin American delegates. It was an unusual role for him to play. He declined to accept the nomination as chairman of the U.S. delegation, insisting that the post be given to Doherty as "Vice-President and Council member," as he put it, "of the largest U.S. trade union organization, the AFL." He served as any other delegate on a convention committee and attended all meetings to the end—well into the night or toward morning, as is the Latin American custom. Even when he finally addressed the congress, he did so with a deliberate pose of humility. It was a strange environment for John L. and I believe he tried to show his sincere respect for his Latin American brothers by speaking with a cautiousness not typical of his renowned oratory in the United States.

At the end of the convention, the delegates were received at the headquarters of Brazilian President Getulio Vargas. The waiting room had no chairs or benches and was stiflingly hot. There was not even a drinking fountain available. For reasons never explained, the delegates were kept waiting one hour. Most of us grew hotter with impatience. Delaney became concerned about Lewis's health and offered to accompany him back to his hotel. John L. wanted none of it. He kept repeating: "We must not be discourteous to the President of the host country." Finally Vargas emerged from his office. With him, like manna from Heaven, came chilled champagne with which we toasted him, Brazil, free labor, and inter-American solidarity.

After a brief exchange of salutations, Vargas approached Lewis, said something in a light vein, and proffered a Brazilian *charuto*. Lewis accepted it and promptly returned the compliment by offering Vargas an American cigar. Thereupon, both lit up and started puffing away like a couple of peace-pipe chiefs. The delegates cheered wildly. Somehow, in a few seconds all seemed to have forgotten the discomfort of the dreary wait.

In attendance at the second ORIT convention were voting delegates from 16 countries, representing 28 affiliated organizations—including the CTM of Mexico, which joined ORIT during the sessions. Observer delegates were present from unaffiliated organizations of Chile, Paraguay, Bolivia, and El Salvador. Twelve affiliates from eleven countries were unable to send delegates but sent messages of support.

The Cubans, in their fight to keep ORIT headquarters in Havana, were far from being isolated, but they lacked the votes and lost the battle. After the convention voted to move the headquarters to Mexico City, the Cubans refused to accept any position on the Executive Board. Aguirre previously had given private assurance he would take the post of President, but he changed his mind and refused to run. However, a few months later, the Cuban CTC resumed normal relations with the ORIT.

As had been unofficially agreed in advance, Luis Alberto Monge was elected to the post of General Secretary—the title being changed from Regional Secretary—after Aguirre announced he would not seek reelection. The Presidency went to Luis Alberto Colotuzzo of Uruguay, a working bricklayer who was an effective and politically sound trade unionist.

Arturo Sabroso of Peru, who had retired as President because he believed the post should be rotated, was rewarded with a post on the Executive Board, along with George Meany, Jacob Potofsky, and John L. Lewis of the United States, and Fidel Velázquez of Mexico. The growing importance of the ORIT membership in the Caribbean area was reflected in the election of F. L. Walcott of Barbados and Leo E. Eleazer of Surinam (Dutch Guiana) to the Board.

The convention's resolutions included condemnation of the dictatorial regimes in Peru, Venezuela, the Dominican Republic, and Spain. Arms shipments to military regimes under the pretext of strengthening hemisphere defense were deplored. A special resolution introduced by a delegation of Argentine trade unionists exiled in Uruguay branded General Perón's government as "a menace to the independence of the Latin American nations and a threat to the peace of the Western Hemisphere."

The most important accomplishment of the Rio convention was the adoption of an ORIT reorganization plan recommended by the Convention Committee on Bylaws, of which I had been elected chairman. The large unwieldy Regional Council was abolished. Field organizers were placed under the control of central headquarters. A secretariat was established to handle administrative matters between meetings of the Executive Board. The Secretariat consisted of the President, the General Secretary, and three Assistant Secretaries, who were Schwarz and myself from the United States, and Alfonso Sánchez Madariaga from Mexico. The years that followed proved beyond doubt the wisdom of the Rio reorganization. The ORIT was put practically under a collective leadership, thus preventing the possibility of another period of quasi paralysis resulting from a General Secretary's inertia.

The new General Secretary, Luis Alberto Monge, did not suffer from inertia. He coped successfully with many problems, showing patience, firmness, and political integrity. He was not a "brick and mortar" official and not a seeker of affiliations at any cost.

Monge felt the strength of ORIT lay in its contribution to the struggle against the totalitarian regimes of Perón in Argentina, Odría in Peru, Jiménez in Venezuela, Trujillo in the Dominican Republic, Somoza in Nicaragua, and later Batista in Cuba. Any trade union gain achieved by even a minimum of contact with such regimes was repugnant to Monge.

Luis Alberto Monge showed a deep affection for me although he and I sometimes had painful disagreements on methods needed to achieve ORIT objectives. Our differences sometimes were threshed out at ORIT Secretariat meetings but more often in personal confidential correspondence. He never aired our differences in public, not even when I wrote veiled criticisms of his policy in the AFL press and in the *Inter-American Labor Bulletin* published from my Washington office. Monge knew that from the first day I met him in Costa Rica, back in 1947, I was deeply impressed with his brilliant mind and captivating libertarian faith. I took advantage of every opportunity to urge him to climb the ladder to higher positions of leadership. He admired the policies of the AFL and George Meany's leadership. Meany so esteemed Monge that he sponsored him for the Geneva ILO post. Time showed that he had the ability, and he is regarded today in Costa Rica as a potential candidate for his country's highest office.

The San José, Costa Rica, convention of ORIT in April 1955 reflected a high degree of cooperation among delegations from all parts of the hemisphere.[1] The Credentials Committee reported the presence of 74 official delegates representing 25 affiliates from 17 countries, and 13 fraternal delegates from 13 organizations from 7 countries. For the first time, every country of Central America was represented at an ORIT convention.

An outstanding welcome was provided by the Costa Rican Administration of President José "Pepe" Figueres, who delivered a speech in praise of ORIT and also took the occasion to urge the United States to help stabilize the economies of its Latin American neighbors. Greetings on behalf of the North American delegates were extended by AFL Secretary-Treasurer William F. Schnitzler, who praised Figueres and the other Costa Ricans who had led the democratic anti-Communist revolution of 1948 and beaten off two attempts at counterrevolution, the latest having been in January 1955 in the form of an invasion from neighboring Nicaragua.

Controversy developed at the convention as an outgrowth of the involvement of several ORIT affiliates—particularly the AFL, the CIO, and the Cuban CTC—in the reconstruction of the democratic labor movement of Guatemala following the overthrow of the Arbenz regime in 1954. Guatemala's new Minister of Labor, Dr. Jorge Arenales, requested to appear before the convention to explain his government's labor policy. The Convention Steering Committee, after some debate, granted the request, despite the objection of ORIT President Colotuzzo. When Dr. Arenales spoke, the Uruguayan delegates, headed by Colotuzzo, left the convention hall as a gesture of protest.

The convention unanimously reelected Monge as General Secretary, selected Ignazio González Tellechea of Cuba as President, and added Arturo Jáuregui Hurtado of Peru to ORIT leadership as Assistant Secretary in charge of the Department of Organization. He had served ORIT from its inception as an organizer. He also was designated as Acting Secretary during Monge's absence from headquarters. Luis Alberto Colotuzzo was retired as President under the terms of the constitution but was elected to the Executive Board.

Until 1954 the ICFTU Secretariat in Brussels left ORIT pretty much alone. During this time the trade union situation in Latin America was not too encouraging and ORIT's main efforts were directed against the dictatorships. It was a hard, relentless fight, which needed occasional European support—and the ICFTU provided it—especially at ILO conferences and meetings of its Governing Body, where complaints for violation of trade union rights were often lodged. But it was a kind of activity that provided little room for accomplishments in terms of obtaining new affiliates—the sort of thing that most interested Brussels.

A few weeks after the 1955 ORIT Convention, General Secretary Luis Alberto Monge went on an extended leave of absence in order to be of service to his close friend "Pepe" Figueres, the President of Costa Rica. Arturo Jáuregui became the ORIT Acting Secretary.

Jáuregui, who was impatient with bureaucratic delays, soon ran into trouble with the ICFTU officers. At the meeting of the ICFTU Executive Board July 2–7, 1956, he stressed the need for better coordination between ORIT and the ICFTU on all matters concerning Latin America and pointed out that ORIT wished to work with greater autonomy because events in the region were developing at such a rapid pace that at times it wasn't possible to wait for consultation with and a decision by ICFTU before engaging in necessary action. He reminded the ICFTU leaders that the inter-American free trade union movement had dissolved the CIT in order to take part in the foundation of ORIT, as a regional organization of ICFTU, and had, therefore, the right to expect that this incorporation would give benefits and not impediments. Jáuregui ended by proposing that a special committee, composed of the President and General Secretary of the ICFTU plus the Executive Board members from the inter-American region, be appointed for the purpose of analyzing the specific instances which in his view indicated lack of ICFTU cooperation. However, this suggestion was not put to a vote nor was it even discussed.

An earlier instance of ICFTU impropriety had been noted by ORIT in April 1955 at its Executive Board meeting in San José, where it was reported that the ICFTU's chief for Latin American relations, Hermes R. Horne—a second-string trade unionist from Uruguay—had gone to Colombia and Peru on a mission without notifying ORIT. Horne reported to the ICFTU on his trip and discussed it with certain labor leaders in the United States but did not inform the ORIT people in Mexico City. The San José meeting adopted a resolution sponsored by the U.S. delegation calling on the ICFTU "to conduct all of its Western Hemisphere activities through the ORIT, in order to achieve closer coordination and in order that the ORIT may be accorded greater credit and recognition." Although a copy of that resolution was sent to the ICFTU congress held in Vienna in May 1955, General Secretary Oldenbroek made no mention of it in his report to the congress.

Further difficulties developed over the question of financial aid to the post-Perón free labor movement in Argentina. Jáuregui had asked for such help at an October 1955 ICFTU subcommittee meeting. Shortly afterwards, several ICFTU missions went to Argentina authorized by Oldenbroek to pledge financial assistance to democratic groups. ORIT's president, Ignacio González Tellechea, followed them in February 1956, authorized in writing by ICFTU to pledge a maximum of $20,000—half of which was to be made available immediately. Tellechea prepared a program based on a joint contribution from ORIT and ICFTU; it was approved by ORIT at once but ICFTU dragged its heels. Almost a year later, in September 1956, the ICFTU-ORIT representative in Argentina finally received an advance from the Brussels headquarters—a meager 10 percent of the amount pledged!

Another source of disagreement was the question of financial help for underground activities in Venezuela. CTV leaders in exile asked the ICFTU in mid-1954 for funds to finance such activities. ORIT agreed immediately but nothing happened until June 1955 when Pedro Bernardo Pérez Salinas, former President of the CTV, arrived in Mexico City after his release from a Venezuelan jail. He brought the plan for assistance up to date on the basis of his personal experience. The ICFTU received the plan and asked for time in order to determine its feasibility. When Jáuregui raised the subject in October 1955, Oldenbroek said that although he approved the proposed operation it would have to be discussed by the ICFTU Executive Board. However, this item failed to appear on the agenda of subsequent ICFTU meetings and it was not until May 26, 1956—*almost two full years after the plan was first presented*—that the ICFTU came up with $2,250, one fourth of its total pledge. ORIT had paid all of its share during this time, permitting the underground work to proceed in Venezuela.

At the 1955 ICFTU Convention in Vienna all organizing activities were assigned to the newly created Office of the Director of Organization. Charles Millard, a Canadian trade unionist and member of the United States Steel Workers of America, was eventually selected to fill the post. Millard, whose credentials as a trade unionist were impeccable, had no previous experience in international labor, and did not speak any language other than English. As far as Latin America was concerned he remained obdurate in his belief that the area's geography, culture, history, ethnic makeup, economic development and labor movement were really no different from Canada's. Yet, at the beginning, properly concerned over the ORIT-ICFTU rift, he managed to bring about a truce. Meanwhile, Luis Alberto Monge, after a leave of absence of eleven months, resumed his post as ORIT's General Secretary on June 12, 1956.

Millard played a key peace-making role in the ORIT-ICFTU differences. During the November 1956 Executive Board meeting of ICFTU, private talks were held by top leaders of the two organizations. Past disagreements were reviewed and it was clear that Millard desired to placate ORIT and reach a workable understanding. During one session, for example, ICFTU decided to make good all of the debts incurred by its regional office in Chile and to place it under the administrative supervision of the ORIT organizer, Rafael Otero Borlaff. The ICFTU also agreed, in principle, to transfer to Mexico City the preparation of its Spanish-language bulletin and other publications in Spanish. José Aguirre, who at that time was on the ICFTU publication staff, was assigned to ORIT headquarters. At the close of the Executive Board meeting Millard, Monge, and González Tellechea had another meeting and agreed that henceforth the ICFTU would channel all of its Latin American financial help through ORIT; that all the ICFTU planning for the Western Hemisphere would be done in cooperation with ORIT, with the Mexico City headquarters having exclusive responsibility for implementation; and that the ICFTU Director of Organization would attend the meeting of ORIT's Executive Board in Mexico City in February 1957, after surveying all South American projects.

But the truce between ORIT and the ICFTU was shortlived. Charles Millard arrived in Mexico City for the February 1957 ORIT Executive Board meeting directly from his South American tour, during which he visited a number of countries accompanied by Hermes Horne, chief of the ICFTU's Latin American desk. It was obvious from the start that the two had something up their sleeves. They provoked a disagreeable discussion by demanding from Secretary General Monge a yes or no reply as to whether ORIT had received any money from the AFL-CIO Free Trade Union Committee. After this matter was clarified, Ary Campista, a member of the Board from Brazil who was regarded as a stooge for the ICFTU Secretariat, started a tirade against the U.S. Labor Attaché in Rio, accusing him of "interference" in ORIT affairs. The purpose of these maneuvers was obviously to attempt to smear ORIT as a puppet of the AFL-CIO and of the State Department.

Millard then presented a plan of action that, he emphasized, "would really put ORIT in the proper shape." He explained the plan orally; no copies were distributed. Its main points were the creation of an "Information and Consultation Center" and a series of local ICFTU offices in South and Central America, plus the appointment of a supervisor for the southern countries who would operate not from ORIT headquarters but from an office of his own, presumably in Brazil. Since Millard had no idea of the real needs of the free trade union movement in Latin America, it was obvious that the plan had been concocted by the ICFTU Secretariat in Brussels and sold to Millard by Horne, with the clear purpose of straitjacketing ORIT and shifting to the ICFTU the ultimate direction and control of trade union activities in the Western Hemisphere.

At the next meeting of the ORIT Secretariat, held in early April 1957 in the Mexican border town of Nogales, Monge submitted a statement on the Millard plan. Monge said he felt it was "improper and inopportune to dispose with such haste of a matter of great importance." He said the Information and Consultation Center was absolutely unnecessary because "its establishment would be a real threat to the international coordination of ORIT's work and would bring about the fragmentation of our administrative machinery." He added that local offices could only be justified for Brazil, because of its size and large population, and for CADORIT, the Caribbean Area Division of ORIT, because of language differences and the colonial status of the islands, and that the establishment of a supervisor for Chile, Argentina, Uruguay, and Brazil was "totally unnecessary." The supervisory work, Monge added, "can be very well carried out by ORIT."

The controversy went on with increased vehemence and bitterness. At the ICFTU Convention held in Tunis, July 1957, Monge was pressured to get in line with the proposed plan and an attempt was made to deny him his right to be seated as a voting delegate representing the Costa Rican Confederation of Labor. After the Convention, Oldenbroek intervened directly and wrote Monge a letter dated October 2, 1957, in which he reiterated in bureaucratic cant that "regional organizations must recognize that we are the parent body, and if there are good reasons for our undertaking a special job in any particular country the final decision must be with us."

On October 23, 1957, Monge wrote me a personal letter detailing further cases of intolerable interference by Brussels in the internal affairs of ORIT. He also apprised me of Millard's latest brainstorm—a proposal to split ORIT in two by creating a regional office for North America (United States, Canada, and possibly the English-speaking Caribbean islands) and another for all of Latin America. This implied the complete reversal of the concept of an integrated Pan-American Labor body enunciated first by the CIT at its Lima Conference in 1948, and later ratified at the Mexico City Convention when ORIT was organized in 1951. Monge concluded his letter on this sad note:

All of this and numerous other details would seem to prove that the last Congress of our ORIT will be the one scheduled for next year. Or at least that is what the people in Brussels propose. I have given a great part of my life to this ORIT of ours. And that is why I cannot resign myself to seeing it turned into a mere bureaucratic office, and much less could I stand to see it cut up into bits.

Monge was not alone in his determination to save ORIT. George Meany, who from the beginning had given ORIT his strong personal support, was infuriated upon learning of such mischievous, destructive plans. Others, such as Fidel Velázquez in Mexico, the Canadians, and the Cuban President of ORIT joined in opposition. In no time, Millard's plan was stopped cold. Meanwhile a drive started by the AFL-CIO to clean out the ICFTU executive leadership culminated in the decision of the X Anniversary Convention held in Brussels, July 1959, to reorganize the ICFTU structure at the top level. Oldenbroek was reelected by a very narrow margin. Soon after, Millard resigned, and early in 1960, Oldenbroek followed suit. ORIT was finally left in peace.

Early in 1958, Luis Alberto Monge passed the word that he would soon be leaving the post of ORIT General Secretary in order to return to Costa Rica to participate actively in national politics. Assistant Secretary Arturo Jáuregui, after three years' service with the old CIT and seven with ORIT, also announced that he was returning to Peru to work in the labor movement. In addition, two other Peruvians, Ricardo Temoche Benítez, who had served for almost three years as Director of Workers' Education, and organizer Leopoldo Pita, resigned from ORIT at that time. Still more staff people left the Mexico City headquarters when the Venezuelan dictatorship was overthrown in January 1958, among them P. B. Pérez Salinas, who was Assistant to the Director of Education; Manuel Méndez, who had succeeded Temoche as Director of Education; and Augusto Malavé Villalba, who was serving as an ORIT-ICFTU organizer last stationed in Argentina.

The ORIT Executive Board at its meeting held in Washington, D.C., January 13–15, 1958, fully realized the impact of these abrupt changes, but rather than proceed hastily to the selection of new personnel, it decided to appoint a subcommittee, to which were referred all the administrative actions of the agenda, including the filling of the vacant posts in the ORIT leadership.[2]

At the first meeting of the subcommittee, held in Mexico City, February 14–16, Monge announced his resignation to take effect on May first. On that date he was going to be sworn in as a member of Congress in his native Costa Rica. As a provisional solution until the next Convention, the subcommittee entrusted the administration of ORIT to the three Assistant Secretaries who were to act in consultation with President Tellechea.[3]

The subcommittee did not confine itself to administrative, financial, and personnel matters. In fact, it redefined the program of ORIT in the light of the downfall of the dictatorships that had occurred from 1955 to 1958 (Argentina, Peru, Venezuela, Honduras, Colombia). The prodemocratic cycle released ORIT from the pressing task of fighting the dictators in order to regain the freedoms needed by the labor movement to function without restraints. Now, although all the Latin American dictatorships had not disappeared, the need for such "political" emphasis no longer existed. It was, therefore, imperative that in the future greater stress be given to the organizational and educational aspects of the ORIT program.

This was accomplished at the IV ORIT Congress which met December 9–12, 1958, in Bogotá. There the ORIT constitution was amended creating an Administrative Committee in place of the former secretariat, authorizing the reelection of the President, establishing separate budgets for the Departments of Organization and Education, and enlarging the scope of the publications and propaganda services. Alfonso Sánchez Madariaga of Mexico was elected General Secretary, Ignazio González Tellechea was reelected President.

The new ORIT General Secretary, Sánchez Madariaga, and the delegates had hardly returned to their homes when the Batista regime in Cuba fell on January 1, 1959. The event shook ORIT from stem to stern. The many admirers of Fidel Castro started pressuring ORIT to go all out in support of the new Cuban revolutionary labor leaders, who had occupied by force all trade union headquarters, replaced all officers not in the good graces of the 26th of July revolutionary movement, and initiated a systematic campaign of slander and persecution against them.

On the other hand, there were a considerable number of individuals and organizations inside ORIT who were dubious of Castro's alleged democratic faith and were not disposed to turn their backs upon the ousted CTC leaders. They could not forsake their longtime CTC brothers just because they were down and out, defeated, defenseless, and at the mercy of mobs manipulated by shrewd Communist agents or naive dupes. However, there are times when a revolutionary wave reaches such a crescendo that attempts to contain it are futile. Cuba, in the early months of 1959 following Batista's downfall, went through precisely one of these periods. The anti-Castro elements inside ORIT were aware of that. They had no choice but to be cautious, patient, and bide their time.

Alfonso Sánchez Madariaga was confronted with a difficult, almost impossible task. On the one hand, could he ignore the new Cuban revolutionary labor leadership that then was proclaiming to the four winds its allegedly democratic, anti-Communist position? And on the other hand, could he repudiate the old elected CTC leadership—as the revolutionaries were demanding? Alfonso chose a middle course, temporizing and giving in a little when such action was advisable, but refusing to budge when the demands implied the commission of a dishonorable act. And this is how he kept the ORIT boat afloat in spite of the breakers that were smashing it from all sides. He had the remarkable distinction of preserving intact his entire ORIT crew, with the exception of the Castro-controlled CTC, which eventually went Communist. But when this latter event happened, it had the salutary effect of consolidating the unity of all the ORIT affiliates. There was no longer any reason to argue over Cuba. It was now definitely in the enemy camp!

Alfonso Sánchez Madariaga had accepted the responsibility of leading ORIT with the understanding that he would not serve more than one term. He was not free to devote to ORIT all of his time because of his obligations to his own CTM, the Mexican Social Security Administration, and the ILO, of which he was titular worker member of its Governing Body. Sánchez Madariaga had to rely a great deal on his top assistants, particularly the Director of Organization.

Because of ill health and partly because of his past connections with the Cuban CTC which were causing him considerable difficulties, Otero Borlaff resigned toward the end of 1959 as Director of Organization. Actually, the organizing department had not functioned efficiently since Arturo Jáuregui had left it to return to Peru. Sánchez Madariaga asked me to "work on Jáuregui" to see if he could be induced to return. I succeeded and, in January 1960, Arturo rejoined ORIT at his old post of Director of Organization.

Soon after Jáuregui's return, Daniel Benedict, ORIT Assistant Secretary in charge of education, left for Europe to take an important post with the International Metalworkers' Federation. Jim Bury returned to Canada, having found it rather difficult to acclimate himself—mainly on account of language difficulties—in a Latin environment. The third North American, who was serving ORIT as organizer in Central America, Andrew C. McLellan, had accepted the post of Inter-American Representative of the International Federation of Food and Drink Workers. Later he moved to Washington as my assistant with the title of Associate AFL-CIO Inter-American Representative.

My involvement in the ORIT administration, which had been heavy during its first ten years, began to taper off in 1958 when North Americans were assigned to ORIT headquarters, and ceased almost completely by 1961 when McLellan moved into my office. He became, in fact if not in name, the liaison man between ORIT and the AFL-CIO. Although lacking a solid Latin background—he was born and raised in Scotland and later moved to lower Texas, on the Mexican border—Andy soon became *muy simpático* in the eyes of the Latinos. He never fell into the trap of adulating them to gain their friendship; instead, he chose the harder but more secure road of frankness, firm criticism, and an open mind.

The return of Jáuregui to ORIT was, however, the strongest factor that reduced my participation in ORIT's administrative affairs. I felt that with his experience, great capacity for work, and unquestionable pride in his job, Arturo would give the General Secretary all the efficient and loyal assistance he needed. Furthermore, he had been absent from the Mexico City headquarters during 1959, the first disillusioning year of the Castro regime. Therefore, Jáuregui could start his job with a fairly clean slate—no direct involvement in previous controversies over Cuba which, especially with Latinos, often leave scars that do not heal easily. I felt that ORIT, with Sánchez Madariaga and Jáuregui at the helm, was now in secure hands and I could safely divert my energies elsewhere.

As the V ORIT Congress was approaching, Sánchez Madariaga announced his intention to step down as General Secretary. His replacement by Jáuregui became a foregone conclusion. The Congress, in Rio de Janeiro August 20–25, 1961, elected him to the post with only one dissenting vote. The services of Sánchez Madariaga were retained, however, by electing him ORIT President. This team is still running ORIT affairs, having been uanimously reelected at the sixth Mexico City Congress, in February 1965.

Jáuregui has had to face a number of problems which, although really minor, were magnified out of proportion by superficial observers who tended to confuse appearance with reality. In actuality, these matters never threatened in the slightest the strength and primacy of ORIT in the Latin American labor movement.

The first of these difficulties stemmed from the efforts of Castroites to organize an inter-American trade union confederation as a rival to ORIT. This plan was solemnly proclaimed at the November 1959 CTC Convention in Havana when the Communists took over and decided to disaffiliate from ORIT. The Chilean Confederation of Labor (CUT), dominated by a Socialist-Communist coalition, was the first to answer the call. There was for a while some speculation that the Venezuelans and also the Bolivians might join. The latter group was then under the influence of radical leftist leader Juan Lechin. To attract recruits to the proposed new organization, Lombardo Toledano's CTAL, which had been dormant for a number of years, officially announced its disbandment. However, when the preliminary meeting assembled in Santiago in September 1960, only the usual well-known Communist faces were around. No neutral or independent organization of any importance was represented. So the group decided to adjourn *sine die;* but over six years have passed since then, and nothing similar to CTAL has been created to challenge ORIT.

The second "threat"—Jáuregui would surely dispute my use of such an expression—came from the Latin American Confederation of Christian Trade Unionists (CLASC). This regional arm of the International Federation of Christian Trade Unions was set up in 1954 in Santiago, Chile. Based on individual affiliation, instead of unions, it has had no difficulty in establishing local groups in practically every Latin American country. But in terms of trade union control, the policing of collective bargaining agreements, the capacity to paralyze entire industries or disrupt economies, CLASC is still in an embryonic stage. Its influence is, therefore, largely of a moral-ideological character, and as such the organization could really perform an important, even historical role if it were possible to bring CLASC into a harmonious relationship with ORIT. Until now, efforts in this direction continue to be in vain. Apparently, rather than be equal partners in a modern supermarket, CLASC prefers to be sole owner of a small corner grocery.

Meanwhile, the largest Catholic or Christian-inspired trade union groups in Latin America, as well as the most prominent Catholic trade unionists, remain affiliated to ORIT with unqualified support. Whatever semblance of challenge to ORIT might have been read into the early clamorous CLASC activities, it has now been reduced to little more than a thorn in the flesh. Even CLASC leaders themselves apparently have no hope of becoming a serious rival to ORIT in the near future.

After the 1961 Rio de Janeiro Convention ORIT entered a new stage characterized by the extraordinary impetus given to its traditional activities, as well as new programs. The latter not only cover trade union, economic, social, and political areas, but also involve ORIT's relations with international agencies, democratic governments, employer groups of liberal or progressive leanings, civic organizations, universities, etc. In short, ORIT's influence now extends to the most varied sectors of society, even including the Rotary Clubs.

Until 1961 the territory under ORIT's jurisdiction, that is, the Western Hemisphere, had frequently been trespassed upon by the Brussels ICFTU officials. But the ORIT Secretary General himself, Arturo Jáuregui, has acknowledged that since he assumed office the earlier difficulties between ORIT and the ICFTU have been resolved. Dissension has been replaced by positive teamwork.

ORIT has come to be regarded as a prestigious consultative organization on the social and economic problems of Latin America. The OAS Commission on Labor Affairs, recently created by the Inter-American Economic and Social Council, as well as other OAS commissions on agrarian reform, housing and, especially, the Technical Advisory Labor Committee (COSATE), all draw upon ORIT's experience and wide contacts for advice on matters affecting labor.

Today, the views of Latin American labor on complex economic and technical matters are receiving more deference than ever before. The democratic governments not only listen respectfully to the voice of inter-American free trade unionism, but they also incorporate the views of ORIT's national affiliates into their development studies and programs under the Alliance for Progress. Dividing the hemisphere into six geographic areas, ORIT has reinforced its team of international organizers with the addition of many representatives in various countries needing technical assistance. ORIT personnel in the field must be organizers, trade union educators and propagandists, while serving as liaison with the workers themselves, their trade union organizations, governmental organs, and international agencies.

ORIT is the most dynamic and successful of the ICFTU's regional arms, carrying out a program of action benefiting the organized workers of the Western Hemisphere. As I was closing this chapter, in the fall of 1966, ORIT's membership had reached 28 million workers, grouped in 52 affiliated organizations located in 39 republics, territories, and possessions of the hemisphere.

Recognizing that its extensive program could not be effective unless it were based on a plan of systematic education, ORIT established, in the early sixties, trade union training courses in practically every Latin American and Caribbean country. But its greatest achievement in this field has been the ORIT-ICFTU Inter-American Labor Institute in Cuernavaca, State of Morelos, Mexico, not far from Mexico City. Its cornerstone was laid on the occasion of ORIT's VI Congress, held in

Mexico City in February 1965. One year later, on Easter Monday, April 11, 1966, the Institute was officially inaugurated. Erected on a gently sloping site at the approach to the resort city, the ORIT school covers an area of 6,000 square meters (approximately one and a half acres). The buildings are modern and there are facilities for thirty-eight resident students and at least half a dozen professors.

The Inter-American Labor Institute is under the direction of Bernardo Ibáñez, the old Chilean war-horse of free trade unionism. He is the most scholarly pundit of Latin American labor history and combines his solid experience with a burning faith in freedom—the *sine qua non* for the growth of any labor movement.

In the Institute ORIT has set an outstanding example for others who have responsibility for educating the leaders of tomorrow. The school is living testimony that ORIT is a powerful force for progress in the social revolution now sweeping the hemisphere.

Notes

1. The AFL was represented by Secretary-Treasurer William F. Schnitzler, International Representative George P. Delaney, President Sam P. Ming of the American Federation of Grain Millers, and the author. Representing the CIO were O. A. Knight, Daniel Benedict, Nicolas Zonarich, and Ernest Schwarz. Paul K. Reed represented the United Mine Workers.

2. This subcommittee was composed of President Ignacio González Tellechea, General Secretary Monge, and William F. Schnitzler and Paul K. Reed for North America and Fidel Velázquez and Luis Alberto Colotuzzo for Latin America.

3. The ORIT Assistant Secretaries were then Jim Bury of Canada, Alfonso Sánchez Madariaga of Mexico, and Serafino Romualdi.

X

Argentina under Perón

PERÓN'S CAMPAIGN to subvert the Argentine trade unions to his own political purposes was well under way by 1947, at which time the AFL broke with the Argentine General Confederation of Labor (CGT) following the visit of our delegation to that country. The cornerstone of Perón's labor policy had actually been laid as early as 1945 with the passage of the Trade Union Organization Law, which in effect dealt the deathblow to labor's right to organize freely. Those unions that refused to bow to the will of the dictator were simply taken over by the government-controlled CGT. Under this "authority," the ORIT-affiliated Workers Committee for Independent Trade Union Action (COASI) was "intervened"—taken over—in December 1949, and its headquarters closed.

Soon after the right to organize was denied, free assembly became virtually nonexistent. Whatever meetings took place were held under heavy police surveillance. Likewise, labor's strongest weapon, the right to strike, was outlawed. All previously accepted definitions of a legal strike were cast aside and it became the prerogative of the regime to determine a strike's legality or illegality.

Of grave concern to the forces of free labor was the extensive use of imprisonment, intimidation, and physical violence as instruments of repression by Perón to assure his full control of the most "recalcitrant" unions.

The actual day-by-day control of organized labor in Argentina was exercised, until 1952 when she died of cancer, by Perón's wife, Maria Eva (Evita) Duarte. She was the real boss of labor in Argentina.[1]

This remarkable woman, who was endowed with a great fanaticism and a magnetism over the masses, was also genuinely loved by the *lumpen-proletariat,* the *descamisados* (shirtless ones) of the industrial belt, and the peons of the *pampa*—especially the women.

One night during the AFL mission to Argentina in January 1947 I paid an unreported visit (thanks to the complicity of my "police chauffeur") to Doña Enrichetta Chiaraviglio, daughter of the many-times Prime Minister of Italy, Giovanni Giolitti. She was a political leader on her own, who had migrated to Argentina with her husband and family out of contempt for Mussolini and his Fascist regime. Earlier, my contacts with her sons and daughter (then married to my friend Gioacchino Dolci) in the Free Italy Association during my anti-Fascist service in Argentina gave me many opportunities to visit with Doña Enrichetta. She was a brilliant intellectual and sociologist of great renown. I wanted this wise woman to explain Evita's popularity. She told me:

"My cook and housemaid, two women much devoted to me, are strong admirers of Evita. A few days ago I said to them: 'Your Eva wears costly dresses, adorns herself with precious jewelry, lives in luxury, and uses the workers to gain power. How can you, working women, adore such a woman?'

" 'Because she is our queen,' they answered. Here is your reason. It is the monarchical spirit that remains latent in our masses. They feel happier as subjects of a resplendent queen rather than as equals to a modest wife of a democratic president!"

In spite of the extent of Perón's control of organized labor and his use of both legal and illegal means to gain complete domination of the unions, from time to time he did encounter strong opposition from groups of workers. They realized the danger to the free organization of unions and were fed up with Peronista demagoguery. Resistance by these groups was countered with still more repression, and this in turn, together with a gradually deteriorating economic situation, incited the workers to direct action.

In mid-1950 the port and maritime workers, in defiance of government pressure to join the CGT, conducted a highly effective six-week strike that was supported by port workers throughout the world. When the strike finally collapsed the unions were "intervened" by CGT "administrators," their leaders were removed from their jobs, and they faced all forms of persecution.

Perhaps the most significant manifestation of labor discontent with the Perón regime began in late November 1950 when the railroad workers' union, the Unión Ferroviaria, the largest affiliate of the CGT, went out on strike. The walkout was ostensibly for a wage increase to meet the rising cost of living, but it quickly took on the aspects of a revolt against the government-imposed union leadership. The government combined its pleas for the strikers to return to work with the imprisonment of many of their leaders and with threats to their job security. When they were promised that their wage demands would be met, the workers ended the strike only to resume it again a few weeks later when it became clear that the government was reneging. Again work was resumed with the assurance that wages would be increased, the administration of the union would be changed, and no reprisals would be taken against the strikers.

When the Unión Ferroviaria went on strike a third time in late January, 1951, because none of the earlier promises were kept, Perón took extreme measures. He mobilized the railroad workers under military control as provided for in the "Law for the General Organization of the Nation in Time of War," a move that was endorsed by the captive CGT. Hundreds of workers were dismissed, and hundreds more disappeared only to be found later in prison. Many of those jailed were held incommunicado for an extended period of time while the strike was being "investigated."

It was at this time that Perón decided to strangle *La Prensa* with the complicity of the government-controlled CGT. This daily newspaper enjoyed enormous domestic prestige and worldwide fame for its independence and devotion to democratic principles. Run by three generations of the Paz family, it was then under the editorship of Dr. Alberto Gainza Paz. After he was forced to go into exile, I was privileged to become his friend and collaborator in the cause of freedom.

Obviously irked by *La Prensa's* impartial reporting of the railroad workers' strike in January 1951, the dictator finally decided to carry out his long-prepared plan of silencing what little remained of Argentina's free press. The only other independent daily, *La Nación,* had already received ominous portents. The News Vendors' Union, a branch of the CGT, was assigned the role of hangman for *La Prensa.*

This union was composed of people who sold papers and magazines at newsstands or at street corners. They sold all available publications under equal conditions, and undoubtedly these could have been improved. But traditional, bona-fide trade union practices call for serving demands for improved conditions simultaneously to all publications concerned. Yet what the News Vendors' Union of Buenos Aires did was to present demands only to *La Prensa*—and these were the demands: suppression of branch distributing centers which *La Prensa* maintained in outlying districts; abolition of the mail subscription list or payment to the News Vendors' Union of 10 cents for each copy mailed directly to subscribers; and payment to the Union of 20 percent of the gross income for classified advertising.

Those demands were served on *La Prensa*'s management the morning of January 25, only forty-eight hours after it had received the required written notice that the union had grievances. Actually, the ultimatum had already expired when the letter was delivered. On the same night (January 25–26) Peronista thugs, aided and abetted by the police, prevented the shipment of copies of *La Prensa* as they were coming off the press. The following day the CGT, which three days before had proclaimed the railroad strike illegal, quickly decided that there was a "legal" strike against *La Prensa* and ordered the members of the printing union to quit work. Picket lines were established to enforce the strike order. *La Prensa* was thus compelled to suspend publication.

The membership of the News Vendors' Union was never called to a meeting to discuss the demands to be served on *La Prensa*. It was never consulted as to the proclamation of the strike. Likewise, no meeting was ever called of union members of *La Prensa*'s mechanical shop, or of its editorial room, or of the delivery and distribution crews. On the contrary, an overwhelming majority joined in demanding prompt government intervention to put a stop to lawlessness and bring about the resumption of publication. Management also appealed to the government several times.

Ten days later, on February 8, the Minister of Labor finally agreed to preside at a meeting of representatives of management and the union for the purpose of attempting conciliation, but at the last moment the meeting was postponed.

Meanwhile, the News Vendors' Union of Rosario (the second largest city of Argentina), at a regular meeting of its membership, denounced the procedure of the officers of the News Vendors' Union of Buenos Aires and demanded that the membership of the Buenos Aires union be consulted and given an opportunity to voice its views on the outrageous tactics employed against *La Prensa*. But no meeting of the News Vendors' Union of Buenos Aires was ever called.

On February 14, more than one thousand employees of *La Prensa* attempted to march to the Ministry of Labor, demanding that something be done to restore them to their jobs, since there was absolutely no grievance between the management and the employees. But the police dispersed the crowd, arresting some of the leaders of the demonstration.

Finally, on February 16, representatives of *La Prensa* and the News Vendors' Union were allowed to meet at the Ministry of Labor. But as soon as *La Prensa* showed a willingness to consider some of the union's demands—although it strongly protested their unfairness—these were quickly revised upwards, thus making an accord impossible.

On February 27 employees of *La Prensa*—after having received assurances of protection by the police—attempted to enter the plant to resume publication. Armed thugs assaulted them, killing an employee, Roberto Núñez, and wounding fifteen others. Nevertheless, over six hundred editorial employees, printers, pressmen, and other craftsmen managed to enter the plant and started working on the next day's issue. But before they were able to send the edition to press the whole crew was summoned to the police station for an investigation, and the following day the plant was occupied by the police, who prevented everybody from entering, even the watchmen.

On March 6, a federal judge ordered the *Prensa* plant returned to the lawful owner, Señor Alberto Gainza Paz, but on the same day Gainza Paz was charged by the government with "violation of state security." Thereupon the police ordered the plant to be closed again.

Meanwhile, the News Vendors' Union and the General Confederation of Labor started a campaign demanding that *La Prensa* be confiscated and run "in the interests of the Argentine people." The charges against publisher Gainza Paz of having violated "state security" led first to his conviction and then to the confiscation of his newspaper. *La Prensa*, as the unfettered voice of Argentine democracy and freedom, had been strangled. It became, tragic irony, the official organ of the CGT!!

Following the third railroad strike, almost every labor opponent of Perón was arrested, particularly those known as independents. Many of them were held without bail while awaiting trial; many remained incommunicado, unable to consult even with their lawyers.

A strike by the powerful union of locomotive engineers and firemen, La Fraternidad, in August 1951 led to still another wave of persecutions against the railroad workers and provided the regime with an excuse to arrest many of Perón's political opponents who had no direct labor connections. Many of those imprisoned following the August railroad strike were kept in jail for almost one year without any specific charge.

A number of Buenos Aires port workers, members of FORA, the old syndicalist labor organization then operating underground, proposed to refuse payment of part of their wages for the erection of a monument to Eva Perón. The idea was unanimously accepted by their fellow workers who acted in unison when the time for action came. Soon, however, the Argentine secret police started a systematic campaign of persecution against the leaders of the "rebellion," arresting some, kidnaping others, or detaining as hostages members of the families of those who managed to escape. A number of port workers were subjected to inhuman tortures, including the application of the electric needle. Six of them, whose names I published in the November 1952 issue of the *Inter-American Labor Bulletin,* had their hands tied behind their backs and were hung from a hook ten feet high for half an hour, during which they were brutally beaten on the sensitive parts of their bodies by police officers. This happened on the first floor of the Boca y Riachuelo precinct of the Police Maritime District.

Congressman Carlos Perette, one of the opposition members of Parliament who was still allowed to circulate, denounced these persecutions and tortures from the floor of the House of Representatives, but his request for detailed information was totally ignored by the Argentine press, and was not even printed in the *Congressional Record.* (Perette was elected Vice-President of the Argentine Republic in 1964.)

Not satisfied with silencing the opposition press and subjugating all sectors of the labor movement, Perón also went after one of the few remaining citadels of intellectual freedom—La Casa del Pueblo (People's House). It was completely destroyed by fire following Perón's harangue of his *descamisados* (shirtless ones) in the Plaza de Mayo on April 15, 1953.

The Casa del Pueblo was situated at Calle Rivadavia 2150, a few blocks from Congress, the Fire Brigade and Police headquarters. Built in 1927 with the help of voluntary contributions, members and friends of the labor movement continued to give financial support for its upkeep. It was a large three-story building with a big basement. On the first floor were the library and the administration and editorial offices of *La Vanguardia.* A complete collection of this journal—founded by Juan B. Justo on April 7, 1894—could be found in its archives. They also contained a wealth of material on the Argentine Fascist movement, dating back to its inception in 1943.

The Juan B. Justo library, founded in 1897, was one of the most important libraries of the country, comprising 60,000 volumes, among them many books which were out of print. Students from all over Argentina had been using the library for their social and political studies for more than fifty years. Another valuable library also lost in the fire was that of the Jockey Club, which contained thousands of valuable volumes as well as a rich collection of original plates.

Following the gutting of the People's House and the headquarters of all the opposition parties—with the exception of the Communists—the Perón government, using as a pretext the explosion of bombs of unknown origin, proceeded to arrest all the known leaders of the opposition still in Argentina. Among them were such veterans of the labor and Socialist movements as Juan Antonio Solari, Alfredo Palacios, and Nicolas Repetto.

The flames that burned down the People's House were hardly extinguished when the Argentine Communist Party Executive Committee published a manifesto. It called upon Perón to broaden the bases of his government to include Communists and thus constitute a "popular democratic front"!

Faced with a disastrous economic situation, Perón sought and received help from the Communists. He accepted their recommendations for an economic plan that included the confiscation of private property and the complete nationalization of all public services. The Communists were clearly prepared to embrace Perón, endorse *justicialismo* and work with it toward their common objectives—in the national and international fields.

The Communist support of Peronismo was not limited, however, to Argentina. When Perón visited Chile early in 1953 a committee of prominent Communists, headed by the poet Pablo Neruda, issued a manifesto urging the Chilean people to attend a lecture by the Argentine dictator. A few days later, at the founding Congress of the new Chilean labor organization (CUTCh), the Communist delegates insisted that Peronista fraternal delegates from Argentina be admitted to the Congress.

Clear indications that the Communist-Peronista entente was not casual but a "party-line" order was the about-face of every Communist group. Witness the following letter by the Young Communists, a facsimile of which appeared in *Resistimos,* the bulletin of the Argentines-in-Exile. The letter reads:

The truth is that in the first Justicialist program—as our comrade Codovila [2] opportunely points out—there are many points which merit the help of our party.

We plan to work assiduously to bring success to these objectives, although we reserve the right to fight any ideas with which we are not in accord.

We have not always been able to work openly because the word "Communist" frightens many of the working masses; but we have continued all the same, without renouncing our political creed, because the most important and urgent thing is to bring about the triumph of our basic program for the workers and the fight against criminal capitalism, and Anglo-Yanqui imperialism.

By means of this standard it becomes constantly more evident that Justicialism and Marxist-Leninism are not enemies. Our points of view were brought into practice through unions and government sectors in which we were able to effect dynamic collaboration and increase our influence. What does it matter if the social revolution is called Justicialism or Communism? The important thing is that the revolution triumph! And it is important that, with the irrefutable logic of historical materialism, we succeed in modifying and adjusting to our democratic-social program, the points which at first we opposed.

General Perón and the working masses have taken notice that the Communist collaboration is offered in good faith. The evidence shown by Comrade Puiggros [3] has proved this conclusively. We propose to continue offering our definite collaboration and to fight to have adopted within Justicialism for the benefit of the people those norms whose merits have been proved in practice by the Soviet Union.

During the many years of Perón's dictatorship in Argentina, the international free labor movement—particulaly ORIT and the AFL and CIO in the United States—never ceased to denounce the repressive measures of his regime and its flagrant violations of human rights. As AFL representative, and in many instances on my own exclusive responsibility, I did my share to expose Perón's crimes and support unreservedly the gallant freedom fighters of that country. I remained in constant contact with Argentines of every walk of life, both inside the country and in exile—trade unionists, political leaders, businessmen, intellectuals, journalists, and clergymen. Therefore, it was no surprise when the official Peronista trade union organ, *C.G.T.*, devoted an entire page to me in its July 18, 1952, issue, replete with insults. I became a favorite *bête noire* of the Peronistas in September 1953. They plastered Buenos Aires with posters denouncing me as "Enemy No. 2" (Spruille Braden was still No. 1) when they learned of my address before the AFL Convention. Apparently, I gained their affection with the following remarks:

The activities of Perón, before and since he became President of Argentina, have proved conclusively that he is our foremost Latin American enemy.

Attempts to appease him—such as the ill-fated loan of $125 million a few years ago—have only served to make him bolder in his demands. The events in Argentina, last spring, are still fresh in everybody's memory. The destruction of the democratic opposition's headquarters; the burning of the newspaper *Vanguardia* and a labor library; and the arrest and torture of thousands of citizens of every walk of life, provoked a feeling of revulsion throughout the world and caused the publication of scathing comments in the leading newspapers of our country. Yet it was precisely at that time, when the ashes of the burned buildings were still warm and the jails of Buenos Aires were full to capacity with Argentina's leading democrats, that the government of our country chose to include Buenos Aires in Dr. Milton Eisenhower's itinerary. But that in itself could have been excused on the ground of diplomatic propriety. However, what cannot be understood by the people of Latin America, by our friends in particular, is the love feast that was staged during Dr. Eisenhower's two-day stay, and the abrupt decision of our government to retain in Buenos Aires, reportedly on Perón's personal request, our Ambassador, after he had been transferred elsewhere. Since this Ambassador is a leading proponent of the policy of letting bygones be bygones, the impression is prevalent now in Argentina that Uncle Sam will soon make another concrete gesture of appeasement.

Meanwhile, documents found by the Allied Forces in the archives of the German Foreign Ministry—just published in book form by a prominent Argentine exile—accuse Perón of having been a paid Nazi agent during the last war; of having actively participated in espionage acts which cost the lives of Allied personnel, and of having finally engineered, on Nazi orders, the June 4, 1943, military coup. The connection of Perón with the Nazis—during the war and after the war—is documented to the last detail. Some of the revelations are truly shocking. All these documents were collected in 1946–1947 by a group of U.S. military officers and were made known to Washington. With this added knowledge of Perón's anti-American record, our government would be making a terrific mistake, on moral as well as political grounds, were it to appease the Argentine dictator again.

As early as January 1948, shortly after the CIT meeting in Lima, Perón conceived the idea of launching a new Latin American trade union organization, mainly in retaliation against the AFL, which had denounced his regime, and the CIT, which had rejected the affiliation of the Peronista CGT. The plan for a Perón-dominated hemisphere labor organization was proposed to a group of Latin American labor leaders invited to Buenos Aires. After several rebuffs, the idea again was publicly announced in Mexico City in January 1951, after the Argentine delegation to the ORIT conference was denied admission.

Following the pattern he had used in Argentina, Perón hoped to establish his hegemony in Latin America by first taking over its labor movement. ORIT and its democratic allies in the hemisphere stood in his road.

During 1951, Argentine labor attachés, the dictator's chief propagandists, and his government-controlled General Confederation of Labor (CGT) spent huge sums of money on publications and broadcasts designed to whip up anti–U.S. feelings and thus divide the free labor movement in Latin America. Large numbers of "labor leaders" from other countries were sponsored on trips to Buenos Aires and other bribes were paid to generate support for an Argentine-sponsored trade union conference in Asunción, Paraguay, in February 1952. All expenses were paid by Perón's Casa Rosada. The Argentine government even applied pressure on some governments to send labor representatives.

As a result of the free spending and pressures, more than a hundred delegates from 18 countries in addition to Argentina attended the Asunción conference. The Paraguayan government forced its reluctant Confederation of Labor—which had been organized in 1951 largely through ORIT efforts—to host the meeting. Most countries sent delegates with little or no influence in their own labor movements. Bona-fide trade union delegations came from only eight countries. Dominican Dictator Trujillo, who tightly controlled his Confederation of Labor, foxily ordered it to stay away. He wanted to see the outcome of the meeting before committing himself.

Although it was convoked to set up a Perón-controlled hemisphere labor organization, the Asunción conference decided to create only a Committee for Latin American Labor Unity, with headquarters in Buenos Aires and top personnel furnished by the Argentine CGT. Speeches and resolutions adopted by the meeting were directed against the United States. They called for a spread of Justicialism and the "third position" [4] throughout Latin America, and the formation of a solid bloc against the "two imperialisms," presumably capitalism and Communism, though neither was named. One resolution "condemned the fact that the people of Puerto Rico are deprived by force of the enjoyment of her sovereignty," and authorized the newly formed Committee to fight for the return of Puerto Rico's full sovereignty.

It was clear the conference in Asunción had attracted those elements that had grievances against the United States but did not openly dare to side with the Communists, although a few Communist delegates came from Guatemala, Peru, and Bolivia. I was convinced that the position of Latin American governments toward the new organization—support or neutrality—would ultimately depend on the reaction of the U.S. State Department. I was particularly worried about Perón's neighbors, Bolivia and Paraguay, since Bolivia was being drawn closer to him for political reasons, and Paraguay for economic ones. If those two governments were to pressure their respective labor movements to maintain an alliance with Perón it might conceivably form a nucleus strong enough to undermine or woo democratic, anti-Communist labor groups throughout the hemisphere.

During 1952 Perón stepped up his anti–U.S. propaganda campaign through his labor attachés. In two articles in the *New Leader* (September 29, 1952, and April 13, 1953) I noted the pattern of this anti-American offensive. In every Argentine Embassy between Patagonia and the Rio Grande there was a special office staffed by at least two labor attachés and several assistants. The CGT set up a school in Buenos Aires for trade union leaders. Dozens of young unionists from every Latin American country were invited to attend. The school openly preached Fascist dogma. Opposition to the tenets of democratic trade unionism constituted the bulk of its curriculum.

In December 1952 Perón created his Latin American Association of Trade Unionists (ATLAS) at a meeting in Mexico City, spending more than an estimated $10,000 just to transport the delegates. Lombardo Toledano himself sent a message of greetings and offered his collaboration. A number of Communist delegates were present at the meeting, including a full delegation from Guatemala. New ATLAS branches thus offered the dictator additional outlets for the distribution of anti–U.S. propaganda. Equally as important, they provided a convenient "cover" to placate local authorities whenever charges of Argentine interference were raised in the press. But despite all its efforts in money and manpower, ATLAS never became an effective rival to ORIT and the free labor movement in Latin America, and after the downfall of Perón it disappeared completely from the scene.

In the final years prior to the overthrow of the Perón regime, the nation's steady economic decline was matched by a corresponding increase in discontent by the workers, and an intensification of their hatred for the government-imposed leaders of the CGT. All attempts to placate the workers with demagogic promises of better things to come were futile. Although the prostituted CGT leadership faithfully obeyed Perón's orders to try to discourage wage increases, the rank and file began to take matters into their own hands. They staged, with increasing frequency, demonstrations of protest. At the same time, the old democratic trade union leaders who had remained under cover in Buenos Aires and other Argentine cities and the new ones who emerged during the Perón era began to establish contact with one another. They formed the trade union branch of the Civic-Military Committee, which, almost openly, was preparing to overthrow the hateful regime.

The June 16, 1955, army revolt did not succeed but it shook the Perón government to its foundations and prompted the dictator to make a last desperate attempt to survive. He dumped some of his closest collaborators, including the most faithful of them all, Minister of Interior Angel G. Borlenghi.

Borlenghi was the real strong man of the regime. As late as March 10, Perón eulogized him in a public meeting with these words: "I am asking Divine Providence to preserve him, because I know what Borlenghi's collaboration means to the success of our government."

His career was filled with acts of treason to the Argentine labor movement. As a labor leader and member of the Socialist Party, he betrayed both when Perón started his meteoric rise to power and looked around for a labor Judas to help him. Borlenghi gave Perón the list of trade union organizations to be taken over, and the names of labor leaders that were to be jailed, exiled, beaten or . . . bribed! Later, he simulated the organization of a plot against Perón, in which many prominent opposition leaders were involved, with the result that at the opportune time the "plot" was discovered and those who had fallen for it were arrested.

As Minister of Interior, Borlenghi had under his command the whole apparatus of the Argentine police. More workers were arrested under him in ten years than in the whole history of the Argentine labor movement, dating way back to the nineteenth century. Under his rule, the most savage tortures were inflicted on labor prisoners, and for the first time even women—a group of striking telephone workers—were subjected to the inhuman treatment of the electric needle. He enacted a special legislation protecting from prosecution and punishment police personnel engaged in acts of violence against prisoners, on the assumption that "they carry out orders," and organized the Argentine Secret Police along the lines of the dreaded Gestapo. Borlenghi was the organizer of all the acts of destruction against La Prensa, the Jockey Club, the headquarters of the opposition parties, the People's House, the Juan B. Justo Library, down to the destruction of Buenos Aires churches and the residences of Church dignitaries—the last straw which prompted the Army to intervene and demand his elimination from the Government.

But the Army also had other vital reasons for demanding Borlenghi's head. Rumors started circulating in May 1955 that Borlenghi was preparing a "counterrevolution" to eliminate Army influence and install a sort of "black bolshevism" with the cooperation of the Communists. In an interview with two prominent Communist leaders, he gave clear hints that a counterrevolution was in the cards.

In 1954 a group of Army officers authorized the distribution in downtown Buenos Aires of a pamphlet against Borlenghi, in which he was called the "Beria of Argentina." Previously, Vice-President Quijano had attacked him during a Cabinet meeting for his illicit financial manipulations. The Minister of the Navy resumed the attack during a Cabinet meeting in the spring of 1955, calling Borlenghi a Communist and criticizing his plan to abolish all religious holidays and replace them with "days devoted to Perón, Eva Perón, the Immortal Martyr, etc." Also, Borlenghi was severely criticized by some of his Cabinet colleagues for having accepted a "gift" from the National Confederation of Commercial Employees, where he still remained as President. The gratuity consisted of a luxurious apartment house in the heart of Buenos Aires, in addition to a costly summer home which he had previously received from the same organization.

Every time one of his collaborators became a liability for his government because of excessive stealing or opposition from the Army or other influential sectors, Perón did not hesitate to drop him. In the case of his brother-in-law, Juancito Duarte, he even arranged his "suicide." But in the case of Borlenghi, Perón's loyalty remained to the end. A revolution was needed to shake the "close bonds of friendship" between the two, and even at that Perón managed to whisk his friend out of the country in time to save him from arrest.

After resigning the Cabinet post, Borlenghi announced on June 30 that he was going abroad on a temporary diplomatic mission as Ambassador Extraordinary, accompanied by his wife, daughter, and brother-in-law. However, two days later, Perón told him to get out of the country at once to avoid arrest. That same day Borlenghi obtained a visa for Uruguay and two hours later arrived by plane in Montevideo, without baggage and without his family. The precipitate departure of Borlenghi signaled that the end was approaching. It finally came, less than three months later, on September 16, 1955.

Notes

1. Eva Perón's trade union role has been described in great detail by Robert J. Alexander in his books *The Perón Era, Organized Labor in Latin America* and *Labor Relations in Argentina, Brazil and Chile.*

2. Vittorio Codovilla, a founder of the Argentine Communist Party.

3. Rodolfo Puiggros, Argentine Communist leader who was first to advocate cooperation with Perón.

4. "Justicialism" was the name given by Perón to his social and economic doctrines based on the concept of "justice" for the workers. It is synonymous with Peronism. The "third position" refers to a policy independent from the democratic bloc headed by the United States and the Communist bloc headed by the Soviet Union. It is distinguished from Neutralism by its readiness to attack verbally both the United States and the Communists and is similar to Nazism and Fascism and, like the latter, has shown a readiness to collaborate with the Communists when it has served its ends.

XI

After the *Revolución Libertadora*

IN DESCRIBING the nature of revolution in Latin America, I have often said that a successful one is regarded as a "creation of God" while a failure gets branded as "the product of the Devil." Judged by this standard, the revolution that ousted Perón was unquestionably *dei gratia*. As such it had its rights to make reforms and, like all triumphant coups, the Argentine *Revolución Libertadora* of September 1955 asserted them—but with one crucial exception. It stopped at the door of the CGT.

Provisional President General Eduardo Lonardi, in my opinion, should have disbanded the Confederation immediately and deposed its entire Perón-oriented leadership. Furthermore, control over every union should have been returned to the democratic rank and file from whom it had been stolen by fraud, bribery, violence, persecution, and direct government imposition during the ten years of the Perón era. Instead, Lonardi conferred with Hugo Di Pietro, the General Secretary of the Confederation of Labor, reassuring him that the CGT would not be dissolved and that the gains of organized labor would be protected. Thus he allayed the fears and rumors, deliberately spread by Peronista diehards, that the change of Government would bring about a loss of trade union rights and the weakening of the protective labor laws. It was recalled that in October 1945, during the first brief eclipse of Perón when he was deposed as Vice-President and Minister of Labor and was confined to prison, employers had hastily proceeded to nullify many provisions of the re-

154

cently enacted labor legislation, thereby causing the workers to join the famous October 17 march which brought Perón back into power.

The argument that in order to protect labor gains it was necessary to retain the Peronista labor leaders remains unconvincing. The revolutionary democratic labor leadership also had a strong interest in protecting labor gains, but within the framework of a free society. And above all, they wanted to prevent a potential counterrevolution from using organized labor as a springboard to regain power. I believe that all the troubles—social, political, and economic—that have plagued Argentina during the last decade stem precisely from that enormous historical mistake: stopping the *Revolución Libertadora* at the door of the CGT.

In spite of many urgings and a natural desire to return to Buenos Aires after nine years of enforced absence, I felt that it would be a great mistake for me or the ORIT-ICFTU to rush down to Argentina on the heels of the victorious army. In a September 21 memorandum to George Meany—only five days after the revolution—I advised against joining a projected ICFTU mission to Argentina "because there are in existence in that country scores of trained labor leaders who will undoubtedly resent this public show of paternalism on the part of the ICFTU." The day before, I had spoken in New York with the former owner of *La Prensa,* Dr. Alberto Gainza Paz—who was about to return to Argentina to resume publication of his newspaper—and he advised me "to let, for the time being, the Argentine democratic trade unionists handle the situation they way they see best, without embarrassing interference from abroad."

In line with the Lonardi directives, the Minister of Labor, Luis Cerutti Costa, followed the policy of leaving the CGT and its constituent unions intact, calling for early trade union elections, and hoping that the changed political situation in the country as a whole would result in a democratization of the labor movement.

Many of the old trade unionists who had been active in the labor movement before the advent of Perón were opposed to this policy of Cerutti Costa's. They were anxious to take energetic measures to oust the Peronistas from control of the unions and to set the process of democratization in motion. These elements seized a number of unions by force in the early days of the Revolution, only to have the government take them back again, in most cases, and turn them over to the same Peronistas who had been running them before September 16, 1955.

Lonardi was ousted early in November and a new government headed by General Pedro Eugenio Aramburu was installed. Fearing that the new regime (which included as Vice-President the strongman of the September revolution, Admiral Isaac Rojas) would be unfriendly, the Peronistas reacted to the change by calling a general strike. But they failed to blackmail Aramburu, and, as a result, the CGT and its affiliated unions were "intervened" late in November. That is, their officials were ousted and "interventors," or administrators, were named by the government to carry out the job of administering the unions until duly elected officials could once more assume office.

Unfortunately, most of the interventors placed in charge of the unions in the first instance were military men. This fact aroused a good deal of opposition to the intervention among the workers. In addition, the military interventors were completely unacquainted with the problems which they were called upon to handle; frequently, they made mistakes which were difficult to rectify.

On May 1, 1956—traditionally celebrated in Argentina as Labor Day—the Aramburu regime announced that the process of electing new officials in the unions would begin on July 1 and would continue through October. This announcement spurred a wild scramble among labor elements to organize in order to compete for control of the CGT and its constituent groups. By mid-1956 at least six such groups could be counted.

The *Comité Obrero Argentino por Sindicalismo Independiente* (COASI) was the group organized in the early years of the Perón regime to oppose the dictatorship in the trade union field. Throughout the Perón period it held high the standard of opposition to the totalitarian domination of the labor movement. It was affiliated directly with ORIT and the ICFTU. Most of its leaders had gone into exile in Uruguay.

The *Movimiento por Recuperación del Gremialismo Libre* (MRGL) was formed immediately after the Revolution by workers who had participated in the revolutionary movement against Perón. However, its principal figures had been working from the early years of the Perón regime against the dictatorship, and did not go into exile. Although not affiliated with ORIT and the ICFTU, it followed the general line of these international organizations. MRGL was friendly to COASI.

A somewhat different current of opinion was represented by the *Comisión Obrera de Recuperación Sindical*. It consisted of a group of old trade unionists of syndicalist persuasion, also working for the reestablishment of free trade unionism. They had certain differences in tactics with the MRGL and COASI, though remaining on friendly terms with them.

Completely outside the CGT and its affiliated unions were the anarcho-syndicalists. The FORA—the earliest central labor organization in the country, and traditionally anarchist—never ceased fighting the dictatorship, and since September 1955 had shown renewed life and vigor. Elements of the FORA were particularly strong among the port workers and plumbers of Buenos Aires, while a similar group, the Federación de Constructores Navales, completely dominated the country's shipbuilding workers.

Then there were the Communists, who had organized a *Movimiento por Democratización e Independencia de los Sindicatos* (MPDIS). It tended to work in the shadows, without giving much publicity to its activities. However, there was no doubt that the Communists were working very closely with the Peronistas. MPDIS maintained contacts with CTAL and WFTU.

Finally there were the Peronistas themselves, who maintained what they called "the clandestine CGT," which sought to return the trade unions to a situation similar to that which existed before the Revolution of September 1955.

There were other extraneous elements in the labor movement who were very active, especially the so-called *Intransigente* wing of the Radical Party; but they had not organized as specific trade union groups. Though they too were working for the reconstruction of a free labor movement, these elements had not taken a position on the future international affiliation of the trade unions. A weekly newspaper, *Palabra Radical,* was considered the mouthpiece of the trade union group inside the Intransigent Radicals, which was led by Arturo Frondizi, who won the presidency in 1958.

In the April 5, 1956, issue of this newspaper there appeared a scurrilous attack against the ORIT-ICFTU and, of course, against the AFL-CIO Inter-American Representative. ORIT General Secretary Luis Alberto Monge issued a press release in which he recorded his dismay that an organ of a democratic party, just emerging from a successful anti-Fascist revolution, should echo the worn-out clichés of the Communist and Peronista slanderers. In his press statement Monge generously asserted that such attacks against me actually were "the best recognition of [Romualdi's] many years of service to the most noble causes and aspirations of the people of the Western Hemisphere."

I was anxious, however, to know what Frondizi had to say about the attack. Although I had never met him I recognized his prestige, ability, and great political potential. To have him in the other corner would have been a serious handicap. Accordingly, I asked my friend Professor

Robert J. ("Bob") Alexander, then in Buenos Aires collecting material for his book *The Perón Era,* to try to see Frondizi and ask him about the article in *Palabra Radical.* On May 31 Bob wrote to me that Frondizi had assured him that he was not responsible at all for what was printed in that newspaper and that he "surely would not countenance such attacks because he knows Romualdi and the work he did in the struggle against Perón."

Writing to me again a few weeks later, Alexander related that a number of trade union leaders, particularly those of the COASI and MRGL, had approached him suggesting that a good-will mission from the AFL-CIO, possibly headed by President George Meany, go to Argentina in the near future. The same suggestion had been made to me by the new Argentine Ambassador in Washington, Adolfo A. Vicchi. Soon an official invitation came from various organizations of the democratic Argentine labor movement. Taking advantage of the fact that he had already accepted an invitation to go to Brazil in November, right after the U.S. elections, President Meany readily consented to extend his tour to include Argentina. He saw in it a fitting epilogue to the 1947 AFL mission.

The AFL-CIO group arrived in Buenos Aires on November 17, 1956. In addition to President Meany, it included Vice-Presidents David Dubinsky and O. A. Knight, and myself. We were received at the airport by hundreds of trade unionists waving flags and cheering. When I set foot again on Argentine soil, after ten years, emotion got the best of me and I wept while scores of old friends almost smothered me under an avalanche of *abrazos.*

At a mass meeting called to pay homage to the visiting delegation George Meany outlined the AFL-CIO hemispheric policy, based on "inter-Americanism without imperialism," uncompromising defense of freedom and equally unqualified opposition to dictatorship. In their response, spokesmen for Argentine free labor expressed gratitude for the report on the evils of Peronism published by the AFL group that came to Argentina in 1947. The report, they said, was the first crushing blow to Perón's international prestige.

The delegation found a confused situation in Argentina, the heritage of the ten-year dictatorship. Nevertheless, the free labor movement was somewhat successful in its efforts to recoup what had been lost under the repressive regime. Many of the responsible leaders who had been forced underground or into exile had resumed their positions of leadership; among these were Francisco Pérez Leiros, again holding the reins of the Municipal Workers' Union; Jesús Fernández, once more in control of

La Fraternidad; and Sebastian Marotta, the veteran leader of the printers. The delegation also met with Alfredo Fidanza and Cándido Gregorio who represented COASI at many ORIT and ICFTU meetings during their exile. They were back in positions of leadership of the democratic sector of the labor movement. We also met with new democratic leaders, formed under the Perón regime, among them Armando March of the powerful Commercial Employees Union.

At the time of the visit, the free trade unions had made a notably strong showing in the trade union elections at the local level. However, they suffered from internal dissension, hostility from military "interventors," and bitter external opposition from both the Peronists and the Communists—the two groups frequently working in concert. The Argentine free trade unionists gained new prestige during our visit. They were invited for the first time to the American Embassy and accompanied us to meetings with President Aramburu and Vice-President Rojas.

When he met Meany, President Aramburu took advantage of the occasion to ask, "Is it true that New York City is a melting pot?" "I guess so," Meany replied. Then he placed his arms around two of the union leaders accompanying him and added: "I'm from Ireland. Serafino Romualdi is from Italy. David Dubinsky is from Poland. And all three of us are New Yorkers."

By the middle of 1956 Argentina was in the grip of a serious inflation. The government had intervened earlier in February establishing minimum wages and ordering a provisional 10-percent across-the-board wage increase. Wage negotiations completed in September and October 1956 resulted in increases averaging about 40 percent. However, these were insufficient to keep up with the zooming cost of living.

The inflation continued to plague Argentina throughout 1956 and 1957, and still does in 1966 at the writing of this chapter. It was undoubtedly a determining factor in creating a mood of disenchantment with and opposition to the provisional government of Aramburu, even among the democratic workers who had supported the *Revolución Libertadora*. In the month of August 1957 I had occasion to question at random some workers in Buenos Aires. The view was almost unanimous that "this Government lacks social sensibility." I could not agree completely with the Argentine man in the street because, having met Vice-President Isaac Rojas and Minister of Labor Dr. Raul Migone, I knew that they certainly did not deserve such a censure. Yet it was a fact that the general economic policy of the government seemed to be oblivious to the inflationary pinch affecting the mass of wage earners. More and more workers began to murmur, "Things were not so bad under Perón," and some joined the chant: *"Ladrón o no ladrón, queremos vuelva Perón!*—Thief or no thief, we want Perón back!"

The Peronista leaders who had drifted back with increasing tempo into trade union activity fanned the flames of discontent and reaped fat benefits. By the time CGT intervertor Navy Captain Patrón Laplacette called the CGT national convention for the purpose of "giving back the Confederation to the workers," the Peronistas were buoyant and confident.

When the CGT Convention assembled early in September 1957 I was still in Buenos Aires attending the Inter-American Economic Conference as adviser to the U.S. delegation. The Communist and Peronist press immediately charged that I had arrived in Buenos Aires to "direct" the strategy of the democratic bloc inside the CGT. I regret that they were wrong; perhaps things would not have turned out so disastrously.

First of all, even the most optimistic estimates did not give the democratic bloc more than a majority of 40 votes, despite its lion's share of the total trade union membership. Unfortunately, the rules called for voting by delegates and not by the membership they represented. It was really unpardonable, in my opinion, for an intervertor appointed ostensibly to purge the labor movement of totalitarian influence to have called the convention at that time and with those rules. A civilian intervertor with a labor-political background would not have committed such a mistake. But Captain Laplacette was a cultured gentleman anxious to be relieved of the whole trade union mess and to return to his Navy duty.

Secondly, the democratic bloc was so torn by jealousies and rivalries that it would have been almost impossible for them to unite behind a single man. Sebastiano Marotta, the veteran leader of the printers, was regarded as the "conscience" of Argentine trade unionism for his immaculate record of noninvolvement in political squabbles. He wanted to crown his honorable career with at least one term as Secretary General of the CGT. On the other hand, Armando March, who represented the young Turks in the labor movement, enjoyed anti-Peronist credentials derived from his active membership in COASI. He was practical enough to have cultivated contacts in one or two political parties that were expected to make a strong showing in the forthcoming February 1958 presidential elections. March would not agree to step aside. And there was a dark horse ready to be drafted in case of a deadlock—Francisco Pérez Leiros. He had all the qualities for outstanding leadership and had been such a consistent, aggressive, and vocal anti-Peronista that it was feared that the reds, the blacks, and the grays (Communists, Peronists, and timid souls) inside the CGT would mutiny in the event of his election.

The Convention, which I followed largely via the press and occasional evening chats with some delegates and observers, was a classic example of totalitarian discipline on one side, and confusion, disunity, and even irresponsibility on the democratic side. On one crucial vote, for instance, the democratic majority became a minority just because forty or fifty delegates were absent. After three days of wrangling the Convention was still unable to get organized. The deadlock had become hopeless. It was, therefore, adjourned and the government intervention continued.

Two well-defined groups emerged from the Convention: The so-called "32 Bloc" with a membership of about 1,500,000; the other, composed of Peronists and other assorted elements, represented 62 federations (the so-called "62 Bloc") with a membership of about 800,000. However, the industrial importance, tactical experience, and discipline of the "62 Bloc" gave it power disproportionate to its size. Later, another group emerged, the so-called "19 Bloc," consisting of some Communist and some independent unions. This bloc was known also as MUCS—Movement for Trade Union Unity and Coordination—and tended to ally itself with the "62 Bloc" in antigovernment policy. These blocs have continued in existence up to the present time, although greatly altered in terms of influence and membership strength. Efforts to reconvene the CGT Convention in 1958 were defeated when the courts upheld the Peronist contention that a convention would be illegal without representatives of the Peronist unions which were then under government intervention.

On February 23, 1958, Arturo Frondizi was elected President of Argentina, supported by a coalition of his own Radical (Intransigent) Party, the Nationalists, the Peronistas, and the Communists. In terms of popular vote, his victory was decisive. Five days later he held an interview with representatives of the "32 Bloc" democratic unions, expressing willingness to cooperate with them and remarking that he undoubtedly would have difficulties with the "62" unions led by Communists, Peronistas, Clericals, etc. In April the Aramburu Government made a final attempt to turn the CGT over to a provisional committee made up of leaders of the twenty largest unions. This was a move that should logically have been made the very same day that the CGT Convention became hopelessly deadlocked and had to be suspended. But a labor tribunal, assuming powers that were never exercised in the history of Argentine labor jurisprudence, declared the provisional committee illegal, began to issue injunctions against it, and appointed an interventor.

On May 10, the court-appointed interventor, aided by armed force, was able to take possession of the CGT headquarters. The reaction of the democratic trade unionists was very strong. On May 13 the displaced members of the administrative committee of the CGT, representing some of the largest unions of the country, visited President Frondizi and served notice on him that they were prepared to call a general strike for Monday, May 26. According to press reports, Frondizi explained that he could not intervene against the decision of the judiciary, but pledged that his future labor policy would be one of nonintervention.

That was surely good news. But two months earlier I had received from my friend "Paco"—a top Argentine labor leader—a letter that cast doubts on Frondizi's sincerity:

Following the February 23 elections, Frondizi has shown a determination to work together with the democratic groups and with the present government, to the extreme that some of his allies have already protested. This attitude has given rise to expectations on one side and disappointment on the other; however, it is hard to place trust in such a Machiavellian attitude full of contradictions. If this attitude were firm and honest, Frondizi could organize a good government which would contribute to the strengthening of democracy. In that case he could refuse to pay the bill that his heterogeneous allies will undoubtedly present, and he could do so without endangering his stability because the free, democratic elements of the Argentine nation would rally to his support. But if he is compelled to pay the bill and to give his election allies some concrete recognition, then we will face a very difficult situation.

Judging from his conduct of the last few weeks and public and private statements that he has made, Frondizi appears to be heading for a realistic position. But whom should we believe, Frondizi of the election campaign or Frondizi after the triumph? With whom does he really want to work—with us or with them?

President Frondizi, who took office on May 1, 1958, proceeded to play a cat-and-mouse game with the Peronists, adopting austere economic policies which angered them, but giving them many advantages in the labor field. For example, he did intervene in trade union affairs, despite his pledge. Shortly after assuming office Frondizi reversed the decree issued by the Provisional Government that provided for an administrative committee for the CGT composed of representatives of the twenty largest unions, pending the calling of a national convention. In lieu of this administrative committee, the Frondizi Government appointed its own interventors. Most of them were former adherents of Perón, thus facilitating the return of the Peronist trade union leadership. Frondizi was confident in his ability to manipulate organized labor through a CGT under Peronist control and thus assure labor tranquillity as well as support for his economic program. And, moreover, having won the election with Peronist support, Frondizi had a debt to pay, and it was this debt that gave form to the trade union policy of his administration.

Under Frondizi the top positions in the Ministry of Labor went to Alfredo Allende, Undersecretary, and Horacio Ferro, Director of Labor. Under their authority a number of the large unions—textile, meat, metal, bank, streetcar, and health workers—which had been "intervened" by the Provisional Government, were restored to their former Peronist leadership.

Thousands of Peronists in the labor field were the main beneficiaries of a government bill to grant amnesty to all those earlier convicted of political or quasi political offenses including those of a trade union nature.

Reminiscent of an earlier period was the use of violence to assure trade union control. Less than a month after Frondizi's inauguration numerous union headquarters were attacked and occupied by Peronist elements, reportedly under the personal direction of Undersecretary of Labor Allende.

The passage of new labor legislation in August 1948 reestablished almost without change the absolute control over organized labor that had prevailed under Perón. Sponsored by the Frondizi Government, the new law was bitterly opposed by the anti-Peronist democratic unions, the Church, business and professional organizations, and most of the press. The democratic unions strongly resented the provision calling for new union elections within ninety days, a move that they had been assured would not be taken. Peronist leaders barred from active trade union participation under the Provisional Government would thus be eligible for election, since their rights had already been restored by the general amnesty. A score of unions elected Peronist slates under those provisions, while a few elections held in prodemocratic unions were declared illegal by the appointed government electoral officers.

The new trade union law was designed to unify the labor movement by imposition from above, rather than through democratic processes. The Ministry of Labor was given the authority to certify a union as bargaining agent, to recognize only one national federation in each industry, and to allow only one national confederation. Only those unions certified by the Ministry could receive members' dues, which were to be collected by the employer through compulsory checkoff. Perón used a series of measures identical to these to manipulate the labor movement and force the trade unions to submit to totalitarian control.

In spite of these restrictive measures, the "32 Bloc" campaigned militantly for free union elections, challenged the constitutionality of the labor law, and refused to accept the jurisdiction of government electoral agents. In an appeal sent to the AFL-CIO and the international labor movement, they pledged "to continue to fight, with all our strength, to preserve freedom and democracy in the labor movement, because without them there cannot be genuine trade unionism."

The "62 Bloc," notwithstanding favors received from the Government, attacked Frondizi's economic policies with repeated appeals to nationalism and Peronist loyalties. Late in 1958 the Bloc threatened a general strike to protest the terms of government contracts with foreign petroleum companies. Frondizi promptly declared a state of siege and arrested some 250 Peronists and Communists. Nevertheless, in January 1959, the "62 Bloc," supported by the "19 Bloc," called a general strike in protest against the austerity program. It was broken by prompt government action; petroleum and transport workers were mobilized into military service and hundreds of Peronist and Communist labor leaders were arrested. Ten important Peronist and Communist-controlled unions were "intervened," and Peronist Labor Ministry officials were replaced by others supposedly nonpolitical. These strikes and later ones were actively opposed by the "32 Bloc" and the independent unions. At the same time, conciliatory elements appeared among this group, whereupon the government began to make overtures of peace to them and to renew promises of union elections under fair conditions.

In January 1959 President Frondizi came to the United States on an official visit. Henry Holland, former Assistant Secretary of State for Inter-American Affairs, who had since become a consultant to foreign oil firms seeking drilling concessions from the Argentine government, informally approached the AFL-CIO to arrange a visit by Frondizi to AFL-CIO headquarters. This was vetoed by President Meany, who authorized me to inform Holland that "such a visit, with the accompanying fanfare and splash of publicity, would be interpreted as a stab in the back of our democratic trade union friends" who were then in opposition to Frondizi's labor policy. However, well aware that the new President was reassessing this policy, and realizing the benefits of a frank conversation, President Meany agreed to meet privately with Frondizi in Miami. The latter was scheduled to be there for one day before leaving for home, in order to speak at the inauguration of the new International Airport.

The meeting took place at the Hotel Fontainebleau and President Meany asked me to go along with him. The conversation with Frondizi was cordial but frank—a characteristic of the American labor chief, especially when he talks to high ranking personalities. We were impressed with Frondizi's analysis of Argentine economic problems and his cool appraisal of the labor difficulties. We therefore concurred with the Frondizi plan for the reorganization of the CGT on the basis of exclusion of Communists and hard-line Peronistas. *Linea dura* was the expression used repeatedly, meaning those who were using the labor movement to try to bring back Perón.

As a consummate politician almost without peer, Frondizi perceived that I would immediately grab the line he had thrown. He knew that the democratic trade unionists of Argentina were anxious to reach an understanding with his government mainly to reverse the growing resurgence of the Peronistas in the labor movement and in the country as a whole.

Meanwhile, the situation in the Railway Union (Unión Ferroviaria), which was led by democratic elements, had become so tense that no immediate progress along the lines hinted by Frondizi in Miami Beach could be expected. At the beginning of November 1958 the Argentine government had decreed total mobilization of the railroad workers and put them under military rule. This was a result of a second railway strike within three months which they had called to enforce their demands for a lump sum payment of back pay increases. The mobilization decree meant the immediate cessation of all trade union activity by the two railwaymen's organizations. A warrant was issued by the military courts for the arrest of the members of the Executive Committee of the Unión Ferroviaria, who had to go into hiding in order to escape imprisonment. In addition to this, thousands of railwaymen belonging to both trade union organizations were sentenced by military courts, in the majority of cases for acts which the Military Code qualifies as "contrary to discipline."

The plight of the railwaymen led to the sending of a joint international free labor mission to Buenos Aires. The government eventually acceded to their request to demobilize the railwaymen and its action greatly contributed to the abatement of the tension. Thus a climate was created favorable to the initiation of a dialogue between the democratic unions and the government concerning the normalization of the CGT. The democratic groups were, however, still hopelessly divided, still raked by jealousies. The result was that nobody took any initiative to do anything.

I celebrated my birthday on Wednesday, November 18, by visiting President Frondizi in his Casa Rosada office. Emerging from the interview I told the reporters who had been waiting outside that the purpose of my visit was "to voice the stand of the international free labor movement against the Argentine Law of Professional Association which does not permit trade union pluralism even if the rank and file desire it."

Actually, the main topic of my conversation with the President was how to bring about the badly overdue normalization of the CGT. Frondizi came forth with a specific formula. "Let the largest affiliate, the Union Ferroviaria, and the oldest one, Fraternidad, issue a call for the CGT convention. And if they manage to get enough delegations to attend, representative of a substantial majority of Argentine organized labor, I will give back to them (*se les entregaré*—he said) the CGT." I promised that I would get to work on that right away.

Less than one hour later I was paying a courtesy call on General Severo Toranzo Montero, Army Chief of Staff, with whom I had become friendly during his tour of duty as Military Attaché in Washington. General Toranzo was a strong anti-Peronista who had differed sharply with President Frondizi on many issues, especially on what he considered Frondizi's protection of the Peronistas inside the labor movement. A few months before, Toranzo had led a successful "show of force" which caused Frondizi to offer his resignation—a gesture spurned by the General, probably to his subsequent regret. The topic of our chat was, as usual, Peronist versus democratic influence in Argentine labor. When I casually mentioned the President's plan just outlined to me, Toranzo could hardly contain his rejoicing. *"Por fin, por fin*—Finally, finally, . . ." he exclaimed. Taking me by the hand he led me across the hall to repeat the good news to Minister of War General Benjamin Larcher, and he too expressed delight over the prospect.

In less than forty-eight hours I was lunching at the home of Crisólogo Larralde, leader of the Radical People's Party and candidate for governor of Buenos Aires province. Also present were Antonio Scipione, head of the Unión Ferroviaria and a member of the Radical Party, and Armando March, leader of the powerful Buenos Aires Federation of Commercial Employees. I started my pitch full of enthusiasm, but Scipione deflated me. He said that time was needed to think the matter over; it would be a risky move, he repeated, to take the initiative in calling a CGT Convention. Scipione noted that elections in the Unión Ferroviaria were still in progress—district by district—and perhaps it would be better to wait until their results were known. However, the railway union chief believed in the soundness and feasibility of the plan, and in parting promised to examine further President Frondizi's suggestion.

Late in the same afternoon I met with Felix Mendoza, a top leader of the Fraternidad. He had no authority to give me an answer, but promised to convey the suggestion to his chief Herminio Alonso, who was then out of town.

In spite of these indecisive results, I was not completely discouraged. I realized that political pressure was perhaps needed from the Social Democrats and the People's Radical Party. They both had considerable influence with the leadership of the railwaymen's unions. And some pressure from inside the labor movement itself was also needed. The same night, at a dinner given in my honor by the Coordinating Committee of the "32 Bloc," I approached a number of the labor leaders and obtained unanimous backing for the plan. Most of them promised to see to it that both Unión Ferroviaria and Fraternidad would carry out their assigned role. In the next few days I contacted a number of political friends, such as Américo Ghioldi of the Social Democrats, and Ernesto Sanmartino and Miguel Ángel Zavala Órtiz of the People's Radical Party. Sanmartino and Zavala later became Ambassador and Foreign Minister, respectively, under President Illía. They all tempered their encouragement with doubts of Frondizi's sincerity.

Well, the plan came to naught, mainly because of the lack of initiative and aggressiveness so characteristic of the Argentine democratic trade union sector. Of course, the stated excuse for the inaction was the hackneyed refrain: "We don't trust Frondizi." Nonsense. They could, at least, have put him to a test. As it was, they left a vacuum that was finally filled in 1961 in a manner that further reduced the influence and strength of the democratic group, allowing the Peronistas to regain absolute unchallengeable control of the CGT.

After July 1960 several discussions were held between the "32 Bloc" and the "62 Bloc" regarding reactivation of the CGT. Agreement was reached at an early stage to exclude the Communist-oriented Movement for Labor Unity and Coordination (the MUGS, or "19 Bloc") from any future CGT. But it was not until March 1961 that Frondizi issued a decree permitting the CGT to resume its functions. A provisional executive committee was established as the ruling body of the CGT, pending the calling of a Congress before the end of 1961. The provisional committee consisted of ten members from the Peronist "62 Bloc" and ten from the democratic "32 Bloc." However, in this last group were included some alleged independent unions, such as Luz y Fuerza (Power and Light) whose representatives were Peronistas in disguise. The ratio, instead of being 10 : 10 was actually 13 : 7.

The democratic, or independent group as it now began to call itself, entered the coalition in a mood of passive acquiescence. They were unable to agree among themselves to do anything else.

It was hoped that a Congress of the CGT would be held in November or December of 1961. Close observers correctly predicted that no Congress would take place because the democratic group would not participate unless it was agreed in advance that the status quo would be maintained. This meant barring from the provisional executive committee all known Communists and retaining the rule requiring a two-thirds vote for any binding action on major problems. A CGT Congress had been rescheduled for March 26, 1962 but it was cancelled by the Peronista election sweep a week earlier, which led to the overthrow of President Frondizi.

An example of the difficulties encountered in achieving labor unity occurred at the time of the Seventh American Member States ILO Conference, hosted by Argentina April 10–21, 1961. To the great embarrassment of the government, the CGT failed to select a worker delegation to represent Argentina. The real reason was inability to agree, after seventy-two hours of continuous debate, whether the titular head of the delegation would be Peronist Augusto Vandor or non-Peronist Riego Ribas. In late May 1962, again after long, heated debate, the CGT selected Vandor as worker delegate to the ILO Conference in Geneva, with the condition that his speech be nonpartisan and prepared by a subcommittee made up of four "62 Bloc" members and four independents.

A few weeks after unity was achieved in 1961, the Peronistas booed Francisco Pérez Leiros—a leader of the "Independent 10"—off the speakers' stand at the May Day CGT celebrations. This happened so frequently that Pérez Leiros, supported by his municipal workers, had ceased to participate in CGT affairs by 1963. Meanwhile, the hard-liners among the "32 Bloc," led by the leader of the Custom House Employees, Juan Carlos Brunetti, declared war on the rest of the group that had rejoined the CGT and created a further split.

The year 1963 was one of sparring and watchful waiting. The provisional regime of President José María Guido was preparing general elections which would presumably decide which way the labor movement would go. The Peronistas, especially those in the labor movement, adopted a democratic posture for electoral ends. The U.S. Embassy in Buenos Aires became convinced that the time had come to make a fresh start with the Peronist elements of the CGT. Since they had become the unbeatable numerical majority, it was argued, why not give them the recognition they deserved?

A series of projects were tentatively launched, including leader exchange grants for top CGT officers to visit the United States. At the same time, International Trade Secretariats were persuaded to drop the ideological barrier that some of them had maintained, and admit to membership Peronist unions. Even ORIT was led to believe that the CGT itself would soon be ready for affiliation. Although guarded and uncommitted in his public statements, ORIT General Secretary Arturo Jáuregui paid a courtesy call on CGT headquarters. The Peronist General Secretary, José Alonso, reciprocated by attending a reception in Jáuregui's honor given by a CGT affiliate.

Ambassador Robert McClintock, on consultation in Washington, came to see me inquiring if the AFL-CIO would receive CGT labor leaders brought to the United States on leader exchange grants. The answer was: "If they ask to pay us a visit, we will be polite and will receive them." After all, our Argentine democratic friends were coexisting with the Peronistas in the CGT. We could not—as the saying goes—be more papist than the Pope.

During my trip to Buenos Aires in November 1963, when I was already in charge of the American Institute for Free Labor Development (AIFLD) the U.S. Labor Attaché urged me to include some CGT trade unionists in the AIFLD Washington course. Until then I had given *becas* (scholarships) only to unions belonging to the "Independent Bloc." Since the local AID Mission was the source for the financing of these grants, I could not, therefore, ignore any reasonable request to broaden the base of our contacts. Accordingly, I agreed to meet with José Alonso, the Peronista labor chief, in the office of the Labor Attaché, Henry Hammond. I had met Alonso at a number of ILO meetings and our relationship was civil. I told Alonso: "You know you will not be able to fool me; and I know I will not be able to fool you. So, let's place our cards on the table."

I finally agreed to give the CGT, on a trial basis, four scholarships for the next AIFLD Washington course scheduled to begin in January 1964. Alonso did actually try to pull a fast one and up to this time I am sure he believes he succeeded. But if he ever reads this book, he will get the surprise of his life.

A couple of weeks after the four Argentines arrived in Washington

Alonso sent them a letter which fate put into my hands after it had been received. He gave them instructions on how to conduct effective Peronist propaganda among the participants from other Latin American countries —a barefaced violation of the "gentleman's agreement" he had made with me in the presence of the U.S. Labor Attaché. Here are some of the passages from that letter (I have a photostatic copy of the original, with signature, etc.) :

During the discussions or debates, never assume a *fanatic position*—listen, explain, rebut, and above all try to stimulate curiosity and gain sympathy for our cause. Fights are often lost if one tries to win them in the first round; on the other hand, victory comes to whoever works with perseverance and vision without rest, but without haste. Make friends, ask questions, and give explanations; I am sure victory will be yours. You will divide yourselves into two groups, and if each group will adhere to these general directives you will not fail.

Alonso then advised his boys to return home from the United States or Europe by the Atlantic route, requesting from the AIFLD an open return ticket with a number of stopovers. Anywhere near Spain, they were instructed to make a quick jump to Madrid where they were to phone Señor Algarbe, at 231-6305 or 231-6306. "He will take care of everything," Alonso assured. "In the event airline connections should go wrong, you will be able to give him [Perón] at least greetings by phone."

Needless to say, none of our Argentine students went to Madrid. Two participated in the Washington course and the other two joined the international travel program in West Europe and Israel. Also, none was ever questioned about the letter, although, of course, they were kept under discrete surveillance. It happened that those four Argentine labor leaders, in spite of their open and ardent Peronismo, were model students, attentive and courteous. They were more interested in learning the ways of democratic labor than in propagating the theories of Peronista trade unionism. Ironically, one of them, Jorge Vicente Tur, was selected class valedictorian for the graduation ceremony and delivered a wonderful address that was much admired and applauded.

Judging by these results, the first experiment with Peronista trainees was not so bad, after all. I decided, therefore, to keep silent about the content of the letter and repeated the offer to the CGT for more grants to another course. But the next group were of a different stripe—quarrelsome, tactless, aggressive. Soon they were ostracized by most of their fellow students from other Latin American countries. At the end of that course we decided that we had had enough of CGT trainees and quietly dropped them from future consideration.

Following the 1964 Presidential election, which brought Dr. Arturo Illía to the Presidency of Argentina and greatly increased the parliamentary strength of the Peronistas, the latent antagonism within the CGT flared up again. As a result, most of the Independents, early in 1965, refused to continue their participation in the affairs of the Confederation. Actually, after considerable indecision, they managed to set up an organization of their own which became, in effect, a parallel CGT. At the same time, the Peronist forces split wide open as a result of the rivalry between Augusto Vandor and José Alonso for the leadership of what was left of the "62 Bloc." Alonso was expelled "de facto" from the CGT when the pro-Vandor majority gave him a vote of no confidence and refused to recognize his leadership. Both groups, however, proclaimed their loyalty to the "Jefe" in Madrid. For Vandor, this was a tactical gesture rather than a true mirror of his feelings.

The regime of President Illía was deposed in 1966 by a military junta headed by ex-Commander in Chief of the Army, General Juan Carlos Ongania. At the start of Illía's brief tenure of office, it was felt that he would move to curb the power of the Peronist unions. However, he established instead a sort of truce with the labor movement, following a policy that he would not move to take away any gains which had been established before he took office.

As I write the conclusion of this chapter in the fall of 1966, it is still too early to conclude what effect the revolution led by General Ongania will have on the future of the Argentine labor movement. A strong ruler, Ongania immediately acted to consolidate his control by issuing orders dissolving Congress, the Supreme Court, and all political parties. He reportedly also has told the CGT that unless it gets in line and gets out of politics it, too, will be dissolved.

XII

With Nixon in South America

MUCH HAS BEEN WRITTEN about Vice-President Nixon's 1958 visit to South America, during which he encountered violent demonstrations in Caracas, and hostile treatment in Lima and other cities. Few people with the exception of those who regularly read the labor press know, however, that many labor groups greeted him warmly during that trip and an earlier one to Central America and the Caribbean in 1955.

The first time I met Nixon and his charming wife Pat was in April 1958, at their home for a get-together of the U.S. delegation to the impending inauguration of President Frondizi of Argentina. I was a member and the Vice-President was heading the delegation as personal representative of President Eisenhower. I already esteemed and admired him for his militant anti-Communist stand since the days of the Alger Hiss affair—sentiments that were shared by most of the staff of the AFL-CIO International Department. As far back as I can remember, especially since he became Vice-President, Nixon consistently supported the overseas activities of U.S. labor representatives on behalf of free trade unionism. But as to his views on domestic labor, it is a known fact that the AFL-CIO leadership had very strong reservations. I clearly remember how Al Barkan—now head of COPE, the AFL-CIO Committee for Political Education—would remark: "I know, I know, Nixon is all for labor . . . outside the United States!"

During his 1955 tour of Central America and the Caribbean, Nixon

172

insisted on meeting with labor groups, listened to their problems and encouraged them to build strong free unions—to the dismay of many American employers and quite a number of host governments. In Cuba he met with a delegation of top leaders from the CTC; in Mexico with a group headed by Jesús Yurén, leader of the powerful CTM Federation of the Federal District; in Guatemala with the railroad workers and the Independent Trade Union Federation. Similar meetings were held in El Salvador, Nicaragua, and Panama. A special reception was arranged in Nixon's honor at the union hall of the Confederation of Labor of Costa Rica. His visit to Tegucigalpa, Honduras, coincided with the promulgation of the labor code, and Junta chief Julio Lozano held a special ceremony and invited a number of labor leaders. Arturo Jáuregui, then ORIT director of organization, headed the trade union delegation and conferred at length with Nixon.

The introduction of trade union receptions in a tour of such a high ranking U.S. official as Vice-President Nixon was a sharp departure from tradition. I was therefore asked by the Office of the Inter-American Labor Adviser at the State Department to cooperate by furnishing background information on organizations and individuals, and to help in the arrangements for the planned labor receptions and interviews. When we discussed the Dominican Republic—whose labor movement was created and controlled by the secret police of the Trujillo tyranny—I strongly recommended that no trade union reception or interview be included in the program for that country. The Vice-President agreed.

When the U.S. official delegation to the inauguration of President-elect Frondizi arrived in Buenos Aires, I learned that the democratic unions of the "32 Bloc" had expressed the desire to have Nixon as their guest of honor at a May Day afternoon celebration to follow the inaugural ceremony and military parade. I naturally began pressuring Ambassador Willard L. Beaulac, Assistant Secretary of State Roy Richard Rubottom, and other members of the delegation to urge Nixon to accept the invitation. I was really excited at the prospect of having the Vice-President of the United States attend and address a May Day trade union meeting.

Everything seemed to go well until powerful voices—reinforced, I learned later, by Henry Holland, Rubottom's predecessor, who was in Buenos Aires on private business—tried to convince the American Embassy and Nixon himself to cancel the union visit because "it would displease Frondizi." At that time there was a fight going on between the "32" and "62" blocs, the latter having supported Frondizi in the presidential election. My position was that, if Frondizi had objections, we as his guests for the inauguration, had no choice but to comply with his wishes. "However," I insistently demanded, "to whom has Frondizi expressed displeasure?" It then came out that Frondizi himself had said nothing, but his close adviser Rogelio Frigerio had spoken to Henry Holland, voicing his belief that Frondizi would be unhappy if Nixon attended the reception of the "32 Bloc." Most of the Embassy and State Department officers by then were of the opinion that it would be better for Nixon to stay away so as not to get involved in any internal labor squabble.

When the issue finally reached the Vice-President he overruled the diplomats and sent word that he would go to the labor reception. That same evening, at a dinner for the members of the delegation and some Argentine guests, he approached me and said: "I have decided to go on account of you. I want to strengthen your position and that of the AFL-CIO you represent."

The reception, the next day, at the Sports Club of the Municipal Workers' Union, was a tumultous, joyous affair. Hundreds of men and women mobbed Nixon, Ambassador Beaulac, and every American in the party, which also included actress Jinx Falkenburg and my wife Miriam. The address of welcome, delivered by Francisco Pérez Leiros on behalf of the host organization, hit the mark just like the expressions of thanks from the guest of honor. Nixon cheerfully answered many questions and forcefully underscored the incompatibility of free labor and dictatorships of either the right or the left. The entire unforgettable affair culminated with the serving of a typical *asado criollo* (gaucho style barbecue). This was Nixon's first taste of it, judging from his delightful description of the *asado* in his book *Six Crises*.

"The violent anti-Nixon demonstrations in Peru and Venezuela, and the others of minor character that took place in Uruguay and Bolivia, clearly indicated a prearranged plan of unquestionable Communist organization and direction." This is what I wrote in the May 24, 1958, issue of the *AFL-CIO News*.

Democratic public opinion, not only in the United States but throughout the hemisphere, reacted with a unity transcending political parties and national borders. There was real evidence of indignation and regret over the outrages even in the countries where they took place. And it was a source of satisfaction, as well as highly significant, that in the demonstrations against the United States organized labor in Latin

America did not take any part. On the contrary, the conversations the Vice-President had in practically every country with groups of labor leaders were cordial, dignified, fruitful. Nixon's interviews gave labor representatives an opportunity to present the workers' viewpoint on their respective country's relations with the United States and to tell him what labor regarded as legitimate grievances against our policies. For example, leaders of Colombia's two ORIT-ICFTU affiliates, the UTC and CTC, told Nixon that the best way to defeat communism was through "the elimination of poverty." This took place at a reception given by Colombian labor in honor of Nixon, during which he presented a 300-volume library on U.S. labor history and related subjects to Colombia's free labor movement.

From Montevideo, Juan A. Acuña, then General Secretary of the Trade Union Confederation of Uruguay, wrote to me after the Vice-President's visit to his country: "Nixon has won a great battle for democracy and friendship with the United States." Another Uruguayan, Alberto Z. Pintos, leader of the Association of Postal and Telegraph Employees, voiced similar sentiments by writing: ". . . The visit of Mr. Nixon was, in my opinion, a great success."

After the Caracas attacks, scores of letters and telegrams of protest were sent to me by labor leaders throughout the hemisphere. Typical of them was the one from the Trade Union Committee that organized the Buenos Aires May Day reception:

The aggressions against Nixon which took place in Lima and Caracas have caused astonishment and profound indignation here. The attitude of Nixon was a sterling example of dignity on the face of injustice and vulgar attacks of which he was victim. We will always remember the visit that Nixon made at our Sport Club and the great favorable impression that he left on the labor movement of our country.

The Confederation of Labor of Peru protested the anti-Nixon demonstration at the University of San Marcos, in Lima, with the following press statement:

The barbarous behavior of the Communists and their allies in the University Square of Lima during Mr. Nixon's visit does not reflect the sentiments of the Peruvian people and particularly of our labor movement, which is inspired by the firm ideals of democracy, freedom, and inter-American trade unionism.

Most significant was the letter from Augusto Malavé Villalba on behalf of the United Trade Union Committee of Venezuela:

I am writing to you, still under the impression of the shameful hostile demonstrations which took place in our country when Vice-President Nixon arrived. What has happened in Caracas has filled with shame all the democratic citizens of our country. Those who took part in the hostile demonstrations were not representative elements of Venezuela, but people belonging to the lower depths of society, who were stirred up by agitators for many days previous to the arrival of the Vice-President. I must also say that many students, especially those of high school age, joined in the demonstrations. The organized workers of Venezuela, however, did not take part in any of the deplorable actions because they have a clear conception of their sense of responsibility. Furthermore, those who promoted the riots knew well in advance that we would not fall for their propaganda tricks.

The overwhelming majority of the Venezuelan people—as represented by the three leading political parties—unreservedly condemned the attacks on Nixon and described May 13 as "a day of sorrow for the Venezuelans." Rafael Caldera, head of the Christian Democratic Party; Jovito Villalba, leader of the Democratic Republican Unions; and Rómulo Betancourt, President of the Democratic Action Party, joined in a nationwide broadcast condemning the mob violence.

In Venezuela other "emotional factors" contributed to making the demonstration against Nixon—the symbol of U.S. policies in Latin America—so violent. There had been a lapse of only one hundred days between the fall of the Pérez Jiménez dictatorship and the Vice-President's arrival in Caracas. The Communists were able to build upon the students' strong resentment over the fact that Pérez Jiménez and his Chief of Police Pedro Estrada were granted visas to enter the United States.

Under Pérez Jiménez the University of Caracas was closed for more than one year while hundreds of students were arrested and tortured by the secret police. It should also be remembered that it was at that time that our government bestowed on the dictator a medal "for his contribution to democracy."

Additional fuel was added to the smoldering resentment with the publication in the Communist daily newspaper in Caracas of a photostatic copy of a congratulatory letter which Fletcher Warren, former U.S. ambassador to Venezuela, wrote to Venezuelan Chief of Police, Pedro Estrada, after he had suppressed the first large-scale revolt against the Pérez Jiménez dictatorship on New Year's Day, 1958. This unfortunate error of judgment on the part of one of our diplomats was fully exploited by the Communists to whip up an anti-American emotional climate.

As I declared in an interview published in the May 22, 1958, issue of *The Machinist:*

The last straw was a rumor last month that the U.S. government planned to restrict imports of Venezuelan crude oil. The demonstrations against Vice-President Nixon are a harvest of the bad fruit of years of neglect in Latin America.

After his return to Washington, Nixon himself took the lead in advocating a change of United States policy in Latin America. According to *The New York Times* of May 18, he declared that "the problem of dictatorship in Latin America is a ball and chain around the neck of the United States." His formula to cope with the problem was: "for dictators the United States should have only a handshake and for free governments a warm embrace." Nixon's comments on the failings of U.S. policy in Latin America were endorsed by O. A. Knight, chairman of the AFL-CIO Inter-American Affairs Committee, as reported in the July 1958 issue of the *Inter-American Labor Bulletin*.

Although it was generally acknowledged that the demonstrations against the Vice-President resulted from pent-up resentment against Washington's Latin American policy, an important dissent was voiced by Professor Kenneth Galbraith of Harvard. In a letter to the editor published in the October 16, 1958, issue of *The New York Times*, he stated that the disorders were mainly caused by "popular hostility against Mr. Nixon himself," adding that "Mr. Nixon is widely regarded in Latin America as an antidemocratic figure." Galbraith cited statements in university circles concerning Vice-President Nixon's early campaigns in California, his characterizations of President Truman, and his alleged defense of the late Senator Joseph McCarthy.

In spite of my admiration for Galbraith's intellectual stature and his penetrating socioeconomic studies of our society, I felt that his appraisal was incorrect. I therefore wrote a letter of my own, which was published in *The New York Times* of November 7. Excerpts from that letter follow:

I have no evidence to dispute Mr. Galbraith's statements insofar as they might be the result of conversations held, as he asserted, in university communities. I would like to point out, however, that in my extensive connections with groups and personalities in the labor and political movements in every country of Latin America, I have never heard any remark which, even remotely, could be construed as substantiating Mr. Galbraith's statement.

Since the so-called Nixon incidents of last May, I have visited Venezuela twice, associating with the highest trade union and political leaders; I have been in Colombia twice; four times in Mexico City; twice in Havana and Panama; and made two trips through every country of Central America. At the AFL-CIO headquarters, I have received scores of labor leaders, newspaper men, and management representatives, visiting the United States under the ICA Technical Assistance Program.

Furthermore, I have had frequent conversations with Latin American diplomats, many of them outspoken democrats. In addition, I receive regularly from Latin America clippings of editorials and news items from every type of newspaper and magazine, all of which I read carefully. In no instance have I ever heard or read any indication that the views expressed by Mr. J. K. Galbraith as to the cause of the so-called Nixon incidents reflect the sentiments of any appreciable sector of Latin American public opinion.

What I have heard and read repeatedly was that the underlying motive for the demonstrations was the accumulated dissatisfaction against the economic and political policies of the United States government in Latin America, such as the denial of adequate economic help and credit facilities and the alleged support of dictatorships. May I add, also, that the Latin Americans with whom I come most often in contact—including outstanding leaders of democratic parties—have had nothing but admiration for the Vice-President's calm behavior in the face of the indignities to which he was subjected, and for the sober appeals to strengthen the bonds of solidarity among the American family of nations, especially in view of the political and economic offensive of the Soviet Union. He is also being credited in almost every quarter for the new emphasis given in our government's high echelon to Latin American problems and for the measures already adopted to correct past mistakes.

It was clear to me that the hostility, heckling, and violent demonstrations experienced by Nixon were expressions of deeply rooted Latin American criticism of U.S. policies in the hemisphere. Among the reformists and populist elements, especially university students, the Vice-President was seen as the *symbol* of these policies and the *target* of the strong criticism, resentment, and hostility. This was one of the findings of an American political scientist who conducted a survey in 1959 among Chilean university students on key inter-American and cold war issues. Over three hundred fifty students from the schools of law, political science, journalism, engineering, economics, etc., participated in the survey. They were asked the following question: "In your opinion, which of the following reasons that have been offered to explain the anti-Nixon demonstrations seems to be most valid?

"1. The Republican Party in the United States opposes the aspirations of Latin American reformists.

"2. U.S. policies in Latin America favor the dictatorships.

"3. Latin American Communists are very strong and they promoted the disorders.

"4. U.S. policies have been neglecting the economic development of Latin America."

Some students gave multiple replies which accounts for the fact that the total adds up to more than 100 percent. Only 16 percent gave No. 1 as their answer, 18 percent selected reason No. 3; 46 percent believed that the U.S. support of dictators in Latin America best explained the anti-Nixon demonstrations; and 68 percent said that it was Washington's neglect of Latin American economic development.

XIII

Mujal and Batista

MY INVOLVEMENT in the Cuban labor situation dates from 1947 when I met with Eusebio Mujal and Francisco Aguirre before they led the revolt against the Communists inside the CTC. That bitter struggle finally culminated in the elimination of the Communists at the CTC Convention in November 1947. But the fight took its toll. Prominent democratic labor leaders such as Felix V. Palu and the Barrera brothers were killed. Mujal himself was shot twice and gravely wounded. The democratic forces were greatly helped by Dr. Carlos Prío Socarrás, then Minister of Labor and later President of the Republic.

Ángel Cofiño, an independent, was elected General Secretary of the CTC in 1947; but at a special convention called in April 1949 he was replaced by Eusebio Mujal, who kept the reins until the end of 1958. Mujal had been active in the Cuban Revolutionary (Auténtico) Party since 1940, when he was elected delegate to the Constituent Assembly. Twice he was a member of the Cuban House of Representatives and in 1948 he was elected to the Senate from Oriente province.

In 1949, Cuban labor suffered a minor split. The independent unions affiliated with CONI (National Independent Labor Committee) under the leadership of Cofiño (Electrical Workers) and Vicente Rubiera (Telephone Workers) went their separate ways. However, in 1951 they returned to the fold and took part in the Seventh Congress of the CTC which met in Havana May 28–31. It was the Congress of democratic labor

180

unity, and was perhaps the biggest demonstration of labor strength ever staged in Cuba; attended by 3,222 regularly accredited and 340 fraternal delegates, representing 1,860 unions. The Congress, which had only a smattering of Communist delegates, went on record giving full support to the UN action in Korea and urged that there should be "no concessions to the forces of totalitarianism that are attempting to subjugate the world."

On March 10, 1952, a military coup by former President Fulgencio Batista overthrew the government of President Carlos Prío Socorrás. The labor movement, however, managed to avoid repressive measures as a result of a compromise worked out between Batista and the CTC. The events leading to this understanding were described in a communication sent by the CTC to all ICFTU affiliates throughout the world. Dated March 18, 1952, it was the first in a series of statements that the CTC was to distribute in an attempt to justify its position in relation to the Batista regime:

The coup staged by the armed forces was a complete surprise and with no resistance on the part of any of the existing political parties, not even those which were part of the government. However, the Cuban Confederation of Labor declared on that day a general strike throughout the country. On the same night of Monday, March 10, the Minister of Labor appointed by the new regime had an interview with Eusebio Mujal, General Secretary of this Confederation, and in the name of his government, offered guarantees that all the present trade union officers would be respected, that all the labor gains would be protected, and that the government would strongly oppose Communist as well as reactionary forces, cooperating in this respect with the Confederation's policy. Furthermore, he guaranteed that the government would not interfere in any way with the union's activities.

Our Executive Board met on the eleventh of March. It considered the proposals of the new government and gave its approval in principle, appointing a committee which was to meet with the Minister of Labor and later with the Chief of State, General Fulgencio Batista. These interviews took place, during which the proposals made previously to our General Secretary were ratified. The Workers' Palace, headquarters of the CTC, and the building of the Federation of Workers of Camaguey—which since the tenth were occupied by armed forces— were returned to their lawful owners. In addition, full guarantees were given for the normal activities of the ORIT, which has its headquarters in the CTC Building in this city.

Our Executive Committee, having taken into consideration the facts described above, resolved to continue our normal trade union activities within the limits accorded by the law, in complete independence of any political party and without any commitment other than to fight for the maintenance of our labor gains and for further extension of the rights of our laboring class.

The reaction in Latin American labor circles to the CTC communiqué was mixed. I would say that, generally, accommodation with Batista was regretfully accepted as a misalliance. The AFL Free Trade Union Committee, however, felt that it was necessary to express strong reservations, and its Executive Secretary, Jay Lovestone, issued a statement which I circulated among ORIT-affiliated organizations, and which read in part:

We disagree with the estimate of the situation given by our Cuban friends. Though we are not seeking to give them any advice as to what they should do in their country, we can't see how we can keep quiet about a situation where force and violence were used in a military putsch to overthrow a legally constituted, democratically elected government. We cannot keep quiet about such crimes in our own backyard when we show much alertness to denounce military usurpers and totalitarian subverters of democracy in other lands. The double standard of morality is not good for international labor policies.

We don't think we should play dumb to the fact that the first one to recognize Batista was Trujillo and the second one Venezuela; nor do we think it is insignificant that antilabor, big business interests were celebrating the return of Batista to power.

Batista "legalized" his power by winning the presidential elections of 1954, almost without a contest. The political opposition was given no opportunity to reorganize its forces. Batista knew that he was not popular with the people and he therefore took no chances. But after 1954 he relaxed his rule, most of the exiles returned to Cuba, and the jails were emptied of political prisoners. Even Fidel Castro, sentenced to a long prison term for leading the attack on the Moncada military barracks in Santiago, on July 26, 1953, was pardoned and allowed to go to Mexico. I doubt if Batista was familiar with Machiavelli's *Il Principe,* or my friend Ignazio Silone's *School for Dictators,* or otherwise he might have handled Castro somewhat differently!

Cuba's economic future looked bright, but the country needed political stability which could only be obtained by returning to constitutional rule via free, honest elections. A group of prominent Cubans, headed by elder statesman Cosme de la Torriente, formed the Sociedad Amigos de la República (Society of Friends of the Republic). Its aim was to bring together Batista and the opposition in order to work out a timetable for the return to constitutional normalcy. The proposal called for the eventual resignation of Batista, the appointment of a provisional president, and the holding of elections by stages—from the municipal level up through Congress and the presidency itself. It would have meant a peaceful liquidation of the dictatorship through an agreement with the opposition. The alternative was bound to be, sooner or later, a violent uprising.

The Cosme de la Torriente group held several meetings during the months of November and December 1955, but it finally had to give up because Batista would not consider any shortening of his presidential term, which still had almost three years to go. Batista was under pressure from a clique of senior military officers and civilian profiteers who urged him not to give an inch. Actually, Batista meant nothing to them—they wanted to preserve their privileges and sources of graft. The opposition had publicized its demands and could not retreat without impairing its moral standing with the people. A go-between was needed—a person of high enough stature and influence to impress Batista. Our Ambassador to Cuba could have played this role. At that very same time, in Peru, the U.S. Ambassador, career diplomat Ellis O. Briggs, was discreetly inspiring contacts between the Government of General Odría and the underground APRA. But our man in Havana, Arthur Gardner, a political appointee, obviously did not understand that the proposal advanced by the Society of Friends of the Republic was the last chance to spare Cuba from the abyss of civil war and bloody revolution. Neither Gardner nor the State Department did anything to inspire, encourage, or nudge Batista toward an agreement with the opposition. And Ambassador Gardner had numerous opportunities during his many evenings spent socially with Batista; they were good pals addressing each other as Archie and Fulgencio. I have had many occasions to state publicly that, in my opinion, the turning point in the recent tragic history of Cuba occurred when the Cosme de la Torriente group failed in its initiative to arrange the peaceful liquidation of the Batista dictatorship. The CTC had wholeheartedly supported this demarche and had issued press statements to this effect.

Those who followed the do-nothing policy justified their inaction by reiterating that Batista was, after all, a good friend of the United States. If he was forced out, they added, the Communist would surely fill the vacuum. Of course, there do arise instances in which a real political vacuum exists, and I am not in favor of ever letting the Communists fill it. But that was not the case of Cuba at that time. On April 4, 1956, I wrote an analysis of the Cuban political situation—prepared for the leadership of the AFL-CIO—in which I dispelled the fear of a Communist take-over:

The present political opposition to Batista is aiming to regain power, the latest by 1958 when a new president is elected, or possibly before as the result of general elections which may be called in order to appease the opposition and divert it from resorting to violence. This opposition is led by people like Carlos Prío, Raul Chibas, Grau San Martín, Pelayo Cuervo, Dr. Lincoln Rodó, Ing. Carlos Hevía, who are strongly opposed to Communism—perhaps even more so than Batista himself. The leader of the underground forces—Aureliano Sánchez Arango—is known for his anti-Communism. Since the opposition to Mujal leadership in the labor movement is made up largely of those who are against Batista—plus a small number of independents, such as Cofiño of the Electrical Workers Union—there is no reason for the time being to worry about the possibility that a change of government may enhance the prestige and strength of the Communists.

As to the relationship of the Opposition leaders with the United States, in spite of occasional angry outbursts designed to show displeasure over isolated actions on the part of our government vis-à-vis Batista, most of them can be counted on to follow the present policy of friendship and cooperation with our country.

The IX National Convention of the Cuban CTC, held in Havana April 27–May 1, 1956, was the last one under the Mujal leadership. It was marked by unprecedented unity and by the firm collective will of the Cuban labor leadership to rely on ballots and not on bullets to bring about the return of democracy and constitutional government to their tormented country.

Among those who attended the meeting was Pedro B. Pérez Salinas, President of the Venezuelan Confederation of Labor (CTV) in Exile and member of the ORIT Executive Committee. He subsequently submitted to ORIT a report which, because of the unquestionable moral authority of its author, who had spend many years in the prisons of the Venezuelan dictator, amounted to a clean bill of health for the CTC.

Salinas emphasized the meaning of the Unity Pact, signed by the principal leaders of the organization representing various ideological currents and overwhelmingly endorsed by the Convention. In this pact they reaffirmed "our democratic conviction in the face of all forms of totalitarianism" and appealed "to all citizens, without distinction, to concentrate on the welfare of the Republic and to find practical solutions which may be not the triumph of any single individual but the success of Cuba, so that our country may be spared days of bitterness and sorrow." The Venezuelan noted that at the urging of General Secretary Eusebio Mujal, the Convention adopted resolutions condemning the dictatorships of Leonidas Rafael Trujillo in the Dominican Republic and Marcos

Pérez Jiménez in Venezuela, and recommended the application of an international trade union boycott against those countries. Pérez Salinas concluded: "The Convention proceedings were conducted on a high plane and were marked by repeated manifestations of prudence and labor-political maturity. In the present Cuban situation the powerful labor confederation is acting as a force for moderation, leading the workers toward a just solution to the problems of the working class and of the people in general, for the good of Cuba as a whole."

The Convention was also attended by fraternal delegates from the AFL-CIO, the ORIT, the ICFTU, and the Mexican CTM. This display of international support was motivated by the CTC's impressive international trade union record. The CTC, in addition to its active participation in the founding of the CIT and later of the ICFTU and ORIT, was the prime mover in the formation in 1956 of the International Federation of Plantation Workers. It financed this International Trade Secretariat with an original contribution of $65,000 and with additional annual contributions until the end of 1958, when the Castroites took over. It joined with the ORIT and the AFL in special organization campaigns in Chile and Guatemala, to which it contributed with separate financial grants and the assignment of some of its best organizers. On its own it also furnished assistance to the labor movements in Brazil, Argentina, Honduras, Peru, Ecuador, and the Caribbean area—particularly in Jamaica and British Guiana. The CTC provided shelter in Cuba to trade union refugees from Venezuela, Peru, and the Dominican Republic, and took the lead at the ICFTU Convention in Stockholm in 1953 in demanding the application of trade union boycotts against the dictatorial regimes of Perón, Trujillo, Pérez Jiménez, Somoza, and Rojas Pinilla.

The first public confrontation of the CTC with Fidel Castro's 26th of July Movement took place in late August 1956. From his Mexican exile, where he was putting the finishing touches on his expedition that was to land three months later in Cuba, Castro issued a manifesto also signed by a representative of the University Students Federation (FEU). It called for the overthrow of the Batista regime through a popular uprising accompanied by a general strike. The CTC's reply of September 3, 1956, declared that a rebellion would not be in the interests of the Republic and reaffirmed its preference for a civic and electoral approach. "We do not need an insurrection," said the CTC reply, "to achieve the triumph of our program," adding that "the Cuban proletariat would never emerge victorious since violence would only encourage a dictatorial regime with the consequent loss of all the liberties and guarantees that the Cuban working class now enjoys." The statement continued with a strong re-affirmation of the political independence of the CTC and with a denial that there existed conditions in Cuba that would justify calling a general strike. "Trade union rights have not been infringed, nor have the unions been closed down. Workers' organizations, from the base to the very top, that is to say from the locals to the Executive Committee, share equally the most absolute guarantees. At no time has the activity of any party— opposition or government—caused injury of any sort to the trade union leaders or their affiliates."

The position of the CTC was correct. Every competent observer of the Cuban trade union scene at that time could reach no other conclusion than that it would have been suicide for the CTC to go along with a call for a general strike, especially one issued from abroad by an opposition political leader and by a student organization whose leadership had gone underground.

The landing of Fidel Castro and his "Gramma" companions on the east coast of Cuba in December 1956 did not have immediate repercussions inside the CTC or for that matter in Cuba itself. For a few months it was even thought in some circles that Castro himself might have lost his life in the brief battle that took place after the landing. Even those who believed that the survivors had holed up in the Sierra Maestra mountains thought that it would be only a matter of time before the whole adventure would be liquidated. But things developed quite differently. The dozen or so survivors were soon joined by others and in no time they became self-supporting, thanks to the help they managed to receive regularly from their friends inside Cuba and from abroad. Meanwhile, the underground was getting bolder, and in March 1957 almost succeeded in killing Batista in the Presidential Palace. Cuba had entered the stage of a full-scale civil war with no quarter given or asked. Although some elements in the CTC, especially at the lower level, began to take an active part in the underground opposition to Batista, the top CTC leadership maintained a position of alleged independence of both Batista and the Castro movement.

Newspaper correspondents from the United States and Europe flocked to Cuba to report on developments. A few succeeded in crossing the military cordon encircling the Sierra Maestra. Most notable for their impact and repercussions were the stories filed from Cuba by Herbert L. Matthews of *The New York Times*. In addition to visiting Castro in his hideout, Matthews roamed the country far and wide and interviewed people from every rank, including trade unionists at all levels. Matthews's implications were that the top leadership of the CTC, although professing neutrality, were in fact helping Batista, and that second-level leaders, on the other hand, and many of the rank and file, especially in the cities, were siding with the rebels.

In order to disprove Matthews's assertions that pro-Castro sentiments were rising inside Cuban organized labor, the CTC sent a long statement to *The New York Times* of which only excerpts were published. However, the full text, occupying an entire page, appeared in the July 4, 1957, issue of *The Havana Post.* It was signed by the leaders of twenty-nine affiliated federations, representing 90 percent of the membership in contrast to four dissenting federations representing 10 percent of the membership—the Electrical Workers of Ángel Cofiño, the Telephone Workers of Vicente Rubiera, the Bank Workers and the Traveling Salesmen. In that statement, carefully drafted by Mujal himself, it was conceded that even within some of the twenty-nine listed federations there were leaders who were not in full accord with the Mujal line, among them some in sugar, building construction, railroads, slaughterhouses, maritime, metal workers, tobacco, and textiles. Nevertheless, the bulk of the CTC leadership and membership was still following the official CTC policy. This was convincingly demonstrated in August 1957, when Castro's call for a general strike failed to gain any appreciable support among the workers.

As the civil war became bloodier, the position of Mujal's CTC was increasingly condemned abroad, especially among pro-Castro democratic elements. Even the late Jules Dubois, well-known Latin American correspondent of *The Chicago Tribune* and chairman of the Freedom of Press Committee of the Inter-American Press Association, who later was an outspoken foe of the Castro dictatorship, wrote me protesting ORIT's inaction against Mujal. The Latin American edition of *Time* described Mujal as Batista's strong supporter. *Life* followed suit in its Spanish-language edition. Every important newspaper in Latin America was echoing the same charge.

Inside ORIT also the policy of the Cuban CTC began to be questioned by some. When Luis Alberto Monge resumed his post at ORIT headquarters in Mexico City in the summer of 1956 after his extended leave of absence, he became friendly with Fidel Castro, who at that time was making preparations from Mexico for his landing in Cuba. They used to spend hours together, mostly in Monge's house, often until early in the morning. They discussed, debated, and planned not only the over-throw of Batista but the future role of a democratic Cuba within the framework of Latin America. No one has ever doubted Monge's honest conviction that the Castro revolution was going to be a truly democratic one. After Castro's landing and his subsequent encampment in the Sierra Maestra mountains of Oriente province, Monge became passionately attached to the 26th of July movement. At that time, to him and many other top spokesmen of the democratic left throughout Latin America, Castro's objective was the reestablishment of a democratic regime, free of corruption and abuses. Monge, accordingly, was among those in ORIT who felt the CTC should end its neutrality and give its support to Castro.[1]

But what could ORIT do? The CTC was a founder of ORIT. One CTC officer was President of ORIT, another was Vice-President of ICFTU. There had been continuity in the leadership of the Cuban organization, legally elected and reelected at succeeding conventions observed by fraternal delegations from abroad who had never made any objection or criticism. Monge fully understood this and in his campaign against Batista he was careful not to involve the CTC directly. But the CTC leadership, particularly Mujal, resented Monge's attitude as a re-buke to them and accused him of interference in violation of his duties as ORIT's General Secretary. The controversy spread to all the ORIT affiliates, with the ICFTU supporting Mujal and most of the Latin American affiliates siding with Monge.

An aura of romanticism had begun to surround Fidel Castro. The Latin imagination was fired at the thought of this young man ostensibly carrying the torch of democracy and freedom, building up strength until he could come down from the mountains, launch a frontal attack and destroy the Batista tyranny with all of its opportunism and corruption. To understand what was going on in the hearts of many Cubans, one must remember that Castro's publicized objectives were then to carry out a democratic, libertarian revolution, purely political in character and scope, involving the elimination of Batista, the reestablishment of the 1940 Constitution, free elections, etc. There was no hint of any social or economic revolution that would lead to Communism or even Socialism. Castro then was simply for freedom. It was, therefore, inevitable that a pro-Castro sentiment should develop, as it did, among some members of the CTC, especially those of middle-class background belonging to the white-collar unions. For instance, my dear friend Calixto Sánchez, leader of the Airline Pilots' Union, joined the underground. When the police began to suspect him, Mujal arranged for him to leave the country. But months later Calixto returned, leading a commando raid in which he lost his life. The CTC voted a pension for his widow, herself an active pro-Castro underground militant.

The CTC leadership was suspicious of the middle-class background of the Castro underground, which was made up largely of intellectuals, students, and politicians. Mujal also detected the Communist infiltration; he had been a Communist in his youth and knew who was still in the Party and who had clearly broken with it. Furthermore, he realized that Batista's military establishment was still strong enough to suppress any general strike and smash the labor movement. For different reasons, both Batista and Mujal had a vital interest in preventing a general strike. The rank and file were enjoying a relatively high purchasing power (the peso was equal to the dollar) and the trade union bureaucracy welcomed Batista's decree making compulsory the union dues checkoff in industry, commerce, retail enterprises, banking, agriculture, transport, etc.

The daily preservation of the bread-and-butter function of the labor movement became the paramount preoccupation of the CTC leadership. Everything they did until the ouster of Batista has to be viewed and judged in terms of this main objective—the salvation of the CTC.

In August 1957 Mujal sent an invitation on behalf of the CTC Executive Committee to the ICFTU General Secretary to visit Cuba and observe on the spot the conditions under which the trade union movement functioned. Oldenbroek could not accept the invitation for various reasons but he asked Charles Millard, ICFTU Director of Organization, to go in his place.

Millard, accompanied by Hermes Horne and Otero Borlaff, a Cuban on the ICFTU payroll as organizer in South America, arrived in Havana on October 10. At the conclusion of their brief visit the group drafted a report which was approved by the ICFTU Executive Board in Brussels, November 4–8, 1957. In its report the mission stated it had found that the CTC was doing a large-scale and effective job within the strictly trade union field, in the performance of which it enjoyed the necessary freedom of association and assembly. On the other hand, the ICFTU group said, the CTC in no way acted in the political field, and this exposed it to attacks from those who thought that a force with such considerable potentialities should not confine itself to purely economic functions, but should play a preponderant role in national life. The ICFTU questioned "whether any manifestation by the CTC, in fields other than those in which it is at present active, would not lead to serious dissensions in its own ranks and to subsequent interference on the part of the government, which is undoubtedly a military dictatorship."

The mission could find no signs of disintegration within the CTC, nor of policy disagreements among its top leaders. It pointed out that many of the CTC leaders were not partisans of the dictatorship, but were acting in line with the general policy of safeguarding the unity and independence of action of the CTC vis-à-vis the government and the political parties.

The mission reported that there "was not a single proof of lack of trade union freedom—on the contrary, everywhere one had the feeling that there were no obstacles to trade union action in the field of demands and social matters. At present, there is no surveillance, either by the police or of any other kind, at trade union meetings, which are held freely and without hindrance, both as regards their procedure and as regards freedom of speech." It concluded that while there undoubtedly existed a very strong opposition to Batista, and that consequently no conclusion reached could be final or permanent, it did not, however, find evidence of violations of the trade union rights universally respected in the free world, nor any sign that would allow any doubt about the CTC's acting within the basic principles of the ICFTU.

The report on Cuba was rejected by ORIT's General Secretary Monge but endorsed by ORIT's President Tellechea—both attending the November 4–8 ICFTU Executive Board meeting. The split between the two top officers of ORIT was accompanied by a personal clash that further aggravated CTC-ORIT relations. Fortunately, it was quickly patched up, but for a few weeks it was a very unpleasant matter for the protagonists. Tellechea, as an officer of the Cuban CTC, was, of course, under the discipline of the pro-Mujal Executive Board.

The ICFTU verdict was naturally hailed by Mujal as a vindication of his stand and it emboldened him to intensify his attacks on Monge. Headlines in the Cuban press—"Mujal will request Monge's expulsion from ORIT," or "Mujal accuses Monge of being responsible for the Communist penetration in ORIT"—were obviously so distorted that Monge refused to believe Mujal responsible for them and therefore refrained from answering.

During the last three months of 1957 I was in constant communication with both men. ORIT was faced with a split and everything possible had to be done to prevent it. This thankless and difficult task at times irritated Mujal to the extent that he accused me of being Monge's "accomplice," and ultimately moved Monge to reproach me, almost in tears, for what he considered my recantation of his position. But ORIT was saved and that was the important achievement of those months of patient, behind-the-scenes work.

The next ORIT Convention had been tentatively set for March 1958. It became obvious that it would be impossible to wait that long to settle the rift over the Cuban situation. Therefore, an agreement was reached to hold a special Executive Board meeting January 13–15 in Washington, D.C.

Mujal knew very well that he could never hope to obtain enough votes to "repudiate" or even "criticize" Monge, and wisely decided not to attend the Washington meeting. The Cubans were nevertheless well represented by a large contingent that included ORIT President Tellechea and the ICFTU Vice-President Francisco Aguirre.

The North American members of the Board reached an agreement prior to the meeting on how they would seek to preserve ORIT's unity. They made it the main objective of the meeting. But the hot Cuban issue precluded unanimity. On every resolution that failed to condemn outright the Cuban CTC there was a minority that voted for condemnation.

The resolution on Cuba was preceded by a long, heated, and at times quite unruly debate. While the discussion was in progress, Mujal sent a cable from Havana in which he stated that as a result of a "meeting with the Cuban government, representatives of CTC have obtained restoration of constitutional guarantees, elimination of press censorship, and reestablishment of freedom of political activities for four government and four opposition parties in preparation for June 1 general elections." The cable added: "Cuban labor shows by this attitude that it is, as in the past, for true democracy and against terror and violence."

The resolution on Cuba was finally adopted by a vote of 8 in favor, 3 against, 1 abstaining and 2 absent. The text read in part as follows:

At the present time Cuba, according to the ICFTU, "is undoubtedly a military dictatorship." It is passing through difficult and turbulent times, which demand great diplomacy, strength, and tact on the part of the CTC.

We are deeply concerned with the preservation of life, liberty, and democracy within Cuba, and with the preservation of the strong and effective labor movement in Cuba. We express herewith our sympathetic understanding of the problems of our affiliate, the CTC, and we reaffirm our historic policy of opposition to all forms of oppression and dictatorship.

We insist that the forthcoming elections in Cuba must be freely conducted along democratic lines, thus providing for the complete restoration of the democratic freedom so greatly desired by the Cuban people.

In the fall of 1957, the AFL-CIO Free Trade Union Committee took the initiative of suggesting to Mujal the preparation of a memorandum entitled "For Democracy and Peace for the Cuban People." The AFL-CIO document, which I sent to Mujal on October 22, recommended that the CTC memorandum be issued in the form of an appeal to the government and the people of Cuba "to stop all civil war and to activate all political parties for strengthening the democratic institutions of the country." It then proposed four or five concrete steps "to be taken immediately by the Batista government in the direction of strengthening the democratic processes and institutions of the country, thus providing the people with assurances of free elections being held at a specifically fixed date." The Free Trade Union Committee also reminded the CTC that regardless of its real strength in Cuba and the soundness of its position, its image abroad was being tarnished. We believed that our suggestion, if carried through, could have the beneficial effect of reestablishing in the minds of the people of Cuba, the Latin American labor movements, and the rest of the international labor movement that the CTC was an independent, bona-fide free trade union organization.

During the months of November and December 1957 the CTC held a number of conversations with Batista and the leaders of the so-called *fuerzas vivas* (civic and business organizations) in an effort to find a formula that would lead to the termination of the civil war. The CTC finally presented to Batista a written document urging the immediate reestablishment of constitutional guarantees and the calling of general elections. On Christmas Eve, following a meeting with labor, civic, and business groups, Batista announced the end of the State of Emergency and assured the country that he would soon call general elections with full guarantees to all political parties. These were the measures that Mujal announced in a cable to the ORIT Executive Board meeting in Washington, D.C., in January 1958 as having been obtained mainly through the intercession of the CTC.

Soon after that, the CTC came out publicly in favor of the suggestion advanced by the Catholic Church hierarchy for the formation of a civilian provisional government. According to Mujal, Batista would have accepted such a solution. However, Fidel Castro, from his Sierra Maestra headquarters, announced that anyone who took part in such a government would be shot as a traitor to the Revolution. The Church proposition collapsed for want of takers. Mujal has also stated that, toward the end of 1957, he and a CTC delegation visited the State Department in Washington looking for support for the idea of a provisional government. The goal of this provisional government would be to reestablish peace in Cuba and "to prevent the victory of Castro," because the "CTC knew that Castro was a Communist." Mujal claims that the State Department there did not accept this evaluation of Castro.

Years later I asked Mujal to give me "the facts" that led him and his colleagues to believe so firmly, as early as 1957, that Castro was a Communist. Following is the substance of his lengthy reply.

The Communist International had signed a pact with Fidel and Raul Castro and other Cuban youth as early as 1949, perhaps without knowledge of the Communist Party of Cuba. Fabio Grobart, the Third International representative in Cuba since 1933, was known to favor the so-called double approach in that country. On the one hand, the local Communist Party follows a line of opposition to the Government in power, while at the same time the Third International through its covert operations from Prague, Paris, or Mexico establishes direct secret contacts —unknown to the official local Communist Party—with individuals or groups and even with elements inside the government itself.

In line with this double tactic, also employed in Argentina and Venezuela, the Communists succeeded in infiltrating the strongly anti-Communist Ortodoxo Party of Raul R. Chibas. Fidel Castro wanted to be a candidate for Congress under the emblem of that Party, but as long as Raul Chibas was alive (he later committed suicide) he was blocked. Chibas used to refer openly to Fidel Castro as "a gangster and a pro-Communist." After Chibas's death, the Ortodoxos split in several factions and that made the infiltration tactic of the Communists much easier.

Cuban Communist leaders headed by Blas Roca—at that time the most powerful Communist tactician in Latin America—were in Santiago de Cuba when Castro assaulted the Moncada barracks on July 26, 1953. Ten of them were arrested, including Blas Roca, Lazaro Peña, Joaquín Ordoqui, Calcines, and Bravo. They were set free after claiming that they were touring Oriente province to celebrate the birthday of Blas Roca, who was a native of Manzanillo. Communists do not engage in such celebrations unless they are meant to cover up for some important political activity.

According to Mujal, it is an historic fact that a few days after arriving in Mexico, following their release from jail on Batista's orders, Fidel and Raul Castro held their famous meeting with "Che" Guevara, Lombardo Toledano, Dionisio Encina (General Secretary of the Mexican Communist Party) and two military attachés from the Soviet Embassy in

Mexico. There they planned the subsequent landing in Cuba. Years later it was revealed that while holed up in the Sierra Maestra, the Castro group received food, clothing, medical supplies, arms, and other equipment from Russian submarines that surfaced at a hidden cove near the Pilón beach below the Sierra Maestra.

While all this was taking place, the Communist Party of Cuba was courting the government of Batista. In its clandestine press deploring Castro's violence, Mario Díaz (Blas Roca pseudonym) was describing Fidel as a petit-bourgeois anarchist type. That was the smokescreen to cover up the double game.

In June and July 1958, according to revelations published in the Magazine *Bohemia* by Amadeo López Castro, a close friend of Batista, a committee of the Communist Party of Cuba, including Blas Roca and Joaquín Ordoqui, had several contacts with Batista. They proposed, as a *quid pro quo* for turning against Castro, four points: legalization of the Communist Party; the control of the CTC; the return to Communist ownership of the daily *Hoy* and the Radio Station 1010-4; and a substantial amount of money to launch the proposed campaign against Castro. According to López Castro, the Communist proposals were rejected by Batista. It is not clear from the account whether the Communists met directly with Batista or used López Castro as intermediary.

In August 1958, after Batista rejected the Communist offer, the official Pact of Alliance between Castro and the Communist Party of Cuba was signed on the island of Jamaica. After the publication of the Pact, the clandestine organs of the Communist Party of Cuba stopped criticizing Castro and his guerrilla tactics and switched to open praise and support. Obviously, the Third International, sensing that Batista was finished, no longer felt any need to employ the double game.

A new U.S. Ambassador, Earl E. T. Smith, had meanwhile arrived in Cuba. I had been among those who were requested by the State Department to give him the benefit of my organization's views on Castro and Cuba. It was customary for the State Department to ask me and other AFL-CIO officials to brief newly appointed ambassadors to Latin America, especially the noncareer men, in order to give them our views on problems affecting labor relations. I distinctly recall, for example, that Ambassador Ellsworth Bunker was given such a briefing before he went to Argentina. He also met in New York with members of the Inter-American Association for Democracy and Freedom, including Argentine refugees. He was thus able to learn firsthand why organized labor and liberal progressive groups were maintaining their opposition to the Perón regime.

Ambassador Smith's debut in Cuba was on the side of human rights. He deplored police brutality in dispersing a demonstration in the city of Santiago composed largely of middle-class women. This auspicious beginning for Smith led to the hope that the United States would embark on a firmer policy toward Batista, trying to persuade him to transfer power to a provisional government that would restore peace and freedom and would, at the same time, keep Castro out. But it did not come out that way, as Ambassador Smith himself subsequently detailed in his book *The Fourth Floor* and at hearings before congressional committees. I want to say, at this point, that Embassy Counselor Daniel Bradford told me, as early as March 1958, that "we, the United States, could never get along with Castro. He is our sworn enemy."

Eusebio Mujal had spent his youth in Oriente province. There he began his political career as a member of the Auténtico Party. It was natural, therefore, that among the early Castro supporters in the Sierra Maestra there were a number of friends or political supporters of Mujal: Celia Sánchez, now Fidel Castro's closest personal aide; Crescencio Pérez, another of Fidel's collaborators; Huberto Matos, famous military commander now languishing in jail; Luis Orlando Rodríguez, and others.

As Fidel Castro enlarged the area under his control it came to include a number of sugar plantations. Representatives of the National Federation of Sugar Workers, the strongest CTC affiliate, had to cross the "front line" daily in order to take care of their normal trade union duties. They were in possession of safe-conducts issued by Castro and the Batista army. These labor representatives, who were neither Batistianos nor Fidelistas, were often allowed to visit Castro's encampments and talk freely with his followers. Once one of these labor leaders went to Havana to confer with Mujal and remarked: "I have noticed a change in the type of books Fidel keeps in his La Plata military camp. Before, they were books by Martí; now he displays only books by Marx, Lenin, and similar Communist authors. Is it that he has now publicly become a Communist?"

It was through such trade union delegates that Celia Sánchez, Huberto Matos, Crescencio Pérez, Luis Orlando Rodríguez and others were sending messages to Mujal trying to convince him to smarten up and come out in support of Castro before the imminent downfall of Batista. Mujal, and other CTC leaders now in exile, have assured me that they took up on different occasions this indirect offer from what they then considered the anti-Communist faction inside the Castro movement; but they unanimously rejected the proposal because of their firm conviction that "Fidel, Raul, and Guevara were in absolute control of the movement" and that they were confirmed Communists.

According to Mujal, he once was approached by Herbert L. Matthews, who in a strictly confidential manner relayed to him a message from the Havana branch of the 26th of July Movement. The substance of the message was that the 26th of July people were aware of Castro's inclination toward Communism, but that if the CTC would join with them, there would then be a solid anti-Communist block inside the movement "and Fidel Castro would not even reach to be chief of the Havana police."

Mujal asserts that he rejected this oblique overture as he had rejected those coming directly from the Sierra Maestra. Furthermore, he adds, in those days the Castro staff had denounced to the Batista police in Santiago de Cuba the noted anti-Communist rebel Frank Pais. When the police went to arrest him, Pais resisted and was killed. That was a typical Communist tactic to get rid of an anti-Communist. It could have been Mujal's fate if he had decided in favor of the proposal. "There is nothing to do but fight to defeat Castro," was Mujal's final answer.

A few weeks later, Mujal received another message, this time from friends in Oriente province who had joined the Castro movement. They told him that a general strike was in preparation and the collaboration of the CTC was being asked in earnest and full sincerity. The emissaries spoke in the name of Hubert Matos, Luis Orlando Rodríguez, and others. Mujal tried to convince them that Castro had firm commitments with international Communism, showed them proofs, and some were even given to them for delivery to Matos, Rodríguez, and the others to convince them to break with Castro while there was still time. "If Castro wins, it means that Communism will win," Mujal told them, "and every one of our friends, Matos, Rodríguez, and all, will be liquidated. Tell them to quit Castro and to look for another solution that would prevent Cuba from falling under the Communist yoke."

But the emissaries were insistent. Finally, to give them some leeway "and to put Castro in a position to demonstrate himself that his commitment to the Communists was irrevocable," Mujal has claimed that he made the following proposal: "Let Castro break publicly with the Communists; let Castro declare that his Revolution is democratic, free, sovereign, without any commitment with Moscow or the Communist Party of

Cuba. If Castro makes such a solemn declaration, then the CTC will reappraise its position."

The go-betweens left for Oriente and some time later returned to Havana to talk again with Mujal. They had spoken to Matos, Rodríguez, and the others, and they in turn had laid before Castro the conditions submitted by the CTC. Castro answered with a clear No. He would make no declaration as suggested by Mujal. If the CTC wanted to join the strike, well and good; but without any previous *guarantees* on the part of Castro and *without any repudiation of the Communists.*

What happened is now history. Mujal was right. The Communists gained complete control, and all his Castroite friends, with the sole exception of Celia Sánchez, are now in jail, in exile, or in the cemetery.

In March 1958 I went to Cuba as a member of a large U.S. labor delegation [2] invited to the inauguration of the Havana Hilton, built by the Cuban Hotel and Restaurant Workers' Union retirement fund. The AFL-CIO Executive Council, in accepting the invitation, made it clear that our presence in Cuba was solely to honor the achievements of a trade union organization, and that we would not appear at the dedication ceremonies if President Batista shared the speaker's stand. As it turned out, Batista stayed away. His wife substituted for him.

The CTC hosted a luncheon in honor of the visiting labor delegations (there were also representatives from Europe and Mexico). Mujal reaffirmed the CTC policy of seeking a peaceful solution of the increasing difficulties facing the country. After the lunch I met privately with him. For the first time I got the distinct impression that he had begun to doubt Batista's ability to weather the storm. He uttered the expression *desengancharnos* (to disengage ourselves) from a situation that was fraught with mounting danger. The CTC, according to him, was still a force to be reckoned with by both Castro and Batista, but the latter's demands on the CTC were getting stronger and more insistent. Before parting from what was to be our last meeting in Cuba, I remarked:

"Eusebio, my wife Miriam went today to your house to visit your wife Nereida. She came back frightened at the sight of so many armed policemen surrounding your home. Is your life in danger? Is the Castro underground after you?"

"*¿Quién sabe?*" he replied. "Maybe I am closely watched not to protect my life, but to protect someone else from me. . . ." [3]

Shortly afterwards, during Easter Week, the Castro forces attempted to pull a general strike, which again failed mainly because the CTC opposed it. Castro sympathizers in the United States "demanded" from the AFL-CIO a public condemnation of the CTC opposition to the general strike. On April 11, 1958, President George Meany issued a statement in which he stated the AFL-CIO position. He said:

> The CTC of Cuba is an affiliate in good standing of the International Confederation of Free Trade Unions (ICFTU) and its Inter-American organization (ORIT). Like all other affiliates, it enjoys a high degree of autonomy, especially in matters affecting national affairs and its internal policy. Therefore, the AFL-CIO is reluctant to pass individual judgment and to assume that it knows better than the CTC how to protect the interests of the Cuban workers and their organizations. This judgment will eventually be passed by the Cuban workers themselves and, if necessary, by the ICFTU and ORIT.

President Meany's statement ended by expressing "sympathetic understanding" of the problems of our affiliate, the CTC of Cuba; reaffirmed the AFL-CIO historic policy of "opposition to all forms of oppression and dictatorship"; and insisted that "elections in Cuba must be freely conducted along democratic lines, thus providing for the complete restoration of the democratic freedoms so greatly desired by the Cuban people."

In the summer of 1958, in the midst of the last stage of the Cuban civil war, the CTC was confronted with an international labor complication that led to the CTC's finest gesture of trade union solidarity. It all started with the refusal of the Canadian Steamship Company in July 1957 to grant wage increases to its maritime workers and the ensuing strike called by the Seafarers' International Union of the United States and Canada.

The strike began on July 4, 1957, and was carried on with grim determination in the face of every effort by the company to break it. In March 1958 the eight ships in question were finally sold to British interests, to be manned by Jamaican crews. However, when apprised that the sale of the ships was a strikebreaking tactic on the part of the Canadian government, the Jamaicans went home, the deal was called off, and the strike continued.

In August 1958, the fleet was again sold—to the Bank of Foreign Commerce of Cuba, this time to be manned by Cuban seamen, members of the CTC. In this instance, unaware that the ships were struck and had been so for more than a year for legitimate economic reasons, the CTC-affiliated Maritime Labor Federation of Cuba proceeded in good faith to sign a contract with the ships' operators, the Browning Company of Cuba. There followed a long series of communications with the CTC, including appeals from the AFL-CIO and the Seafarers' Union, urging that the Cubans recognize the strike effort of their fellow maritime workers and refuse to work the ships.

A unity agreement was reached between the Cubans and the Seafarers' International Union at a meeting at the AFL-CIO Maritime Trades Department in Washington on September 19, 1958, which I chaired. Following the agreement, the crews were ordered back to Cuba. This decision was taken in spite of strong opposition by the Batista government, which had invested a considerable amount of money in the purchase of the ships. The deal had been advertised as the first concrete move toward the creation of a big Cuban merchant fleet with opportunities for employment and additional revenues. This attitude on the part of the CTC was favorably received in U.S. and Canadian labor circles and received praise from the ICFTU and the International Transport Workers' Federation.

Contrast the attitude taken by Mujal and the CTC with the position adopted a few months later by the leadership of the Revolutionary CTC after Castro seized power. The National Maritime Federation of Cuba, in a telegram signed by its provisional President and by the new CTC General Secretary, David Salvador, urged the AFL-CIO to facilitate the transfer to Cuban registry of the eight strike-bound Canadian boats still being held up in Halifax, Canada. I tried to explain to them with telegrams and telephone conversations the true facts surrounding the case. They were even invited to come to Washington for a conference with AFL-CIO Maritime Trades Department, but we waited in vain for their arrival. Instead, David Salvador declared in a press interview that the Revolutionary CTC would not resume relations with the AFL-CIO until we gave back to them the ships that he said "rightly belonged to Cuba." To the best of my knowledge, Castro is still waiting. The ships wound up in the shipyard for scrap.

The IV Congress of ORIT, held in Bogotá December 9–12, 1958, was marked by tension over the Cuban issue. Only the frequent and firm "out-of-order" rulings of the ICFTU General Secretary, who acted as parliamentarian, kept the controversial aspects of the situation in Cuba out of the plenary sessions. The Batista regime was crumbling. The Cuban delegation representing the CTC felt that the end was approaching and managed to walk a narrow tightrope—voting for the resolution that reaffirmed "continued opposition to the dictatorial regime in Cuba" and obtaining in return the exclusion from the sessions of a group of self-appointed labor representatives of Castro who came to Bogotá without bona-fide trade union credentials.

Early New Year's morning, 1959, I was awakened by a telephone call from Havana. It was Nereida Mujal informing me, in a voice that betrayed intense fear, that Batista had fled the country and that her husband had taken refuge at the Argentine Embassy. That very same day Mujal's house was sacked by an infuriated mob egged on by a group of known Communists, who were systematically attacking the homes of all prominent anti-Communists, especially those with whom the Party, as in the case of Mujal, had old scores to settle. Most of the other prerevolution CTC leaders, including ORIT President Tellechea, also went into hiding or, in many cases, were jailed by the revolutionary forces. Mujal's wife and children were able to go to a safe refuge, where they were protected by one of her nephews, Regino Botti, a prominent member of Castro's entourage and later a member of his Cabinet.

A couple of weeks later Mujal was allowed to leave Cuba for Argentina on a safe-conduct pass issued to those who had been granted political asylum in a foreign embassy. As soon as he reached Buenos Aires he immediately obtained air passage to the United States, being in possession of a valid visa issued to him by the U.S. Embassy in Havana late in December. Had Mujal flown directly to the United States, without interruption, his arrival would probably have gone unnoticed, since his documents were in perfect order. However, his departure from Argentina had come to the attention of our State Department, which in no time tracked Mujal aboard a PanAm plane flying to New Orleans.

Ben Stephansky, then labor adviser of State Department's Inter-American Bureau, phoned me that Mujal's visa had been revoked because his admission into the United States, at that time, "would have been contrary to our national interests." I must say that I agreed with him.

Mujal elected to go to Belgium, where he was aided by the leadership of the ICFTU in obtaining temporary residence for himself, and later for his family. As the situation was rapidly changing in Cuba, a number of people, including Stephansky and myself, felt that the reasons that were invoked earlier to keep Mujal from entering the United States were no longer valid. He was therefore advised to apply for an immigrant's visa, but before it could be granted it was necessary to obtain the concurrence of the new U.S. Ambassador to Cuba, Philip Bonsal, who took the matter under long, careful consideration.

At the end of 1959 Ambassador Bonsal came to Washington for consultation, and among the many actions he took was to review Mujal's visa status. I was invited to confer with Bonsal, and I endorsed his willingness to lift the ban on the visa. A few weeks later, Mujal and his family arrived in the United States.

Notes

1. After Castro had established his regime, Monge visited Cuba, became disillusioned with what he saw, and joined the ranks of those opposing the Cuban dictator.

2. The delegation included AFL-CIO Vice-Presidents Emil Rieve, Paul Phillips, and A. Philip Randolph; President William Lee of the Chicago Federation of Labor, Vice-President David Ramos of the National Maritime Union, William H. Bowe, field representative of the Brotherhood of Sleeping Car Porters, and Arnold Beichman, ICFTU press representative in New York.

3. In the summer of 1958, Mujal's family—wife, children and maid—came to the United States for the ostensible purpose of putting the children in a summer camp so as to become more conversant in the English language. However, Mujal's family absence was interpreted by some of his enemies in the Batista entourage as an indication that Mujal himself was planning to flee Cuba. An "alarm" was sounded in some newspapers, and the Mujal family returned in a hurry to Cuba.

XIV

Labor Under Castro

THE DOWNFALL of the Batista dictatorship was welcomed by the international free trade union movement. The ICFTU immediately issued a press release expressing deep satisfaction with the end of the dictatorship, but also concern "that the CTC might be the object of measures of force." It appealed to all democratic trade unionists to help maintain the unity of the Cuban labor movement and "the right to elect their own leaders by democratic procedure." Alfonso Sánchez Madariaga, General Secretary of ORIT, issued a statement on January 3, 1959, in which he said: "We hope that an authentically democratic regime, facilitating the free and full exercise of trade union rights, will be established in Cuba as soon as possible."

Sánchez Madariaga dispatched Luis Alberto Monge to Cuba on a special fact-finding and good-will mission. Monge arrived in Havana with a member of the ORIT staff, remained five days, and summed up the Castro coup in a report issued from Mexico City on January 17: "The victory of the revolution has been absolute, unique in the political history of Latin America." The ORIT representatives found that the trade union scene was being dominated by the hysterical issue of "Mujalismo." All former collaborators of the ex-CTC chief, even those who became openly anti-Batista, were being deposed from responsible trade union positions or were prevented from resuming them. Monge found very few revolutionary labor leaders willing to consider a rapport with ORIT, unless they could impose their own conditions.

Luis Alberto saw many of the top leaders of the revolution but not his old buddy and former house guest, Fidel Castro. It must have been quite a shock for gentle Luis Alberto to be treated in such a shabby manner. The editor of *Revolución*, Castro's mouthpiece, asked Monge to answer a written questionnaire on Eusebio Mujal and other deposed leaders "knowing of the controversy you had with the ex-Secretary of the CTC," the questionnaire slyly suggested. Their object, Monge stated, "seemed to be to provoke an attack by us on the former CTC leadership." The questionnaire was not answered because, as Monge put it in his report to ORIT, "we felt that it would have been ignoble on our part." Although attacked and even insulted by Mujal in the course of their differences, Monge now refused to throw stones against the fallen leader who had saved his life only by taking refuge in the Argentine embassy. On the other hand, Mujal was being disowned by those who had been his faithful sycophants when he was CTC chief.

The AFL-CIO's first pronouncement on the revolution came in the form of a telegram sent by George Meany in answer to a message of greetings from David Salvador, the new head of the CTC. Dated January 20, 1959, the telegram stated: "Our organization having consistently fought dictatorial regimes rejoices over prospects of consolidation of democracy in Cuba through strengthening of independent democratic labor movement free of any totalitarian control or influence. We stand ready to cooperate in any way possible. Best wishes."

The ORIT Executive Committee met in an emergency session over the Cuban situation in Mexico City, February 3–4, under the chairmanship of Claude Jodoin, President of the Canadian Labor Congress. At the conclusion of the meeting, the Committee issued a statement in which it expressed "fervent hope that Cuban society will now organize itself along genuinely democratic lines"; urged that "trade union members should have the exclusive right to elect their own leaders on every level and in full freedom"; and expected that "with the least possible delay such elections will be organized at the local and national level, to be followed by a Congress to elect the leadership of the national trade union center." The free labor movement was thus proffering its hand of friendship to the Cuban revolutionary labor movement, but it did so on the clearly stated premise that democratic procedures would be applied.

All trade unions, at every level, came under the control of the United National Labor Front (FONU), in which all revolutionary groups were represented. Later, the FONU was reorganized with elements pertaining exclusively to the 26th of July Movement, most of whom were not Communists but were, as events eventually proved, either under Communist influence or afraid to tangle publicly with them.

Some democratic leaders who had fought from exile against the Batista dictatorship were also completely eliminated from trade union leadership. Ángel Cofiño, former leader of the electrical workers, on returning to Havana was not only prevented from resuming his trade union activities, but was suspended from his functions as trade union leader for ten years. Vicente Rubiera, who had also distinguished himself by his anti-Batista attitude, was eliminated from the leadership of his trade union (telephone and telegraph workers), and replaced by "26th of July" elements. The same applied to Pascasio Lineras, of the Textile Federation, and Marcos Hirigoyen, leader of the Bus Drivers' Union.

Early in February, George Meany received from the new CTC leadership an invitation to visit Cuba. He asked me to go to Cuba in his place, as a sort of advance scout to see what was going on and how things were shaping up, reserving the option to go himself later if the circumstances were favorable. Our position was that as long as there was an opportunity to help steer the Cuban revolution along democratic lines we should not refuse to do our part in the field of our jurisdiction—organized labor.

I arrived in Havana in the early afternoon of February 6. A delegation from the CTC greeted me at the airport and took me to the Havana Hilton. The CTC had paid for the round trip air ticket and I was regarded as their guest. But at the hotel I waited and waited in vain for an interview with the CTC leaders. Instead, I received a total snub, aggravated by an insulting story that appeared the following day on the front page of *Revolución*. The paper was then edited by Carlos Franqui, a prominent pro-Communist journalist. In that article I was linked to Mujal and was called "a millionaire" and "a gangster." The non-Communist leaders of the CTC got cold feet and refused to see me— although I was supposed to be their guest. So I took the first available plane home.

Although the rebuff suffered by his personal representative was deeply resented by George Meany, he did not allow this incident to influence the AFL-CIO position on Cuba. This was reiterated in a statement, issued on February 19, reaffirming the AFL-CIO desire to cooperate with the CTC of Cuba in their task to strengthen democracy and freedom in their country. It also urged the U.S. government not to grant asylum to former Dictator Batista and to cooperate with the Cuban government in making possible the return of huge sums of stolen money sent to the United States for safekeeping by the former dictator and his cronies.

Forces inside both ORIT and the AFL-CIO who wanted to weaken the influence in inter-American relations of the former AFL staff in favor of militant leftist elements were urging the new CTC leadership not to quit ORIT. As a matter of fact, they envisaged the possibility of reorganizing the whole ORIT structure around the revolutionary Cuban movement. It must be emphasized, however, that these people were convinced that the Cuban revolution would remain democratic. When Communist control of the CTC became apparent, they turned outspoken anti-Castristoites like the rest of us. But at that time they went to extreme lengths to appease the revolutionaries.

The non-Communist CTC leaders indicated their desire to remain members of the ORIT, but they presented a set of conditions that ORIT could not, and did not, accept. For example, at the meeting of the ORIT Administrative Committee which took place April 9–10 in Mexico City, Reinol González, chief of the Foreign Relations Department of the CTC and a member of the Young Catholic wing of the 26th of July Movement, demanded my removal from any position of responsibility in the ORIT; the purge from ORIT membership of all those organizations that did not meet the "democratic standard" set by the Cubans; the elimination of pro-Mujal leaders from top posts in the international free labor movement; and the convocation of a special Convention of ORIT in Havana.

The request that I be excluded from any important ORIT position was based on my past friendship and collaboration with Mujal. At the Mexico City meeting I told Reinol González that it did not make sense to single me out unless this treatment was extended to all ORIT/ICFTU officers and affiliated organizations who without exception maintained friendly relationship with Mujal. It simply indicated their unwillingness to oppose the Communists on this issue; for the last fifteen years they had made me their number-one target in Latin America.

On the other hand, González pledged certain actions and reforms inside the CTC that could not be ignored by the ORIT leadership. As explained in a letter from Madariaga to George Meany, dated April 23, 1959, Reinol González pledged:

(a) That elections in all trade union sectors to be held to replace the provisional officers now in charge, will be conducted in full respect of the will of the majority of the assemblies and in the presence of ICFTU-ORIT observers;

(b) That, upon his return to Havana, he would at once undertake negotiations for the release, as soon as possible, of ORIT President Ignacio González Tellechea;

(c) That the former CTC leaders shall have all the guarantees enjoyed by other Cuban citizens; and with regard to their trade union position, this shall be subject to the decisions made by the assemblies of their respective unions or federations. This would apply to all except those indicted for common crimes.

News coming from Cuba indicated that things were taking a turn for the worse, not for the better. José Figueres, who had been among the most outspoken and effective opponents of the Batista regime, had been booed while on a visit to Havana. Members of the Cuban Cabinet with a record of outspoken anti-Communism were being forced out. However, in the labor movement the Communists as such were unable to develop any real rank-and-file support.

The continuation of contacts and talks between ORIT and the non-Communist leaders of the CTC was, therefore, to be accepted as good policy, provided that we kept constantly on the alert and never underestimated either the resources or the tactical ability of the Communists.

Early in April 1959 I drafted and distributed an analysis of the Cuban situation that contained the following conclusions:

(1) The policy of physical liquidation of the militant opponents of the Castro revolution, as manifested in the still-mounting number of executions, reminds me of the methods adopted by the Communists in every one of the so-called popular democracies in Eastern Europe and in Asia. It seems to me that some strong force, behind the scene, is urging Castro to go on deeper and deeper with his "war crime trials" so as to make impossible the regrouping of any anti-Castro military force in the present as well as in the future. The field will thus be clear for the military monopoly on the part of the 26th of July army which is under the control of elements who are very friendly with—if not completely under the discipline of—the Communist Party.

(2) The policy pursued in the labor movement shows a disturbing parallel with the Army policy described above. Every one of the anti-Batista trade union leaders, unless an active member of the 26th of July movement, has been purged. I am not referring to those who are in jail as a result of charges of misappropriation of funds. I have in mind labor leaders of democratic extraction such as Rubiera, Hirigoyen, Linares, Balbuena, and many others who have been eliminated by the simple trick of declaring them ineligible for a period of many years—in some instances up to ten years. The so-called trials of these leaders were conducted at membership meetings which had been packed with outsiders and which were conducted without regard to normal procedure and in an obvious atmosphere of coercion and intimidation.

It is significant that while this show of intolerance did not appear in the first few weeks after the triumph of the revolution, when it could have been to a certain extent understood and excused, it was applied with an ever mounting severity in a second period precisely when it became obvious that these democratic elements were about to regain the upper hand in most of the unions.

(3) It was announced, in the latter part of January, that the top provisional leadership of the Cuban Confederation of Labor (CTC) had been purged of Communist elements. The fact remains that 29 of the 33 federations comprising the CTC are still in the hands of provisional committees packed with Communists. Furthermore, it is now obvious that of the 26th of July people who compose the present provisional committee of the CTC, most of them are under Communist influence, if not secret members of the Communist party.

The statements attributed in press reports to David Salvador indicate a marked increase of Communist influence over his thinking in matters affecting international relations. As late as last week Salvador stated that unity with the Communists would continue, that no relations were contemplated with the AFL-CIO or the ORIT-ICFTU, and that Cuban labor has adopted a neutral position in the struggle between East and West.

(4) Members of the present leadership of the CTC are touring Latin America in an effort to rally support for a projected Latin American Confederation of Labor. This confederation aims at separating Latin American labor from the AFL-CIO and the Canadians. This is precisely the current Communist line. In order to detach Latin American unions from ORIT, the Communists advocate a "neutral position," implying that they are willing to stay separate from the WFTU also. Although I am confident that this project will not succeed, it is nevertheless an indication of the growing Communist influence in the present Cuban trade union leadership.

(5) The non-Communist elements in the CTC leadership appear unable to carry out their program of rapprochement with the United States labor movement and the ORIT itself. These non-Communist leaders include Reinol González, Conrado Bécquer, and others who either are members of the Young Catholic Labor Movement (JOC) or who were in the past affiliated with the Auténtico Party of former President Prío. These people apparently are afraid to tangle openly with the Communists, and they wind up by doing exactly what the Communists want.

I concluded my analysis by supporting, at least for the time being, the continuation of our efforts to establish normal relations with the non-Communist elements inside the CTC. However, I did strongly advocate that free labor organizations "cease the issuance of public statements which might indicate complete, unreserved approval of what is going on now in that unfortunate country."

The attitude of the AFL-CIO toward Cuba and its willingness to co-operate with the Cuban labor movement "in whatever effort might be required to maintain it truly democratic, free and independent, and solely responsible to the will of its members," was reiterated in a resolution adopted by the AFL-CIO Convention in San Francisco, September 17–23, 1959. The resolution also demanded "prompt and fair trials for the many former leaders of the Cuban Confederation of Labor and affiliated unions who have been detained in jail for over six months without the benefit of reasonable bail and—in some instances—without specific charges."

The Convention of the Cuban Confederation of Labor was scheduled for the month of November. Elections in the various federations indicated overwhelming support for the anti-Communist forces inside the 26th of July movement. The leaders of the democratic bloc were not so sure, however, that in case of a showdown and pressure from above, meaning Castro, the bulk of the delegates would maintain an anti-Communist line. Therefore, they intensified efforts to get support from abroad. Above all, they wanted to resume friendly relations with the AFL-CIO. Thus, Reinol González went to Mexico City early in August to secure ORIT support for "a mission of the CTC headed by Salvador to visit Washington, or a mission of the AFL-CIO headed by George Meany to visit Cuba." After an exchange of correspondence, it was finally agreed that the top leaders of the two organizations would meet October 14, at the Commodore Hotel in New York City.

The group from the AFL-CIO included President George Meany, Secretary-Treasurer William F. Schnitzler, Chairman O. A. Knight of the Inter-American Affairs Committee, Vice-President William C. Doherty, and Inter-American Representative Serafino Romualdi. However, the CTC group did not include its leader David Salvador, nor its Secretary of International Relations Reinol González. The delegation consisted of José Pellón, CTC Treasurer and General Secretary of the Brewery Workers; Luis Moreno, General Secretary of the Tobacco Workers' Union, and Pedro Forcade, General Secretary of the Chemical Workers' Federation. Meany and Schnitzler, after greeting the visitors, left the meeting. The second level of the team from Cuba had obviously displeased them. I found out, later, that the Communists within the CTC top leadership vetoed, at the last moment, Salvador and González's trip to New York.

The three-hour meeting was presided over by ORIT General Secretary Alfonso Sánchez Madariaga, assisted by Daniel Benedict, ORIT director of Education. It was made clear from the beginning that the Cubans had no power to commit the CTC to anything. Their mission was to listen and to request instructions. In the course of the discussion, however, a number of points were cleared up. Most important, the visitors conceded that the treatment to which I had been subjected in Cuba as the representative of President Meany was "perhaps not the proper one." Pellón stated: "You can be sure this will not happen again."

Both Knight and Doherty insisted, however, that until the charges against Romualdi were withdrawn, there could be no resumption of relations. The following exchange took place:

DOHERTY: "It appears to me, however, that in the absence of Salvador and González we cannot obtain the withdrawal of the charges that have caused our rift."

PELLÓN: "You are right. I cannot withdraw the charges. However, I will make a recommendation to the Executive Board of the CTC upon my return to Cuba that they examine the convenience of doing so."

ROMUALDI: "I want to be realistic. I see that you people hesitate to promise a public statement of apology or even a public announcement of withdrawal of charges because of attacks on the part of Communists, especially now on the eve of your convention. I want to make it easy for you. If I can help you in your fight against the Communists by dropping the request for a public statement, I will be glad to do so. This will be my contribution to your desire to remain members of our family. I suggest, therefore, that you send a letter signed by the responsible officers of the CTC to President George Meany expressing your regret for the incident connected with my visit to Cuba last February, and informing him that you will not press the request for my removal as substitute member of the ORIT Executive Board."

Pellón replied that the delegation would convey the suggestion to the CTC Executive Board. He then expressed the hope that the AFL-CIO would be represented at the CTC Convention in November. After a brief discussion on this point, it was agreed that an invitation would have to be confirmed in writing to President George Meany before any action could be taken.

Finally, Pellón declared: "Before ending this meeting, I wish to emphasize that a violent campaign is waged against us from various camps. We need the help of the AFL-CIO to defend the Cuban revolution from the attacks of the reactionaries. I assure you that there is no Communist control in Cuba and that there will be no Communist control in the future. We are only anxious to be masters of our own destiny, and to achieve that, we expect and need your cooperation."

No letter of apology or simple explanation was ever sent to President

Meany, nor did he receive the invitation to attend the Convention. Nevertheless, President Meany sent to the Convention, which opened in Havana on Novmber 16, a telegram of greetings and encouragement which reiterated the AFL-CIO position toward the Cuban revolution and the CTC:

Your tenth convention meets at a crucial moment in the life of your nation. Your deliberations and decisions will affect profoundly the efforts of your country to secure a stable and prosperous democracy cooperating on the basis of equality with our country and the other freedom-loving peoples.

We of American labor have hailed the overthrow of the Batista dictatorship as a severe blow to despotism throughout the new and old world. This defeat for dictatorship can become full and final victory for democracy only if the working people build powerful free trade unions cooperating with free world labor and capable of defending workers' interests and promoting human dignity, liberty and social progress.

The AFL-CIO extends best wishes to your convention in the sincere hope that its decisions will serve democracy and the well-being of the workers and the entire Cuban nation and strengthen Cuban labor's bonds with the free trade unions organized in the ORIT and under the banner of the ICFTU.

We pledge to you our firmest solidarity and support toward the achievement of these great goals.

The Convention started with the 26th of July Movement having the overwhelming majority of the delegates. The Communists had less than 15 percent. Another group composed of leaders belonging to the Auténtico (Democratic) Party commanded the allegiance of a sizable number of delegates, all experienced trade union leaders. But its effectiveness collapsed when the 26th of July leadership imposed from above a policy of collaboration with the Communists.

Three known anti-Communists, who had been serving on the CTC executive board since January 1959, were dropped from the final slate drawn up by David Salvador. They were: Conrado Bécquer, Reinol González, and J. A. Plana. All three had been prominent in the underground struggle against the Batista dictatorship.

In order to save the appearances of "unity," those who managed the convention from behind the scenes had to leave on the thirteen-man executive board at least one known anti-Communist. They chose Octavio Loit, the most outspoken anti-Communist at the convention, secretary of organization and the No. 2 man in the former directorate; but they relegated him to the window-dressing position of "delegate to official and employer organizations," where he would wield no significant power or influence.

The convention resolved to withdraw its affiliation with the Inter-American Regional Organization of Workers (ORIT) and announced its intention of setting up a new Latin American confederation of trade unions with headquarters in Havana under the direction of the CTC. This was precisely what the Communists had been advocating.

The convention demonstrated that democratic anti-Communist sentiment was very strong among the rank-and-file Cuban trade unionists. However, in an atmosphere of psychological violence such as that which prevailed throughout the convention—where every word of disagreement with the policy laid down by Fidel Castro and his henchmen was termed "treason" to the fatherland and the revolution—these democratic forces had no chance to prevail. It must be said, however, that the battle was long and bitter. Time and time again the Convention refused to accept alliance with the Communists. Fidel Castro intervened in person, speaking twice. He threatened the delegates, accusing them of being "Mujalistas." Then his brother Raul came with armed militiamen who took positions in the balcony. Finally, at 4 o'clock in the morning, with the delegates completely exhausted, a suggestion was made by a Castro spokesman:

"Let us stop arguing and fighting. Let's give David Salvador full power to make up a slate of new officers."

The Convention agreed. And that is how the anti-Communists went out and the Communists came in.

The period following the delivery of the CTC to Communist control saw the steady deterioration of the economic and personal benefits for which the Cuban workers had struggled. It also saw their gradual enslavement by the Communist regime, with the loss of all individual dignity and freedom. Moreover, a series of actions over the next three years completely eroded both the structure and the function of the CTC, destroying the tradition of democratic trade unionism so long associated with that organization.

On January 7, 1960, the new Executive Board of the CTC, in the presence of the President of the Republic and the Minister of Labor, adopted a resolution proposed by the pro-Communist Director of Organization Jesús Soto, empowering the CTC leadership to purge any official or member of any affiliated organization whom they considered counterrevolutionary. As subsequent events indicated, this power was used to eliminate all the leaders who at the November 1959 Convention had shown anti-Communist feelings.

Among those purged was Luis Moreno, general secretary of the Tobacco Workers' Federation. He was one of the leaders who gained power with the Castro revolution and was one of the three CTC delegates who had conferred in New York with AFL-CIO representatives in October 1959.

In January 1960 other trade union leaders were purged for criticizing the deduction of 4 percent from the workers' earnings to finance the industrialization plan of the Castro regime. The same month the CTC announced that all union members, particularly "hundreds of thousands of farm workers," would receive compulsory military training.

On March 12, 1960, the Cuban Cabinet issued an order prohibiting workers to change jobs without government authorization and also forbidding them to obtain employment without the approval of the Government Labor Exchange, controlled by the Department of Labor.

The same month David Salvador, CTC General Secretary, announced that the 4 percent contribution to aid the industrialization plan of the Castro government would continue for the next five years. He said that this 4 percent contribution would amount to about $40 million a year. Premier Castro announced that the government would give each worker a savings certificate for the amount contributed to the industrialization plan. He said the certificate would begin to draw interest after five years. Needless to say, these certificates were never issued.

On March 21, 1960, the Castro regime promulgated Law 762, which made obligatory the following contributions, amounting to 17¼ percent of the gross income: 3 percent income tax: 4 percent for the government industrialization program; 4 percent for the purchase of arms "to defend the country from Yankee aggression"; 5 percent for social security; 1 percent for compulsory union dues, and ¼ percent for maternity tax.

At the end of 1959 Fidel Castro had eliminated the so-called sugar "differential," which was that portion of sugar workers' wages that was paid them above a fixed minimum on a sliding scale geared to the average price of raw sugar in the U.S. and world markets. It amounted to a loss of about $25 million for that year, and by April 1960 serious discontent was apparent among sugar workers. Besides their 1959 loss, they were being forced to hand over the Castro government 17 percent and even more of their earnings as different types of "voluntary contributions."

In the same month of April, the Castro government issued a decree extending the 3 percent income tax to all earnings, from one peso up. Before, those earning 100 pesos or less were exempt from paying the income tax.

Article II of Resolution No. 16782, issued by the Minister of Labor on August 20, 1960, authorized the management of the nationalized enterprises—already comprising 90 percent of the Cuban economy—to establish new wage scales, regardless of the schedules established by existing collective labor agreements.

Labor Law 647, promulgated early in 1960, had a paragraph which reads as follows: "The Minister of Labor, at his pleasure, is empowered to take over the control of any local union or national federation and is also authorized to demote and remove from office union leaders and appoint substitutes in their places."

The leaders of the Construction Workers' Federation, Luis Penelas and José Fernández, incurred the displeasure of the Minister of Labor for their opposition to the Communist policy of the CTC Secretary of Organization, Jesús Soto. At a special meeting of the Havana Construction Workers' Union called by the Minister of Labor, Penelas and Fernández were removed from office. The meeting was packed with Communist outsiders and was marked by fist fights. The Acting Secretary General of the CTC, Noelio Morel (David Salvador was at that time traveling abroad) declared the meeting illegal and refused to recognize the new leadership elected as a result of violence. He was supported by the majority of the CTC Executive Committee. Thereupon, the Minister of Labor, supported by the Soto group, ordered the armed occupation of the CTC in order to enforce his will.

In May 1960, the internationally known Cuban labor leader Francisco Aguirre was arrested in a suburb of Havana while trying to defect by plane. The pilot hired for the rescue mission was ambushed and killed by the Cuban police before he could take off. For his attempted escape, Aguirre was sentenced to nine years in jail. On August 15, 1967, Francisco Aguirre, his weight down to a bare ninety pounds, died of untreated illness and malnutrition in La Cabaña jail.

Ignacio González Tellechea, former President of ORIT, who after having been in jail several times had obtained asylum in the Mexican embassy, was allowed to go to Mexico on a safe-conduct permit.

Jesús Artigas Carbonell, former Secretary-Treasurer of the CTC, was also allowed to leave Cuba on safe-conduct after he had obtained asylum in the embassy of Costa Rica. Artigas was jailed for fifteen months under charges of mishandling of the CTC funds. He was, however, acquitted by a Castro tribunal on the strength of evidence attesting to his honesty.

David Salvador, who from the beginning of 1959 was Castro's right arm in the labor movement, fell into disgrace when, following the CTC Convention in November 1959, he tried to resist the pressure of the Communist clique. On the eve of May Day, 1960, Salvador left the position of General Secretary following a clash in the Presidential Palace with Labor Minister Martínez Sánchez. He went into hiding, but was captured while trying to leave Cuba and was imprisoned in La Cabaña Fortress, accused of betraying the revolution. Later the same fate struck Reinol González. At this writing both are still languishing in Castro's jails.

The collective contract, fundamental to democratic trade unionism, clearly has no meaning under the Communists. A labor law decreed by the Castro regime in March 1960 took the right to negotiate with employers away from the union and gave it to the Ministry of Labor, which acquired full authority to settle any labor controversy. In the next two years a series of laws further extended the jurisdiction of the Ministry of Labor into all aspects of labor-management relations, including work conditions, organization, and wages. The destruction of the collective contract concept was completed in April 1962, when the Ministry was authorized to suspend any collective agreement which, in its judgment, infringed upon any socioeconomic legal ordinances. In September 1962 Minister of Labor Martínez Sánchez stated publicly that the system of collective contracts had been transformed into a means of guaranteeing the fulfillment of production plans.

On December 9, 1960, two thousand employees of the nationalized Cuban Electric Company, led by their president, Amaury Fraginals, marched on the Presidential Palace, shouting "Cuba yes, Russia no!" Another thousand of the union's members remained at their headquarters to guard it against threatened Communist seizure.

Amaury Fraginals, who was an original leader of Castro's 26th of July movement and a militant opponent of Batista, had to seek asylum a few days later in a foreign embassy. Most of the workers who took part in the demonstration were arrested or found refuge in the embassies of Argentina, Brazil, Peru, and El Salvador.

In this atmosphere, the members of the Electrical Workers' Union were called to a second meeting at the headquarters of the CTC for the purpose of removing the "counterrevolutionary" leaders. Heavily armed militia units surrounded the CTC headquarters, while rifle-carrying guards diverted traffic for two blocks to prevent disorder. The meeting was attended by a small number of electrical workers, less than one thousand out of a six-thousand membership. It was highly infiltrated, as the press reported, by students, armed militiamen and over two thousand Communist members of other unions. Also present were the Minister of

Labor and Fidel Castro himself, who, in the course of a very angry speech, threatened the *"paredón"* (execution squad) for any union leader who committed counterrevolutionary acts.

A few dissenters who came there to voice their solidarity with Fraginals were immediately arrested. Afterwards, the meeting "unanimously" expelled Fraginals and all the members of the Executive Committee who supported him, and voted into office a new directorate composed exclusively of Communists.

Two months later three members of the Electrical Workers' Union, William Lex Sante, Julio Casielles Amigo, and Orlirio Méndez Pérez were executed in Havana. They had cooperated with Amaury Fraginals in opposing the surrender of the union to Communist officers.

As a result of this wave of terror against the dissenting leaders of the Electrical Workers' Union, Ángel Cofiño, former leader of the union and for many years a member of the governing body of the ILO, also took asylum in the Argentine embassy. The same precaution was taken by Vicente Rubiera, former leader of the Telephone Workers' Federation and Executive Board member of the Postal, Telegraph, and Telephone International. Both eventually came to the United States.

On March 2, 1961, United Press International reported from Havana that Fidel Castro's new wage scale for sugar cane cutters had brought down their earnings to about 50 percent of the previous year's level. The Cuban government, by using the traditional formula by which sugar wages are keyed to the price at which Cuban sugar is sold abroad, fixed them on the basis of 4 cents per pound for the first 4 million tons and 2.5 cents for the balance of the harvest.

In 1960, the sugar cane cutter, by producing 300 arrobas daily (about 760 pounds) was making about $128.70 per month on the basis of 22 working days. In 1961, with Castro's new wage scale, for the same weight of cut cane a sugar worker was getting only $69.96, which was further reduced to $56.76 when the new wage scale for the balance of the harvest went into effect.

The situation was further aggravated by the fact that before the "revolution," Cuban workers were contributing only a total of $7\frac{1}{4}$ percent of their wages to the union and to social security, while now the fixed contribution and the "voluntary" contributions for various "revolutionary" causes increased the total by another 10 percent.

Under the authority granted to the Ministry of Labor in June 1960 to "intervene" worker organizations, the Communists seized control of the unions and restructured the entire labor movement. They forced non-

Communist leaders who had been freely elected to relinquish their positions. The unity of the Cuban labor movement was completely destroyed by the Law of Syndical Organization of August 3, 1961. Under its provisions, all workers at the same establishment—mine, factory, shop, etc.—must belong to the same organizational unit, regardless of occupation. In addition, the "unions" of two or more places of work were prohibited from uniting.

At the CTC Convention held in Havana during the month of November 1961, Communist leader Lázaro Peña again became General Secretary of the organization. This was the same Peña who in 1947 was displaced by the successful anti-Communist revolt led by Mujal and Aguirre. In that Convention, which was held in the usual doctrinaire Communist fashion, where only unanimity is tolerated, the number of federations was reduced from 33 to 25. Members of the 8 federations abolished were simply redistributed arbitrarily by the Communists. The 1961 Convention made history with its sweeping decisions. Under the guise of "voluntary action" it wiped out all the benefits that the Cuban workers had gained during a generation of struggle.

The Convention resolved to give up the following benefits that Cuban workers were enjoying, either as a result of their pre-Castro collective agreements, or of specific provisions in the Constitution or the Labor Code:

(a) *30 days of paid vacation* (Constitution of 1940) .
(b) *9 days' paid sick leave* (Social Legislation) .
(c) *26 days of extra pay, at the rate of 4 hours per week.* The workers gained this when the working week was reduced to 44 hours but pay remained at the rate of 48 hours.
(d) *Annual Christmas bonus.* The majority of Cuban industrial and commercial establishments for many years had given a Christmas bonus of 15 days' pay. In some cases, it was as high as 30, 60, and even 90 days.
(e) *Extended summer weekend.* During the four months of torrid Cuban summer, one and one-half days were added to the weekend. This amounted to 26 days of paid vacation resulting from the shorter work week.
(f) *4 days of national holidays* (Constitution of 1940)
(g) *4 days of other optional holidays which were, as a rule, uniformly granted.*

The delegates to the CTC Convention also "voluntarily" gave up overtime, which was computed in the following way: When the working day was 12 hours, which frequently happened under the pressure of harvesting, the workers before Castro would get 8 hours of straight time plus 4 hours at time-and-a-half—a total of 14 hours at regular rate pay. Now the workers were to receive 8 hours straight time; for the 4 hours overtime, 2 hours would be considered as a "gift" to the national economy and the other 2 hours would be paid at the regular rate. This makes a total of 10 hours of regular rate pay while before it amounted to 14 hours.

In addition to all these "voluntary" sacrifices, the Convention agreed to continue the taxes that had been imposed since the Castro regime, for various "revolutionary" causes, such as the industrialization program, the agrarian reform, the purchase of arms, etc.

At the beginning of 1962 it was estimated that the average wage of the Cuban worker was only about 40 percent of what it was before the Castro regime. His purchasing power and standard of living, as compared with the rest of Latin America, had almost reached the bottom of the scale. Statistics show that while before Castro the average wage scale of Cuban workers was 13 percent higher than the average in the neighboring countries of the Caribbean, at the beginning of 1966 it had plummeted to 15 percent lower.

On June 29, 1962, the then Minister of Industry "Che" Guevara declared that basic to the development of Communism was the increase of production and productivity, regardless of the sacrifices involved. Several months later, Blas Roca, Secretary General of the Cuban Communist Party, was quoted as saying that previously the basic function of the trade union had been the struggle for the immediate demands of the workers; now its *raison d'être* had become the struggle for increased production and productivity. Thus it fell to the working class to bear the yoke of the Communist objective in Cuba. The regime has attempted to increase production at the lowest possible cost by measures designed to drive the workers at maximum speed without rest. Norms established by the Ministry of Labor determine both the quality and quantity of work to be produced by an individual in one day. If the predetermined quota is not completed, the worker is not paid at all. The union at the shop has the responsibility to see that quotas are filled—and also to denounce management in the event a boss eases up on a worker who is unable to fulfill his assignment.

Under the Third Organic Law, of May 1962, all workers are required to carry work cards. Fourteen pages in length, these "cards" provide complete and detailed information on each worker, including his attitude toward his work, the regime, and the Communist indoctrination to which he is subjected. In order to work each person must have a card. Thus the worker who is known to be against the regime is denied a card and thereby effectively blacklisted. Moreover, workers do not have the right to change jobs at will.

The "voluntary" forgoing of overtime at the 1961 Convention soon was extended to mean not only extra hours each day without pay but also work on Sunday without pay. In effect, all workers were required to "volunteer" this extra day—not just at peak periods but on a permanent basis. It is commonplace for a worker to go for years without so much as a Sunday off. Furthermore, a strict system of fines for tardy arrival at work and absenteeism was instituted in August 1962.

By 1962 the steady decrease in food production was matched by increasing dissatisfaction among the *campesinos*. In the beginning, Castro had won the peasants' support with promises of land of their own. Of course, this promise was never kept. All the farm and pasture land in Cuba now belongs to INRA (National Agrarian Reform Institute). State latifundium has replaced private ownership. The INRA now controls millions of acres of the arable lands existing in Cuba. Small farmers (where permitted to exist) must sell their produce in the state-controlled markets and at prices set by INRA, which also dictates what may and may not be planted. A peasant needs a permit from INRA to slaughter his own animals. There is no incentive to produce in excess of the farmer's needs, as the Communist government appropriates the surplus.

The regime has continued to encourage "voluntary" salary reductions. For example, on February 2, 1963, Radio La Habana announced that construction workers in Las Villas, Matanzas, and Pinar del Rio provinces had accepted "voluntarily" a 5 percent reduction in wages, and expressed the hope that construction workers in all the other provinces would follow suit. On the other hand, according to a 1962 resolution, a worker who is promoted can receive only 25 percent of the difference between his previous salary and the new one. The same law also declared that there would be no salary increases without the prior knowledge and approval of the Ministry of Labor.

Finally, to drown thoroughly and completely any small spark of opposition from the workers, the Castro regime has prohibited the use of labor's most effective weapon—the strike. In January 1961 strike action was declared "counterrevolutionary" and any workers involved were subject to dismissal and criminal charges. It is significant that in Law No. 1022 of May 1962, which deals with the administration of labor justice, the word "strike" is never once used.

Press liberty died completely in Cuba when the last of the opposition dailies, *Prensa Libre,* was shut down. The means used were the same as previously utilized against *Diario de la Marina, Avance, Excelsior, El Mundo,* and *El Pais,* the same that the dictator Perón used when he strangled *La Prensa* and the rest of the free press in Argentina, the same as all dictatorial and totalitarian states use to silence any free expression from the opposition.

The direct instrument used to silence the free press was the printing trade unions. Having been previously captured by Communist leaders, these unions became "goon squads" for the suppression of even a whisper of opposition to the ruling clique. Their members were instructed to refuse to print anything that was critical of the government or the Communist Party.

Sensing that the May 17, 1960, edition of *Prensa Libre* would be the last one, assistant directors Humberto Medrano and Ulisses Carbó drew up a manifesto to the Cuban people. But it was never read, because the Castro printers refused to set the type and the paper itself was suppressed. But I obtained a copy of it and published it in full in the June 1960 issue of the *Inter-American Labor Bulletin.* The following are excerpts from its two concluding paragraphs:

Today we appear before you, Cuba, to denounce an outrage, a crime against our liberty and our democracy. Dark forces that obey foreign orders have incited and conspired with elements who wish to capture the channels of expression in order to destroy us. . . . These elements attack us for having our own viewpoint . . . for combating the sinister international conspiracy, directed by Russia, against our land and against the solidarity of the American continent.

If this crime is committed against us, against you, beloved Cuba, then let it be known in every Cuban family, in every Cuban heart, that we have sacrificed our all, our property, our personal security and that of our children, because we did not submit to those who wish to replace our symbol of the lone star with a red rag.

In order to justify their revolutionary measures as a "painful but necessary operation," the Communist propaganda apparatus has peddled the legend that Cuba was "backward, economically underdeveloped, and a victim of American imperialistic exploitation." It is amazing how the Communists and their fellow travelers managed to feed their unsupported statements to a variety of naive individuals, including some of the highest officials of the United States government. The statistics present, however, a different story.

According to the U.N. Economic Commission for Latin America

(ECLA) and the National Bank of Cuba, the per capita income in Cuba was $339 in 1956, and $360 in 1957—far above the average for all Latin America. Cuba ranked third in number of newspapers and magazines, paper consumption, telephones, automobiles, and per capita consumption of electric power. According to a U.S. government report published in 1962, the Cubans were "among the better-fed people of the world. . . . Farm output in the late 1950's was twice the 1935–1939 level with an average annual growth of 3.5 percent over the two decades, significantly higher than average population growth of about 2.3 percent for the same period."

Statistics published in 1960 by the International Labor Organization in Geneva show that the average wage of Cuban agricultural workers in 1958 for an eight-hour day was $3, excluding fringe benefits. When adjusted to compensate for differences in purchasing power this compares with $4.06 for the United States, $2.70 for Belgium, $2.86 for Denmark, $1.74 for France, and $2.73 for West Germany. These same ILO figures show that Cuban workers received 66.6 percent of the gross national income compared to 73.4 percent for Great Britain, 70.1 percent for the United States, and 68.5 percent for Canada. As compared to Latin American countries, Cuba was ahead of Argentina (57.2 percent) and Brazil (47.9 percent).

Concerning foreign investments in Cuba, particularly from the United States, the following figures, from the same official sources, are also revealing. For instance, U.S. investments in Cuba, which were $1,066,-555,000 in 1930, had decreased to $800 million in 1958, while they increased in practically every other Latin American country. In 1939, the sugar plantations and refineries owned by North Americans accounted for 55 percent of Cuban sugar production; in 1958 the percentage had gone down to 36.65 percent. Put in a different way, Cuban-owned sugar mills increased from 56 plants in 1939 to 121 in 1958, more than 100 percent, while American-owned sugar mills decreased 46 percent during the same period.

Even more revealing are the Organization of American States figures which show that in 1958 Cuban industries represented a capital investment of $3,268,887,823, of which only 20 percent was foreign capital. The percentage of sugar in these overall figures of Cuban national products was only 29 percent, which should dispose once and forever of the legend that Cuba was a "monoculture" country, largely dependent on foreign capital, especially from the United States.

The Cuba that Fidel Castro seized in January 1959 was *not,* on the strength of the above-mentioned official figures, the underdeveloped, hungry, and illiterate country that Communist propaganda is trying to make the world believe it was in order to justify Fidel Castro's "liberating" revolution.

XV

The Bay of Pigs and After

ON MAY 4, 1960, the AFL-CIO Council adopted a statement on Cuba, drafted by its Inter-American Affairs Committee, in which it reviewed the successive steps which had led to the establishment of a totalitarian police state in that country, including complete suppression of trade union independence, political opposition, freedom of the press, and all other democratic rights. The statement also analyzed the "intensive violent campaign of hatred and scorn against the United States," and the repudiation by the Castro regime of the treaties which are the foundation of the inter-American system. The Council concluded that "the disruptive activities of the Cuban government can no longer be lightly dismissed as outbursts of inexperienced, youthful leaders swept by the upsurge of economic nationalism. They have all the earmarks of a well-planned strategy designed to make Cuba an advanced outpost of the Soviet Union's drive to infiltrate the New World."

The AFL-CIO warning, belittled by perennial appeasers of Communism, was taken seriously in many other quarters, including the highest echelons of our government. Senator William Benton, in his book *The Voice of Latin America,* written when the Communist character of the Cuban regime was already flagrant, paid tribute to the AFL-CIO for its "perceptive statement."

The Cuban situation was analyzed again by the AFL-CIO Council at its February 28, 1961, meeting, in a resolution which stated that "It is now clear to all that Cuba has become a Soviet satellite and that it is being openly and boastfully used as a staging area for the internal subversion and ultimate control of all Latin America." The AFL-CIO, therefore, urged the Organization of American States (OAS) to undertake collective action against the Castro regime, including the breaking of diplomatic relations and the imposition of economic sanctions.[1]

As indicated in previous chapters, I never expressed, publicly or in private, anything resembling approval of Castro and his movement. In addition to the revelation of my brief visit to Havana on February 7, 1959, I was apprised of the true strength and strategy of the Communists inside the Castro movement by Aureliano Sánchez Arango, leader of the underground "Triple A" movement which had fought heroically against Batista. I saw Aureliano in Caracas later in February of the same year at the time of Rómulo Betancourt's inauguration as President of Venezuela. To my conjecture that Castro might eventually be able to eliminate the Communists from his movement and government, Aureliano answered:

"Don't cultivate illusions, Serafino. *Ya lo tienen todo en sus manos*— They already have everything in their hands!"

My friend Robert C. Hill, then our Ambassador to Mexico, with whom I had frequently shared doubts on Castro's democratic professions, had written to me on January 21, 1959: "Do watch the Cuban situation carefully and give the Department the benefit of your views because I see grave trouble in the area for a considerable time ahead."

In fact, I had been doing that for quite some time, both as AFL-CIO Inter-American Representative and because of my mounting personal concern over the trend of events in Cuba. I had a feeling, however, that I was viewed as too much of an alarmist. Only Ben Stephansky, then Labor Adviser in the American Republics Area (he was later appointed Ambassador), seemed to heed my deep concern.

On or about April 5 or 6, 1961, I spent two hours with Ambassador Hill at the American embassy, briefing him on the Communist infiltration in the Castro government. When I offered to brief the U.S. Ambassadors in the Caribbean area in their conference in San Salvador, April 9–11, Ambassador Hill sent a confidential cable to Assistant Secretary Roy R. Rubottom in which he told him about our conference and the important information that I had and my availability to brief the Ambassadors. Hill told me later that when he arrived in San Salvador on April 8 he spoke to Rubottom again and he said he did not think it was appropriate for me to brief the Ambassadors, that he doubted very much that I had any additional information not already available to the Department of State.

By the time of the May 1960 statement of the AFL-CIO, charging Cuba with being "an advanced outpost of the Soviet Union," I had become a strong advocate of the hard line against Castro. Among those who showed a sympathetic response to my arguments and warning was Vice-President Nixon, who, on April 9, 1960, wrote to me:

> I read with great interest the report which you attached to your letter to General Cushman of my staff.
> This is one of the most realistic appraisals of the Castro regime that I have seen. I must say that I share many of your views on the situation. You can be sure that the facts you have presented will be most helpful to me as I participate in discussions within the Administration on our policy toward Castro and Cuba.

When news of a possible landing in Cuba of anti-Castro patriots began to circulate in the fall of 1960, I made it a practice to ascertain, for my own edification and guidance, the Latin American reaction to such a move. I must say, emphatically, that I never met a Latin American labor, political, or governmental leader of democratic affiliation who did not express to me the hope that the job would be done soon and well. People in Latin America understood that the very ultimate survival of the United States as the leader of the democratic world would have been endangered by the consolidation of a Communist regime in Cuba. They took it for granted, therefore, that we, with the cooperation of the OAS according to the terms of the Caracas Pact, or alone if the collective action was not forthcoming, would do something about it. The Latinos are very realistic, and as they had tended to justify certain action taken by Soviet Russia in order to safeguard her protective belt of satellite or "neutral" states, they likewise would have understood any energetic action on the part of the United States to protect the Western Hemisphere and, particularly, the Caribbean area from Communist infiltration.

"What about Trujillo?" I would often hear, meaning: how can you justify your action against a Communist dictator and leave alone the Fascist dictator next door? For instance, in a conversation I had in November 1960 with President Betancourt of Venezuela, he agreed with me that action against Castro was necesary. His only request was that we help him dispose first of Trujillo and then he would help us or even take the lead in organizing help for the Cuban patriots set to overthrow Castro. I mentioned this conversation to our Chargé d'Affaires (later Ambassador)

C. Allan Stewart, who told me that he already knew President Betancourt's attitude.

On March 13, when I was at the White House for the ceremony which launched President Kennedy's "Alliance for Progress" in Latin America, I chatted with a number of Ambassadors with whom I had had long, friendly acquaintance. The favorite topic was the impending Cuban invasion. One of them, Victor Andrade of Bolivia, took me aside and said. "Why do you Americans insist on getting written permission for hunting in a private preserve? Go ahead and do it on your own. You know that we, the wardens, will look the other way."

The trade union section of the Cuban Liberation Committee was composed mainly of members of FORDC (Cuban Democratic Revolutionary Labor Front). It was a group of exiles led by the early supporters of the Castro regime who had left Cuba disenchanted—many of them for the second time, the previous one because of Batista—when Communists began to take over. Few of them had had any prominent role in the pre-Castro labor movement, but no one could question their patriotism and readiness to sacrifice their lives for Cuban freedom. I had never been close to them although I had maintained friendly relations with a few. I felt that the competent and experienced leaders of the old CTC, even if they were still *mujalistas* (followers of Eusebio Mujal), should have been included in the group that was being formed to take over the Cuban labor movement. But no one in the top political and labor leadership of the Cuban exiles would then even consider accepting any leader tainted with *mujalismo*. They refused to consider evidence indicating that inside Cuba the workers reportedly were becoming nostalgic over the "not-so-bad, after all, old days of the Mujal leadership," and were angry not only at Castro and his Communist stooges but also at those who had helped Fidel establish his tyranny. My views were rejected and I was therefore "out." Those "in" as counselors were a group of U.S. labor subleaders, most of whom were associated with the CIO before the merger and who had a reputation of being "democratic leftists." As far as trade union policy was concerned, it is obvious that the intelligence contacts with the Liberation Army could not possibly be accused of having favored "conservative or right-wing" elements. They put all their eggs in the FORDC basket.

A small group of FORDC leaders, headed by Pascacio Lineras, were infiltrated into Cuba a few days in advance, and when the landing began at the Bay of Pigs they had already entered Havana. There, amidst the general fear that followed mass arrests and the collapse of the invasion, they wandered about seeking refuge and safety. Old CTC workers, forgetting past differences, opened their doors and their arms to their brother trade unionists who had for the second time risked their lives in the cause of freedom, and sheltered them until they could seek asylum in some friendly Latin American embassy.

The day the Cuban patriots landed, April 17, I was in Buenos Aires as U.S. worker delegate to the ILO Regional Conference of American States. Three days later I was having lunch at the University Club, in Calle Tucumán, with a group of Argentine political leaders and newspapermen: Juan Antonio Solari; Américo Ghioldi, editor of *La Vanguardia;* Dr. Manuel Ordóñez, leader of the Christian Democratic Party; Dr. Julio Noble, spokesman for the Democratic Progressive Party; Juan Valmaggia, editor in chief of *La Nación;* Dr. Adolfo Lanus, editorial writer of *La Prensa;* Santiago Núdelman, of the daily *Crítica;* Dr. Curio Chiaraviglio, and others. They represented different political views, from Social Democrat to Liberal Conservative. News from Cuba indicated the impending failure of the invasion. Everyone present expressed regret and wondered why the United States was not furnishing sufficient military support to avoid defeat. There was not a word of recrimination.

The following day, Friday, April 21—a day that will remain impressed on my memory as long as I live—from early morning until late at night, every person of importance whom I met was expressing unrestrained rejoicing over the statement made the night before by President John F. Kennedy, speaking before the American Society of Newspaper Editors, to the effect that Cuba would not be abandoned to Communism. Two top labor leaders, one of them the Latin American Vice-President of the International Confederation of Free Trade Unions, were so outspoken in their support of President Kennedy's pledge that I took them to see Ambassador Rubottom so that they could repeat to him what they had told me. Ambassador Rubottom, of course, expressed the hope that I would convey such information to Washington, which I naturally did.

A few days later, on April 29, I visited Governor Carlos Lacerda of Rio de Janeiro, accompanied by Deocleciano de Hollanda Calvacanti, head of the Brazilian Confederation of Industrial Workers, and a member of the ICFTU Executive Board. Governor Lacerda expressed the hope in no uncertain terms that we would, perhaps with different methods, make another attempt to overthrow Castro, adding the recommendation to make sure that the next time we would not fail. Everywhere I found the same reaction. I did not meet any Latin American of democratic affiliation who expressed regret that we had helped the ill-fated Cuban invasion. The only regret that they expressed was that we did not go all the way and assure the victory of the enterprise.

What greatly disturbed me, and many other Latin American observers, was the fact that our failure to give the Cuban patriots the military support which was generally expected was attributed, in the Latin American interpretation, to our fear of Khrushchev's retaliation. This to them was an indication that we had become, to all intents and purposes, a second-rate power. An example of this was given by Francisco Julião, well-known pro-Communist leader of the farm workers of northeast Brazil, who, before leaving for Havana to attend the May Day demonstration, gave a press interview, which I read in the Rio de Janeiro newspapers, stating that after Cuba, Venezuela would be next, and then Brazil. "It is now clear," said Julião, "that the United States is a second-rate power and is no longer in a position to stop our march toward socialism."

Subsequent statements by Administration spokesmen, such as those of Senate Majority Leader Mike Mansfield, Senator J. William Fulbright, and Undersecretary Chester Bowles, to the effect that Cuba, after all, did not represent a vital threat to the United States and that the only thing to do was to isolate it by propping up the economy of the rest of Latin America, created the widespread impression that we had actually given up Cuba as lost.

The AFL-CIO reacted strongly to this "nuisance" theory with an Executive Council statement issued June 28, 1961, which supported "unreservedly the pledge made by President John F. Kennedy on April 20, that the U.S. would not abandon Cuba to Communism and that efforts would be continued to arouse the inter-American community to the realization of the Castro-Communist danger." It also joined "wholeheartedly with the democratic labor movement of Latin America in rejecting all attempts to sidetrack the Cuban Communist issue, under the specious argument that it does not represent a danger to the Western Hemisphere."

Less than ten days after the Bay of Pigs fiasco came May Day, celebrated throughout Latin America with parades, demonstrations, mass meetings, addresses, statements, and other populist manifestations. Condemnation of the role played by the U.S. government in the Bay of Pigs affair could have erupted in many ways—slogans, posters, resolutions, attacks on U.S. embassies, etc. Generally, the May Day 1961 labor assemblies were noted for their overwhelming anti-Castro sentiments.

The few anti-U.S. and pro-Castro demonstrations that a noisy minority of Communists and fellow travelers were able to stage here and there were duly reported with an abundance of details by the wire services. But by failing to report in full the more numerous anti-Castro turnouts the impression was created in the U.S. press that Latin American labor had reacted overwhelmingly in favor of Castro.

In an attempt to assess the situation accurately I carefully gathered, with the help of ORIT, accounts of the May Day demonstrations in each country. After checking them carefully with unclassified reports prepared by the State Department and USIA, I published them in the July 1961 issue of the *Inter-American Labor Bulletin*. This was the picture:

Demonstrations against the United States were staged in Santiago, Chile, with fewer than 3,000 in the crowd. But on the same day anti-Castro rallies were held by democratic unions in Antofagasta and Tocopilla. In Montevideo, 6,000–8,000 demonstrated in favor of Castro on April 21, the day the Bay of Pigs failure was announced; but anti-Castro rallies, under the auspices of the local ORIT affiliated unions, were held April 25 in Montevideo (4,000), April 26 in Paysandú, Uruguay's second largest city (2,000) and on May Day in Rivera, a city of the interior (4,000).

A number of rallies were held on May Day in Buenos Aires. The one by the newly united CGT, which attracted about 10,000 people, ignored the Cuban issue altogether. The FORA meeting (anarcho-syndicalists), with 3,000 participating, was a pronounced anti-Castro affair, and so were the separate meetings under the auspices of the Social Democrats and the Christian Democrats, which attracted a total of about 6,000 workers. One meeting organized by Communists, Marxist Socialists, and assorted fellow travelers—which was strongly pro-Castro and anti-U.S.—drew about 5,000 persons. Of the reported 25,000 that attended May Day meetings, in a city of over three million, only about one-fifth went to the pro-Castro rally.

In Bolivia, where the leadership of the Labor Confederation (COB) was sympathetic to Castro, the May Day rally turned into a rousing anti-Communist demonstration. There were disorders and fistfights, with the anti-Castro elements finally gaining control of La Paz's Central Square where the rally was taking place. A similar thing happened in Venezuela where the anti-Communists, supporters of the democratic administration of President Rómulo Betancourt, finally gained control of the parade and subsequent mass meetings.

In Peru, the only May Day demonstration of any significance was the one organized in Lima by the CTP, where Arturo Sabroso was the main speaker. It was clearly anti-Castro. The CTP was the pioneer in repudiating the Cuban revolution after it fell under Communist domination. The same situation prevailed in Colombia, where the CTC and UTC—ORIT affiliated organizations that comprise about 90 percent of the organized workers—denounced the small Communist group that attempted to stage anti-U.S. street demonstrations. Colombian labor has always been noted for its marked democratic stand.

The May Day demonstration organized by the Communist-controlled Confederation of Labor of Ecuador did not attract more than 1,000 people, including students and truckloads of Indians transported to the capital from the interior. The democratic unions held a series of indoor meetings with a cumulative attendance far superior to the Communist rally. The ratio of the demonstrators in Panama was 400 pro-Castro in Panama City and Colón, against over 5,000 anti-Castro in David and the banana plantations in Puerto Armuelles and Bocas del Toro. All Panama City newspapers reported them as the largest labor rallies ever held in the country. In Costa Rica, more than 10,000 workers assembled in front of various city churches where appropriate meetings were held. The traditional Communist May Day parade did not attract more than 500 people. When they attempted to hold a meeting in San José's central square they were chased out by anti-Communist workers, members of the Confederation of Labor "Rerum Novarum." In Honduras, a Communist meeting in Tegucigalpa drew only a few hundred, including students and fellow travelers. In contrast, the meetings held under the auspices of democratic unions were attended by 8,000 people in Tegucigalpa, 20,000 in San Pedro Sula, and over 5,000 in La Ceiba.

In Mexico City, students and some radical left-wing unions, particularly the teachers, were able to stage some noisy demonstrations in support of Castro, thus creating the impression that a strong anti-U.S. sentiment was sweeping the Mexican people. The May Day parade, however, gave a true picture. More than 500,000 workers passed in review before the President of the republic. The parade lasted four hours. No slogans or placards offensive to the U.S. were to be seen anywhere. Only six pennants out of thousands in the parade had expressions supporting Castro. They were borne by contingents representing six well-known left-wing unions. Parades in other large cities of Mexico had the same characteristics as the one in the capital.

Of particular significance were the May Day demonstrations in Brazil, where pro-Communist elements were being coddled by the government, and particularly by the then Vice-President, João "Jango" Goulart. The rally organized by extreme left-wing and Communist elements in Rio de Janeiro was such a dismal failure that Goulart, who was featured as the main speaker, failed to show up when he was informed of the small size of the crowd. On the other hand, the rally that was addressed by Governor Carlos Lacerda, a leader of the Brazilian anti-Communist forces, drew an impressively large audience. It was a clear-cut anti-Communist and anti-Castro demonstration.

Of all the national labor organizations affiliated to ORIT throughout the Western Hemisphere, representing an aggregate of 25 million members, only one—the Canadian Congress of Labour—censured the United States government for the part played in support of the Cuban landing.

The August 1961 Inter-American Conference at Punta del Este, Uruguay, was called for the specific purpose of launching the Alliance for Progress. Not many people remember, however, that Cuba took part in that Conference—held less than four months after the Bay of Pigs— because she was still a member of the OAS. I attended the Punta del Este Conference as a member of the AFL-CIO delegation of observers. The others were William C. Doherty, Sr., and Stanley Ruttenberg, then Director of the AFL-CIO Research Department, who later became Assistant Secretary of Labor.

The leading roles at Punta del Este were played by Ernesto "Che" Guevara, head of the Cuban delegation, and Richard N. Goodwin, whose title then was Deputy Assistant U.S. Secretary of State. Because of his ties with the White House, sharp intellect, and aggressive personality, Goodwin was unquestionably the key "political" member of the U.S. group. The titular head was Treasury Secretary Douglas C. Dillon, who was primarily concerned with the economic and financial aspects of the Alliance.

"Che" Guevara, in his very first address to the plenary session, excoriated the United States in the most vicious and insulting language, not even sparing the person of President Kennedy. He and his deputies in the various committee meetings kept up the barrage for three days. Any other delegation would have protested, would have threatened to leave the Conference, and would have demanded a public manifestation of desagravio (apology). I have seen Latin American delegations at international conferences do precisely that for much lesser offenses than those committed by Guevara. But our delegation said nothing, did nothing. They just sat there smiling. Obviously, they had orders not to reply, not to fight back. What was the impression created among other delegates by such a naive passivity? Instead of admiring our forbearance they pitied our weakness. Instead of *machismo* (pride and manliness) which the Latinos respect and expect from all political leaders, the U.S. delegation was trying to atone with humility, ashes, and sackcloth for our Bay of Pigs adventure.

My old friend Arturo Morales Carrión, another Deputy Assistant Secretary of State, was the chairman of the committee on social, labor, and cultural affairs. The Cuban member of that committee even tried to outdo his chief Guevara in his vitriolic anti-American tirades. At one point I approached the chairman, pleading with him:

"Arturo, you are a Latin. You understand that if we do not answer these criminals we will lose face with our friends." As an observer I could not address the plenary sessions and was chafing at the bit.

"You are right, you are right," he replied. And then, with a resigned defeatism and choking voice he added: "But we have orders! . . ."

Stanley Ruttenberg, economist par excellence, was very busy analyzing, discussing, and trying to improve the many Conference documents dealing with Alliance aims, structure, and immediate practical objectives. He was doing a first-rate job, so Bill Doherty and I decided not to bother him too much with our frettings about Uncle Sam's loss of face. Doherty felt the same way I did about the passivity of the U.S. delegation. We were good friends of our Ambassador to the OAS, de Lesseps S. ("Chep") Morrison, who was also a member of the delegation. We asked for an appointment at the Cantegrill Country Club, where he was staying.

Ambassador Morrison confirmed that the delegation had received instructions not to fight back, but he shared our dismay over the unfavorable political and psychological consequences of our nonchalance and joined us in exploring how to repair the damage. "Chep" hit on the idea that perhaps I could persuade some of my good friends in the Costa Rican, Peruvian, or Venezuelan delegations to take the floor at the plenary session and introduce a motion or make a speech deploring Guevara's intemperate language. It was a random suggestion expressed in vague terms, but I cut him short:

"Chep, in this part of the world, national honor cannot be defended by proxy!"

When the astute "Che" Guevara realized that the U.S. delegation had instructions not to fight, he interpreted this as an implicit offer to "start talking." Accordingly, he changed his tune and, playing the role of a reasonable fellow, started impressing upon some delegates of Latin American countries (particularly Argentina, Brazil, Bolivia, and Mexico) that Cuba was anxious to enter into peaceful coexistence if only the United States would "kiss and make up."

In a typical Latin American atmosphere, such as the one which prevailed at Punta del Este during the Conference, every social gesture on the part of a prominent delegate was regarded as having a definite meaning; thus, when "Che" Guevara made it known that he had sent a box of fine Havana cigars to Mr. Goodwin, accompanied by a note full of humble and friendly expressions, ending with a proffer of the hand, tongues started wagging and speculations flew in every direction. Therefore, when a Goodwin-Guevara meeting took place on Wednesday, August 16, it was absolutely and unequivocally interpreted as an indication that Uncle Sam was willing to "talk sense" with Fidel as a prelude to the "kiss and make up finale" that "Che" Guevara had so assiduously cultivated.

What followed this meeting, which was not as casual as Mr. Goodwin later told the Senate Foreign Relations Committee, is well known. Argentine Foreign Minister Dr. Adolfo Mújica arranged for Guevara to meet with President Frondizi, while Brazilian Foreign Minister Afonso Arinos did the same with President Quadros. Both countries had repeatedly suggested that they act as honest brokers between the United States and Cuba—a suggestion which was politely but firmly rejected by the U.S. State Department. Now, however, that a first contact between a representative of Castro and a representative of President Kennedy had actually taken place, the Argentine and Brazilian Foreign Ministers found a good opening to resume the initiative for mediation with a good chance for them to get credit for any eventual positive results.

When President Frondizi met with general condemnation for his clandestine meeting with Guevara, he quickly sacrificed Mújica as a scapegoat and "apologized" to the country on a radio-TV appearance. A new Foreign Minister, unfriendly to Castro, was subsequently appointed.

Brazilian Foreign Minister Afonso Arinos was faced with a wave of indignation as a result of the Quadros-Guevara meeting and the conferring on the latter of the highest Brazilian decoration for meritorious service. He, too, tried to justify his actions on the basis of the Goodwin-Guevara meeting. In a press statement issued August 23, which I read in the August 24 issue of the *Correio da Manhá* of Rio de Janeiro, Arinos asserted that the Goodwin-Guevara meeting took place in the presence of a Brazilian diplomat, that the Brazilian Foreign Office was fully informed of what was aired (*ventilado*) in the course of such a meeting, and that it was "very cordial."

The impression created among the Punta del Este delegates that the United States was embarking on a less firm policy toward Castro was so strong that Secretary Dillon found it necessary to issue a forceful statement denying such a possibility. However, the seed had been planted. It sprouted in no time!

Our stay at Punta del Este was not completely fruitless. We were fairly treated by the members of the U.S. delegation and were given every opportunity to advance suggestions. We were, thus, able to include in the final draft of the Declaration specific mention of the advisability of using labor and management representatives in a consultative capacity in the drafting and execution of Alliance for Progress national development plans. However, Richard N. Goodwin at first resented my suggestion to include management alongside labor, because he thought that "free enterprise" had a bad connotation in Latin America, being too often confused with imperialism and exploitation by American firms.

It was not without significance—at least to me—that Secretary Dillon himself, in his keynote speech at the conference, took care not to mention, even once, this scare expression, "free enterprise." To even the score they took care, also, to eliminate every reference to "free labor." I was told that some countries, such as Argentina and Chile, objected to the word "free," which in their countries, they alleged, was used by opposition groups. The argument was specious, but the U.S. delegation swallowed it, and so we emerged simply as "labor and management," shorn of the annoying adjective "free."

A large contingent of observers representing business were also at the Conference. I remember among them the veteran Latin American expert Henry W. Balgooyen, now President of American and Foreign Power, and neophyte C. Rodman Rockefeller, Vice-President of International Basic Economics Corporation. I never saw a group of more "forgotten" capitalists than those who assembled at Punta del Este. They were really way "out," but I could not say that we, the proletarians, were very much "in." However, we at least got a foot in the door and were honored with a get-together luncheon where our host, Secretary Dillon, gave us an opportunity to express our viewpoint on a number of subjects related to the Conference. But the "capitalists" . . . they were left out in the cold.

The AFL-CIO Executive Council, at its meeting in Bal Harbour, Florida, February 26, 1962, expressed full support of the Punta del Este conference of American Foreign Ministers—held in January, 1962—which declared the Cuban-Communist regime "incompatible with the principles of the American political system" and therefore excluded it from the Organization of American States.

The statement also urged the OAS and its individual member states "to put into effect as rapidly as possible all the measures agreed upon in principle, especially the application of diplomatic and economic sanctions against the Castro regime, and the adoption of effective measures to stop and roll back the Castro-Communist offensive, which, now more than ever, is determined to undermine, subvert, and conquer the whole of Latin America."

However, after the missile crisis of October 1962, official U.S. policy accepted the Castro regime in Cuba as an irreversible reality, an unpleasant fact of life. We pledged to contain it and to prevent it from promoting infiltration and subversion against democratic regimes in Latin America, especially in the Caribbean area. Even the AFL-CIO could no longer realistically demand in its statements the overthrow of Castro either by the United States alone or through OAS collective action. It therefore concentrated its demands on effective measures to stop the "unchecked expansionist activities of the Castro regime." This policy was spelled out in detail in the statement adopted by its Executive Council at the February 1964 meeting in Florida:

We believe the time has come for the American community of nations to make a new appraisal of the serious danger posed by the unchecked expansionist activities of the Castro regime and to assume collectively and firmly the responsibility of terminating these activities. The defense of the democratic representative institutions of the Western Hemisphere cannot be the task of the United States alone, or of any other particular country whenever it is threatened by imminent danger. There are sufficient inter-American treaties unanimously adopted and ratified by the OAS member states to cope with the present Cuban danger. These treaties must be invoked and action taken before it is too late.

But if the Castro regime was to be regarded as fairly stable with little likelihood of being overthrown by an internal upheaval could we continue to refuse indefinitely to try to normalize relations?

Taking cognizance of the overtures made by Castro for negotiations with the United States, the AFL-CIO Council, meeting again in Chicago, on August 4, 1964, suggested the following conditions as a prerequisite to any such talks:

(1) Castro should fulfill his original promise to implement the 1940 Political Constitution of Cuba.

(2) In line with Castro's pledge when he first took power, a specific date

should be set for the free election of a representative government no later than six months after the acceptance of these conditions.

(3) The elections should be supervised by the OAS.

(4) Complete freedom should be restored to the trade union movement.

(5) Immediate release of all trade unionists and other political prisoners.

(6) Immediate removal of all Soviet personnel, rockets, and other war-making material.

Castro and his Russian masters have, of course, no intention of restoring any tolerable semblance of freedom or allowing any free elections supervised by the OAS. They have instead proclaimed again to the four corners of the world, in the solemn Tri-Continental Conference held in Havana in January 1966, their iron-clad resolve to continue and to intensify at any cost and with all the means at their disposal their offensive to achieve a Communist victory in the Western Hemisphere. As the AFL-CIO warned in 1961, Cuba "is being openly and boastfully used as a staging area for the internal subversion and ultimate control of all Latin America."

Notes

1. The AFL-CIO Inter-American Affairs Committee which initiated all the inter-American resolutions adopted by the Council, was composed of President George Meany, Secretary-Treasurer William F. Schnitzler, Director Michael Ross of the Department of International Affairs, and Vice-Presidents David Dubinsky, William C. Doherty, Sr., Joseph A. Beirne, James Suffridge, David McDonald, and Emil Rieve. Its Chairman was O. A. Knight and Serafino Romualdi was its Executive Secretary.

XVI

Bananas and Coffee Beans

CENTRAL AMERICA, to which this chapter is devoted, comprises five countries—Guatemala, El Salvador, Honduras, Nicaragua, and Costa Rica. But
in the structure of ORIT, Panama and British Honduras (Belize) belong
to the same group. All these countries are commonly referred to as a conglomeration of Banana Republics. I have added "coffee beans" to the
title because coffee is actually Central America's largest money-making
crop. The farms (called *fincas*), where the coffee beans are cultivated,
harvested, dried, and packed employ the largest number of farmhands
(*peones*) —even more than cotton, sugar, and bananas combined.

Much has been written about banana plantations, especially about
their largest owner-operator, the United Fruit Company; but little has
been said about the coffee producers, with the possible exception of the
so-called sixteen families of El Salvador, all of them owners of extensive
coffee farms, who are alleged to dominate the economic and political life
of that little country. The barefooted *peones* of the coffee *fincas,* however,
have been practically forgotten—the tourists seldom see them, and the
political writers rediscover them only when there are revolts or revolutions.

The story of organized labor in Central America, particularly the
story of the exploited Indian *peones,* has been a story of blood, sufferings,
suppression, political and economic exploitation, revolts, revolutions,
defeats, and recovery. It has also been a long tragic story of quest for
economic and political freedom—that burning, almost unattainable ideal
which too many economic "experts" and sociologists deny exists at all in

236

the aspirations of the starving barefooted Indians. But it is there; it exists! And I dare say that if the totalitarians, Communists and Peronistas, have failed to gain the enduring alliance of the Central American *campesinos*, it is because they underestimated their natural attachment to freedom, even if in their lack of sophistication the *campesinos* do not fully understand or feel freedom's true spiritual values.

The libertarian aspirations of the free labor movement's slogan "Bread and Freedom" are perhaps better understood in Central America than in any other part of the Western Hemisphere, because in Central America there has been, always, almost a total lack of both. How many times "Pepe" Figueres and Luis Alberto Monge in Costa Rica, and Villeda Morales in Honduras—to cite three friends who have played such an outstanding role in the defense of freedom in Central America—have joined me in condemning the tendency prevailing among United States "experts," including some in the labor movement itself, to assert that what "the people down there" (and they never fail to add "especially the *campesinos*") need most is to fill their stomachs, relegating the quest for freedom to the bottom rung of their aspirations' ladder.

I experienced an instance of this type of approach while taking part in the Yale Law School Forum on "Social Revolution in Latin America—What Role United States?"—which took place in New Haven, Connecticut, March 14, 1961.[1] One of the panelists belittled my statement that the absence of freedom in a number of Latin American countries was the main aspect of democracy's crisis there, by saying that, in his opinion, lack of material things, mainly food, was at the root of all trouble. To stress his point, he repeated Napoleon's adage that "an army marches on its stomach." To which I retorted with vehemence: "Don't forget that if the stomach is hungry, so is the soul. And the food for the soul is freedom."[2]

It is not my intention to write in this chapter a detailed story of the labor movement in each Central American country. It has already been well done by others.[3] I shall rather limit myself to a number of significant episodes and sketches, mostly involving my activity as United States trade union representative and my dealings with humble labor people, political personalities, and even some of the eighteen Chiefs of State whom I have met in the course of my Central American journeys.[4]

British Honduras

This colony, which will probably adopt the name of Belize when it gains full independence from Great Britain,[5] was occasionally the first stop of my Central American tours, being on the direct airline from New Orleans to Guatemala. A country about the size of Massachusetts, but with less than 100,000 inhabitants, one-third of them in the capital city of Belize, British Honduras never had an industrial proletariat of any size, its income deriving mostly from timber, citrus fruits, bananas, and agriculture. Nevertheless, it developed, in proportion to its population, a large and strong labor movement, militant and self-supporting. When ORIT was organized in 1951, the General Workers' Union (GWU) of British Honduras was among its charter members. At that time, the GWU had close to 10,000 members.

Linked to Jamaica, once largest British Caribbean colony, by geographical proximity and direct air connection, the political and trade union movements of the two countries developed a close relationship. When I went to British Honduras for the first time in April 1953, I also visited Jamaica. I found that the People's National Party of Jamaica, led by Norman Manley, and the People's United Party (PUP) of British Honduras, led by George Price, had a good chance of gaining—as they actually did—the majority in their respective next general elections. The Jamaica group, older in tradition and experience and with a large reservoir of mature leadership, had not aroused any fear of reckless experimentation or constitutional complications. The Honduras party, on the other hand, perhaps because of the youth of its leadership and some constitutional pronouncements which were motivated more by impatient nationalism than political realities, was being attacked both at home and abroad as "another British Guiana" [6] or even was accused of being under the influence of the pro-Communist regime of bordering Guatemala.[7]

I arrived in British Honduras with open eyes, having been tipped off to be on the lookout for possible Communist influence. I found that nothing could have been further from the truth. The officers and members of the GWU, who also constituted the bulk of the PUP,[8] were convinced anti-Communists, mostly of the Catholic faith. They had never been involved in any domestic or international "peace" trap, nor had they any contact with Guatemalan Communists.

In their desire to obtain a greater degree of independence, they had clashed rather bitterly with local British authorities and had adopted, as their emblem, the United Nations flag rather than the Union Jack. All this was the result of nationalistic, anticolonial aspirations (with which the people of the Western Hemisphere were in general sympathy) but not of Communist infiltration or domination.

Whenever I think of my first visit to British Honduras, several episodes come fondly back to my mind, all indicative of the economic and spiritual conditions of the workers of that country. On the day of my arrival, Friday, April 24, I addressed a GWU open air mass meeting at Yarborough Green, in Belize, in which some 2,000 people participated. In the midst of my address, we were suddenly dispersed by a typical tropical downpour of short duration. When the rain stopped, I again mounted the platform ready to resume my address, but Nick Pollard, the GWU General Secretary and chairman of the meeting, signaled me to wait. He went to the microphone and invited the crowd to kneel with him and pray, "to thank God for having stopped the rain so that Brother Romualdi could resume his address."

The following day, a party of GWU leaders and I went to Stan Creek, the country's second largest town, way down the coast. The GWU boys traveled in a small fishing boat but they urged me, instead, to charter a plane as the sea was rather rough and they were afraid that I would get awfully seasick. The suggestion of chartering a plane became associated in my mind with a rental cost much beyond my travel allowance; but I finally consented when I found out that Colonial Airways was quite reasonable. For $34.50 they took me, in a two-seater, to Stan Creek and returned me the following day to Belize.

In Stan Creek we visited the citrus fruit plantations and conferred with a number of local labor and political leaders. In the evening, just before it got dark, there was a big mass meeting in the town square, followed by a dance. At one point I was asked whether I wanted to eat something—a request that as far as I was concerned, was hours overdue. I was taken to a small back room, lit by an oil lamp, where a kind old woman, full of courtesies and apologies, served me two fried eggs and some baked breadfruit. I noticed that a dozen or so of my friends were standing around, not eating. I asked them why. Somewhat embarrassed they told me:

"We brought with us plenty of cocoanuts; didn't you see them when we left the boat? That's all we can afford to eat. Besides, there are no restaurants in this town and no house would have enough food for all of us . . . even if we had the money to pay for it."

There was a great deal of merriment at the dance, with plenty of local rum going around. I soon got tired and asked where I was assigned to sleep. They took me to a boardinghouse, upstairs, in a sparsely furnished room without lights. Just the same, I could see my way around, because it was a bright night with a full moon. Before leaving, my friends pointed through the window to a shed, across the back yard, behind some bushes, and told me: "There is a toilet there, if you need it." Before dawn, I made an attempt to get there, but a huge dog, obviously scenting a stranger, barked furiously at me and came uncomfortably close. I beat a quick retreat and had to rely on my ingenuity, which fortunately never failed me in such emergencies.

Following the 1953 events in British Guiana, which culminated in the dissolution of the Communist-controlled People's Progressive Party and the suspension of the newly granted Constitution, newspaper correspondents, mainly from Great Britain, began to concentrate their attention on British Honduras. They "discovered" a situation "similar to the one in British Guiana," owing to alleged Communist infiltration in the country's two largest organizations, the General Workers' Union (GWU) and the People's United Party (PUP). Particularly disturbing were the accusations of being under Communist control made against the GWU and the PUP by T. S. Steele in *The London Daily Telegraph* of November 2 and 3, 1953, and subsequently in *The London Daily Mail*.[9]

When I visited British Honduras the second time in 1953, on November 2 I discussed in my public address at Pound Yard Bridge the situation in British Guiana and the destructive role played by the Communist-controlled PPP, warning the people of British Honduras to keep the country free of Communism. Philip Goldson, Assistant General Secretary of the GWU, replied to me by giving public assurance that "the people of British Honduras were opposed to Communism politically, but that they were more opposed to it spiritually." He added that, if necessary, "the people would lay down their lives to keep Communism from taking root in their country."

On his part, George Price, leader of the PUP, issued statements[10] joining the GWU leadership in repudiating Communist charges in the strongest possible terms. So deep was their despair in the face of such unfounded and unfair accusations that they sent an official request to the British Colonial Office to appoint a Royal Commission of Inquiry and to include none other than Senator Joseph McCarthy of Wisconsin!

Guatemala

The American Federation of Labor rejoices over the downfall of the Communist-controlled regime in Guatemala, brought about by the refusal of the Army to serve any longer a Government that had betrayed the democratic aspirations of the people and had transformed the country into a beachhead of Soviet Russia in the Western Hemisphere.

This was the opening paragraph of the statement issued on June 30, 1954, by AFL President George Meany on the overthrow of Guatemalan

President Jacobo Arbenz Guzmán. Unlike other organizations, including the CIO and the ICFTU, which either opposed the victorious insurrection led by Colonel Castillo Armas or took an indifferent position, the AFL set forth its stand in unequivocal terms. Aware, however, of the peril that the anti-Communist revolution might degenerate into a reactionary, antilabor restoration of the old order which was swept aside by the democratic revolution of October 1944, President Meany expressed "fervent hope that the new Provisional Government will restore as quickly as possible absolute respect for civil liberties and human rights" and urged the government of the United States "to exercise all the influence and pressure in its power to strengthen the democratic forces of Guatemala, now emerging from a long period of suppression and persecution." [11]

The AFL had closely followed for years the political and labor events in Guatemala and on repeated occasions had voiced its alarm over the pro-Communist policy of President Arbenz. For instance, on February 5, 1954, President Meany sent to President Arbenz, with the approval of the AFL Council meeting in Miami Beach, Florida, an open letter in which he denounced "with profound apprehension the extensive subversive activities of the Guatemalan section of the world Communist party in your country," and gave three specific demonstrations of this Communist influence.[12]

The labor movement of Guatemala had begun organizing following the October 20, 1944, revolution which was supported by the overwhelming majority of the Guatemalan people with a group of students and professors in the vanguard, none of whom were Communists.

In the elections held in December, 1944, Dr. Juan José Arévalo, a University professor who had spent sixteen years of exile in Argentina, was elected President. He took office on March 15, 1945. Under his administration, labor received every facility to organize, a Labor Code was promulgated, minimum wages and the eight-hour day were introduced, and the Labor Courts were established. Arévalo was a typical leftist-oriented Latin American intellectual, but he was not a Communist.[13] However, he did not know how to defend himself and his regime from the boring-from-within tactics employed by the Communists in the labor, intellectual, and political sectors. Furthermore, Arévalo did not understand (a weakness of many intellectuals turned statesmen) the importance and the role of organized labor as a potential pillar of a democratic society or, conversely, as a potential bulldozer for its destruction. Yet, in spite of all their efforts, the money at their disposal, and the trained leadership they brought back to Guatemala from Russia, the Communist-controlled Confederation of Workers of Guatemala, affiliated to the CTAL-WFTU, remained very small during the entire period of the Arévalo regime. In fact, strong anti-Communist unions sprang into existence, forming three distinct national central labor organizations.

Colonel Francisco Xavier Arana, a staunch anti-Communist and a participant in the October 1944 democratic revolution, was being groomed by the Army and a strong segment of the civilian population as a successor to Arévalo. One Sunday afternoon, July 19, 1949, while crossing the narrow Puente de la Gloria, near Lake Amatitlán, Colonel Arana was ambushed and killed by a band of Communist conspirators. A faction of the army, outraged by this crime, which it attributed to the laxity of the Arévalo administration, revolted against him and laid siege to the Presidential Palace. Arévalo was about to surrender when a cease fire, arranged through the intervention of the Apostolic Nuncio and American Ambassador Richard C. Patterson, Jr., provided a providential respite. Meanwhile, a general strike had been called. The Communists reinforced the loyal army units in the capital by bringing up truckloads of armed *campesinos* from the coffee farms and the banana plantations. The fighting was resumed and the rebel units were defeated.

After the elimination of Colonel Arana, the leftist forces and the Communists supported the candidacy of Lieutenant Colonel Jacobo Arbenz Guzmán, who easily won the November 1950 presidential elections. He took office March 15, 1951. From the very beginning Arbenz acted as a willing tool of the Communists. Seven months after his inauguration, the various Guatemalan unions were pressured, under the pretense of unity, to take part in a so-called Unity Convention, held in October 1951, where they agreed to merge into a General Confederation of Workers of Guatemala (CGTG). The Communists obtained 70 percent of the key positions.

Soon after the achievement of this unity, the Communists started a campaign of slander against the older leaders of the labor movement with the view of taking away from them the support of the workers. Trusted and experienced labor leaders were thus forced out and were replaced with young, inexperienced leaders whose only qualification was blind submission to the will and dictates of the Communist Party. With the constant support of the government, a veritable Communist trade union dictatorship was thus built up in Guatemala.

In 1953, anti-Communist leaders of a Defense Committee formed to protect the interests of 4,000 unemployed workers were accused by the

Communists, who had vainly tried to capture that organization, of being "antipatriotic elements." As a result, all the leaders were arrested, the headquarters of the Committee were destroyed, and the organization itself was forced out of existence. A similar fate was suffered by a group of Catholic leaders who had organized a Central Committee of Anti-Communist Workers.

Also in 1953, a group of democratic trade unionists, aided by the ORIT and the AFL, organized the National Union of Free Workers of Guatemala (UNTL). Based on the principle of free, independent trade unionism, it opposed government domination and interference from political parties. It advocated a type of constructive trade unionism that was in open contrast with the destructive policy employed by the Communists. The UNTL began to organize unions of factory workers as well as agricultural laborers.

Harassment and persecution, including arrest of its leaders under the false accusation of carrying arms, were first employed by the Communist-infiltrated Judicial Police to cow the UNTL into submission. That having failed, on the morning of January 25, 1954, a band of Communists armed with machine guns assaulted the UNTL headquarters, destroyed the furniture, burned the AFL and ORIT literature, stole what money they found in the safe, and arrested all the leaders who were present. These they tortured in the most barbarous fashion to make them confess that they were plotting with the international free trade union movement against the government of Guatemala.

Meanwhile, the Communists successfully completed their infiltration of political parties. Every one of the so-called "democratic" parties had one or more of its key officers secretly belonging to the Communist Party or under its absolute influence. By the spring of 1954, the Communist control of Guatemala was complete. Although the members of the Guatemalan Congress belonging to the Guatemalan Labor Party (the name adopted by the Communists) were only four, the Congress declared a minute of silence in reverence to the memory of Joseph Stalin—the only "non-Communist" legislative body in the world to do that. Also, Guatemala was the only "non-Communist" country in the world where, according to its President Arbenz, it was "subversive" to be anti-Communist.[14]

The Army, however, still remained the one big force capable of blocking the Communist road to total power. To checkmate the Army, the Communists began to organize along military lines. They received from Europe heavy shipments of arms which were smuggled through the Panama Canal and were then landed on the Pacific coast of Guatemala.

Trucks belonging to the National Agricultural Department, whose Agrarian Reform Division was under the absolute control of the Communists, were used to carry the arms to various distribution points.[15]

During the third week of June 1954, a so-called Liberation Army—to which the National Union of Free Workers of Guatemala contributed all of its leaders who were in exile—crossed the Honduras-Guatemalan border and marched to victory under the leadership of Colonel Carlos Castillo Armas. After the resignation of President Jacobo Arbenz Guzmán and the succession of three military juntas, Castillo Armas assumed sole power on September 1. I spent most of the months of July and August in Guatemala as representative of the AFL, helping the free trade unionists to reorganize their forces and, occasionally, advising the new Government on various aspects of its labor policy. Daniel Benedict of the CIO, Raul Valdivia of the Cuban CTC, and Otero Borlaff from the ORIT joined me in the mission.

The people of Guatemala were solidly behind Castillo Armas and a strong wave of anti-Communism was sweeping the country. The discovery of scores of corpses of victims of the Red terror, the stories of tortures told by the released prisoners and the revelations concerning the huge sums of money stolen by Arbenz and his cronies during the last weeks of his regime, greatly contributed to inflame popular indignation and passions.

Unfortunately, this wave of anti-Communism threatened to sweep away the labor movement itself. The monopoly which the Communist Party had had in the labor movement and the use the Communists had made of unions for their political purposes had led many Guatemalans to look upon unionism as a synonym for Communism. A major task in Guatemala, therefore, was to persuade the people by argument and through experience that free trade unionism was the main means of preventing the resurgency of the Communist danger.

My colleagues and I realized that the free trade union movement needed trained leaders and experienced organizers. The Communists had taken over all of the leader posts in the old unions, and since the ousted leaders had gone into exile or underground, a vacuum was left. Nevertheless, we were able to bring together a group of people, mostly young elements, representing over twenty unions, in the capital city, and formed a National Committee for Trade Union Reorganization.

Another group of trade unionists, under the leadership of a prominent Catholic layman, attorney José García Bauer, former labor judge, organized the Federation of Independent Unions, with a program based on the social teachings of the Catholic Church.

Upon returning to the United States from my Guatemalan mission, in

September 1954, I wrote an article of impressions and comments which appeared in the *American Federationist* of the same month, in which I stated:

It is obvious that there are two opposite currents within the new government in regard to trade unionism, one that would like to reduce it to a minimum if not to suppress it altogether, and another that believes in organized labor's usefulness and constructive possibilities and is therefore in favor of strengthening it. All evidences so far indicate that President Castillo Armas himself favors the development of free trade unionism.

For a few months the issue was still in doubt, but early in 1955, after the defeat in January of a military attempt to overthrow his regime, Castillo Armas took some concrete steps to put into practice his free labor policy. But the reactionary forces eventually gained the upper hand when they pressured him into issuing, on February 1956, a decree amending the Labor Code in a way that made it much more difficult for a trade union to operate and exist.

I had already learned, in the course of my previous visits to Guatemala, that the employers, with the connivance of the governmental authorities, had resorted to wholesale dismissals of every active trade unionist whom they classified as agitators. Agricultural workers were brought back to conditions of servitude if not actual slavery. I found out that in the Ixcán region workers were being paid 50 cents a day and were forced to work 84 hours a week. Although representatives of the workers appealed to the Director General of Agrarian affairs, the government bureau informed them that they "must obey the instructions of their employer."

On another occasion I learned that fifty-eight Indian *campesinos* employed on a coffee farm in San Martín Jilotepeque, had been arrested under charge of being Communists and brought handcuffed to the jail in Guatemala. I asked Luis Balcárcel, then head of the Federation of Independent Unions (FAS), which had organized the arrested workers, to explain to me what actually happened. Balcárcel told me that the owner of the farm had further reduced wages and increased the hours and had also raised the quota of production for each worker to impossible levels. Fifty-eight of them wrote a protest to the President (or rather had a Union representative write it for them because they were all illiterate) and signed it with crosses. But the employer learned of the move, and before the protest could reach the Capital had them arrested immediately under charges of being "Communists."

Hardly able to contain my indignation, I asked Balcárcel: "Who has the protest?." And he told me: "I still have it here, in my pocket." We decided on the spot to go straight to see Dr. Carlos Cifuentes Díaz,

Private Secretary to the President, who was supposed to be in charge of "measures to prevent the resurgence of Communism." We were admitted to his presence without much difficulty, but when I told him what we knew of the reasons behind the arrests of those poor fifty-eight illiterate Indians, he shouted back: "This is impossible." I turned to Balcárcel, almost white with fear, and asked him to show the Secretary the petition-protest signed with the fifty-eight crosses. Whereupon Dr. Cifuentes Díaz abused me, calling me a bad subject and a dangerous agitator, and citing as the source of his information none other than . . . Trujillo's Embassy in Guatemala! For a moment I really thought that he was going to put me in jail; but the magic of an American passport was then working wonders in Guatemala!

Serious incidents occurred during the May Day, 1956, celebration in Guatemala City. The workers took advantage of the parade and mass meeting to show their dissatisfaction with the labor policies of the Castillo Armas Government. ORIT asked me to make another hurried visit to Guatemala with the view of bringing the deteriorating situation to the attention of the President himself and urge him to take some remedial steps before it was too late. In my interview with President Castillo Armas, to which I went accompanied by labor leaders Mario Mencos and Felipe Balcárcel, the President conceded that many of the amendments to the Labor Code could actually make difficult, if not impossible, the normal development of democratic trade unionism. He therefore agreed to appoint one of his legal advisers, Dr. Ernesto Zamora, to work with the unions in order to prepare a draft of a final, all-inclusive revision of the Labor Code to be submitted to Congress with a Presidential message urging its adoption.

The study was initiated, time passed, in 1957 Castillo Armas was assassinated, Guatemala went through another period of turmoil, then came the Presidency of Ydigoras Fuentes, more meetings, more interviews, more promises, a little relaxation here and there, but nothing substantial really happened. The major difficulty was, in my opinion, the fact that the Guatemalan employers, including some from the United States, influential newspapers, top government advisers, government officials stationed in the outlying districts, and some members of the Cabinet itself had failed to realize the absolute need of a free, independent, strong, democratic labor movement as an essential prerequisite for the reconstruction of a democratic society. The vigilance against the return of Communist trade union leadership was commendable and worthy of support; but what good was this vigilance exercised by political and judicial authorities, if on the other hand the government was feeding the Communist underground with an ever increasing stream of issues as a result of the curtailment of trade union rights and the whittling down of the Labor Code? And how could anyone in his right mind hope to defeat the Communists' renewed underground agitation as long as Guatemalan labor courts continued to side openly with management, allowed violations of law to go unpunished, and ignored the persecution of peasants by farm owners?

The answer to these agonizing questions was finally given by Colonel Enrique Peralta Azurdia, the last Guatemalan President with whom I discussed these problems at length, in 1964. He was moving in the right direction and by the time his successor, Dr. Julio Cesar Montenegro, took office in 1966, labor had regained hope and was looking to the future with renewed confidence. But it was still really too soon to tell.

El Salvador

Years ago, in the early thirties, El Salvador was the testing ground of Communist revolutionary propaganda and experiments. It cost dearly in the number of lives lost and property destroyed. I am referring to the revolt and the subsequent massacre of the Indian *peones* which took place under the administration of General Maximiliano Hernández Martínez. One day in 1956, while traveling with the leader of the Confederation of Labor of El Salvador, Rafael ("Chele") Fernández Saravia, along the road from the capital city of San Salvador to the port of Acajutla, on the Pacific Coast, I passed through a number of places and towns where the bloody massacre had taken place almost a quarter of a century before. I started talking with "Chele" about those days and asked him to tell me all he knew about those tragic events, the antecedents, and the consequences, not sparing any of the gruesome details. What came out was a story which is almost impossible to believe. As soon as I had a little time at my disposal I jotted down some notes, which I carefully preserved for ten years. In August 1966 "Chele" came to the United States to attend a labor training institute at Front Royal, Virginia. I compared those notes with him, explaining that I was thinking of using them for a story for this book. "Chele" volunteered to put them in order and to type them for me. He finished just before entering Washington's Doctors Hospital, where he died a few days later, on September 8, following an operation.

Rafael Fernández Saravia was a worker who had had little opportunity to go to school. He was a self-made man, like many other leaders of labor in Central America. The notes he gave back to me, typed in Spanish, lacked punctuation, grammar, and syntax—yet I found them one of the most moving documents on the sufferings, struggles, aspirations, and defeats of the poor Indian *peones* of El Salvador. In making the translation, I have tried to remain as close as possible to the construction of Saravia's original Spanish text. I wanted the story to be, also, a sort of tribute to his memory.

"Already at the turn of the century," wrote Saravia in his introductory background, "there were in El Salvador some manifestations of labor discontent, but it was not until 1924 that a Regional Federation of Workers was organized. It was under the leadership of known Communists and it became affiliated to the Red Trade Union International with headquarters in Moscow. At that time, the President of our country, Alfonso Quinones Molina, was mostly interested in persecuting his personal political enemies and did not bother to look into the labor situation at all. His successor, President Pío Romero Bosque, allowed the exercise of some political freedom, but he too showed no interest in labor-social problems. President Romero, however, permitted real free elections and the Communists took advantage to enter the presidential campaign by supporting the candidacy of Dr. Arturo Araujo, leader of the Labor Party, who won overwhelmingly on a firm pledge to put into effect an agrarian reform. President Araujo took the oath of office on March 1, 1930, but the second of December of the same year he was deposed by a military coup headed by the Vice-President of the Republic and Minister of War, General Maximiliano Hernández Martínez."

"How come that Martínez was the Vice-President of a Government headed by the leader of the Labor Party?" I asked. "Was he a progressive-minded general?"

"Not at all. He was a very calculating and ambitious man, thirsty for power. He had founded a small political party of his own, but at the last moment he managed to join forces with the Laborites and the price of the switch was the vice-presidency.

"The condition of the *campesino*," continued Saravia, "was at that time one of incredible poverty and exploitation. Just imagine, the Civil Code still permitted the punishment of *peones* who were disrespectful to their employer with up to twenty-five lashes. Their salary was 18 cents of colon (the Salvadorean monetary unit, worth 2½ to the U.S. dollar) for a day's work of from eight to ten hours—in all, 7 U.S. cents. I know that this may seem incredible, but I can prove it with documents.

To this salary, there was added their food which consisted of two tortillas (small pancakes made of cornmeal) and some beans *sancochados* (boiled in water and salt). Plates were not in existence. In order to get some juice with the beans, the *campesino* cupped the tortilla on his palm."

"And what else?"

"Just that—tortillas and beans, in the morning, at noon, and before going home. . . . Since I have mentioned home, let me explain that it consisted of a one room hut, called *rancho*, with the bare ground for floor, and the walls and ceiling made of palm leaves. One room for the whole family, sleeping on straw or Indian *tapexcos* (made of rustic tree branches), exposed to the mosquitoes which abound in our countryside, sooner or later falling sick of malaria. But to make things even worse, the *peones* were paid in scrip, which could only be redeemed at the *tiendas* (stores owned by the farm owners themselves), where there was no control over prices. The fact was that the *campesinos* never had a cent to their name."

"And how did the massacre start?"

"The *campesinos* had believed in the promise of an agrarian reform, which to them meant nothing of the newfangled things now associated with this expression. They expected a little more money, a little more food, and perhaps a more human treatment. But the government under Martínez forgot all about the promises made by the Labor Party during the 1930 campaign. Communist agitators, mainly coming from the University, roamed the countryside, inciting the illiterate masses to revolt. Some sporadic cases of violence occurred. A number of farm owners were attacked, a few killed. For three days the *campesinos* spread the revolt from the western plain to the eastern valleys. That was in 1932. Then the Army intervened and the repression began.

"The first thing the Government did was to capture the known leaders of the revolt, those who were known as Communists, and execute them. They were Augustín Farabundo Martí, law student and son of a well-to-do family in Juayua; Mario Zapata, also a law student and schoolteacher; and another student named Luna. They were executed in a public square in San Salvador. For the next five days, all over the countryside, squads of soldiers shot down the *campesinos* on sight. More than 25,000 were killed in five days. Some said 30,000. The exact number was never known." [16]

We were approaching the hamlet of Guyagualo. There, Saravia related, the *campesinos* from the countryside used to get together on Sunday. On the Sunday of the massacre they were surrounded by troops and machine-gunned to death. Then we approached the hamlet of Ateos. "There too," Saravia added, "the government troops made another *carniceria* (carnage) ." Then we reached the town of Armenia.

"In this town," Saravia resumed, "five hundred *campesinos* were executed. By express order of the dictator, the bodies were left exposed in the open so that the people left alive could see and 'learn the lesson.' This macabre exposition lasted for eight days. Armed guards did not permit the relatives of the victims to get closer than 50 yards. The guards were lined up along the edge of the road. Way in the back there were another type of guards that prevented the people from getting close to the victims—the vultures. After satiating themselves, the vultures would remain over the human carcasses, with their wings spread to the sun, waiting to be hungry again. And the people passing by were watching with horror this horrible spectacle and were crying. That was the only thing they could do. Just cry . . . !"

After a while, during which "Chele" drove the union's station wagon in silence, and I tried to regain my composure, we reached the city of Izalco. There, too, hundreds of *campesinos* died during the massacre. As we entered the square, Saravia resumed:

"Do you see that ornamental tree, in the center? The local leader of the *campesinos,* Feliciano Ama, was hanged from that tree. The officers who commanded the troops crowded around the dead body, still hanging, some pulling his hair, others pulling his legs. While doing that, laughing, a picture was taken, as a sort of a trophy, as hunters do with their bag of game.

"I told you, at the beginning, that in some places the *campesinos* committed acts of atrocity against the owners of the *fincas.* But the repression was so brutal and so extensive that entire zones where no *campesino* violence had taken place were also affected. In some cases, whole *caserios* (hamlets) were put to the torch during the night, and the poor peasants who tried to escape the flames were shot down like savage animals. Some isolated ranchos, too, were set on fire, with whole families perishing inside, their bodies charred."

Saravia also wrote a post-scriptum to the story. "Today, after thirty-four years, there still are, as mute witnesses to the massacre, the mass graves of the victims, dug deep into the blooded land. Coffee has been planted over the graves, and the land is now rich and the harvest is very good. Human bodies make good fertilizer. . . ."

The life of the *campesino,* in El Salvador, although it still leaves much to be desired, has vastly improved. Scrip has been outlawed; all the *campesinos* must now be paid in currency. The working day has been fixed at eight hours, with a compulsory day of rest every week; and the minimum wage has been set at 2 colones a day, equivalent to 80 cents of the dollar. The food has been improved, and when the owner cannot provide it for some valid reason, he must compensate the worker in cash. Of course, the *peones* still do not have the right to form unions, but there are labor tribunals to take up their grievances and complaints. The situation has greatly improved, no question about that.

The labor situation in El Salvador began to change for the better with the December 14, 1948, revolution which brought to power a junta composed of young military officers and civilian professionals. They set their mind and enthusiasm to remake El Salvador into a modern, developing country, with constitutional guarantees for all the citizens, freedom of press, religion, and assembly, vastly improved education, and a favorable climate for the investment of domestic and foreign capital. The process, although not yet fully completed, is way ahead of other Central American countries. And it has continued, uninterrupted, for almost twenty years since the 1948 revolution. One member of the military-civic junta, who actually dominated it through the strength of his popularity and the magnetism of his personality, was Major Oscar Osorio. On December 14, 1950, Osorio became Constitutional President of El Salvador.

As late as 1950 the Communists had almost complete control of the unions in that small republic. At the beginning of its term, the Osorio government thought it could fight the Communists by indiscriminate use of police power, and by labeling as Communist anyone who was fighting for the improvement of the working class. The present General Secretary of ORIT, Arturo Jáuregui, was once deported from El Salvador, in the middle of the night, as a dangerous "Communist."

However, the government of El Salvador soon changed tactics. I was privileged with an invitation to discuss with President Osorio himself the "best way to fight Communism and build up a genuine democratic labor movement." Intelligent cooperation was also given by Minister of Labor Héctor Salazar, and by the then Undersecretary of Labor, later Private Secretary to the President, and finally Minister of Labor himself, Dr. Fernando Basilio Castellanos.

The dialogue with the President and his collaborators continued for a number of years; difficulties had to be straightened out; misunderstandings had to be cleared up; and above all, a democratic leadership had to be developed, because the Communists were numerous, able, and strong, and to defeat them—and defeated they eventually were—equally dedicated and able democratic leaders were needed. But the problem was not solely one of organization—social measures on the part of the government itself were required, and to get them the other sector of the population, in addition to the workers, had to be convinced.

I made a light survey of the conditions prevailing among agricultural and rural workers, which I often used as a basis for my recommendations. In the early fifties, although 63 percent of the population of El Salvador was rural, the peasants and agricultural workers were excluded, along with domestic servants, from the protection of the country's social legislation. No fewer than 230,000 agricultural laborers were engaged during the coffee harvesting season—two to five months—and when their work was done, they were left without employment and without income. During the "season" their wages varied from one colon to a colon and a half a day.

The government undertook the construction of houses for the workers, who could purchase them over long periods of time. However, housing remained a tremendous social problem, which continued to face the country for many more years, up to the present time. The problem of rural housing was of growing seriousness, since agricultural laborers did not remain in one place for long, and could not permanently acquire a house.

Illiteracy and drunkenness were widespread. About 57 percent of the urban population could not read and write, and about 64 percent of the inhabitants of rural areas were also illiterate. Drunkenness was used by employers as a pretext to refuse wage increases, whereas in fact the peasants took to drink because of their precarious economic situation. Today, with economic conditions improved and illiteracy reduced, drunkenness among the rural population has taken a downward plunge.

The conditions of the urban workers varied from place to place. Those in the Monte Cristo mine, located some 156 kilometers from the capital city, for instance, were distressing. Though the workers had a union, it had not been able to help them to any great degree. The workers earned only 80 cents (U.S.) per day. There were no sanitary services nor bathing facilities available to them. The firm did not provide either housing for the workers, or company stores where the workers could buy their minimum needs at cost prices. There were no recreation facilities and there was only one small medical dispensary available for their use, which was open for only two hours a day, when there was a nurse on duty.

Another mine which I had the opportunity to visit together with Paul K. Reed of the United Mine Workers—El Divisadero, in the eastern part of the country—filled me with a feeling of helplessness. It was a gold mine, but its methods of operation were so antiquated that we could not see how any profit could be made, even less if wages were raised. We found out that a number of workers could no longer work because they were suffering from silicosis or tuberculosis. The company was giving a small subsidy to those who were ill and no longer able to work, but it was so pitiful that it was not sufficient to buy the minimum amount of food to spare them the pangs of hunger. So physical weakness increased and with it more illness, more tuberculosis. Some workers insisted on telling us, in all seriousness, that even the dogs had gotten tuberculosis.

In 1952, after having finally succeeded in defeating the Communists in the key unions of the country, Saravia became General Secretary of the General Confederation of Trade Unions (CGS). By then other capable leaders had emerged in the cities and in the countryside. With the tacit approval of the government, organizing campaigns were initiated, especially in those places of employment where conditions had remained unchanged for many years. One such place was a match factory in Santa Tecla, where the company refused to discuss wage conditions in spite of the fact that they had remained unchanged for almost twenty years. A strike was called.

I happened to arrive in El Salvador when the strike had progressed for over five weeks without any prospect of settlement. I was told by Saravia that the number of workers involved was less than 100. The majority received an average wage of 60 to 70 cents (U.S.) a day. Piece-work rates for filling match cartons were still the same as twenty years before, while the selling price of the cartons had gone up 450 percent. At the union's request, I went that evening to Santa Tecla to address the strikers.

The meeting hall was poorly lit, there was no furniture, save for a table and a couple of chairs for the speakers. The strikers, men and women, stood around us, barefooted all of them, with their clothes in tatters, their faces emaciated. I just could not speak to them in the usual way. I simply asked them how long they could continue to resist. "We are hungry," they replied. "If we could only have some corn and beans, for ourselves and our families, then we could stay out indefinitely. . . ."

I made a mental calculation, and then solemnly announced that the union brothers from the United States had sent me down to give them $100 and to assure them that there would always be money to buy corn and beans as long as the strike continued. I had not finished when they, recovering from the unexpected announcement and realizing what it actually meant, rushed to embrace me, shouting *"Viva los Americanos,*

Viva AA-EFFE-ELLE!" The following day, my pledge was ratified in a statement to the press. Within twenty-four hours, the employers got together with the union, granted a wage increase, signed a collective agreement, and called for a workers-employers celebration at which I was the honored guest. Of course, I had actually given the strike committee $100, gambling on the AFL Secretary-Treasurer's understanding to reimburse me (which he did), but as to the rest, I had bluffed, counting on the psychological impact on the employers. At any rate, that is how a strike was won with $100!

During one of my interviews with President Osorio, exactly the morning of November 4, 1954, I heard martial music from the outside, something like a military band. The President told me that the new Ambassador from the United States was being escorted to the Presidential Palace to present his credentials. I made a move to leave, so as not to interfere; but President Osorio motioned me to stay. Minutes later, we heard footsteps from the antechamber, and then the Chief of Protocol entered to inform the President that the party was waiting outside. I again made a move to exit by a side door, but President Osorio took me gently by the arm and led me through the main door into the reception room where I faced Ambassador Robert C. Hill.

"What are you doing here, Serafino?" asked Bob as we greeted each other. But before I could answer, President Osorio said with a smile:

"The Ambassador of the workers and the Ambassador of the government—both at the same time. *Que bueno!"*

Honduras

Until the spring of 1954, Honduras was the only remaining country in the Western Hemisphere without unions, without a labor code, without minimum-wage legislation, without even a compulsory weekly day of rest. But in the brief space of a few months the panorama changed radically. On May 3, 1958, the banana workers employed on the vast plantations on the north coast of Honduras owned by the United Fruit Company went on strike for better wages and working conditions. The government and the company were not prepared to cope with the emergency and it took a long time before some concrete steps were taken to end the strike. Finally, on July 9 an agreement was signed, calling for an increased daily minimum wage, vacations with pay, and other fringe benefits, as well as a tacit recognition of the union subject to the enactment of ad hoc legislation by the Honduras government. The labor organizations in the United States, particularly the American Federation of Labor, played a considerable part in bringing about the strike settlement.[17]

The successful conclusion of the strike on the United Fruit Company's plantations sparked a wave of union organization which spread to the Standard Fruit Company's banana farms in La Ceiba and to a number of manufacturing plants in San Pedro Sula and Tegucigalpa. Never before had so many thousands of workers in such a short period rushed to join the unions. It reminded me of the NIRA times in 1933–1934 in our own United States.[18] However, this sudden spurt of trade unionism in Honduras posed a problem of leadership. The Communist elements and their fellow travelers, aided and supported from nearby Guatemala, where, when the Honduras strike started, the Communists were still in control, had managed at the beginning to influence the strike committee, but were later ejected by a strong anti-Communist group which succeeded in establishing firm control. A combination of local and international factors, including the Communist defeat in Guatemala at the end of June, contributed to the Communist failure. But it was to be expected, as I wrote in the January 1955 issue of *The American Federationist*, that they would soon renew their attempts to bore from within and to attack from without—which they did, especially in 1956, but with limited transitory success.

Following the strike settlement, the United Fruit Company adopted a policy of dealing on a permanent basis with bona-fide organized labor. An expert, Alfredo Giardino, who now heads the New York City Board of Education, was hired, according to a statement of the Company's President himself, "primarily to set up a modern system of labor relations and to teach the Company's personnel how to deal and live with the union." On the other hand, the ORIT sent one of its seasoned organizers, Augusto Malavé Villalba, to help advise the labor movement in Honduras. Malavé spent most of his time with the United Fruit Company's union, on the North Coast, where he did a remarkable job. But it was obvious that while it would take time until the employers, and particularly their subordinate supervisors, learned how to deal with the union and forget the old system of arbitrary decisions "which were to be accepted in silence, or else, . . ." it would also take time for union representatives to learn how to operate effectively without losing patience and becoming unduly discouraged. Democratic responsible labor leadership could not be improvised overnight, yet there was in Honduras a very promising element, which with a little more training could give a good account of itself. In this connection, the United States Embassy in Honduras lent its full cooperation by arranging with the Foreign Operations Administration in Washington the setting up of a special labor training course at the University of Puerto Rico for a group of twelve young Honduras trade unionists. After three months in Puerto Rico and two in the United States, the group returned home in June 1955. With a better understanding of the role of organized labor and the added training and experience acquired abroad, these young leaders provided an effective and efficient leadership in their respective unions.

A serious political crisis developed in Honduras early in 1956. The President of the republic, Julio Lozano, had pledged free elections, but a group around him, headed by Minister of Labor Dr. Mariano Guevara, was pressing for Lozano's continuation in office. A good section of the military was in that group, and so were the Communists, who were playing their traditional game of allying themselves with the reactionary forces in the hope of getting a free hand in the labor movement. All the forces around Guevara had one main preoccupation and objective in mind—to deny the Presidency to the Liberal Party leader, Dr. Ramón Villeda Morales. He was very popular, especially among the organized workers on the North Coast, who regarded him as a reformer; but for this reason he was opposed by the landowners and the reactionary business interests who regarded him as a "Communist."

To weaken the strong hold of the Liberal Party over the newly organized masses, the government first resorted to political bribery by offering a number of labor leaders a place in the government-sponsored list of candidates for the constitutional convention, scheduled for the fall of that year; but when these leaders refused, they were arrested, in La Ceiba and La Lima (headquarters of the Standard Fruit and United Fruit Companies, respectively). This took place during the month of February.

Alarmed by the prospect that a wave of government persecution might wipe out the still young and inexperienced unions in Honduras, Arturo Jáuregui (then ORIT Acting General Secretary) and I went to Honduras during the month of April 1956 to see what the real situation was and to offer our services for the establishment of a *modus vivendi* that would save the unions' integrity and independence.

We were surprised to learn how deep was the resentment of the rank and file against the labor policy of the government, particularly the tactics used by Minister of Labor Guevara, in causing the arrest of those leaders who, for one reason or another, did not agree with him politically.

In our conversations with the leaders of SITRATERCO (Union of

Workers and Employees of the Tela Railroad Company—the corporate name of the United Fruit Company in Honduras) we learned that the arrest of the union leaders during the second half of February and their detention for more than one week had caused widespread discouragement among the rank and file. Continuous government propaganda accusing the union leaders of being "Communistic" and the persecution on the part of the police aggravated the situation. The presence of the troops in the whole banana zone made the union activity increasingly difficult.

On the morning of April 20 we met with the management of the United Fruit Company in the presence of members of the union's Executive Board. The conversation was confined to general terms, but it was instructive because it revealed that the main cause of the difficulty between the company and the union seemed to be confined to a series of irritating incidents partly due to abusive language on the part of union representatives and partly to arbitrary, vindictive actions on the part of the field supervisors.

During my stay in the North Coast banana zone, I gathered considerable evidence of renewed Communist activity and of the readiness on the part of the Communists to cooperate politically with the government at the price of getting a free hand in the unions. Unfortunately, the Minister of Labor seemed to have fallen for such a trick. Therefore, I found it advisable to collect documents and testimony on this apparent collaboration between the Communists and the Minister of Labor and to present them to the President and to the United States Ambassador when I would meet with them.

At the meeting with President Julio Lozano, which took place on Saturday morning, April 21, I spoke to him freely about what I considered grievous mistakes on the part of the government. I criticized it, first, for having arrested the union leaders on flimsy pretext, and, second, for having described them as Communists while at the same time protecting the true Communists just because they had made a political deal to support the government candidates. I told him, also, that the ORIT and the unions from the United States could not maintain indefinite silence about this situation. I repeated, however, that we were ready, as in the past, to mediate a sort of compromise that would make possible the resumption of normal relations between the government of Honduras and the banana unions of the North Coast.

The President acceded to my suggestion and agreed to invite the union leaders for a conference. For a while the situation improved considerably, but then, on July 9, 1956, Dr. Villeda Morales and most of the leaders of the Liberal Party were forcibly expelled from the country and deported to Costa Rica. Hundreds of active trade unionists were arrested. Many sought asylum in the embassies of Costa Rica, Mexico, and Argentina. From Costa Rica, Dr. Villeda Morales came to the United States.

The Liberals were not allowed to contest the 1956 presidential elections, and the result was the "overwhelming" victory of President Lozano. But shortly after, a bloodless coup removed him and a military junta was installed. The Liberals were allowed to return and to resume political activity. Villeda Morales was appointed Ambassador to the United States, where he remained until August 1957, when he resigned to return to his country to take part in the political campaign as presidential candidate. The elections held September 22, 1957, were free. The Liberals won and Dr. Villeda Morales assumed the presidency.

I had established a very cordial personal relationship with Dr. Villeda Morales. Upon assuming the presidency he asked me to visit Tegucigalpa to give him some advice on labor relations policy. During his administration the democratic elements in the labor movement were left free. The employers, domestic and foreign, were told by the President, in no uncertain terms, that the law would be applied to protect the unions in the fulfillment of their legitimate activities. Likewise, he told the union leaders that the law would be equally applied to protect management in its rights and prerogatives, and that the government would not tolerate any activity unfairly directed against foreign companies. Honduras's economy depended on their investments and President Villeda Morales was determined, if possible, to increase them.

Relations between organized labor and the employers had reached a stage of mutual respect, but there was no social contact between them. Of this I became well aware on the occasion of the inauguration of the new headquarters of SITRATERCO (built by the union on land donated by the company), which took place on March 27, 1959. President Morales was the main speaker at the inaugural ceremony. Other speakers included representatives of organized labor from Honduras and other countries, and an officer of the United Fruit Company. Afterwards the President asked me to accompany him to a buffet luncheon at the house of retired Colonel López, who was a company official. I pointed out that I would rather stay with the union leaders unless they, too, had been invited. They had not been, but the invitation came forthwith. The union leaders, however, were reluctant to accept. They had never entered the home of a company official and felt that it would really be "a terrible thing to do." But finally they relented; "This is after all our *fiesta*," they said, "and our President is asking us to go along. . . ." And so, for the first time, Honduras trade unionists joined a social affair in the house of an employer. Timid at first, then relaxed, they had two or three drinks, ate a delicious *lechón asado* (barbecued pig) and other native victuals, and then let go and did some real fraternizing. A lot of jolly good time was had by all!

The country that once starved for capable trade union leadership now has a surplus of them to the extent that Hondureños often lend a helping hand to the labor movement in nearby countries. One man who, in my judgment, typifies the best there is in them as to probity, capability, patriotism, and devotion to the cause, is Oscar Gale Varela. He was elected Secretary General of SITRATERCO in 1956, succeeding his friend, Celeo González, another respected democratic labor leader who became head of the North Coast Labor Federation (FESITRANH) of which SITRATERCO is a part. The two still work closely together.

Under Oscar Gale and Celeo González, tremendous advances have been made in labor-management relations, not only in the banana plantations but all over the growing industrial zone of the North Coast. Since SITRATERCO was formed, five collective agreements have been negotiated without a work stoppage. The last two came after direct negotiations without the need of any outside mediation.

A company carpenter in 1954 when the general strike occurred, Oscar Gale first battled the Communists, who had initially taken hold of the strike, and then helped drive them out and form the new anti-Communist union. Well aware of what Oscar Gale's success can do to their cause, the Communists have done their best to bring about his downfall. They failed, as Oscar responded to their attempts with a minimum of demagoguery and a maximum of hard work. "The best way to combat Communism," believes Gale, "is to work hard. Communists come and offer everything but do not deliver. But this leadership of the union delivers." [19]

A man with limited formal education but vast native intelligence, Oscar Gale is known and respected throughout Central America. Under his leadership, SITRATERCO has gained a reputation as one of the best-run and most responsible labor organizations in Central America. The officers of the United Fruit Company would be the first to concede that. And because of Oscar Gale's leadership SITRATERCO was the first union in Latin America to receive a direct loan from the Agency for International Development (AID) without it being first filtered down through a government. A $400,000 AID loan, approved in 1963, was used for the construction of two housing projects, totaling 187 units, in the company headquarters town of La Lima and in the coastal city of Tela.

In 1967, Oscar Gale in cooperation with Celeo Gonzalez, President of the North Coast Workers Federation of Honduras (FESITRAHN), arranged a loan for $2,270,000 from the Inter-American Development Bank for the construction of approximately 1,000 low-cost workers' houses in a suburb of San Pedro Sula. This loan to the federation was the first loan made directly to a trade union organization by the IDB. The project, which is being carried out with AIFLD technical assistance, has the support of local businessmen and the Chamber of Commerce of Cortés has agreed to finance the urbanization of the site. At a Central American labor institute held in San Salvador in 1964 Oscar Gale Valera was one of the speakers. This powerfully built man of forty-three, speaking calmly but in direct terms, with no pretense at oratorical flourish (a trait perhaps inherited from his grandfather, an American engineer who settled in Honduras), was relating how in 1958, following the devastation of a hurricane and the spread of a banana disease, he felt that the company was in real trouble. "Perhaps the company's threat of eventually being forced to leave Honduras was not an empty one," said Oscar Gale. "In that year the labor agreement was to be renewed. My members expected an increase in wages, which they deservd and was badly needed. But I felt that of more importance to them and to the country was to protect their jobs, to help the company remain in Honduras. And so I signed an agreement in which for the first time I had to give more than I could take. . . ."

Don "Pepe's" Costa Rica

The labor movement of Costa Rica was completely dominated by the Communists until the year 1944, when the Catholic Church promoted the organization of the Confederation of Labor "Rerum Novarum." Its founder and first President was Father Benjamin Núñez, who had studied sociology at the Catholic University in Washington.

The AFL established contact with the "Rerum Novarum" as early as May 1946, during the ILO Regional Conference in Mexico City. In 1947, Luis Alberto Monge became president of the "Rerum Novarum," and remained in this post until 1950 when he went to Geneva with the ILO.

It was in 1947 that I visited Costa Rica for the first time. On that occasion, the Communists distributed leaflets protesting my presence in that country and declared me *persona non grata*. However, I got an apology from President Teodoro Picado when I paid him a courtesy visit accompanied by Father Benjamin Núñez.

Costa Rica was then being conditioned for a popular front experiment. As successor to President Picado, a leftist coalition, of which the Communists were the prime movers, presented the candidacy of Dr. Rafael Calderón Guardia, chief of the National Republican Party, who had already served during the 1940–1944 term. He was opposed by newspaper publisher Otilio Ulate Blanco supported by a coalition of center forces and a group of young democratic, reform-minded intellectuals of whom an American trained engineer, José "Pepe" Figueres, was the spokesman. The "Rerum Novarum" trade unionists went along with them.

To give an example of how great was the dependence of Dr. Calderón Guardia on the Communists, I will cite the demonstration that took place on September 15, 1947, Costa Rica's Independence Day, sponsored by the Communist-controlled labor Confederation (CTCR) to observe the fourth anniversary of the promulgation of the Labor Code and the social security legislation. The meeting degenerated into a political rally during which the "Rerum Novarum" and the political parties opposed to the leftist coalition were violently attacked. During the entire demonstration Dr. Calderón Guardia shared the spotlight with Manuel Mora Valverde, founder and chief of the Communist Party of Costa Rica, then called Vanguardia Popular.

The election, held February 8, 1948, was a bitter one, but in the end Otilio Ulate won, his victory being attested by a majority of the National Election Board. However, Congress, which was under the control of Calderón's followers, nullified Ulate's victory. On March 12, from his farm named *La Lucha* ("The Struggle") José Figueres led a revolt in support of Ulate. After a month of civil war, President Picado and Dr. Calderón Guardia fled to Nicaragua and Dr. Santos León Herrera assumed power as temporary President. On April 28, Figueres and his troops entered San José, the capital of Costa Rica. On May 8, the Constitution was nullified and the "second republic" established. León Herrera retired in favor of a governing junta of which Figueres became the President.

A Constituent Assembly met on January 16, 1949, restored political liberties, drew up a new Constitution, and on November 8 of the same year retired in favor of an elected Legislative Assembly. Figueres and his revolutionary junta resigned, and President-elect Otilio Ulate was inaugurated.

Figueres's 1948 revolution, whose objective was not the conquest of power for the victorious rebels but to restore to the Presidency the man who had been freely elected by the people, represented the first instance in Latin America in which the forces defending freedom and political honesty had risen, arms in hand, to defeat a coalition of Communists and political opportunists who had stolen an election and were attempting to set up a dictatorship.

In 1953, José Figueres—who was already being referred to by friends and foes alike as "Don Pepe"—was elected to the Presidency by a two-thirds' majority of the voters. In his first public statement after the election Figueres pledged loyalty to democratic ideals, and friendship for the United States. He advocated continuation of the Technical Assistance Program and other measures that enable the United States to help develop in Latin America a healthy economy. But he warned against the continuation of privileges for big foreign corporations and said that these privileges would have to be taken away. He said, in fact, that certain private investments in Latin America were more dangerous than beneficial, and used for the first time the slogan, "No more economic occupation!"

From the moment he was inaugurated President on November 8, 1953, at a colorful ceremony in San José Stadium which I was privileged to attend, Figueres was under attack from the regime of Anastasio "Tacho" Somoza, the dictator of neighboring Nicaragua, and powerful economic interests opposed to his "socialistic" plans. The Communists, on their part, did their best inside Costa Rica to stir up discontent and to sabotage Figueres's administration. Meanwhile, across the border, in Nicaragua, Figueres's internal enemies, organized by the Picado—Calderón Guardia combine, were preparing an armed invasion.

On the morning of January 11, 1955, the invaders struck. They crossed the border, occupied a number of lightly guarded frontier posts, and started marching toward San José. The Figueres regime was in real danger, but it was saved by the prompt intervention of the Organization of American States (which authorized the United States government to furnish Costa Rica adequate military aircraft to stop the invaders) and the spontaneous solidarity of the democratic and labor forces in the United States and all over Latin America.[20]

From the day I first met him, in February 1949 when he was President of the Provisional Junta, I have cultivated with "Don Pepe" a mutual friendship which has extended to our respective families. We have visited with each other in San José and in Washington; we have taken part together in a number of international conferences and seminars; we have exchanged countless letters on political matters and inter-American policy. In every major activity in which I was involved since 1949, I have had the cooperation and support of "Don Pepe." I have come to like him very much, to respect his views, to admire his courage and intellectual honesty. Of course, "Don Pepe" has his own way of saying and doing things, his own style; and I did not always subscribe *in toto* to all his views and proposals.

My observation of the man has led me to believe that Figueres gets deeply immersed in whatever he is saying or doing. He wants to be thorough, precise, exact; every angle has to be explored, nothing can be left out. Thus, faithful to his style, at a plenary session of the 1950 Havana Conference of the Inter-American Association for Democracy and Freedom (see Chapter XXV), Figueres spoke for many hours, so much that at one o'clock in the morning the session was recessed for a half hour so that the delegates could stretch their legs and obtain some nourishment. But all went back when "Don Pepe" resumed, so interesting and truly fascinating were his historical excursions, his philosophical asides, his pointed barbs, and his deeply felt vision of how truly great Latin America could be if the forces of darkness were vanquished by the concerted efforts of the freedom-loving members of the American family of nations.

Figueres was—and I believe he still is—a convinced believer in collective intervention for the preservation of human rights and freedom. While we were both taking part in the Sixteenth American Assembly devoted to Inter-American Relations, held in October 1959,[21] Figueres advocated a policy of intervention to support democratic regimes threatened by totalitarian forces. "If government is ignorant, corrupt, and illegitimate, your first duty is to change it," he said. And then he added: "As a friend of the United States, I would rather see you accused of doing something, if it be a noble something, than accused of doing nothing." [22]

"Don Pepe's" preoccupation and intense identification with the political and economic problems of Latin America, especially since he left the presidency in 1958, gave him the *de facto* role of spokesman for Latin America. At any rate, at times he acted as though he were the duly chosen and anointed one. But to "Don Pepe" being the spokesman never meant voicing the views of the majority. On many occasions, he was a minority of one, as when he refused to attend, in 1954, the Inter-American Conference in Caracas, Venezuela, because that country was then ruled by one of the most brutal dictatorships ever to appear in the Western Hemisphere. "But what counts is the truth," he would say "and the truth is not decided by a majority of one."

In a letter to Senator George Smathers of Florida, written June 27,

1956, in comment on Senator Smathers' proposed amendment to the foreign aid bill in which he recommended that a special fund up to $100 million be established to help the economic development of Latin America, President Figueres stressed the concept of "parity" level for international prices.

It must not be forgotten that Latin America's first economic need is the stabilization of prices, at fair levels, for its exports; that is, adequate compensation for the work of its people and for the use of its natural resources.

Internally, in the United States, the struggle of the farmer for "parity" prices—whatever the mistakes incurred and the comparatively small waste provoked—has brought about an even distribution of the national income, and has benefited the urban population by enlarging the rural market for industrial and cultural products.

Latin America is today "the farmer" of the hemisphere. We live on our exports of primary articles to the industrial nations, and we consume their products, only to the extent that our income permits. By allowing our prices to be low—by buying cheap—the whole hemispheric economy has been hindered in its growth.

The ideal "parity" level for international prices—which is still distant, despite the advances of the last fifteen years—would be one that would afford the same economic and educational standards for the different peoples engaged in international trade.

Now that I have given my impressions of "Don Pepe" as a thinker, fighter, statesman, and self-appointed conscience of the Americas, one may want to ask: What kind of man is he? And my answer would be: José Figueres is a Spartan who has never learned the joy of relaxation the way I understand relaxation should be. The prospect of a good dinner does not excite him a bit; and if you offer him a drink he is apt to say "Yes, give me a glass of milk"!

INCAE

One interesting and successful experiment in training business and industrial managers for the complex responsibilities of the modern industrial society in the developing countries is the Instituto Centro-Americano de Administración de Empresas—Central American Institute for Management Training (INCAE), a Research Project of the Harvard Business School, launched in 1962 under the guidance of George Lodge, former U.S. Assistant Secretary of Labor for International Affairs. INCAE, which now has its own permanent school and administrative headquarters in

Managua, Nicaragua, started its activities by holding resident seminars in different localities. Since one of the objectives of INCAE is to stimulate on the part of management the study and understanding of the role that constructive trade unionism can perform in a democratic society, George Lodge adopted from the beginning the policy of inviting visiting labor lecturers to address the INCAE seminars. I was selected to speak at the seminars held in 1964 at the University of San Carlos, in Antigua, Guatemala, and in 1965 at the mountain resort El Boquete, near the town of David, in Panama. In both instances my lectures provoked a genuine interest on the part of the participants, mostly young unversity-educated owners of family enterprises or managers of larger concerns.

I incorporated in my INCAE lectures the concepts which I advanced for the first time in my address before the United States Inter-American Council, in Philadelphia, December 10, 1959, and which I have found extremely effective on numerous subsequent occasions in creating among the employers the psychological and mental preconditions for the establishment of a permanent dialogue with the representatives of democratic labor.

A "dynamic approach," I said in those lectures, can save Latin America for democracy—the democracy of the free people, the democracy of free labor and free enterprise. The Communist movement, in all its ramifications, aims to control unions so as to destroy free enterprise.

A characteristic of the propaganda employed by the Communists in order to win the support of the masses is the widespread use of demagogic promises, which in most cases cannot be fulfilled without endangering the economy of the country. The Communists create in the minds of the lowest sectors of the working class, devoid of civic consciousness and social culture, the belief that the quick and revolutionary action of the masses can solve all economic problems. They preach against the slow but steady cooperative effort on the part of capital and labor, through constructive trade union action, which will in the end benefit the workers and the people in general. The tragic effects of the demagogic policies of the Communists will eventually expose the fallacies of their program and open the eyes of their blind followers. But do we always have the time to wait for the awakening of the people? And will the Communists, once they seize power, give the freedom-loving people a chance to come back?

Management is not doing enough, or perhaps is doing it in the wrong way—I usually added—to demonstrate that democracy is superior to Communism. Perhaps capital needs to undergo a reexamination of its relation to society and its objectives.

In my conclusion I urged management to attach to the profit motive the function of helping people "attain a higher standard of life, morally and economically, socially and politically. Give to your capital a social dynamism," I said in ending my INCAE lectures, "give it a mission; the mission to help make the world safe for the democratic way of life—the life as we understand it, where man can exist in freedom and plenty, in dignity and peace."

Notes

1. Taking part in the discussion were, in addition to the author, Brantz Mayor, managerial expert with the International Basic Economic Corporation and formerly with *Time and Life International;* Igor Gordevitch, editor in chief of *Visión* magazine; Professor Stanley J. Stein, History Department, Princeton University, and Professor Lloyd Reynolds, of the Yale Economics Department, who moderated the panel.

2. This was a paraphrase of the motto "Bread and Roses—*Ex Pane Rosae"* of the Italian Dressmakers' Union, Local 89, ILGWU, which the author served for a while as director of its educational radio program. It was coined by Local 89's founder and leader, Luigi Antonini, to signify man's striving for the material and the spiritual. Its inspiration came from poet Arturo Giovanitti's epigraph: *"Se hai due pani, vendine uno e comprane un fiore, poiché anche l'anima ha fame—*If you have two loaves of bread, sell one and buy a flower, because the soul too is hungry."

3. In his book *Organized Labor in Latin America,* Professor Robert J. Alexander has included a detailed account of the origins and history of the trade union movement in each country of Central America.

4. Exclusive of mere shaking of hands on the receiving line at formal or informal receptions, the author has had personal dealings, interviews or correspondence, with a total of fifty-seven Presidents or Chiefs of State, divided as follows: Cuba, 2; Haiti, 1; Dominican Republic, 2; Jamaica, 2; Guyana, 2; Barbados, 2; Mexico, 1; Guatemala, 3; British Honduras, 1; San Salvador, 3; Honduras, 3; Nicaragua 2; Costa Rica, 4; Panama, 2; Colombia, 3; Venezuela, 2; Ecuador, 4; Peru, 1; Bolivia, 2; Chile, 2; Argentina, 3; Uruguay, 3; Brazil, 2; Italy, 3; United States, 2.

5. At the time of this writing, no date had yet been set for British Honduras's independence. It was predicted, however, that it would probably take place in the latter part of 1967 or early 1968.

6. The People's Progressive Party of British Guiana, under the leadership of Dr. Cheddy Jagan, won the general elections in the spring of 1953 and formed the Government. Later in the same year, the British accused Dr. Jagan of leading the country towards a Communist totalitarian dictatorship, dissolved his government, and suspended the Constitution. (See Chapter XX)

7. In 1953, Guatemala was governed by a pro-Communist regime headed by President Jacobo Arbenz. It was overthrown in 1954. Guatemela, regardless of its type of government, claims that British Honduras (Belize) is part of its national territory.

8. George Price, leader of British Honduras's People's United Party, was also, at that time, President of the General Workers' Union.

9. Following the publication in the British newspapers of the articles on British Honduras, the Associated Press sent to Belize its correspondent Paul Sanders. In a dispatch describing the conditions he found in that British colony, Sanders wrote in part the following:

The economic and social structure is a capsule of trouble but the Jesuit priests from North America who make up most of the colony's clergy see little or no evidence of Communist influence.

A campaign for independence is being carried on by the People's United Party (PUP). This party is so noisy and demands so many reforms that some of the elements loyal to Britain accuse it of coming under Communist influence. But they find it difficult to back up the charges.

10. George Price, leader of the PUP, replied to the Steele charges with a letter which was published in the Belize *Billboard* of November 16. It is interesting to note the line of defense of this supposed Communist or dupe of the Communists. He wrote:

The PUP's statement of policy contains a resolution condemning Communism, Colonialism, Fascism, and all other undemocratic systems of government.

The PUP is probably the only political party in the world which begins and ends its public and private meetings with oral prayers.

The colonial conditions which would ordinarily cause Communism do exist in this country, but the threat of Communism does not exist here because the Christian leaders of the PUP came to rally the masses and give them a practical solution to their economic, social, and political problems before any Communists could appear and win the people's misguided confidence.

11. The full text of the remaining paragraphs of President Meany's statement read as follows:

We express the fervent hope that the new Provisional Government will restore as quickly as possible absolute respect for civil liberties and human rights and will preserve the social gains codified in the Guatemalan labor and agrarian legislation enacted as a result of the democratic revolution of 1944.

The leaders of the National Union of Free Workers of Guatemala, who were forced into exile by the regime of deposed President Arbenz, at the instigation of the Communists who had seized control of organized labor, are now returning to their country determined to rebuild the labor movement on a firm basis of independence from Government or political party control. The American Federation of Labor, which has extended moral solidarity to the Guatemalan free trade union leaders during their exile, stands ready to assist them in this difficult task or reorganization, directly and through the medium of the Inter-American Regional Organization of Workers (ORIT) with which it is affiliated.

We urge the Government of the United States to exercise all the influence and pressure in its power to strengthen the democratic forces of Guatemala, now emerging from a long period of suppression and persecution, so that they may successfully resist any attempt on the part of reactionary, pro-Fascist forces to turn the clock back to the pre-1944 feudalistic dictatorship. It would be a calamity with serious repercussions throughout Latin America, if the overthrow of the first Communist-controlled regime in the Western Hemisphere were not to be followed by the establishment of a strong democratic regime that would bring Guatemala back into the family of truly democratic American nations.

12. The full text of President Meany's open letter to Guatemalan President Jacob Arbenz was published in the February 1954 issue of the *Inter-American Labor Bulletin*. The three specific instances of Communist influence in Guatemala cited by President Meany were thus described:

In the first place, it is shown by the way in which newspapers that are associated with the parties supporting your Administration take every possible opportunity to attack the United States, to accuse it unfairly of such monstrous crimes as germ warfare and generally to picture our country as a grasping and money-mad tyranny, while at the same time supporting such Communist moves as civil war in Indo-China and the fraudulent Communist peace campaigns.

The second way in which the Communist influence is demonstrated is in the affiliation of many of the leading figures in your Administration with the various international Communist drives and organizations. Bogus peace campaigns, Communist "youth" congresses, "cultural" gatherings and other Communist front organizations count among their members leading figures in the Government parties of Guatemala.

Thirdly, Communist influence is shown through official patronage to the Communist-dominated labor bodies and discouragement of attempts to organize bonafide democratic free trade unions. Recently, the latter was demonstrated in the arrest of the leaders of the Union Nacional de Trabajadores Libres. We are certain that were it not for the continuous Government support of the Communists' control of the organized labor movement, many workers' groups would be willing and anxious to break the shackles of Communist domination.

13. The author was told by Rómulo Betancourt that in 1946–1947, when he was President of Venezuela, Arévalo asked him twice whether he could deport to Venezuela twenty or so Communists who were creating trouble for his administration in Guatemala—a request that Betancourt declined on account of having his hands already full with his own Venezuelan Communists.

Dr. Samuel Guy Inman, specialist on Latin American Affairs, visited Guatemala for three weeks in June and July, 1950. Arévalo granted him an interview in the course of which, after denying his government's sympathies with Communism, he declared that, "The people and government of Guatemala recognize and understand their complete solidarity with the people and government of the United States. We hope, of course, that the situation in Korea will not lead to a new world conflagration; but if it should come, we have only one loyalty, and that is to the American Continent."—*Dr. Guy Inman's mimeographed press release,* July 18, 1950.

14. *The New Leader,* April 13, 1953: "Is Guatemala Communist?" by Daniel James.

15. The *Boletin del CEUAGE,* issued by the Committee of Guatemalan Anti-Communist University Students in Exile, No. 5, August 27, 1953, published a detailed account of the distribution in nine Departments of 28 machine guns, 1400 rifles, and a large assortment of pistols, supplying the names of the individual Communists who in each locality received the arms and giving also the names of the training camps where Communist militiamen were instructed in the use of the arms by a corps of instructors under the supervision of Guatemalan Colonel Carlos Aldana Sandoval. These arms had been obtained through Miroslav Pisov, an agent of the Skoda factory: Oswald Rehquate, Guatemalan representative; Colonel Julian, known as the "Black Eagle," of Harlem, arms salesman from the United States; and Czechoslovak citizen Frank Polasek, who was living in Guatemala.

16. After leaving the Presidency, Dictator Martínez spent the rest of his life in exile in Honduras. In 1966, at the age of eighty-four, he met violent death at the hands of his chauffeur, who stabbed him seventeen times. Years before his death, General Martínez was interviewed by a *Visión* magazine correspondent who asked him whether it was true that his troops killed 25,000 during the 1932 *campesino* revolt. "That was an exaggeration of the foreign press . . . only 15,000 died," replied the general. *Visión,* June 10, 1966, page 46.

17. Acting upon an urgent request from the anti-Communist leaders of the striking banana workers, President George Meany of the American Federation of Labor on June 22, 1954, sent a telegram to Mr. Joseph Montgomery, Executive Vice-President of the United Fruit Company, in San Pedro Sula, Honduras, in which he urged the company to reach an honorable settlement with the anti-Communist strike leadership

and grant them union recognition. "Failure to strengthen the position of those openly defending the cause of democracy and freedom," said President Meany in his telegram, "will play into the hands of Communist totalitarians with further disagreeable consequences in respect to our country's position in Latin America." Telegrams along the same lines were sent also by the presidents of the Congress of Industrial Organizations and the United Mine Workers of America.

Mr. Kenneth H. Redmond, President of the United Fruit Co., replied by telegram on June 25, saying in part: "I am pleased to state that from the outset of the problem in Honduras commencing May 3, we have continuously endeavored to resolve our differences with our employees through collective bargaining on a basis comparable to your suggestion and to this end we have consistently cooperated with the Honduran Government. Our earnest efforts to reach a mutually satisfactory settlement have been continuously frustrated by Communistic intrigue and influence in local areas. Negotiations are continuing and we believe prospects for settlement are brighter today than at any time."

Further delays, mainly caused by the refusal of the company to accept the terms suggested by the specially appointed Government Mediation Board, prolonged the strike for another two weeks. Alarmed over the economic and political consequences that would inevitably affect the position of the United States all over Latin America if the strike settlement was further postponed, AFL President George Meany renewed his demands for the United States government's indirect intervention and on July 8— the day before the strike was finally settled—sent to U.S. Ambassador Whiting Willauer in Tegucigalpa, Honduras, the following telegram:

> While appreciate fact that State Department cannot dictate to UFCO settlement of current Honduras strike nevertheless AFL is most concerned over protraction such conflict and over reports received from strike leaders that Company is unwilling to accept mediation proposals. Would appreciate hearing from you any additional information that may guide AFL planning further steps.

18. With the promulgation of the National Industrial Recovery Act (NIRA) in the first year of President Roosevelt's administration, the labor movement in the United States received a tremendous impetus, which, in less than two years, led to the addition of millions of workers to the ranks of the AFL.

19. Quoted from an article by Don Bohning in *The Miami Herald* of March 29, 1965.

20. Statements in support of the Costa Rican democratic government were issued by CIO President Walter Reuther, the United Mine Workers of America, and the AFL. A joint committee representing these three U.S. labor organizations watched the proceedings of the OAS and urged individual government representatives to that organization to vote prompt measures in support of the Figueres government. In addition, Matthew Woll, chairman of the AFL International Relations and Free Trade Union Committees, sent an appeal to the government of the United States in which he said:

> It is not enough to wait for the fruition of the laudable course pursued by the OAS. The AFL strongly urges our government to spare neither effort, nor energy, nor resources in enabling the progressive Republic of Costa Rica, where the free trade unions are a bulwark of its dynamic democracy and determined opposition to Communism and all other forms of dictatorship, to beat back all aggression, regardless of its source of instigation.

21. The American Assembly was founded by President Eisenhower when he was president of Columbia University as a means of bringing together leaders in various fields to compare opinions on questions of general importance. Its meetings are held in Arden House, Harriman, New York, which was donated to the Assembly in 1951 by former Governor W. Averell Harriman.

22. As quoted by Sam Pope Brewer in *The New York Times* of October 18, 1959.

XVII

From Getulio to Castello Branco

In 1946, following the end of the dictatorship of Getulio Vargas, the trade union movement of Brazil underwent a period of reorientation and reorganization. The labor situation there was unique because Brazil was the only Latin American country where the government had made a full-fledged attempt to organize the trade unions within the framework of a corporate state. This was done during the Vargas dictatorship (1930–1945), when much social legislation was enacted and put into practice. During the last few months of his government, in order to build among the workers a strong sentiment in favor of his continuance in office, Vargas accentuated this pro-labor policy and encouraged strikes and increases in wages. He also promoted the organization of a Labor Party, which was a mixture of his personal followers and labor leaders of the government-controlled unions. The birth of the Partido Trabalhista coincided with the reestablishment of political liberties and the recognition of the Communist Party as a legal organization.

The Communists lost no time in getting extremely busy in the government-controlled trade unions. Since they appeared to favor the continuation of Vargas in power, they got from him, if not actual encouragement, certainly unlimited freedom in executing their offensive in the labor field. When on October 29, 1945, Vargas was finally compelled to step aside, and the provisional government headed by the Supreme Court's President Linhares took control, complete freedom of labor organization was established. The Communists, with their cells in almost every industry, were ready to seize their opportunity and soon emerged as the controlling force in many important unions. Their Brazilian Communist leader, Luis Carlos Prestes, was released after nine years in jail, and the Reds polled over half a million votes to become the fourth largest party. The old government-appointed trade union leadership in many instances enjoyed very little popularity, and there were no forces to challenge the Communists.

The Linhares regime was of brief duration. The government of General Gaspar Dutra, which emerged from a fairly democratic and orderly election, soon reestablished as an emergency measure the old trade union law of the Vargas regime and froze all trade union administrations until a Constituent Assembly should enact a new labor code. However, although many attempts have since been made to amend the basic Vargas labor law, especially the clauses that regulate dues collection and the government's political-administrative control of the unions, no really substantial progress has been made up to the time of writing of this chapter.

As described by Professor Robert J. Alexander,[1] the Brazilian trade union structure and the method for settlement of labor-management conflicts were made part of the corporate state established in 1937 under the name of Estado Novo. The New State was generally regarded as a copy of Mussolini's Italy and Salazar's Portugal. Under the Brazilian system, the demands of the workers' unions are usually settled not by collective bargaining but by Brazil's unique labor courts. If the employers will not negotiate an increase in wages, the union presents a demand to the local labor court, which then hears both sides and decrees an increase which it thinks just.

The labor courts not only deal with annual wage demands, but also treat with those matters which in the United States are usually settled through union-management grievance procedures. When a worker thinks that he is being mistreated by his employer he will generally go to the labor court instead of to his union, or if he goes to the union he will do so only to obtain legal aid to present his case to the labor court. Since the law regulates with great minuteness the way in which an employer must treat his workers, the labor courts' decisions are usually made on the basis of some statute or legal regulation.

Another remnant of the Estado Novo is the extensive control which the government has over the workers' organizations. Each March every union in the country must submit to the Ministry of Labor a complete auditing of the money which it has received and spent during the preceding year. In addition, every June the unions must present to the Ministry a budget for the following year. If, during the course of the year, a union wishes to change this budget in any substantial manner, it must first obtain permission from the Ministry.

The supposed justification for this government control over the finances of the unions is the existence of the so-called *imposto sindical,* or trade union tax. This amounts to one day's pay a year which every worker must contribute, whether or not he belongs to the union of his trade or industry. Sixty percent of this tax goes to the local union in the workers' trade; 15 percent goes to the state or national federation of unions in that trade; 5 percent goes to one of the national labor confederations— industrial workers, commercial workers, land transport workers, etc.; 20 percent goes to the Social Trade Union Fund, administered by the Department of Labor under a tripartite supervision in which labor, government, and employers are represented. The Fund was supposed to be spent only for aiding those workers without union protection, or those unions that were financially weak. However, it was largely used for purely political purposes and was considered a sort of slush fund which the Minister of Labor used to strengthen his control over the trade unions. This social Trade Union Fund was abolished soon after the 1964 revolution but the other allotments of the tax continued.

The reestablishment of governmental control over the Brazilian unions decreed by the Dutra regime was motivated by the desire to halt the Communist sweep and freeze them in a minority position. But in July 1946, reporting on my first contacts with the unions of Rio de Janeiro and São Paulo, I wrote that ". . . the Communist threat is still real, and if the non-Communist elements do not change policy and methods the Communists may still win the battle for control of Brazilian labor." I was referring mainly to the prevalence of *peleguismo,* a typical Brazilian expression to describe the type of leadership appointed from above, supported by the proceeds of the *imposto sindical* and spending most of their time in their offices or the anterooms of the Ministry of Labor or its regional and state branches. These leaders never bothered to establish contact with the rank and file, but were always careful to follow the instructions of the government and the political directions of the Partido Trabalhista (Labor Party), to which at that time most of the non-Communist labor leadership was affiliated.

During the Dutra regime, which lasted until the return to power of Vargas in 1951, there was a strong tendency on the part of the labor leadership, including a considerable number of *pelegos,* to advocate

R. y J. Caruso

With Count Carlo Sforza in Uruguay, after the Free Italy Convention in August 1942. Behind Sforza is Don Tomás Beretta, who later became President of the Republic

At the ILGWU summer resort, Forest Park, Pa., June 1946. *L. to r.*: Luigi Antonini, First Vice-President ILGWU; Congressman Ivan Matteo Lombardo, then Secretary of the Italian Socialist Party; Congressman (now President of the Italian Republic) Giuseppe Saragat; Congressman ... Martire of the martyred Italian Social-Democratic leader; Serafino Romualdi

Felix A. Knight, Chairman of the United States Labor delegation that visited Argentina in January 1947, tries to make peace after the quarrel between Perón and Serafino Romualdi. *L. to r.:* Romualdi, Knight, Foreign Minister Attilio Bramuglia, Interior Minister Angel Borlenghi, President Juan Domingo Perón, Mrs. Eva Duarte Perón.

Vice-President Richard M. Nixon with members of the Union of Municipal Workers and Employees of Argentina, New Day, 1958.

Sam Reiss from *Inter-American Bulletin*

President Adolfo Lopez Mateos of Mexico with AFL–CIO delegation at the Waldorf-Astoria, October 1959. *L. to r.:* O. A. Knight, President, Oil, Chemical and Atomic Workers; President Lopez Mateos; William C. Doherty, President, National Association of Letter Carriers; AFL–CIO President George Meany; Jacob S. Potofsky, President, Amalgamated Clothing Workers; and Serafino Romualdi, AFL–CIO Inter-American Representative

Merkle Press

In the Rose Garden of the White House, August 1962. Serafino Romualdi, then Executive Director of the American Institute for Free Labor Development, introduces the participants in the first AIFLD class to President John F. Kennedy. At the extreme left is Jesse A. Friedman, the

The Free Italians Congress in Montevideo, Uruguay, August 1962. To the right of the speaker, Italian novelist Mario Mariani, is the President of Uruguay, Don Tomás Beretta (with folded arms), and to his left is Serafino Romualdi. Also in the front row are the heads of participating delegations: Don Emilio Frugoni (Uruguay), Juan Cappello M. (Chile), Don Torcuato Di Tella (Argentina), Trento Tagliaferri (Brazil), Salvatore Amodei (Paraguay)

The original picture has President Kennedy's signature and the following inscription by Betancourt:

Para Serafino, amigo de siempre, con el afecto de Rómulo Betancourt
Miraflores, Caracas
1 Mayo, 1963

United States Delegation to the ORIT's II Convention in Rio de Janeiro. *L. to r.*: John L. Lewis, Cathryn Lewis, William C. Doherty, Sr., George P. Delaney, Emil Mazey, Ernst Schwartz, Serafino Romualdi

Serafino Romualdi, AFL–CIO Inter-American Representative; Dr. Eduardo Santos, former President of Columbia and Editor of *El Tiempo,* which resumed publication after the fall of dictator Rojas Pinilla; and Luis Alberto Monge, ORIT General Secretary. The occasion was the presentation to Dr. Santos of the annual award of the Inter-American Association for Democracy and Freedom

Serafino Romualdi with Nicaraguan President René Shick

Americans from varied states and nations saluted twenty-five potential leaders from a dozen countries at the ninth graduation ceremonies of the American Institute for Free Labor Development in the AFL–CIO auditorium. *L. to r.:* David Dubinsky, President of the ILGWU, Ambassador Celso Pastor de la Torre (Peru), AFL–CIO President George Meany, Governor Nelson Rockefeller (R-N.Y.), Ambassador Juracy Magalhaes (Brazil), AIFLD Executive Director Serafino Romualdi, Samuel F. Pryor, Vice-President of Pan American World Airways radical changes in the Brazilian labor code. A deep, sincere desire to bring about a transformation of the Brazilian labor movement along the lines of democratic self-government and political independence was discernible. In 1946 an agreement was reached by some of its leaders "to work for the establishment of a Brazilian Confederation of Labor that will seek to cast aside, gradually if necessary, every form of governmental control and domination."

Although I had previously visited Brazil during my wartime service, my first contact with organized labor there took place in 1946. From the beginning, I refused to be a party to the government's domination of labor. The following paragraph from my July 1946 report to the AFL shows how careful I was to avoid any appearance of support:

On Saturday, June 29, I was invited as guest of honor to a banquet celebrating the tenth anniversary of the Maritime Workers' Federation. However, the fact that the Minister of Labor and the Chief of Police of Rio were also listed as speakers prompted me to stay away, pleading sudden illness. My presence alongside such government officials of dubious labor record would have exposed me to damaging criticism.

The purpose of my mission to Brazil was explained to the public through a press interview. This was arranged by William A. Wieland, our Embassy Press Attaché, and Edward J. Rowell, our Labor Attaché, and was distributed by the Brazilian Press Association in Rio and other cities. The Communists reacted immediately with a bitter editorial against me which appeared in their leading daily *Tribuna Popular*.

On Monday, July 1, the Cuban Communist leader, Blas Roca, arrived in Brazil. In his first interview with the press he betrayed his worry about our work in Latin America by launching a bitter attack against the American Federation of Labor and particularly against President William Green, whom he falsely depicted as a millionaire and great property owner. Blas Roca strongly urged the Brazilian workers not to pay attention to my statements and assured them that "the AFL is a small minority organization by far surpassed in numerical strength by the CIO."

From Rio I went to São Paulo, where, thanks to the splendid cooperation of my old friend Cecil Cross, U.S. Consul General, I was able to establish in only four days a frank understanding with the labor leadership of that city. Our relations have remained, up to this day, unbroken and have provided free labor with a solid core of true friends.

The majority of São Paulo trade union leaders belonged to the Labor

Party. Most of them, however, desired the evolution of trade unionism toward full independence from government or party control. I met with a group of about fifty leaders headed by Deocleciano de Hollanda Cavalcanti, who later became President of the National Confederation of Industrial Workers and member of the Executive Board of the International Confederation of Free Trade Unions. At that meeting, Cavalcanti was appointed provisional correspondent with the AFL and other Latin American labor organizations pending the organization of a Brazilian Confederation of Labor—a goal that twenty years later is still waiting to be achieved.

On the Fourth of July, I was tendered a banquet by a group of labor leaders representing twenty federations of the state of São Paulo. They presented me with a *"Livro de Ouro"* (Golden Book) in which there was inscribed a message of greetings and solidarity to the American Federation of Labor, and the organized workers of North America. The concluding paragraph of the message read:

May the simple words of this message of friendship, appreciation, and solidarity be the interpreters of our feelings toward the North American workers and of our ardent wishes that all the workers of the Americas be united in the struggle against reaction, Fascism, and the Communists, freeing man from fear and want.

After an initial period of friendship with the Dutra government, the leadership of the various federations and confederations, largely affiliated to the Brazilian Labor Party, reverted to active support of Getulio Vargas. They worked hard to bring about his victory in the presidential elections of October 1950. To that end, they organized a "National Labor Campaign Front" which became a decisive factor in Vargas's victory.

Getulio had gained the support of the working class during his previous administration as a result of his comprehensive program of labor legislation. It gave the workers rights that they had never enjoyed before, and also gave them a feeling of political power. The questionable aspects of the Vargas dictatorship, particularly its administrative corruption and the suppression of civil liberties, were of no concern to the trade union leadership (the *pelegos*) and the great mass of politically inert Brazilian workers. Deocleciano de Hollanda Cavalcanti, by then President of the National Confederation of Industrial Workers, wrote to me about Vargas's victory:

The results of the election of October 3 completely vindicated our stand. Elected by the people in order to govern in the name of the people, Vargas is today, as he was yesterday, the hope of Brazil. He has promised us more rights and a fair compensation for our work. He will keep this promise as he has kept all of his promises in the past.

In his May Day, 1951, address to the Brazilian people, Vargas advocated a massive organizing campaign that would add millions to union ranks. It was his typical gaucho appeal to the workers. However, he did nothing to introduce trade union freedom and democratic institutions. A São Paulo labor leader, Angelo Parmigiani, had defied his Labor Minister at the 1949 ILO Montevideo Conference by voting with me to censure the governments of Venezuela and Peru. Following Vargas's address, Parmigiani addressed a message to him that went straight to the roots of Brazilian trade union difficulties. It said in part:

I don't believe that it is possible to obtain the unionization en masse of the workers of Brazil unless they are convinced that labor unions are independent organisms whose only purpose for existence is the protection of the working class. Labor unions controlled by the government have never been able to attract workers to their ranks. Please, Mr. President, give us in the next National Congress, labor unions built on the spirit of modern democracy, guaranteeing liberty of association, liberty of trade unions, and liberty of action, and we, the workers, will guarantee you a unionization en masse which will contribute to the welfare of the nation as a whole. But right now, what's the use of telling the worker that labor unions are his friends when the unions are really government agencies for the collection of dues?

Meanwhile, the Communists, by again putting into effect the policy of "boring from within," had succeeded in gaining control of a number of unions. Masquerading as members of the Brazilian Labor Party, they received indirect support from Vargas's heir apparent, a young, rich politician from Rio Grande do Sul, João (Jango) Goulart. He had made his debut and political apprenticeship as Minister of Labor with tactics reminiscent of Juan Domingo Perón. In fact, it was insistently rumored that there existed a secret understanding between the two.

In 1954 Goulart was forced out of office as Labor Minister by a combination of military leaders and industrialists in retaliation for his "demagogic" policy of advocating the doubling of the minimum wage. From that time on he became a "hero" to the working class.

Jango's policies and other factors such as political corruption, usurpation of power, and virtual economic paralysis prompted the Brazilian armed forces to ask on August 23, 1954, for Vargas's resignation. The last straw was the attempt on the life of opposition Congressman Carlos Lacerda. Perpetrated by henchmen of the Vargas regime, it resulted instead in the killing of an Air Force major. Vargas, refusing to resign, retired to his office and early the following morning shot himself.

The period that followed, until the presidential elections of October 1955, plunged Brazilian labor into a state of uncertainty. Most of the leaders and rank and file were embittered by Vargas's tragic departure from the political scene. A few, however, began to nurture the hope that the provisional regime of President João Café Filho might lead to the emergence of a democratic regime that would free labor of the stifling governmental control. They also hoped that the end of Vargas would also bring the end of the *peleguismo* which Getulio had created. Things, however, developed in a different way. In Brazil the voters cast their ballots separately for President and Vice-President. Goulart, as leader of the Labor Party, paired as candidate for Vice-President of the Republic with Dr. Juscelino Kubitschek, candidate for President of the Social Democratic Party (which had no similarity, even remote, to the Social Democrats of Europe). Kubitschek and Goulart won the October elections.

I arrived in Brazil, together with ORIT director of organization Arturo Jáuregui, when the ballots were still being counted. The dominant question in labor circles was: What would be the role of the Communists vis-à-vis the new administration, which they had helped to elect although their party itself was illegal?

An overwhelming majority of the trade union leaders had supported the victorious ticket. However, a significant group of leaders had actively supported Adhemar de Barros, candidate for President of the liberal Socialist Progressive Party, and Danton Coelho, former Labor Minister and Labor Party (PTB) leader, candidate for Vice-President. Coelho, an open enemy of João Goulart within the PTB, entered the race during the last two weeks of the campaign with the avowed intent of cutting into Goulart's vote and possibly bringing about his defeat. A third group of labor leaders had supported the Christian Socialist candidate, General Júarez Tavora, and his running mate, Milton Campos. These two were also the candidates of a large coalition group including the National Democratic Union, the Socialists, and all other anti-Vargas forces.

The optimists could not believe that the Kubitschek-Goulart administration would tolerate the Communists. As I wrote in a report dated October 27, 1955, most of the leaders of the national trade unions insisted that both Kubitschek and Goulart would concentrate on attempting to solve the basic problems facing the country, such as inflation, lack of adequate transportation, insufficient energy and power, the extraction of oil, etc. "They need the cooperation of the United States," was the refrain. "They will not jeopardize the interests of the country by playing up to the Communists."

Another group of Brazilians, supported by the Navy and Air Force and inspired by Carlos Lacerda, who, in addition to being a vocal opposition Congressman was an influential journalist (*Tribuna da Imprenta*), wanted to prevent the transfer of power. They accumulated impressive proof that the election was tainted with widespread fraud, that Kubitschek and Goulart had a pact with the Communists, and that the "Vargas oligarchy" had in fact regained power. They wanted an extralegal solution, culminating in the annulment of the election.

President João Café Filho, who had taken leave of absence on account of illness, had been succeeded by the next in line, the President of the House of Representatives, Dr. Carlos Luz, who leaned toward the extralegal solution. However, on the morning of November 11, 1955, the Army staged what was described as a coup to prevent the violation of the Constitution, deposed Carlos Luz and installed in his place, with the concurrence of Congress, the Vice-President of the House of Representatives. Carlos Luz took refuge, together with his Cabinet and Carlos Lacerda, in a warship. Later they were transferred to the Cuban Embassy and went into exile abroad. The new government suspended constitutional guarantees until the elected Kubitschek and Goulart were sworn in, January 31, 1956. After four months of turmoil, the constitutional crisis was settled in true Brazilian fashion—without bloodshed.

The events in Brazil during the last four months of 1955 had indicated the growing influence and danger of the Communist movement in that country. The Communists had succeeded in entering a sort of popular front which elected the Kubitschek-Goulart regime, they had taken to the streets to support the Army in defense of the "Constitutional succession," and their penetration into the labor movement had become strong and determined. Communist resources were great. Secret training schools existed in key industrial cities. Hundreds of free visits for Brazilian workers to the Soviet Union were arranged each year, and scores were receiving special training there in infiltration tactics and industrial conflicts. To counteract this, Brazilian labor, aided by the ICFTU-ORIT, planned a national labor seminar in Brazil for the early part of 1956. The national labor confederations, such as the CNTI (Industrial Workers) and CNTT (Land Transport Workers), organized new labor leader training programs of their own for their union members.

At a special session with U.S. Ambassador James C. Dunn and Labor

Attaché Irving Salert, Brazilian labor leaders accompanied by myself and Jáuregui discussed the impact and effectiveness of the Point IV and the Labor Leaders Exchange Program. The Brazilians were encouraged by the deep concern for the future of their trade union movement shown by our Ambassador, his complete support for the Point IV labor projects, and his pledge of continued interest in a program to help develop a genuine trade union democracy in Brazil. Arrangements were made for dozens of young labor leaders to visit the United States in order to study the structure and functioning of our trade union movement. Our goal was the development of a corps of labor leaders who, by commanding the enthusiastic support of the rank and file, could turn back Communist attempts to capture the Brazilian labor movement. A short-term program was devised with extensive educational seminars at the local and national levels. ORIT affiliates, which included the labor movement of the United States, were considered as the best sources of assistance.

In regard to its attitude toward the Kubitschek-Goulart regime, the free labor movement of the Western Hemisphere, including the newly merged AFL-CIO, decided to follow the lead of the ORIT Brazilian affiliates. The latter were anxious to go along with the new administration, which they had helped elect, hoping that international commitments and trade union pressures would keep it in line. It was worth the gamble and, on behalf of the AFL-CIO, I played it to the hilt. However, as will be shown in the following pages, fortune looked the other way.

Goulart was elected Vice-President of Brazil by a majority vote, in contrast to President Kubitschek, who received only a plurality. It was feared that Kubitschek would favor the Communists as a sort of payoff for their nonrequired support during the campaign. However, he selected as Minister of Labor—a position allotted to him at the time of the pre-election deal—a man of known democratic tendency, a strong Catholic and a decided anti-Communist. Furthermore, he announced open support of the ICFTU-ORIT affiliates and expressed publicly the desire to visit the United States "in order to observe U.S. labor organizations and workers' training programs."

Soon after the Kubitschek-Goulart administration took office on January 31, 1956, a new law was enacted, reportedly under Goulart's pressure. It permitted union members to determine in their own way, with their own votes, who should be their elected leaders and for how long and how many terms they should serve, and allowed elected officials to take office immediately upon being certified, without awaiting Ministry of Labor approval. In addition, some very important changes in the

Consolidated Labor Laws were also included in the new legislation, which gave trade union organizations a lot of additional freedom.

As I wrote in the April 1956 issue of *The New Leader*, this favorable turn of events "was attributed largely to the conversations Kubitschek had in Washington with AFL-CIO President George Meany and in Brussels with ICFTU General Secretary J. H. Oldenbroek. Credit was also being given to Vice-President Nixon's February 2 visit to the head-quarters of Brazil's free unions, during which he praised the democratic policies of the ORIT and ICFTU. Nixon was accompanied by AFL-CIO Vice-President William Doherty and U.S. Ambassador James Dunn, and his remarks were widely publicized." Nixon and Doherty were in Rio as members of the official U.S. delegation to the inauguration of the new government.

While in Rio, Vice-President Nixon extended to Goulart a formal invitation to visit the United States. Doherty assured Goulart that he would get an opportunity to meet the leaders of our labor movement and get acquainted with our trade union structure and methods of operation. The visit was set for the first three weeks of May 1956. There were misgivings in some AFL-CIO circles concerning Goulart, and the desire to receive him and show him around was definitely not unanimous. The main complaint against him was that he was a political opportunist, ready to play ball with anyone, including the Communists, who could advance his ambitions. Outstanding among the anti-Jango group were Jay Love-stone of the Free Trade Union Committee and Charles Zimmerman of the ILGWU. I shared the view of the Brazilian trade union leadership, strongly supported by our Embassy in Rio and the State Department, that if Goulart were given a chance to come and see for himself he might decide to make a clean break with the Communists. My position was eventually supported by AFL-CIO President George Meany.

Before leaving Brazil for the United States on April 26th, Vice-President Goulart gave a press interview during which, according to the United Press, he condemned Communists and said, among other things, the following:

My paramount interest is to defend the working class. My foremost wish during this coming trip to the United States is to establish contact with the trade union leaders of that country. I represent the Labor Party of Brazil, whose policy is clear and well defined against the extremists of the right, as well as those of the left. We advocate better understanding between capital and labor. We are opposed to the concept of the class struggle. We want better living and working conditions for the wage earners of Brazil because we know that this is the best way to fight Communism, which grows on the misery and suffering of the poor people.

During his stay in the United States, Vice-President Goulart visited the new AFL-CIO building on Sixteenth Street in Washington. He was also entertained at a luncheon during which he delivered to AFL-CIO President Meany a message of greetings from the Metal and Electrical Workers' Union of Brazil, signed by all eighty-two delegates to their recent Convention at Volta Redonda. Goulart delivered a brief talk in Portuguese in which he pointed out that Brazilian workers have the same ideals of peace and liberty as their counterparts in the United States.

That same evening Vice-President Goulart was guest of honor at a dinner tendered by President William C. Doherty of the National Association of Letter Carriers, which was attended by Cabinet members, Senators, Congressmen, and a large number of representatives of the labor movement.

Continuing his tour, Goulart visited Detroit, where he conferred with AFL-CIO Vice-President Walter P. Reuther, and Atlantic City, where he was introduced by President David Dubinsky to the Convention of the International Ladies' Garment Workers' Union. It was here that a number of ILGWU officials walked off the platform to signify their displeasure with Goulart's appearance. President Dubinsky emphasized during his introductory remarks the anti-Communist record of the ILGWU. When Goulart was through with his message of greetings, Dubinsky asked him some pointed questions, finally succeeding in extracting from him an indirect denunciation of Communism. I was there as translator.

For a number of years George Meany had toyed with the idea of making a tour of South America. Goulart gave him the proper opening when he extended to him an invitation to visit Brazil. Thus came the decision to make the trip which would also include Uruguay, Argentina, Peru, and Panama. As already mentioned in previous chapters, Meany went accompanied by Vice-Presidents David Dubinsky and O. A. Knight, and myself. Other members of the party were Mrs. Meany, Mrs. Dubinsky, AFL-CIO Public Relations Director Philip Pearl, and AFL-CIO Radio Consultant Morris Novick and Mrs. Novick.

We left for Brazil two days after the 1956 presidential elections. From the first moment we arrived in Rio to the last minute before our departure from São Paulo, it was an uninterrupted series of receptions, press interviews, official visits, labor meetings, conferences, etc. We had many opportunities to compare notes with key Brazilian labor leaders on the structure and functions of trade unions in our respective countries. In the course of these conversations, we were struck by the lack of self-reliance on the part of the Brazilians. It was a condition that apparently had its roots in the already described system of dues collection which facilitated strong government control of union affairs. Lacking adequate research and workers' education programs the Brazilian unions clearly had much to learn in the area of collective bargaining.

While in Rio, Meany visited Vice-President Goulart, who honored him with an official reception to introduce him to the labor leaders of the country. Goulart told the AFL-CIO leader that he would have to apologize for his wife's absence from the official reception, because Mrs. Goulart had just been taken to the hospital to have a baby. Meany promptly offered the following toast to the Vice-President's lady: "In New York we have a special word for such occasions. In fact, it's two words—'Mazel tov.'"

In his public statements, President Meany took the opportunity to debunk Communist claims that they were responsible for any significant labor gains, but he backed the strong currents of nationalism sweeping the country.

Time magazine reported on Meany's visit in its December 10, 1956, issue as follows:

> In Brazil, where Communists often try to claim credit for labor gains, Meany hammered at the theme that in Red "satellite countries, workers are shot down by the hundreds for daring to lay down their tools and demand bread." But George Meany went along with Brazilian nationalism, which is most often expressed, in reaction to foreign offers to develop Brazilian oil, by the slogan, *O petroleo e nosso* (The oil is ours). Agreed Meany, in halting Portuguese: "*O petroleo e vosso* (yours)."

The AFL-CIO delegation was equally conscious, however, of the impact of the visit on the rank and file and was responsive to their needs.

In Rio de Janeiro, President Meany received a letter from Osvaldo Ferreira, President of the local union of Brazilian railway workers in Catanduva. The letter was written in crude English, but the pathos and sincerity of the Ferreira family shone through every line. The father had worked on the railroads for thirty years, and his wife was a schoolteacher. They had a son, José Pedro, who was born with an uncommon case of extra-heavy eyelids which made it almost impossible for him to see. In order to get any vision at all, little José had to hold his head way back. At that angle, he could see straight ahead through a narrow gap.

His parents had read that operations to cure this condition were being done in the United States. But how to finance the trip? There were eight Ferreira children, the oldest of them sixteen. As Mr. Ferreira wrote, even with "maximum sacrifice," we have no "economy."

Deeply moved by the letter, Meany asked AFL-CIO officials in New York to ascertain the cost of the operation needed by the boy. The estimate came to about $4,000 for hospital, surgical and medical fees, transportation for mother and child, etc.

At this point, the Community Services Department of the AFL-CIO stepped in. Dr. Raymond Pfeiffer, a leading surgeon at the Eye Institute of the Columbia Presbyterian Medical Center, agreed to do the operation without charge. The hospital agreed to cut costs to the bone. The AFL-CIO agreed to "pick up the check" for the remaining amount, which was still several thousand dollars.

The story had a happy ending. When Mrs. Ferreira walked out of the hospital with her boy, she said:

"It is wonderful. Nobody stares at little José any more when we walk down the street."

I met Carlos Lacerda for the first time in New York City in the spring of 1956. He was anxious that I convey to the leadership of the AFL-CIO his misgivings about Vice-President Goulart, whom he considered a conscious tool of the Communists. He also put me on guard against the alleged anti-Communism of the *pelegos,* whom he described as ready to sell their own mother in order to retain their profitable positions of leadership in the labor movement. I developed a strong liking for Lacerda. I admired his forceful, yet sensible, opposition to Communism and every form of totalitarian dictatorship; I appreciated his belief in a truly independent labor movement; and I shared his concept of dynamic democracy and contempt for conformity, particularly the conformity he described as the "ritualistic totalitarian liberal left."

The conversation with Lacerda was, in effect, a series of monologues during which he expounded on every conceivable subject. At the end I managed to ask:

"What are you doing here in exile? Why don't you go back home where you belong, to fight for what you consider right?"

He liked my remark. Years later he always reminded me, and those within listening range, how much he appreciated my blunt suggestion.

A few weeks later Lacerda returned to Brazil, took his position in the forefront of the anti-Communist, anti-government-corruption struggle, built up a political machine inside and outside the UDN (National Democratic Union Party) and in 1960 was elected Governor of Guanabara, the state that comprises the city of Rio de Janeiro.

Some newspaper correspondents have acquired the habit of labeling Lacerda a rightist, perhaps because of his uncompromising anti-Communist stand and his increasing distaste for the demagogic policies of Vice-President Goulart. Yet those who have taken the trouble to read his books and addresses, or have conversed with him at length, or have listened to him speaking at labor rallies and at international gatherings such as the 1961 ORIT Convention and the Postal, Telephone, Telegraph Workers' Inter-American Conference in 1963, could not fail to admire his progressive economic views, especially his support of free labor. Of course, he also believes in free enterprise and adheres to a sane concept of economic nationalism, but he also believes in cooperation with, not subservience to, the United States as leader of the Free World combating aggressive Communism.

In 1961 Governor Lacerda sent me an article for publication in the AFL-CIO press entitled "The Communist Idea-Weapons." In the following excerpts from that article the philosophy of this controversial Brazilian is clearly articulated:

As its principal adversary, Communism has chosen the United States of North America, which is the strongest bulwark of the democratic world, in the sense of materialistic well-being at least, of economic stability, military power, and educational development. Communism has concentrated all its efforts against the United States; it is attempting to mobilize all resentments against this country, and to attribute all ills to it, and thus alienate all sympathy from it.

. . . By sins of commission or omission, by whetting hatreds, by pointing up antipathies, by neutralizing friendships, by fostering misunderstanding, exploiting traditions, exaggerating errors, soliciting followers, infiltrating sectors of influence, paralyzing resistance movements, intimidating the craven and terrorizing the bold, and by inciting demagogues to action, Communism has succeeded in weaving a tissue of lies. . . .

In view of the situation which prevails today, we believe that the price of freedom is a precise defining of our position. From such a definition we can evolve the only effective defense against Communist envelopment: the isolation of Communism by a clear distinction between its methods and our methods, between its goals and our goals. . . .

The idea that economics is at the base of all things . . . is an absurd concept which the practical facts of daily living disprove. . . .

I consider nationalism—defined as the doctrine which seeks to place the Nation above all else—as a totalitarian concept. . . . A Nation is simply one of man's creations. . . .

Anticolonialism is thus being turned into a pretext to justify the intervention of a new imperialism, hotheaded and enslaving, totalitarian in principle and in form, totalitarian in its means and its objectives. . . .

For my part, I avow that I am not afraid of the type of imperialism which can be met with competition and honesty; but that I am opposed to that type of imperialism which not only wishes to take over the people's money, but also to possess itself of each individual's conscience. . . .

Let us face up to our adversary, who is less numerous than we but is to be found wherever lack of purpose and confusion exist.

In the presidential elections of 1960, Governor Lacerda supported the candidacy of Janio Quadros, the Governor of the State of São Paulo. Quadros rose to prominence and popularity on the strength of his colorful personality and successful administration in São Paulo. The symbol of the broom—a promise to get rid of the crooks and the incompetents— swept him into office with a huge plurality. But together with Quadros, Jango Goulart also managed to be elected again as Vice-President, this time with the open support of Communists and fellow travelers.

After the initial period of the Kubitschek-Goulart regime, during which the latter played the role of anti-Communist democrat, the Communists again found the road to favors and protection. The Ministry of Labor, under Goulart's tight control, helped eliminate the non-Communist majority from the leadership in a number of unions, specifically among maritime workers, bank clerks, steel and manufacturing, particularly in the Rio de Janeiro area. In June 1959 a sector of the Brazilian press reported that the Vice-President had signed an election pact with the Communists, opening the Brazilian Labor Party ticket to their candidates.

Janio Quadros was elected with the votes of most of the Brazilian middle class and the majority of organized labor. Trade unionists were seen everywhere displaying buttons "Jan-Jan," meaning vote for Janio (President) and for Jango (Vice-President). Once installed in the Presidential palace in Brasilia, Quadros started disappointing his supporters, including trade unionists from his home state of São Paulo. It is not yet clear what actually happened in Quadros's mind. He accentuated his anti-Americanism, started flirting with the Communists, and above all became impatient of any criticism, taking issue with Congress and, last but not least, engaging in a running feud with the Governor of Guanabara, Carlos Lacerda—who had been one of his most enthusiastic and most important supporters.

When I arrived in Rio de Janeiro August 20, 1961, for the V ORIT Convention, the country was already seething over the split between President Quadros and the Governor of Guanabara, based on Lacerda's accusation that the President's foreign policy was becoming more and more pro-Soviet. The ORIT Convention was scheduled to open that afternoon. The Minister of Labor, Dr. Francisco Castro Neves, was to speak at the opening ceremony as a representative of President Quadros. Governor Carlos Lacerda, by previous arrangement, was scheduled to speak the following Friday, at the closing session of the convention. Lacerda phoned me requesting my intervention to make it possible for him to speak that very same day at the opening ORIT session, because he was considering resigning in order to lead "from the streets" the fight against the pro-Communist policy of Quadros. Lacerda's request was granted.

The following day Governor Lacerda came to see me at the hotel and gave me confidential information on the worsening of the national crisis and the probability of an attempt by Quadros to set himself up as a sort of dictator. On August 24, the Governor gave an official reception for the ORIT delegates, at which he announced that he was not going to resign after all, but reiterated, in even stronger terms, his determination to fight to prevent the absorption of Brazil into the Communist orbit. He took me aside and informed me that he was going on TV the same night to denounce a plot by Janio Quadros to dissolve Congress. He invited me to visit him again the following day at 3:00 P.M.

At the appointed hour, I was again at Guanabara Palace. After an unusually long wait, I was finally ushered into the Governor's office. There was an air of great excitement, with aides—civilian and military— going in and out. Governor Lacerda, who was visibly agitated, apologized for talking to me standing and in such a hurried manner. He told me that the President had just resigned and confided in me his suspicion that it was a move calculated to cause an uprising of the population to carry Quadros back with unlimited power.

The Governor's Labor Secretary, Helio Walcacer, and I reviewed the strategy on how to defeat the expected Communist call for a general strike. We felt that the overwhelming majority of the union leaders in São Paulo and Rio had already become disenchanted with Quadros's policy and would not go on strike to bring him back into power. It was, nevertheless, agreed that the top leaders of the labor movements in those cities—who were attending the ORIT Convention—should immediately be contacted in order to make doubly sure that they did not fall into any Communist trap. This was done so effectively that, in retrospect, I feel justified in stating that democratic labor played a decisive role in that fateful day for Brazilian history. At one conference we had with some leaders of the São Paulo delegation, AFL-CIO Secretary-Treasurer William F. Schnitzler was also present. This fact added considerable weight to our pressure.

The following day, August 26, the Communists issued the expected general strike order. But first the Maritime Workers, then the Central Committee of the Railway Unions, and finally the powerful Trade Union Committee for the Defense of Democracy, which less than a month before had assembled in São Paulo 820 democratic union leaders representing over four million workers, went into action and caused the general strike to fail.

After my return to the United States, I received a letter from Jorge E. Sierra, ORIT representative in Brazil, informing me that Castro Neves, Quadros' Minister of Labor, had prepared an administrative decree outlawing ORIT's operation in Brazil. This was done as an intended reprisal for the alleged complicity of ORIT with Governor Lacerda's antigovernment plans and it had not been issued only because of the unexpected resignation of Quadros. It is noteworthy, however, that Castro Neves figured prominently among those Brazilian leaders who, during the crucial twenty-four-hour period following Quadros's resignation, tried desperately to promote, together with the Communists, the success of a general strike with the view of bringing Quadros back into power.

Army and Air Force elements gained control of the situation and tried to prevent the accession to power of Vice-President Goulart, who was then abroad visiting Communist countries. However, their revolt was short-lived. Backed by the Army garrison of Porto Alegre, Jango managed to reenter Brazil from the Uruguay border and soon reached Brasilia, where he was finally able to take office as President.

In line with his opportunistic bent, Goulart played the role of moderate in the initial period of his administration. To prop the sagging economy Goulart desperately needed loans from Washington. Thus he assumed the posture of democratic reformer, claiming that he was going to do in Brazil what President Kennedy was doing in the United States. In the field of labor, he made overtures to the democratic leadership, urging them to coexist with the pro-Communist forces that had already heavily infiltrated the National Confederation of Industrial Workers. As Minister of Labor he appointed Franco Montoro, a leading Christian Democrat, who was definitely out of sympathy with Communism.

ORIT, again at the urging of its Brazilian affiliates, tried to reach an understanding with Goulart. Early in 1962 an ORIT mission headed by General Secretary Arturo Jáuregui, Mexican Senator Manuel Pavón, and myself went to Brasilia to confer with Goulart. Arrangements had been made in advance through Labor Minister Montoro. He waited for us at his office and from there he telephoned the Planalto (the Presidential Palace) to announce that we were ready. But no answer came during the entire morning. The performance was repeated in the afternoon, but again no answer concerning our appointment. The Minister was visibly embarrassed. He suggested that we remain in Brasilia overnight, but I pointed out that, according to press reports, the following morning the President was scheduled to leave early for Belo Horizonte to address a meeting of farm workers (*camponeses*) organized by the well-known Communist Francisco Julião. Montoro then made a final attempt to get word from the Planalto.

"With whom have you spoken?" I asked.

"Presidential Secretary Assyr," he answered.

"Then we may as well go home. Assyr is a known Communist stooge. He will surely block our interview with the President."

Months later when President Goulart visited the United States he approached me in New York, during a reception in his honor given by Governor Rockefeller.

"My dear Romualdi," he said. "When are you coming to visit me in Brasilia?"

I told him the story of our fruitless wait in Montoro's office. Goulart pleaded ignorance and was full of apologies.

Goulart was accompanied to the United States by the new President of the National Confederation of Industrial Workers, Clodsmidt Riani. He was a bitter anti-American, pro-Communist agitator. Goulart was trying to get Washington's support for a reorganized inter-American labor movement along "neutralist" lines, to include all ideologies and without affiliation to either the WFTU or the ICFTU. When he broached the subject with Secretary of Labor Arthur Goldberg he was quickly discouraged from pursuing the matter any further. Goldberg let him know that the AFL-CIO would never buy that. Obviously, Goulart—like Peron before him—had not realized that the labor movement in the United States was not taking instructions or even suggestions from the government.

This time Jango was not received at AFL-CIO headquarters as in his 1956 visit to Washington. Instead, he invited AFL-CIO President George

Meany to have breakfast with him at Blair House. Meany took along a number of Council members and advisers, including myself. The conversation rambled along until Meany asked bluntly:

"What is your stand, Mr. President, on cooperation with the free labor movement of the ICFTU, as opposed to dealing with the Communist-controlled WFTU?"

The answer was ambiguous. Meany pressed again, in plain language. Goulart finally suggested that a committee of the AFL-CIO stay to confer with Riani and presidential labor adviser Gilberto Crocket de Sa on technical arrangements to bring about closer cooperation. Walter Reuther and I remained. Walter was overly optimistic and explained in detail the activities of the International Trade Secretariats, particularly his own Metal Workers' International Federation. He pointed out what they could do for the labor movement of Brazil. On the other hand, I regarded the talk as an exercise in futility, certain that once back home Riani would do exactly what the Communists would allow him to do—and that clearly would not include cooperation with the AFL-CIO or any other free labor group.

The help given Brazil by the United States and the international lending agencies was not able to check a runaway inflation that from 1958 to 1963 had produced a 600 percent increase in the cost of living. Criticism against Goulart inefficiency mounted. Industry, commerce, the military, and the Church became alarmed at the direction in which Jango was leading Brazil. He began to rely more and more on the support of the Communists. A new Minister of Labor with extreme leftist tendencies was appointed. Although a good number of important unions were already controlled by the Communists and their fellow travelers, Goulart was not satisfied. He wanted total control. In clear violation of the law he promoted the formation of the General Workers' Command (CGT) as a legal entity, with the view of gradually bringing under his control all Brazilian trade unions. Goulart's deliberate effort to lend to the CGT the prestige of his office was strictly opportunistic. The CGT was financed in part by the National Confederation of Industrial Workers (CNTI) and partly by the illegal Communist Party of Brazil, which provided its orientation. The CGT was thus serving as an instrument of the Communist Party.

By late 1963, the Communists were maneuvering deliberately to create an atmosphere of utter political chaos which would culminate in a putsch and the suppression of all forces opposed to them. In such a situation, the

Communists would control the legislative branch of the government through its executive and then rule by decree. This would enable Goulart to remain in office beyond the limits provided by the Constitution and lay the foundation for a totalitarian regime. The CGT was to play a prominent role as coordinator in the contemplated coup.

Goulart was supremely confident that no force was left in Brazil strong enough to stop him. He had juggled the army command in such a way that the key garrisons were safely on his side—at least that was what he thought. As to the governors who strongly opposed him—particularly Carlos Lacerda in Guanabara and Adhemar de Barros in São Paulo—he was preparing "incidents" that would justify their removal through the appointment of "interventors." However, Goulart obviously underestimated the resources of his adversaries. Particularly, he failed to perceive the growing aversion of the middle classes to the mob rule that he was fostering as a springboard to absolute power.

In the fall of 1963, accompanied by Berent Friele, an old Brazilian hand belonging to Nelson Rockefeller's entourage, I visited Governor Adhemar de Barros. He confided to us that plans were already under way to mobilize military and police contingents to counter any attempt by Goulart to establish dictatorial control by force. Adhemar complained that the U.S. Embassy was not "listening." Berent Friele and I decided to acquaint U.S. Ambassador Lincoln Gordon with the substance of Adhemar's statements. I drafted notes for the attention of Labor Attaché John Fishburn. The Embassy's reaction was, of course, noncommittal.

Governor Lacerda's life was in constant danger. Several attempts had already been made to kill him. However, he told me he was confident that Goulart would make a fateful *faux pas* that would give the Brazilian armed forces the right and the duty to intervene.

I knew that a substantial sector of labor's rank and file, particularly in São Paulo and Rio, was fed up with the Goulart regime and was ready to take to the streets, if need be, to bring it down. In the first three months of 1963 the American Institute for Free Labor Development, of which I was the Executive Director, trained in Washington a special all-Brazilian class of thirty-three participants. Ten of these union leaders were later taken to West Europe and Israel under my personal supervision to learn more about the techniques and practices of democratic labor. When they returned to their country, some of the trainees were sent to the interior on internships to organize and conduct education seminars; others served their unions in Rio, São Paulo, Santos, and other industrial centers.

The crisis came to a head in March 1964. On March 13, Goulart staged a rally in Rio de Janeiro designed to provide a popular base for his extralegal acts. At this rally, Jango signed two decrees in plain contempt of the Congress—land expropriation and the nationalization of all private petroleum refineries. These measures, if carried out, would have pushed Brazil further down the road to a socialist state. As Ambassador Gordon aptly described the process, it was not a case of subversion but rather of "superversion"—the social, political, and economic order being undermined from above.

Later Goulart tried to undermine the Army's authority over its troops by addressing a meeting of mutinous sergeants and other noncommissioned officers. This triggered the successful March 31 military revolt, supported by democratic Brazilian governors.

At the peak of the crisis, the CGT declared a nationwide strike to defend Goulart's mandate. The government-controlled national radio hookup served the CGT strike effort by broadcasting CGT subversive orders calling for a strike and asking the people to go to the streets to defend, and if necessary fight to preserve, Goulart and the "Constitution."

Primarily affected by the CGT action were the strategically important transportation and petroleum refining industries. The response of the workers in the key areas, however, indicated lack of support for the CGT strike order and the effect of the strike call was minimal. Also lessening the impact was the appeal from a number of democratic leaders calling on their membership to ignore the CGT orders. Later, the same democratic trade union leaders were among the organizers of the great mass demonstrations in the streets of Rio, São Paulo, Belo Horizonte, and other cities hailing the downfall of the hated, corrupt, incompetent, pro-Communist Goulart regime.

After a brief period of provisional rule, the Brazilian Congress elected General Humberto Alencar Castello Branco to serve out the term of Goulart. Speaking at a May Day rally in São Paulo, Castello Branco pledged that ". . . the Revolution will not be a step backwards but a march ahead in the just and legitimate conquest of the workers." Democratic labor supported the revolution, and pledged to go along with the austerity measures designed to stop the inflation and bring about economic recovery. Of course, it is too early for a final judgment on the success or failure of the Brazilian 1964 Revolution. However, two years later the Castello Branco government had lost the support of many of its civilian backers, including Carlos Lacerda and Adhemar de Barros. The latter was removed as Governor of São Paulo and deprived of his political rights for ten years.

In an article published in the *Jornal do Brasil* to commemorate the second anniversary of the anti-Goulart revolution, Carlos Lacerda, who ended his term as Governor of Guanabara in October 1965, reiterated his opposition to the Goulart regime. But he also made clear that he considered the original aims of the Revolution as having been betrayed by Castello Branco. He proclaimed that the Revolution needed to be rescued and predicted:

The Brazilian mass will make the revolution. It will be anti-American to the extent that the Americans help the Castello Branco government. It will be anti-militarist to the extent that the Army lets itself be identified with the Castello Branco government. It will be totalitarian to the extent that the Castello Branco government discredits democracy in the eyes of the people.

Disenchantment with the military regime spread also to the ranks of democratic labor, both in and outside of Brazil. The AFL-CIO echoed the dissatisfaction in a resolution adopted at its December 1965 San Francisco Convention:

. . . The Castello Branco administration has recently become an authoritarian regime. It has curtailed civic and political rights and liberties, and the Brazilian labor movement has again been forced back to its original status—an integral part of the state.

The Presidential election of 1966, conducted under an ad hoc electoral law which made inevitable the victory of the candidate supported by the government, brought to the Presidency General Arturo da Costa e Silva. In his Inaugural address the new President abounded in liberal-slanted pronouncements and pledged to lead Brazil toward eventual full restoration of constitutional structure and freedom.

The labor leaders of Brazil received President da Costa's pledges with renewed hopes that unfettered trade union freedom would some day be reestablished. But the road is still a long and difficult one.

Notes

1. *Inter-American Labor Bulletin,* May 1956.

XVIII

Peru and Haya de la Torre

THE LABOR MOVEMENT in Peru, as in other Latin American countries, was initiated by the anarcho-syndicalists, and received considerable impetus from World War I. In 1918, it successfully called a general strike for the establishment of the eight-hour day. However, in the post-World War I period, the emerging labor leadership was shaped by the student–trade union alliance established by Victor Raul Haya de la Torre, who later founded, in exile, the Peruvian political movement known as the Alianza Popular Revolucionaria Americana (APRA). Arturo Sabroso emerged as the outstanding young labor leader in Peru of that period.

Another young Peruvian, José Carlos Mariategui, who had studied in Europe after World War I and had become a dedicated Marxist, founded the Socialist Party of Peru, which established a "fraternal" affiliation with the Communist International. In 1929, the Comintern ordered the Peruvian party to change its name to the Communist Party of Peru. This was done (Mariategui meanwhile had died of tuberculosis) and Eudocio Ravines became its first General Secretary.

During the turbulent period that followed the return of Haya de la Torre to Peru (1931) until the assassination of President Sánchez Cerro (1934), the Peruvian labor movement was split into two factions. The larger group, controlled by the Apristas, suffered the brunt of government persecution; the smaller segment, controlled by the Communist Party, was treated more tolerantly by the government of Sánchez Cerro.

292

Thus began in Peru the rather anomalous situation of a Communist minority enjoying government tolerance and even support under authoritarian military regimes while the Aprista majority was being persecuted. This resulted from the bitter feud between the Apristas and the Army, which grew out of a bloody clash in the city of Trujillo in 1932 where many lives were lost on both sides. Under the regime of General Oscar Benavides, members of the non-Communist sector of the labor movement continued to be arrested, exiled, and otherwise persecuted.

Benavides's successor, Manuel Prado, chosen by the Peruvian military, was elected with the open support of the Communist Party. Juan P. Luna, the principal Communist labor leader, head of the Chauffeurs' Federation and a colleague of Lombardo Toledano in the CTAL leadership, was elected to the Chamber of Deputies on the Prado ticket.

Although President Prado from the very beginning allowed a much wider degree of freedom to organized labor and tolerated a few Aprista-controlled unions—such as the Textile Federation headed by Arturo Sabroso—his administration was openly on the side of the Communist-led unions. In order to place events in proper perspective, it should be understood that the Communists were then openly and loudly in favor of all-out efforts to win the war and that they were causing no "embarrassment" to the government. When Lombardo Toledano visited Peru in 1942, ostensibly to stimulate greater labor efforts to help win the war, he was received by the President and succeeded in persuading him to permit the organization of a new central labor confederation under the leadership of the Communists. On May Day 1944, the Confederación de Trabajadores del Perú (CTP) came into being, with Communist Congressman Luna as its first General Secretary. It immediately affiliated with CTAL.

As long as the Prado administration remained in power, the Communists continued to dominate the labor movement. Their leading position was due partly to support from officials of the Ministry of Labor who feared the Apristas.

Prado's term came to an end in June 1945 and under his successor, José Luis Bustamante y Rivero, Apristas received complete political and trade union freedom. In no time they took control of the CTP from the Communists, with Arturo Sabroso becoming Secretary-General.

As already indicated in a previous chapter, I first met Victor Raul Haya de la Torre, the founder and chief of the APRA Party, in August 1946. While I retained from the very beginning serious reservations concerning the vertical structure of APRA, I developed a strong admiration for Haya de la Torre as an intellectual and a leader. He was unquestionably a phenomenon typical of Peru. He was worshiped by his followers, and those in the labor movement were among the most loyal. A combination of the traditional Latin-American *caudillo* and the modern type of mass movement leader, not averse to authoritarian practices and the cult of personality inside his own party, Haya's mere suggestions became an order to his party members.

APRA's economic program, as explained to me by Haya himself in the course of our first meeting-lecture, was daring, but not based on any class-struggle concept. As a matter of fact, I heard from him, for the first time, the expression *policlasista*—meaning a political party based on the concept of a pluralistic society. Thus the APRA party had separate sections composed of workers, peasants, businessmen, professionals, employers, civil servants, etc.

Haya de la Torre believed that Peru was greatly in need of foreign capital to advance its industrialization program, without which, he proclaimed, there was no chance to improve the standard of living of the Peruvian masses. He fathered the Peruvian Economic Council based on the tripartite representation of labor, capital (domestic and foreign), and government, whose task was to study, plan, and supervise the execution of economic and industrial projects. He was still strongly anti-imperialist, but he had shifted his focus to the Communist imperialism, regarding it as a real threat to the security of our continent and its democratic institutions.

Haya de la Torre rejected the narrow conception of nationalistic self-sufficiency, which he declared was the favorite slogan of Nazi-minded demagogues. "There are no Peruvian, Colombian, Chilean, or Brazilian economic problems," he declared, "but only Peruvian, Colombian, Chilean, or Brazilian *aspects* of the wider inter-American economic problem."

Haya visited the United States for a series of lectures at various universities and colleges—some of which I helped to arrange—in 1947 and 1948. Addressing the symposium on "Conditions of Peace—1948" organized by Yale Law School, Haya de la Torre advanced the suggestion of an Inter-American Economic Conference with the participation of labor, management, and government—a concept which has now become a standard feature in the pronouncements of the inter-American labor movement, but which at that time represented a sharp departure from the noncollaborationist policy of most Latin American trade unions.

While Haya was in the United States for his second visit (mid-January to mid-May, 1948) things were not going so well for APRA in Peru. Its enemies, sparked by the military, were getting ready to suppress it again. I got word from a friend of mine, the Italian Ambassador in Lima, to warn Victor Raul of grave dangers facing him and his party. "Tell him to be very careful, in words and in actions, because at the first opportunity they will drown in blood the whole APRA movement."

Haya de la Torre's last speaking engagement in the United States, during the first week of May 1948, was in Washington, D.C., when he addressed a luncheon of Americans for Democratic Action. When he left for home, I went to the airport to bid him farewell. The late Pierre Loving, a reporter for INS, was with us. I had a premonition that something terrible was soon going to happen to Victor Raul. I relayed to him the warning of my friend, the Italian Ambassador. But Haya was supremely confident. "We will never permit a military coup," he asserted. Again, a few weeks later on the night of May 27, before a crowd of one hundred thousand followers, who paraded before the People's House on Avenida Ugarte in Lima to celebrate his return from the United States, "We will not tolerate a dictatorship," he thundered.

And thousands upon thousands of men and women, waving white handkerchiefs, their APRA symbol, shouted back their reply:

"No! Never! We will not stand for it!" [1]

The revolt of the Peruvian Navy at the port of Callao, the morning of October 3, 1948—which the government of President Bustamante y Rivero blamed on the APRA party with the alleged complicity of the CTP—was followed later in October by the overthrow of President Bustamante by his Minister of Interior, General Manuel Odría. The coup ushered in another long period of persecution for the Aprista-led labor movement. The Odría dictatorship arrested most of the CTP leaders, including General Secretary Arturo Sabroso. They were held in prison for more than a year, when their release was brought about largely by pressure from abroad, especially from the United States. Meanwhile, rank-and-file members belonging to the APRA party, or suspected of sympathy with it, were fired en masse from their jobs.

The extent of the persecution suffered by the CTP was revealed in an "Appeal to the Workers of America," issued November 20, 1948, by the clandestine leadership of the CTP under the signature of the acting General Secretary Luis Negreiros Vega, and published in full in the January 1949 issue of the *Inter-American Labor News.*

A more dramatic description of the suffering to which the arrested leaders of the CTP were subjected by the police of the military junta came to me in the form of a letter from the Lima Penitentiary, which I received through underground channels. The letter, which was published in the CIT press,[2] is herewith reproduced in full:

I am writing to you so that you may know, and let other people know, all about the atrocities of which a group of people who had nothing to do with the events of October 3 are innocent victims.

From Sunday, October 3, until Tuesday, October 5, at 5:30 P.M. we had nothing to eat. At that hour they gave us a piece of bread. It was on Wednesday, October 6, that they finally permitted us to receive food and blankets from our own families. We had to remain, therefore, without food for three solid days, sleeping in rat-infested, dirty cells made of cement, without even a sheet of paper to protect us from the cold and the humidity. As a result of these conditions, our Arturo [Arturo Sabroso Montoya, General Secretary of the Peruvian Confederation of Labor] got seriously ill, and the leader of the student group, Carlos Valle Huayta, got so sick that he died after a few days.

Senator Luis Haysen has been with us in this prison since the fourth of October. He badly needs medical attention, as a result of an infection in his left wrist caused by a tight handcuff when he was arrested. The case of Senator Haysen indicates how vengeful are the reactionary feudalists of Peru. They want to punish him for having faithfully associated, for twenty-six years, with Haya de la Torre in his work of democratic social education and enlightenment. For a while we thought he had been sent to the prison hospital, but then we found out that he is still confined, together with twelve other members of Parliament, in a small cell of only twelve square meters. They are exposed to the cold humidity of the cell without the opportunity of seeing the sun—not even for one hour daily—and this has been going on for more than two months.

We had also with us a seventy-two-year-old trade union leader, Leonidas Calderón, with ruined lungs, who suffered in painful agony. We asked that he be sent to the police hospital, but the director answered that the hospital is reserved for the members of the police force and their families, and not for the Apristas. So they sent him to the sixth wing, with the lowest type of criminals, and he is still held there incommunicado.

Of course, they refuse to give us any food. It is up to our families to feed us with whatever means they can scrape together, and this has been going on already for eight weeks.

I, myself, am very ill. In spite of the fact that two police doctors, who have visited me, have requested my immediate hospitalization, and that such transfer has already been approved by the Police Chief, the higher-ups have refused because, as they said, I am a "dangerous agitator" not deserving any consideration.

Not knowing whether this letter will safely reach your hands, I am not signing my name. So that you may know who I am, I will say that I am the one who wrote to you concerning the per capita payment of the CTP to the CIT and received from you a postcard from San Francisco, at a time when I was already ill.

Good-bye, my dear friend, and let us hope that the workers of the Americas may come to our rescue by using strong pressure so that we may soon be put on trial. If judged in a fair way, we know we will be released because we are innocent.

On the night of March 23, 1950, agents of the Odría military government assassinated Luis Negreiros Vega, the acting clandestine replacement for the arrested Arturo Sabroso as General Secretary of the CTP, while on his way to attend a secret labor meeting. Negreiros had been President of the Street Car Workers' Union and was a member of the CTP Secretariat. I had met him in Mexico City at the April 1946 ILO meeting, which he attended as one of Sabroso's labor advisers.

Several days before the assassination the ad hoc court which had tried political and labor leaders for their alleged part in the Callao Navy revolt of October 1948 rendered its verdict acquitting all the accused labor leaders, including Sabroso. However, they were not immediately released. Negreiros, who until then had remained out of sight and had moved cautiously at night from one hiding place to another, interpreted the acquittal verdict as a sign that he was no longer in danger of being arrested. Thus he dropped all precautions.

During the many months that he acted as Sabroso's replacement, Negreiros had previously been surprised three times by the government's political agents. Each time, owing to his daring and courage, he had successfully avoided capture. Orders were therefore given from higher-ups to capture him "dead or alive" wherever he might be. Unknown to Negreiros, political police agents were waiting for him outside his hiding place. As he emerged, they followed him in several cars until they reached an area of parks and open ground. There, at a road intersection, Negreiros's car was stopped and, at the command "hands up," he got out. He offered no resistance. There were a few words exchanged between Negreiros and the police; then a burst of fire, then another. Negreiros fell. Even as he lay on the ground and still gave signs of life, two final bursts were fired at him. It was about 11 P.M.

The body was taken to a police building for autopsy. Medical orderlies who were members of the CTP stated that twenty-eight bullet wounds were found in the body, in vital parts, causing almost instantaneous death. The greatest number of bullets were found in the head and neck, which proved that the crime was premeditated. If the police had wished to capture Negreiros alive, and wanted to be sure that he would not offer any resistance, they would have fired at his legs or arms. No member of the police arresting squad suffered even a scratch. In spite of this, the police communiqué stated that the police fired in self-defense, after Negreiros had opened fire first.

For four days, thousands of Peruvian workers, defying the government, filed before Negreiros's body, at Police Headquarters, to pay him their reverent and affectionate silent homage. Then an impromptu mass meeting with several thousand workers participating was held in a square. After the meeting, a column of workers, with Negreiros's relatives at the head, marched to Police Headquarters to reclaim the body of the martyred leader in order to give him a proper burial. But the police refused to release his body. They finally buried Negreiros's remains in the middle of the night and only after many days informed the family of the place where he had been interred.

News of Negreiros's assassination caused deep shock and consternation in labor circles throughout the world. On March 30, the AFL wired David Morse, ILO Director General in Geneva, a strongly worded protest urging him to initiate investigative proceedings against the Peruvian government for violation of trade union rights. This request was supported by the Inter-American Confederation of Workers (CIT) in a statement issued April 1, from its headquarters in Havana, Cuba, and by most of its affiliated organizations. Formal charges were later submitted by George P. Delaney, AFL International Representative and worker member of the ILO Governing Body, who on May 30, 1950, presented a paper to the ILO Fact Finding and Conciliation Commission of Freedom of Association in which, in addition to the Negreiros murder, he listed the following important facts in corroboration of his charges:

> The present regime in Peru has passed a law, called "Home Security" Law, which brutally attacks civil and trade union rights and even goes to the extreme of forbidding "the attempt to strike."
>
> The funds of the Peruvian Confederation of Workers (CTP) have been seized by order of the authorities.
>
> The premises of this organization, situated in the city of Lima, have been closed down. The same thing happened to all its branches, as for example, the Trade Union Federation (Unión Sindical de Trabajadores) of the North, with its seat in Chiclayo, the Trade Union Federation of the East, with its seat in Iquitos, and of Junín, with its seat in Huancayo, and the Trade Union Federation of the South, with its seat in Arequipa.
>
> All the press organs of the CTP and its branches have been wholly closed down, among them its official organ Cetepe.

A strike called by the trade unions in the sugar-producing region in the north of Peru, covering workers on the Cartavia, Paramonga, Chiclín, and Casa Grande plantations, was put down violently by the police, who shot and wounded a number of workers.

Hundreds of union members and leaders have suffered and are still suffering from police persecution, which has obliged them to go into hiding to escape assassination or imprisonment. Many trade union leaders have been detained on one or more occasions; some have been expelled from the country after months in prison, and, finally, many remain in prison without trial.

[Delaney's paper contained long lists of names of labor leaders in hiding, in exile or in jail.]

The day of the Callao revolt, October 3, 1948, Victor Raul Haya de la Torre went into hiding in order to avoid capture. The government claimed that he had masterminded the revolt. When, later in October, General Manuel Odría assumed power as head of the military junta, the search for Haya became a manhunt. A special police detail was organized to capture him. Moving at night from place to place, with his top lieutenants arrested or in hiding, Haya was finally persuaded to seek asylum by the inner core of his loyal supporters who had managed to remain in contact with him. On January 3, 1949, he was admitted to the sanctuary of the Colombian embassy.

In Latin America for nearly a century, the right of asylum has been recognized as a protection for the lives of those men who, in fighting for the social, economic, political, and cultural progress of the people, have often been victims of governmental persecution. This same asylum has served in many cases to protect the lives and personal security of the dictators and their servants on occasions when the liberties and rights of the citizens have been restored.

The Peruvian government refused to grant the Colombian embassy's request for safe-conduct for Haya de la Torre to leave the country, as is customary in such cases, on the allegation that Haya de la Torre was not a political refugee but a "common criminal." The dispute was finally submitted for final disposition to the International Court of Justice of The Hague, in accord with the Pact of Rio de Janeiro, which governs the relationship between members of the American family of nations.

It was a long wait for Haya—over five years. During all this time, the Colombian embassy in Lima remained under constant military surveillance, day and night. Every exit was guarded to prevent any possible attempt to escape. Every visitor to the embassy was questioned and many were searched. Every person leaving the embassy was likewise checked to uncover any possible disguise.

During the first few weeks of his asylum, Haya was treated like a transient guest, expected to receive at any moment the requested safe-conduct that would allow him to go abroad. But when the Odría government repeatedly refused to allow Haya to leave, he settled down for a long stay, was given his own private quarters, and was allowed to take daily exercises in the small embassy garden. Haya the agitator reverted to Haya the thinker, the scholar, the writer. The world had again become his province, every country of Latin America the object of his special analysis and observation; every social current caught again his passionate interest. From his confinement Haya managed to establish a regular exchange of correspondence with me. It meant that somehow, he broke the rules of the right of asylum . . . but only when he and his friends became convinced that the Odría government was acting arbitrarily and illegally by refusing him safe-conduct. My letters went in, and Haya's letters came out, through a crack in Odría's security wall which APRA, schooled in decades of underground work, was soon able to open. I thus became Haya's unofficial confidant and representative here in the United States. His letters were signed "The friend of Jesse" (my son).

In May 1949, Victor Raul sent me a 5,000-word memorandum discussing (1) the political situation in Latin America in general and in Peru in particular, and (2) the Latin American policy of the United States. Nearly two decades later, de la Torre's opinions of 1949 still have great relevance.

Haya de la Torre pointed out that the Communists often use a pincer's strategy in Latin America, seeking to crush "middle" forces between the cynical demagoguery and active subversion of the Communists on the one side and harsh and corrupt military dictatorships on the other.

Communist tactics are entirely destructive, he wrote, and then (as now) were directed toward the following objectives:

1. To destroy among the masses all hope of seeing true democracy under existing governments.

2. To provoke the United States to intervene in Latin America in support of military dictatorships threatened with chaotic conditions.

3. To cause the masses to believe that U.S. leaders are hypocrites, that their democratic promises are false, that the World War II slogans of the Four Freedoms were only for show, and that the United States has thrown overboard all principles of democracy which enabled it to attract the Latin American peoples to its cause during World War II.

4. To foment resentment and hatred against the United States by

cooperating in the anti-North American propaganda campaigns of the Peronistas and certain other militaristic groups.

5. To use the working people and intellectuals as blind instruments for sabotage and economic and social resistance against the United States and North American corporations as a consequence of the prevailing atmosphere of pessimism, despair, and cynical disillusionment.

Subversion, sabotage, and terrorism are "invincible when they are inspired by resentment, hate, and the destructive fanaticism which is created by disillusionment and despair among peoples who consider themselves to have been defrauded and who no longer believe in anything," according to de la Torre. The Communists' temporary goal is a destructive nihilism which can be a "psychological weapon of great power against the United States," he emphasized.

Russia well knows that Latin America is the backyard of the United States, hence the Communist program of penetration is well studied and carefully calculated. As it did in China, Communism takes into account the "ignorance of the masses, their racial suspicions, oppression, and misery, and the possibility of corrupting key military leaders," he continued, adding:

"It is very significant that much Communist activity is directed at the large mass of Indians and at generating among them racial hate toward the United States."

If the Communists succeed in bringing about chaos and anarchy among disillusioned masses, they then can follow up with the capture of those masses through demagoguery, Haya suggested. (Years after Haya wrote this, Fidel Castro used such tactics in winning control of Cuba.) In Argentina, where Peronism had a large popular base, Haya de la Torre wrote in 1949, it was evident that many disillusioned people lost to Perón were won by the Communists.

Even as the Communists openly attack "Yankee imperialism" and "Wall Street" and the North American corporations with investments in Latin America, they secretly provide clandestine aid to *certain* military dictatorships. They disregard "public" attacks made on them occasionally as political camouflage by those same dictatorships, Haya de la Torre wrote.

In Argentina, he noted, Perón censored all the democratic, liberal, and socialist press but only made public declarations against the Communists and permitted them to publish their daily, *La Hora,* in the same establishment which printed *Noticias Gráficas,* the Buenos Aires daily owned by Eva Perón.

In Venezuela, he continued, the military dictators attacked Communism in their speeches but carried on cordial relations with Russia and the Communist Party and cooperatively fought and persecuted the democratic party, Acción Demócrata, and the anti-Communist labor organizations. He added:

"What does it matter to the Peruvian Communists if General Odría declares Communism 'illegal' while permitting the Communists to operate freely among the workers so long as they work with the militarists against the Apristas and carry out an antidemocratic and anti-U.S. campaign among the indigenous masses of Cerro de Pasco, Oroya, Cuzco, etc.?"

Odría, as Minister of Government, signed a decree prohibiting the Inter-American Confederation of Labor (CIT) from maintaining offices in Lima. The AFL protested repeatedly, but both Odría and the Communists united against the democratic Confederation of Peruvian Workers, finally suppressing it and managing to get its leaders into prison.

The captive press in Argentina, Peru, and Venezuela did not publish statements from the 1949 ILO Conference of Montevideo protesting against persecution of democratic and anti-Communist workers in those countries, but it did publish speeches of Gromyko and other Communist delegates at the United Nations in defense of the "oppressed Indian masses of Peru" and the workers of Bolivia and Venezuela. These speeches, attacking North American corporations as "Yankee imperialists" have a tremendous effect as used by the Communists, Haya de la Torre said.

The Communists depict U.S. leaders as hypocrites who oppose some dictatorships but arm others. And when the United States provides arms, this places the recipient nation under an increasingly heavy economic burden to support the armies set up under the "pretext" of continental defense, the Communists contend. Haya added:

"Our masses are not like those of Europe. Our masses' explosiveness and passion are less reasoned. A propaganda based on resentment and rancor is an emotional factor of great force in our countries."

The United States is presented as a privileged and despised nation, profiting as an armory of the world's military tyrannies. Latin Americans, Haya de la Torre also stressed, frequently give greater importance to political phenomena than to economic conditions. It is characteristic of both the Spaniards and the Indians, he wrote, to prefer the enjoyment of certain liberties to the attainment of economic necessities. This is illustrated by the Spanish proverb which says: "I wish to be free to do as I please, even if I die of hunger."

U.S. government circles generally overlook the fact that Latin Americans attach great importance to "isms" and theories, Haya de la Torre wrote. The slogans of President Franklin D. Roosevelt (the Good Neighbor Policy, the Four Freedoms, etc.) were much more effective in winning friends for the United States "than all the loans and economic aid which Latin America received from the United States prior to Roosevelt's administration," he said. Consequently, when the slogans were not put into effect after World War II, a great disillusionment set in among the people.

The standard arguments of the United States are well known: respect for the sovereignty of the Latin American states and nonintervention in the internal affairs of those countries. To this, the Communists respond by saying that the United States intervenes when it "superarms" certain military dictatorships yet refuses to intervene on behalf of democracy when the arms are used against the people.

The United States entered World War II not to gain territory or destroy economic competitors but to intervene in and to destroy antidemocratic regimes threatening the freedom of humanity, Haya de la Torre wrote, adding:

"President Roosevelt was very clear when he stated that the North Americans would destroy tyranny and totalitarianism in every part of the world. . . . How may the tolerance of the United States toward the tyrannies of this hemisphere be explained in the light of its policy in Europe and Asia? Are the Latin American people unworthy of democracy and liberty?"

If, in the name of "absolute sovereignty" and "nonintervention," democracy in Latin America is permitted to perish under dictators, we shall see then that the most dangerous form of intervention has won the battle against freedom, Haya continued.

If the dictators find they are not opposed in the United Nations or in the Organization of American States, and if the protests against them are diplomatically stifled, hopes for democracy on the southern continent become increasingly doubtful, he added.

The only defense of democracy in our countries, and the only means of defeating Communism, which is advancing at a "fearful rate among our peoples," he asserted, "is to bring about a solid system of freedom of expression, of the vote, of conscience, and of the right to live without fear." He concluded:

"Action by the United States on behalf of democracy in Latin America is a part of the defense of the United States itself against the totalitarian and Communist influence in our countries. It is in support of this supreme defensive necessity that immediate action must be taken in the same way as was done in Europe against Hitler and Mussolini."

The Peruvian government spared no efforts to blacken Haya's reputation. Through its myriad agents and accomplices, and often through the gullibility of American newsmen always looking for the sensational, Haya was depicted as a Communist and a dope peddler. These accusations, clearly baseless to anyone acquainted with Haya's political history and personal character, greatly aggrieved him. He pleaded with me to help him rebut the charges. Particularly offensive to me was a story by Roger Stuart which appeared in the *New York World Telegram* of September 28, 1949. Two days later I sent a letter to the editor of the offending paper, vindicating Haya's anti-Communist stand. It was not published, so I had it printed in the October 1949 issue of the *Inter-American Labor News*. It read in part:

To call the APRA Party of Peru a Communist organization is simply ridiculous. The fact is that the Apristas have been the pioneers in fighting Communism in Latin America even when, during the recent war, the Communists were accepted as democratic partners. Haya de la Torre and the Confederation of Labor of Peru have been among the first to line up with the American Federation of Labor in fighting Communism in Latin American organized labor and in smashing the Communist-controlled CTAL.

If your staff writer had taken the trouble to check the Communist newspapers of the last ten years, including *The Daily Worker,* he would have found that Haya de la Torre has been the object of constant, virulent attacks on the part of the Communists. He would also have found out that the Communists, out of their deep hatred for Haya de la Torre and his democratic, anti-Communist, anti-Fascist movement, are supporting the present military, totalitarian government of Peru.

The dope peddler charge was so cleverly woven out of a tissue of innuendos, out-of-context quotations, and outright falsehoods, that the government of Peru included it in its documentation submitted to The Hague tribunal to prove that Haya was "a common criminal" and not a "political refugee." The accusation started with the publication in the Peruvian press, and in some American news media such as *The New York Journal* and *The Saturday Evening Post,* of a report allegedly linking Haya and his brother, Edmundo, with dope-smuggling traffic carried on by one Eduardo Balarezo. This patently false charge was given wide publicity in the Lima newspapers in February of 1950. According to their account, the U.S. General Supervisor of Narcotics for the New York District, Garland H. Williams, had sent letters to the Peruvian Ambassador in Washington stating that Victor Raul Haya de la Torre had met Balarezo in New York in September of 1948, had visited his Long Island home, and had traveled with him by boat between Peru and the United States.

Haya expressed his deep hurt and indignation that such a charge, which the Communists and his political enemies in the Odría dictatorship exploited to the fullest, should be made by an official of the U.S. government which he had held in such high esteem as leader of the democratic forces. Newspapers in both Peru and the United States said that Williams's charge had been supported by New York's Attorney General, Joseph Martin. Haya indignantly denied that he had seen Balarezo during his visit to this country and sent me a detailed account of his travels and lecture engagements while here which showed that the alleged meeting was quite impossible. He also pointed out that he had traveled to and from the United States by Pan American Airways and not by boat—a fact readily confirmed. Later, Balarezo's wife, who was in Peru, told the press that Haya had not met her husband in New York, but only once in Peru when he was introduced by Águila Pardo, second in command of the Peruvian ship *El Callao,* who later led the Navy revolt of October 3, 1948. He was a friend of Balarezo and the latter had returned to Peru on his ship in 1948 on the voyage that Haya was falsely accused of making with him.

I learned that after the Navy revolt failed, Odría's secret police sent to the United States a man named Mier y Terán to accuse Balarezo of being an Aprista. He and other agents spread the stories linking Haya de la Torre and his brother to Balarezo and were the source of the allegation that Attorney General Martin had backed Williams's charges. Martin repudiated his support of these falsehoods, pointing out that it was a police agent from Peru that had told the press he had done so, and declaring that he had never made the accusation himself. The Peruvian press, however, did nothing to correct the false accusations, and Haya was deeply hurt that the U.S. Ambassador to Peru, Harold H. Tittmann, who had been informed of Martin's denial and been given evidence that Williams's allegations could not be correct, did not speak out to set the record straight. In the absence of a disclaimer from Tittmann, Haya felt that the Williams letters appeared to be an accusation against him by the U.S. government.

Because this same impression was widely held by many of the democratic leaders and the vast number of Peruvian workers who held Haya in such cherished esteem, I felt that some action was imperative to have our government set the record straight. Accordingly, under date of April 11, 1950, I addressed the following letter to Edward G. Miller, then Assistant Secretary of State in charge of Latin American matters:

I have been reliably informed that *Ultima Hora* on February 3, 1950, and *El Comercio* on February 9, 1950, both of Lima, published what were alleged to be letters dated May 27 and August 30, 1949, from Mr. Garland Williams, the Narcotics Supervisor of the New York District to Mr. H. J. Anslinger, the U.S. Commissioner of Narcotics. These letters contained statements that Edmundo Haya de la Torre was "closely associated" with the Peruvian cocaine traffic and implications that Victor Raul Haya de la Torre was likewise involved. I note certain obvious inaccuracies in the letters. For example, Victor Raul Haya de la Torre did not "visit the United States aboard an unidentified Peruvian battleship," but arrived and departed by Pan American World Airways and Peruvian International Airways, as can easily be verified.

With respect to the contents of the letters therefore, they clearly contain both inaccurate and unverified statements. Apart from those Peruvians referred to in the letters who have been tried and convicted in the United States courts, the letters in turn unfairly and inaccurately impugn the reputation of prominent Peruvians, with whom the American Federation of Labor has had pleasant and helpful relations over a number of years.

In order that the reputation of eminent Peruvian friends of the American Federation of Labor may not be unjustly impaired by the publication of the letters referred to above, I would like to know if my understanding of the letters, as expressed above, is substantially correct.

Under date of May 1, 1950, I received a letter from Miller in which he declared, "I am informed that the interpretation of the situation, as given in your letter, is substantially correct." Haya was delighted when he learned that the State Department had taken this stand. "This," he wrote me, "will be enough, I think, to pull the coat of hair off of the wolf!" My letter to Miller and his reply, properly authenticated according to international juridical requirements, were sent to the Hague Tribunal which was considering the Peruvian government's charges that Haya was a criminal and not entitled to asylum.

In the fall of 1950 the World Court unanimously decided that Haya de la Torre was a political exile and rejected the assertion of the Peruvian government that he was guilty of common crimes. However, the International Court also asserted that Colombia had acted wrongly in granting him asylum and that it must cease doing so. This contradictory decision was immediately used by the government of Peru to demand that Colombia surrender Haya, a request that the Colombian government indignantly and persistently refused to accede to.

The case of Victor Raul Haya de la Torre threatened to throw Latin America into one of its worst political crises in modern history. The decision of the International Court of Justice, by which Haya de la Torre was expected to be surrendered to the government of Peru, aroused so much indignation that as a reprisal a number of Latin American countries were expected to refuse ratification of the Bogotá Inter-American Agreement, in which the International Court of Justice is specifically mentioned as the juridical agency to which disputes will be referred for settlement. If he was surrendered to the Odría government, only a miracle would save Haya de la Torre's life; at best, he would get a long-term imprisonment from which he would probably never emerge alive. If this were allowed to happen, the democratic forces of Latin America would be humiliated and discouraged, thus creating a situation from which only the totalitarians, Communist and Fascist, would profit!

Furthermore, it was being freely predicted by those familiar with the Latin American scene, that if Haya de la Torre were handed over to the government of Peru, it would be impossible for a long time to expect any harmonious collaboration in the international field between the bloc of Latin American states that would side with Peru, and the prodemocratic bloc that would side with Colombia. Parliaments in a number of countries, among them Uruguay, Guatemala, and Cuba, had already gone on record demanding safety for Haya de la Torre. If their hopes were not realized, the relationship of these countries with Peru might reach the breaking point. And what good would this do to the United States, which at that time was involved in the Korean War and needed the unanimous and harmonious support of the Latin Americans in the United Nations?

At the urgent request of Haya himself, I joined with a number of his American friends in drafting and circulating among high U.S. government officials a memorandum in which there was made the following specific suggestion:

It is obvious that a way must be found to persuade the government of Peru to settle peacefully this disagreement with Colombia over the fate of Haya de la Torre, by allowing him—through some form of face-saving compromise—to leave the country. The impending political crisis would thus be avoided, and the unity of the American states would be preserved.

It is also obvious that at this stage of the crisis the United States is the only government that can bring about a peaceful solution, perhaps through a personal appeal from President Truman to President Odría asking him, for the sake of Latin American unity, to allow Haya de la Torre to leave the country.

The founding ORIT Convention, held in Mexico City during the month of January 1951, adopted a Statement and Resolution on the Right of Asylum, devoted largely to the case of Haya de la Torre, in which it was resolved "to support the position of Colombia in this issue, which is also that of the democratic working class forces of the continent," and "to express our satisfaction over the offer of mediation made by the governments of the United States and Mexico to avoid the breaking off of diplomatic relations between Colombia and Peru—a move which has been unanimously applauded throughout America."

But it took three more years for the mediators and the conciliators to succeed. Finally, one day in 1954, Haya was "surrendered" to the Peruvian government, which in turn, by previous arrangement, immediately allowed him to go to Mexico.

One of Haya's first acts was to visit the Mexico City headquarters of ORIT in order to express—as he himself said—his gratitude and solidarity with the free labor movement of the Americas. I was there to receive and embrace him, to shed with him tears of joy, to renew pledges of continued collaboration.

"And what do you intend to do, now, Victor Raul?" I asked.

"Resume the fight for all the good causes. This is the destiny and duty of all free men!" he replied.

From Mexico, Haya de la Torre went to Europe. I received a letter from him, dated Copenhagen, December 15, 1954, which greatly pained me. Haya was bitter and resentful at the way he had been treated by the Consular and Immigration authorities of the United States. He had gone to the U.S. Consul in Mexico City, asking for a transit visa, for which he presented all the necessary documentation, including fingerprints; but it was denied with the simple explanation that "just to go through, without stopping, it was not really needed." At Miami International Airport, Haya was treated like a prisoner, escorted from one plane to another by a guard, denied permission to write postcards, and was only allowed to have breakfast—at his own expense, of course. "I had to pay $12 to my police escort," he claimed, "and I am still waiting to get this money back."

Haya concluded that all this was part of the hostility displayed against him by U.S. Ambassador Tittmann while he had been holed up in the Colombian embassy, and was "proof" of his contention that President Eisenhower was "a moral supporter of the American tyrants." Haya ended by stating that he would never come to the United States as long as "the

Republican dictatorship" continued. He also felt sure, on the basis of alleged statements by Ambassador Tittmann, that his APRA party would continue to remain illegal, hinting that this would be the desire of the U.S. government and American business interests in Peru.

While not sharing the pessimism which had obviously overcome Haya's mercurial character, I nevertheless shared his indignation over his having been subjected to such deplorable treatment. In my reply, dated December 29, I wrote him:

> The treatment to which you were subjected by the U.S. Consular authorities in Mexico City and the immigration officials in Miami is almost incredible. However, we must confess, with shame, that such things have been happening with embarrassing frequency within the last few years. Although I am sure you did not want me to do so, I went deliberately to the State Department where I managed to convey to Henry Holland, Assistant Secretary of State for Inter-American Affairs, my strongest resentment and protest for the treatment accorded you. When later I discussed the matter with Jay Lovestone, he said to me, in a tone of despair, that the stupidity of these actions must lead us to suspect that perhaps there is still some cleverly disguised Communist influence around. When I put your episode together with others of similar nature that have happened recently, it appears as if there is in our government a concerted move to force all the liberal democratic elements of Latin America to become enemies of the United States. As you rightly observe, who could profit from it but the Communists?

I could not let go unchallenged, however, Haya's unfortunate expression about a "Republican dictatorship." So, I included in my reply the following paragraph:

> In spite of your and our justified opposition to the Eisenhower Administration, I do not think that it deserves to be called a "Republican dictatorship," as you specify in your letter. We are still enjoying our civil liberties and it is pretty sure that we will succeed in preserving them. I hope, therefore, that you will change your mind about coming to the United States and will make plans to visit with us as soon as possible. If the stupid bureaucrats of the Consular Service should raise difficulties concerning your visa, you can rest assured, my dear Victor, that we will fight like hell and will leave no stone unturned. When you come you will see for yourself that since the last time you were here, in May 1948, the forces that believe in democratic freedom and oppose the totalitarian dictatorship of Communism and Fascism are still strong and are ready to do battle at every turn.

Haya soon made peace with the United States and became one of the strongest voices in support of our policy during the long period of the cold war. But somehow he never managed to come again to the United States, in spite of the fact that every time I mentioned the subject, he invariably answered:

"Of course, of course; I am anxious to come, as soon as I get a chance. . . ."

The Odría regime did not want to allow the democratic reestablishment of a unified labor movement, fearing quite rightly that it would probably come under the control of the Apristas. There were two principal political groups which were given freedom to operate in the labor field during this period—a Communist faction and the Peronistas.

Juan P. Luna returned to importance in the labor movement during the Odría regime. Officially, he had quit the Communist Party a few weeks before the overthrow of the Bustamante government. Consequently, he was technically eligible to run for office in the 1950 election. Luna was elected Senator on the single pro-Odría ticket which participated in the "contest." Previously, Luna had succeeded in regaining control of the Chauffeurs' Federation when its Aprista leaders were arrested.

Under the leadership of pro-Luna Communists and Peronistas, several attempts were made to reestablish the CTP. However, Apristas continued to enjoy a majority among the union delegates who participated in these meetings. As a result, the government refused to approve the legal reorganization of the CTP. It continued to operate as a *de facto* organization with Arturo Sabroso as General Secretary.

On May 1, 1951, the CTP issued a manifesto which contained the following significant sentences:

All the CTP leaders indicted for participation in the Callao mutiny were absolved, after an exhaustive examination of evidence which included—at our request—the Constitution of the CTP. The decision of the court established the complete innocence of the CTP leaders who *never will risk the fate of the unions in a coup d'état.*

The manifesto then complained that "some leaders of affiliated organizations are still under indictment and are even held in prison." It deplored that "certain restrictions on the activities of the unions still persist in spite of the declarations of the President of the Republic and high Labor Ministry officials that trade union liberty would be restored." Finally, the manifesto ended with this statement of policy:

We are facing a period of reorganization, which we began only recently when our headquarters were returned to us and it was once more possible to hold meetings. With activity again under way, we are aware of the necessity of convoking a Congress which will renew once again the dynamic life of the CTP, directed by leaders freely chosen by the workers.

The CTP leadership has decided to stay in Peru. They did not want to go abroad and become another Confederation of Labor in Exile, at least not so long as they were able to enjoy enough freedom to be of some service to their members. It was our duty, in turn, not only to respect their decision but also to resume our AFL and ORIT open contacts with them, to put behind them the full weight of the inter-American democratic labor movement.

In October 1951 I went to Peru. The visit was openly advertised as being made on behalf of the ORIT, of which I was Secretary of International Relations, and the AFL, of which I was the Inter-American Representative. I was met at the airport by Sabroso and other CTP leaders, mostly members of the Textile Workers' Union. We started our talks immediately. It was obvious that the trade union situation in Peru was still far from normal. Some Peruvian labor leaders who were in exile had warned me against supporting any "appeasement." However, I did not see—at least for the time being—any other solution than continuing to support the policy of compromise which our people inside Peru had adopted. This policy called for stressing trade union independence from any political party (meaning specifically the APRA Party) without surrendering to the government, but maintaining normal relations with the Ministry of Labor so that unions would be allowed to act freely in their own sphere. Sabroso insisted in his talks with me that this policy was the only one that would give our unions a chance to survive and to combat effectively the Communist movement.

I had conversations with Senator Victorio Casagrande, Director of Labor, who was very influential in the government, and with other officers of his Department. From the conversations I gathered that they were firmly opposed to the spreading of the Communist-controlled trade unions.

They pointed out that at the trade union convention of the Southern Districts of Peru a proposal to join the WFTU and the CTAL was blocked by government hints that such a move would be resisted on account of the Communist domination of these two international organizations. On the other hand, I was assured that the Peruvian government had no objection to affiliation with the ICFTU and the ORIT. As a matter of fact, they pointed out that Sabroso had been allowed to leave the country to attend meetings of the ORIT, and would be allowed to do so without restriction in the future.

As soon as I arrived in Lima I found myself under surveillance by the police. In fact, two of them remained outside my hotel room door throughout the night and they followed me constantly during the day wherever I went. At 11 o'clock at night Sabroso was arrested as he was leaving my room and was kept in jail until the following day, when he was released with apologies for the "misunderstanding." It appears that the police had me classified as a "dangerous Communist" who had arrived in Peru with "dangerous intentions." The matter was cleared up thanks to the intervention of the American Embassy and the officers of the Ministry of Labor. The fact that the police kept following me until I left Lima was explained by them as a "precautionary measure" for my safety.

The ORIT Executive Board meeting in Miami, Florida, January 24, 1952, took cognizance of the trend toward liberalization of the labor policy of the Peruvian government, and encouraged it by including, in its Statement on the Trade Union Situation in Peru, the following:

We hope that the Peruvian government has reached the conclusion that popular support organized by Communist elements has no value whatsoever; furthermore, such Communist contacts would damage the political interests of the government itself, which as a member of the international community of democratic countries, is committed to follow a policy of democratic orientation in its national affairs, especially in relation to trade union freedom, without which any social security legislation would be void of any real meaning.

The ORIT statement demanded the repeal of the so-called Law for Internal Security, which, especially in the countryside, was used to oppose legitimate trade union activity. It also urged the government to allow *all democratic unions* to function without crippling restrictions as was still the case among agricultural and sugar workers, and ended with a solemn pledge of continued solidarity with the Peruvian Confederation of Labor in its efforts to achieve complete trade union freedom.

The new Peruvian policy of ORIT was being sharply criticized then by a number of Peruvian political exiles who believed that the labor movement should have been used to harass the Odría regime in any way possible to the extent of rejecting any concessions that would allow greater measures of trade union freedom. ORIT took cognizance of such criticism by emphasizing in its January 1952 statement:

Our position opens the possibility for further progress and for clarification of the Peruvian trade union situation which is misrepresented by elements opposed to a really free trade union movement. ORIT, respectful of the political autonomy of its affiliates, leaves entirely to our brothers of the Peruvian Confederation of Labor the task of solving this particular aspect of their national problem.

In August 1952 I went back to Peru accompanied by Paul Reed, International Representative of the United Mine Workers of America, and Angelo Verdu, staff representative of the United Steel Workers. We had been to Chile, where, at the invitation of the Copper Workers' Confederation, we had made a survey of labor-management relations in the mining industry. We felt that a brief visit to Peru would give us an opportunity to see on the spot how the normalization of the trade union movement was progressing. We also wanted to offer the moral support of ORIT, the ICFTU, and the whole labor movement of the United States to the CTP, which was then battling to repel the attack of Communist and Peronist elements which had joined forces with the view of capturing the CTP. The year 1952 was the time of the great Peronist drive to destroy ORIT. In Peru they had obtained the support of a renegade Aprista, Tomás del Piélago, who, with the lavish support of the Argentine Embassy, had opened an office and started a well-financed campaign to win converts.

We arrived in Lima, Peru, on the afternoon of August 7, and were met at the airport by a labor delegation headed by Arturo Sabroso. The following day we talked with U.S. Ambassador Harold Tittmann, with Santiago Salines, Director of the Ministry of Labor, and other labor officials. In the evening we were honor guests at a dinner given by the Textile Workers Federation, at which we were presented with a scroll with the signatures of many leaders representing all the branches of the textile labor movement in Lima and nearby localities.

In the afternoon of Saturday, August 9, we went to Cantera de Atocongo, where we visited the cement factory "Portland-Sol" and addressed an impromptu meeting of the workers. It was the first open meeting in many years that the workers had the opportunity to attend. They listened to our addresses with visible rapture. After our speeches, for more than one hour we answered questions dealing with the structure and policies of the U.S. labor movement and its role in international affairs. We left Lima the same evening, and a large group of trade unionists were at the airport to see us off. Labor in Peru was again feeling free.

But it was too good to be true. A few months later the government again tightened the screws—under the pretext that a number of strikes had political rather than economic origin. By September 1953 the situation had become practically as bad as it was three years before, especially for the elements that had belonged in the past to the Aprista Party. Almost the only unions which were allowed a certain degree of freedom— not to strike but to meet in their headquarters and to deal with the government and employers—were those that for one reason or another had five years before supported the anti-Aprista coup of General Odría. In this group were included the Socialists, who were now in the opposition, and the so-called Luna Communists, the followers of "loyal" (read "domesticated") opposition leader Senator Luna. The "Stalinist" Communists were, however, out of favor, while the Peronistas continued to enjoy considerable freedom, although their stock had decreased since Perón had received, early in 1953, the plaudits of some Aprista leaders exiled in Chile and conferred with them when he visited that country.

Outside of Lima, particularly in the sugar plantations of the northern part of the country, the situation of the trade union movement became absolutely impossible. The workers had reverted to the state of peons. In the October 1953 issue of the *Inter-American Labor Bulletin,* I published a story on the conditions prevailing in the plantations of the Gildemeister Company, entitled "A Case of Colonial Exploitation in Peru." It had international repercussions and moved the government of Peru to give private assurances "that the situation would be corrected." I wrote:

The Gildemeister Co. in Peru controls 80 percent of the sugar production of the Valley of Chicama, which is the chief sugar producing area in the country. It has under sugar cultivation almost 50,000 acres of land. It has some of the world's largest sugar mills. It has its own railroad, two hundred miles in length. All of this makes Gildemeister one of the most potent economic and political forces in all of Peru.

On the front of the Gildemeister offices there is an inscription dating from 1873 which has served as its motto in social and labor matters: *"Tace, ora et labora,"* which means "Keep quiet, pray and work." However, as a corollary to this motto the company might have another: "High-priced sugar, cheap peon labor."

The company pays scandalously low wages. Yet it is able to sell its product at the same international price as that of Cuban sugar, which is produced by workers receiving relatively high wages. The sugar workers receive but few benefits of the country's social security system, and their families receive none of these benefits at all.

Because of the infamous wages paid the Gildemeister workers, the annual profits of this powerful firm in 1951 amounted to 61.5 percent on the total invested capital.

In September 1952 the workers of Gildemeister went on strike for an increase in their miserable wages. This strike lasted four weeks and in spite of police repression the workers won a moderate victory, forcing an increase which though small could not have been obtained at all without the unity and spirit demonstrated by the workers. The increase amounted to about 9 cents (US) per day, so that the present minimum wage is 55 cents a day.

The National Federation of Sugar Workers of Peru has been outlawed by the military dictatorship, and its leaders are in hiding or in exile. The General Secretary of the Federation, Leopoldo Pita, after several years of arbitrary imprisonment without charges being brought against him, was deported and is now in exile in Costa Rica.

After Haya de la Torre was allowed to leave Peru, in 1954, the APRA Party entered a period of tacit normalization. Its General Secretary, Ramiro Prialé, almost openly engaged in activities and negotiations leading to what I have already described as the peaceful liquidation of the dictatorship. The party was still technically outlawed, but government agents simply looked the other way. They pretended not to know what was going on. In a sense, the APRA Party went through the same process of gradually emerging from the underground as it had in the war years 1943–1945, when friends of Haya de la Torre coming to visit him from abroad were met at the airport by "mysterious" representatives who would escort them to Haya's "secret hideout."

The labor movement also benefited from this normalization trend encouraged by the government, reportedly under the discreet but effective prodding of U.S. Ambassador Ellis O. Briggs. In October 1955 I decided to travel again to Peru, mainly for the purpose of meeting the new Minister of Labor, Carlos d'Ugart—formerly an employee of the ILO in Geneva—and to try to impress him with the necessity of settling the few outstanding grievances of the free labor movement against his government. Foremost of these grievances was the inability of Arturo Jáuregui, Acting General Secretary of ORIT, to visit Peru, and the refusal of the Peruvian government to allow the return of a texile workers' leader, Lucio Sandoval, who had been deported three years before. I told the Minister that unless some immediate action was taken we would be compelled to issue a public protest, possibly at the AFL-CIO unity convention scheduled for the following month of December 1955. I also discussed this matter with other members of the government, with the U.S. Embassy, and with Arturo Sabroso and other trade union leaders.

As a result of my intervention, Jáuregui received permission to go back to Peru. After an absence of eight years, he visited Lima early in November and met freely with his family and trade union associates. Lucio

Sandoval went back in late October, with the government paying his return passage.

Odría's term came to an end in 1956. Manuel Prado returned to power, winning the elections mainly as a result of Aprista votes that were given to him at the last moment, after he agreed to legalize their party.

During the six years of the second Prado administration the country enjoyed more political freedom than at any other time of its history. The labor movement, in particular, was allowed to organize freely and to negotiate collective agreements with employers. Moreover, such unions as the sugar workers, which had been destroyed under Odría, were allowed to reorganize.

The labor movement was almost completely in the hands of the Apristas during the Prado government. They dominated the CTP, which was reestablished in 1956 under the leadership once again of Arturo Sabroso. They controlled almost all national industrial unions, the only important exception being the Federation of Bank Clerks, which was dominated by the Communists and their allies during most of this period.

Haya de la Torre returned to Peru, where he resumed active leadership of his party. His influence in the CTP continued undiminished and was an important factor in the consolidation of its anti-Communist leadership. During the long period of the Odría regime a few secondary APRA leaders, inside Peru and in exile, had succumbed to the left-wing, pro-united front maneuvers of the Communists. Their objectives were to undermine Haya's leadership and to detach the CTP from ORIT and the AFL-CIO. They were soon read out of the APRA Party or reduced to a condition of impotence.

Apprised of the impending visit to South America of the AFL-CIO mission headed by President George Meany, the CTP extended a cordial invitation to add Peru to his itinerary. President Meany readily accepted. We flew to Peru directly from Argentina in the latter part of November 1956. It was thrilling to see our old friend Arturo Sabroso once again in command of the CTP and to witness the support and admiration of the rank and file that he enjoyed. Just as the free trade unions played a major role in the election of Prado, so also were they continuing, under the leadership of Sabroso, to make a real contribution to the efforts to develop the economy and the social structure of Peru.

When he reached Lima, Meany got an explicit challenge from a local union chief, who contended that U.S.–owned companies there paid their Peruvian workers less in a day than they paid U.S. workers in an hour. He asked: "Why don't you help us fight them?" Pulling on a cigar, Meany said: "It is entirely up to you to create the conditions necessary to stand up and fight for your rights. You have to do what we have done: organize. Once you are organized, whenever you need our assistance in a just claim against your American employer, we will not hesitate to help you."

The Lima visit included a mass meeting and a number of social events, among them a reception at the U.S. embassy. It was attended by the President of the republic, members of the Cabinet, diplomats, political leaders, newspaper editors, representatives of business, and a large number of trade unionists. It was the first time that workers were admitted in such a large number into the elegant halls of the Embassy's residence. Mrs. Claire Timberlake, the wife of our Chargé d'Affaires, acted as hostess. At one point, in the receiving line, she extended her hand to greet a plainly dressed middle-aged woman; but as she suddenly recognized her, she warmly embraced her with exclamations of delight. Her guest was Gregoria Choque, leader of the Domestic Workers' Union, and one-time cook in the Timberlake household. In aristocratic, class-consicous Lima that vivid demonstration of American-style democracy was surely something!

Another sudden crisis, caused by the military coup of 1962, plunged the Peruvian labor movement into a period of turmoil, fear, and confusion. Haya de la Torre, presidential candidate of the APRA Party, obtained a plurality of votes but was short of the percentage needed to be proclaimed President. The election was thrown to the newly elected Congress, where none of the three candidates (the other two were General Manuel Odría and Dr. Fernando Belaunde Terry) commanded an absolute majority. Negotiations and horse trading followed for about a month. At that time, Haya de la Torre considered Belaunde, who had formerly been with APRA but was now supported by the military and the Communists, as his worst enemy. In the end, he managed to reach an understanding with Odría. The logic would have been to have Odría's followers combine with APRA Congressmen and elect Haya, but this would most likely have met with a military veto. So Haya pledged APRA's votes to elect Odría, hoping the military would tolerate him as being after all one of them. However, the military, bent on having their own man or nothing, deposed Prado, annulled the elections, and assumed absolute power.

At a convention held almost a year before, the CTP had adopted a resolution binding its leadership to immediately call a general strike in the event of a military take-over. However, when this actually took place, the labor leadership was hampered by a lack of communications because of a telephone workers' strike and, even worse, was almost paralyzed by the unexpected turn of events in the extremely unpopular APRA-Odría alliance. They hesitated. They debated. Finally, a few days later, they issued the call for a general strike; but it was too late. The military junta had had time to consolidate its power. The strike was a pitiful failure.

The Communists rushed to the support of the military junta, staged demonstrations condemning the Aprista-led general strike, and attempted to occupy by assault the CTP headquarters. A Committee to "reorganize" the CTP was hastily assembled. It was under clearly recognized Communist control. Its promoters were more than confident that the military junta would eventually recognize it as the legitimate voice of Peruvian organized labor.

At both ORIT and AFL-CIO headquarters the Peruvian chain of events caused consternation. President Kennedy broke diplomatic relations with Peru and recalled Ambassador James Loeb—a friend of mine of many years' standing. I spoke with him almost as soon as he reached Washington. His report deepened my fear that the democratic, anti-Communist CTP was in danger of being supplanted by a Communist-controlled labor group, friendly and subservient to the military junta. I decided to do something, quickly. With George Meany's immediate approval, I took a plane for Lima, where I arrived incognito.

Within twenty-four hours, through the good offices of friendly elements, mostly Americans, I was talking alone to General Juan Bosio, Minister of Interior of the military junta. The resentment against the CTP leadership for having called the general strike was strong. I had found it also widespread among American and Peruvian friends with whom I had talked the very first morning of my arrival. Of course, had the general strike been successful, it would have been quite a different story. General Bosio flatly stated that giving control of the CTP to Communist elements, as some of his military colleagues blinded by anti-Aprista hatred were inclined to do, would have been disastrous.

"I have been head of the SIM (Military Intelligence Service) for a number of years," he said. "And I know who they are, and what they are up to. As long as I am Minister of Interior, the Communist seizure of the CTP will not be permitted."

Reassured on this score, I moved to the People's House to see Ramiro Prialé, General Secretary of the APRA Party. The building had been attacked and partly sacked by Army elements during the first few hours of the take-over. But then, on orders from the authorities, it was returned to APRA with the pledge that they would pay for the damages. A quick inventory had been made. Ramiro himself took me around to see the doors of the padlocked, damaged rooms, with strips across reading *Revisado*—checked. It was clear that the military junta wanted to rule with soft gloves, without outlawing any opposition party, bent on having its way through the holding of new elections, one year hence. Furthermore, they badly needed to be recognized by the government of the United States and they rightly felt that a posture of moderation would be of help.

When I later talked with Sabroso and other trade union leaders, I found them calm, confident that the worst was over. I acquainted them with the results of my personal contacts. They were pleased, but urged me to keep up the international pressure at full steam. Then I took Sabroso aside:

"Why did you call for a general strike, when it was obvious that the unions would not respond, because it was too late and the issue was confused? After all, it was a general strike to protest the Army's intervention that had prevented not *Haya*'s but *Odría*'s accession to the Presidency."

"Perhaps you are right, Serafino, but the pressure was too strong. The order came, and we had to obey it."

"From whom, from the Party, from Haya de la Torre himself?"

Sabroso did not answer. He was visibly embarrassed. At times, silence is more eloquent than words.

As Minister of Labor the military junta appointed Air Force General José Gagliardi Schiaffino. His anti-Aprista credentials were as good as those of any other military chief, but he was wary of the Communist maneuvers and from the very beginning he established formal, if not too cordial, relations with Arturo Sabroso and the CTP leadership. In the *modus vivendi* that was worked out, the CTP was recognized as the most representative voice of Peruvian labor, with certain acknowledged limitations. The military junta also gave approval to a plan, originally accepted by the Prado regime, to set up a labor leadership training center—called Centro de Estudios Laborales del Perú—under the advisory supervision of representatives of management, the CTP, the Ministry of Labor, and AID, the latter furnishing the major share of funds. The direction of the Center was later given to the American Institute for Free Labor Development, whose structure and functions are described in Chapter XXIV.

During the Peruvian military junta interlude, I visited twice with Haya de la Torre. I got somewhat the impression that being allowed to move around freely under a military regime was almost embarrassing for Haya. It was something foreign to his established mode of life—which he had lived in exile, in underground activity, or in unbounded freedom with huge masses to be harangued. He then had no such excitement, at least for a while. But when elections were called and the campaign started, Haya de la Torre, again the candidate of APRA, plunged into the contest headlong, confident that this time the presidency of Peru would not elude him. Haya sensed that this was undoubtedly his last chance. He and his people campaigned in truly heroic form. But again they failed. The defeat was narrow but decisive. Belaunde Terry won, with the support of the Army and the Communists.

The Apristas feared that the new government might use its influence to break their control over the CTP. Their fears were well founded, as I found out myself in a long, exhausting interview with Belaunde's first Minister of Interior, Dr. Oscar Trelles. The Communists, through their spurious Committee for the Reorganization of the CTP—the same Committee that was set up after the military coup the year before—had high hopes. A date for their own CTP Congress was set. Some inconsiderate actions by Belaunde's Minister of Labor lent credence to the rumor that the President himself would attend the Congress. But I was able to intervene in time. Thanks to the help from Dr. Celso Pastor, President Belaunde's brother-in-law and later Ambassador to Washington, and the cooperation of U.S. Ambassador John W. Jones and other influential sources aware of the perils of letting the Communists assume control of organized labor, I was finally able to convey to my CTP friends the firm commitment that the trade union *status quo* would remain unaltered. At the same time, the General Secretary of ORIT, Arturo Jáuregui, himself a Peruvian and a member of the Aprista Party, established personal contacts with President Belaunde and gave him assurance of international labor support.

In retrospect, Haya's strange support for Odría in 1962 appears to have accomplished his basic goal of preventing a Communist take-over of the CTP. Haya was convinced that Belaunde's election at that time would have put the Communists in power. Although Belaunde also got the Communist vote in the next election, he had made no commitments to them and meanwhile he also had made an alliance with the Christian Democrats. After his election, events forced him to crack down on the Communists because of their guerrilla tactics.

The CTP Aprista leaders have mellowed with time and have adopted a policy of cooperation and collaboration with management. They have dropped from their lexicon any reference to nationalization of private property or socialization, and have established friendly "technical relations" with the Belaunde government, thus reducing to a minimum strikes and industrial conflicts that would otherwise have damaged the economic progress of the country.

Haya's birthday falls on February 22. On that day, in 1966, he became seventy years old. Close to one hundred thousand people paraded through the streets of Lima, past the Casa del Pueblo, APRA's headquarters, chanting "Victor Raul! Victor Raul!" They were Indians from the uplands, slum dwellers from the *barriadas,* workers, peasant, students, intellectuals, professionals. *El Jefe* stood for hours on the reviewing stand, waving the white handkerchief, held aloft in a crooked arm, in the traditional party salute of APRA. To any observer not familiar with Peru's modern history, the sight of the huge demonstration might have presaged the coming victory of a revolutionary movement swept to power by an upsurge of popular fervor. But to those who knew, it had quite a different significance—it was the supreme tribute to a leader who had entered the autumn of his life and was now resigned to fade away.

But then, was Haya's struggle in vain? Was he actually a defeated man? I do not think so. In forty years of struggle, suffering, bloodshed, exile, and underground work, Haya has given a new meaning, a new dimension, to the concept of social revolution. He has kept it, in his own Peru, and elsewhere by the power of example, inside the boundaries of freedom; he and his movement have been the strongest bulwark that successfully resisted the infiltration and capture of the social-revolutionary concept by the Communist totalitarians. Peru is now considered by most competent observers off the danger list. But where would Peru be today, I ask, if Haya de la Torre and his APRA Party had not been on the scene?

Notes

1. *La Tribuna,* May 28, 1948.
2. *Inter-American Labor News,* January 1949.

XIX

Labor and Communism in Chile

THE COMMUNIST SUCCESS in infiltrating and controlling the labor movement in Chile has been, in my considered opinion, the main cause of the economic instability with consequent inflation that has plagued that country since the immediate postwar period. It is also the main obstacle in the path of President Eduardo Frei's current effort to achieve a peaceful social revolution.

The first significant manifestation of Communist influence in Chile took place in 1922 when the Socialist Labor Party (PSO) joined the Communist International and its labor arm, the Chilean Labor Federation (FOCh), affiliated with the newly organized Red International of Labor Unions.

After President Arturo Alessandri returned to power in Chile in 1925, a commission was appointed to write a new constitution. The principal labor organizations and the Communist Party were represented on the commission. No other country in Latin America saw the emergence of the Communist Party as a national force as early as Chile.

One of the first acts of the regime of Colonel Carlos Ibáñez del Campo, who ruled Chile from 1927 to 1931, was to implement the 1924 Labor Code which provided for the registration and legalization of unions. Communists and anarcho-syndicalists were opposed to such a law, fearing extensive government control over union matters. Consequently, they bitterly opposed the Ibáñez del Campo regime and as a result suffered

322

serious setbacks. By the time of the September 1931 overthrow of Colonel Ibáñez, the Communists had been considerably weakened. However, a few years later they recovered their strength. These ups-and-downs of the Chilean Communists happened several times, always ending in a Communist upswing.

The short-lived Socialist Republic of Chile established in 1932, first under Colonel Marmaduque Grove and then 100 days under Carlos Dávila, gave rise to the reorganization of the Socialist Party a year later. In the following years it grew in strength and became one of the largest political parties of the country. Under its influence the various labor groups that had split along ideological lines (Stalinists, Trotskyites, Socialists, and Anarcho-Syndicalists) joined together in a national convention out of which emerged, in January 1937, the Confederación de Trabajadores de Chile (CTCh) with a Socialist (Juan Díaz Martínez) as General Secretary and a Communist (Salvador Ocampo) as the No. 2 man.

The victory of Don Pedro Aguirre Cerda's Popular Front in the 1938 elections gave the Communists an opportunity to strengthen their hold on organized labor and to begin their process of infiltration into important government agencies. How this was accomplished is described in revealing detail by Eudocio Ravines, then the Comintern's commissar in Chile, in his book *The Yenan Way*.

During World War II the Communists increased their influence over Chilean labor but refrained from any move that would have compromised unity inside the CTCh. However, as soon as the war ended, they managed to obtain the support of Radical and the so-called *Falangista* [1] labor leaders and challenged the leadership of Bernardo Ibáñez, who had meanwhile assumed control of the Socialist trade union forces, becoming General Secretary of the CTCh in July 1939.

Two explanations are needed in order to understand the reasons for and the consequences of this move. Bernardo Ibáñez, in addition to being General Secretary of the CTCh, was also a leader of the "democratic" wing of the Socialist Party. He had always opposed the Communists, and had already formed personal friendly relations with AFL labor leaders— to such an extent that at the 1944 Philadelphia conference of the ILO he allowed himself to be nominated against Lombardo Toledano for membership in the ILO Governing Body. Naturally, the Communists marked him for liquidation at the first opportune moment.

But why did the Radicals and the Falangists join with the Communists in this move against a moderate Socialist? The explanation lies in the fact that in Chile each political party decides, through its own trade union department, the policy to be followed by its members inside the labor movement—under pain of severe disciplinary measures against the violators. These party trade union departments, almost without exception and up to the present time, have followed a policy of servile collaboration with the Communists inside the labor movement.

The break between Bernardo Ibáñez and the Communists became final, as already indicated in a previous chapter, during the month of February 1946. Organized workers, under Ibáñez's leadership, went on a nationwide general strike in order to defend union rights threatened by a government decree. They later defeated a Communist attempt to capture the government by using the weapon of a general strike of indefinite duration for political purposes.

The poor health of Chile's President Juan Antonio Ríos compelled him, early in January 1946, to give up his office, delegating all presidential prerogatives to Vice-President Alfredo Duhalde, member of the moderate wing of the Radical Party. Simultaneously the Communists launched a campaign for the reorganization of the government, demanding Communist participation. It was the first time that the Communists had declared their willingness to enter the Cabinet, a responsibility which they had consistently refused in the past, even when during the war they were loudly championing national unity. They reached an understanding on a common plan of action with the majority of the Radicals and other left-wing groups, but not with the Socialists, who, in 1945, had left the so-called Democratic Alliance, proclaiming their independence of action. The Socialists had accused this Alliance of being unable to do anything constructive for the welfare of the working people while it was embroiled in endless political maneuvers and plots for the benefit of one of its component groups.

Meanwhile, two serious labor conflicts developed in the northern nitrate districts of Mapocho and Humberstone. The government, ill-advisedly, revoked the *personeria juridica* (juridical status) of the two unions involved, claiming that they had engaged in illegal strikes under Communist pressure to embarrass the government. Nevertheless, the Chilean Confederation of Labor, under the leadership of Bernardo Ibáñez, took prompt defensive action to protect its right to strike.

On January 28, while thousands of workers were assembled in Bulnes Square for a protest meeting, there was a clash between demonstrators and Federal police, resulting in several casualties. The CTCh immediately proclaimed a protest general strike throughout the nation for January 30. The government replied with a proclamation of martial law and the appointment of several military leaders to key government positions in place of a number of Ministers who had resigned in protest against police brutality.

Chile was suddenly plunged into a situation that took on all the aspects of imminent civil war. Orders for the arrest of Ibáñez and other labor leaders were issued, but the general strike called for January 30 went on just the same and it was the most complete national stoppage ever to occur in Chile. Not a wheel turned, not a hand worked, not a place of business was open.

The 100 percent success of the strike greatly impressed government circles, which, already alarmed by the rising dangers of civil war (for it was common knowledge that military elements ideologically tied to the Perón movement in Argentina were making preparations to stage a coup), sought to establish negotiations for the solution of the crisis.

At this point the Communists launched their plan for a general political strike of indefinite duration, in order to force Acting President Alfredo Duhalde to transfer the government to the left-wing Alliance, which included the Communists. This proposal was opposed by Bernardo Ibáñez and his friends in the Executive Committee of the CTCh at a meeting on February 1, as nothing less than a maneuver to exploit organized labor to gain political power for the Communists and their allies. "We struck two days ago all over the country in order to safeguard the rights of organized labor, and we are ready to do it again if the circumstances should require it," declared Ibáñez, "but I will never give the order to strike for the purpose of helping a political combination to gain its political objectives."

During that same night acting President Alfredo Duhalde dismissed the military government, lifted martial law, restored juridical status to the two labor syndicates of Humberstone and Mapocho, and entrusted to a new Government, composed of four Socialists, two moderate Radicals, one Democrat, and two representatives of the armed forces, the task of putting into practice the program of economic reforms previously demanded by the CTCh.

Democratic labor had won. The general strike of January 30 had had its effect. Civil war had been averted. But the Communists, having received the order to enter the government of Chile at any cost, insisted on their plan for a general strike in order to force the government to yield to their demand. Ibáñez pleaded in vain for hours. Others did the same. The

Communists insisted, and over the head of the legally constituted authorities of the Chilean Confederation of Labor issued the strike call. Without hesitation, Ibáñez countered with an appeal to the workers to refuse to obey the Communist strike order but to rally instead around the new government.

The Communist general strike was almost a complete fiasco. After seven days they had to give it up. But it brought a series of charges and countercharges that irreparably compromised the unity of organized labor. In typical Communist fashion Ibáñez was called a "traitor" and was "demoted" from the post of General Secretary of the CTCh. But he continued unperturbed at his post, now openly welcoming this opportunity to clean house and reorganize the Chilean labor movement on a more stable and sound basis, which—as he stated before 15,000 cheering workers at Caupolicán Theater on February 10—"would never permit the interests of the working class to be exploited for the benefit of a political party or a combination of parties, including my own party, the Socialist."

The Socialists, with a small group of the Democrats and a few independents, continued their activity under the name of CTCh. The Communists and their allies did the same. The rivalry continued for six years, until 1952. Meanwhile, the sudden death of President Juan Antonio Ríos had caused the calling of Presidential elections on September 4, 1946. Gabriel González Videla, candidate of the Radical Party and a revived Popular Front, which included the Communists, won the election. During the first months of González Videla's administration, with three Communists in the Cabinet, Bernardo Ibáñez's CTCh was definitely on the defensive and would have disappeared had it not been for the help received from the AFL.

After the Communists were ousted from the González Videla Government, the fortunes of the moderate Socialist CTCh improved to the point that it soon regained control of most of Chilean organized labor. Steps were also taken, with assistance from ORIT and ICFTU, to call a unity congress of all the democratic labor forces with the view of reconstituting —on a broad basis and free of political party control—a central Chilean labor organization. The congress was scheduled to be held in the latter part of 1952, after the September presidential elections.

In 1952 the Copper Workers' Confederation of Chile elected a democratic leadership headed by Manuel Ovalle, who extended an invitation to the AFL, the CIO, and the United Mine Workers to send a delegation to Chile for a visit to the mining centers, particularly those of the U.S. copper enterprises (Kennecott and Anaconda) at Chuquicamata, Potrerillos, and Sewell. When the Executive Board of ORIT gave approval to such a visit, the U.S. trade union groups appointed Paul K. Reed, International Representative of the United Mine Workers of America; Angelo Verdu, staff representative of the United Steel Workers, for the CIO; and myself, for the AFL. We arrived in Santiago July 20, welcomed by the mayor, many labor leaders, and the Chilean press.

Accompanied by Ovalle and a three-man team, we began our mission by going south to the Concepción area, visiting the Lota and Schwager coal mines, the Huachipato steel plant, the Penco sugar refinery, and the Braden copper mines (Kennecott) at Sewell. Returning to Santiago we were honored at a dinner at the Moneda Palace given by President González Videla and conferred with Ambassador Claude G. Bowers. During the one-week trip to the north we visited the Anaconda mines at "Chuqui" and Potrerillos, the smelter plant in Paipote, and labor groups in Antofagasta, Barquito, and Copiapó. Before leaving Santiago on August 7 we saw González Videla and Bowers again and talked to the Minister of Labor and the press.

In all our interviews, conversations, meetings, and addresses we repeated the basic purpose of the mission: to strengthen relations between the workers of Chile, especially the copper workers, and the American labor movement. For years pro-Communist and Peronista propaganda had partly succeeded in driving a wedge between the labor movements of the United States and Chile. We hoped to eliminate or reduce some of the misconceptions regarding the international role of American trade unionism and its basic philosophy. For example, we repeatedly stressed its nonpolitical stand in "rewarding friends and defeating enemies." Because Chile is so highly politicized, this subject aroused the greatest interest among the workers and union leaders. In our meetings we emphasized that labor in the U.S. is based on complete independence from any political party, foreign ideology, or government control.

Our hosts were greatly impressed with the cardinal features of American trade unionism: collective bargaining methods and gains, labor legislation provisions on wages and hours, social security, industrial relations, union educational activities, the aims of our legal, research, welfare, and engineering departments, etc. We also noted the active role of American labor in the worldwide struggle for the defense of democracy against totalitarian aggression.

Following are some of the observations in our report submitted to ORIT:

General Characteristics of the Chilean Labor Movement. There was no central confederation under democratic leadership with enough support to influence labor policy at the national level. Though lacking industry-wide or national coordination, the labor movement was fairly strong at the unit or plant level. In addition to two groups each claiming title as the Confederation of Labor of Chile (CTCh), there were a number of independent unions and federations at the national level. Of these the Confederation of Copper Mine Workers was one of the strongest, representing more than 95 percent of all workers employed in the copper mining, milling, and smelting industry. This Confederation was composed of 18 local unions of blue- and white-collar workers, all belonging to the three Kennecott and Anaconda companies at Chuquicamata, Sewell, and Potrerillos.

Chilean Labor Legislation. Though the right of the worker to belong to the union of his choice was protected, the labor legislation imposed so many restrictions that it generally tended to weaken rather than strengthen day-to-day union operations. For example, labor leaders were—and still are —required by law to be actually employed by the company whose workers they represent. Thus, it is impossible to appoint or elect full-time union officers. We found the legislation also weak in protecting labor leaders from possible persecution by management because their right to their jobs was not guaranteed.

Working Conditions and Living Standards. The mission did not have the time to make a full study of wages and working conditions in mining centers outside the copper industry. However, we gathered some data at Lota (coal) Huachipato (steel), and Paipote (smelter). Coal production methods were obviously antiquated and new machinery on the surface and underground was urgently needed. Many of the coal miners lived in squalid, unhealthy quarters. Though the productivity in the modern plants at Huachipato and Paipote was fairly high, wages and living conditions appeared to be far below the economic capacity of these new industries.

In the copper industry, wages and various fringe benefits—such as family allowances, free housing, hospital services, commissaries, and bonuses—had lifted living standards higher than those prevailing in other Chilean industries. These gains had been achieved through the direct efforts of the Copper Mine Workers' Confederation. However, there was much to be accomplished in housing, recreation facilities, and other welfare services. The barren, isolated mining camps require special facilities for the worker and his family.

Labor Relations. Conversations with many workers, union officials, and the local management of the Anaconda mines strongly indicated that this company had been slow to recognize the need of a solid labor-relations policy. The union apparently had not yet been accepted as a necessary and constructive force in society, except as prescribed by law. There was no real collective bargaining between Anaconda and the Confederation, as it is understood and practiced in the United States. Constant harassing tactics by management had convinced the workers that the company sought to weaken the union and possibly destroy it. Naturally, we were very distressed by this situation because by preventing the establishment of harmonious labor relations the prodemocratic, anti-Communist position of the union leadership was jeopardized. We noticed that where cordial industrial relations were being practiced and grievances were speedily settled, productivity tended to rise and the average worker was generally free of anti-U.S. sentiments.

Communist Penetration of Chilean Labor. The Communists exercised an influence disproportionate to their numbers in the labor movement and controlled several important unions in the coal and nitrate industries. Together with their Peronista allies they made repeated attempts to disrupt our trip and conducted a full-scale propaganda campaign in the press and on the radio, even calling for our expulsion from Chile. These attacks actually proved to be counterproductive and helped to expose the international character of the Communist movement.

We returned to Washington via Lima, fully satisfied that our mission to Chile had helped to establish closer relationships and a better understanding between our labor movements. Specific programs were planned with the leaders of the Copper Workers' Confederation to strengthen the union in its efforts to attain higher wages and improved working conditions.

A few words are also needed to summarize the coal mining conditions we investigated. In the year 1952 Chile produced 1,900,000 metric tons of coal. Since then, production has decreased steadily, amounting in 1964 to about 1,370,000 metric tons. Coal mining, concentrated in the towns of Coronel and Lota, in the vicinity of Concepción, is mostly controlled by the Lota-Schwager Coal Corporation, which accounts for 80 percent of output. Paul Reed, who learned mining in the coal fields of West Virginia, was simply appalled at the conditions he saw in the Coronel and Lota mines. The latter, located at the edge of the Pacific Ocean, has about 100 miles of tunnels, many underneath the sea. Miners were then working on their knees behind compressed-air drills for hours on end. The quality of coal was poor and the machinery antiquated. Reed made copious notes and compared them with union and management officials. He remarked that the productivity of the average U.S. coal miner was about eight to ten times higher than that of his Chilean counterpart—mostly because of modern machinery and equipment. As a result, wages were unbelievably low.

Fourteen years later, in 1966, a long overdue program of modernization was finally getting under way. But wages, even after an upward adjustment of 35 percent, were still about $1 a day for beginners for a full shift underground, going up to about $2 a day for highly experienced miners. Chilean copper workers averaged 4 to 10 times more.[2] Even a common laborer in Santiago was getting a minimum wage of $2 to $2.50 a day.

It is also my belief that our visit to Chile, and particularly the section of our report dealing with the labor-relations policy of the Anaconda Copper Company, was one of the factors that later induced this particular company to completely change its labor-management relations practices and put it in the forefront of firms with an enlightened labor policy.

The results of this program of changes in working and living conditions were described, ten years later, by Robert J. Alexander in an article published in the May 1962 issue of the *Inter-American Labor Bulletin*. Some excerpts follow:

In the first place, the town was provided with all the exterior attributes of a permanent city. The streets were paved and trees were planted along the streets to improve their appearance and to add some green foliage to the brownish-gray of the desert in which Chuquicamata is located.

The community's social services were expanded and improved. In 1957, a new 300-bed hospital was completed. The school system was expanded to better handle the increased number of young people living in the town.

Another fundamental aspect in the transformation of Chuquicamata into a permanent city is the improvement in the workers' houses. The objective of the program is to provide each family with a house containing at least three bedrooms, a living room—which can double as a bedroom—a kitchen, and a bathroom. More than 1,500 of these houses had been constructed by 1962. Hundreds more have been added since.

Another aspect of the program to make Chuquicamata a permanent place of residence for its workers has been the company's policy of placing more Chilean personnel in administrative and technical positions. The Industrial Relations

Department was placed in the hands of a Chilean citizen as soon as it was created, and other administrative positions were also given to Chileans.

When the U.S. labor mission left Chile, prospects for the consolidation of the free labor movement were indeed good. Maritime workers, copper workers, most of the government employees, public service unions, sundry manufacturing and mining local unions, were enlisted in what appeared to us to be a determined move for a democratic labor unity. Progress was also made in the coal and nitrate industries. However, the victory of General Ibáñez del Campo in the Presidential elections of September 1952 dashed all our hope.

Bernardo Ibañez, who for many years had led the traditional Socialist Party of Chile, lost control of it to a faction headed by leftist Senator Salvador Allende. In the presidential campaign of 1952 Ibañez supported the democratic candidate of the Radical Party. Shortly after the election he retired from active political and trade union activity in Chile and went to Geneva to work with the ILO where he remained for ten years.

The defeat of the democratic candidate supported by the outgoing González Videla government stemmed basically from the appalling inflation, which had reduced living standards to intolerably low levels. Although for five years Chile had received considerable U.S. aid, which enabled it to build such things as modern electric power plants, and revenues from U.S.–owned copper mines had increased to the point where they accounted for 50 percent of the national budget, these achievements never benefited the working man. In fact, he was much worse off than before.

In the course of our visit to Chile during the months of July and August 1952, just preceding the elections, I noticed that the main topic of discussion was the revolt of the people against the Government in power and, generally speaking, also against the traditional political parties of all shades. One sensed widespread reaction resembling the political nihilism typical of Italy and Germany preceding the rise of Fascism and Nazism. On this popular resentment General Ibáñez del Campo, who had been dictator of Chile from 1927 to 1931, rode back into power. During the 1930's he had played around with the Chilean Nazis and in the 1940's he was the fair-haired boy of Perón in Chilean politics. However, it was obvious from the very beginning of his term that Ibáñez del Campo came to the presidency this time determined to live down his reputation of being a dictator and a Fascist. Nevertheless, his administration was a failure because he did not realize the real significance of his own victory—

a popular mandate for a sweeping change in the Chilean political and economic scene.

The Partido Socialista Popular of Chile (PSP), headed by Senator Raúl Ampuero—a splinter group from the Socialist Party led by Senator Salvador Allende—supported the candidacy of Ibáñez del Campo. After the victory, Ampuero became the trade union spokesman for the administration. The first thing he did was to advocate the return of the Communists, as well as any other trade union group, to a reunited house of labor. The slogan was "unity." Everyone opposed to "unity with all" was branded a sectarian, a traitor to the working class, a lackey of Yankee imperialism. Besides, it was emphasized, the Communists would only be a minority. "It is better to have them inside, where they can be watched and controlled, than outside," it was argued.

Chilean delegates to the ORIT convention which took place in Brazil in December 1952 were warned not to fall into this Communist "unity" trap. But pressure at home was stronger than pressure from abroad. The unity Congress took place in early 1953, and everything went as predicted. The Communists packed the meeting with phantom delegates representing paper organizations and ended by gaining control of the new organization, the Central Única de Trabajadores (CUT)—a control that today, even after the 1964 victory of Christian Democratic leader Eduardo Frei, is stronger than ever.

In 1956 an ORIT-ICFTU office was opened in Chile. With the cooperation of the AFL-CIO and the Cuban Confederation of Labor it launched a full-fledged campaign designed to rally the independents around a program of nonpolitical, nonsectarian trade unionism, strongly opposed to the Communist-dominated left alliance. In view of our previous failures with the anti-Communist labor elements in Chile, I was at first reluctant to recommend the investment of additional AFL-CIO funds. In a memorandum sent to President George Meany in March, 1956, I wrote:

In order to understand my cautiousness in relation to Chile, I must remind you that the AFL, as early as 1946, contributed substantial amounts of money to the "anti-Communist" elements in Chile; that the CIT kept its headquarters in that country for two years devoting a large share of its income and personnel to the support of the local "anti-Communists"; that later the ORIT and the Cuban CTC sent organizers and spent many thousands of dollars in similar work; that the United Mine Workers contributed likewise thousands of dollars; and that finally the ICFTU, after keeping its Latin American representative in Chile for several months, installed an office and allotted to its maintenance a considerable amount of money. All these efforts have produced nothing more than a series of uninterrupted failures, disappointments, bickerings, and resentment, for various reasons that would be too long to enumerate. Nevertheless, if we find that this time there is really "a will to fight" I am in favor of giving all the support we can muster.

We reached the conclusion that there was really a "will to fight." This belief was reinforced by the apparent willingness of the Christian Democrats to break away from CUT and join forces with the ORIT-ICFTU. In May 1956 Senator Eduardo Frei, with whom I had maintained cordial personal relations since the early forties, visited the United States and had an interview with President Meany to which I was also invited. Following the interview, I sat down with Senator Frei and worked out some possible practical approaches to the reaching of an understanding in Chile between the not-yet-too-strong Christian Democratic trade union forces and the ORIT-ICFTU forces, which were going through a period of bullish activity and self-confidence.

Upon his return to Chile, Eduardo Frei shared his United States experiences with William Thayer Arteaga, his adviser on trade union matters. Both wrote me a letter, dated June 7, 1956, in which they pointed out the controversial issues that needed to be cleared up before a lasting cooperation between the Christian Democrats and the ICFTU forces could be achieved. They urged me to come to Chile in order to "exchange ideas and experiences" that might lead to "more promising bases for an understanding."

In my answer, dated June 21, 1956, addressed to William Thayer Arteaga, I was very specific: "The organization drive," I wrote, "which ORIT-ICFTU, with the help of the AFL-CIO, the CTC of Cuba, and other trade union bodies have resolved to launch in Chile, will need, in order to succeed, the effective cooperation of all democratic elements including, especially, the Social Christians. To help achieve in an effective way this unity, I recognize the need to have private preliminary discussions. For this reason, I have decided to include Chile in the itinerary of my forthcoming visit to South America. It will be my specific purpose to have interviews with a number of trade union leaders and especially with you and Senator Frei."

I arrived in Santiago, Chile, on July 27 and remained there until August 2, 1956. In spite of apparent good will and good intentions on every side, nothing concrete came out of my conversations and interviews. The Christian Democrats insisted on certain requirements including a delay in the affiliation of the proposed new labor central to any international trade union center, although they were willing to let the component unions of the new national labor center affiliate on an individual basis. The ORIT-ICFTU spokesmen, on the other hand, insisted on the affiliation of the national federation to their body as a *sine qua non* for organizing aid. It was for them a question of understandable prestige. Furthermore, the Chilean ORIT-ICFTU elements then did not believe that the Christian Democrats had any real trade union or political future in Chile. As has already been explained in a previous chapter, relations between ORIT and ICFTU were rather strained in 1956 and there was also a reluctance on the part of the ICFTU representative in Chile to follow any suggestion under what might have appeared to be pressure from the AFL-CIO. The ICFTU was then practically going its own way in Latin America, issuing directives that took into little or no account the recommendations of either ORIT or the AFL-CIO inter-American representative.

A group of labor leaders representing shoemaking, printing, chauffeurs, and a few other unions abandoned CUT in 1957 and formed the National Confederation of Labor (CNT), which became affiliated to the ORIT and the ICFTU. The independent maritime workers also joined the international family of free labor. But in spite of ample support from abroad, the CNT never achieved a position of real strength. Opposition inside CUT was left to the emerging Christian Democrats.

During General Ibáñez's second administration, the Communists' main objectives were, in addition to the consolidation of their power inside CUT, the repeal of the "Defense of Democracy Law," enacted under the regime of President González Videla, and the transformation of the So-cialist-Communist alliance into a permanent Popular Action Front (FRAP). The latter was officially launched in February 1956 and the "Defense of Democracy Law" was finally repealed in August 1958, on the very eve of the presidential elections that gave victory to Jorge Alessandri, the candidate of the Center-Right coalition.

As a result of the increasing deterioration of the country's economy, with inflation and a further decrease of the wage earners' purchasing power—which the Alessandri government was unable to reverse or even to stop—the FRAP registered a series of electoral successes that almost brought it to power—400,000 votes in the congressional elections of March 1961; 600,000 votes in the municipal elections of April 1963 (30 percent of the votes cast); and 982,000 votes in the presidential elections of September 1964 (38.5 percent of the total).

Inside the CUT the Communists abandoned any pretense of "trade union political neutrality"—the false posture they had adopted during the early stage of coexistence with the Christian Democrats. CUT became a subsidiary of the political aims of FRAP. This was made clear at the Second CUT Convention, held in Santiago, December 1959. In the words of Christian Democrat Cesar Vergel Lozano, who attended the Convention as fraternal delegate from the Labor Confederation of Venezuela, ". . . Socialists and Communists, employing typical totalitarian methods, imposed their monopolistic control over CUT. . . . The Communists call for unity with the sole objective of adding forces to their sphere of influence. When they feel strong enough and safe, they bring these forces under their monopolistic control and keep them in subjection through their known methods of trade union dictatorship." [3]

The increasing Socialist-Communist use of CUT to enhance the political objectives of FRAP was resented by rank-and-file trade unionists of the Christian Democratic Party and by those leaders who were in charge of local unions and provincial and national federations. They began to revolt against the policy of continued affiliation with CUT that was still advocated by the Party's trade union bureau. Talks were again resumed, first informally and then officially, between representatives of ORIT and Christian Democratic trade union leaders, including officers of CLASC— the Latin American Confederation of Christian Trade Unionists—with the view of breaking the Christian Democratic unions away from CUT at its III Convention scheduled to meet in Santiago, August 1–5, 1962. However, at the very last moment, even after everything had been agreed upon, the Christian Democrats backed away. Here is how the events developed.

Preliminary talks were held between Julio Etcheverry Espínola, then ORIT Representative in Chile, and José Goldsack, President of CLASC. An agreement was reached in principle, but CLASC asked to finalize the matter with a top officer of ORIT. On July 29, Morris Paladino, then ORIT Assistant General Secretary, arrived in Santiago. On August 1, a meeting between representatives of ORIT and CLASC was held at the Hotel Carrera.[4] It adjourned after having reached the following agreements:

(1) In the event the Communists, who controlled the Convention Credential Committee, refused to accept the credentials of about four hundred delegates representing agricultural workers' unions that were bitterly opposed to the Communists, the democratic forces would leave the Convention en masse. All expected the Communists to refuse to validate these credentials because they represented the balance of power.

(2) To strengthen the democratic forces inside the Convention, it was agreed that COMACh, the Federation of Taxi Drivers, and *other* democratic unions would take part in the Convention with voice and vote. To make this possible, the ORIT representative agreed to pay the arrears in dues owed CUT by these organizations. The CNT also agreed to send out immediate instructions to all its affiliated organizations to regularize their situation with CUT so as to be able to take part in the Convention and thus increase the democratic strength.

(3) If they abandoned the site of the CUT Convention, which was to meet in the Caupolicán Theater, the democratic delegates would assemble in another hall, to be selected by CLASC, but whose rent would be paid by ORIT.

(4) A new National Democratic Labor Confederation would be launched. The convention itself would decide whether it should join the ORIT or CLASC. It was agreed, however, among the participants in the Hotel Carrera meeting, that they would recommend, for the time being, independence from both—in other words, the solution advanced six years before, in 1956, which was then dropped because of opposition from the ICFTU. To defray the immediate urgent expenditures for the planned operation, Paladino authorized Etcheverry to give Goldsack an advance, for which he signed a receipt.

On that same afternoon, however, Goldsack received orders from the Christian Democratic Party leadership not to break with the CUT Convention. For several days Etcheverry and Paladino were unable to contact him, not even by phone. After the CUT Convention ended, with the Communists in solid control as before, Goldsack did tell Paladino the whole story of how he had been prevented by orders from the Party from going through with the agreement.

On September 10, 1964—six days after his election to the presidency of Chile—Eduardo Frei received me at his home in Santiago. I was accompanied by my friend William Thayer Arteaga (who was latter appointed Minister of Labor by Frei). The purpose of my visit was to congratulate an old friend on his victory and to discuss with him in what way the American Institute for Free Labor Development, which I was then directing, could be of service in strengthening the democratic trade union movement in Chile. Inevitably, the conversation expanded to include the Communist-Socialist (FRAP) influence in the labor movement, their domination of CUT, and what I expected—and said so frankly—the probable Communist use of CUT to sabotage Frei's administration and his "Revolution in Liberty" program.

"They are going to make your life miserable," I kept repeating. "You must build up your own labor support if you want your government plans to succeed."

My visit to Frei threw the Communists into an uproar. In the September 11 issue of their daily newspaper *El Siglo* they published a scathing attack against me. They returned to the charge with a full-page spread, double headline, in the September 12 edition, condemning Frei for having spoken to me, and claiming that I was attempting to divide the labor movement of Chile. Finally, they devoted a full page to me in their Sunday, September 13, supplement, defending Chilean labor unity "threatened by the imperialist agent Romualdi."

Actually, the Communist fears were well founded. I had made no mystery of my firm belief that the "unity" of Chilean labor under FRAP domination was a disservice to democracy, served only to promote the political interests of the Communist movement, and would eventually become a poisonous thorn in the flesh of Frei's Christian Democratic government. The democratic labor forces in the United States and all over Latin America had rejoiced over Frei's victory and we were justifiably worried about any potential threat, such as the Communist control of CUT, to the success of his administration. Unfortunately, influential elements inside the Chilean Christian Democratic Party, especially those controlling the Party's Trade Union Bureau, held different views. They considered coexistence with the Communists inside CUT preferable to the creation of a dual trade union movement under democratic control.

Frei had won with 56 percent of the vote as against 39 percent for Senator Salvador Allende, the candidate of FRAP. The rest went to the candidate of the Radical Party. As between Allende's type of revolution à la Cuba [5] and Frei's "Revolution in Freedom," the Chilean electorate had given decisive preference to Frei.

The basic objective of Frei's program was a radical structural change of the Chilean society that would eliminate centuries-old social injustices and would give the workers and peasants a convincing demonstration that they could attain a better economic status without sacrificing their freedom.

High priority was given to combating inflation [6] through a gradual application of anti-inflationary measures while at the same time guarding against the danger of drastic deflation that would probably have caused an economic recession with its incalculable political liability. Thus, Frei advocated increased production and encouraged foreign investments. In this respect, he avoided any measure, especially in his approach to agrarian reform, that would have resulted in decreased production. For instance, his agrarian reform bill limited the size of land holdings but advocated taking over only idle land so that it could be put into the most suitable form of agricultural use.

Chile's farm production had lagged behind the growth of population. Against the export of only $30 million worth of fruits and grapes, Chile still imported, in 1965, $155 million worth of foodstuffs. Frei's program called for Chile's self-sufficiency in milk, wheat, and beef by the end of his term in 1970.

Better housing and education, a change in the tax structure, and greater government efficiency were also parts of Frei's program. But the item that gave it distinction and focused on it the attention of the democratic world —and conversely caused the bitterest opposition on the part of the Communist-Socialist left—was the so-called Chileanization of the copper industry. Against the nationalization proposed by Allende and his supporters, Frei's Chileanization called for a twenty-five-year partnership with the U.S. companies (the old, established Anaconda and Kennecott, and the newly established Cerro de Pasco), under which the increased revenues would be devoted to the financing of the government program of public works and agrarian reform. Under the plan, the country is to get over a period of five years new foreign investment of $536 million and copper production is to be raised by 400,000 tons annually.

The leftists went all-out to sabotage the copper program. They employed obstructionist tactics in the Senate, where Frei's Christian Democrats lacked a majority, and launched a series of strikes, mostly political in nature, through their present control of the Copper Workers' Confederation.

After sporadic wildcat strikes that occurred at intervals in every one of the major mines, the Communist leadership closed the El Teniente mining complex, 50 miles south of Santiago, belonging to the Braden Copper Company, a subsidiary of the U.S.-based Kennecott Copper Company. Then in March 1966 they spread the walkout, under the guise of a sympathy strike considered illegal under the Chilean labor code, to the El Salvador mine of the Anaconda Copper Company, in the northern part of the country. The strikers, led by a number of Communist Congressmen, provoked a fight with the police which resulted in eight persons' being killed and about thirty wounded. This was what the Communists wanted —blood and martyrs to blame on Frei. They called a general strike of protest, with the aim of causing a national commotion that, they hoped, would force Frei to deal with them and to accept their proposal for the reorganization of the government on a left base that would include the

Communists themselves. In other words, they hoped to make Frei their prisoner. But Frei struck back with determination and vigor. Addressing the country on national television, he said:

We are witnessing a decided and premeditated attitude of subversion by a minority which, defeated in democratic elections, has gone over to violence and illegal strikes. The extremist leaders do not seek the improvement of the workers. They seek the failure of the government.

He then ordered a return to work at all mines, except El Teniente, where legitimate negotiations for wage adjustments were under way. By the end of March a new contract for miners at El Teniente was negotiated, calling for a 34-percent wage hike. And on April 1, 1966, Congress finally passed the copper bill, the first major legislative victory of the "Revolution in Liberty." But the cost was high.

A well-informed source, with access to government and industry statistics, put the total loss of copper production in Chile caused by strikes since Frei took office until the end of March 1966 at 263,754,000 pounds, divided as follows: Chuquicamata and El Salvador mines (Anaconda) 134,474,000 and El Teniente mine (Kennecott) 129,280,000. Government officials estimated that losses in copper export earnings caused by strikes during the six-month period September 1965–February 1966 amounted to $60 million.[7] Another source [8] estimated that more political strikes in the copper industry took place in one year under Frei than during the entire six-year period of the preceding Alessandri administration, with a total loss in foreign exchange revenues, by March 1966, approaching $90 million—almost enough to finance the entire agrarian reform program.

At the August 1965 CUT Congress, the first after the election of Eduardo Frei to the presidency of Chile, the Communist-Socialist coalition made a clean sweep of all offices, leaving the Christian Democrats without a post in the Executive Council. Nevertheless, the order from the Trade Union Bureau of the Christian Democratic Party was still to remain inside the CUT in order not to violate the "sacred principle" of labor unity. It must be noted, however, that an increasing number of rank-and-file Christian Democratic trade unionists have rebelled against this policy and are trying to have it changed. But the final decision rests with the Party, and perhaps with Frei himself. Until such time as the Party officially orders its members to leave the CUT and organize a new national labor body—and puts the weight of the government behind it, as has been done in other countries—the stranglehold of Communist control over Chilean labor will remain unbroken. On the other hand, without the collaboration of the Christian Democrats, the other non-Marxist forces in the Chilean labor movement are too weak to create an effective national trade union organization of their own.

At the Christian Democratic Convention, August 25–28, 1966, the left-wing, anti-U.S. faction managed to obtain majority approval of a resolution prohibiting membership in, and any type of collaboration with, the ICFTU, ORIT, and the American Institute for Free Labor Development. Many top labor leaders belonging to the Christian Democratic Party, such as Wenceslao Moreno, resigned from the Party in protest and launched new activities to reorganize the free and democratic trade union forces. The possibility of a united labor movement comprising all the anti-Communist forces in Chile has been made impossible because of the intransigence of the Christian Democrats. As a result, the Communist-controlled CUT remains the single labor confederation and, paradoxically, the major obstacle to the success of the reform program advocated by Chile's Christian Democratic President.

Notes

1. Although called *Falangistas,* this group had no connection, organizationally or ideologically, with Franco's Spanish Falange.
2. Allen Young, *The Christian Science Monitor,* January 7, 1966.
3. *La Razón,* Caracas, January 3, 1960.
4. Present at this meeting were: For ORIT, Paladino, Etcheverry, Carlos Ibáñez King, President of the Chilean ORIT affiliate CNT, and Wenceslao Moreno, General Secretary of COMACh (maritime unions) and member of the ORIT executive board; for CLASC, Goldsack, Fulgencio Barreiro, member of its Executive Board, and Fernando Frías, member of the Trade Union Bureau of the Chilean Christian Democratic Party.
5. Senator Allende was one of the participants in the Tri-Continental Conference which the Communists held in Havana in January 1966.
6. According to the Research Department of the Central Bank of Chile, the cost of living index had gone up from 138.6 average in 1959 to 443.7 in December 1964.
7. *Visión Letter,* March 16, 1966.
8. William P. Lineberry, *New Leader,* May 23, 1966.

XX

Caribbean Excursions

IN AMERICAN trade union parlance, the Caribbean area means the conglomeration of islands and territories that were, or still are, under British, Dutch, or French administration, stretching from Jamaica all the way down to Surinam, formerly known as Dutch Guiana. Under this definition, the Spanish-speaking countries surrounded or bathed by the Caribbean Sea are not part of it.

The trade union movement in the Caribbean area assumed strength and distinctive characteristics in the year 1937. Dr. Rawle Farley, Staff Tutor in Industrial Relations in the University College of the West Indies, has described 1937 as "the watershed year in the development of trade unionism." The Caribbean labor movement thus is hardly one generation old—much younger than the labor movement in some of the countries in Latin America. Before 1937 there were a number of protest movements which gained occasional victories, but the labor movement itself was sporadic, lacking in continuity and consistency. Dr. Farley relates:

In 1842, for instance, in British Guiana, the workers, just four years ex-slaves, organized and staged a general strike against a unilateral directive by management that wages should be reduced. The workers won, but no continuous organization emerged. In 1848, when they attempted similar action, they lost. Their ranks were divided and circumstances had so changed that unity was even more necessary than before. In Trinidad, in 1897, we find a Trinidad Workingman's

Association. It was a protest movement, but not a fully developed trade union. This was the situation in many islands. Political protest groups existed championing the cause of the working man, but no distinct trade union movement as such emerged.

After a series of upheavals in the early thirties, there emerged in 1937 a number of strong unions that still exist today, such as the British Guiana Labor Union and the Man-Power Citizen's Association, in what is today Guyana. Five unions were founded in Trinidad, among them the Oilfield Workers Trade Union; and sugar workers began organizing in Jamaica and in Barbados.

Intellectuals, interested in launching labor-oriented political parties in preparation for the day when full independence status would be achieved, realized the need to get the backing of strong labor unions. They took the lead in promoting their organization and lent to the task their time, prestige, and leadership. Outstanding in this group of intellectuals were Sir Grantley Adams, who subsequently became Premier of Barbados and of the short-lived West Indies Federation, and Norman Manley, leading Jamaican barrister and Premier before independence.

The trade union movement in the Caribbean area is today an accepted and respected feature of its socioeconomic life. It is a type of constructive trade unionism that believes in and practices collective bargaining with a degree of responsibility and realism matched by a corresponding attitude on the part of the employers. It also is a labor movement that in a number of places grew up under the protective shadow of a proliferation of political parties, mostly patterned after the Labour Party of Great Britain. Today the tendency is to separate the role and the leadership of the unions from those of the political party—although much still remains to be done in this respect.

In the beginning, as in most other places, the labor movement in the Caribbean area had strong idealistic traits. Today, it bases its strength, survival, and progress on pragmatic leadership, effective organization, efficient administration, technical assistance, research, negotiating techniques and education. This last activity, which has enabled a new generation of trade union activists to assume the leadership handed down to them by the intellectual-type pioneers of the early thirties, was effectively promoted by the University College of the West Indies, the British Trade Union Congress, Colonial Development and Welfare, the ICFTU, the Caribbean Area Division of ORIT (CADORIT) later transformed into the Caribbean Congress of Labor, various International Trade Secretariats through their North American member unions, and lately the

American Institute for Free Labor Development, which supports two resident institutes in Jamaica and Guyana as well as a number of short-term courses in other localities.

CADORIT was organized in Barbados June 4–7, 1952, following a call issued by ORIT to all its affiliated organizations in the area.[1] I was the only non-Caribbean in attendance and this was my first conference experience in the Caribbean area. The thing that most impressed me was the orderly manner in which the delegates went about their business. There was nothing of the clamor, confusion, lengthy speeches and long sessions that were, and still are, the trademark of labor assemblies in Latin America. Everything was conducted according to Robert's Rules of Order. Little or no attempt was made to substantially change the reports of the various committees when they were submitted to the Conference. All the reports were confined to matters of immediate concern and the recommendations were attuned to the modest resources of that fledgling organization. For instance, the committee dealing with problems of trade union education and legislation to guarantee individual liberties and freedom of association, recommended:

(a) the starting of radio educational programs and the publication of a bulletin;

(b) the establishment of training courses for trade union leadership; lectures on various topics of interest to trade unionists; and the establishment of small libraries for each affiliated union;

(c) the exhibition of films on trade union matters; and

(d) the establishment of effective coordination with the ICFTU, the ORIT, and the specialized UN agencies such as the ILO and UNESCO, for the promotion and carrying out of an effective program of workers' education.

The committee also presented a resolution which deplored the violation of freedom of association in territories such as Curaçao, Aruba, and the Bahamas; attributed this state of affairs mainly to pressure on the part of large business enterprises, national as well as foreign; and recommended an intensive campaign for the promulgation of laws protecting freedom of association and containing severe sanctions against those who violate it.

During its first years of existence CADORIT maintained headquarters in Barbados; later they were moved to Trinidad. It was my task to guide CADORIT activities while I remained in charge of ORIT's International Relations. I saw it grow steadily until it established itself in every island, from Aruba to the Bahamas, from Bermuda to St. Vincent. Of course,

British Guiana, Trinidad, and Jamaica held the spotlight in terms of size, activity, and number of affiliates, and I visited those three places more often. But no less important was the work done in smaller islands, where we were at times called upon to perform tasks that were more in the nature of Red Cross activity. One illustration of that was given in a report from the island of Dominica, which appeared in the August 1953 issue of the *Inter-American Labor Bulletin*. It described the successful mass meeting held on the night of June 12 in Roseau, capital of Dominica, B.W.I. The people attended by the thousands and unanimously approved two resolutions, one asking for an urgently needed increase in wages so that the agricultural workers could earn at least enough to eat, and the other asking for the introduction of an adequate pension system for all workers who were old and unable to continue to work.

At the same mass meeting the workers agreed to publicize in the labor press throughout the world the incident which led to the demolition of a number of workers' houses causing untold suffering to the displaced occupants. The story, as furnished us by the Dominica Trade Union, was as follows:

Sixty-two occupants, almost all trade unionists, were evicted from 11 houses which they occupied on Highland (approximately two acres of land), a part of the 1500-acre Geneva Estate. The houses had been handed down from slave times, about eighty years ago. The eviction was ordered by a new landlord who bought the estate in 1949.

The tenants failed to quit because they had nowhere to go. They explained their situation to their legislative council representative, Hon. R. St. Luce, who, together with leaders of the Dominica Trade Union, made representation to the government on their behalf, requesting the allocation of two acres from thirty acres owned by the government in that same village, Grandbay, to place those houses. They were denied this privilege and were brought before the Magistrate, who specified a period in which to leave.

The time having expired by March 23, 1953, the government dispatched a van of policemen to Grandbay to demolish those houses. What was worse, there was among the evicted occupants a sick child. That child was simply placed under a tree.

The destitute, being rendered homeless, then became wanderers in the village. Many of the villagers were weeping at their distress. Some were given temporary refuge by the village sympathizers pending government help. One or two were sheltered in the same manner at the trade union branch office. Further representations followed by means of an interview with the Administrator of Dominica by trade union leaders, but no redress was given, and no sign of same is shown up to date.

Surinam (Dutch Guiana) I visited only twice. The first visit took place on May 4–6, 1952. It was thus reported in the June 1952 issue of the ORIT's English-language publication:

Right after his arrival at the Paramaribo airport, Romualdi was taken to the Luxor Theater which was overflowing with workers. Loudspeakers were set up outside for the benefit of those who could not get in. It was estimated that 3,500 people were present. The meeting was organized by the unions affiliated to the ORIT as well as the Progressive Workers' Organization (Catholic) and the Surinam Workers' Federation (Protestant). It was a very colorful affair because of much choreographic show put on by members of the respective unions who wore different costumes and headgear. The trade union sentiment in Paramaribo is so strong that most of the bicycles and automobiles seen on the streets have a flag of one labor organization or another.

Romualdi spoke for over one hour in English, a language which is well understood by most of the Surinam people. Other speakers were: Leo E. Eleazer, ORIT leader in Surinam, who presided; R. Schoonhoven, secretary of the Surinam Workers' Organization; Father Weidmann, for the Catholic Union; Rev. S. F. Helstone, for the Protestant Union, and a number of miners' representatives, among them V. Sweet of Paranam who presented the visitor with a bauxite paper weight which he himself had made. A similar meeting was held the following day in the mining center of Paranam, where Romualdi had occasion to ascertain the cordial relationship existing at present between the management of the Company (an Alcoa subsidiary) and the union. The visitor spoke also for fifteen minutes over the radio on the eve of his departure.

I might add that my departure from Paramaribo took place in the very early hours of the morning, when it was still pitch dark. Because of the intense heat, I had slept with the windows open, under the protection of a sleeping net. But when I switched on the lights to get up, a dozen huge angry bats swarmed through the open window, causing me to take cover in the corridor in dishabille, calling for help to cope with a most unexpected situation.

Dr. Cheddi Jagan, who was three times Prime Minister of British Guiana before his country won its independence in May 1966, has on repeated occasions accused me of having committed acts hostile to his regime [2] and of having conspired to overthrow it. The latter charge was included in a letter to *The New York Times,* in July 1963. Dr. Jagan's letter claimed that "local (Guianese) trade unionists known to be hostile to the Government—and none others—have been trained by the American Institute for Free Labor Development to overthrow my government.

Serafino Romualdi, head of the Institute, has declared his opposition to my government."

I never tried to deny Dr. Jagan's charges. As a matter of fact I publicly acknowledged the fact that, having become convinced of Dr. Jagan's subservience to the Communist movement since my first visit to British Guiana in 1951, I did everything in my power to strengthen the democratic trade union forces opposed to him and to expose Jagan's pro-Communist activities from the day he was elected Prime Minister, following the general elections of April 27, 1953.[3]

When, early in 1953, British Guiana was granted a constitution which called for a wide degree of self-government, there was only one political party that was well organized and ready to take part in the general election for members of the newly established House of Assembly. This was the People's Progressive Party (PPP), launched about five years before by Dr. Jagan and his United States–born wife, the former Janet Rosenberg of Chicago, who was an active member of the Young Communist League and was instrumental in converting her husband to Communism. The Jagans and some of their collaborators were confirmed, 100-percent Communists, who never deviated one iota from the Stalinist line, either in their writings or in their utterances.

The PPP was a kind of popular front designed to attract groups and individuals that were not Communists but had political and economic grievances against the British colonial government. As such, it had a good number of prominent members and even leaders who were non-Communists.[4]

Until the PPP came into power, the dominant trade union organization in British Guiana was the Man-Power Citizens' Association (MPCA), which held bargaining rights in sugar and rice plantations, in the bauxite mines, and in other industries. The MPCA was a member of the International Confederation of Free Trade Unions and was among the founders of ORIT.

Against the Man-Power Citizens' Association, the Communists set up the Guiana Industrial Workers Union (GIWU), which affiliated with the World Federation of Trade Unions. All attempts on the part of the GIWU to wrest control of the Guiana workers from the MPCA had failed in the past. But as soon as the Communist-controlled new government took over, its first objective became to destroy the MPCA with every means at its disposal. Cabinet members, including Minister of Health and Housing Dr. Lanchmansingh—who was also president of the GIWU—spent most of their time visiting the sugar estates, arousing the workers with demagogic promises, and preparing them for a general strike.

The political atmosphere of British Guiana suddenly reached a stage of revolutionary tension. Plans for economic development and expansion, which were well under way when the Communist Ministers took over, were ignored or sabotaged.

In the 1953 May Day parade, pictures of Stalin, Malenkov, Mao, and other Communist bigwigs were carried by leaders of the PPP. Literature extolling the virtues of the "people's democracies" behind the Iron Curtain flooded the country. The ban on the entry of West Indian Communists was lifted. The Minister of Education announced his intention to discontinue the churches' participation in the educational system.

After the return of Dr. Jagan, his wife, and other PPP leaders from visits to the Communist satellite countries—where they conferred with Soviet leaders and undoubtedly received instructions and support—branches of the World Federation of Democratic Youth, the World Peace Council, the Women's International Democratic Federation, the Pioneer Youth League, and other cloaks for Communist activities were set up all over British Guiana. An open Communist Party was never established. But those who know how Communists operate quickly realized that this was not necessary because the PPP had obviously proved a good, reliable, and safe substitute.

Early in September 1953, the GIWU called a general strike on the sugar estates with the alleged goal of forcing the employers to break the contract with the MPCA and recognize the Communist-controlled union. No real economic demands were attached to it. But when Governor Sir Alfred Savage himself offered to mediate the strike and a fair formula was presented for the revision of the collective bargaining representation, the strike leaders refused to cooperate unless they first obtained complete surrender. They wanted nothing less than absolute and total control of all the unions in order to strengthen their political plans. Every form of intimidation was used to force the workers to strike.

After twenty-five days, with workers losing more than a million dollars in wages, in addition to loss of bonuses and other benefits, the GIWU ordered the workers to go back to work, promising that meanwhile the government would obtain by law what they had been unable to obtain from the British Governor and the employers through the pressure of the prolonged strike. The Minister of Labor promptly introduced in the House of Assembly an Industrial Relations Bill, which the *Labour Advocate,* official organ of the MPCA, described as "infamous," intended "to collar the workers into government unions."

The Communist Ministers attempted to set aside the rules of the House of Assembly to get this bill passed at once, without debate. The opposition members were intimidated with threats and abuses. A frenzied crowd of hundreds of people filled the entrance of the Assembly Chamber and staged demonstrations which compelled the Speaker to suspend the session. It was a clear attempt to impose mob rule in violation of the constitution, which was then not even six months old.

When the Governor and the Speaker refused to surrender, the Ministers of the government and members of the majority party walked out of the House of Assembly. An open appeal was made to the police force—which had already been infiltrated by disloyal elements—to refuse to carry out the Governor's orders. Workers were being organized into shock troops, called People's Police. Members of the State Council as well as the leaders of the democratic opposition, alarmed by such doings, which reminded them of the Communist inside conquest of Czechoslovakia, urged the Governor to take firm steps before it was too late.

On October 9, 1953, after the landing of British troops that had been secretly summoned from the West Indies, Governor Savage announced that the British government had decided "that the constitution of British Guiana must be suspended to prevent Communist subversion of the government." Every Communist Minister was fired. The House of Assembly was dissolved. The British government also published a White Paper enumerating the reasons that led to such a measure. The White Paper pointed out that the PPP, through its members in the government, had created a "revolutionary atmosphere" which the Communists planned to exploit for their ultimate design to capture the country through a *coup d'état*.

Soon after the removal of the Jagan government and the publication of the White Paper, I went to British Guiana, where I made an extensive investigation of the events leading to the crisis. I was the only outside trade unionist to go to British Guiana to lend moral support to the democratic labor movement of that country. Nobody came from the British Trades Union Congress or from the ICFTU or from any other organization. Jagan had succeeded in misleading world labor-liberal opinion, and particularly the British Labour Party, into believing that he was nothing more than a reformer unjustly branded a Communist.[5] The findings of my investigation were published in the *AFL News Reporter* of October 30, 1953, and in the *International Free Trade Union News* of December 1953. In the latter I wrote:

Every fair-minded person interested in the preservation of democracy in the Western Hemisphere, who has followed events in British Guiana since last May, when the Communist-controlled People's Progressive Party emerged victorious at the first general election, must agree that the suspension of the constitution, decided upon by the British government on October 9, was the only recourse left to prevent the setting up of a Communist totalitarian state.

Only those who believe, or pretend to believe, that the Communists' only interest in British Guiana was to promote "agrarian reforms" and that their trained and tested leaders were nothing more than "left-wing democrats" may have ground to deplore the strong action taken by the British government. But these people would then be, consciously or unconsciously, dupes for the latest action of the international Communist conspiracy.

After the British government reinstated a modified constitution which limited the power of the elected government, Dr. Jagan won the 1957 election (by plurality, not majority) and again formed the government. Mrs. Jagan entered the Cabinet as Minister of Labor.

In 1958, Harry H. Pollack, then AFL-CIO Associate Inter-American Representative, visited the country at the request of the British Guiana Trade Union Congress (BGTUC). Upon his return, he published a report in the September 19, 1958, issue of the *Inter-American Labor Bulletin* in which he stated ". . . this time [the Jagans] were obviously prepared to act much more subtly and carefully. Jagan, his wife Janet, and other leaders of the PPP, assumed the guise of responsibility and the role of latter-day statesmen."

Nevertheless, Pollack reported, "several attempts were made on the PPP's part to dominate the free trade union movement, particularly the Man-Power Citizen's Association, which had organized the bulk of the sugar workers in the country. Their attempts, however, failed, mainly because the MPCA, under the new leadership of Richard Ishmael, had improved its position with a significant increase in membership and the right of checkoff, together with other benefits." The Jaganites, therefore, resorted to what Pollack described as a ". . . far more devious, and therefore more frightening, new tack."

In order to eliminate, to all intents and purposes, the usefulness of the union, Mrs. Jagan in her role of Minister of Labor, Health, and Housing, suggested the establishment of a Wages Council in the sugar industry with statutory powers to fix wages and working conditions.

The free labor movement bitterly opposed this measure because, once introduced into the sugar industry (with the consequent elimination of the union), it would eventually have been extended to the bauxite mines, the waterfront, and other industries. The measure never became law.

A further revision of the constitution, enacted just before the expiration of Jagan's four-year term, introduced full administrative autonomy with the British government retaining only responsibilities of Defense and Foreign Affairs. It was also stipulated that negotiations leading to complete independence would be initiated after the new government assumed power.

In the general elections of August 1961, Cheddi Jagan and his People's Progressive Party obtained a majority of seats (20 of 35) in the Parliament. However, he got only 42.7 percent of the votes cast, a drop of 5 percent from 1957, while the opposition People's National Congress got 41 percent of the votes, an increase of 6 percent over 1957. Had it not been for the emergence of a third group called the United Force, who received about 16 percent of the votes, Jagan would surely have been defeated.

After his third installation as Prime Minister, Jagan did not lose any time in showing his admiration for Fidel Castro and the Cuban Communist regime. In a memorandum submitted to the ICFTU in the fall of 1961, Richard Ishmael, President of the Trade Union Council, reported, among other things, the following:

> Jagan has said at a weekly news conference which he holds that "Castro is the greatest liberator of the Western Hemisphere" and he "admires him tremendously," while the Chairman of the PPP, Brindley Benn, during the debate in the Legislative Council on Freehold vs. Leasehold (collectivism) was agitated into making the vicious statement "It is easier to stop tomorrow than Communism."
>
> Quite recently a number of Cuban Ministers, so-called businessmen and experts, have been visiting British Guiana, and a number of PPP activists have been sent to Cuba and behind the Iron Curtain for training, presumably.
>
> Heavy printing machinery originating from behind the Iron Curtain has recently arrived in British Guiana through Cuba. This will be used to commence their daily newspaper.

The Hon. Brindley Benn, Acting Premier of British Guiana during the absence of Dr. Jagan, who had gone abroad in quest of financial help, delivered an address to a mass meeting at Bourda Green in which, according to the October 15, 1961, issue of the *Georgetown Sunday Argosy,* he boasted that his Party had deposed the Archbishop of the West Indies and said many more like him would have to be deposed. He said many more heads would roll if the government and people were to march forward to success. The acting Premier named Richard Ishmael as one whose head would soon be rolling.

Meanwhile, the People's Progressive Party, with the support of the government, launched a new Guiana sugar workers' union, again with the purpose of displacing the MPCA. The British Guiana Trade Union Council, in a statement issued October 15, 1961, considered the attack by acting Premier Benn and the formation of the new sugar union deliberate attempts to create disruption in the labor movement which would result in its "domination or destruction."

The statement, signed by BGTUC President Richard Ishmael, declared that, "The Caribbean Congress of Labour, ORIT, and the ICFTU have been informed of these moves by Government, and these bodies have been requested to consider the situation and to join in a defence of the Free Trade Union Movement to avoid the unfortunate situation which the Movement faced in Cuba repeating itself in British Guiana, since the Movement does not intend to be dominated by Government or by a political party and will never permit itself to be Castroized."

The opportunity for the world's free labor movement to come to the aid of the British Guiana trade unions in their battle to resist the Jagan Government's encroachment came during the eighty-day general strike of 1963, one of the longest strikes in labor's history. The strike, which came close to toppling the Jagan regime, was called to protest the introduction on March 27, 1963, of a Labour Relations Bill, identical in its objectives and reasons to the one Jagan introduced in 1953, which had been one of the factors that caused Great Britain to remove Jagan from office after his earlier election.

The provisions of Jagan's bill would have empowered the Minister of Labour to take action to decide which trade union was "representative" of any unit of workers as a bargaining unit and would have compelled employers to deal with that union alone.

Throughout the crisis, the democratic trade unions of the country, backed by ORIT-ICFTU, the AFL-CIO, and the democratic world labor movement, maintained a solidarity of opposition despite great sacrifices. The solidarity efforts were ably coordinated by Andrew C. McLelland, my successor as AFL-CIO Inter-American Representative.

The strike brought to a standstill all sectors of the economy. The cost to the country was estimated at $40 million—more than its anual budget. Loss in government revenues alone was estimated at $4.5 million.

In an effort to offset the effect of the British Guiana peoples' protest, Jagan increased trade with Communist nations. Cuba and Russia acted as strikebreakers by shipping oil, flour, and other essentials to Jagan. Cuban supplies in particular, by preventing critical shortages, saved the Jagan Government from collapse during the crisis.

As Jagan's Communist ties were thus made more evident, the British

Guiana workers only stiffened their determination to continue the walk-out, which itself had been provoked by the totalitarian nature of the labor legislation the government had proposed.

In the end, the workers of British Guiana, and the free labor movement of the world which supported them, scored a great victory when the Jagan government signed an agreement withdrawing the Labour Relations Bill.

The role I played in that general strike was a minor one, yet it infuriated Prime Minister Jagan to the extent of moving him to issue angry denunciations against me. I simply put at the disposal of the strike committee the services of six graduates of the American Institute for Free Labor Development, of which I was then Executive Director, who were working as interns with various local unions. They performed so well that one of them, David Persaud, later was elected President of the BGTUC.

As a preliminary condition to the granting of full independence, Great Britain promulgated in 1964 an amendment to the election procedure in British Guiana which established a system of proportional representation. At the election later that year, the People's National Congress of Forbes Burnham, supported by the BGTUC, won a plurality. Combining with Peter d'Aguiar's United Force, Burnham obtained a majority in Parliament and became Prime Minister. His victory was cause for widespread rejoicing, especially in trade union circles in the United States, where Burnham had won friendship and respect. I had the privilege of becoming one of his friends. When I last visited British Guiana, in February 1965, on the eve of its becoming the sovereign state of Guyana, Forbes Burnham, who was already Prime Minister, came to the farewell party which the BGTUC gave in honor of myself and my wife. He also put at our disposal the only plane the government owned, so that we might fulfill my long-cherished ambition of flying over the majestic Kaieteur Falls, way over the Merume mountains, close to the Brazilian border—one of the natural wonders of the world that today still can only be reached by air!

It has become a sort of obbligato overture, when writing about Jamaica, to state that its political scene is dominated by two men—William Alexander Bustamante and Norman Washington Manley. One may add that these two men also dominate the labor scene. The noted inter-American labor expert, Robert J. Alexander, thus described the impact of these two personalities:[6]

Organized labor in Jamaica traces its history back to the depression years of the late 1930's. The price of sugar, the country's principal crop, was low, the workers' wages were lower, and there was widespread economic discontent in the Island. In addition, there was a growing feeling of national self-consciousness on the part of the people of the Island.

These two movements of economic discontent and nationalism found expression in a two-pronged movement headed by two men: William Alexander Bustamante and Norman Manley. Bustamante and Manley were cousins, but in most other ways were poles apart: Bustamante being an imposing-looking, white-haired man with more than a touch of demagoguery in his makeup; Manley being a soft-spoken athletic man, who had become the Island's leading lawyer.

In the beginning, the two men divided the work between them, with Bustamante concentrating principally in the field of trade union organization, and Manley in the field of political agitation and organization. The upshot was that there developed the Bustamante Industrial Trade Union (BITU) and the People's National Party (PNP). For several years they worked together.

A split between the PNP and the BITU occurred in 1944, resulting in the formation of the Jamaica Trade Union Congress (JTUC), which in 1945 joined the World Federation of Trade Unions. The JTUC was dominated by Richard Hart and the brothers Ken and Richard Hill.

There was widespread feeling that the Hill brothers and their friends had become too friendly with the Communists. This was indicated in 1949, when, after the withdrawal of the British TUC and the American CIO from the WFTU, and the formation of the International Confederation of Free Trade Unions, the Hill leadership of the JTUC refused to withdraw from the Communist-dominated World Federation. The struggle over this issue resulted in the suspension of Hill and his associates from positions of leadership in the People's National Party, which favored withdrawal from the WFTU, and finally, under much pressure, Hill agreed to have JTUC quit the Communist group.

This, however, was regarded only as a tactical maneuver by the anti-Communist sector inside the JTUC, led by Florizel A. Glasspole and other Social-Democrats who were members of the PNP. In March 1952 Glasspole, supported by leaders of the PNP (including Norman Manley), broke away from the JTUC and on April 2, 1952, organized a new group, the National Workers' Union (NWU).

The move was criticized in some European trade union circles as being too precipitate and even unnecessary, the chief argument being that Ken Hill's claim of not being a Communist should have been taken at its face value. I did not agree with such reasoning. At the Barbados Conference that led to the formation of CADORIT, Ken Hill was present, but he was refused seating as a delegate and was only given the status of observer. In the course of the Conference I had opportunities to talk to him, and came to the conclusion that, if he was not a full-fledged Communist, Ken Hill was surely a fellow traveler. The way he was defending the policies of Jagan's PPP in British Guiana led me to believe that he was advocating a similar line for Jamaica, which had already obtained a measure of self-government with Bustamante as Chief Minister.

One of CADORIT's first organizational tasks was to assist in the development of the Jamaica NWU. At its first Convention, held in Kingston, November 23, 1952, I brought greetings on behalf of the AFL and ORIT, while Frank L. Walcott, President of CADORIT, pledged the support of his organization. The Convention unanimously decided to join ORIT-ICFTU.

The NWU grew rapidly. In its first months it gained exclusive bargaining rights in several important firms. Some of the important organizations of the JTUC, including the Kingston Port Workers Union, joined the new group. In April 1953 I journeyed again to Jamaica to assist the NWU in negotiating an agreement with the Kaiser Bauxite Company. Later, the Cuban Confederation of Labor gave a helping hand in launching an organization campaign among the sugar workers. By the time of the second Annual Convention, October 31–November 1, 1953—which I again addressed—the NWU had doubled its membership to over 10,000, having scored remarkable progress in almost every field, particularly in organizing bauxite, textile, sugar, and government workers.

As Jamaica approached its independence, the attention of the labor movement was focused on three major issues which were also of direct interest to the AFL-CIO. These were immigration policy; the allocation of a sugar quota to help Jamaica dispose of some of its 70,000-ton annual surplus; and the Island's desire for an increase in the number of British West Indies workers recruited for seasonal farm work in the United States. While the issues of sugar and immigration quotas have been disposed of by subsequent legislation passed by the U.S. Congress, the issue of the West Indies farm laborers is still an open one.

The British West Indies labor program began in 1943, as a means of providing a supplemental supply of workers to meet shortages in the United States resulting from World War II. Originally, it supplied workers for both industry and agriculture and was administered by the War Manpower Administration and the War Food Administration under trilateral agreements between the United States, the United Kingdom (Great Britain), and the Caribbean governments involved, negotiated under Public Law 75. When this wartime law expired in 1947, the program was continued to supply farm workers only under agreements negotiated directly with U.S. agricultural employers by the British West Indies Central Labour Organization, as representative of the various participating governments, under the terms of our immigration laws. General supervision of the contracts and the standards which growers must meet in order to be eligible to use the program is vested in the U.S. Department of Labor. The use of these workers was confined largely to Florida and the eastern states and involved mainly workers from Jamaica and Barbados, with lesser numbers coming, at different times, from the Windward Islands, British Honduras, the Leeward Islands, Trinidad, and British Guiana. The government of the Bahamas also ran a separate program, contracting with U.S. employers directly.

The number of workers involved was always small when compared with the Mexican Contract Labor Program and reached its peak on June 30, 1945, when the total of both Bahamian and BWI agricultural workers was 23,978 and the number of industrial workers totaled 16,346. Use of the program declined rapidly after the war, reaching a low of 2,765 workers employed in 1949. The program thus never was large enough to be a cause of major concern to the American labor movement, which had generally grouped it with the Mexican Contract Labor Program in its criticism of "foreign" contract labor programs.

When Norman Manley was elected Premier of Jamaica in 1955, he sent Florizel Glasspole, his Minister of Labor, to the United States to confer with both the AFL and CIO and urge that they support greater use of BWI workers in the United States as a means of helping Jamaica's ailing economy. He pledged strict administration of the program to insure that all of the labor standards negotiated in the contract with employers would be scrupulously observed. President Reuther of the CIO assigned Milton Plumb, Secretary of the Joint U.S.–Mexico Trade Union Committee on which the AFL-CIO United Mine Workers (Independent), and the Railway Labor Executives' Association were represented, to investigate the BWI program, and to prepare a recommendation to submit to the AFL-CIO after merger. Since he had worked on the problems of the Mexican labor program for many years and knew agricultural labor conditions throughout the country, Plumb was in a unique position to compare the conditions under which BWI workers were employed with those existing elsewhere in American agriculture. He set out on an extensive field trip, visiting the various BWI labor camps both alone and later with state and BWI officials, and submitted a report which recommended that, because of the superior compliance work being done by the BWI officials administering the program, the labor movement should favor the use of BWI workers over Mexicans in states east of the Mississippi River. He made clear that, because of inferior enforcement and working conditions he had found in camps under the Bahamian program, his recommendation did not include the Bahamian workers. At this time, the American labor movement, while generally supporting the Mexican labor program as better than the "wetback" [7] situation which had prevailed previously, was highly critical of the inadequate compliance staff which the Labor Department had available to oversee its operations.

I was in complete agreement with Milton Plumb's findings because they were in accord with my own knowledge of the BWI and Mexican labor programs as I had watched them closely over the years. Moreover, I had meanwhile received, in addition to Glasspole's assurances, a pledge from Harold Edwards, the Chief Liaison Officer in charge of the program, that the high labor standards and the strict compliance procedures would continue to be followed and improved. I discovered that the BWI Central Labor Organization required all employers to provide full workmen's compensation protection for their BWI workers, thus benefiting American workers, who had to be given the same coverage by their employers. I also learned that the BWI worker was covered for accident and sickness off the job by a group insurance policy which dated back to 1948 and which was the first policy of that nature written in the United States for migrant agricultural workers. Therefore, when the proposal from President Reuther for an expansion of the BWI program was received by AFL-CIO President Meany shortly after the merger of the two labor bodies in December 1955, I recommended that he submit it to the U.S. Section of the Joint U.S.–Mexico Trade Union Committee for consideration. This group considered the report early in 1956 and adopted a resolution which, while opposing the program of importing workers for agriculture from Japan and the Philippines, urged that greater use be made of BWI workers to fill bona-fide shortages. This became the official position of the American labor movement in regard to the BWI labor program. Although this stand has been the subject of some controversy, I remain convinced that it was a wise decision that, in addition to aiding the development of Jamaica and other Caribbean nations at a crucial time in their history, has also been to the advantage of the United States. Although never involving more than a peak of 14,000 workers in the post-World War II years, the program has nevertheless met essential shortages of agricultural labor arising out of the Korean War and, particularly, our need to rapidly expand domestic sugar production following Fidel Castro's take-over of Cuba.

Since Congress terminated the Mexican Labor Program in 1964, the number of BWI workers admitted has declined and there have been increasing pressures to end the program completely, which has already happened to the Bahamian program. As this is written, in the fall of 1966, it appears that the chief use of BWI workers in the immediate future will be in the harvesting of cane sugar crops, where shortages of workers continue to exist despite all efforts to recruit domestics for this work.

Premier Norman Manley, who in 1955 had succeeded Bustamante as head of the government, in March 1962 invited AFL-CIO President George Meany to visit Jamaica. I was also asked to go along. Meany discussed the labor issues that were uppermost in the minds of the Jamaicans with Manley and other government officials, with the leader of the political opposition Sir Alexander Bustamante and his top aides, and with the leaders of the NWU. At a press conference called at the conclusion of his visit, Meany pledged the AFL-CIO's support, especially on the questions of the sugar and immigration quotas. He stressed the AFL-CIO's belief that every possible aid should be given to underdeveloped nations and said that since organized labor was interested in helping countries in Asia, it would be even more interested in U.S. assistance to "our neighbors" in the West Indies.

Jamaica's independence was set for August 6, 1962. At the election that preceded it [8] Manley's PNP was narrowly defeated by Bustamante's Labor Party.[9] Sir Alexander went back into power as Prime Minister and presided over the great celebration for independence. Among the guests who assembled in Kingston for the occasion there were Princess Margaret, as representative of the Queen of England, and then Vice-President Lyndon B. Johnson as personal representative of President John F. Kennedy. AFL-CIO Vice-President William C. Doherty and I were also there—he as a member of the official U.S. delegation [10] and I as a special invited guest of the Jamaican government.

On the afternoon of August 6, Prime Minister Bustamante held a labor rally at a downtown square, to which Vice-President Johnson was also invited. Busta (as the Jamaicans called him for short) was in a jolly, exuberant mood. He spoke glowingly of the labor plans of his administration and then invited Doherty and me to take the microphone. Just before ending the rally the octogenarian Busta addressed himself to Vice-President Johnson asking him to convey to President Kennedy—"to that wonderful boy . . . after all, he is still a boy, you know . . ." (these were his exact words) the sentiments of admiration and support expressed by the Jamaican workers.

As Busta said "that wonderful boy . . ." I looked at Vice-President Johnson's face, which became frozen in a stony, sphinxlike expression.

Notes

1. The Conference was opened by the Governor of Barbados, Sir Alfred Savage, in the Legislative Council Chamber. The Governor was introduced by the Hon. Grantley Adams, leader of the Barbados Labor Government and member of the Executive Board of the ICFTU. The author, as representative of ORIT, was elected Conference Chairman; Cecil P. Alexander, President of the Waterfront Workers' Union of Trinidad, and Grantley Adams, were elected Vice-Chairmen, and F. L. Walcott of Barbados was the Secretary.

The conference was attended by 26 delegates representing 17 affiliated organizations divided as follows: 6 from Trinidad and Tobago; 3 from Surinam; 2 from British Guiana; 2 from Sta. Lucia; and one each from Barbados, Grenada, Dominica, and British Honduras. In addition, representatives of the Trades Union Congresses of Jamaica and British Guiana, whose applications for membership in the ICFTU were pending, were admitted as observers.

2. Cheddi Jagan, *The West on Trial*, p. 186.

3. *Inter-American Labor News*, January 1951. *Inter-American Labor Bulletin*, May 1952.

4. Most prominent of the non-Communist members of the PPP was Forbes Burnham, who in 1955 broke with Cheddi Jagan, formed his own party, the People's National Congress, and in 1965 succeeded in being elected Prime Minister. Testifying before the Commonwealth Commission of Inquiry, set up as a result of the riots which took place in Georgetown in February 1962, Burnham was questioned by the Commission's Counsel (p. 1820 of the official transcript):

Q. MR. LUCKHOO: "Now, could you tell me why you broke with him (Jagan), Mr. Burnham?"

A. MR. BURNHAM: Yes, sir, because I found he was more interested in peddling the latest Moscow line than in looking after the particular and peculiar problems of Guiana."

5. Dr. Cheddi Jagan's adherence to the beliefs and practices of Communism were confirmed in the course of the above-mentioned inquiry. Page 1877 of the transcript show the following:

Q. MR. LUCKHOO: "Dr. Jagan, I do ask you—just answer me—you know the tenets of Communism?"

A. DR. JAGAN: "Your definition of Communism may be different from mine."

CHAIRMAN: "That will not do. You have admitted to knowing the tenets of Communism. You are now asked, having regard to those tenets, do you believe in them? You must answer yes or no."

A. DR. JAGAN: "I believe the tenets of Communism to be 'from each according to his ability, to each according to his need.' I believe in that."

Q. MR. LUCKHOO: "That is your conception of the tenets of Communism and you believe in that?"

A. DR. JAGAN: "Yes."

Q. MR. LUCKHOO: "That represents your Communist belief?"

A. DR. JAGAN: "Yes."

Q. MR. LUCKHOO: "Dr. Jagan, are you an admirer of Fidel Castro?"

A. DR. JAGAN: "I have said so, yes."

Q. MR. LUCKHOO: "Had you declared him to be the greatest liberator of the twentieth century?"

A. DR. JAGAN: "Yes."

Q. MR. LUCKHOO: "Are you an admirer of Nikita Khrushchev?"

A. DR. JAGAN: "Yes."

Q. MR. LUCKHOO: "And you have publicly proclaimed this?"

A. DR. JAGAN: "I have publicly said so, yes."

Q. MR. LUCKHOO: "You are not aware of those policies (of Khrushchev). Well, the policies which you know—is there any that you can think of to which you do not subscribe?"

A. DR. JAGAN: "I cannot think of any at the moment."

CHAIRMAN: "I think you may take it Mr. Luckhoo, that you have established that he [Dr. Jagan] is an avowed Communist.

6. "Organized Labor in Jamaica," *Inter-American Labor Bulletin,* January 1953.

7. "Wetback" was the term given to Mexican farm workers who entered the country illegally, often with the help of farm employers who sought to escape the minimum labor standards imposed by the Mexican Contract Labor Program. Workers under the latter were called *"braceros"* to distinguish them from the illegal entrants. At one time, over one million "wetbacks" were rounded up by the Immigration Service in a single year. The term originated from the assumption that the illegal workers got "wet backs" crossing the Rio Grande, but most of them actually entered at various points along the border where they did not even get their feet wet.

8. The dominant issue of the election was whether Jamaica should remain part of the West Indies Federation or secede to become an independent country. Manley advocated remaining in the Federation, while Bustamante was opposed to it.

9. In terms of social-economic platforms, Manley's PNP, which is affiliated to the Socialist International, is more to the left than Bustamante's Labor Party, which firmly supports the free-enterprise system.

10. William C. Doherty was later named the first U.S. Ambassador to Jamaica.

XXI

Haiti—The Forgotten Tyranny

PUBLIC INTEREST in the Caribbean world has been concentrated in the most recent years on events in Cuba and the Dominican Republic. Haiti, the little country sandwiched in between, has faded into the background. Whenever it makes the front page, it is usually in stories describing the damage of this or that hurricane and dramatizing the plight of the sick, starving population.

Haiti is a very poor country. According to Lester Velie,[1] Haiti's per capita income in 1950 was about $60 a year. In 1957, after $77 million in foreign aid, it was still about the same. Five years later, the situation was even worse. The people, undernourished, discouraged, ill, worked at only 20 percent of capacity.[2]

Little Haiti has been reduced to this incredible state of economic paralysis and starvation by a succession of incompetent, corrupt, dictatorial governments. A ray of hope appeared on the horizon with the January 7, 1946, popular democratic revolution that swept out of power the tyrannical regime of President Lescaut. The elections held later in that year brought into power President Dumarsais Estimé. He encouraged the labor movement and took the first steps to bring Haiti into the twentieth century. Labor unions actually came into existence under the guidance of labor specialists, directed by Clément Jumelle, a U.S.–educated official of the newly created Haitian Department of Labor.

Jumelle and I became friends during the April–May 1949 ILO Regional

Conference in Montevideo, which he attended as government delegate from Haiti. He also had brought along with him a worker delegate, Molière Compass, a young fellow who was still a novice in the labor field and who had never been out of Haiti before. Molière was excessively vain, and he arrived with a generous supply of calling cards on which there was printed in boldface the fact that he was a worker delegate to the conference.

The large Peronista delegation which attended the Conference (see Chapter VI) focused their attention on Compass and persuaded him to go with them to Buenos Aires, just across the Plata River from Montevideo, for the May Day celebration. I learned of this Peronista scheme on the afternoon of April 30 when by a mere coincidence I saw Molière Compass, in the courtyard of the Miramar Hotel, the seat of the conference, surrounded by a group of Peronistas who were marching him out to a waiting automobile. Molière, who had not said a word to me about his decision to go to Buenos Aires, looked at me and lowered his eyes as if ashamed, while his "captors" smiled at me with an air of triumph.

Dark forebodings crowded my mind. I envisaged Compass being paraded at the Buenos Aires May Day celebration, and even speaking at the Peronista rally, as a sort of prized Negro trophy, "rescued" from the influence of the Yankees. There were no limits to the possibilities of Peronista exploitation of Compass's voyage to Buenos Aires. Something needed to be done, immediately, to prevent that. I rushed to Jumelle. Together we devised a plan to keep Compass away from the Peronista celebration. It worked perfectly.

Jumelle phoned the Haitian Ambassador in Buenos Aires urging him to find Molière Compass, to lure him to the embassy and to keep him there, by all means, until after the May Day celebration. The possibility of "complications" that would endanger the foreign policy of Haiti, then basking under a newly acquired democratic respectability, should Molière appear at a Peronista rally, galvanized the Ambassador into quick and effective action. When the Argentine delegation returned to Montevideo to resume their place at the conference it was my turn to greet them with my version of a triumphant smile.

My first visit to Haiti took place on June 4, 1949. During my brief stay of only two days I delivered at least ten addresses, visited the headquarters of the Haitian Federation of Labor and other trade union organizations, established contact with all the newspapers of Port-au-Prince, had conferences with the Minister of Labor and other government officials, was received by the President of the Republic, Dumarsais Estimé, and spoke at one large meeting of union members. I also met with leaders of the independent transport and port workers and the building trade unions. They were all young and enthusiastic, some inexperienced, but anxious to learn. Later, a few were given U.S. government grants to come to our country to study the structure and functions of our labor movement.

The Haitian Federation of Labor joined the CIT. The port and transport workers also came in later that same year at the time of the Havana CIT Convention. The labor movement of Haiti was solidly behind President Estimé with the exception of a small group of Communists who had some measure of control over the sugar workers. However, Estimé attempted to use organized labor as a political weapon on behalf of his regime, and that caused the disintegration of the movement when in 1950 Estimé was overthrown by a *coup d'état* engineered by General Paul Magloire.

The new regime did not make the same mistake, meaning that it did not try to coordinate and regiment organized labor for the government's benefit. However, Magloire was opposed to the free exercise of trade union rights and made it difficult for organized labor to exist. This policy drove the young and untested democratic trade union leadership to desperation and exposed them to the siren song of underground Communist propaganda.

The policy of the newly organized ORIT, as well as that of the AFL, was not to drive our Haitian trade union friends to an open break with the government. We decided to mark time in the hope that somehow the government of Haiti could be persuaded to adopt a different policy. That task was assigned to me.

In April 1951 I went back to Haiti and after considerable difficulty I managed to gather together under the same roof a large number of trade union representatives, including some I had never met before. I reported on the result of my behind-the-scenes approaches to the government of Haiti and announced that I had received assurances that a measure of trade union activity, divorced from political party connections or interference, would be permitted. The response was overwhelming. A Committee for Trade Union Coordination was formed on the spot. It later became the National Union of Haitian Workers (UNOH) and affiliated to the ORIT and the ICFTU. All those present subscribed to a statement of policy which proclaimed that "unions must be democratic in character and oppose Communism and any other form of totalitarianism."

The regime of General Magloire tolerated the existence of the labor movement in Haiti, but never gave it any official blessing. Nevertheless, the result was that a vigorous labor movement, depending only on its own strength, began to take shape. It was poor, but honest and respected. I recall one occasion when, at the home of the General Secretary of UNOH, Nathanael Michel, the labor movement gave a party in my honor where they served homemade cookies and soda pop. Liquor, even the local cheap rum, was beyond their means! Women began to take part in labor activities, especially in the tobacco factory and the retail stores. By the time the end of President Magloire's term approached, in 1956, the UNOH had become a solid member of ORIT and was playing its part in inter-American labor activities. It had also learned how to play its political role in winning greater democratic strength in its own country without getting involved in internal party politics. When I went to Haiti in August 1956 the leaders of UNOH told me that Clément Jumelle, who was a member of President Magloire's Cabinet, was considering whether to run for the presidency and that organized labor was going to support him almost to a man.

I was elated at the prospect of Jumelle's becoming President of Haiti. He was a true friend of the United States, strongly anti-Communist, yet a deep believer in the need for radical social and economic reforms that would give the Haitian masses a chance to rise slowly but steadily from the depth of misery, ignorance, and disease that was still their tragic lot. I inquired from our Ambassador, Roy Tasco Davis, what, in his opinion, were Jumelle's chances. I really wanted to know whether President Magloire was, in Ambassador Davis's view, disposed to leave the presidency at the expiration of his term and allow free elections—in which case Jumelle would win without much difficulty—or would resort to a last-minute scheme in order to remain in power. Ambassador Davis, a cagey old career diplomat endowed with a captivating, friendly personality, was of course evasive, but not enough to convince me that he had no prejudices against Jumelle. As a matter of fact, I left the interview with a feeling that Ambassador Davis did not like Jumelle on account of his "left-wing"—as the Ambassador repeated—democratic views and his alleged "unfriendliness" toward the United States; these were descriptions unfortunately too often attached then to almost any Latin American nationalist political leader who was not disposed to jump every time the United States Ambassador cracked the whip. In any event, the small but influential American business community was openly averse to Jumelle while it was full of praise for Magloire's authoritarian "no-nonsense" regime.

On October 18, 1956, Jumelle wrote me a letter announcing his resignation from the Magloire Cabinet in order to run for the presidency of the republic as a candidate of the National Haitian Party (PNH), which he himself had founded. In that letter, Jumelle reiterated to me his program of reforms which we had discussed together during my visit to Haiti the previous August.

The "doubts" about Jumelle expressed to me by Ambassador Davis were also shared in Washington by the career officers at the State Department's Haitian desk. I decided, therefore, to do something a bit extraordinary—that was to make an explicit endorsement of Jumelle's candidacy. On November 1, 1956, I replied to him—authorizing him to make public, if he so wished, the content of my letter—in the following words:

Your statement reaffirming your intention to create and support a climate favorable to the development of a strong labor movement has been received with deep rejoicing in the AFL-CIO circles. Although we do not wish to interfere in any way in what is purely an internal affair of the people of Haiti, yet I am glad to say to you, in the most emphatic manner, that the labor movement of the United States and the whole of Latin America hopes that next April you will be elected President of Haiti.

I regret that this expression of moral support is the only thing I can do on behalf of your candidacy. May it help you in your determination to advocate during the campaign the program of social and economic development with which you have been identified in the past.

Meanwhile rumors began to circulate in Haiti that the government of the United States would not object to Magloire's remaining in power after the expiration of his mandate. Whether the rumors were true or false, the fact is that on December 6, 1956, President Magloire went to the radio to announce to the people that he was leaving office. But as had been planned, the Army refused to let him go. Magloire "bowed" to the Army's request and announced that he was going to stay. All this took place in less than one hour!

The population of Haiti reacted to this brazen military ploy by going on strike. Everything was shut down. On December 12 Magloire gave up and went into exile. The President of the Supreme Court, Nemours Pierre-Louis, became Provisional President of the Republic.

During the following ten months, Haiti had five different governments [3] representing different coalitions of the diverse and conflicting forces jockeying for power. The Army wound up by seizing power on June 14, 1957, and ruled the country with a military junta headed by General Kebreau. This general made an alliance with Dr. François Duvalier, an

obscure politician who had been an inconspicuous Minister in a number
of previous governments, and managed to have him elected President at
the general elections of September 22, 1957. Those elections were a complete farce. They were preceded by acts of wholesale intimidation and
violence to the extent that Jumelle's National Party abstained and the
opposition headed by Senator Louis Dejoie was only allowed nominal
and token participation in the electoral process. Most of his representatives were arrested and imprisoned on the eve of the election, which, in
any case, took place under a stage of siege. The whole nation was indignant and the Army had to repress by arms the protest of the citizens.
A general strike in Port-au-Prince was broken by the force of bayonets. On
October 22, 1957, Duvalier took office.

Nobody thought that Duvalier was going to last. The operetta-style
political confusion prevailing in Haiti during most of the year 1957 had
accustomed the people to view with disenchantment the crumbling of
their feeble and unstable political structure. To them, no solution could
be permanent. The main worries of the people were by now the absence
of jobs, the absence of food, the absence of everything needed to exist. On
the other hand, foreign observers—among them the U.S. press corps and
diplomats—were by now so frustrated and so disillusioned that the only
solution they envisaged for Haiti was the emergence of a Messiah, a man
who would have the will and the strength to put the Haitian house in
order by any means and at all costs.

Dr. François Duvalier, superstitious believer in voodoo and magic, disappointed those who looked upon him as another passing chief slated to
go in a few months' time and fulfilled with a vengeance the expectations
of those who hoped for a strong-willed Messiah. He put the Haitian
house in order, all right—the order of the cemetery. And he did so by
imposing on poor hapless Haiti one of the bloodiest and cruelest dictatorships in modern history.

Duvalier realized very quickly that power won against the will of the
majority of the people and with the complicity of a part of the military
which he had corrupted was extremely precarious. He therefore undertook to defend himself against the people and the Army by creating a
secret police. For that new institution, established outside of any legality
and functioning without any known regulation, he called upon the dregs
of the population of the cities and villages, enlisting the habitual criminals and other lawless and vicious elements. He cleverly managed to
deprive the Army of arms and ammunition, and he set upon the whole
population the masked secret police, called *cagoulards* (the hooded

ones) who, generally speaking, operated only at night. The masked men of Duvalier broke into private homes, pulled citizens from their beds, kidnapped them, and left them half-dead in isolated spots.

In a document submitted to the Foreign Ministers of the American States, meeting in Santiago, Chile, August 1959, Roger Rigaud, spokesman for the Haitian National Party in exile, asserted:

> Duvalier anticipated any articulate reaction on the part of the opposition. He invented plots; his secret police exploded bombs at night, they set fire to thickly settled poor sections of towns, and then denounced to the police citizens whom the government wished to imprison. Prisons were crowded, in the capital as well as in the provinces. All the substantial citizens (in politics, business, industry, labor, liberal professions) became worried. Some were apprehended, humiliated, tortured, and then sent home; others were beaten, tortured, and thrown into medieval jails. Many did not survive the tortures and ill treatment; several were incapacitated for life. In order to sap the morale of the accused, who were never arraigned before any judge, they were taken away from their families and friends and imprisoned in the more distant and putrid jails of the Republic.
>
> Respectable women were arrested and thrown into jails with common prostitutes. Some were stripped of all their clothing and humiliated and beaten by the secret police. Even expectant mothers were subjected to the same brutal treatment. The three sisters of Clément Jumelle, the Founder and Head of the Parti National Haïtien, were taken as hostages while their brothers were actively sought by the secret police, to be killed.
>
> In order to justify the suppression of the opposition leaders, the government exploded, on April 30, 1958, some bombs in a suburb of the capital. Then the government arrested some friends of Senator Louis Dejoie, the President of the National Industrial and Agricultural Party, and a price was put on his head. Dejoie took asylum in the Mexican embassy. President Duvalier sent, during the night, for the Mexican Ambassador, threatened him, and demanded that he turn Dejoie over to him. Naturally, the diplomat refused. Duvalier sent his secret police to violate the diplomatic mission, but its courageous Chief, helped by a few colleagues, declared himself ready to meet violence with violence. Dejoie finally received a safe-conduct.

Elected in the same scandalously fraudulent circumstances as Duvalier, most of the Senators and Deputies comprising his Parliament backed his regime, declaring that their fate was closely linked to that of the President. There were, however, in both chambers a few voices to protest the government's action against liberty. One of the Deputies of the capital city, Frank Séraphin, was arrested on May 2, 1958, while in Parliament, and in spite of his immunity was thrown into prison. The government brought false witnesses against him, accused him, had him judged by a military tribunal, which condemned him to five years in prison. Senator Thomas Désulme, a former Minister, went into exile. Senator Jean P. David was arrested as he was going to the Parliament, was then driven to the airport and exiled, to New York. In September 1959, contrary to the Constitution, Duvalier dismissed six Senators: Thomas Désulme, Jean P. David, Jean Béligaire, Emmanuel Moreau, Luc Stephen, and Jules Larrieux. They are, all but one, living in exile.

Duvalier illegally removed or replaced judges who did not protect the interests of his friends or who refused to condemn his enemies. The Chief Justice of the Supreme Court of Haiti, Théodore Nicoleau, who upheld a legal principle displeasing to the President, was removed from office the following day. At the same time, Duvalier removed another career judge, Émile Sainclair, because he was a friend of the Chief Justice.

The Duvalier regime also carried out its tyrannies against religion. In 1960 some priests of the Roman Catholic Church were expelled from Haiti and the Archbishop of Port-au-Prince was threatened with arrest. The Superior of the Congregational College was called in by the Minister of Religion and Foreign Affairs in May 1960 and threatened with imprisonment because of a sermon which Duvalier did not like. The Christian religion is generally held in very low esteem by Duvalier, whose wish and intent is to establish Vaudou (voodooism) as the national religion.

As in any dictatorship, the opposition press in Haiti soon went out of existence. This is how it happened:

The newspaper *Indépendence* had its printing plant sacked by the secret police after its editor in chief, Georges Petit, had been arrested, together with other editors. Petit had been an active newspaperman for more than thirty years.

Albert Occénard, the Director of *Haiti Miroir,* and his principal collaborator, Daniel Arty, were imprisoned and the newspaper's printing plant was destroyed. Messrs. Petit, Occénard, and Arty were later judged and condemned to five years' imprisonment by a military court.

One morning in June 1958 some members of the secret police hurled grenades into the plant of the newspaper *Le Patriote* and later arrested the editor, Antoine Petit, who was tortured and kept in prison for over seven months without ever having been brought to trial.

Augustin Clitandre, the editor of the newspaper *Le Soleil,* was arrested on the street in broad daylight by the secret police, and his wife has not had any news of him since, the authorities having declared that they knew nothing of him.

Hébert Magloire, the editor of the newspaper *Circuit Artibonite,* one of the leaders of the provincial press, was imprisoned for about nine months without ever having been charged with any crime.

All these newspapers and many others have discontinued publication.

No sooner had Duvalier come to power than he began to persecute the labor unions and to force their leaders on the road to exile.

On December 20, 1957, a leader of the Haitian transport workers, Lydéric Bonaventure, was arrested by the police and lodged in jail without the benefit of a trial or even of a hearing before the magistrate.

On January 5, 1958, the General Secretary of UNOH, Nathanael Michel, was also arrested. On the same day, the police forcibly entered the headquarters of UNOH, ransacked the place, took away the archives and the keys, and closed it.

The general secretaries of ORIT and ICFTU, upon learning of Michel's arrest and the closing of UNOH headquarters, expressed their concern in telegrams addressed to President Duvalier, offering to send to Haiti an ORIT-ICFTU mission in order to ascertain the facts and to cooperate in bringing about a satisfactory solution. Both telegrams, however, remained without an answer.

On January 28, 1958, Nathanael Michel was released from jail and brought to Cressier, a little locality 11 miles from the capital city of Port-au-Prince, with orders not to leave the place and to report twice daily to the police. At the same time, he was dismissed from his job as teacher at the Central School of Arts and Trades in the capital city. Thus deprived of any means to earn a livelihood, Michel and his family would have faced starvation had it not been for some emergency financial help which ORIT and ICFTU were able to send him.

The international free trade union movement was determined to wage a worldwide campaign to protest these violations of trade union rights and individual freedom committed by the government of Haiti, and contemplated the filing of strong complaints with the International Labor Organization and other international bodies of which Haiti was a member. However, at a conference held in Washington, early in February, with the participation of officers from ORIT, ICFTU and the AFL-CIO, it was decided to make a final attempt to discuss the situation with President Duvalier himself by sending to Haiti, on a confidential mission, Michael Ross, Director of the AFL-CIO Department of International Affairs.

Michael Ross, who spoke French fluently, arrived in Haiti on March 14, 1958, and stayed for one week, interviewing government officials, labor leaders, and President Duvalier himself. From the labor leaders he learned that the price demanded by Duvalier for leaving them in peace was complete submission to the control of the police. From Duvalier and his Minister of Labor, Ross received "assurances" that there was complete trade union freedom and that only "Communists" were being detained by the police and deprived of their trade union posts. Apparently Duvalier had well learned the lesson—cover the suppression of freedom with the excuse of fighting the Communists and everything will be all right. That this was so appeared to be well illustrated by praise heaped upon Kebreau by U.S. General Shepherd, who visited Haiti in March 1958. Shepherd's statements so infuriated our democratic friends in Haiti that Michael Ross brought back to me a strong letter of protest signed by Roger Rigaud, Jumelle's right-hand man, to which I replied, in order not to further aggravate the situation, in the following rather charitable terms:

I am unable to attribute to the visit of General Shepherd and his rather unfortunate statements in praise of Kebreau any more significance than past statements made by other high American military officers in praise of Odría, Jiménez, Perón, etc. Although I cannot accurately interpret the views of our government on this particular incident, I am willing to bet that the State Department is rather annoyed at this sally into the international field by our good General Shepherd.

Duvalier's claim to being a pillar of anti-Communism in the Caribbean area is exposed as a barefaced lie when one considers that he was a signatory to a Communist manifesto in Mexico City during World War II. Duvalier openly defended and collaborated with Communists in Haiti. His private secretary and brother-in-law, Lucien Daumec, is a member of the Haitian Communist party and has even been refused a visa for transit through the United States.

One of Duvalier's most intimate advisers is Felix Dorléans Juste, President and founder of the Haitian Communist Party. Jules Blanchet, personal adviser to the President, former Minister Without Portfolio, President of a Superior Court of Record (Cour Supérieure des Comptes), is a founder and member of the Popular Socialist Party, the Haitian version of the Communist People's Socialist party of Cuba. Herve Boyer, at one time Minister of Commerce and Industry in the Duvalier Cabinet, and his wife, who was an instructor in a Parisian Communist school, are—according to highly respected Haitian sources—both members of the French Communist Party.

Duvalier has recalled to Haiti all the young Communists living in

France or in the Iron Curtain countries who, prior to his assuming the Presidency, had been denied entry into Haiti. Rodolphe Moïse, a member of the Haitian Communist Party, and his Hungarian wife received personal letters of invitation from Duvalier to come to Haiti. They were put in charge of a school in the Kenscoff area, where they instruct Haitian peasants in Communist doctrine; the school is sustained by Duvalier. Roger Gaillard and his wife, formerly university professors in Bulgaria, were appointed professors at the Haitian National University. Edriss St. Amand, who was a founder of the Haitian Communist Party, a militant Communist in France and the author of a Communist novel published in Paris, was named professor at the School of Advanced International Studies, an institution supported by the Haitian government.

Most former members of the Haitian Communist Party and the Popular Socialist Party are officials, functionaries, or protégés of the government, living peacefully in Haiti, methodically pursuing their subversive activities. None is in exile. In contrast, democratic political groups and free labor organizations have been ruthlessly crushed, their leaders killed, imprisoned, or forced into exile.

Duvalier is also apt at using the Communist issue to blackmail the U.S. government. In a published speech delivered June 21, 1960, for instance, he threatened to put Haiti into the Moscow camp if he did not receive extensive financial assistance. At the January 1962 Punta del Este Conference of the Organization of American States, Haiti withheld its crucial decisive vote to condemn Cuba and suspend it from the OAS until Duvalier's delegate was able to extract from the United States, in behind-the-scenes trading, assurances of continued financial support.

Duvalier's Communist advisers have managed to influence his policy in order to generate a violent dislike and hatred of Americans. They prepare things so that when Duvalier inevitably falls—as all dictators sooner or later do—the people will give vent to their anti-U.S. anger and put a Communist–anointed "popular democracy" *à la Cubana* into power.

During the month of June 1958, ICFTU, ORIT and the AFL-CIO received a communication from UNOH, signed by a new General Secretary, Fritzner Sainvil, informing us that a new leadership had been elected. None of the old democratic leaders with whom we had been in contact for years was included. We all got suspicious and decided to make an on-the-spot investigation. ICFTU asked me to go to Haiti as soon as possible.

On July 5, 1958, I arrived at Port-au-Prince from Puerto Rico, but as I entered the immigration office I was detained by the police and forced to reboard the Miami-bound plane. An officer of the United States Embassy in Haiti, who had come to the airport to meet me, was not permitted to talk to, or even approach, me—a procedure which was in clear violation of the established custom of allowing diplomatic representatives to assist citizens of their respective countries when they have difficulties with the immigration or police authorities. A large group of trade unionists who had come to the airport to receive me were disbanded by the police and some of them were arrested.

Upon learning of this arbitrary action against me, AFL-CIO President George Meany, on July 17, sent a letter to Secretary of State John Foster Dulles urging him to lodge a strong protest with the government of Haiti. In his letter, President Meany stated:

For over twelve years, Mr. Romualdi has distinguished himself in his fight against Communism and any other brand of totalitarianism in Latin America— earning the respect and approbation of leaders in every walk of life in Latin America, as well as in the United States. The behavior of the present govern- ment of Haiti against a representative of the free, democratic labor movement can only result in the strengthening of subversive totalitarian forces which we are trying to defeat, and is strongly resented by the American Federation of Labor and Congress of Industrial Organizations.

In view of these events, the continuation of U.S. financial help to Haiti, which in the past fiscal year amounted to $3½ million, cannot fail to arouse the type of resentment which U.S. representatives have been experiencing when visiting Latin America. It may lead to the incorrect assumption that our government favors undemocratic regimes which violate civil liberties and trade union rights.

I urge you, Mr. Secretary, to lodge with the government of Haiti the strongest possible protest against the unwarranted action taken against Mr. Serafino Romualdi, and to request a prompt reversal of this unfriendly attitude so that he may be permitted in the near future to go to Haiti in the pursuance of his legitimate mission.

On July 30, 1958, Undersecretary of State Christian A. Herter replied for the Department of State declaring that "I share your concern over this incident." He further said that "our Embassy at Port-au-Prince has been instructed to request an explanation for the Haitian authorities' action in not permitting Mr. Romualdi to enter their country on July 5 despite the fact he possessed a valid entry permit."

Our Embassy's request for explanation did not deter the Haitian gov- ernment from continuing and intensifying its suppression of the free trade union movement. Equally ineffective was the complaint filed on July 29 with the International Labor Organization by the ICFTU, charging that the Haitian government was engaged in repressive actions against trade unions.

At the same time, in order to destroy the opposition, Duvalier—whom his acolytes had started calling "Papa Doc"—began by striking at the leaders of political parties. On May 3, 1958, Duvalier seized the properties of Clément Jumelle, former presidential candidate and leader of the opposition National Party, and also those of his brother, Ducasse Jumelle, a former professor of law, a former Senator of the republic and former Minister of Justice and of the Interior. On May 19, 1958, without any justification, he outlawed these two personalities and undertook to implicate them, twenty days later, in the explosion of a bomb.

During the night of August 28, 1958, Ducasse Jumelle and his brother Charles—a nonpolitical man who was managing the family affairs—were shot and killed in the street, in the heart of a residential quarter, after being arrested in a house where they had taken refuge to escape persecution. They were chained together and machine-gunned in cold blood by police major Clément Barbot [4] on orders given personally by Duvalier, who was present at the scene, together with Majors Daniel and Jean Beauvoir, two pillars of Duvalier's military support, whom he later promoted to colonel.[5] Also under Duvalier's orders, the owner of the house where the Jumelle brothers had been granted sanctuary, Jacques Monfiston, was murdered at the same spot.

A few evenings later, "Papa Doc" gave a banquet to a selected group of his henchmen. As two roasted pigs were brought to the table, "Papa Doc" said:

"We are starting with two Jumelle pigs. I am confident that the other two, Clément and Dr. Gaston, will soon be served at another banquet. . . ."

Dr. Gaston Jumelle was able to reach safety at the Mexican embassy [6] while Clément went deeper in the underground to lead the resistance as leader of the National Party. But his luck ran out, and a third pig was actually served at another banquet, almost one year later.

As the wave of violence and murder mounted in Haiti, the situation of Nathanael Michel and other labor leaders was increasingly worrying me. I felt that their lives were now in real danger. The only solution would be to bring them to some Latin American embassy in Port-au-Prince for political asylum. During the month of September I went to

Caracas, where I was able to enlist the help of Dr. Rómulo Betancourt. He obtained definite advance approval from the Venezuelan provisional government that Michel would be granted asylum. Now it was only a matter of organizing a safe journey for Michel and his family from their hiding place to the Venezuelan embassy.

On my way back from Venezuela to Miami, I stopped for about a half hour at the Port-au-Prince airport in the hope of meeting some member of Michel's family, whom I had notified in advance. Unfortunately, new regulations restricted passengers in transit to a small room with no possibility of mingling with the public in the regular waiting room, as is customary in other airports. However, I was able to talk to a trusted friend from the American Embassy who had access to the restricted area, and through him I sent word to Michel that someone would shortly contact him and take him to a safe place from where he could later leave the country.

From the same source I also learned that the new leadership of UNOH had been put into office by the police and it was composed of elements unworthy of any consideration from ORIT-ICFTU. It had been conclusively established, for instance, that it was Fritzner Sainvil, the new General Secretary of UNOH, who upon learning of my arrival in Port-au-Prince on July 5 (and he was the only one to know that) went to the police and urged them to bar me from entering the country. On the other hand, Michel and other displaced leaders conducted themselves honorably and, in spite of tremendous difficulties, remained loyal to the principles of free trade unionism. They enjoyed the unqualified support of the rank and file, although this support could not be manifested in any organized way.

Early in February 1959, ORIT General Secretary Alfonso Sánchez Madariaga received a letter from the Haitian Ambassador in Mexico, assuring ORIT that complete freedom had been reestablished in the country, that a number of prominent opposition leaders had been pardoned and released from jail, and that a policy of social harmony and economic progress was being pursued energetically by the government of President Duvalier.

The ORIT Executive Board asked me to go to Haiti to reestablish contact with the democratic labor leaders who were still in hiding in the hope that the new climate of freedom, as announced by the Haitian government, would permit them to reorganize the National Union of Haitian Workers (UNOH), from which they had been illegally eliminated the year before as a result of government interference and police intervention.

On February 25, 1959, accompanied by my wife Miriam, I arrived in Haiti. This time I had taken precautions to fool the airport police, and was able to go through immigration and customs without any difficulty.

It took me only a few hours to realize that the situation was as bad as— or even worse—than the one that had prevailed the previous year. The pledges of full reestablishment of freedom uttered by President Duvalier were a dead letter as far as the Haitian people were concerned. Nathanael Michel, the General Secretary of UNOH, whom I first tried to contact, had sought asylum a few days earlier in the Venezuelan embassy, together with his wife and three children. He decided on this desperate move after he became convinced that his life was in real danger. Another labor leader, Lydéric Bonaventure, head of the chauffeurs' union, was also in the Venezuelan embassy. He sought asylum after another man, Dieudonne John, was mistaken for him and murdered on the night of January 25.

Dacius Benoît, President of the longshoremen's union, and a dear old friend of mine, was in hiding with both health and mind broken after his arrest and torture by the police. I was told that he was doused with gasoline and then set on fire. For a few days he hovered between life and death on account of his severe burns.

During the two days I remained in Port-au-Prince, the city was in the grip of terror. Rumors that the democratic opponents of Duvalier were about to stage an invasion of the republic had made the government jittery. Duvalier was no longer satisfied with jailing his opponents. He was resorting simply to their assassination. Thus, at the end of January, Télémaque Guerrier, a prominent leader of the opposition, was arrested at 4:30 P.M. on Magloire Ambroise Avenue and was executed during the night in Bonne-Foi Street. On February 17, hardly a week before my arrival, Franck Hogarth was killed with five bullets as he was returning to his home.

Clément Jumelle was in hiding. Word reached me at the hotel, where a trusted member of the underground opposition was working, that arrangements had been made for me to see him at an undisclosed place. I would get directions from a downtown bookstore clerk. Later, as I was talking to this clerk, my back was turned to the street while the clerk had a clear view of the store entrance and the street beyond. Suddenly, without altering voice or posture, my contact said to me:

"Now, be calm. A car full of *cagoulards* has just stopped before the store. I think they are looking for you. Do you have a taxi?"

"Yes, it is parked just across the street."

"Then I suggest you go out immediately and order the taxi driver to go straight to your embassy."

The clerk handed me a book so as to prove that I had gone into the store for a legitimate purpose, and calmly said good-bye.

At a quick but unhurried pace I reached my taxi and in a loud, clear voice I said: "À l'embassade américaine!"

The *cagoulards* followed me but did not dare enter the embassy compound. Once inside, I was advised to leave the country immediately. We checked with Pan American Airways and found that I still had enough time to catch the afternoon southbound plane. An Embassy car was sent to the hotel (the phone would have been too risky) to ask my wife to pack, pay the bill, and come to the embassy. Later, the Labor Officer, Virgil P. Randolph, III, and his wife took us to the airport in an Embassy car and kept us under their constant protection, in a safe place, until it was time to board the plane. That was the last time I saw Haiti.

After I returned to Washington, I sent Randolph the following letter:

> Mrs. Romualdi and I wish to express to you and your charming wife our most sincere appreciation for all the courtesies and attention extended to us during our recent brief visit to Haiti. Although it was short, I have a feeling that it was to a certain extent rather fruitful.
>
> I do not know when circumstances will permit me to come back again. I surely would like to do that as soon as possible.

My letter was definitely an understatement. I wanted to address that young aristocratic scion of a distinguished New England family and his cultured young wife in different terms, but I was aware of necessary diplomatic limitations. Yet I can say, now, that I have met many brave State Department career officers, young and old, but none equaled, in my experience, Virgil Randolph, III, in courage, daring, and imagination. I had dealings with him for a number of years, practically during his entire tour of duty in Haiti. When in doubt whether they could do this or that, he and his wife used to reassure themselves by saying: "Our country stands for democracy and freedom. Anything we can do to further this cause, we guess will be helping our country too."

There are many so-called "cookie pushers" like Virgil Randolph, III, in the State Department and the many other agencies with personnel abroad, who without recognition are effectively and courageously serving the highest and purest ideals of democracy that have made our country truly great.

The end of Clément Jumelle came on April 12, 1959. Sick in body, racked by diseases contracted up in the mountains where he often slept on the bare ground, with insufficient food and lack of medical attention, Jumelle was taken at night, delirious with fever and in a semiconscious state, to the Cuban embassy. There he died a few hours later.

The funeral was scheduled to take place on April 14. Thousands of Haitians, many simple barefooted peasants from the countryside, congregated at the Cathedral, where a Requiem Mass was to be held. But a group of armed *ton ton macoutes* [7] suddenly intercepted the cortege, dispersed the people with clubs, pistols, and machetes, stole the casket from the hearse, and took it away. The corpse of Clément Jumelle was found days later outside the city, thrown into a ditch, minus the heart and certain organs of the body generally used in voodoo ceremonies of which "Papa Doc" Duvalier is a practitioner.

With the death of Clément Jumelle the political opposition inside Haiti was completely crushed. Only one party was allowed to function—Duvalier's own personal "National Unity" Party. Daniel Fignole, former Senator Louis Dejoie, and Dr. Gaston Jumelle, leaders of the three opposition parties, were in exile. With them, also in exile, were more than one thousand outstanding citizens of the republic—businessmen, professionals, technicians, former senior officers of the Army, brilliant and long-experienced diplomats, labor leaders, and others. All of them were waiting for the opportunity to return to their country, to which they were patriotically devoted. But years passed with no change in sight.

In April 1961, "Papa Doc" Duvalier pulled a fast one that did not go well with the government in Washington and other capitals in Latin America. Having been "elected" in September 1957, Duvalier still had two years to go; but he took advantage of a so-called Parliamentary election by having his name printed on top of the single and only ballot allowed. There had been no announcement that he was a candidate for anything, but after the electoral farce was over, Duvalier announced that he had been unanimously reelected for a second term—two years ahead of time. His inauguration took place on May 22, 1961. Most of the Western Hemisphere countries, including the United States, shunned the ceremony or sent the lowest-ranking Embassy officer that protocol would allow. This, however, did not deter Duvalier. Two years later, on June 22, 1963, he announced that, "by proclamation of the people," he had been elected President for life. [9]

The government of the United States as well as governments of at least a dozen other countries in the Western Hemisphere, began to show in many ways short of outright intervention their disapproval of the Duvalier tyranny. For instance, in the spring of 1963, the OAS Commission on Human Rights, at the request of the Dominican Republic, held hearings on the charges submitted by a Committee of Haitian citizens representing the opposition political parties in exile. The OAS voted to send to Haiti an ad hoc committee to investigate, but the Haitian government refused to admit the committee and rejected every request for information or cooperation.

Pierre L. Rigaud, a former Haitian ambassador, thus described Duvalier's reaction to the OAS move: [9]

A night watchman entrusted with guarding a store of materials and equipment belonging to the Ministry of Public Works in the capital of Haiti was bound with barbed wire and hanged in the main entrance to the depot. At Pétionville, a suburb of Port-au-Prince, another patriot was crucified with his feet and hands transfixed by nails. More than fifty cases of disappearance have been reported, and illegal arrest and political persecution are sowing fresh panic among Haitian families. So much for Duvalier's response to the resolution adopted by the Commission for the Rights of Man sponsored by the Organization of American States, which, for the first time, seems disposed to examine the Haitian problem.

In the spring of 1963, the democratic elements inside and outside Haiti joined forces and formed the Union Démocratique Nationale (UDN) Haïtienne with the view of overthrowing by force the tyrannical regime of François Duvalier. The support was wide and encouraging. Labor people were also involved. Through them I learned that inside Haiti there were cells within the Army, the Coast Guard, the militia—including the *ton ton macoutes*—and even the highest echelons of the government itself, all working for Duvalier's overthrow.

General Léon Cantave, a courageous and dedicated patriotic Haitian Army officer who had gone into exile, was selected as commander of the invading army. His deputy, in charge of the political aspects of the operation, was Roger Rigaud, a close friend of mine who was also one of the executive leaders of the National Party founded by the late Clément Jumelle, and of which Dr. Gaston Jumelle was still the titular head. It was planned that from a base in the Dominican Republic the Haitian Liberation Army would just cross over into Haiti and from there proclaim the insurrection. The leaders calculated that victory would require not more than thirty days. Recognition of a Provisional Government by a number of Latin American countries was anticipated if the operation succeeded.

Although the government of the United States, especially since the advent of John F. Kennedy to the presidency, had given repeated demonstrations of its dislike of Duvalier and his bloody regime, there still prevailed among the Haitian refugees, whose number by then had gone up to many thousands, a feeling of frustration and resentment against the United States. They were becoming dangerously anti-American in their utterances. They claimed that past U.S. financial, economic, moral, and military support had been largely responsible for keeping Duvalier in power. It was true that Washington had finally withdrawn its military mission in March 1963, but by then—claimed the refugees—Duvalier had consolidated his militia and had reduced the Army to virtual impotence. The leaders of the Haitian political emigration also claimed that the government in Washington, through its officials in charge of relations with Haiti, had maintained toward them, individually and collectively, an attitude of arrogance and smugness. I myself had been a witness of actions indicating the truth of this charge, which I attributed to lack of sympathetic and intelligent understanding of conditions, trends, and developments in Haiti by our foreign service personnel concerned with that country.

Of course, officials at the State Department's Haitian desk were afraid of complications from Cuba, which had just emerged from the October 1962 confrontation with the United States with a stronger internal political stability that had enabled Castro to intensify his subversive forays into the Caribbean as far as Venezuela. Besides, they used to tell me at the State Department, the refugees are not really united and, judging from past Haitian history, most likely "they will not be much better than Duvalier." Why then, they argued, should the United States take a chance?

Actually, the permanence of Duvalier in power was creating, in my judgment, the conditions favorable to an eventual Communist take-over, especially by those elements close to Duvalier who had always been well disposed toward Communism. Furthermore, there were 80,000 Haitians established in Cuba, largely in Oriente province across the strait from Haiti. Some four hundred of these Cuban-Haitians had been indoctrinated and especially trained for a possible quick return to Haiti in case of an emergency. Actually, a number had already found their way back into Haiti, prepared and ready for any eventuality. If Duvalier were to be overthrown and supplanted by a regime composed of democratic elements friendly to the United States, the potential Communist danger from Cuba could be more easily forestalled.[10]

I had known the leaders of the Haitian UDN for years. I felt that they were the best elements available for leading their country back to a civilized and responsible form of government. I had also every reason to consider them trustworthy. Andrew C. McLellan, who had succeeded me as AFL-CIO Inter-American Representative, was of the same mind. He told me repeatedly that Roger Rigaud and his friends were to be trusted completely. For this reason, I lent the Haitian democratic revolutionists my full moral support.

Another consideration, of wider international impact, led me to hope that Rigaud and his friends would win the battle. Haiti, as the oldest "African Republic" and the second oldest sovereign nation in the Western Hemisphere (second only to the United States), could become, once restored to the democratic cause, a useful bridge to and interpreter of the Western World with the new African nations. Many Haitian intellectuals and technicians, refugees from Duvalier's tyranny, were serving in Africa with a number of French-speaking newly independent states, under individual contracts with the United Nations. They were primarily employed in the fields of medicine, sanitation, agronomy, education, law, and government administration. Some of them, like my friend Lydéric Bonaventure, were in Africa on trade union missions on behalf of ICFTU. They all were Western-oriented and firm believers in cooperation with the United States. What an opportunity if these people could become the leaders of post-Duvalier Haiti! But fate, again, was not on the side of the angels.

On August 5, 1963, General Cantave entered Haiti with an initial contingent of 120 men. The original plan was to move in from the sea in order not to embarrass the Dominican government, but at the last moment the unmarked boats which were promised failed to arrive. The Dominican Army, which was fully cooperative, made available a number of trucks with which the border was crossed. The trucks returned immediately to Dominican territory and Cantave's group proceeded on foot to take Fort Liberté, which had been evacuated by the Haitian garrison. The plan called for the occupation of Cap-Haïtienne, the second city of Haiti, by 6 o'clock that evening. With the possession of that airfield and the radio station, Cantave would have addressed the Haitian people at 8 P.M., urging them to join the revolt. He would also have proclaimed the formation of a Provisional Government. However, Cap-Haïtienne's military garrison, unlike that of Fort Liberté, put up a stiff resistance while troops from Port-au-Prince, the Haitian capital, were moving up to strengthen the defending garrison. General Cantave, to avoid entrapment, split his forces into two groups with the intent of carrying on guerrilla warfare from the mountains. However, they were outnumbered by regular soldiers, who wiped out one of the two groups (only one man survived). With the remnants of his forces, Cantave returned to the Dominican Republic with the view of launching another invasion later on, after his forces had been reorganized and equipped.

The Dominican military leaders, however, forced General Cantave to move ahead of time. He was not yet in possession of sufficient arms and ammunition to engage Duvalier's forces, which in the meanwhile had been reinforced. The ultimatum served on Cantave by the commander of the Dominican garrison closest to his camp threatened immediate arrest of him and all his troops unless they crossed the frontier and without delay made the attack on Fort Onanaminthe as Cantave was preparing to do.[11]

At 1 A.M. on September 22, 1963[12] Cantave's ragged army, composed of about one hundred men, crossed the border and attacked Fort Onanaminthe. The battle lasted until 11 A.M. of the following day, when Cantave realized that he was beaten. His exhausted and ill-equipped fighters were being mowed down by machine guns and forced back toward the border of the Dominican Republic. Those who made it, Cantave included, were promptly taken into custody by the military, and interned. Cantave was allowed to go abroad after a few days; the others were set free and eventually found means of livelihood in the Dominican Republic or abroad. Weeks later, I asked one of the men who took part in the operation what had actually happened. In a sort of post mortem lamentation he answered: "Our situation could be compared to that of a group of deaf and dumb men, at night and without lights, hunting for vicious rats in a strange cellar!"

Like the Cuban liberty-loving patriots of the Bay of Pigs invasion before them, the Haitian patriots of Cantave's army resumed the bitter wanderings of the exile, proud of having demonstrated that there are Haitians, as there are Cubans, with the will and the courage to take active steps, at the risk of their lives, and extreme danger to their families, to liberate their homeland from the bloody clutches of tyranny.

"Quod Est Dictum"—*The Washington Post* of Saturday, February 19, 1966, carried the following item, from Geneva, Switzerland:

The International Commission of Jurists yesterday accused Dr. François Duvalier, the president of Haiti for life, of "flagrant disregard for the elementary notions of democracy" in his country. In one of the strongest statements it has ever issued, the Commission said the security of ordinary Haitians "depends only on the arbitrary will of the tyrant" because of "arbitrary arrests, persecutions, summary executions in which whole families have been exterminated, the constant extortions and sinister activities of the police, the notorious Ton Ton Macoutes."

Notes

1. Lester Velie, *The Readers' Digest,* March 1962.
2. Lester Velie, *ibid.*
3. The Nemours Pierre-Louis Provisional Presidency was succeeded on February 7, 1957, by a provisional coalition government headed by Franck Sylvain. From April 6 to May 25 Haiti was ruled by a collective regime composed of thirteen members, followed by a coalition government headed by Daniel Fignole. On June 14 the Army sent Fignole into exile and installed the military junta headed by General Kebreau.
4. Clément Barbot in the summer of 1963 broke with Duvalier and organized a plot to kill him, but was betrayed and died in an ambush.
5. The Beauvoir brothers' turn came on November 11, 1966, when they were suddenly dismissed from the Army on suspicion of plotting against Duvalier. The following day they took refuge with their families in the Brazilian embassy.
6. Dr. Gaston Jumelle, a physician, was later allowed to go to Mexico and then came to the United States, where, after the death of his remaining brother Jumelle, he assumed the leadership of the National Party in Exile.
7. *Ton ton macoutes* (boogeymen) was the nickname given by the Haitian people to Duvalier's private army of thugs, formerly known as *cagoulards* (the hooded ones).
8. *Time* magazine has published that like any other voodoo mystic dictator François ("Papa Doc") Duvalier has his good-luck day: the twenty-second. He was elected "President" on September 22, 1957, inaugurated October 22, then inaugurated for the second term on May 22, 1961, then installed as "President for life" on June 22, 1963. Some Haitians even credit his occult powers with the November 22, 1963, assassination of President Kennedy, a longtime foe. But on January 22, 1965, Duvalier's luck suddenly seemed to turn when one of his two DC-3s crashed on Haiti's southern peninsula, crippling his rickety little air force. Haitians hopefully spread the word that Duvalier might be in trouble with the spirits.
9. *Inter-American Labor Bulletin,* July–August, 1962.
10. The latest Communist line vis-à-vis the Haitian government of François Duvalier —as gathered from their shortwave broadcasts in Creole, beamed to Haiti—is to advocate the overthrow of Duvalier as "part of the struggle against the United States" and through an alliance of all the "popular, anti-imperialist forces," etc. The July 29, 1966, broadcast over the Prague station blamed the United States for the continuation of Duvalier's power and for the conditions now existing in Haiti, even going back to the landing of the Marines at the time of World War I.
11. What reasons prompted the Dominican Republic army leaders to give General Cantave the ultimatum "move, or get arrested," probably never will be fully known. One version widely credited in Haitian circles implicated in the affair related the ultimatum to Dominican Republic internal politics. The Army had made up its mind to overthrow President Juan Bosch. The coup was slated to take place during President Bosch's visit to Mexico in September 1963, but nothing happened. Defense Minister General Viñas Román, who had accompanied President Bosch, upon returning to Santo

Domingo was simply furious. According to the same Haitian source, Colonel (soon afterwards promoted to Brigadier General) Elías Wessin y Wessin masterminded the ultimatum, well aware of the fact that it would result in Cantave's failure. However, this would give the Dominican military a pretext to blame Bosch for having implicated the country in an international adventure. A few days after Cantave's defeat at the battle of Fort Onanaminthe, Bosch was overthrown.

12. Another 22, Duvalier's lucky number.

XXII

Unions in Trujilloland

FOR OVER thirty years General Rafael Leonidas Trujillo[1] ruled the Dominican Republic, the eastern half of the Island of Hispaniola, as his personal property. His dictatorship was perhaps even bloodier than the tyranny of François Duvalier in neighboring Haiti. It is not generally known, however, that Trujillo, throughout his long rule[2] managed to get a considerable measure of labor support from the Dominican Republic Confederation of Labor (CDT), over which he installed loyal puppets who served him faithfully and became his accomplices in many crimes.

After the assassination of Trujillo, on May 30, 1961, it was hard to find in the whole Dominican Republic any labor leader who would admit that he willingly served Trujillo. All had excuses that they were forced to do this and to do that under threat of arrest or worse. Yet the fact remains that the labor movement in the Republic continued in existence under the long regime of Trujillo; maintained its organizational structure intact, and even improved it; was able to enjoy some material privileges; and received subsidies and a number of other benefits. Of course, all this was paid for with absolute submission and subservience to the dictator's will. Cases of heroic resistance were numerous, and long is the list of leaders of the workers who paid with their lives for having dared to oppose Trujillo. But the number who submitted and gave the CDT a veneer of legitimacy was nevertheless considerable, to the extent that the Dominican labor movement was for many years recognized as "legitimate" by the

World Federation of Trade Unions and its Latin American branch, the CTAL, and paid regular dues to both. Later, the CDT tried to join the CIT and even the ORIT-ICFTU, but the vigilance and strong opposition of the AFL and a considerable number of Latin American free labor organizations, led by the Cuban CTC, frustrated these attempts.[3]

For a while, inside the Dominican Republic, the CDT even collaborated with the Communists because Trujillo found it convenient to deal with them in order to demonstrate that he was a "democrat" who was tolerant of the opposition.[4] Of course, Trujillo thought that he would be able, in the end, to fool them, while the Communists, on their part, thought that they could take advantage of the opportunity to bore from within, and eventually take over the labor movement.

As CIT Secretary for International Relations, I naturally developed a keen interest in the Dominican Republic labor situation. Since it was not possible for me to visit that country, I established close relations with a number of refugees, especially those with trade union backgrounds. I thus learned the odyssey of other martyrs of the Latin American labor movement, the worker heroes and victims of the Dominican Republic, whom I adopted as my own, as I had already done with the leaders of the authentic trade unions of Argentina, Peru, Venezuela, and other countries ruled by dictatorships.

In 1930 when General Trujillo seized power, he dissolved the Confederation of Dominican Workers. A demonstration of workers, mainly chauffeurs, which was held in Santa Barbara Square in the capital city was machine-gunned, and several workers were killed. As a result of widespread protests throughout the Americas the government subsequently allowed most of the unions to function again, although under severe restrictions.

On January 21, 1936, the government decreed a "Trade Union Day." This decree apparently amplified the right of trade union organization, but it put all the unions under the absolute control of the provincial governors; in smaller towns this control was exercised by the municipal officials. Each union meeting or convention was presided over or controlled by these functionaries, who were usually accompanied by policemen.

In spite of these conditions, the Dominican working class continued to struggle. In 1942 there was a strike of the workers of the Santa Fe and Romana sugar mills. It was suppressed by 600 soldiers and three airplanes, commanded by Colonel Frank Felix, and the sugar workers' leader, Francisco Lantigua, was killed. His body was strung up in front of the machine shop of the Romana mill, with a sign on it, THIS WORKER COLLECTED HIS WAGE INCREASE. Chichi Montes de Oca was hanged in the Ozama fortress, as were Luis Ogando and Juan Deolio. Ramón Espinal and several others were killed by the rural guards at the Romana sugar mill.

A general walkout throughout the sugar regions occurred in January and February 1946. As a result of this strike two leaders were assassinated, two imprisoned, and three forced to flee the country clandestinely. [5] Other workers' revolts took place in 1947 with the number of victims still increasing.[6]

The bloody repression of the trade union movement in the Dominican Republic, which the CIT press made known throughout Latin America, created a wave of indignation and caused the CIT to appeal to the ILO Commission on Freedom of Association. The complaint, dated September 29, 1950, was signed by four Dominican labor leaders in exile—Justiniano José del Orbe, Ángelo Miolán, Hernando Hernández, and Mauricio Báez. After listing all the crimes against freedom of trade union association committed by the Trujillo dictatorship, they asked for the following actions under the terms of Article 5 of the Statutes of the ILO:

1. Transmit this present statement to the Commission on Violation of Freedom of Association for investigation as to the veracity of the charges we make;

2. Independently, we ask that the executive organ of the ILO send an official commission to the Dominican Republic so that they can prove on the spot the existence of these depressing labor conditions, as was done in the case of Venezuela; and

3. Bring the situation to the attention of the Dominican government, urging that it establish full guarantees for the labor movement to function, free of police interference, and that it put into effect the ILO conventions and agreements which it has signed.

The complaint was strengthened with the following significant comments:

An unquestionable fact in our statement is that the government is authorizing the functioning of a group called the Dominican Confederation of Workers which is not given entry into any international democratic labor group. All of the working-class organizations of the world know perfectly well that there is no Dominican trade union movement, nor the conditions under which one could develop. The few international labor groups into which these puppets have been able to sneak have immediately expelled them. The leader of these puppets is Julio César Ballester, the present General Secretary of the CDT. He was an accomplice of the assassins of Hector Quezada, Emeterio Dixson, and other workers during the strike at La Romana in 1946. He is considered by the Dominican workers as the closest collaborator with the hangmen who are now persecuting and assassinating the workers.

The Dominican government has regarded as of great importance the conferences of the ILO and has never missed an opportunity to send a spurious workers' delegation there to give the impression that trade union freedom exists in that country. In this, they have had the cooperation of the Communists, who have always enjoyed governmental assistance. In spite of this cooperation with the Communists, the government labels any protests by the workers as Stalinist, in order to confuse public opinion and justify reprisals. The same weapon is used for purposes of propaganda abroad. Basically the Communists aid the plans of this government as they do those of the despotic regimes of Peru, Venezuela, Nicaragua, etc.

The facts which we have presented are all true and to confirm them we are willing to return to our country in the company of a mission of the ILO, before which the truth could not be hidden. However, we should request an absolute international guarantee that our lives and liberty would be respected and that we would be able to come abroad once more.

In my address delivered before the AFL's 69th Annual Convention in Houston, Texas, October 1950, I emphatically denounced the crimes of the Trujillo regime and called upon the governments of the Americas, especially the government of the United States, "to demonstrate with words and deeds that we are on the side of the oppressed and not on the side of the oppressors." Shortly afterwards, Trujillo's Consul General in New York, Felix Bernardino, well known for having participated in countless episodes of violence in the Dominican Republic as chief of Trujillo's personal guard, received instructions to denounce me as a Communist. He obeyed and sent a letter to AFL President William Green in which he charged that I was associating with "known Communists" and that I had been repudiated by the Confederation of Labor of the Dominican Republic. He added that the Confederation "has always admired the AFL and could not understand how such a marvelous organization could be represented by such a Communist stooge as Romualdi." Of course, Consul Bernardino in due time got the answer he deserved.

My reply to Bernardino was eventually brought by a third party to the attention of Dr. Juan Bosch, the President of the Dominican Revolutionary Party (PRD) in Exile, whom I had met for the first time in Havana. Dr. Bosch wrote me a letter in which he commended the tone of my reply, and expressed "warm congratulations and enthusiastic gratitude."

One of the signers of the memorandum to the International Labor Organization asking for an investigation of the suppression of trade union liberties in his homeland, Mauricio Báez, a founder of the CDT and leader of the Dominican trade unionists in exile, was kidnaped on December 10, 1950, as he emerged from his home in Havana. Báez has never been seen since that fateful morning. He disappeared without trace, just as many others among Trujillo's opponents did before and after him.

The commotion caused by Mauricio Báez's disappearance spread all over the world. The ORIT founding Congress, meeting in Mexico City in January 1951, urged all affiliated organizations "to denounce the monstrous kidnaping of Mauricio Báez before the working classes of their respective nations as an act of governmental gangsterism; and to make representations to the Dominican government and to international organizations, demanding the return of Mauricio Báez, and holding the Trujillo government responsible for his disappearance."

In connection with the trade union situation in the Dominican Republic, ICFTU General Secretary Jacob H. Oldenbroek informed the Congress that the previous July he had been visited by Julio C. Ballester, who, on behalf of the CDT and in order to facilitate its eventual admission to the ICFTU, had "extended an invitation to visit the Dominican Republic" to the ICFTU in order to verify that "freedom and democracy involving the whole labor movement existed in his country." The invitation was discussed at the September 1950 meeting of the ICFTU Executive Board, where it was decided to refer it to the founding Congress of the Regional Organization. "It might be a good idea," suggested Oldenbroek, "to take the CDT at its word and accept the invitation." The Congress agreed and empowered the Executive Board to act in consultation with ICFTU. After the latter ratified the agreement at its Emergency Committee meeting in Brussels, February 20–24, 1951, the ORIT Executive Board proceeded to select the Commission, which was to include one representative from the ICFTU, one from the United States and two from Latin America.

When, however, the CDT was notified of the steps taken and was asked to make all necessary arrangements so that the Commission could go to the Dominican Republic as soon as possible, Ballester blandly replied that the CDT had never extended such an invitation and had no intention of doing it now. In a bristling reply dated April 27, 1951, addressed to Ballester, J. H. Oldenbroek cited names and dates to prove that such an invitation had been extended and concluded by saying "your action speaks for itself—you have something to hide."

Meanwhile, one member of the intended mission, George Woodcock, who later became General Secretary of the British Trades Union Congress, had arrived in Havana, where he joined Francisco Aguirre, ORIT General Secretary, in an attempt to obtain a visa and go to the Dominican Republic. But they were turned down. Woodcock issued a statement in which he said:

I am convinced that under the present circumstances, the Dominican Confederation of Labour cannot possibly be a free and independent trade union movement. My limited observations do not enable me, however, to express a firm opinion on its exact status. At the very worst, it may be no more than a part of the executive branch of the dictatorship. At the best it may well be nominally a distinct and separate organization but in fact entirely subservient to the dictator. I think that it occupies this latter position. Its limited freedom of action exists only insofar as its actions do not conflict with the policies and the wishes of the dictator.

The matter, however, did not rest there. At the ILO annual Conference held in June 1951 in Geneva, Switzerland, contacts were reestablished between Ballester and ORIT Regional Secretary Francisco Aguirre, who was assisted by me as ORIT Secretary for International Relations. This contact later prompted an exchange of correspondence between Aguirre and Ballester, which I am now going to summarize because it gives some insights into the labor movement in the Dominican Republic, helps one to understand the CDT subservience to Dictator Trujillo, and spells out in clear terms ORIT's uncompromising opposition to Dictator Trujillo to which it remained faithful until Trujillo's death.

Under date of October 9, 1951, Ballester wrote Aguirre commenting upon a report in the ORIT publication, *Noticiario Obrero Interamericano,* that the recent Convention of the Cuban Confederation of Labor (CTC) had adopted a resolution "condemning the dictatorship of General Trujillo in the Dominican Republic and the repression of freedom of association in that country," as well as a statement by CTC General Secretary Eusebio Mujal that "The CTC is always ready to help the workers of every country to regain their freedom, even to the extent of supplying them with arms, as would have to be the case in the Dominican Republic." Ballester wrote:

Both articles indicate, in our opinion, a lack of knowledge of the true conditions under which the workers of the Dominican Republic live. Freedom of association in the Dominican Republic is guaranteed by our Constitution and is fully enjoyed. As to the progress of the trade union movement, I am enclosing for your information a copy of the Labor Code, which will be put into effect the twenty-fourth of this month.

As to what Mujal stated in his "Answer to the CGT of Argentina," I wish to say that the workers of the Dominican Republic do not need any help in the defense of their dignity.

Now I want to ask you, distinguished brother, how long do we have to wait until the leaders of the labor movement in our hemisphere stop serving political interests and dedicate themselves to the true and exclusive interest of the workers?

I believe the time has come to abandon this attitude because, as far as we are concerned, we want everybody to know that our social legislation, our trade union freedom, and our efforts have brought us to a position which we wish could be enjoyed by the workers of all other countries.

Aguirre responded under date of November 8, 1951, in a long letter, of which the following are excerpts:

Your letter indicates that in spite of our differences it is possible to discuss the true status of the labor movement in the Dominican Republic. Nevertheless, I remember that some time ago you promised the ICFTU that the Dominican government would permit a visit of an ICFTU Commission for the purpose of studying the trade union organization in your country. You repeated the same promise to me in Geneva, in June of this year, but nothing came of it.

I am therefore justified in asking: if there is so much trade union freedom in your country, why then this insistence to keep away a committee representing the free trade union movement of the world? And why are there hundreds of trade union leaders who live in exile and who are prevented from going back home in spite of their desire to do so? . . . There is no doubt that these facts contradict your statements. . . .

When you state in your letter that "the workers of the Dominican Republic do not need any help to defend their dignity" you contradict what is a present-day reality for the labor movement of every country. Many problems are international in character, and therefore the labor movement of a country, especially a small one, needs the cooperation of the labor movements of other countries. This is the basis of the international labor movement. It occurs to me that in making this statement that you are self-sufficient, you are giving a convincing proof of the true status of the labor movement in your country. In fact, you are attempting to isolate it from any contact with democratic labor abroad, knowing very well in advance that you would not be admitted in any international democratic trade union organization since you are completely dominated by your government. . . .

In the last paragraph of your letter you emphasize that "our social legislation, our trade union freedom, and our efforts have brought us to a position which we wish could be enjoyed by the workers of all countries." Very well. If this is the true status of the labor movement in the Dominican Republic, then I challenge you to support our request to allow a visit to your country of a Commission composed of two representatives of the ICFTU and two from the ORIT (one from the United States and one from Latin America) so that this Commission could verify the truthfulness of your statement. . . .

I do not wish to end this letter without establishing very clearly the position of ORIT versus the government of Trujillo. As long as he denies political and trade union freedom and withholds from the people the benefits of democracy, we shall be firmly against him. The trade union policy of both ICFTU and ORIT is very clear in this respect: We shall stay away from political involvements; we shall not discriminate on account of religion, political views, race, or color; but we shall defend to the limit the right of the workers. Should we become convinced in the future that we were wrong in our opposition to the government of the Dominican Republic we will be ready to rectify our stand, because what we seek is the truth.

The debate continued when, on November 28, 1951, Ballester sent Aguirre an even longer letter of reply. He began by denying that he had ever promised to obtain facilities for an ICFTU Commission to investigate labor conditions in the Dominican Republic, said that he thought the continuous attacks upon the Trujillo government by ORIT-ICFTU leaders were "responsible for the difficulties that prevented the acceptance of the Commission," and denied as "unfounded and slanderous" my statement to the last AFL Convention that the Dominican jails were full of workers. "Do you think it would be wise on our part," he asked, "to invite to our country trade union leaders who, although they know nothing of the true situation here, openly express themselves against our government?" He added:

Years ago, in order to show the leaders of the CTAL that there was trade union freedom in our country we willingly allowed a CTAL Commission, composed of trade union leaders from Cuba and Mexico, to come here. They even became members of the Organization Committee of the Workers Congress which was held in 1946. They took advantage of our hospitality to maneuver our rank and file in favor of the Communist position, even going to the lengths of promoting the organization of a Communist Party, using for this purpose the files of the labor unions, from which they freely took names and addresses of prospective members. We went through periods of great difficulties, after the Communist Party was declared illegal, in order to show that our members had no connection with it. All this was the result of the underground activities of the emissaries from Cuba and Mexico. We have not forgotten that experience, as a result of which we have become rather skeptical of emissaries from abroad.

Ballester said he thought Aguirre exaggerated the number of Dominican workers "who have chosen, of their own free will, to live abroad in exile" and said they were not returning because "they have been convicted in civil court of crimes that have no relations whatsoever with the labor movement." Taking note of the attacks upon ORIT and ICFTU by the World Federation of Trade Unions, he said that he did not believe them and that these accusations were "contemptible." In the course of his letter, however, Ballester asked a number of questions intended to cast doubt upon the existence of free trade unionism in Cuba and, even, in the United States and declared that the "so-called free trade union movement of the world" . . . "is no more free than we ourselves are."

Aguirre acknowledged this letter briefly under date of December 5 and had the final word in a lengthy letter of February 15, 1962. He repeated again that ORIT did not retract any of the denunciations by its Congresses of the Trujillo regime's suppression of trade union freedom, but he made it clear again that we were willing to revise our views if an investigation proved them to be false. Stating that he did not doubt the report of the material progress of the workers and the industrial advances pointed out in Ballester's letter, Aguirre added:

But, compañero Ballester, there is a celebrated expression which history attributes to a revolutionary of the past, which symbolizes the aspirations of the citizens of the world: "Give me liberty, or give me death." Does the liberty of the people of Santo Domingo march equally with the progress of industry and agriculture? On this important matter you have given me no data.

At its third meeting on January 24, 1952, the ORIT Executive Board endorsed the firm stand of its Regional Secretary in dealing with the Dominican Republic Confederation of Labor and decided to continue to try to establish contacts.

In November 1951 Ángelo Miolán, on behalf of the Dominican trade unionists living in exile in Cuba, announced formation of a Democratic Trade Union Committee for the "purpose of leading the fight, independent of any political group, for the restoration of trade union and political freedom for the workers of the Dominican Republic." The Committee decided to apply for affiliation to ORIT and ICFTU.

Upon learning that ILO's Committee on Freedom of Association had agreed to investigate the charges submitted to it by the four Dominican trade union leaders with their memorandum of September 29, 1950, the surviving signers on February 3, 1952, sent to Paul Ramadier, chairman of the ILO Committee, the following additional information and charges:

The three survivors have already fully informed the ILO of the circumstances of the kidnaping, and probably murder, of our friend Báez. The workers of the Dominican Republic, Cuba, and of all Latin America have the moral conviction that Mauricio Báez was eliminated by paid agents of Rafael Trujillo as a reprisal for our original protest to the ILO.

To amplify the available information concerning the disappearance of Báez, we wish to add that since his disappearance from his home at No. 8 Cervantes Street in the El Sevillano district of Havana, the police of Cuba as well as the Cuban workers and ourselves have all done our utmost to find him but there are no clues as to his whereabouts. Furthermore, when two of us, Justino José del Orbe and Ángel Miolán, went to Mexico to present the case of Báez to the founding Congress of the Inter-American Regional Organization of the ICFTU in January 1951, we were menaced by anonymous telephone callers with the same fate as befell "the other one" if we did not desist from going to Mexico. This and much more evidence which it would be tedious to relate account for our firm conviction that Mauricio Báez was physically eliminated by the Dominican government so as to deprive the Dominican working class of its principal leader and our people of one of the most earnest fighters for democracy.

Since we first requested that you investigate the condition of the Dominican working class, the situation has gotten increasingly worse. Using openly Fascist methods, the government of Trujillo has intensified the terror and exploitation of the workers in our country. We have trustworthy reports that wages in the sugar industry (the basic industry in the Dominican Republic) have been reduced by more than 50 per cent. Because of his dual position as employer and chief of state (Trujillo owns the two most productive sugar mills in the country) the dictator has been active in trying to reduce as far as possible the labor costs of the industry.

Furthermore, Trujillo has worked against the interests of Dominican workers by importing several thousand Haitians a year at even lower wages. At the same time he has made it impossible for the workers to protest, for those that do are subjected to jail terms, torture, and even death. Thus we have recently learned that sixty workers from another of Trujillo's plantations, La Caobera, near the capital city, were jailed and tortured because they suggested that wages should be raised. In the Las Pajas and Consuelo sugar mills the same fate befell two hundred workers less than a month ago.

We have also learned, through very reliable sources, that two workers have lost their lives in a police cell as a result of the infamous water torture. They are Abelardo Acevedo and Alejandro Mencia, Jr. The body of Acevedo was delivered to his widow without any explanation by agents of the Federal Police Department.

The decision of the ILO Committee on Freedom of Association to take jurisdiction over the charges leveled against the government of the Dominican Republic caused a reaction inside Trujilloland. Julio C. Ballester on February 25, 1952, dispatched to David Morse, ILO Director General, the following cablegram (translation mine—S.R.) :

We have learned through an United Press cable of the recommendation made by the Special Committee concerning alleged violation by Dominican government of our trade union rights. We ask you to convey to the ILO Governing Body our disagreement with such recommendation. The government is respecting our freedom of association guaranteed in our Constitution. The Confederation of Dominican Workers invites the ILO to send to our country a Commission of your choice to ascertain objectively the true situation of our workers.

And so another invitation, this time to an intergovernmental agency of which the Dominican Republic itself was a member, was sent in the obvious hope that somehow it would either bring a whitewash of the Trujillo regime or cause the investigators to issue one of those reports that say very little or nothing and can always be interpreted favorably by the interested party. But things came out quite differently. The ILO Governing Body, meeting on June 26, 1952, agreed to accept the invitation to send an investigating committee under two conditions:

(1) That the Director of the ILO receive formal guarantees that the Commission would enjoy complete liberty to carry out its studies;
(2) That it be understood that the Commission would make a report to the Director of the ILO, which would in due course be published.

But that was not the way Trujillo intended to play the game. The ILO mission was barred from entering the Dominican Republic, and on November 24, 1952, the invitation and the previously granted permission to enter were withdrawn by Trujillo himself. ORIT, in a statement issued by General Secretary Luis Alberto Monge, commented:

Trujillo's refusal to allow an ILO mission to go to the Dominican Republic clearly exposes him as a dictator with an iron curtain of his own and bloodshed to hide. We call upon the ILO to hold hearings and take evidence from the democratic opponents of Trujillo and to examine the serious accusations made against his regime.

The kidnaping, disappearance and subsequent death of Professor Jesús de Galíndez, attributed to Dictator Trujillo, caused a sensation that shook the Dominican dictatorship to its very foundation. In a way, it could be compared to the kidnaping and murder of Giacomo Matteotti which in June 1925 almost toppled Mussolini's regime. Jesús de Galíndez, with whom I had collaborated for many years in our common opposition to Fascism and dictatorship, was a Basque Republican refugee from Spain who had lived six years in the Dominican Republic and then moved to New York, where he headed the Basque Republican groups in exile and earned his living by writing and teaching at Columbia University. Galíndez was about to publish a 700-page doctoral thesis entitled *The Era of Trujillo*. On March 12, 1956, after having finished his day's classes at Columbia University, he was kidnaped as he was entering a subway station and was forcibly taken to an airport near New York City from which he was flown to the Dominican Republic and to his death.[7]

The AFL-CIO joined the protest with a statement of condemnation adopted by its Executive Council at the May 1956 quarterly meeting. The statement also reiterated previous charges of complete suppression of trade union freedom in the Dominican Republic.

A few days after the statement was circulated by the press services throughout Latin America, AFL-CIO President Meany received a telegram of "protest" from the Dominican Republic, signed by Julio C. Ballester, General Secretary, and other leaders of the CTD, in which they extended to him an invitation to visit the Dominican Republic in order to "ascertain the inaccuracy of the information"—as they claimed—on which the AFL-CIO had based its recent statement condemning the dictatorial policy of the Dominican Republic government.

In his reply, dated June 19, 1956, President Meany recounted the particulars of the two previous invitations, later withdrawn, extended to the ICFTU and the ILO, and stated:

Charges against the government of your country for violation of trade union rights and civil liberties are not new. At every international trade union convention since 1949 such charges have been repeatedly and amply documented. It would be highly desirable that an opportunity be finally given to an international body to look into the situation, present a dispassionate report, and suggest some remedies. Two international bodies such as the ICFTU and the ILO have already been invited to carry out such an investigation, but, as I have indicated above, your government at the last moment backed out. Frankly, I don't see the point in your issuing a third invitation to me when you already have the other two still pending. My suggestion, therefore, is that you ask your own government to allow the ICFTU and the ILO to send their mission and I can assure you that, if necessary, the AFL-CIO would participate with a representative of its own.

One would think that Meany's reply would have settled for good the invitation game. But that was not the case. Trujillo was reeling under the impact of world criticism and indignation as a result of the Galíndez crime and the thousand others that had come to light in countless newspaper and magazine articles. He desperately needed a whitewash, but realized that it would be difficult to get it from the ICFTU or the ILO. So he hit upon the idea of having the University of the Dominican Republic—completely dominated by him as was the case with every other institution in the country—extend an invitation to a group of distinguished Americans to undertake "an investigation of labor conditions." On paper—he surmised—they would look good. Professors would concentrate on studying the labor code; lawyers would interrogate CDT labor leaders who would swear that Trujilloland had become a veritable workers' paradise; political questions would be kept out as not germane to the investigation of labor conditions; nobody would talk about persecution, torture, and murder, and if by chance some mention did crop up here and there, it would be sternly denied, and a public challenge would be issued to bring forth witnesses and proofs. Besides, if under the worst circumstances some case could not possibly be denied, there would be plenty of people to testify that the victim was a Communist caught in the act of sabotaging the security of the state.[8] It was, all considered, a gamble worth taking. But to succeed, Trujillo needed at least one universally respected labor leader among the members of the proposed investigating group. Had not George Meany written to Ballester that the AFL-CIO would participate, if necessary, with a representative of its own in either the ICFTU or the ILO investigating group? Why not, then, try to get him to join the group suggested by the University?

One day, December 4, 1956, to be exact, I received a telephone call from one Judge Cayton who told me he was planning to see George Meany the following day "in order to discuss the advisability of accepting an invitation to join a committee set up to investigate labor conditions in the Dominican Republic under the auspices of the University of Ciudad Trujillo."[9]

It had been reported to Judge Cayton, he said, that "President Meany is in agreement with this proposed investigation." While I could not speak for President Meany in setting the record straight, I urged Judge Cayton to ascertain the facts directly from him. Judge Cayton did see President Meany, the following day, and that was the last I heard of the proposed committee.

Trujillo then took a different course. Through his Ambassador in London he sent word to ICFTU in Brussels that, after thinking the matter over, he realized that it was a mistake not to have allowed the ICFTU mission to visit the Dominican Republic in 1951, and that he was now willing to let them come without any restriction.

At the ICFTU Executive Board meeting which preceded the ICFTU Convention in Tunis, July 1957, it was decided, subject to certain conditions, that the ICFTU should "proceed with the mission to the Dominican Republic." This decision was hotly debated among Latin American delegates present in Tunis. ORIT General Secretary Luis Alberto Monge was strongly opposed to the idea; nevertheless, the ORIT Executive Board, meeting August 26–27 in Mexico City, registered no official objection, although it decided not to appoint any official ORIT representative to serve in the mission.

On October 14, 1957, after having received certain assurances on behalf of his government from the Minister of Labor of the Dominican Republic, a mission composed of ICFTU Board member Francisco Aguirre, ICFTU Director of Organization C. H. Millard, Raul Valdivia of Cuba, and Hermes Horne of the ICFTU Secretariat arrived in Ciudad Trujillo. Daniel Benedict of the AFL-CIO International Affairs Department, whom President Meany had appointed to the mission at the specific request of Millard, was not able to serve because of an error in the wording of the telegram requesting his attendance.

Before leaving Havana, where they had assembled, all members of the mission agreed that the short time that could be spent in the Dominican Republic would only permit a preliminary survey and that if it were found that conditions would allow a more detailed study, this would be made.

After the completion of their *preliminary survey* (italics mine—S.R.) the members of the mission submitted a report to the ICFTU Executive Board meeting in Brussels, November 4–8, 1957. The report stated in part:

From contacts and meetings with many of the leading trade unionists, as well as a number of local members and branch officers in and near Trujillo City, it appeared that unions and their federations, both provincial and national, do have considerable freedom of organization and collective bargaining, though the latter function is severely handicapped by mandatory conciliation and arbitration services. It is freely admitted that the National Federation CDT is heavily subsidized by the government. However, the organizational structure, including the collection of fees and dues, seems to be dangerously defective.

While in conference with the Assistant Secretary of Labor, it was asked whether or not the government would have any objection to a continuing delegation staying longer and making a more detailed study of the whole field of trade union freedom, legislation, and economic and social conditions. In reply to a question as to the number making up such a delegation, also the probable time involved, it was stated that there probably would not be more than two persons and the time would be one month or less. The mission was later informed that the President had stated that there would be no objections and the continuing mission would receive the fullest cooperation of the government departments concerned.

As a result of their visit, members of the mission are under the impression that regardless of conditions which may have caused the present lack of healthy growth and development of the trade union movement in the Dominican Republic, the suggested continuing mission should take up the work which has been started and go to that country as soon as possible.

The ICFTU Executive Board received the report and approved it with the following significant clarifying statement:

The Board wishes to underline the fact that the present document does not in any way endorse the present government or the situation affecting trade unions in the Dominican Republic.

The Board then approved the recommendation to have a continuing mission, composed of Daniel Benedict and Raul Valdivia, return to the Dominican Republic, took note of the fact that this move had been made in full agreement with the Dominican trade unionists in exile, and instructed that in the report to be submitted by the continuing mission the background of the Trujillo regime should be included.

Valdivia and Benedict remained in the Dominican Republic from November 16 to December 3, 1957. Being familiar with the history of the Dominican Republic, with the circumstances that led to the establishment of the Trujillo dictatorship, and with the allegations of violations of trade union rights as presented by the Dominican trade unionists in exile, they knew what questions to ask and where to go to find true answers. Furthermore, both spoke Spanish fluently and had therefore no need of an interpreter. Here are the highlights of the report which Valdivia and Benedict submitted to ICFTU:

The majority of the Dominican Confederation of Labor affiliated organizations can with difficulty be considered as trade unions. The local leaders are often managers and foremen, who constantly affirm that the workers are satisfied with their wages.

The regional federations receive no information from the national center about wages in the rest of the country. The CDT leaders show no signs of caring about the civil liberties of the workers.

For this situation to be changed, it would above all be necessary for an atmosphere to be created in the Dominican Republic in which the workers feel free to negotiate their working conditions themselves rather than leaving this task to the National Salary Committee and the Conciliation Service. In other words, the preliminary conditions for a change in the trade union situation in the Dominican Republic consists in the introduction of a system making possible genuine and not merely theoretical collective bargaining, especially in the big companies.

The general conclusions to be drawn from the report of the ICFTU mission is that freedom of association does not exist in the Dominican Republic. Indeed, the trade unions in that country are not genuine trade unions but are linked on the one hand with the employers and on the other with the government. Collective bargaining does not exist in the Dominican Republic. Furthermore, the mission found that forced labor was practiced in certain sisal plantations, and it was informed that forced labor also existed in the rice fields.

On the basis of the mission's report and its conclusions, the ICFTU decided, at the meeting of its Board held in April, 1958:

1. To communicate to the government of the Dominican Republic the above general conclusions, asking it to create the conditions whereby genuine trade unions, independent of the employers and the government, can develop. To this end, it would be necessary that:

(a) the workers be able to elect freely, with adequate safeguards, the responsible trade union leaders, so as to avoid these latter being linked with the enterprises and the government;

(b) the employers recognize the trade unions as the representative bodies of the workers;

(c) the workers' right to collective bargaining and to strike be clearly established and genuinely applied;

(d) all the necessary conditions be established for the application of all those provisions of the Labor Code which are in conformity with freedom of association.

2. To inform the government of the Dominican Republic that, under the conditions existing at present, the ICFTU sees no possibility of giving its support to the development of free trade unions in the Republic, and considers itself free to undertake any necessary action, unless the government takes steps in the direction indicated under paragraph 1 above.

The Trujillo regime was stunned. It reacted to the ICFTU report with complete silence.

The AFL-CIO Executive Council meeting in San Juan, Puerto Rico, in February 1959, branded the Trujillo dictatorship as "a blot on the honor of the American family of nations" and urged the government of the United States "to take the lead in the Organization of American States to bring about the suspension of the Dominican Republic from membership." In this way, the Council asserted, "our country will give to the people of Latin America another demonstration of our sincerity in actively promoting the cause of freedom and human dignity throughout the world." The Council added:

The collective conscience of the Americas considers the continued existence of the Trujillo tyranny not only a blot on the honor of the American family of nations but a constant threat to the peace of the hemisphere. We therefore urge the Organization of American States (OAS) to isolate diplomatically the Dominican Republic, as well as the other dictatorships, by suspending their membership until such time as a democratic regime, freely elected by the people, is installed in their place. Such action, now widely demanded by the democratic public opinion of Latin America, would be consistent with the charter of the OAS, which declares that its membership consists of representatives of legitimate democratic governments.

This blast must have infuriated Trujillo no end. Julio César Ballester, who in the past had been given instructions to maintain a posture of consideration and respect whenever addressing the AFL-CIO, and particularly its President, George Meany, was handed the text of a fiery telegram of protest which he sent over his own signature. It makes rather interesting reading:

On seeing in the press of Puerto Rico the absurd petition addressed by the AFL-CIO to the Organization of American States from San Juan, Puerto Rico, asking that the Dominican Republic be expelled from the said organization we, the Dominican workers, express our amazement at the ridiculous and biased part played by your organization under the influence of Luis Múñoz Marín and José Figueres brought into the AFL-CIO by Serafino Romualdi and Luis Alberto Monge (Stop) Be warned that you are being miserably deceived by agents of international Communism infiltrated into your organization and we repeat that we the Dominican workers justly repudiate the proselytizing and other Communist-type work carried out against our country by the AFL-CIO in San Juan under pressure from the Governor (Stop) Furthermore it is shameful to see the AFL-CIO give such an outstanding demonstration of juridical ignorance and lack of union spirit by adopting such a censurable resolution.

The government of Venezuela, under the presidency of Rómulo Betancourt, on February 7, 1960, submitted a complaint to the OAS Council that the denial of human rights in the Dominican Republic threatened the already precarious peace in the Caribbean.

The Council referred the matter to the Peace Committee. This group, originally created in 1940 but inactive since 1956, had been reactivated in August 1959, at the Inter-American Foreign Ministers Conference in Santiago, Chile. It received the added power to "investigate the relationship that lack of representative democracy and the suppression of human rights and civil liberties in one country may have with the threat of invasion from abroad."

After a four-month investigation, the Inter-American Peace Committee [10] made public June 8, 1960, a report which accused the Dominican Republic of "flagrant and widespread violations of human rights." The violations, the committee said, included "the denial of free assembly and of free speech, arbitrary arrests, cruel and inhuman treatment of political prisoners, and the use of intimidation and terror as political weapons." The Peace Committee also reached the conclusion that the Dominican Republic by its denial of human rights had aggravated tensions in the Caribbean area. When the five-nation Peace Committee asked to visit the Dominican Republic for an on-the-spot inquiry, it was refused permission by the Dominican government. The committee interviewed refugees, former Dominican government officials, and newspapermen.

The action taken by the OAS Committee fully vindicated the position of the AFL-CIO. The free labor movement had repeatedly demanded that nonintervention in internal affairs of other countries should not be invoked as a cloak to condone suppression of civil liberties and violation of human rights, specifically protected in the charter of the OAS.

Never before had the Organization of American States or any of its bodies publicly excoriated a country for such indignities. The committee's uncompromising indictment of the Trujillo regime unquestionably marked a milestone in the inter-American system. It was bound to have far-reaching consequences as it established a precedent to be used for collective condemnation of other dictatorships whose disregard of civil liberties and human rights was greatly disturbing, and is still disturbing, the democratic forces of the Western Hemisphere.

By the summer of 1960, a showdown with the Dominican Republic was fast approaching on two fronts. The OAS, acting on another complaint of the Venezuelan government, which accused Trujillo of complicity in the attempted assassination of President Rómulo Betancourt, decided to convene a special meeting of Foreign Ministers. At the same time, the free labor movement took concrete steps leading to the proclamation of a worldwide transport boycott against Dominican goods.

On July 13 the Union of Free Dominican Workers in Exile, with headquarters in Puerto Rico, asked the AFL-CIO in Washington and the longshoremen of Puerto Rico for moral support in their plan to picket a German boat that was reported to arrive in San Juan with a cargo from the Dominican Republic. AFL-CIO President Meany wired the President of the Port Workers Union in Puerto Rico and the Commonwealth Federation of Labor urging their membership "to refrain from unloading such ship in any island port as a gesture of international labor solidarity in support of Dominican fighters for freedom." President Meany's telegram further stated that this action was in line with the well-known AFL-CIO policy of opposition to the Trujillo dictatorship and the action taken in the past by ORIT-ICFTU and the International Transport Workers' Federation.

The picketing of the German boat *Iserlohn* was very successful and received wide publicity throughout Latin America. A few days later, a similar action was repeated in the port of Mayagüez, where two coastal boats from the Dominican Republic were prevented from unloading their cargo.

The AFL-CIO also sent an appeal to Governor Múñoz Marín of Puerto Rico urging him to take action that would deny the use of commonwealth-owned as well as private piers to Dominican boats.

The AFL-CIO Council, at its meeting in Chicago on August 16, 1960—the very day on which the American Foregin Ministers' Conference opened in San José, Costa Rica, for the purpose of considering the threat to peace represented by the aggressive actions of the Dominican Republic regime—sent to Secretary of State Christian Herter a telegram that reaffirmed its strong condemnation of the Trujillo dictatorship for repeated violation of human rights, civil liberties, and trade union freedom, and reiterated its previous demands that the Dominican Republic be condemned and subjected to sanctions.

After the San José conference recommended the adoption of economic sanctions against the Trujillo regime, President Meany called upon the U.S. Congress to give President Eisenhower the authority to cut the sugar quota of the Dominican Republic.

The effect of all these measures was beginning to be felt inside the Dominican Republic itself. Members of the CDT began to shake off the fear that had paralyzed them for so many years and managed to establish contacts with some Dominican trade union leaders in exile. Political opposition, long dormant under the crushing blows of the dictatorship, began to stir. There were signs all around that Trujillo had reached the end of his rope. The AFL-CIO helped to set up a special training course for Dominican trade unionists in exile at the Labor Relations School of the University of Puerto Rico; they were readied to go back home at the opportune moment and take charge of the reorganization of the CDT under democratic leadership. In New York, hundreds of Dominican workers banded together and formed a branch of the Union of Free Dominican Workers in Exile. Alfonso Sánchez Madariaga, ORIT General Secretary, and I were invited to address an assembly of Dominican democratic labor and political forces which took place at 2645 Broadway, in upper Manhattan, on Friday evening, May 26, 1961, under the auspices of the Free Dominican Workers Union.

At the end of my address, swept by the enthusiasm of the audience and by a premonition that Trujillo's end was really approaching, I exclaimed: *"A notte più profonda, alba più vicina*—Darkest the night, closer is the dawn." Four days later, a band of patriots put an end to the life of Dominican Republic's Generalissimo and Benefactor Rafael Leonidas Trujillo Molina.

Postscriptum: *El Caribe* of Santo Domingo, in its April 13, 1965, issue, published the following item:

The North American labor leader Serafino Romualdi yesterday received from the hands of Dr. Donald J. Reid Cabral, member of the Government Triumvirate, the decoration of the Order of Duarte, Sánchez y Mella with the grade of Knight Commander. The ceremony, which took place at the National Palace, was attended by the other Triumvir Ramón Cáceres Troncoso; by the Ambassadors of Italy, Roberto Venturini, and of the United States, William Tapley Bennet; by the Dominican Ambassador to Washington, Dr. José Bonilla Atiles, and a large number of Dominican trade union leaders including the representative of ORIT.

In presenting the decoration to Mr. Romualdi, Triumvir Reid Cabral said: "The government of the Dominican Republic wishes to reward, with this highest decoration at its command, your lifetime services on behalf of the free trade union movement.

"We, the Dominicans assembled here, especially myself and Ambassador Bonilla, were in close contact with you during the difficult days of our country's history. You helped to transform into free democratic trade unions what had been a slave labor movement. We are glad for this opportunity to give recognition to what you have done to bring back freedom in our country."

Mr. Romualdi answered: "I consider it a great honor to receive this decoration. I accept it with deep emotion, not only for what it means to me as a person, but because it is actually a recognition of what the labor movement of the United States and the free trade unions of Latin America have done in defense of freedom in the Dominican Republic as part of the wider struggle to defend freedom in every part of the world."

Notes

1. Trujillo's full name was Rafael Leonidas Trujillo Molina. During his career he acquired a number of other titles besides General or Generalissimo, including "Genius of Peace," "Hero of Labor," "Paladin of Democracy," "The Chief," and "Benefactor of the Fatherland." The last, "Benefactor," became a sort of official one, being used in all documents, addresses, etc.

2. Trujillo took over the presidency of the Dominican Republic on August 16, 1930, following a revolution which earlier in that same year had put the country under his absolute control. Trujillo was assassinated on May 30, 1961. During this long period he gained, in addition to complete autocratic political control, virtual ownership, in his name or that of his family, of most of the country's industries and sugar estates, and amassed a fabulous personal fortune. Thus the Dominican Republic became known as Trujilloland and its capital city, Santo Domingo, was renamed Ciudad Trujillo.

3. At its founding Convention in London, in December 1949, the ICFTU unanimously rejected the credentials of H. Calderón Jiménez, a diplomat disguised as a "labor attaché" whom the Dominican Government had audaciously sent as a "delegate."

At the 1948 Lima Conference, where the CIT was founded, the Dominican Republic delegation was given the status of "fraternal," without voice or vote.

4. In 1946 Trujillo allowed a number of Dominican Communists to return home, authorized them to form a Dominican Republic's Communist Party, gave them facilities to organize meetings, and allowed them to infiltrate the unions. But in 1948, when the Cold War started, Trujillo suppressed the Communists and gave orders to the CDT to withdraw from the WFTU and the CTAL.

5. The labor leaders assassinated were Emeterio Dixson, General Secretary of the Factory Union, and Hector Quesada, Organizing Secretary of the Federation of Workers La Romana. The two leaders arrested and kept in jail for over one year, and then confined to the town of Hato Mayor, were Manuel Tuma, Sr., and his son Manuel, Jr., both Executive Committee members of the Federation of Workers La Romana. The three leaders who were forced to leave the country clandestinely, after having saved their lives by taking timely refuge in the Mexican embassy, were Mauricio Báez, General Secretary of the Federation of Workers of San Pedro de Macorís; Hernando Hernández, General Secretary of the Federation of Workers at La Romana, and Alfredo Brito, General Secretary of the Port Workers' Union.

6. Those killed included Luis Espinosa, President of the Sugar Workers Union of Montellano sugar mill; José López Castillo, President of the Mechanics' Union of Santo Domingo; Francisco Medina, worker of the Porvenir sugar mill; José A. Pérez, President of the Port Workers' Union of San Pedro de Macorís and Assistant Secretary of Organization of the Provincial Federation of Workers.

Other murdered workers included Luis Guillen, President of the Port Workers' Union of the capital; Jaime Onill, Organizing Secretary of the Federation of Workers of

Santo Domingo and Secretary General of the Brewers' Union; Alberto Larencuent, Secretary General of the Port Workers' Union of Puerto Plata.

7. The Galíndez case was the subject of a protracted press coverage that extended for many months until the various pieces were put together and it was conclusively established that the crime was committed at Trujillo's orders. The pilot of the plane, Gerald Lester ("Gerry") Murphy of Eugene, Oregon, was murdered, and so were other accomplices. A comprehensive presentation of all the facts and evidences related to the Jesús de Galídez case is contained in the book, *Trujillo—Little Caesar of the Caribbean,* by Germán E. Ornes, publisher and editor of *El Caribe,* Santo Domingo's leading newspaper. This book also gives a complete background of Trujillo's rise to power, lists the crimes attributed to him, relates how he amassed a fortune valued at half a billion dollars, and explains the totalitarian techniques that enabled him to stay in power.

The Galíndez murder did not represent Trujillo's first foray on foreign soil to silence his enemies. The Dominican political leader Dr. Sergio Bencosme and the novelist-writer Andres Requena were shot and killed in New York by Trujillo's agents in 1935 and 1952, respectively.

8. Johnny Abbes García, dreaded chief of Trujillo's Military Intelligence Service (SIM), was interviewed in Haiti, where he now lives, by the American newspaperman Jeremiah O'Leary. Asked to explain the murder of the Mirabel sisters, Minerva, Patria, and Antonia, for which a Dominican court has convicted four of his guardians, Johnny Abbes replied, "They were Communists." (*The Washington Star,* November 16, 1966.)

9. Quoted from a memorandum to George Meany from Serafino Romualdi, dated December, 1956.

10. The members of the committee were the United States, El Salvador, Mexico, Uruguay, and Venezuela. The chairman was Ambassador John C. Dreier of the United States. For the investigation of the Dominican Republic, Colombia was designated a substitute for Venezuela.

The Venezuelan Ambassador to the OAS, Dr. Marcos Falcón Briceño, presented the charges on behalf of his government. He submitted an impressive documentation concerning violation of human rights, suppression of civil liberties, denial of free trade unionism, and continuous interference in the affairs of the neighboring democratic countries, particularly Venezuela, even to the extent of helping plots to overthrow the constitutional regime of President Rómulo Betancourt.

XXIII

The New Face of the Church

When I finished speaking, Monsignor Gallego, Bishop of Barranquilla, came forward with outstretched arms and exclaimed: *"Lo felicito, compañero Serafino—*Congratulations, comrade Serafino!" That was in 1956, at the UTC Convention in Cali, Colombia, to which I had brought greetings from the AFL-CIO.

In the course of my address I had commented with approval on the presence in the section reserved for the public of a half-dozen bishops and scores of priests and friars—all moral advisers to the UTC branches in their respective localities. "This is an eloquent demonstration," I declared, "that the Church wishes to play an active role in the social changes now taking place all over Latin America. The Church wants to be on the side of the exploited and not of the exploiters."

Then I related an episode that I had witnessed a few years before in San Salvador, as indicative of the changes that had been taking place inside the Catholic Church. Young Father Tomasino, the brother of a trade unionist, a friend of mine, was celebrating his first Mass. Following the service, his family, superiors, fellow seminarians, and friends gathered for a little luncheon celebration. Being in San Salvador on a trade union mission, I, too, was invited. The affair called for speeches—mainly from Father Tomasino's professors and superiors. They extolled the young man's moral virtues and offered their good wishes for the success of the spiritual mission to which he had pledged his life. No mention was made, however, of the opportunities to work for greater social justice for the hungry and the exploited poor. Then, unexpectedly, I was called upon to say a few words and, being a trade union representative, I urged the young priest to help put into practical application in the parish to which he had been assigned the teachings of Pope Leo XIII's encyclical *Rerum Novarum*. Although I made the remark with a bit of oratorical emphasis, the reception was unresponsive. Later Father Tomasino approached me and inquired: "What does the *Rerum Novarum* encyclical say? They never mentioned it at the seminary."

The contrast between what was there before my eyes, at the UTC Cali Convention, and what I had related of my San Salvador experience, was a dramatic proof that the Catholic Church was acquiring a new social face in Latin America—no longer did it appear as the defender of the *status quo,* but now it was an active front line participant in the trade union efforts to help the exploited workers and *campesinos* attain a better life.

The role of the Catholic Church in modern industrial society had been in my mind, as a fixed preoccupation, since the early years of my life. As I recall, my first trade union activity took place in 1914 in the Tiber Valley of Umbria in support of a strike of farmhands—a strike which was inspired by a pioneer of the Italian Catholic trade union movement, Father Busone Rossi of Gubbio. I could say, also, that I grew up with the Church, and for a while within the Church, having spent two years in the Diocesan Seminary of Assisi, which I entered on a scholarship in the fall of 1910.

It was in the seminary that I was introduced to Modernism—a movement inside the Church which Pope Pius X termed heretical and stamped out with a strong inflexible hand. Not that the seminary itself was expounding the Modernist doctrine, but a group of students, older in age, whom we called the refugees from Perugia, had been "tainted" with it and were trying to gain converts. The seminary in Perugia had been closed, at the end of the 1910 school year, in an attempt to stamp out the Modernist heresy which had been spread by some of its professors. That seminary had been noted for years for its progressiveness, both social and theological, since the time Cardinal Vincenzo Gioacchino Pecci, who later became Pope Leo XIII, was Archbishop of Perugia. When the seminary was closed, for only one year, as a sort of prophylactic measure, half of its student body were sent home for good and the other half, those believed safe, were scattered in small groups in various seminaries of the province. About a dozen came to Assisi.

I was actually too small, just ten years old, to understand what Modernism's objectives were, but I was attracted by the aura of subversion and conspiracy which surrounded the activities of its propagandists; and so I managed to join. The task assigned to me was to be the keeper, in my footlocker, of the forbidden literature. I never went much beyond that.

Being the youngest and the smallest of the seminarians, I was made Bishop Ambrogio Luddi's *reggicoda*—holder of his cape's train during the processions or when the Bishop was making a solemn entrance from his residence into the Cathedral. I liked to be admired by the faithful watching from the sidelines. I did so well that in 1912, at the time of the great week-long celebration of the seventh centenary of the founding of the Poor Clares, held in their mother church of St. Clara of Assisi, I was chosen to hold the train during Mass of Cardinal Van Rossum, the Papal Legate to the celebration. But soon my exalted position of *reggicoda* came to an inglorious end.

It happened on a Sunday morning, later in the same year. For reasons I can't recall, a large group of boys about my age from my own native town of Bastia, with whom I had played games and other school boys' diversions, were in the Cathedral. When they saw me entering behind the Bishop holding his train, they made fun of me, sticking out their tongues and making other grimaces. I, of course, returned their mocking gestures, but in doing so I slowed my pace and suddenly stopped. The train became taut and the Bishop was jerked back, losing his balance. Only the quick support of his *camerlengo* (chamberlain) saved him from falling to the floor. Imagine the commotion! I was promptly dragged by the ear to the sacristy, demoted on the spot, and punished with a period of silence.

Whenever the opportunity presented itself, during the years I spent traveling in Latin America, I always sought interviews with Church dignitaries and influential Catholic leaders to discuss primarily the potential contribution of the Church to our efforts to contain and reverse the Communist tide by strengthening democratic trade unions organized on a nonpolitical, nonsectarian basis. One of my earliest contacts was with Monsignor Francisco Vives, rector of the Catholic University of Santiago, Chile, who introduced me to a group of brilliant Catholic intellectuals and professionals, among them Eduardo Frei and others who are today the country's political rulers.

In 1947 I met Monsignor Victor Sanabria, Bishop of San José, Costa Rica, who was a great admirer of Don Luigi Sturzo's work and writings. Bishop Sanabria granted me an audience of almost two hours. As I wrote to Don Sturzo after the interview, "He is certainly a remarkable man, with a broad and progressive social vision almost unequaled." It was Bishop Sanabria who sent to the United States a young Costa Rican priest, Father Benjamin Núñez, to study the structure and the program of our labor movement. When he returned to Costa Rica, Father Núñez became the prime mover in organizing, as a counter to the Communist-dominated trade union movement, the Confederation of Labor "Rerum Novarum," now the dominant labor group in his country.

In the ensuing years I came into contact in different Latin American countries with many more priests, all actively engaged in assisting in the organization of democratic, antitotalitarian trade unions. One who was outstanding in this work was Monsignor (now Bishop) Ramón Bogarin in Paraguay, who at a critical moment prevailed upon the trade union members of the Catholic Workers' Youth (JOC) who were delegates to the Paraguayan Confederation of Labor Convention, to vote in favor of joining ORIT instead of the Perón-dominated ATLAS. In Brazil, the free trade union movement is greatly indebted to the Capuchin Frai Celso of São Paulo, Father J. Veloso of Rio de Janeiro, and the Reverend Pedro Crespo of the Northeast, as well as others. They were greatly responsible for the breakthrough in the farm areas, where Catholic-inspired unions succeeded against many odds in organizing the agricultural workers, called *camponeses*. Perhaps the most successful of all, however, has been the Jesuit Father Vicente Andrade Valderrama of Colombia, who almost singlehanded took under his wing in 1946 the minuscule UTC (see Chapter V) and transformed it by his leadership into one of the most influential and most militant trade union organizations in all of Latin America.

In tiny British Honduras, which despite its small size and underdevelopment has a strong labor movement, the labor unions owe their origin and growth to the help they received from the Jesuit priest Father Marion Ganey, who actually founded the labor organization there and was responsible for its affiliation to ORIT. He was also active in founding credit unions. The most outstanding leader of the credit union movement in Latin America, however, is Father Daniel MacLellan, who established hundreds of credit unions in Peru with assets running into many millions of dollars. *Fortune* magazine, in its issue of February 1962, mostly devoted to Latin America, published under the title of "Private Allies for Progress" a portfolio of twelve North Americans who had contributed the most to the economic and social development of contemporary Latin America. Father MacLellan was included along with ten business leaders and AFL-CIO representative Serafino Romualdi.

Because of its new militancy for social reform, many observers of the Latin American social and labor scene, especially in the United States, have acquired the impression that the Church is actually advocating a violent upheaval of the social order, a sort of quasi-Communist revolution with indiscriminate expropriation of property and even bloodshed. I strongly disagree with such views. Actually, my observations have led me to the conclusion that the Church in Latin America wants social evolution in depth, with radical reforms where needed, but within the framework of the free enterprise system—nothing less, eventually, than the democratic economic transformation which was brought about by the free enterprise system in the United States.

The wrong impression as to the methods advocated by the Church to attain its objectives of radical transformation of the present social and economic structure in the developing countries has been caused partly by a widespread misunderstanding of the relationship between CLASC (Latin American Confederation of Christian Trade Unionists) and the Church hierarchy.

CLASC is not an arm of the Catholic Church [1] as some people believe. CLASC's program and objectives are difficult to define. According to one of its spokesmen, CLASC is "anticapitalist and anti-Communist because it feels that neither one or the other system represents the best arrangements for the workers and for man as a human being." [2]

We are living in a revolutionary, deep, intensive and extensive process in Latin America. Christian trade unionism is on the side of those forces which seek revolution in Latin America. We cannot remain outside of this revolutionary process because it is necessary to give it the constructive ferment of the thought, action, and mystique of the authentic Christian presence.[3]

Speaking at the XV World Congress of the International Federation of Christian Trade Unions (IFCTU), Emilio Maspero, considered CLASC's most outstanding leader, thus explained the differences between ORIT and CLASC:

ORIT sees the problem of Latin America in the form of an alternative between the Communist world and the free world. By the latter they mean a system of free enterprise such as the one now practiced in the United States. On the contrary, CLASC can accept neither one nor the other system as the solution for the problems of Latin America.[4]

Maspero concluded his address by stating that CLASC wants "Total and integral revolution on the economic, social, political, moral, and psychological scale."

It is easy to see how CLASC's pronouncements lead to confusion and misunderstandings. One could make a good case for the claim that CLASC wants to supplant the Communists in the leadership of the violent revolution that would end with the destruction of Capitalism. But also one could probably argue more correctly that CLASC's pronouncements are nothing more than verbal excesses intended to dramatize the need for evolutionary reforms which in many countries are long overdue—excesses to be explained by the youth of CLASC's leadership, which will probably mellow with age and experience.

An action on the part of CLASC which caused misgivings and repudiation by the Catholic hierarchy in Colombia was its support of the sincere but mentally unstable Colombian priest, Father Camilo Torres, who left the Church, joined a guerrilla band of Communist rebels, and was killed, in 1966, in an encounter with the military police.[5] The Catholic Bishops of Colombia, in a statement approved at the Bishops' Conference in 1965, had warned the faithful against Father Torres's errors and had denied the necessity for violent revolution. This statement was interpreted in some quarters abroad as an indication that the Catholic Church was opposed to social reforms. This interpretation is wrong. Some random examples should suffice to prove the contrary.

In the early fifties the Church in Colombia undertook a vigorous campaign to correct the deplorable conditions under which coal miners were working in the Department of Cundinamarca. I happened to be present, in January 1953, at a membership meeting of the coal miners' union in Suesca, at which 400 workers were present. The meeting had been called to discuss a list of demands to be presented to the employers and to honor the local mine union leader with the medal of "Miners Fraternity" given by John L. Lewis, President of the United Mine Workers of America. During the meeting I was given a copy of a report, prepared by a committee of the regional clergy, in which the Church attacked some of the most glaring social and economic injustices then prevailing in the country.

The report charged that "thousands of coal miners in Cundinamarca, especially in the regions of Guacheta and Nemocón, have the lowest social and economic standards existing in the country. In addition to low wages, they are denied by most of the employers the minimum social assistance to which they are entitled by law. Furthermore, the workers complain of unsanitary conditions, of poor food and uncontrolled use of alcoholic beverages. These conditions have favored the spread of tuberculosis, with a high percentage of mortality, and other similar diseases."

The committee's report added that "hundreds of women and children are employed in the coal mines, especially for the transportation of heavy crates of materials down in the tunnels. The spread of illness is accentuated among the women and children, because of their physical weakness. The children also become victims of hernia which disables them for the rest of their lives."

The report concluded that "employers, on the other hand, do not pay any attention to the social legislation, violate its administrative rulings, and seem to be unconcerned about any adverse reports of the so-called labor inspectors. Wages are kept to the very minimum allowed by law and the workers employed under the piece-rate system often work as many as 15 to 20 hours a day. The employers do not provide any of the social assistance measures prescribed by the law and indulge in all kinds of abuse against their workers."

In 1957, when Venezuela was still under the dictatorship of General Marcos Pérez Jiménez, Archbishop Rafael Arias Blanco, the country's highest prelate of the Roman Catholic Church, wrote in a pastoral letter that workers in Venezuela would get a fair share of the country's growing wealth only if they organized free labor unions and if employers assumed their responsibilities.

In his pastoral letter, the Archbishop said, "Our country's wealth is increasing with astonishing rapidity. But no one can say that this wealth is being distributed in a way which enables all Venezuelans to share it, since a very large number of our people live in conditions that can hardly be called human."

Among the social evils condemned by Archbishop Arias were Venezuela's widespread unemployment and extremely low wage rates. The letter also deplored the nation's lack of schools to give its children the "culture and education to which they have a right."

To improve their lot, the Archbishop said, the workers must unite. The Church, he added, has always fought for the right of workers to organize labor unions.

These actions on the part of the clergy in Latin America had been recommended the previous year at the Fourth Convention of the Inter-American Catholic Action Confederation held at Cuernavaca, Mexico, in

April 1956. The convention passed a resolution declaring that, "For healthy industrialization, Latin America needs to build strong labor unions controlled by the workers themselves—and not by the government, the employer, a political party, or any other outside group."

In addition to being charged with blind support of the existing unjust socioeconomic order, the Church in Latin America is still described, in some quarters, as being antidemocratic and thus partial to authoritarian and even totalitarian regimes, especially those of the right. While I am not stating that this criticism is undeserved in every Latin American country, I want to emphasize, nevertheless, that a close examination of events in the last twenty years would indicate that in a number of countries influential prelates and in some cases the Church hierarchy *in toto*, have actively opposed the dictatorial regimes and have even contributed to their downfall.

For instance, in July 1956 His Eminence Crisanto Cardinal Luque, Archbishop of Bogotá and Colombia's Primate, wrote a personal letter to the then dictator General Rojas Pinilla, in which he rejected Pinilla's efforts to organize a "Third Force" in the labor movement and told him that "the oath of personal allegiance he had demanded of Colombian army personnel and civilians is invalid and thus not binding." [6] The Cardinal charged that the "Third Force," which President Pinilla was trying to organize against both the Conservative and the Liberal parties, included within its ranks Marxist and Peronist elements which the Bishops had previously condemned.

Concerning the oath of allegiance which Dictator Pinilla was demanding of the armed forces and the citizens at large—an oath of allegiance to one person in the sense that it committed affiants to carry out his orders without restriction of any sort—Cardinal Luque declared: "It is not legal to demand an oath of this sort," and then added:

It is proper to recall here that which the Sovereign Pontiff Pius XI wrote in the Encyclical *Non Abbiamo Bisogno* in reference to the oath demanded by the Fascist regime . . . of those who joined the government's party, to carry out without question the orders of the Duce and to defend with all their strength, to the point of bloodshed, the cause of the Fascist revolution. The Sovereign Pontiff wrote on that occasion: "This oath, as it is written, is not licit."

Less than one year later, in May 1957, dictator Rojas Pinilla was overthrown by a military coup preceded by a nationwide general civic strike in which the Church and the labor unions played a decisive role.

A more recent example of the Church's opposition to military rule, and particularly the military denial of right of assembly and trade union freedom, took place in the Northeast of Brazil. In August 1966 the seventy-two bishops of that region, led by the Most Reverend Helder Pessoa Camara, Archbishop of Recife and Olinda, issued a declaration condemning what they termed "widespread violations by factory and plantation owners in the Northeast of legal provisions for payment of minimum wages, severance pay, and vacation and family allowances, and on the allocation of family garden plots to rural laborers." [7]

Students who had tried to hold an antigovernment meeting in Belo Horizonte, State of Minas Gerais, Brazil, escaped arrest by the military by obtaining asylum in the Franciscan cloister of that city. The asylum provided by the Franciscans was supported in public declarations by the prior of the Dominican order of São Paulo, Friar Francisco de Araujo, who said in a sermon that "Christ would cry if he were in Brazil today against the violences being committed." [8]

My friend Monsignor Luigi G. Ligutti, Executive Secretary of the National Catholic Rural Life Conference, invited me to attend, in April 1955, the Rural Life Congress which was held in Panama City, Panama. It was a gathering of over two hundred missionaries, Church dignitaries, and laymen from the United States and twenty Central American and Caribbean nations and territories.

As related by Monsignor Ligutti himself,[9] while he was waiting for the meeting to open he was approached by a Mexican journalist who said to him:

"Is this to be a liturgical congress?"

"No," Monsignor Ligutti replied emphatically. "It is to be a gathering of leaders who will discuss the problems of landless people, their low material, social, and religious status. It will explain the teaching of the Church on the subject. It will hear reports on what has been done and through democratic discussions it will suggest remedies."

The journalist was surprised. Apparently, he did not expect priests to be dealing with such concrete problems. A group of humble peasants participating in one of the round tables that were organized in connection with the Conference showed similar surprise. They were asked:

"Would you expect a priest to take an interest in your working conditions, wages, and housing?"

"No, we would not expect him to," was the reply, "but we wish he would."

Monsignor Ligutti's comment was sharp and incisive: "There have been and still are too many priests, brothers, and sisters taking care of the 'better class'—developing a so-called 'elite' that has never produced the hoped-for results. It is far wiser and far more Christian to go to the poor and try to lift them up."

As my own final comment on this subject, I would like to add that "to lift them up" is also commanded in that great stanza of the *Magnificat* which as a youngster I used to sing in Church with a mixture of religious rapture and budding rebel fervor: *"Deposuit potentes de sede et exaltavit humiles!—*He has put down the mighty from their thrones and has exalted the lowly."

Notes

1. On April 23, 1963, Emilio Maspero, founder and most outstanding CLASC spokesman, speaking at Notre Dame University, South Bend, Indiana, thus defined CLASC's relationship to the Church and its use of the name Christian:

> In the term, Christian Trade Unionism, the noun is trade unionism, the adjective is Christian. . . . The term Christian, as we use it, has no sectarian, religious, ecclesiastical, theological, or dogmatical implications. We use the term to refer to the social philosophy and ethic of Christianity as they are projected on the trade union plane. . . . Our unionism is based on some very fundamental ideas, attitudes and morals which are common to all men of good will. Through action and reality we have elaborated our own ideology, the ideology of Christian trade unionism. . . . Christian trade unionism is not in any way sectarian, it is not dependent on any ecclesiastical authority, nor does it assume for itself the specific apostolic goals of official Catholic action. . . . Our interest is simply trade unionism . . . oriented by the social philosophy and ethic of Christianity. . . .

2. *Cuaderno No. 3, p. 9,* Publication of the Christian Trade Union Movement of Peru (MOSICP).
3. *Cuaderno No. 1, pp. 5–6.*
4. *Labor* (official organ of the ICFTU), No. 4–5, 1964.
5. Father Camilo Torres's difficulties with the Catholic Church's hierarchy, his "pro-Communist" activities and his tragic death are described by Father Vicente Andrade in two articles, "Rebel Priest in Colombia" and "The Death of Camilo Torres," which appeared in *America*, September 18, 1965, and March 12, 1966, respectively.
6. *NCWC News Service* (Foreign), August 27, 1956.
7. *Juan de Onís, The New York Times,* August 11, 1966.
8. *Ibid.*
9. *America,* June 25, 1955.

XXIV

AIFLD—An Experiment in Labor Education

THE AMERICAN INSTITUTE for Free Labor Development, better known by its initials AIFLD, was, chronologically speaking, my last full-time assignment in the field of inter-American labor activity. I became its first Executive Director in March 1962 and remained its chief executive officer and spokesman until September 1965 when I resigned on the eve of my retirement.

Today, AIFLD is a successful institution, with a multi-million-dollar budget and branches in practically every country of Latin America and the Caribbean area. It is engaged in a variety of activities, from education to low-cost housing, credit unions, labor banks, cooperatives, and community services. Its origins were, however, quite modest. As a matter of fact, at the beginning AIFLD was confined mainly to labor education, and even that was on a sort of experimental basis.

In this chapter I relate how all this came about, why this novel experiment has proved to be so successful, and what the AIFLD has accomplished in terms of practical benefits to the workers and to the cause of freedom and democracy in the Western Hemisphere.

The Institute came into being as the result of a very personal experience. The man involved was Joseph A. Beirne, since 1947 President of the AFL-CIO Communications Workers of America, and for five years before that head of the independent union which was its predecessor. In 1957, Beirne was flying over the Andes mountains in South America, en route from Santiago to Buenos Aires. As related by Beirne himself to the late American journalist Milton Bracker,[1] during the flight his oxygen supply was not operating properly and it was an uncomfortable flight. But somehow, the inhospitable Andean peaks below—and sometimes above, on both sides—made him think of the misery of those thousands who for centuries had tried to draw sustenance from the great western spine of South America and some of its slopes. He remembered particularly seeing children in the barren fields around Cuzco, and others sleeping huddled together with adults in the slums of Lima.

"I suddenly realized that this would never be cleared up," Beirne recalled later in Washington, "unless it could be put in the minds of these people to change their outlook, their view of the world."

In one word, this meant education. Returning to this country, Beirne and his union invited sixteen Latin American communications workers to come to the United States for a three-month stay. They spent it taking training courses at the Communications Workers' Educational Center, also known as the Front Royal (Va.) Institute. After the visitors returned home, they were assisted financially for nine months by the Postal, Telephone and Telegraph International (PTTI), one of the International Trade Secretariats, of which Beirne was one of the leaders. Most of the "graduates" are still in the labor movement, and some are professionals. The project seemed to have borne fruit.

Beirne was pleased but regarded it as a "drop in the bucket." Looking to an expanded program, in August 1960, he obtained the approval of the AFL-CIO Executive Council—and a $20,000 appropriation to be used as a sort of seed money to study the feasibility of launching a labor leadership training program that would benefit all the branches of the labor movement, particularly in the underdeveloped areas of Latin America.

The money was transferred to the Union Research and Education Project Center of the University of Chicago through the National Institute of Labor Education. John McCollum, already on the staff of the University, was made director of this project. He had had only limited experience in the trade union movement of Latin America and therefore wisely decided to draw upon the suggestions of many experts, inside and outside the labor movement. As AFL-CIO Inter-American Representative, I was often consulted by McCollum and worked with him in the planning and execution of the needed organizational steps. He was also helped by an Advisory Committee which met in Washigton, D.C., in early May 1961.[2] This meeting recommended the setting up of a non-profit organization to be known as the American Institute for Free Labor Development (AIFLD).

Following the filing in August 1961 of the Certificate of Incorporation of the AIFLD in the State of Delaware, County of Kent, there took place in October 1961 at the Commodore Hotel in New York the first meeting of the Board of Trustees, at which the officers of the Corporation were elected [3] from labor, management, and the academic community.

The fact that AIFLD sponsorship included, in addition to labor, a selected group of business leaders exposed it to criticism and doubts from various sources, including some trade union sectors, particularly among professional United States labor educators and their friends in the academic world and even in some agencies of our government. They considered as a sort of unpardonable heresy even the simple thought that employers could be represented in the management of a labor education program. Other people now assert, however, that were it not for the fact that both labor and management are represented in the AIFLD Board, it would have been exceedingly difficult to get funding from the U.S. government. This is true. But to me, and to the AIFLD top officers, another paramount consideration entered into the decision to make the AIFLD a joint labor-management-goverment venture.

In the United States as well as in every country of the Western Hemisphere the old concept of confining organized labor's role to matters pertaining to wages and working conditions and, above all, fighting against the employer, is being supplanted by the new concept of labor as a full-fledged partner in a national society, able to work constructively with the government as well as with the employer, offering to both its own contribution toward making social and economic progress feasible and obtainable.

There was a time when a Latin American labor leader's primary qualification was his ability to sway listeners to his point of view through oratory. Today, he is becoming a source of constructive contributions for the development of the national economy, enabling wage earners to receive a greater share of the ever-growing fruits of their labor. This new type of labor leader cannot be improvised. To begin with, he must have deep within himself a burning desire to serve his fellow workers and, through them, his own country. But he must also acquire a great deal of technical knowledge and this requires specialized education and intensive study.

A desirable technical development that can aid the emergence of a strong independent labor movement in the Latin American countries now going through the process of economic and social development requires an atmosphere of representative democracy in which all elements of society are encouraged to contribute actively to the general welfare. The concept of the various economic power elements in a free society working together, instead of in opposition, became the most fundamental credo of the Institute. The idea of labor and management pulling together was seen as a necessity for the continued growth of a democratic society. And it was in tribute to this concept that business representatives were asked to join with labor in the management and support of the Institute.

Furthermore, labor in the United States does not subscribe to the concept of the class struggle. It believes in the free enterprise system, subject to limitations and controls designed to prevent dangerous monopolies and abuses, but a free enterprise system nevertheless. George Meany, the AIFLD President, in an address delivered April 2, 1965, before the Council on Latin America, thus defined this viewpoint:

We believe in the capitalist system, and we are members of the capitalist society. We are dedicated to the preservation of this system, which rewards the workers, which is one in which management also has such a great stake. The investors of risk capital also must be rewarded. It is, perhaps, not a perfect device, but it is the best that the world has ever produced, and it operates effectively in a free society. We are not satisfied, no, but we are not about to trade in our system for any other. We are content to keep on trying to make our methods work a little bit better in behalf of the people.

The other AIFLD top officer, Chairman of the Board J. Peter Grace, echoed Meany's sentiments in an address delivered at the International Trade Week, Houston, Texas, September 16, 1965. He said:

Essentially I believe there is a great deal to be gained by business, labor, and government working together for the common good of the United States at home and in defense of American interests abroad. Certainly there is much more advantage to be had by all concerned through cooperation for achievement of common goals rather than by working separately, or in competition with each other.

All three—business, labor, and government—quite obviously believe in the democratic form of government, and in the capitalistic system, in private initiative and in promoting the general well-being of the individual. And again quite obviously it is much better that they should all work together along common lines.

Joseph A. Beirne, Institute founder and Secretary-Treasurer, was even more specific and concise:

If we are going to export the concepts of our society, all of the elements of that society must be represented. The Institute, therefore, had to find its support not only in labor, but the Federal government, business management, and the professions as well.[4]

On January 18, 1962, President John F. Kennedy warmly endorsed the aims of the Institute. In a letter addressed to AIFLD Board Chairman J. Peter Grace, President Kennedy wrote:

Achieving the objectives of Latin America and the rest of the Free World requires the support of the workers and their trade unions in these countries. Support will be forthcoming only when workers have opportunity for full participation in the affairs of the nation. Effective and responsible leaders are essential in gaining the participation of the unions in the social and economic life of these nations and in making such participation meaningful to workers.

Other letters of commendation and support came from Luis Múñoz Marín, Governor of Puerto Rico; Rómulo Betancourt, President of Venezuela; José Figueres, former President of Costa Rica; Adlai Stevenson, U.S. Ambassador to the United Nations, and New York Governor Nelson A. Rockefeller. Governor Rockefeller wrote:

This Institute is one of the most daring and far-reaching plans I have seen for attacking the problems of Latin America—it is worthy of our interest and support.

The resignation, for personal reasons, of John McCollum in early 1962, caused the AIFLD leadership to search for a new Director. A number of professional labor educators were asked if they would like the job. No one wanted it. Some of the people felt that they would be going against their conception of "trade union principles" because management was a part of the Institute. Others worried about "what the Communists would say." This ritualistic response on the part of these professional labor educators, many of whom held responsible teaching positions in the labor-management departments of a number of our universities, greatly irritated me. I felt these people, who mostly had only a book knowledge—often outdated —of Latin America had allowed their dogmatism to obscure the magnitude of the great opportunity opened to them to help build a strong, independent, and constructive trade union movement in Latin America. I voiced my disappointment to George Weaver, who had been recently appointed by President Kennedy to the post of Assistant Secretary of Labor for International Labor Affairs, during an airplane trip from Texas to Washington. Weaver suddenly said: "Why don't you take the job, Serafino?"

At first I demurred, but then I reconsidered and was quickly won over by the challenge. I had supported Beirne's idea from the beginning because I myself, through my own Latin American trade union experience, had reached the conclusion that a center for labor leadership training had become a necessity. As a matter of fact, in the early fifties, I met with Nelson A. Rockefeller and his Latin American adviser, the late Frank Jamieson, to argue in favor of setting up a sort of Inter-American Council for Labor-Management Relations. The idea did not prosper then, because of the still existing split between the AFL and the CIO. But now the situation had changed. I made known to Meany and Beirne that if they were unsuccessful in finding a qualified successor to McCollum, I would be ready to help. In March 1962 I was drafted for the job of AIFLD Executive Director, though remaining for all administrative purposes a member of the AFL-CIO International Department staff.

In January 1962 the Bureau of Internal Reveune granted the AIFLD tax-exempt status. It was thought that this would open the door of many foundations from which AIFLD promoters had confidently expected to receive the bulk of its financing. It soon became apparent, however, that the foundations were not too eager to help the AIFLD. Of the two dozen selected foundations approached by John McCollum, only one answered in the affirmative with a generous but nonrecurring contribution. The problem of financing the AIFLD was accordingly brought before the newly established Labor Advisory Committee to the Alliance for Progress, composed of a selected group of labor representatives and government officials under the chairmanship of George Meany. The Advisory Committee endorsed the suggestion for government's participation in the financing of the AIFLD, but we would have to wait a number of months before funds could be made available. Talk of the impending activities of the AIFLD had been going on for quite some time and we wanted to get "this thing off the ground," as President Meany expressed himself when he gave me the appointment, "as soon as possible." We were finally able to do that, thanks to help from Secretary of Labor Arthur J. Goldberg, who obtained for us an advance of $100,000 from the President's Emergency Fund. Afterwards, the Agency for International Development included our organization in its regular annual appropriations to the extent that at the present it provides by far the major share of the AIFLD's financial requirements. The AFL-CIO and a number of its affiliates also contribute to the Institute's support, as do American businessmen. In regard to the latter, Board Chairman J. Peter Grace took the initiative of gathering at a dinner meeting at the Link Club in New

York City, October 2, 1962, scores of business associates and friends who gave a sympathetic reception to arguments in support of business participation in the AIFLD programs presented by Grace himself, the Secretaries of Labor and Commerce, AFL-CIO President George Meany, and this writer in his capacity as AIFLD Executive Director. When I left the AIFLD, about sixty firms were contributing an aggregate amount somewhat less than the contribution from the AFL-CIO. The two sources add up to about 15 percent of the AIFLD annual budget. The balance comes from AID regional and country funds.

With the $100,000 Secretary Goldberg delivered to me in person, I opened an office, hired a skeleton staff, and proceeded to select the participants in the first course, which was composed almost evenly of Spanish-speaking and English-speaking trainees from Central America and the Caribbean area, respectively. Classes started in June 1962.[5] The classroom was a small, dark, converted street-level store a block up the street from the AIFLD office, at 1925 K Street, N.W., Washington.[6] Three months later, on September 13, 1962, the first class graduated. President Kennedy, who on August 8 had received at the White House the AIFLD officers, staff, and student body, sent to the graduates a personal message of congratulations in which he said:

> The Institute is a formal acknowledgment of the fraternity of spirit to which all who choose freedom belong. American trade unionism, the beneficiary of an open political system and an accomplished economy, can impart to its brother trade unionists from other lands its technical know-how and its experienced methods. But it receives something in return—the refreshing reminder that these things have come into being and exist for the welfare of the individual and the advance of human dignity.
>
> The free man anywhere seeks an end to poverty and deprivation everywhere; he seeks equality in opportunity for all persons, and justice in the rewards a man receives for his labors on earth. Above all, he believes so truly in his own dignity that he cannot deny it to others.

When the AIFLD endeavor first began, the program consisted only of the training course in Washington. The courses and the people chosen to attend them were considered in terms of a "multiplier" effect, that is, that the Institute would train those who had a capacity for training others. But this approach proved inadequate on two counts.

In the first place, the Institute was not obtaining a sufficient uniformity in the background experience of students to give the courses continuity. Second, the Institute was not moving fast enough in enabling its trainees to take care of themselves. The Institute did not want to entrench itself in these peoples' native countries, but simply to offer them the experience gathered in the decades of trade union activity in North America and then to withdraw to let them move their countries forward as they saw fit.

The Board of Trustees felt the best answer to these problems would be the establishment of training programs in Latin America itself, programs which, as soon as possible, would be completely operated by local union leaders.

In the early months of 1963, such programs were started in Peru, Colombia, and Venezuela. The response was so positive that by the end of the year other local programs had been set up in Ecuador, Brazil, Argentina, Bolivia, Honduras (for Central America), the Dominican Republic, Chile, and Uruguay. Other education programs were organized in Mexico and Jamaica (for the Caribbean area) early in 1964. At the time of this writing AIFLD labor leadership training programs are operating in every country and territory of Latin America and the Caribbean area, with the exception of Haiti, Paraguay, and, of course, Cuba.

The national education programs that developed during my AIFLD stewardship varied according to the country. Where conditions were especially favorable the Institute was able to establish a national center, whose resident program of eight to ten weeks was patterned after the Washington school's full-time curriculum. In other countries short-term seminars were held in a variety of industrial and agricultural complexes. At the present time the Institute is endeavoring to establish both kinds of programs in each country.

In setting up the several levels of trade union education, the Institute has been able to give its curriculum a definite hierarchy. The best of those trained in the short-term seminars are selected as candidates for the resident courses at the national centers. The best of the national center graduates further their knowledge by attending the Washington school for an additional twelve weeks of training. So far, more than 40,000 men and women have attended these AIFLD field program courses.

In Washington, the school's twelve-week program was divided into two class groups. The first devoted the full period to studies and field trips to industrial centers in the eastern United States. The second group (of about ten students) spent several weeks in Washington and then studied in Europe and the Middle East in a travel program.

The Washington-based group covered the following subject areas:

• American government and democratic institutions. Traditions and means of a free society, with illustrations from the American system; explanation of the functioning of the American government.

· Labor history and American labor movement. Origins and development of present-day American labor organizations; their role in the democratic process. Trade union structure; techniques of organizing.

· International labor. The significance of international cooperation and exchange of information by labor groups and the roles played by different international labor organizations, such as the United Nations International Labor Organization, the International Confederation of Free Trade Unions and ORIT, its regional arm in the Americas.

· Labor education techniques. Application of the techniques of teaching, conducting conferences, and of audio-visual aids; planning programs and preparing labor education seminars; trade union public relations.

· Collective bargaining. Labor-management relations and the process of collective bargaining. Negotiation strategy, grievance procedures, union security issues and labor-management cooperation.

· Threats to unionism and democracy. Communism and other forms of totalitarianism. Analysis of the strategy and tactics of subversion and its effect upon democracy and trade unions. Defense tactics and safeguards.

· Labor economics and the economic problems of industry and agriculture. Analysis of the functioning of the labor market and its manpower implications on wages, employment, unemployment, and underemployment. Economic effects on industry and agriculture, with special emphasis on problems of developing nations.

· Special Latin American issues, including analysis of Alliance for Progress, Organization of American States, Latin American Free Trade Area, and the economic integration of Latin America.

· Other special issues, including cooperatives, workers' housing, credit unions, and community development programs.

· Role of unions in a modern industrial society. The economic, political, social, and cultural functions of trade unions in a democratic setting.

The European travel program began with the first class of 1964. The participants first spent three weeks in the United States at the Washington school to acquire a basic knowledge of the structure and functions of the United States labor movement and its role in the nation's economy. The students then studied for three weeks in Israel, two weeks in Italy, two weeks in West Germany. One additional week was spent in short visits to the ILO office in Geneva, the Organization for Economic Cooperation and Development, the office of the AFL-CIO European Representative in Paris, and the ICFTU headquarters in Brussels.

In Israel, the three-week program was under the supervision of Histadrut, the country's General Confederation of Labor, in conjunction with the Afro-Asian Labor Institute in Tel Aviv. The curriculum included classroom work and field trips, with the general objective of observing how a cooperative economy can coexist with free enterprise and how state-run services can operate in an atmosphere of freedom, pragmatic interdependence, and competition.

The program in Italy, worked out in cooperation with the Italian Confederation of Labor Unions (CISL), consisted of one week of lectures at the CISL Center for Trade Union Studies in Florence, with a field trip to a nearby cooperative center and one week of visits and round table discussions at the Center for Labor and Social Studies in Rome. The main objective of the Italian program was to expose the visitors to the causes and effects, good or bad, of "trade union pluralism" even at the shop level and to the division of the labor movement almost exclusively along political and ideological lines.

In West Germany, the travel program was supervised by the Friedrich Ebert Foundation of Bonn. The three main objectives of this program were:

(a) To obtain from the spokesmen of management and labor first-hand information on the operation of the codetermination policy;

(b) To observe how public services can be operated profitably and efficiently regardless of private or public ownership;

(c) To bring the visitors to West Berlin, and possibly to East Berlin, in order to see for themselves the dramatic and ultimate contrast between the worlds of democracy and totalitarianism.

At the end of their European program the participants returned to Washington, where they rejoined the class for a final week of evaluation and exchange of information and impressions with their fellow students and the staff before their graduation.

The program was initiated with the view of giving to a specially selected group of young Latin American labor leaders a multinational exposure to the problems, structure, functions, and achievements of democratic labor, thus broadening their horizons and experiences in preparation for their future positions in their native countries.

As part of its educational program the AIFLD launched in 1965 a pilot project leadership training for *campesinos* (rural workers). It was conducted in Central America, jointly with ORIT and the AFL-CIO Inter-American Representative, under the direct supervision of the Central American Institute for Labor Studies (IESCA), located in San Pedro Sula, Honduras. About thirty trainees participated, coming from every Central American country and the Dominican Republic.[7]

The basic purpose of the program was to develop, as speedily as possible, a *campesino* corps large enough to expand the training to as many rural communities as possible. What distinguished this *campesino* program from other labor leadership training schools was the amount of field experience, comprising the major portion of the time, which the participants were able to undertake.

At the conclusion of the program, the IESCA trainee teams were asked to file reports on the projects in the field to which they were assigned. These reports served to determine whether the participants were now ready to undertake on their own the launching and supervision of similar projects in their respective countries. Excerpts from two such reports will suffice to describe the effectiveness and the novelty of the AIFLD approach to the training of *campesino* leadership. The team that worked in the community of El Porvenir, Honduras, wrote:

This team met with the local mayor and members of the community, touring the district in order to convince the people that the construction of an artesian well could solve their water problem.

Various committees representing the community then agreed to go ahead with the construction, and they approved the following work plan for the two-week period: the construction of four school stairways, two latrines, three doorways, the fencing in of two school areas and the acquisition of 160 writing desks.

Financial contributions were made by the local community, the township, and IESCA. The student team rolled up their sleeves, carrying out their work plan with the help of the local community. In addition, the team had a meeting with the local fishermen, arranging for the presence of a co-op specialist who was asked to return to El Porvenir in order to help them organize a fishing co-op.

The other team, assigned to the community of El Cacao, also in Honduras, reported:

Upon arriving in this community the student team asked the mayor to arrange a meeting with the local people in order to explain the aims of the AIFLD, IESCA, and its pilot *campesino* program in Central America.

After ascertaining the needs of the community, a collection was taken up for the purchase of writing desks for the school. A community services committee was organized. A lecture was given on cooperatives and a team member showed the farmers how to increase their sugar cane output.

Other meetings dealt with health problems, housing, agrarian reform, agricultural extension services, etc. With the help of the townspeople, awnings were built to shade the school. The team made specific recommendations on potable water and other type construction.

Similar undertakings were also conducted in the communities of Yaruca, Esparta, Santa Ana, San Juan Pueblo, and Las Palmas. Local "Committees for Community Progress" were established with the local members electing their own officers and determining the various projects to be undertaken with AIFLD trainee help. These *campesino* programs are now a regular feature of the AIFLD field work. In the impoverished Northeast regions of Brazil they have been so successful that AID funds have been made available for the staffing of a separate Northeast AIFLD branch headquarters and a number of subsidiary centers.

My successor in the management of the AIFLD, with the new title of Administrator, is William ("Bill") Doherty, Jr., who became associated with the AIFLD in the very first months of its operation as Director of the Social Projects Department. Previously, he had worked with me for many years—when I was AFL-CIO Inter-American Representative—in a number of trade union projects in Latin America, where he served first in Mexico and then in Brazil, as Regional Director of the Postal, Telephone and Telegraph Workers' International. He had also pioneered in the field of labor leadership training and had worked for a while at the Brussels headquarters of the International Confederation of Free Trade Unions. Although different from me in many ways as a result of his relative youth and ebullient personality, Bill and I have never disagreed in our interpretation of the role of democratic trade unionism in our modern pluralistic society, in our belief in free labor as a component and interdependent part of a free society, and in the necessity of promoting a cooperative constructive relationship between labor and management.

When Doherty came to the AIFLD on April 15, 1962, he had almost nothing to start with—just an incredibly small cubicle which we hopefully called an office, a telephone extension, and a part-time secretary. A proposal for a contract was submitted to the Agency for International Development in the latter part of that same month and a contract in the amount of $210,000 was signed on August 9, 1962. The general intent of the AID contract was to allow the Social Projects Department to hire sufficient staff to assist the Latin American democratic labor unions to develop and submit feasible projects in the field of housing, credit unions, training centers, workers' cooperatives, etc. Separate office space was immediately acquired on the same floor as the general offices of the Institute. A professional and clerical staff, consisting of eight full-time persons and three technicians serving in a consulting capacity, was employed in the first few months.

From the very beginning, the Social Projects Department was on a relatively autonomous basis. The August 1962 Memo: *AIFLD—Aims, Objectives and Program,* thus described the SPD scope:

A Department of Social Projects was established at the suggestion of the Labor Advisory Committee on the Alliance for Progress. This Department, through the process of education, will try to assist free trade unions of Latin America in the establishment of low-cost housing, credit unions, cooperatives, workers' clinics, vocational and adult education, and similar institutions. However, unlike the Institute's other educational program, which seeks financial support from private foundations, the Social Projects Department will rely upon the U.S. Agency for International Development for the major part of its funds on a project basis.

In a speech at the National Conference on Economic and Social Development in Chicago on July 19, 1962, Bill Doherty said:

The principle that free unions are necessary to economic, political and social development has been widely endorsed. In fact, the Congress of the United States, when appropriating Alliance for Progress funds, recognized the need for strengthening the free labor movement. It was the express intention of Congress when authorizing the establishment of the AID, that the free democratic labor movement would be aided and supported. Part III, Ch. 1, General Provisions, Section 601 (a), of Public Law 85–195 AID Act of 1961, states *inter alia:* "The Congress of the United States recognizes the vital role of free enterprise in achieving rising levels of production and standards of living essential to economic progress and development. Accordingly it declared to be the policy of the United States to . . . *strengthen free labor unions.*" [8]

The accomplishments of the Social Projects Department, as of mid-1966, were summarized by Bill Doherty himself in an article which appeared in the July 1966 issue of the *AFL-CIO Free Trade Union News:*

AIFLD has to date completed over 3,400 units of workers' housing in five countries: Mexico, Honduras, Peru, the Dominican Republic, and Uruguay. The total amount of loans for these homes is almost $11 million. In addition AIFLD has provided temporary dwellings for earthquake victims in Chile and assisted in completing a worker housing project in Ecuador. At the present time construction is under way on an initial 280 units in Colombia, more units are being completed in the Dominican Republic, and ground is soon to be broken for 488 units in São Paulo, Brazil.

These units under construction, plus other projects for which financing totaling $30 million has been committed, will provide 6,146 units in eight countries. Seven additional projects are in earlier stages of preparation and will eventually produce about 10,000 units in seven countries, using loans totaling about $31 million more.

In all these housing projects, down payments amount to 10 percent, monthly mortgage payments are kept within one-fourth of the worker's monthly income, and in about twenty years the individual worker owns his own home. Borrowing organizations are generally housing cooperatives set up by the trade unions. Sources of lending vary, with AID and the Inter-American Development Bank providing some loans, and the largest portion coming from pension and welfare funds of AFL-CIO unions, under AID guaranty.

In Lima, Peru, AIFLD has established the first workers' housing bank in Latin America. Known as ASINCOOP, it opened in July 1964, under trade union control. By the spring of 1966 ASINCOOP had amassed $1,256,000 in worker savings, most of which has been loaned out to build houses. By the end of 1965, 88 houses were completed, with 161 more due for completion within a few months. All of this has been done through the initiative of the workers themselves, without drawing upon the $5,000,000 in Alliance for Progress put at the disposal of the bank by the AID and the government of Peru. AIFLD plans more worker banks in Latin America, and has completed a feasibility study for a union-operated bank in Nicaragua to provide consumer credit and to finance trade union cooperatives.

The emphasis of the AIFLD Washington courses, since they have been moved to the residential institute at Front Royal, has been changed from direct union leadership training to teacher education. In this way—according to Administrator Bill Doherty—AIFLD hopes to achieve a greater "multiplier effect" when the trainees return and pass on their training in local classes. The international program has been discontinued. By the end of 1966 a total of 480 trade unionists had passed through courses in the United States of either the old or new type.

Almost one-half of the Washington graduates have received full-time, nine-month paid internships. The main purpose of the internship program is to enable financially weak unions in Latin America to utilize the full-time services of our Washington graduates for educational and administrative duties. The internships are requested by Latin American labor organizations at the time that the labor leader begins his Washington instruction, and the intern works under the discipline and policy direction of his own Latin American union.

These Institute graduates are showing their strength in many countries.

Although, for example, "fighting Communism" is not the sole purpose of AIFLD, its graduates have found in several cases that they had to fight it if they were going to continue to work for the development of the free labor movement. Graduates already have been challenged by Communist agitators in Venezuela, British Guiana, Honduras, Brazil, Bolivia, and Chile. In each case the challenges were met head on; the graduates not only held their own but eliminated totalitarian elements from a number of important unions.

For instance, in August 1963 two graduates were able to bring a Honduran union that had been solidly under Communist control back into the democratic camp, but only after a nine-month fight in which the family of one of the men was savagely beaten in the street by known Communist toughs.

In other positive action, a number of Brazilian graduates from the Washington school have trained their fellow countrymen in short-term seminars reaching more than six hundred people. In Peru, of the twenty-seven men that graduated from the first national resident course there, seventeen have become general secretaries of their unions. In Bolivia, one of the Washington graduates is serving as second in command of the AIFLD seminars.

In Colombia, a graduate has become the first general secretary of the National Federation of Oil and Refinery Workers. In Chile, a tenth-class graduate of the Washington school was recently elected President of the Valparaiso Railroad Workers Union. In newly independent Guyana a first-class graduate has been elected President of the country's trade union council. AIFLD trained leaders are now leading important unions of Brazil and Peru. Another is President of the Central American Labor Federation.

As it was to be expected, the AIFLD is constantly attacked by the Communists, their fellow travelers, and many who are dragged along by the transmission belts of Communist propaganda. From Moscow, and from Prague and other Communist satellite centers, radio broadcasts in Spanish beamed to Latin America carry frequent attacks directed at the Institute. Because such attacks indirectly reflect the effectiveness of the AIFLD program, I am quoting in part the following broadcast in Spanish from Moscow on October 4, 1965, as typical of such Communist propaganda:

AFL-CIO USES INSTITUTE TO OVERTHROW REGIMES

(Radio Peace and Progress anonymous commentary: "A Center for the Preparation of Strikebreakers in Latin America")

In Washington on the fourth floor of the marble palace of AFL-CIO, which incidentally is situated in front of the White House, is the office of Jay Lovestone, leader of the international section of the AFL-CIO. An obdurate enemy of Communism, he heads a group of people who, following the orders of AFL-CIO President George Meany, are fighting all over the world against Communist influence in the trade union movement.

Close to the marble palace is situated a building which houses the beloved creation of Meany and Lovestone—the American Institute for Free Labor Development. Among its leaders there are not only trade unionists but also representatives of those same corporations against which many Latin American trade unions are fighting. Thus, the President of the Institute is George Meany, and the Chairman of the Board is Peter Grace of W. R. Grace & Co. In Latin America this Yankee monopoly owns shipping companies, sugar plantations, sugar refineries, textile mills, and other enterprises. The Vice-President of the Institute's Council is Berent Friele, protégé of the oil magnate Nelson Rockefeller. Among the directors are Charles Brinckerhoff, President of Anaconda, Juan Trippe, President of PAA, William Hickey, President of the United Corporation, and others. The fact that such persons are on the Board of the Institute shows that its objectives are very far from genuine trade union struggle, a struggle for workers' rights to which the trade unionists trained at the Institute should devote themselves.

In planning course programs and in selection of trainees, anti-Communism is the criterion. Apart from studies purely in trade union work, classes are given on the U.S. government system, on questions of American trade union policies, on the question of anti-Communist struggle in Latin America, and other topics. Analyzing the syllabus of the Institute, even the American magazine *The Nation* expressed doubts as to how Latin American activists armed with such knowledge would be able to carry out their revolution against the oligarchy.

The Institute operates fourteen training centers in Latin America where more than 20,000 people have been trained, and 317 have taken their course in Washington. In the fight against the progressive labor movement, the Institute's graduates use any method to achieve their chief objective, which has been placed before them by the reactionary leadership of the AFL-CIO headed by Meany.

In Brazil it did quite a lot for the overthrow of the Goulart government. After the April coup last year, William Doherty, Jr., head of the Department of Social Projects at the Institute, was saying in a triumphant tone that many trade union leaders, several of them trained at the Institute, had actively participated in overthrowing Goulart.

This same role of betrayal has been played by the Institute in the Dominican Republic. Here the AFL-CIO and the Institute were operating through a trade union called CONATRAL. A week before President Juan Bosch was overthrown, CONATRAL published a statement in which the population was hypocritically exhorted to rely on the armed forces for defense against Communism. In other words, it was openly exhorting the overthrow of the government and establishment of a military dictatorship.

The virulence and misrepresentations in the foregoing broadcast are so obvious that I am sure they do not need to be answered here. The growing effectiveness of the AIFLD program throughout Latin America is, of course, the most effective refutation of the Communist attacks. Unfortunately, unbelievable as it seems to me in the light of my knowledge of the activities of the Institute, some of these Communist-inspired attacks on the AIFLD have been repeated by writers for the liberal press in this country and even have been echoed by some sincerely anti-Communist but misinformed labor leaders. The operations of the Institute were fully examined—at the request of its Secretary-Treasurer, Joseph A. Beirne, himself—by the AFL-CIO Executive Council at its August 1966 meeting in Chicago, Illinois. After hearing full reports on its activities in helping to develop a free trade union movement in Latin America and on the campaign of vilification which has been carried on in the Communist press and other publications, the AFL-CIO Council by a vote of 23 to 2, with one abstention, adopted the following resolution:

The Executive Council commends the American Institute for Free Labor Development for their work in carrying out the policies of the AFL-CIO in the international field and rejects out of hand the campaign of vilification that has been conducted against the AIFLD.

A recent study of 398 graduates of the Washington school is, to my mind, convincing proof of the real effectiveness of the AIFLD program. Its findings show that three-fourths of these former students have either retained or advanced their trade union positions since completing their studies, and one-third of them have actually moved upward in the leadership of their unions.

The foreign trade unionists who have worked with AIFLD programs, in either the education or the social projects fields, are truly men who are their own masters. Many of their beliefs differ from ours. They take from the Institute only what they themselves feel will benefit their fellow countrymen. The United States labor movement offers its experience; then they are on their own again. But in the eyes of the Institute, and the AFL-CIO, they stand stronger, straighter, and taller, better able to do the job their people expect of them.

Notes

1. *The Grace Log,* Spring issue, 1963.
2. Present at this meeting were, in addition to labor representatives such as AFL-CIO President George Meany, Joseph A. Beirne, and the staff of the AFL-CIO International Affairs Department, representatives of management such as Eric Johnston, President, Motion Picture Association of America; J. Peter Grace, President, W. R. Grace & Co.; and educators and economists such as William Benton, Chairman of the Board, Encyclopaedia Britannica; Kenneth Holland, President, Institute of International Education; and Berent Friele, Senior Vice-President, American International Association for Economic and Social Development.
3. AIFLD officers and Board of Trustees members, as of March 1967, were: George Meany, President; J. Peter Grace, Chairman of the Board; Kenneth Holland, Vice-President; Berent Friele, Vice-Chairman of the Board; Joseph A. Beirne, Secretary-Treasurer. Board members, in addition to the officers were:

From Labor: I. W. Abel, President, United Steelworkers of America; William C. Doherty, Jr., Administrator, AIFLD; David Dubinsky, Vice-President, AFL-CIO; Oscar Gale Varela, President, Tela Railroad Company Workers' Union, Honduras; José González Navarro, President, Confederation of Labor of Venezuela; A. F. Grospiron, President, Oil, Chemical and Atomic Workers' International Union; George M. Harrison, President Emeritus, Brotherhood of Railway and Steamship Clerks; Arturo Jáuregui H., General Secretary, Inter-American Regional Organization of Workers (ORIT); Paul Jennings, President, International Union of Electrical, Radio and Machine Workers; Joseph D. Keenan, International Secretary, International Brotherhood of Electrical Workers; Ernest S. Lee, Assistant Director, AFL-CIO Department of International Affairs; Jay Lovestone, Director, AFL-CIO Department of International Affairs; Andrew C. McLellan, AFL-CIO Inter-American Representative; Lee W. Minton, International President, Glass Bottle Blowers' Association of the United States and Canada; Wenceslao Moreno Ávila, General Secretary, Maritime Confederation of Chile; A. Philip Randolph, International President, Brotherhood of Sleeping Car Porters; William F. Schnitzler, Secretary-Treasurer, AFL-CIO; James A. Suffridge, International President, Retail Clerks International Association;

From Business: Charles Brinckerhoff, Chairman of the Board, The Anaconda Company; William M. Hickey, President, The United Corporation; Ambassador Robert C. Hill, Director, Merck & Co.; Juan T. Trippe, Chairman of the Board, Pan American World Airways; Henry S. Woodbridge, Chairman of the Board, True Temper Corporation.

From the Academic Community: Dr. José Barbosa de Almeida, President, Labor Cultural Institute, Brazil; George C. Lodge, Beverly, Massachusetts.

The Latin American members are rotated every two years. Among those who served in the past are: Rómulo Betancourt, former President of Venezuela; Professor Luis Alberto Sánchez, Rector, San Marcos University, Lima, Peru; Juan Antonio Solari, General Secretary, Social Democratic Party of Argentina; William A. Thayer Arteaga, labor lawyer, Santiago, Chile; José Figueres, former President, Costa Rica; Celio González, General Secretary, Trade Union Federation of the North Coast of Honduras; Guillermo Videla V., Executive Director, Community Development Corporation, Chile.

4. Quoted from *Buttressing Democracy in the Americas,* an AIFLD promotional pamphlet.
5. The first director of the AIFLD Washington School was Jesse A. Friedman, a graduate of the New York School for Industrial Relations, Cornell University, who was on leave from the AFL-CIO Department of International Affairs. He was succeeded at

the beginning of the second class by Samuel Haddad, a member of the United Steelworkers of America.

6. In September 1963 the AIFLD Washington School moved to 1860 Nineteenth Street, N.W., in a building formerly occupied by the School for Advanced International Studies of Johns Hopkins University. In March 1966 courses were moved to the residential Front Royal, Virginia, Institute where the Communications Workers' of America conducted the first pilot PTTI Inter-American labor leadership training school.

7. The program was directed by one of the ablest AIFLD regional representatives, Jesús Artigas Carbonell, formerly Secretary-Treasurer of the Cuban Confederation of Labor before the advent of the Castro regime. He is now the director of the AIFLD Front Royal Institute.

8. Speech by William C. Doherty, Jr., at National Conference on Economic and Social Development, Chicago, Illinois, July 19, 1962. *The Alliance for Progress—A Revolution That Can and Must Succeed*, p. 3.

XXV

Rómulo Betancourt—
The Man and the Fighter

Rómulo Betancourt and I look so much alike, in height, corpulence, complexion, and physiognomy, that I was often mistaken for him in photographs, at gatherings, and even while driving through the streets of Caracas—a circumstance that has brought me occasional undeserved cheers but could also have resulted, in the light of the events I am going to relate, in something less pleasant. The friendship that has developed between the two of us has led to what I believe is the most fruitful political collaboration of my life. I admire in him the idealist, the fighter, the practical statesman, and also the human being, with all the virtues, and perhaps the defects, of a "regular guy" who comes from the people and who has never ceased to be identified with the feelings and the aspirations of the people, especially when he reached the summit of power in his own country and the apex of renown abroad.

We have been together in many places, in a number of countries, while he was President of Venezuela, then when he was in exile, then again in Venezuela during his stormy second presidency, and then again out of his country while he was resting, writing, and meditating over the meaning of his past rich heroic life, perhaps to accumulate new physical and intellectual energy to reenter the arena and finish off the last quarter of the task that history has assigned to him. For he believes that life is

434

synonymous with action and, as he often said to me, "Action is the destiny and duty of a certain breed of men. . . ."

The first time I talked to Rómulo Betancourt was on June 20, 1946, when he was Provisional President of Venezuela. I had gone to that country (see Chapter III) to urge the Confederation of Labor of Venezuela (CTV) to join in our efforts to organize a democratic, inter-American trade union movement opposed to the Communist-controlled CTAL. Our interview at Miraflores Palace was cordial, but somewhat reserved. Yet I left with a strong admiration for the clarity of his views, for his calm presentation of his program of government, and for the strength of his determination to go through with it.

Upon returning to my hotel I typed some notes on our conversation, which I have carefully preserved to this day. He made remarks and observations against the maneuvers and intrigues of the Communist movement and expressed the hope that an inter-American labor federation or alliance might be formed in the near future without Communist domination or interference.

As to the labor policy of his government, which was well known to be strongly favorable to organized workers, Betancourt concurred with the idea of educating Venezuelan labor to be independent not only of government but also of political parties, although he remarked that without the direct interest of the Democratic Action Party which came to its rescue, Venezuelan labor would probably still be under Communist domination.

President Betancourt lamented that his program of social reforms and land resettlement, which constituted the No. 1 economic problem of Venezuela, was being sabotaged by reactionary influences which had so far, if not completely prevented, certainly greatly slowed down to an insignificant trickle the export from the United States of war surplus farm implements and machinery for which Venezuela was willing and ready to pay. He stated that while chambers of commerce, industrial associations, agricultural concerns, banks, etc., had united in petitioning the Washington government in favor of this release of material for Venezuela's agricultural improvement, U.S. organized labor so far had done nothing in that respect. I assured him that the American Federation of Labor would do everything within its power and influence to obtain from the government of the United States a more favorable attitude. Little did I know that that first pledge was to be the beginning of a long and fruitful era of cooperation between the labor movement of the United States and the democratic forces of Venezuela, which was marked by loyalty and mutual comprehension during the following years of struggle, defeat, resurgence, and triumph!

What was the life history of this man, who still in his thirties had evoked so much enthusiastic support and yet so much hatred from the reactionaries and the Communists? It took me some time to put together events and dates, and I was able to succeed only after many talks with Rómulo himself, in subsequent years.

In 1930, Rómulo Betancourt, aged twenty-three, was studying law and working against the dictatorship of Juan Vicente Gómez. He later told me that at that time, when he was a student at the Central University of Venezuela, he had no defined political ideology. He was an idealist hoping to see more liberty and dignity among his people. His activities led him to a term in jail. Later he escaped from Venezuela, but without a passport. He took refuge in Curaçao and made contacts enabling him to obtain a passport under the name of Carlos Luis Eizaguirre.

Using this passport, he traveled to Haiti, Santo Domingo, and Puerto Rico. U.S. immigration authorities sent him back to Santo Domingo, apparently knowing his documents were false. He spent about a year in Santo Domingo, then went to Trinidad, Costa Rica, Colombia, Peru, and back to Costa Rica, where he resumed law studies, at the Costa Rican School of Law. There he joined the "Workers' and Farmers' Bloc" (Bloque Obrero y Campesino), which had Communist sympathies but no open connection with the Third International (Comintern) headquartered in Moscow, he told me years later.

In 1936, Betancourt returned to Venezuela. By that time, he had severed relations with Communism. He became an organizer and later director of the ORVE Party (Organización Venezolana). This was a reformist party without ties to the various Communist groups.

Shortly afterwards, Betancourt helped organize the Democratic National Party (Partido Democrático Nacional). It openly opposed the Communist Party in 1937, when the latter was becoming strong enough to come out from underground and use its own name and symbols.

The government outlawed the Democratic National Party and exiled several of its leaders. Betancourt, however, managed to hide out and continued organizing clandestinely for his Party. He was captured and exiled to Chile in 1940, whereupon he helped organize the First Congress of Democratic and Popular Parties of Latin America. The Congress was assisted mainly by the Mexican ruling party (PRM), the Chilean Socialist Party (which had three members as Ministers in President Aguirre

Cerda's Cabinet), the Peruvian Aprista Party, and similar organizations. The Congress took a strong stand against Fascism, opposing the Communist line that for the moment called for "neutralism" with respect to Hitler's aggressions.

Betancourt was permitted to return to Venezuela in 1941. In a statement for the daily *Ahora* of Caracas (March 20, 1941), Betancourt said, "It interests me much to affirm what I have always said: that I am not a Communist. That sector of the Venezuelan Communist movement which is affiliated with the Third International wrote of me as follows in No. 3 of its clandestine leaflet "The Hammer" (*El Martillo*) in June 1938: 'Rómulo Betancourt no es Comunista, no es miembro del Partido Comunista y no ha militado nunca en sus filas.' (Rómulo Betancourt is not a Communist, is not a member of the Communist Party, and has never belonged to its ranks.) "

Betancourt's statement said Venezuela urgently needed a major renovation of her political, economic, and social structure. To have any guarantee of permanence, such changes would have to be brought about by "a great democratic party, in which will be congregated, around a concrete program and subject to a unified party discipline, all of the socially productive and creative classes, not just the working class." He added:

Furthermore, I reject the Communist Party with all the force of my intransigent Venezolanismo, because the Party's dependence on Moscow makes it a simple bureaucratic appendix of the Soviet state. If we reject Nazism, which acts globally according to Hitler's dictates, then equally we must reject the Communist Party, which acts globally according to Stalin's dictates.

Shortly afterwards, on June 22, 1941, Hitler invaded Russia. On June 24, *Ahora* published an article Betancourt wrote on "The German-Russian War and the Position of the Communist Parties." Betancourt noted the "pacifist" line the Communist Parties followed during the Stalin-Hitler pact and added:

The Venezuelan Communist Party was attacking me as follows in the April issue of its secret leaflet, *The Hammer:* "It is certain that many will find it difficult to consider Betancourt as a traitor. . . . But in connection with the imperialist war, to cite just one case, he does not shrink from helping the Yanqui bankers and tirelessly runs errands for the politicians tagging the Roosevelts and the Rockefellers." And in another leaflet circulated in Caracas May 8, the Communist referred to me as a "delegate of Yanqui imperialism in Venezuela." This repetitious diatribe, circulated clandestinely, has been hurled at us since we declined to hide our anti-Fascism after the Nazi-Soviet pact was signed, because never have we looked to Moscow for signals by which to orient our course.

After the Soviet Union joined the fight against Nazism, it became fashionable in many circles to be friendly with the Communists. In Venezuela, those were the times of the most volatile disputes between the Democratic Action Party (AD) and the Communist Party of Venezuela. Betancourt, as General Secretary of the AD, led and oriented this ideological battle.

The CP of Venezuela later allied itself with the Democratic Venezuelan Party (not to be confused with Betancourt's party), and for this and other reasons Betancourt found himself in opposition to the government.

Following a military *coup d'état* which deposed the government of President General Isaias Medina Angarita, Betancourt's Democratic Action Party won leadership of the country. From October 19, 1945, to February 14, 1948, Betancourt was Chief of State. His administration's conduct indicated his party's strict adherence to democratic ideals. Human rights were respected. The first free election under a universal suffrage system was held. Several social reforms were put into effect as a result of an equitable levying of taxes, augmenting huge royalties paid by the petroleum companies and other big industries. Land was given to farmers, and schools, hospitals, roads, and houses were built for the people.

That was a period of feverish activity in Venezuela. The AD party, supported by the labor movement, wanted to recover in a few years from the decades of neglect and stagnation that had marked the preceding governments, especially the long Gómez dictatorship. Betancourt and his young collaborators were perhaps too anxious and moved perhaps in too many directions at the same time. Mistakes were inevitably made, but they were the mistakes of honest ambitious youth, impatient of delay, anxious to achieve. I remember in this connection an encounter with Augusto Malavé Villalba, in June 1948, in San Francisco, during the ILO annual conference. I had to spend my limited free time going around with him visiting stores and shops to see what there was of use that the Venezuelans themselves could begin to produce. At that time Venezuela was importing practically all manufactured household and farming implements, in addition to canned food, eggs, etc. And so we went driving up north of San Francisco, in the so-called egg basket of North America, to study the operation of poultry farms, and then visited canning factories, especially those devoted to baby food. "The babies of our workers," lamented Malavé, "cannot have this imported healthy food because it is too expensive. We must produce it ourselves in Venezuela. . . ."

The Communist Party, legalized before Betancourt took office, bitterly opposed him and his successor, Rómulo Gallegos. In the presidential election of December 14, 1947, the Communist Party won only 37,000 out of more than 1,200,000 votes cast. Betancourt optimistically told me: "They are asphyxiated in the climate of democracy."

Meanwhile, Communists holding important positions in the Venezuelan labor movement were ousted. The Federation of Petroleum Workers took such action early in 1947. In his farewell message to Congress (February 12, 1948), Betancourt congratulated the Federation, saying it had excluded persons who were unable to conceive of the solution of labor-managemnt problems without abusing the right to strike.

In April 1948 Betancourt headed the Venezuelan delegation to the Ninth Inter-American Conference, in Bogotá, Colombia. At Bogotá, Betancourt backed the main anti-Communist resolution but called for its amendment to include "every other form of totalitarianism" as well.

During the thirty months of his Provisional Presidency, Betancourt was faced with frequent attempts on the part of the military to interfere with his prerogatives. A number of conspiracies to overthrow the government were also discovered. Rómulo used tact, diplomacy, and, when necessary, force to contain the military. He learned how to bend, occasionally, in order to gain time to readjust the situation later. But Betancourt's successor, the popularly elected President Rómulo Gallegos, *El Maestro* (The Teacher) as the Venezuelan workers, peasants, and intellectuals affectionately called him, adopted a rigid, uncompromising posture. When the military served him with an ultimatum, President Gallegos refused to negotiate. On November 24, 1948, a military coup deposed him and installed a three-man military junta, headed by Colonel Carlos Delgado Chalbaud.[1] Venezuela had entered another priod of dictatorship which was to last almost ten years.

Rómulo Betancourt was the first Venezuelan democratic leader whom the military junta exiled. In January 1949 he settled down with his wife and daughter in a small modest home in the northwest section of Washington, D.C., within easy commuting distance from my apartment in Virginia. We began to visit each other quite frequently. What impressed me most in our conversations was the absolute absence in Rómulo of any feeling of depressing defeat, of any brooding tendency, so common among political exiles, to blame others for the reverses suffered by his Party. Betancourt had no time for that. He felt, quite realistically, that the struggle to regain freedom in Venezuela would be a long and bitter one; but he was sure that his Democratic Action Party, supported by the masses of organized workers and peasants, would someday return to power. He was also sure that AD democratic opponents inside Venezuela, who had been led by political partisanship to rejoice over the overthrow of the Rómulo Gallegos administration, would themselves soon fall victim to the heavy hand of the dictatorship and would find it necessary and desirable to seek a rapprochement with the AD group.

Betancourt realized, also, that the survival of democracy in Latin America could no longer be left to the initiative and strength of the democratic forces in each threatened country. He felt that in order to survive the democratic forces would have to fight on a hemispheric basis, with close cooperation between Latin America and the United States. Thus was born the idea of calling a conference, sponsored by a distinguished committee of leading political figures, intellectuals, and labor leaders, which would give them for the first time an opportunity to get together in order to discuss and plan, free from governmental pressure or diplomatic limitations, what the people of the Americas could do together to fight totalitarianism and strengthen democracy and freedom.

One person who had already distinguished herself in the efforts to link together the democratic forces of the Western Hemisphere was Miss Frances Grant of New York, President of the Pan American Women's Association and leading figure in the International League for the Rights of Man. She responded enthusiastically to the idea of an inter-American democratic conference. The three of us—Rómulo, Miss Grant, and myself —went to work with the determination of making something of real lasting historical value. We agreed that Havana would be a convenient seat for the Conference, not only because of its geographical location but also for the support we confidently expected from the Cuban government of President Carlos Prío Socarrás. We decided, also, that the month of May 1950 would offer the most suitable date.

Toward the end of January 1950 Rómulo Betancourt went to Havana to explore the situation and to make the necessary arrangements. On February 10, he sent me the following encouraging letter:

I am pleased to inform you that the Cuban government has accepted the idea to hold here the proposed democratic conference. President Prío Socarrás has expressed to me his enthusiastic support and his determination to cooperate in order to assure its success. I have also had interviews with Minister of Education [Aureliano] Sánchez Arango and with other elements not connected with the government but who are nevertheless influential in Cuban public life. Also, I exchanged impressions with labor leaders [Eusebio] Mujal and [Francisco] Aguirre, who immediately lined up in favor of the conference. The situation appears so favorable that I am sure I'll be able to leave behind a widely based Reception and Organization Committee of great political and intellectual prestige.

The arrangements that Rómulo made, we later learned from him, could not have been better. Minister of Education Aureliano Sánchez Arango had offered to underwrite the hotel expenses for all the delegates during their stay in Havana; had provided a grant to finance the secretarial work of the Conference Organization and Reception Committee, and was even able to offer air passage to those Latin American delegates who otherwise would have been unable to attend. However, the conference would have lost much of its anticipated political significance and influence without the participation of a large representative delegation from the United States. Much progress was made toward obtaining attendance of a good number of Congressmen and many distinguished personalities representing various sectors and political beliefs of the American people. However, most of the prospective participants, although assured that all expenses in Havana would be provided for, were in no position to pay out of their own pocket the considerable cost of the round trip air ticket. We were thus threatened with the prospect of too many "regrets," which would have greatly thinned the ranks of the U.S. contingent. If we had asked our Cuban friends to provide the passage for the North Americans too they would undoubtedly have responded in the affirmative, but I ruled out this solution as too humiliating and politically dangerous. Fortunately, my friend Nelson A. Rockefeller, to whom I confided the plight we were in, came to our rescue with a generous grant which enabled us to pay for all the needed airline tickets and for some of the other expenses connected with the preparatory work of the conference here in the United States.

In April Betancourt went back to Havana to take personal charge of the last phase of the arrangements. Invitations to prospective participants from the United States and Latin America were sent by the organizing committee.[2] The invitations were accompanied by a memorandum which emphasized the growing menace of the totalitarian forces both from the right and from the left, and warned that "the recent rise to power of authoritarian governments within several American republics constitutes a critical menace to the free exercise of fundamental human rights."

Although only a couple of months were given to the preparation of this conference, and in spite of the fact that the promoters had to contend from the very beginning with open hostility on the part of Communists and the half dozen or so military dictatorships and ultra-reactionary Latin American governments—not to mention the "fear" and the "concern" on the part of other governments anxious not to hurt the feelings of the pro-Fascist dictators on this side of the Atlantic—close to one hundred fifty delegates assembled in the Capitol at Havana on the night of May 12, 1950, for this historic meeting. They came from Argentina, Uruguay, Chile, Peru, Colombia, Panama, Venezuela, Costa Rica, Nicaragua, Guatemala, Mexico, Puerto Rico, Dominican Republic, Cuba, and the United States.[3] Some of them were outstanding intellectuals, political leaders, and labor men living in exile; others were Congressmen, Senators, Cabinet Ministers, journalists, university professors, and labor leaders from countries where democracy was strong and secure. Three former Presidents of Latin American Republics, each one of them a sterling champion of progressive legislation and labor rights, joined in the parley —Eduardo Santos of Colombia, Rómulo Betancourt of Venezuela, and José Figueres of Costa Rica. Among those who in later years were elected to the highest office in their respective countries were Dr. Ramón Villeda Morales of Honduras, Eduardo Frei of Chile, and Dr. Carlos Lleras Restrepo of Colombia.

Messages of greeting were received from President William Green of the American Federation of Labor, Mrs. Eleanor Roosevelt, Senator Herbert Lehman, Senator Hubert Humphrey, former Attorney General Francis Biddle, President Philip Murray of the CIO, former President of Venezuela Rómulo Gallegos, Governor Múñoz Marín of Puerto Rico, and Dr. Max Ascoli, publisher of The Reporter.

President Dr. Carlos Prío Socarrás of Cuba was represented at the inaugural ceremony by the President of the Senate, Dr. Miguel Suárez Fernández, who presided and delivered the keynote address. Congressman Chet Holifield spoke for the United States group.

The conference was primarily conceived for the two-fold purpose of demonstrating inter-American democratic solidarity against every form of totalitarianism and to set up a permanent organization that would coordinate future work not only within the Western Hemisphere, but, if necessary, with similar organizations in other parts of the world. Both purposes were well achieved.

The democratic solidarity of the people of the Americas was admirably expressed and proclaimed in the Declaration of Havana, the major policy statement of the conference in which the slogan of the Act of Chapulte-pec [4] was reaffirmed as a solemn act of faith and a collective pledge— "America cannot live without justice. Nor can America live without freedom."

The Declaration of Havana condemned in strong language Communism, Fascism, Falangism, and Nazism; proclaimed the necessity of raising the standard of living of the people in order to make democracy work; advocated the unfettered enjoyment of political, trade union, civic, and religious rights; reaffirmed the policy of nonintervention in the internal affairs of a sovereign state, but raised the issue of recognition of those *de facto* governments that are the result of military insurrection against constitutional regimes.

It was fortunate, indeed, that the United States delegation was so numerous and so representative of the progressive, labor, and liberal elements of our country. The Latin Americans had no difficulty in getting along with them and, I hasten to say, in becoming real friends. There was no feeling of suspicion, no indication of studied reserve. The result was that the conference was free of the old stereotyped and rancid slogans on Yankee imperialism, which no longer served any useful purpose except to furnish ammunition to the Communists. On the other hand, the conference was unanimous in advocating honest and sound measures to strengthen the democratic way of life against totalitarian infiltration and aggression and to protect the people against the ravages of economic and political imperialism, whether from the Colossus of the North, the Bear of the East, the Caudillo of Madrid, or the Demagogue of the Plata River. To accomplish these aims, the conference unanimously resolved to set up the Inter-American Association for Democracy and Freedom, with central headquarters in Montevideo, Uruguay, but with a permanent committee in the United States, with offices in New York.

One of the first acts of the Venezuelan military junta upon seizing power in November 1948, was to dissolve the Confederation of Labor (CTV) and all its state branches. The CTV, organized at a national labor convention in 1947, was solidly under AD control. Some of its leaders had also been elected members of Congress and the Senate. Originally, the labor movement of Venezuela was strongly under Communist influence, but at the Second Workers' Congress which met in Caracas in the middle of 1944, with CTAL President Lombardo Toledano in attendance, the

AD forces felt strong enough to prevent the election of a Communist leadership. They rapidly gained control of the most important unions, especially after the regime of General Medina Angarita, who had been partial to the Communists, was overthrown in October 1945. The military junta realized that unless the democratic unions were smashed, its regime would be highly insecure.

After the CTV, the military junta dissolved forty-seven oil workers' unions which made up the Federation of Oil Workers of Venezuela; their funds, property and files were attached and their leaders taken into custody.

At about the same time the National Federations of Farm, Construction, Textile, Garment, and Dock Workers and the Printers' Union of the Federal District were also dissolved.

A decree of the Minister of Labor on March 9, 1949, ordered new elections in all local unions, setting up limitations for the eligibility of the new Boards which were a clear violation of trade union rights. As a result of these limitations, no member who had served in previous administrations could be elected.

The government hoped through this device to gain control of the Venezuelan labor movement, but it failed. In almost every local where elections were held, elements loyal to the democratic leadership of the dissolved Confederation of Labor gained control of the administration. The government then resorted again to arbitrary measures, such as confiscation of funds and property, padlocking of headquarters, disbanding of meetings and arrest of leaders, which made it impossible for the unions to continue to exist.

In every city and town and in the oil fields hundreds of labor leaders were arrested. Many of them remained in jail for many years without charges. Among them were Pedro B. Pérez Salinas, President of the CTV; Luis Tovar, President of the Petroleum Workers Federation; José González Navarro, President of the Federation of Workers of the State of Miranda and the Federal District; Hermenegildo Borromé of the Federation of Workers of the State of Monagas; Alcides Rondón, leader of the same Federation; Jesús Amundaráin and González Castillo, leaders of the petroleum unions.

Five hundred prisoners, among them the leader of the Printers' Federation, Raul Acosta, were removed to Guasina Island, at the delta of the Orinoco River, a very unhealthy place with no buildings and nothing that could assure a minimum of safety.

On Columbus Day, 1951, isolated groups of citizens staged violent protests against the continued suppression of civil rights. Following these protests many of the arrested labor leaders were subject to brutal physical torture in the cells of the prison at Caracas and in improvised torture chambers of the National Security Police. Here are some of the most glaring examples of such tortures.

Salom Meza, leader of the National Association of Commercial Employees and ex-member of the Caracas Municipal Council, had his arms and legs dislocated, his eardrums were broken, and he developed serious nose and mouth hemorrhages.

Trade union leaders Humberto Hernández and Lucas Pérez were kept incommunicado for three months in a dark, solitary cell. They were beaten repeatedly and subjected to the "wet treatment" of having buckets of water thrown over them.

Gustavo Ravelo, Crisólogo Ravelo, Desiderio Martínez, Rafael Ángel Prieto, Efrain Colina, and other Venezuelan trade union leaders were subjected to severe beatings for ten consecutive days at the headquarters of the National Guard and fed only bread and water. One of the prisoners, Lino Núñez, suffered such severe cuts that he had to be taken to the Emergency Hospital of Caracas.

Another group of workers were kept for four days completely naked in a solitary cell, compelled to sit on blocks of ice, beaten repeatedly, and subjected to electric shocks. A well-known trade unionist, Eloy Martínez Méndez, was beaten so severely that he fell into a coma. A shoe worker, Armando Díaz, was hung by his feet for two days, as a result of which he suffered several bone fractures in his right foot.

During the long police interrogation labor people were often subjected to a special torture called "tortol," which means that ropes were tied around the victim's wrists and tightened until he lost consciousness. Complete details of these tortures were recorded in *Informaciones Venezolanas,* a clandestine publication circulated by the democratic political and trade union opposition.

The labor movement throughout the world reacted quickly against the antilabor policy of the Venezuelan government.

The first protest was voiced by the labor members of the ILO Governing Body on December 10, 1948. From then on hardly a month passed without such protests being registered from different parts of the world. President William Green of the American Federation of Labor was one of the first to pledge complete solidarity of the free labor movement of the United States with the persecuted trade unionists of Venezuela. Every

AFL convention from 1949 on, as well as every international trade union gathering, consistently added its voice of protest.

Following the approval of a resolution at the ILO's Western Hemisphere regional conference in Montevideo in May, 1949 (see Chapter VI), in which an investigation of labor conditions in Venezuela was demanded, a committee of the ILO visited that country for seven weeks during the summer of 1949 and published a report in which violations of labor's rights were attested and condemned.[5] Nothing, however, was done by the Venezuelan government to remedy the situation.

In June 1950, at the ILO Conference in Geneva, the spurious worker delegate appointed by the Venezuelan military government was denied admission by unanimous recommendation of the Credentials Committee.[6] This stinging rebuke was administered in the hope that the Venezuelan government would finally mend its ways, but again nothing was done.

From time to time the Venezuelan dictatorship issued statements alleging that the democratic political and labor opposition was cooperating with the Communists. These statements were issued with the intent of confusing international public opinion and gaining the support of the democratic governments of the West, particularly the United States, which were already engaged in what was then considered a fight to the finish with the international Communist conspiracy.

The truth of the matter was that no group in Venezuela had been or was more opposed to the Communists than the CTV and the Democratic Action Party. In 1945 the Communists took up arms in order to fight in the streets of Caracas the democratic forces which had organized the provisional government headed by Betancourt.

After the military coup of November 1948, the Communists openly supported the military government, receiving in exchange complete freedom of action, especially in the field of labor, where they attempted to supersede the democratic leadership.

In the middle of 1949 the open support of the Communist elements became a liability to the military government of Venezuela. The Communist Party then was disbanded, but this was done mainly for reasons of international opportunism. A Communist splinter group, known as "Black Communists," was never disturbed and remained almost to the end the main prop of the military government in the so-called leftist sector of the nation. Legal recognition was extended to a rump group under Communist control in Caracas, the so-called Federation of Workers of the Federal District, under the leadership of Rodolfo Quintero, a leader of the Black Communists. Quintero was official delegate to the

World Federation of Trade Unions Congress in Milan in the summer of 1951. Subsequently he was taken on an all-expense tour of "People's Hungary" by the Communist rulers of that country.

Quintero headed a Venezuelan delegation to the 1953 Congress of the Communist-controlled CTAL of Lombardo Toledano in Santiago, Chile, and was elected there to the Executive Committee of the CTAL. Upon his return home, in May 1953, he held a Convention of his Federation in Caracas. The Convention, which was preceded by a mass meeting, could have been held only with the overt support of the military dictatorship. According to reports of observers present at the meeting, it had all the earmarks of a semiofficial gathering.

The Communists loyal to Moscow, known in Venezuela as "Red Communists," were never completely prevented from being active throughout the country and from freely traveling abroad to attend conferences of the Communist International, the World Federation of Trade Unions, and other fellow traveling groups. When not engaged in gathering signatures for the Moscow inspired peace appeals, the Venezuelan Communists concentrated their fire against AD and its trade union leadership, which they accused of being "agents of Yankee imperialism." *Venezuelan News,* the so-called clandestine publication of the Communists, devoted five of eight pages of a 1951 issue to a violent attack against Rómulo Betancourt and his Democratic Action Party, as well as the labor leaders allied with it, whom the Communists accused of "getting ready to seize power in order to serve the interests of the warmonger oil barons."

The VI National Conference of the Communist Party of Venezuela, held in the spring of 1951, reaffirmed that "the duty of the Communists is to fight without quarter the political movement headed by Rómulo Betancourt and the trade union movement headed by Augusto Malavé Villalba." This was reported in the April 1951 issue of the clandestine Communist paper circulated in Caracas. On May 18, 1951, Radio Moscow approved the decision of the VI National Conference of the Venezuelan Communist Party, emphasizing the pledge of "continued opposition to the Democratic Action Party and the Confederation of Labor."

In order to dispel any possible doubt as to the anti-Communist sentiments of the opposition movement in Venezuela, the leaders of AD, in conjunction with the leadership of the CTV-in-Exile, in November 1951 issued a strong statement—which was widely circulated in Venezuela—reaffirming their uncompromising opposition to the Communist Party, which they rightly termed as nothing else than a tool of Soviet imperialism.

On November 13, 1950, the military junta of Venezuela went through a bloody reorganization. Its President was assassinated by a member of the Security Police, who declared that he had acted under orders of junta member Colonel Marcos Pérez Jiménez. The assassin, "General" Rafael Simón Urbina, was in turn shot to death by the Security Police before he could be brought to trial. Under pressure of public opinion, which pointed to Colonel Pérez Jiménez as chief inspirer of the double assassination, a civilian, Dr. Germán Suárez Flamerich, assumed the presidency of the junta, but the real power rested in the hands of Jiménez, who started preparations for an "election" that would make him "legal" President. As a further step toward this goal, Pérez Jiménez at one point sent his junta partners abroad and declared himself Provisional President.

This move on the part of Pérez Jiménez was the direct result of the growing strength of the AD-CTV clandestine operations. From his exile in Havana, where he had gone from the United States in the fall of 1950, Rómulo Betancourt had organized a near-perfect system of communications with his underground lieutenants. Augusto Malavé Villalba, also in Havana, was maintaining contacts with the outlawed labor movement, including the scores of top leaders who were in jail. Dr. Leonardo Ruiz Pineda, General Secretary of the AD Party underground apparatus, had succeeded in establishing a mobile clandestine radio station, "La Voz de la Resistencia," from which constant contact was maintained with the rank and file in every corner of the republic.

On October 18, 1950, the clandestine radio broadcast the following fiery appeal sent by Betancourt from his Havana exile:

We have fulfilled our duty to resist, and we have done it without vacillation. Thousands of our members have gone to jail, where they withstood incredible tortures. Hundreds of others have faced with prideful dignity the test of exile. Scores of labor, political, and student leaders are risking their lives daily, without fear, in order to direct the clandestine activity of our Party. Day after day, men and women belonging to our organization are defying all kinds of persecutions, inspired by the mystic love for Country and Freedom which, after that magnificent display of collective energy which was our long and bloody struggle for our Independence, appeared to have vanished in Venezuela. But if we have shown our ability to discharge our duty when it was time to prove to the rampant barbarism that there was in Venezuela a reserve of democratic resistance, we would be accomplishing only half of our duty toward Venezuela if we were now to reveal ourselves incapable of giving the final push to destroy this putrid creaking hulk which calls itself the Governing Military Junta. We shall discharge this duty also. It would be an exercise in irresponsible adventurism if we were to determine in advance the method and the time limit to accomplish this objective. We are neither a band of professional conspirators nor a confraternity of bureaucrats who have lost their jobs. We are a political party, the first great mass party ever organized in Venezuela with a coherent platform and a realistic program of action. (Translation mine—S.R.)

Pérez Jiménez answered the militantly defiant attitude of his labor and democratic opposition with increased terror. Arrests were multiplied. The political inmates in the concentration camps in the Orinoco River delta and in the jails of Venezuela reached into the thousands. The international free labor movement was frantically trying to stop this veritable genocide. The International Confederation of Free Trade Unions decided to denounce the Venezuelan military regime to the United Nations Commission on Human Rights. It gathered impressive supporting material with a complete list of hundreds of trade union prisoners, mostly supplied by Rómulo Betancourt and his groups in exile. Here in the United States, we felt that the time had come to file an official protest with the government of Venezuela itself. Accordingly, on March 1, 1951, a committee composed of Anthony Boyle, representing the United Mine Workers of America,[7] Dr. Ernest Schwarz, of the Congress of Industrial Organizations, and myself, on behalf of the American Federation of Labor, visited Venezuelan Ambassador Dr. Antonio Martín Araujo. We delivered to him a memorandum which read in part:

We have received information from Venezuela that a number of trade union leaders have been arrested and are being detained in the Cárcel Modelo of Caracas, and in the Penitenciaria of San Juan de los Morros, without any formal charges and without having had the opportunity to appear before a judge so that they might learn the reasons for their detention.

While we do not wish to appear as interfering in the internal affairs of the Republic of Venezuela, we feel, nevertheless, that it is the duty of the labor movement of this country, as well as the labor movement of any other free country, to express solidarity with our brothers in Venezuela and offer them a helping hand so that they may soon regain their freedom.

We would be very grateful to Your Excellency if you would convey to your government the sincere preoccupation of the labor movement of the United States over the status of the organized labor movement in Venezuela and particularly of those labor leaders who are in jail. Since it is obvious that they have not committed any crime, otherwise there would have been specific charges against them, we hope that they will be set free without delay.

The interview with Ambassador Araujo lasted more than one hour. At the beginning, he adopted a cold and reserved attitude, interrupting often to state that Venezuelans could not accept lessons from anybody on matters of internal policy. Later, however, he put aside the official posture and spoke to us off the record, admitting that he too was very much preoccupied with the trade union situation in his country, and promised to do his best to convey to his government the concern of the international democratic trade union movement for the repressive antilabor measures adopted in Venezuela. He also added that he was in favor of letting the democratic trade unionists resume their normal activities, but remarked that he was perhaps the only Venezuelan official to advocate such a conciliatory policy.

The tone of the off-the-record conversation baffled me. What was the meaning of his rather unusual remarks? The answer came almost one year later, from the Ambassador himself, when he phoned me for an interview.

"I'll come to the Embassy, right away," I answered.

"No, not at the Embassy," he replied. *"La commedia è finita*—The comedy is over. I have resigned! . . ." [8]

Whenever I had the opportunity, in Washington, Havana, Costa Rica, Puerto Rico, and Venezuela itself, I always tried to induce Rómulo Betancourt to relax a little, even to indulge in a bit of gastronomic enjoyment which most times consisted of spaghetti with sauce "a la Romualdi," [9] preceded, accompanied, and followed by good, clear, first quality red wine. On some occasions, a selected number of friends would join; and when Luis Múñoz Marín, the Governor of Puerto Rico, and his lovely, artistically minded Doña Inez were in the party, the evening always turned out perfect. We would invariably start by pledging "no politics tonight—just good eating and a good time," and just as invariably would wind up eagerly discussing the whole spectrum of inter-American events, personalities, trends, mistakes, remedies, with occasional forays into literature and art, philosophy and religion, and frequent relapses into plans and plots! Of course, Rómulo and the other guests well knew that to make me happy, the obbligato parting remark at the end of the evening would have to be the well-deserved: "Your spaghetti is always excellent, Serafino; but tonight it was really superb!"

But one night in Costa Rica there were no such compliments, and for good reason. My wife Miriam and I had returned to Rómulo's modest and cold flat late in the afternoon. Nevertheless, it was decided to have spaghetti, even if that meant delaying the supper for at least three hours. All those who could be of some help were invited by Doña Carmen, Rómulo's wife, to come to the kitchen to help—chopping onions, carrots, celery, and parsley, opening cans, gathering spices. Then some guests came in, among them Dr. Raul Leoni (the same Leoni who, in 1964, succeeded Betancourt to the presidency of Venezuela) and his wife Doña Menca. Leoni barged into the kitchen and started tasting the sauce which had barely begun to simmer.

"It's ready," he said. "Let's raise the water to a boil and put the spaghetti in. I am hungry as a horse."

"No," I replied insistently. "The sauce must simmer for at least two hours. You are the son of a Corsican, and whoever heard of a Corsican being an authority on spaghetti sauce?"

But in the end the pressure became irresistible. I surrendered to the clamor of the hungry ones. Of course, the process of blending the various ingredients in the sauce into a pleasant, aromatic whole was far from being completed. And when that sauce was finally eaten, the experts (Rómulo and I, for instance) did not hum any Ohs!!! of pleasure nor did they smack their lips. That night, my culinary reputation was almost ruined!

Notes

1. The other members of the junta were Lieutenant Colonels Llovera Páez and Marcos Pérez Jiménez.
2. In Latin America, the preparations for the conference were carried on by the Junta Americana de Defensa de la Democracia, with headquarters in Montevideo, Uruguay. The Latin American Organizing Committee included:

Francisco Aguirre, General Secretary, Inter-American Confederation of Workers, Member Cuban House of Representatives
Dr. German Arciniegas, Columbia University, former Colombian Minister of Education
Dr. Gonzalo Barrios, former Venezuelan Minister of Foreign Affairs
Dr. Rómulo Betancourt, former President of Venezuela
Juan Bosch, Dominican writer
José Figueres, former President of Costa Rica
Eduardo Frei, Member of Congress, Chile
Dr. Emilio Frugoni, Member of Congress and leader of the Socialist Party of Uruguay
Bernardo Ibáñez, Chile, Vice-President for Latin America, ICFTU
Dr. Jorge Manach, University of Havana
Dr. Levi Marrero, Cuban educator and author
Dr. Ángel Morales, former Ambassador from the Dominican Republic to the United States
Senator Eusebio Mujal, General Secretary, Confederation of Labor of Cuba
Dr. Fernando Ortiz, Cuban author
Dr. Herminio Portell Vilá, University of Havana
Miguel Ángel Quevedo, Editor, *Bohemia,* Havana
Senator Valmore Rodríguez, former President of Congress, Venezuela
Dr. Eduardo Rodríguez Larreta, Editor, *El Pais,* Montevideo

Dr. Lincoln Rondón, President, Cuban House of Representatives
Ernesto Sanmartino, former Member of Congress, Argentina
Dr. Aureliano Sánchez Arango, Minister of Education, Cuba
Dr. Luis Alberto Sánchez, Rector, University of San Marcos, Lima
Senator Manuel Seoane, Peru
Dr. Miguel Suárez Fernández, President of the Cuban Senate
Congressman Adolfo Tejera, Uruguay

The United States Organizing Committee which signed the invitations included:

Dr. Max Ascoli, Editor-Publisher, *The Reporter*
Roger Baldwin, Chairman, International League for the Rights of Man
Pearl Buck, Nobel Prize winner for Literature
Leon M. Birkhead, Director, Friends of Democracy, Inc.
Francine Alessi Dunlavy, Pan American Women's Association
Frances R. Grant, Chairman for Latin America, International League for the Rights of Man
Professor Sidney Hook, New York University
Dr. Alvin Johnson, President Emeritus, New School for Social Research
Charles M. La Follette, National Director, Americans for Democratic Action
Archibald MacLeish, former Assistant Secretary of State
John Mundt, Jr., New York Young Republican Club
Serafino Romualdi, Latin American Representative, American Federation of Labor
Dr. Ernst Schwarz, Secretary, Committee on Latin American Affairs, CIO
Walter White, Secretary, National Association for the Advancement of Colored People

3. The Delegation from the United States included three representatives of the American Federation of Labor (George P. Delaney, Charles Zimmerman, and Serafino Romualdi), Dr. Ernst Schwarz of the CIO, Congressmen Clifford Case, Republican of New Jersey; Chet Holifield, Democrat of California; Clinton C. McKinnon, Democrat of California; and Charles Howell, Democrat of New Jersey; representatives of Americans for Democratic Action, among them James Loeb, Alfredo Giardino, Professor Arthur Schlesinger, Jr., of Harvard, and Professor Bryn Hovde, of the New School for Social Research; Walter White, of the National Association for the Advancement of Colored People; Robert J. Alexander, of Rutgers University; Roger Baldwin and Frances Grant, of the International League for the Rights of Man; Norman Thomas of the Socialist Party; John Mundt, Jr., for the Young Republicans; Robert Hastings Lounsbery, for the Young Democrats; Sol Levitas, Executive Editor of *The New Leader*, and the noted writer Waldo Frank. Also there were Mrs. Francine Alessi Donlavy of the Pan American Women's Association; Clarence Senior, for the League for Industrial Democracy, and Emanuel Demby, for the Friends of Democracy, Inc.

4. The Inter-American Conference on Problems of War and Peace, meeting at Chapultepec in Mexico City, February 21–March 8, 1945, adopted a set of principles governing the reorganization of the inter-American system, embodied in an agreement entitled the Act of Chapultepec.

5. The ILO Committee, headed by Jef Rens, ILO senior Assistant Director General, stated in its report that "freedom of association in Venezuela is far from being complete. The Venezuelan unions do not at present enjoy a freedom of action and organization comparable to that enjoyed by countries in which the functioning of workers' organizations is protected from legal or administrative restrictions."

6. Members of the Credentials Committee were Mario Cingolani of Italy, chairman; Julio B. Pons of Uruguay, representing the employers, and George P. Delaney of the United States, representing the workers. Their report was approved by the Conference with 95 votes in favor, 4 against, and 50 abstentions. The negative votes were cast by

the Venezuelan government (2 votes), and the Venezuelan employer and worker delegates (one vote each).

The worker delegates present at the session when the vote was taken were 33 and they were unanimous in support of the recommendation of the Credentials Committee. Fifty government delegates voted in favor, among them those of Canada, Chile, Cuba, Guatemala, the United States, and Uruguay. The employer's group largely abstained. Of the 12 who voted in favor only one (Pons of Uruguay) was from the Western Hemisphere.

7. Anthony Boyle succeeded John L. Lewis to the presidency of the United Mine Workers of America.

8. After the downfall of the Pérez Jiménez dictatorship, Ambassador Araujo rejoined the Venezuelan diplomatic service. At the time of this writing he was Ambassador to Canada.

9. Briefly, this is how the Romualdi spaghetti sauce is made for a serving of eight: Put four good-sized chopped onions with parsley and a few garlic cloves in hot olive oil in a large iron pot. When browned, add chopped lean beef reinforced by either Italian pork sausages or kosher salami cut in very small pieces, depending on the dietetic preferences of the guests. Stir constantly to permit browning but prevent burning. Then add half a cup of cooking sherry, and, a few minutes later, one large can of Italian peeled tomatoes, one small can of tomato paste and an equal amount, using the empty small can, of hot water. Add two carrots, two celery stalks and half a green pepper, all finely chopped by hand. Blender is tolerated for carrots but not for the celery and green peppers. Lower the heat to simmer. Add spices consisting of salt, pepper, monosodium glutamate, oregano, basil, Italian seasoning, paprika, cayenne, a dash of tabasco, two spoonfuls of sugar or sucaryl. Quantity is determined by experience and touch; perfection is reached only through trial and error. However, always be careful with the pepper, cayenne, and tabasco. Let simmer for at least two-and-a-half hours. Stir frequently.

XXVI

The Jiménez Dictatorship

A CLANDESTINE PAMPHLET, circulated in Caracas by the underground AD on January 2, 1951, warned that Pérez Jiménez was plotting the assassination of Rómulo Betancourt. The story charged that $300,000 had been put at the disposal of a group of international gangsters to carry out the plan. Since by then it was abundantly clear that Pérez Jiménez was using assassination as a normal method of operation to eliminate friendly rivals and bitter foes alike, the warning stirred considerable concern over Rómulo's safety. Cuban President Carlos Prío Socarrás ordered a detail of plainclothesmen to watch Betancourt's residence in Havana constantly and to accompany him whenever he went outside. But despite the government-assigned guards, Betancourt liked to go out alone sometimes because, as he explained to me in answer to my concern, "One feels as if he were confined to a moving jail when he is constantly accompanied by bodyguards."

On the afternoon of April 10, 1951, Betancourt was coming out of a clinic in the Vedado district of Havana and preparing to enter his car when he heard rapid footsteps behind him. Before he could turn, a man grabbed him and Betancourt felt a pricking in his left arm. As Betancourt swung around, the assailant, a tall, shabby mulatto, dropped the assault weapon, a homemade brass syringe, and ran off down the street. Betancourt picked up the syringe and went straight back to his doctor and got a shot of antitoxin. The doctor said that the needle had bent while being

454

inserted and none of the liquid in the syringe had entered Betancourt's bloodstream. A police analyst later reported that the hypodermic contained "hiperita," which he described as a liquefied poison gas, developed in Germany, which can kill in a matter of seconds.[1]

The attempted assassination of Betancourt caused commotion throughout the world, particularly inside Venezuela. But Rómulo himself was not shaken. With an iron, determined calm, he told interviewing newspapermen that "this attempt was planned, organized, and financed by the military junta in Venezuela," and vowed that the struggle for its downfall would continue unabated. To me he wrote, on April 30:

> You know me. I will not lower the flag of battle. I will continue to stand more determined than ever at the front of my ideological trench. And if I should ever waver, the thought of those who are fighting with sublime valor against the dictatorship inside Venezuela should be enough to dispel any possible doubt.

The answer of the Venezuelan workers to Pérez Jiménez's murderous attempt was given on May Day. Tens of thousands of workers paraded peacefully through the streets of Caracas, carrying slogans demanding the release of labor and political prisoners, the reestablishment of constitutional guarantees, and the right to strike. Also, for the first time there appeared a placard with the legend *"Viva ORIT*–Long Live ORIT." The police intervened, clubs and guns were given free play, and the demonstrators were dispersed after dozens were arrested. Betancourt sent me clippings of the May 2, 1951, edition of the Caracas daily *El Nacional*, containing detailed accounts of the demonstration, complete with pictures of the placards carried by the workers. He commented in a letter to me of May 10: "The great objective of the demonstration was achieved: to mobilize the workers and reawaken in them the consciousness of their immense power in the service of freedom."

Starting in 1952, the Venezuelan dictatorship began to organize its own labor movement for the purpose of getting control of the trade unions and preventing their being used by the groups opposing the dictatorship. A so-called Movimiento Sindical de Trabajadores (MOSIT) was established, and the government constructed a luxurious Trade Union House for it in Caracas, with smaller buildings of the same type in several interior cities.

MOSIT made its international debut at the V Conference of American States members of the ILO, which was held in Petropolis, Brazil, on April 17–30, 1952. The Venezuelan worker delegation [2] was selected from its ranks. Their credentials were challenged on the basis of a detailed documentation showing numerous cases of violation of trade union rights and interference on the part of the government with the independent development of the trade union movement. However, the objection was later withdrawn, at the insistence of the Conference's Workers' Group, on the basis of a signed statement offered by the Venezuelan workers' delegates in which they "pledged to fight for the reestablishment of trade union rights, for the release of labor prisoners detained in jail without any specific charge, for the reestablishment of the Venezuelan Confederation of Labor through the holding of a national labor congress, and for the alignment of Venezuelan labor with the worldwide free trade union movement."

The decision of the Workers' Group to withdraw the challenge was preceded by a long and bitter debate, but in the end it was approved because those who wanted to press the charges simply did not have the votes. The ORIT and ICFTU General Secretaries, Francisco Aguirre of Cuba and Jacob H. Oldenbroeck of Brussels, respectively, who were attending the conference, pressured the Workers' Group with the argument that the Venezuelan delegates had received from their government a genuine mandate to make such pledges. They wanted to seize what they considered a good opportunity to influence the Venezuelan government toward releasing the hundreds of labor prisoners who were languishing in jail. However, the net result of this move was to give Pérez Jiménez, although only briefly for sure, the aura of a man of "good intentions," while our friends within Venezuela misunderstood the ICFTU-ORIT action and for a while reacted violently against it.

A telegram formally challenging the credentials of the Venezuelan worker delegates to the 1952 ILO Conference was sent by Augusto Malavé Villalba on behalf of the Venezuelan CTV in exile. However, the Workers' Group failed this time to act on the challenge submitted by the CTV—a failure which angered the CTV no end and for a while weakened their allegiance to ORIT-ICFTU.

The reason given by the spokesmen for ORIT-ICFTU in attendance at the ILO annual Conference in Geneva for their failure to press for action on the latest Venezuelan complaint was purely technical—the challenge arrived too late to be acted upon. Perhaps it was so; but it was also a fact, made undeniable by subsequent events, that European trade union leaders, supported by some of their colleagues from Latin America, were getting annoyed and tired by the frequent challenges coming from exiled labor groups whom they regarded as acting from political animosity rather than from true concern for the welfare of the labor movement.

The functional mentality prevailing at ILO Geneva headquarters considered the material bureaucratic structure of the trade unions a more important aspect than their adherence to the ideological struggle for the recovery of freedom and civil rights. The latter was often classified as political activity, perhaps to be tolerated but only when it did not lead to trouble with the government involved. In the specific case of Venezuela, the attitude prevailed that while it could not be denied that grave violations of trade union rights were still being committed, it would be best not to press the government too hard, in order to give it a chance gradually to restore trade union normalcy. It was wishful thinking pure and simple, but nevertheless convenient, because it helped gain time and it avoided the "annoyance" of another fight.

This attitude was being artfully encouraged by the government of Venezuela itself and by the spokesmen of the captive MOSIT, who by then proclaimed—in words, at least—their willingness to work for the unity of the Venezuelan labor movement (under their leadership, of course) and even to join ORIT and ICFTU—a prospect which somewhat appealed to the respective general secretaries, Aguirre and Oldenbroeck. However, after ORIT headquarters were moved from Havana to Mexico in January 1953 and Luis Alberto Monge succeeded Aguirre as General Secretary, the brief interlude of vacillation and wishful thinking came to an end. In this we were much helped by the leaders of MOSIT themselves, who in September 1952 publicly expressed solidarity with the military junta following the antigovernment uprising in the town of Maturín,[3] and who again came out in support of Pérez Jiménez after his brutal theft of the presidential elections of November 30.

The March 10, 1952, Batista *coup d'état* that overthrew the constitutional government of Cuban President Carlos Prío Socarrás forced Betancourt and his family to pack their meager belongings in a hurry and leave for another country. The day after he left Havana, just in time, Betancourt's house in Almendares was entered by the police with the pretext that they were looking for hidden arms! Betancourt chose Costa Rica, but in order to go there from Havana, he had to change airplanes in Miami. There, in spite of the fact that he had a valid visa for Costa Rica, he was stopped by an immigration inspector who held him for questioning. Rómulo managed to get in touch with Thomas Mann, at the State Department in Washington, and was finally allowed to proceed the following day. Rómulo wrote me as soon as he arrived in Costa Rica:

In spite of the fact that there was no scene, and no strangers were present to listen to the conversation and thus learn the nature of the incident, the press of the military junta in Venezuela published that I had been arrested in Miami. I am not committing even a venial sin of malice in supposing that some immigration officers informed the Venezuelan consulate. I am sending Miller [Edward, Assistant Secretary of State for Inter-American Affairs] a protest. I do not expect it to be answered. Just for the record.

Betancourt's wife, Carmen, was Costa Rican-born, and in addition to relatives on his wife's side Rómulo found in his new asylum a friendly democratic atmosphere and a public opinion, from President Otilio Ulate down, that surrounded him with respect, consideration, and understanding. He was soon able to write to me:

I have already recovered from the shock of the sudden flight. I am again working on my articles and books, and I am studying and preparing myself for the day when I may have to discharge again the responsibility of government.

News reaching Rómulo from Venezuela was greatly encouraging to the extent that it reflected the unbreakable will of the AD political and labor leadership to continue the struggle for freedom until the bitter end; but the price paid in suffering and blood was reaching frightful proportions. On April 13, 1952, hardly two weeks after his arrival in San José, Rómulo sent me a copy of a clandestine report he had received from Venezuela, dated the month before. The report said that in Caracas and Maracaibo the torture applied by the police to arrested suspects to force them to reveal the whereabouts of the AD leaders had reached inconceivable extremes. Thus a number of prominent underground political and labor leaders had been captured. "There are still 450 of our people in the Guasima camp, living in the worst possible conditions, without a change of clothing for over five months, sleeping on the bare ground, eating only fish and what they can hunt, without medical assistance, with three inmates already gone insane and two in advanced stage of tuberculosis." And the report went on to add that, "those in the Trujillo jail, more than three hundred, are literally starving and are kept locked up in their cells for twenty-four hours without a break, denied visits from their own relatives. . . . In San Juan de los Morros there are over two hundred, some of them for more than two years . . . in San Carlos thirty of our women are still there . . . more than two hundred fifty in Maracaibo, most of them subject to daily torture . . . three hundred more in the Obispo jail of Caracas and three hundred fifty in the Cárcel Modelo."

In the spring of 1952, giving in to national and international pressure, Pérez Jiménez made a cautious move to allow the "legalized" political parties, such as URD and COPEI, to conduct a minimum of public activity. But when URD held a mass meeting at the Nuevo Circo the AD underground forces attended in great number and helped transform the rally into a huge anti-government demonstration. People were shouting: "Guasima, Guasima, Guasima! . . ." The government answer was to intensify the arrests and the persecutions, especially among the AD labor leaders who had until then escaped the police net.

In the fall of 1952 ICFTU made an on-the-spot survey of the trade union conditions prevailing in Venezuela, by sending a mission composed of Francisco Aguirre, ORIT General Secretary, and Adrian Vermuelen, prominent leader of the Netherlands Federation of Labor and member of the Workers' Group of the ILO Governing Body. At the conclusion of that visit—which the Venezuelan democratic trade unionists did not oppose, although they had strong reservations as to its timing, just before the "elections" called by Pérez Jiménez—Aguirre and Vermuelen reported that the Venezuelan regime promised that before the elections scheduled for November 30, 1952, the jailed trade union leaders would be released and normalcy would return to the nation's labor movement by reestablishing freedom of trade union association. As will be amply demonstrated farther on, none of the promises were kept.

In the month of October 1952 the leader of the underground AD, Dr. Leonardo Ruiz Pineda, was machine-gunned in the streets of Caracas during a police raid. It was a murder in cold blood. World public opinion reacted with an angry protest. ORIT from Mexico City, as well as unions in the United States, expressed their indignation. For a moment, Rómulo felt almost prostrated. He wrote me:

The assassination of Leonardo has had a tremendous emotional impact on me. He grew up at my side, when he was studying at the University and I was building the party in the underground. For many long years we were bound by a close, loyal friendship. Yet, I must suppress the pain of this personal loss. War is war. I am continuing the struggle with the determination you well know.

After four years of dictatorial rule, Pérez Jiménez and his Venezuelan military clique thought that it would be safe to risk an election. Of course, the Democratic Action Party, the majority party of the country, was not allowed to participate. But the democratic forces, legal or illegal, rallied around the candidacy of Dr. Jovito Villalba, and when the votes were counted on the night of November 30 it became clear that the government had been defeated by a majority of more than two to one. So, at three o'clock in the morning, all the polling places were seized and the ballot boxes impounded, a strict censorship was imposed, and the leading members of the opposition party were arrested and the victorious candidate forced into a government plane and exiled to Panama. The count continued in secrecy, and two days later the government announced that Colonel Marcos Pérez Jiménez had gained the majority. Workers reacted with sporadic strikes of protest here and there. In Caracas, printers refused to work for several days; in Anzoátegui the oil workers struck for ten days; similar stoppages took place in the El Tigre oil fields. But the brutal intervention of the police and the military succeeded in repressing every form of protest. Two respected professionals, Castor Nieves Ríos and Dr. Germán González, were shot and killed at police headquarters. J. A. González, a teacher, was tortured and finally killed in jail.

During the first months of 1953, the police of Dictator Pérez Jiménez stepped up the arrests of those trade union leaders who had managed to remain at liberty in their underground activities. Among those who fell in the hands of the police were Ramón Quijada, acting president of the CTV since the arrest two years before of President Pedro B. Pérez Salinas; José A. Vargas, who was shot and wounded and had to be rushed to the hospital; Juan Herrera, Pedro J. Flores, Pedro Torres, and others. Also rearrested was Dr. Alberto Carnevali, who the previous year had been liberated from jail in one of the most sensational exploits of the AD underground. Carnevali had succeeded Dr. Ruiz Pineda in the leadership of the underground AD. A few months after his arrest, Carnevali died of cancer in the hospital of San Juan de los Morros.[4] Dr. Eligio Anzola had taken Carnevali's place; but he too, in turn, fell into the hands of the police.

On June 16, 1953, Rómulo wrote me:

Another tragic news from Venezuela. Dr. Antonio Pinto Salinas, the successor of Anzola as chief of Democratic Action, has been ambushed and killed by the Security Police. In a few weeks I have suffered two bitter blows—the death of Carnevali in jail, and now the murder of this young comrade-in-arms, valiant writer, promising economist, a man with all the qualities for the country's future leadership. Another man has taken his place. The struggle will continue unabated.

Early in 1953 the OAS decided to hold in Caracas, Venezuela, its X Inter-American Conference. The agenda included, among other items, the adoption of measures designed to strengthen the democratic process threatened by totalitarian forces. The Venezuelan democrats, inside and outside the country, could hardly believe that their military dictatorship had been selected to be host to the American States. They reacted with frustration bordering on despair. Betancourt, however, although hardly able to conceal his indignation, took the position that rather than promote a boycott of the Conference, with the prospect that only a handful of countries would perhaps agree to such a move, the democratic countries of the Americas should be urged to demand, as a condition for their participation, that the government of Venezuela (1) release the political prisoners, even if that would have meant their deportation to other countries, and (2) reestablish a minimum of democratic freedom. In other words, the democratic nations should ask the military regime of Venezuela to demonstrate that it was able and willing to honor the international commitments which obligated it to respect human rights and civil liberties.

This plan, in order to succeed, needed concerted action to arouse public opinion in the United States as well as in Latin America. A demarche with the Venezuelan government by one or more Latin American countries was essential as the opening move that would lead to preliminary discussions and an eventual accord. There was, after all, a precedent which Rómulo related to me in writing. In 1949, Uruguay was ready to charge Venezuela before the United Nations with violation of human rights. Uruguay had already obtained pledges of a majority of votes. However, the Uruguayan chief delegate, Ambassador Domínguez Campora, became the object of strong pressure from Brazil and the United States to desist, on the ground that the submission of such charges would open the door to Russia to meddle in inter-American affairs. Why not try, instead, to obtain from Venezuela a quiet pledge to set free the political prisoners? Negotiations took place, and Ambassador Warren Austin, then permanent U.S. delegate to the United Nations, showed Campora in advance the list of prisoners that were to be liberated. Betancourt wanted, in substance, the repetition in 1953 of the move that had obtained some results in 1949.

To promote such a movement, Betancourt visited, in April–May, 1953, Bolivia, Chile, and Uruguay. Everywhere he found unqualified support. The Senate of Chile, after a prolonged debate, unanimously adopted a resolution urging its government to request the liberation of political prisoners as a preliminary gesture that would permit the democratic states to meet in Caracas. The Uruguayan Foreign Office consulted the U.S. State Department and other chancellories to ascertain what they were prepared to do in this respect.

During the visit to South America undertaken in June–July 1953 by Dr. Milton Eisenhower and John Moors Cabot, Assistant Secretary of State for Inter-American Affairs, they were exposed to demonstrations by students and labor groups as well as to editorial comments in Colombia, Bolivia, Ecuador, Chile, and Uruguay, demanding action on the part of the United States to pressure the government in Caracas for the release of political prisoners.

The free labor movement of the Western Hemisphere had protested from the very beginning the OAS decision to meet in Caracas. On June 18, 1953, a trade union delegation, of which I was one of the members, visited Secretary Moors Cabot and left with him a memorandum in which we urged the government of the United States to demand from Caracas solid guarantees that political prisoners would be set free and civil liberties restored. We told him that the argument of no intervention in the internal affairs of other countries, raised by influential voices friendly to the Pérez Jiménez Venezuelan dictatorship, had no basis because what we were asking from Venezuela was simply the honoring of obligations to respect human rights undertaken by every state member of the UN and the OAS, just as we were then often reminding Russia and her satellites of those obligations in debates at the UN.

The position of the free labor movement in respect to the Caracas Conference was reaffirmed by the ORIT Executive Board at a meeting in Mexico City during the month of August, and by the AFL at its 1953 convention in St. Louis, Missouri, during the month of September, following the presentation of the Venezuelan case which I made at a plenary session. Labor organizations in other countries took the same position. Pamphlets were distributed and petitions circulated. In the end, a vague unofficial promise on the part of the dictatorship that "prisoners would be liberated" was seized on as a sort of victory which saved the face of those democratic governments that had pledged to Betancourt to take a firm position and then bogged down in the morass of diplomatic niceties and compromises. In the end, only little Costa Rica abstained from participating in the Caracas Conference. By then José "Pepe" Figueres had again become its President.

The much advertised liberation of political prisoners was limited to about two hundred. By the time the American delegations reached Caracas, an equal number of newly arrested citizens had already filled the empty cells. However, the harsh realities of the Venezuelan situation were dramatized, for the benefit of the delegates, in demonstrations and public incidents which led to shootings and arrests. Furthermore, during the night of February 14, 1954, the walls of the Conference building were painted with slogans demanding the liberty of political prisoners.

The X Conference of American States managed to adopt a strong condemnation of the Communist conspiracy and its attempts to undermine democracy in the Western Hemisphere. It was a much needed and much justified step. However, the Conference shied away from its duty to adopt collective measures to protect civil liberties and human rights against governments guilty of violating them. The delegates preferred to hide behind the stone wall of nonintervention. A rather significant episode was the effusive congratulations offered by the Guatemalan Foreign Minister Guillermo Toriello Garrido to Pérez Jiménez after he spoke against "any form of collective action." As representative of the Communist-controlled government of President Jacobo Arbenz, leftist Toriello had every reason to thunder against any thought of collective intervention. For different reasons, the two extremes, Fascism and Communism, were once again joining hands.

The delegates to the X Inter-American Conference had hardly left Caracas when the secret police of Pérez Jiménez resumed the wave of terror and murder. Now they felt free to take revenge against the democratic underground that had caused so much noise and disturbance during the Conference. One of the labor leaders who was rearrested was Luis Hurtado. In the early hours of the morning of March 15, 1954, the police broke into Hurtado's home and took him away from his wife and seven children without even permitting him to change from his pajamas to his street clothes. He disappeared without trace. When his wife attempted to find out what had happened to him, she was warned that she too would be jailed if she persisted in asking questions. It was only years later, in March 1958, after the fall of the dictatorship, that Daniel Colmenares, a secret service agent known as "Suelespuma," while under investigation at the La Planta barracks, told all he knew of the fate of Luis Hurtado. This led to other confessions which permitted the reconstruction of how this trade union leader met his martyrdom.

Luis Hurtado was taken away by a group of eleven agents of the Political Division of the National Secret Service, commanded by "El Loco Hernández" and "Pachequito," the latter known for his angel face and bestial instincts. They put Hurtado in a black Chevrolet and took him to the dreaded building of the National Security. Miguel Silvio Sanz, chief of the Political Division, was waiting. Seeing Hurtado, he exclaimed with relish: "Finally, I've got you!" Then, as he was accustomed to do before "processing" the new arrivals, he went to the bar and got almost drunk.

"Give him some good beatings. He is big enough to take plenty of it," Sanz ordered the agents who were holding Hurtado, awaiting instructions.

The eleven men began the "routine" performance of beating the prisoner with clubs until he lost consciousness and fell to the floor. He was revived, beaten again, while Sanz, screaming, demanded:

"Where are Conrado and Vargas Acosta?" [underground leaders].

But Luis Hurtado, although beaten almost to a pulp and bleeding copiously, refused to talk. His teeth remained clenched, his face impassible.

Sweating and raging, Sanz then ordered his men to take Hurtado to a place called "El Junquito."

"If he does not talk up there, I don't want him to come back," he shouted. In the secret police lingo, that was equivalent to a death sentence. And so it was.

The agents beat Hurtado savagely until he died. Then they brought back his body to the Security Police headquarters for instructions as to its disposal. Braulio Barreto, a police handyman, volunteered to bury him.

The body was hastily thrown into a small truck and sped to the cemetery. Braulio did not know the identity of the dead man. But when he was about to lower him into the ground, he noticed that the body was still warm. Moved by curiosity, Braulio looked at his face, and then almost choking with emotion and terror, screamed: "Luis Hurtado!"

Braulio was his friend. He liked him very much. Seized by panic and horror, he abandoned the macabre task and ran away. Someone else eventually buried Luis Hurtado, but up to this time, nobody knows where.

The election of José Figueres to the presidency of Costa Rica sparked a new round of intrigues and conspiracies on the part of Nicaraguan Dictator General Anastasio ("Tacho") Somoza, Figueres's irreconcilable enemy. The anti-Figueres campaign now took the turn that he was under the influence of Rómulo Betancourt, whom the Somoza press—echoed by the organs of the dictatorships in Venezuela and the Dominican Republic —persisted in describing as *nefasto agente* (ominous agent) of the Communist International.[5] In order to relieve his friend Figueres of the burden of these attacks, Rómulo decided to move again—this time to Puerto Rico.

During the month of April 1954 Allan Stewart, First Secretary of the U.S. Embassy in Costa Rica,[6] visited Rómulo in his home in San José and informed him that should he desire to leave Costa Rica he was authorized to offer him political asylum in the United States. Subsequently, Stewart suggested that in order to comply with the requirements of the McCarran Immigration Law, it would be advisable for Betancourt to submit a memorandum detailing his anti-Communist activities during the previous five years. The two agreed, also, to keep the conversation in strict confidence so as not to upset Figueres, who did not even want to hear talk about Betancourt's possible departure from Costa Rica under political pressure.

In compliance with Stewart's suggestion, Betancourt delivered to the U.S. Embassy a memorandum documenting his anti-Communist activities way back to 1936 (not only five years, but eighteen years). On July 26, 1954, Rómulo received a visa for ninety days, with the assurance that it would be extended by the immigration authorities upon his arrival in U.S. territory. On August 6, already in San Juan, Puerto Rico, Betancourt sent to the State Department in Washington, through Allan Stewart, a memorandum in which he formally requested the extension of his ninety-day visa.

As soon as Betancourt arrived in Puerto Rico, the press serving the dictatorships of Venezuela, Nicaragua, and the Dominican Republic launched a concerted campaign protesting his presence in the territory of the United States. That was the beginning of a long, but fortunately never completely successful, agitation to induce the government of the United States to expel Betancourt from its territory.[7]

Governor Múñoz Marín, with the frankness, determination, and courage that have always distinguished him in his remarkable political career, answered the attacks against Rómulo with the following declaration which appeared in the August 15, 1954, issue of the San Juan daily *El Imparcial:*

I am not expressing judgment, because it would be improper for me and unnecessary, over the political situation in Venezuela. But I do wish to express my views on Rómulo Betancourt, whom I consider a distinguished exponent of democratic principles in America, worthy of esteem and respect from all free men. I am absolutely convinced that he is unequivocally opposed to Communism.

Betancourt had made plans, long before he left Costa Rica, to visit New York and Washington, tentatively after Labor Day. But toward the end of August, Henry Holland, who just before the Caracas Conference had been appointed Assistant Secretary of State for Inter-American Affairs replacing John Moors Cabot, telephoned the Secretary of State of the Commonwealth of Puerto Rico requesting that Rómulo Betancourt be persuaded, as a gesture of cooperation, to postpone for a while his planned visit to New York and Washington—not that there was anything illegal about it, but just in order not to give any pretext to Somoza to delay the settlement of his pending differences with Figueres. In addition, Holland suggested that constant police protection be accorded to Betancourt in order to safeguard his life.

On November 12 Betancourt was asked to appear at the Immigration Office in San Juan, where he was told that his visa had expired October 24 and that he had to leave. However, they allowed him to file a request for a six-month extension, on the basis of the formal official pledge given to him at the Embassy in Costa Rica and in view of the impending marriage in San Juan of his daughter Virginia, scheduled for the end of December. The answer from Washington, phoned four days later by Deputy Assistant Secretary of State Robert Woodward, was that in order to extend Betancourt's visa, it would be necessary for him first to leave the territory of the United States; however, in consideration of his daughter's marriage, he was allowed to stay until the end of December.

We were prepared to move heaven and earth to prevent Rómulo's departure from the United States, fearing that once out, every pretext would be invoked to keep him from coming in again. But Rómulo asked, in a letter to me dated November 20, that no issue be made of his case. "Try to obtain discreetly a change in the ruling," he said. "If not successful, I shall go without any public comment. I am not accustomed to dramatize, in the political struggle to which I am dedicated, my personal misfortunes. Of course, I will go disappointed and not without rancor, but I shall keep these sentiments all to myself. We are engaged in a struggle which will not be settled in a matter of days. But the day will come—of this I am sure—when certain functionaries of the United States government will find it very embarrassing to recall the attitude they now adopt toward me."

But suddenly, without any special known intervention, Rómulo received by mail a notification that his visa had been extended to April 1955.

In the year 1955 the Venezuelan dictatorship of President-Colonel Marcos Pérez Jiménez suffered the worst diplomatic defeat of its career at the hands of the international free trade union movement. As the result of the denunciation of the dictatorship by Adrian Vermuelen, worker member of the Governing Body of the International Labor Organization, followed by his expulsion from the country, the Fifth Conference of the ILO Petroleum Committee, meeting in Caracas, April 25, 1955, was summarily adjourned.

The original decision to hold the ILO Petroleum Conference in Venezuela, at the invitation of the government of that country, was made by a majority of the members of the Governing Body of the ILO. The worker members voted unanimously to reject the invitation. But they were outvoted by a majority of government and employer representatives. As a result, the international free labor movement represented by ORIT and ICFTU—largely as a result of the extraordinary missionary work done by Rómulo Betancourt and his Venezuelan trade union friends in exile—called a boycott of the meeting. The U.S., Mexican, and Canadian labor movements refused to name worker members of their country's delegation to the Conference.

In a joint statement issued March 14, 1955, by AFL President George Meany and CIO President Walter Reuther—the first joint statement on record by the top two leaders of the American labor movement on an international labor issue—they related all the efforts made since 1949 by the international free trade union movement to obtain from the Venezuelan government respect for civil liberties and trade union rights. "But all these attempts were ignored by the military dictatorship," said Meany and Reuther. They then announced that the AFL and the CIO, in concert with ORIT, ICFTU, the International Federation of Petroleum Workers, the Oil Workers' Union of Mexico, and the Canadian labor organizations, had decided against participating in the Caracas ILO Petroleum Industrial Committee conference. They concluded:

We appeal to the conscience of all liberty-loving peoples in the Western Hemisphere to join with us and the other democratic trade unions in urging the reestablishment of civil liberties, trade union rights, and the dignity of free labor in Venezuela and the release of the imprisoned free trade unionists.

The Caracas conference opened with a speech by the Venezuelan Minister of Labor, Dr. Carlos Tinoco Rodil, who launched an indirect attack on the international free labor movement, denouncing "interested parties" which claimed that the Venezuelan regime did not permit freedom of organization to the workers of the country. However, the Minister apparently did not expect the immediate reply which Delegate Vermeulen gave to his speech.

Vermeulen in his discourse outlined the history of the relations between the Venezuelan dictatorship and the International Labor Office. He recounted that none of the promises made by the government in 1952 had been fulfilled, that trade unionists still remained in jail—he named several of these—and trade union freedom had not been restored. Finally, he made three specific demands of the Venezuelan regime:

1. That it put at liberty all of the trade unionists who were not accused of actual crimes, and allow them to leave the country if they desired to do so;

2. That those charged with criminal acts be given a fair trial as soon as possible;

3. That the government declare that it was going to provide real trade union liberty by legislation conforming to procedures laid down by various resolutions of the International Labor Organization.

The Venezuelan government delegate to the meeting, Dr. Victor Álvarez, replied, claiming that Vermeulen had interfered in the internal affairs of the country. More drastic action was taken by the notorious Pedro Estrada, head of the National Security Police. He gave orders that Vermeulen be summarily deported from the country, on the same grounds on which he had been denounced by Álvarez. The next morning Vermeulen was on the Dutch island of Curaçao.

As an aftermath of Pedro Estrada's action, the Governing Body of the International Labor Organization decided to cancel all further sessions of the Petroleum Conference in Caracas, on the grounds that the meeting could not continue under conditions which provided no guarantees of the freedom of speech and personal safety of the delegates. The meeting adjourned *sine die.*

As a direct result of the embarrassment which it suffered during this Petroleum Conference, the Pérez Jiménez dictatorship announced its decision to withdraw from the International Labor Organization. This step was taken soon after the closing of the Conference.

Livid with rage, Pérez Jiménez and his Police Chief Pedro Estrada lost no time in exacting vengeance against the democratic trade unionists in Venezuela. Within the space of a few weeks, labor leaders Ramón Alicio García, José Lino González, and Victor Alvarado were assassinated. Many others suffered imprisonment, exile, confinement, and torture, among them Dionisio Álvarez Ledezma, leader of the Bus Drivers' Union; Rafael Amayo, leader of the Trade Union Federation of the Federal District, and Moises Camero, a trade union leader from the State of Falcón. They were denied sunlight, fresh air, decent food, and were constantly kept in a cramped cell in the Obispo jail.

Five trade unionists were brought to the Cárcel Modelo of Caracas, including Daniel Naranjo, a petroleum workers' leader who only six months before had been released from prison after four and a half years of being held without a trial. A few days after being again imprisoned, Naranjo and a young student leader, Carlos Múñoz Oraa, were brought out into the center of the prison, where two lines of policemen, armed with machetes, were drawn up. The two men were made to run back and forth between these lines until they dropped, being beaten on each side by the machetes of the police. Both suffered wounds all over their bodies. Armando González, leader of the workers of the State of Carabobo, received an open wound as a result of barbarous tortures to which he was subjected. He was incarcerated in the Ciudad Bolívar jail, where the conditions were similar to those of the notorious Guasima concentration camp.

At the same time, Pérez Jiménez, now convinced that MOSIT was a complete flop and that in spite of luxurious buildings, fleets of automobiles and a legion of well-paid organizers and functionaries, the workers of Venezuela refused to follow MOSIT leadership, took a different approach to the whole trade union situation. He announced that all the unions outside MOSIT could now organize a national center of their own—Communists ("red" and "black"), Christian Democrats, independents, and even those of AD! The man selected for the job of organizing the "opposition" labor organization was Rodolfo Quintero, leader of the "black" Communists, who was notoriously on the payroll of Pérez Jiménez. The line that both the "black" and "red" Communists had brought back from the 1953 WFTU convention in Vienna was to work for the creation of a single, unitary Confederation, including MOSIT; but for the time being Quintero devoted his efforts to the organization of the "opposition" group, reserving for a later date the task of amalgamating all the trade union forces. The Venezuelan Embassy in Washington took pains to announce, in letters and press releases, that "complete trade union freedom was being enjoyed in Venezuela by all, government supporters as well as opponents."

The Christian Democrats, who had their own COFETROV, declared that after the disillusionment experienced in September 1953, when they joined in a united front in the petroleum industry, they had had enough of "unity" with the Communists. But reliable sources informed me that elements of "what was left of AD labor" had also agreed to join, and that an "AD trade union office" had been opened, with government permission, at Number 89 of Glorieta a Pilita, in Caracas. The sources hinted that perhaps that group of AD labor people did not have the authorization of either the clandestine CTV or the AD. "It is imperative," I wrote to Rómulo on February 15, 1954, "that I be given the opportunity to put out an immediate denial. I have always given positive assurances that the AD labor people would never allow themselves to play the role of 'domesticated opposition' which the Pérez Jiménez dictatorship now tries to obtain through the efforts of Quintero."

Rómulo conferred immediately with Augusto Malavé Villalba, leader of the CTV in exile, and on March 16, 1954, answered me in these precise terms:

I read with consternation your letter of February 15. I have immediately proceeded to establish contacts with our people inside Venezuela. I am convinced that our trade union people will realize the grave national and international danger of working with such an unscrupulous adventurer as Quintero is. But all this has deep roots. On one hand, as you well know, the most experienced and authoritative AD trade union leaders have been in jail for many years, while the Communist leaders enjoy complete freedom of action and movement. On the other hand, Quintero and his people, with newspapers and platforms at their disposal, are exploiting the rising national popular resentment against the United States policy in Latin America.

Rómulo took the matter most seriously. Later he informed me that three of his most experienced trade union lieutenants had received orders to infiltrate back into Venezuela with the specific task of stopping any possible move toward collaboration with the Communists. Furthermore, it was agreed that Professor Robert J. Alexander, of Rutgers University, who was scheduled to visit Venezuela in the summer to do some research for another of his books, would talk to the AD labor leader who had allegedly agreed to join the united front, and would bring back his impression of the whole situation. In addition, it was also agreed that I too would go to Venezuela, mainly to talk with our Labor Attaché and other people at the U.S. Embassy in order to give them straight and without equivocation the thinking of the AFL on this important issue. But when I arrived at the Maquetia airport, the immigration officer found my name in a thick black book which contained the list of undesirable aliens, arrested me on the spot, confined me to a windowless, stiflingly hot cubicle, and after about one hour of waiting, took me out and put me aboard a B.W.I. plane bound for Trinidad.[8]

A few weeks later, Rómulo wrote to me that the AD labor leaders in Venezuela had sent him assurances—confirmed by Robert J. Alexander—that no alliance with the Communists had been contemplated. Added Rómulo:

Our line of conduct remains unaltered. No matter what happens, we must reject the alliance with the Communists, in any and every field. And not because we wish to be on good terms with anybody, but because we want to be true to our people and our own conscience. We know enough of this sect, which has elevated treason to the dignity of a religion, and has made a philosophy of their vulgar opportunistic maneuvers.

Rómulo Betancourt's six-month visa was due to expire in April 1955. Weeks before, I inquired at the State Department what needed to be done in order to obtain an extension. On March 25, John Fishburn, Labor Adviser to the Assistant Secretary of State for Inter-American Affairs and a personal friend of Betancourt, phoned me the following explanation and instructions which I immediately relayed in writing to Betancourt in Puerto Rico:

It is impossible, in Fishburn's opinion, to obtain an extension, because you were admitted to Puerto Rico under an emergency permit extended to you by the Attorney General on the basis of your desire to attend your daughter's wedding. According to the law, you have remained in Puerto Rico illegally and it was only as a special consideration, on account of your personal status, that the immigration authorities granted an extension when you applied for it last fall.

According to Fishburn—who undoubtedly has received his information from official government sources—the best thing for you to do is to apply for a defector visa, which is, according to the law, the only way a person who, by his own admission, has at sometime in his life been a Communist or flirted with the Communists, can be admitted to the United States for either permanent or temporary residence. It is an annoying procedure but in your case there is no doubt that the outcome will be favorable.

Betancourt did not like the suggestion at all. On March 31 he replied with one of the most moving letters I have ever received from him. Rómulo felt that he was being victimized, that the State Department had acted in bad faith with him. In support of this belief, he recounted for my benefit all the negotiations with Allan Stewart that led to his departure from Costa Rica in the summer of 1954, and then concluded:

In summary: (1) I was offered, spontaneously, without any request on my part, *political asylum* in the United States; (2) it is not true that I came to this country exclusively to attend the marriage of my daughter, but because I wanted to take advantage, in good faith, of the *political asylum* offered; and (3) of these two things one is valid: either I was the victim of a disloyal maneuver to get me out of Costa Rica, or the offer to give me political asylum was a sincere one but was later twisted when the dictators, especially Pérez Jiménez, began to pressure the government in Washington against me.

My decision has been taken. I shall send a letter to Mr. [Henry] Holland and a specific, factual memorandum to the State Department for their files. And then I shall leave this country with the firm intention of never coming back as long as there are in the higher government echelons people capable of such schemes or of such complacency with the dictators. I have no intention to issue statements or comments. Around the twentieth of April, four days before the deadline set by the Immigration authorities, I shall take a plane. I do not know yet where to, but I will go. I am trying to get some advances from the newspapers to which I sell my articles, so as to be able to pay the cost of the airplane fares. The few pieces of furniture which we had bought to furnish our apartment are already up for sale.

As for the rest, I remain in a spirited fighting mood as ever. I am being harassed because I refuse to give up the struggle. But in the end, we shall win in Venezuela. I will again be at the head of the government if they do not kill me, first, along the road back. There is not a single day that I do not work hard to achieve this end. And if I personally shall not govern again, there is always someone from Acción Democrática who will.

I do regret, however, that this sudden departure will not permit me to renew old acquaintances in New York; to admire once again Raphael's *Madonna della Candelabra* in Baltimore's Art Gallery; and to enjoy the fraternal hospitality and the spaghetti of the Romualdis in their little home in D.C. . . . But it will be another time, I am sure.

Rómulo's letter caused deep consternation. I went again to the State Department, where I was given the same story, that in Betancourt's case, under the McCarran Law, the application for a defector's visa, to be made outside the country, was a condition *sine qua non* for gaining permanent or temporary admission to the United States. I also got the definite impression that there would be no trick, that Rómulo would get the visa, without delay, once he fulfilled the requirements of the law. Múñoz Marín came to Washington, and he too was given the same assurances. Arturo Morales Carrión, then Puerto Rico Secretary of State, was called by Henry Holland himself, by phone, to assure him that everything was ready in Nassau. Finally Rómulo acceded, went to Nassau, and obtained the visa to enter the United States as a permanent resident, without restrictions.

The alliance of Latin American dictators headed by Pérez Jiménez swallowed hard when they learned of Betancourt's admission for permanent residence in the United States; but they did not give up the attempts to harass, smear, falsely accuse and even assassinate him. What happened to Betancourt in Mexico proves that.

From Nassau, Rómulo went to Mexico City to pay his respects to the widow and the orphans of his intimate friend and Venezuelan democratic statesman, Andres Eloy Blanco, who died there in exile; to discuss with his Mexican publisher his forthcoming book *Politics and Petroleum;* and to spend some time together with a group of Venezuelan deportees just arrived, among them the two top labor leaders José González Navarro and Pedro B. Pérez Salinas, who had finally been set free after having spent about six years in jail. Rómulo wrote to me from Mexico about these two: "Their morale is magnificent. They have improved tremendously. In jail they organized courses in labor and political training, learned foreign languages, read a lot." For the "Chief" there was no time to commiserate over past suffering of two of his most trusted captains. He preferred to rejoice, instead, over the fact that they had returned to the front lines in good form, morally stronger and mentally better prepared for the battles of tomorrow.

While Betancourt was in Mexico, there appeared in the newspaper *El Universal* a report, false from A to Z, that he had presided over a series of meetings attended, among others, by former Mexican President Lázaro Cárdenas, Charnaud McDonald (representing former Guatemalan President Jacobo Arbenz), a brother of Costa Rican President Figueres, the Mexican labor leader Lombardo Toledano, Dionisio Encinas, leader of the Communist Party, and other pro-Communist types. At those meetings, according to *El Universal,* Betancourt was elected chief coordinator of an alleged conspiracy to start revolts and revolutions in those countries ruled by military dictators. The Attorney General and the Minister of Interior of Mexico issued a statement asserting that the information had been published in bad faith *(mala fé)*. Rómulo himself sent a letter to all the Mexico City newspapers affirming that the information was false from beginning to end. However, the United Press, which had sent out the original story as it appeared in *El Universal,* failed—according to Betancourt—to carry the denials of the Mexican Cabinet Ministers and of Betancourt himself.

What was the purpose of this false alarmist story? Obviously it was to revive the old canard of Betancourt being an agent of the Communist International, now about to set on fire Central America and the region of the Antilles—a dangerous man deserving to be eliminated as a preventive measure to preserve peace.

During the night of June 18, 1955, Rómulo received an urgent telephone call from the Assistant Director of Mexican Federal Security, Dr. Gilberto Suárez Torres, who wanted to talk to him immediately. Dr. Suárez told Betancourt that he had "evidences" that during the same night an attempt would be made against his life. Rómulo remarked:

"You do not have to tell me by whom—agents of Pérez Jiménez, no doubt." From that moment on two police cars, with agents selected from the personal guard of President Ruiz Cortínez, stood constant watch over Rómulo. But this meant to Rómulo—as he was prone to say—"being enclosed in a walking jail." And so he quit Mexico and went back to Puerto Rico.

In order, perhaps, to recover from the blow received in April 1955 at the time of the ILO Petroleum Conference, the Venezuelan government began maneuvering to induce the United Nations Educational, Scientific and Cultural Organization (UNESCO) to hold in Caracas the Conference on Cultural Integration planned for the latter part of that year. UNESCO agreed, but organized labor in all parts of the world, including the AFL and the CIO in the United States,[9] immediately launched protests against holding any international conference in a country so beset by dictatorship as Venezuela.

On January 16, 1956, the AFL-CIO received a communication from Max McCullough, Executive Secretary of the U.S. National Commission for UNESCO, Department of State, which read as follows:

In view of the protests which both the American Federation of Labor and the Congress of Industrial Organizations have made with regard to the proposed UNESCO meeting in Caracas, I am sure you will be glad to hear that it is now scheduled for the period April 20–30 in Mexico City.

This decision of UNESCO to shift the meeting from Caracas to Mexico City, an important victory for the free trade union movement, greatly enhanced the morale of the democratic trade unionists of Venezuela.

The political climate in Latin America was improving. Perón had been deposed in Argentina, the Odría dictatorship was in the process of peaceful liquidation in Peru, the OAS had effectively intervened to help the democratic regime in Costa Rica repel an invasion from Nicaragua, and the liberal elements were gaining ground in Honduras. In Venezuela itself, dictator Pérez Jiménez was being pressured by a group of young army officers (it was reported that they actually served him with an ultimatum) to empty the jails of political prisoners, to decree an amnesty, and, most significant, to get the army out of politics. In fact, Pérez Jiménez did set free about one hundred political prisoners and vaguely announced an amnesty that would include the granting of visas to those exiles who wished to return home.

Pérez Jiménez's announcement was greeted by Betancourt with a statement [10] in which he said: "This news deserves to be received with appreciation for what it may contain with respect to the reestablishment of conditions that would permit all Venezuelans to live together again in their own country. A civilized country which belongs to the 'free world' cannot live indefinitely under a state of siege with all constitutional guarantees abolished." Betancourt added that "the amnesty, to produce salutary effects, must be wide enough to empty the jails of all political prisoners and must allow all the Venezuelan exiles to return to their country."

The Venezuelan dictator had the effrontery to announce that a visa to return home had also been offered to Rómulo Betancourt. All this, of course, was designed for external consumption, to impress world public opinion, the State Department and the chancellories of other Latin American countries that Venezuela was taking concrete steps toward a return to constitutionality. The proof of this duplicity came in early February, when Rómulo received from sources inside the Venezuelan police apparatus information that Pérez Jiménez had sent abroad two members of his secret political police, Ángel María Zapata and Rafael Antonio Monsalve, with instructions to make an attempt against Betancourt's life. Chief Sanz of the Political Department of National Security, executor of all crimes ordered by Police Chief Pedro Estrada, was sent to New York to coordinate the plans for Rómulo's elimination. Informed of the plot, Governor Múñoz Marín ordered his police to take precautionary measures so extensive that they made it impossible for the would-be murderers to enter the island.

Leaders of the Inter-American Association for Democracy and Freedom felt that the time was favorable for calling another inter-American Conference, not so large as the first one held six years before in Havana, but rather limited to a selected group of personalities of great prestige and influence in the Western Hemisphere. Since the President of Costa Rica, José Figueres, was scheduled to make an official visit to Puerto Rico in the middle of February 1956, it was agreed that Miss Frances Grant and I would also go to Puerto Rico so as to have an opportunity to discuss in conversations with Figueres, Betancourt, Múñoz Marín and a few others, the preliminaries of such a Conference and its most convenient location. But the trip was cancelled when we suddenly learned that Rómulo Betancourt had left Puerto Rico for a nearby island, at the insistence of Assistant Secretary of State Henry Holland, who did not want him to meet with Figueres when the latter arrived in San Juan, perhaps for fear

476 | PRESIDENTS AND PEONS

that the meeting would "upset" the government of Venezuela. Rómulo's reaction was the reaction of a true statesman. Conscious of the affront committed against him, a former (and most likely, future) President of a friendly country; against Figueres, President of another friendly Latin American country, and Múñoz Marín, the Governor of the Free Commonwealth of Puerto Rico, he could have caused an international scandal; yet he wrote to me that he was not going to say a word, that there would be no publicity about "this most disagreeable event." The statesman had well learned that what one cannot change one must endure, at least until better times come around. Frances Grant and I, in compliance with Betancourt's wishes, said nothing about the incident, made no attempt to lodge protests or to seek explanations from the State Department. This, however, was not the attitude adopted by Figueres. While he decided to go through with the visit to Puerto Rico in order not to embarrass his friend, Governor Múñoz Marín, he nevertheless instructed his Ambassador to Washington to convey to Holland his strong resentment and pointed out the fallacy of the policy pursued by the State Department, of appeasing the dictators at the expense of democratic friends.

Emboldened by what was interpreted as a weakening of the State Department's concern about Betancourt, the Venezuelan regime got ready for the kill—an accusation against Betancourt of having masterminded and organized from Puerto Rico an attempt against Pérez Jiménez's life. On August 10, 1956, Pedro Estrada made the announcement in Caracas, replete with details and names of the supposed conspirators. He ended the announcement with this significant remark: "We are most surprised that Puerto Rico, which is part of the territory of the United States, a friendly country, has been allowed to be the place from which such an attempt was instigated with impunity." That was letting the cat out of the bag. The clear aim of Estrada's remark was to scare the United States into expelling Betancourt. Then Estrada would finally get the long-sought opportunity to do away with Rómulo's life. But the attempt to have Rómulo expelled failed again.

Instructed by AFL-CIO President George Meany, who had received an urgent appeal from ORIT General Secretary Luis Alberto Monge to intervene on Betancourt's behalf, on August 20 and 21 I visited the State Department, where I was authorized to convey to the labor organizations that had shown interest in the case, as well as to Rómulo Betancourt himself, the following statement:

No information has until now reached the State Department or any other governmental agency that Betancourt has violated any law of the United States.

In the event that such accusation should be raised against him in the future, the charges and the supporting proofs will be carefully examined and, if necessary, Betancourt will get plenty of opportunities to present his side of the story.

Ten days later I went back to the State Department, talked with many friends there at length, and came away with the definite impression that nobody there had taken Pedro Estrada's accusations against Betancourt seriously. Most were rather convinced that the whole thing was just another frame-up of the dictatorship.

On his part, Betancourt not only issued strong denials that he had even thought of resorting to the methods of the dictatorship, but he explained in a letter to me how such a move would have been self-defeating. On August 13, 1956, he wrote:

My deep-rooted ideological convictions and principles have led me to question the political efficacy of attempts against the life of any individual. As I have argued for this position in the past when dark was the Inter-American panorama and many Venezuelans were on the verge of desperation, it is with greater reason that I advocate this position now that I see on the horizon the possibility of favorable solutions to the Venezuelan crisis. Next year, there will be elections. Among military and civilian supporters of the present regime the idea is gaining ground that a solution *a la Peruana* [11] must be found to the grave situation facing the country. I have learned from trustworthy sources that a group of military officers have plainly told Pérez Jiménez that they will not go along with any adventure he might scheme to continue himself in power. In these conditions, the idea of an attempt on the life [of Pérez Jiménez] would make even less sense.

A number of innocent people were implicated by Pedro Estrada in his horrible frame-up. Most of them were AD labor and political leaders, either living abroad or still in Venezuela, having been recently released from jail during the brief thaw staged for international consumption. There were also people in the business community, in the professions, and especially in journalism, who were made to pay for doing or saying things that were displeasing to the government.[12] Some of those arrested died as a result of the tortures to which they were subjected, among them Marcelino Rivero, Financial Secretary of the Petroleum Workers' Union of El Tigre, State of Anzoátegui, who died in the jail of Barcelona after six consecutive hours of beatings and tortures, and Mario Pérez Pisanty, distinguished industrialist, never identified with any political activity, who died in the Cárcel Modelo of Caracas. Unable to stand any longer the tortures inflicted on him, Pisanty, who had already suffered a coronary thrombosis while in jail, cut his own wrists in a desperate effort to end it all by committing suicide. Rómulo actually cried when he heard of Pisanty's death. As in previous instances when under the impact of such emotional blows, and as a way of alleviating his physical and spiritual pains, Rómulo immediately wrote to me of his friend Pisanty:

> He was a very loyal friend of mine, a man completely divorced from any political activity. They implicated him in this alleged plot only because of his friendship to me. He was a man of extraordinary human kindness. Born in Italy of a Sephardic Jewish family, he migrated to Venezuela when he was already an adult. There he quickly became assimilated, amassed a fortune, raised a family. His death has deeply affected me. When a labor or political militant falls in battle, that too causes pain, but then one reflects that whoever enlists in the struggle against regimes such as the one now in Caracas knows in advance that his life is in constant jeopardy. But it is absurd, incredible, that a person without political activities or preoccupation should lose his life for the only crime of being a personal friend of an opponent of the regime.

In December 1956 Rómulo Betancourt and his wife visited the United States to spend the Christmas and New Year's vacations with their married daughter Virginia, who was completing her studies at the University of Chicago.

On Thursday, December 27, Betancourt visited the headquarters of the AFL-CIO and conferred at length with President George Meany and Secretary-Treasurer William F. Schnitzler. They discussed particularly the plight of Venezuelan trade unionists, who, after being in jail for a number of years, without trial or indictment, were being released, but immediately deported by force to other Latin American countries and left stranded without resources. In response to Betancourt's plea, President Meany, with the support of the AFL-CIO Executive Council, addressed an appeal to all the affiliated unions for assistance.

On January 12, 1957, under the auspices of the Inter-American Association for Democracy and Freedom, and with the active cooperation of a number of AFL-CIO unions, Dr. Betancourt was honored with a public luncheon at Carnegie International Center, New York City.[13] There was, also, the inevitable family reunion at my house in Bethesda, Maryland, with the obbligato dish of spaghetti, topped with the by now famous "Romualdi sauce," which Rómulo dutifully proclaimed "really superb, better than ever before."

During his stay in the United States, Rómulo and I had many opportunities to go over the Venezuelan situation, from many angles. There was no longer any doubt in our minds that the prospects for a favorable political solution in the near future were indeed good; but we felt that the Communist infiltration in the underground had assumed alarming proportions. This was confirmed in a memorandum which Betancourt sent me on February 27, soon after his return to Puerto Rico. One section of that document, which in the light of what actually happened years later in Venezuela had prophetic overtones, read as follows:

I have had the opportunity to meet here, since my return, with a number of AD co-workers, some of whom I had not seen since 1948. They went through the test of the clandestine work, of Guasima, of the tortures suffered in jail; yet their spirit is high, they maintain undimmed their faith in our cause and their will to continue the struggle. I learned from them the harmful influence that the copious Soviet propaganda, which enters and circulates freely in Venezuela, has had on some young workers and students. I was so disturbed by such news that I have decided to write an essay ("Crisis in the Soviet World—From the XX Congress of the Russian Bolshevik Party to the Hungarian Massacre") to be published in *Cuadernos Americanos* [14] with reprints to be introduced later in Venezuela. We must take advantage of every opportunity to hit hard at Russian totalitarianism. I have remembered what you told me with respect to the situation of our Peruvian Aprista friends who now have to contend with a local Communist movement stronger than the one they had in 1948. The truth is— and I am saying this not as tactical argument but as an undeniable fact—that right-wing dictatorships offer a favorable breeding ground for the fanaticism of the ultra-leftists, and that Soviet propaganda finds a more attentive audience in those countries where the people are exasperated by their reactionary dictator- ships than in those countries where people enjoy public liberties and free political play. This is what the shortsighted chancellories refuse to see. They appear to act like the French king—"Apres moi, le déluge!"

The press in the United States widely reported that when Dictator Marcos Pérez Jiménez met with his fellow dictator and neighbor General Gustavo Rojas Pinilla of Colombia [15] in January 1957 they reached an agreement to both seek the continuation of their respective presidential mandates due to expire during that year. A group of military and civilian cronies, headed by Minister of Interior Vallenilla Lanz, supported Pérez Jiménez in his plan for *continuismo* (the continuation of the mandate), but a strong section of the Army, and even some civilian members of his government apparatus, openly opposed him. The President of the so- called Senate, who was holding office by Pérez Jiménez's fiat, publicly declared that before January 1958 there must be elections for the presi- dency of the republic and for Congress.

The sudden overthrow of Rojas Pinilla [16] considerably disrupted Pérez Jiménez's plans for *continuismo* and emboldened a group of mili- tary officers who no longer made a secret of their determination to prevent

Pérez Jiménez's reelection. Meanwhile, the labor and political cadres of AD, convinced that elections were becoming inevitable, were working hard inside Venezuela to organize a wide democratic front, with the sole exclusion of the Communists, with the view of concentrating on a single candidate all the votes of the civic opposition forces. The AD Party inside Venezuela had recovered from the serious losses suffered in the preceding years, its clandestine newspaper *Resistencia* was again circulating and so were the publications of the democratic trade unionists and of the AD Youth Section. Similar approaches toward the constitution of a democratic united front were being made abroad. During the month of June 1957 Rómulo Betancourt went back to New York, where he met, among others, with former President Rómulo Gallegos and Gonzalo Barrios of his AD Party, and with Jovito Villalba and Luis Arcaya of the Democratic-Republican Union (URD) Party. They reached agreement on a draft declaration to be submitted to the Christian Democratic Party (COPEI) and other civic forces of Venezuela for their approval and adherence to the united democratic front. The manifesto, in summary, advocated a political, evolutionary solution of the Venezuelan crisis, to be achieved through the calling of free elections.

While Betancourt was in the United States, an incident occurred which greatly annoyed him but also gave me an opportunity to learn that the State Department had come to the conclusion that Pérez Jiménez's days were approaching an end. What happened was described by Betancourt himself in the following letter which he sent me on June 14 from Chicago:

Agents of the FBI came to see me in my house in Puerto Rico, just before my trip. They only asked for Carlos Andres Pérez.[17] I told them the truth: that he had not been in Puerto Rico since February 1956. I thought it was only a routine investigation, but I have just learned from Venezuela, through friends in the Security Department, that Pérez Jiménez, as well as [Police Chief] Estrada, are boasting that the FBI is keeping me under severe investigation. Is there a way to find out if it is true? If it is so, I would rather move away from Puerto Rico immediately, without creating a public scandal, in order to avoid a displeasure to our friend Múñoz Marín. This matter of the investigation would be something worse than a crime, a stupidity, "une bêtise," quoting a phrase from Talleyrand. But since I do not have to rush things, I would rather act with care and consideration; so I am asking you to do me the favor to try to find out about this particular and to inform me.

I was glad to reply to Rómulo, on June 28, 1957, that "there is absolutely no change in the attitude of the State Department toward you. They consider you a most welcome guest who until now has caused no inconvenience to our government. They refuse, therefore, to take seriously the braggings of Pérez Jiménez and Pedro Estrada." And then I added that I had exchanged views on this subject, at a dinner at the Honduras Embassy, with Allan Stewart, then Director of the Central American and Caribbean Section of the State Department, and our mutual friend Adolf A. Berle, and they both assured me that "there is a change in the official U.S. government attitude toward you, in the sense that the Department is now 'courting' you, because there are indications of drastic changes in the political scenario of Venezuela."

Having failed to involve the State Department in their defamatory campaign against Betancourt, the two Caribbean dictators, Pérez Jiménez and Leonidas Trujillo, started working on the Legislative branch of the U.S. government in the hope of provoking an investigation of Betancourt's alleged connections with the Communist movement.

On August 2, 1957, Congressman Charles O. Porter inserted in the *Congressional Record* the text of a confidential document which emanated from the Dominican Republic Embassy in Washington. It contained instructions on means to influence U.S. public opinion in favor of the Dominican Republic regime, and the following significant paragraph on Betancourt:

The "Great Guru" label can be fixed squarely on Rómulo Betancourt. His relationship to New York and Washington groups should be made clear. A few well-aimed shots at Mr. R. will probably sink him and his admirers will be discredited along with him.

Worse happened, however, three weeks later when, on August 21, 1957, Senator Olin D. Johnston of South Carolina released the text of a report to the Subcommittee on Internal Security of the Senate Committee on the Judiciary, in which Betancourt was described as a pro-Communist. The Johnston report then suggested that the Subcommittee initiate an investigation of Betancourt's "dangerous activities." Later, rumors began to circulate that the Subcommittee would soon go to Puerto Rico, where Betancourt had returned, to hold such hearings.

The Johnston report was criticized in the daily press on grounds that it falsely called Costa Rica "the known hotbed and headquarters of Communist activities in Latin America," while praising the Dominican Republic as "the rock of stability in the turbulent Caribbean."

William C. Doherty, AFL-CIO Vice-President and member of its Subcommittee on Inter-American Affairs, and a personal friend of Senator

Johnston, wrote him a letter in which he stated that "Betancourt has proven himself to be a strong advocate of democratic trade unionism dating back to 1946. He is also a firm believer in collaboration with the United States. The staff officers of the AFL-CIO who specialize in Inter-American relations, as well as leaders of the labor movements in Latin American countries with whom I am in contact have acquainted me with a number of instances indicating Dr. Betancourt's strong opposition to Communism and to any other form of dictatorship. I, therefore, urge the Subcommittee to insert in its record this statement, with the view of helping to dispel any doubt as to Dr. Rómulo Betancourt's stand on Communism."

Senator Johnston, who privately admitted to Doherty that he had been misled by Trujillo's paid lobbyists in Washington, officially replied that "the statement on Betancourt will be considered by the Committee."

Not fully satisfied with Johnston's reply to Doherty, I then contacted the Senate Committee's Chief Counsel, Robert Morris, and the Director of Research, Benjamin Mandel. On November 8, I reported to President Meany the result of my conference in these terms: "Both showed surprise at the accusation against Rómulo Betancourt and assured me that some steps would be taken to do him justice." Meanwhile, hearings which were announced for early November to investigate the allegations contained in Senator Johnston's report were postponed indefinitely.

Events in Venezuela then began to unfold at a faster pace. Reports reaching Betancourt in Puerto Rico indicated that unless Pérez Jiménez stepped down an upheaval was inevitable. The plan to take part in the presidential elections with a single candidate representing the united democratic opposition came to naught when Pérez Jiménez refused to restore freedom of press and assembly and insisted on running himself for another five-year term. On December 15, 1957, there took place a fraudulent plebiscite in which Pérez Jiménez ran for the presidency without opposition. But that was his final fatal miscalculation. The plebiscite met with so much repudiation in all sectors of the population that people, no longer afraid, began to agitate publicly for an end to Venezuela's tragedy. The expression "This is a shame!" became a sort of password.

Rómulo Betancourt, meanwhile, had returned to the United States. On December 27 he sent me from Chicago this laconic, eloquent message: "—I need to talk to you. Now I know for sure that that man is going to fall."

By the end of the year popular discontent in Venezuela had won over the military. A revolt was attempted on New Year's Day, but it failed. Yet, Rómulo soon learned that the real big push was still to come. Days of feverish activity followed. Anxiety, yes; but never despair. He held constant meetings with the leaders of the exiled democratic opposition, who had all moved to New York—Jovito Villalba, Rafael Caldera, and others. Betancourt had rented a room, always full of people, in the small Hotel Paris on Manhattan's Upper West Side. From there he phoned me almost every day, keeping me posted with the progress reports now coming out of Venezuela in defiance of the censorship. And finally, late in the evening of January 23, 1958, he called me at my house in Bethesda, choking with emotion:

"I want you to be the first to know it, Serafino. It is all over. Hemos ganado—*We have won. Now I am going home!"*

Notes

1. On November, 1951 the Cuban National Secret Police submitted a confidential report on the results of their investigation of the attempt at Betancourt's murder, a copy of which the author still has in his possession. The report stated that the liquid in the syringe was not "hiperita" but cobra poison. It also charged that the crime was committed by three paid gangsters from Tampa, Florida, hired by a Dominican, Carlos Torres, a resident of Miami, who had at his disposal for the job the sum of $150,000 given to him by the military junta of Venezuela. The three gangsters were Joe Wilson, actual executor of the frustrated assassination attempt, who subsequently repaired to Venezuela; Joe Cachatore (or Cacciatore) who was later apprehended in Florida for another crime and sentenced to thirty years in jail; and a third person who arrived in Havana with Wilson and Cachatore and was later killed in Tampa by Cachatore for reasons unknown. The three gangsters left Havana and went back to Florida aboard the SS *Florida* three days after the attempted crime. A fourth person, Enrique Pietro, was also implicated in the conspiracy but he never went to Cuba. He owned a farm in the vicinity of Tampa and was engaged in disposing of counterfeit bills.

2. Members of the Venezuelan workers' delegation were Humberto Ochoa, delegate; Francisco Fernández, Frank Hernández, and Alejandro Brizuela, advisers.

3. The revolt of Maturín, a town in the eastern part of Venezuela, was the first major indication that young military officers had joined the ranks of the opposition. The leader of the revolt, Captain Rojas, was promptly executed by a military squad. Another officer, Captain Wilfredo Omaña, suspected of being implicated in the anti-Jiménez military conspiracy, was machine-gunned in the streets of Caracas.

4. The Foreign Minister of Bolivia, Victor Andrade, asked the U.S. State Department to convey to the government of Venezuela, with which Bolivia did not maintain diplomatic relations, a petition to release from jail, for humanitarian reasons, Dr. Alberto Carnevali, who was already in virtual agony. The State Department refused to convey the Bolivian request and suggested instead that such mission be entrusted to either Colombia or Brazil.—*Rómulo Betancourt's letter to the author, March 19, 1953.*

5. From an editorial in *El Caribe* of Ciudad Trujillo as reproduced in the August 15, 1954 issue of *El Imparcial* of San Juan, Puerto Rico.

6. Allan Stewart subsequently became U.S. Ambassador to Venezuela and served there during the best part of Betancourt's 1959–1964 term.

7. *Visión* magazine published that Pérez Jiménez personally requested of Henry Holland, Assistant Secretary of State for Inter-American Affairs, when he was passing through Caracas, that Betancourt be "expelled from Puerto Rico." Pedro Estrada, the dreaded sanguinary chief of the Venezuelan National Security Police, before departing for an official visit to Washington in November 1954, boasted that he "would force Betancourt to leave the United States."

8. When I went back to Venezuela in the spring of 1958, following the downfall of Pérez Jiménez, my name was still in the immigration black book. The prompt intervention of some labor leaders waiting outside obtained my release. Apologies were later offered by the Minister of Interior of the Provisional Government in Caracas, with assurances that my name would be removed immediately. But when I went back to Caracas a few months later, my name was still in the black book. Fortunately, a number of prominent Venezuelans waiting for me at the airport vouched for me and obtained my admission. The next time I deplaned, my name had finally been removed.

9. In the United States, the protest was made at a meeting of the U.S. National Commission for UNESCO in Cincinnati in November 1955 by John Connors, director of the AFL Department of Education, and Frank L. Fernbach, of the CIO Department of Research. They cited the antilabor record of the Venezuelan government with its accompaniment of brutality, murder, and imprisonment of hundreds of labor leaders without trial.

10. *El Mundo,* San Juan, Puerto Rico, February 6, 1956.

11. The "Peruvian solution" was based on a firm accord between President General Odría and the opposition, represented by the APRA Party, that there would be honest elections, with the opposition supporting a moderate candidate pledged to restoration of full constitutional rights.

12. The wholesale arrests and violations of human rights to which the government of Venezuelan dictator Marcos Pérez Jiménez resorted following the fabricated attempt on his life were protested October 4, 1956, in a letter and memorandum addressed to the Secretary General of the United Nations, Dag Hammarskjold, by Roger Baldwin, Chairman of the International League for the Rights of Man, and Frances R. Grant, Secretary General of the Inter-American Association for Democracy and Freedom. Among the victims named in the memorandum addressed to Hammarskjold were Luis Alfaro Ucero, former Representative in the National Congress; Professor Manuel Vicente Magallanes; Dr. Ramón Velásquez, lawyer and noted journalist; Rafael Serfaty, well-known industrialist of Caracas; José A. Rey, journalist; José Gerbasi, journalist, editor of the Economic Page of *El Nacional* of Caracas; Dr. Rafael Ignacio Cabrices, physician; Dr. Dario Rodríguez Méndez, engineer; Dr. Alberto Aranguren Zamora, lawyer; Jorge Magna, businessman; Horacio Chacin Ducharne, radio operator.

13. Among those who spoke at the Carnegie International Center's luncheon, extolling the contributions of the distinguished guest to the cause of inter-American democracy and freedom, were Norman Thomas; former Ambassador Claude Bowers; Dr. Andres Townsend, member of the Peruvian Delegation to the United Nations; Serafino Romualdi; Roger Baldwin, Chairman of the International League for the Rights of Man; and O. A. Knight, Chairman of the AFL-CIO Committee on Inter-American Affairs and President of the Oil, Chemical and Atomic Workers International Union.

14. *Cuadernos Americanos* is a bi-monthly political-literary magazine in the Spanish language published in Mexico City.

15. On June 13, 1953, General Gustavo Rojas Pinilla, chief of the Armed Forces of Colombia, seized the presidency. In July 1954 the national Constituent Assembly, which superseded Congress after Rojas Pinilla's coup, convened to legalize his position and elected him President for the 1954–1958 term. Although, on seizing the presidency,

Rojas Pinilla promised to restore civil liberties and to lift press censorship, he soon adopted the methods of the military dictatorship and almost three years later Colombia was still in a state of siege and experiencing occasional antigovernment riots.

16. On May 8, 1957, the national Constituent Assembly of Colombia reelected President Rojas Pinilla, but there was so much opposition to this move, inside the assembly itself and throughout the country, that two days later he was deposed by a military junta led by Major General Gabriel París.

17. Carlos Andres Pérez, young AD leader, was a sort of private secretary to Rómulo Betancourt during his Costa Rican exile. Years later, Carlos Andres became Venezuelan Minister of Interior under Betancourt's second presidency.

XXVII

Rómulo Betancourt—The Statesman

THE FALL of the Venezuelan dictatorship came about as a result of the union of all the political and social forces of the country, including the army and the clergy. The workers and the peasants played a decisive role by staging a successful general strike. The government was taken over by a junta, composed of military personnel and civilians, headed by Admiral Wolfgang Larrazabal, which pledged early elections. Pérez Jiménez fled into exile in the Dominican Republic.

Rómulo Betancourt's return to Venezuela early in February 1958 assumed the proportions of a veritable triumph. Not only the members of his AD party, but all the democratic leaders and their followers joined in paying tribute to the man who had become the symbol of the true Venezuela and who had so valiantly led his people, during the long night of the brutal dictatorship, toward the dawn of victory and freedom.

A few weeks after his arrival in Caracas, I got a letter, dated February 24, in which he described the endless, staggering round of meetings, interviews, conferences, and work to which he was subject day and night. He stressed that the "deceased party," as the dictatorship used to refer to AD, had bounced back with an unbelievable degree of vitality and strength. Then he referred to the Communists:

> They who were so crestfallen in 1948, the last year of the democratic government, are now raising their head. They are everywhere, manage to get involved in everything, and know how to seize positions of command. This is the result

of the anti-Communist mask displayed for ten years by the totalitarian dictatorship. However, I don't have the slightest doubt that the democratic forces, when able to engage the Communists in clean contest, will defeat them and will become the ones who will dominate and direct every aspect of our political scene.

Venezuela was facing grave political and economic problems. It was obvious that a degree of unity among the political and labor forces which had worked together during the underground struggle, and had joined in the final battle that toppled the dictatorship, was essential and unavoidable. The slogan of unity became very popular. It was being advocated, with singular force, by the Communist Party, which meanwhile had managed to gain a degree of respectability, was loudly supporting the civilian-military junta, and had joined the other leading political parties —AD, COPEI, and URD—in signing a political truce banning recriminations and binding the participants in fighting together in the defense of the revolution against any possible coup by the supporters, especially military, of the deposed regime.

Communist leader Gustavo Machado, on February 17, 1958, barely a week after his return from a seven-year exile, issued a statement in which he predicted that the political truce might last for years, felt sure that his party at the next elections would double the votes obtained in 1947, and asserted that the four political parties supporting the junta would present a single presidential candidate and a single list of candidates for Congress.

This Communist prediction was echoed in a story about Venezuela, entitled "Power Stall," which appeared in the March 3, 1958, issue of *Time* magazine. According to that story, Rafael Caldera and Jovito Villalba (leaders of the COPEI and URD parties), who had preceded Betancourt's return by only a few days, had already agreed to sponsor a single list of candidates for President and Congress, to be apportioned among the three leading national parties—AD among them, of course— roughly about 20 percent each, with the remaining 40 percent allotted to distinguished representatives of different sectors of national activity. *Time* magazine added the significant comment that the only party which was resisting the popular call for a show of "national responsibility" was the AD, allegedly at Betancourt's instigation, while the Communists, the story said, had shown a high degree of "national responsibility" by being the first ones to come out for a single list of candidates for President and Congress.

The story published by *Time* was quickly disavowed by Caldera and

Villalba themselves, yet it was symptomatic of the great efforts that were being made to prepare the ground for acceptance of the single-candidate theory, whose most energetic supporters were the Communists. Their true objective was to prevent the victory of the AD presidential candidate (that is, Rómulo Betancourt), who in an open contest they felt would win by a large majority.

On March 14, I wrote to Betancourt expressing preoccupation over the advance that the popular-front idea was making in Argentina, Chile, and other countries. I also voiced the hope that if a united front with the Communists in Venezuela appeared inevitable under the momentum generated by the collaboration in the underground struggle, it would be of "transitory character." With his usual forthright manner, Rómulo replied on April 14, 1958:

> I share your preoccupation concerning the progress of the popular-front slogan, behind which one can easily discern the tactic of the Trojan Horse. Here in Venezuela, too, this siren song is being played up; but as far as AD is concerned, there is no possibility whatsoever that we may be fooled by this melody. We well know what is hidden behind this smoke screen and we have already firmly outlined our future course.

At the end of the general strike which contributed so effectively to the overthrow of the Venezuelan dictatorship, the Strike Committee declared its function as such at an end and convoked a meeting of labor leaders to decide the course for the future. As was natural, the political unity forged among all the forces that struggled against Pérez Jiménez was immediately reflected in trade union circles, and the result was the constitution of the United Trade Union Committee, which became the *de facto* central labor body of the country. Its first declaration stated that the function of the United Committee would be to orient the trade union movement until such time as a proper organ to direct the trade union activities of the Venezuelan workers should be constituted. On this basis, local unified committees for trade union reorganization were set up all over the country. In these local committees, representation of the four currents in the labor movement—AD, URD, COPEI, and the Communists —was mandatory. In one small locality in the state of Aragua, I learned later with considerable amusement, there was no one belonging to COPEI that was qualified to be elected a member of the Executive Board of the local united labor committee. Unwilling to violate the directives handed down from Caracas, the chairman of the meeting called to elect the officers adjourned it so that he could consult and devise a way out of the impasse. When the meeting was resumed one of the AD members solemnly announced that he had decided to join COPEI. He was immediately elected and the impasse was broken.

The participation of the leaders of the old CTV in a united front which included the Communists was supported by a joint ORIT-ICFTU mission headed by Charles Millard, ICFTU Director of Organization, that visited Venezuela early in February. There were, however, many in the family of international free labor, especially in the United States, who remained quite apprehensive over the ultimate effect of this united front. To allay their misgivings, justified by past experiences in other countries, Pedro B. Pérez Salinas, the last President of CTV who had worked with ORIT after he was released in 1955 from his six-year confinement in the Venezuelan jails, sent to this organization a report, dated February 19, 1958, in which he stated:

At present we cannot act as the CTV, even when everyone knows that within the united trade union front we represent that policy and as such have belligerency and participation. We, for our part, are willing, when the circumstances warrant it, to arrive at the constitution of a single trade union central body, with minorities represented proportionately, the leaders of the upper and middle levels to be designated from below rather than from above. This does not cause us concern, for we know that we have the majority of the country's workers. Already in the initial work of organization the policy of the majority has been made plain, and this is the representative policy of the CTV.[1]

Pérez Salinas also added that meetings had been held with the Federation of Chambers of Commerce and Production with a view to reaching a labor-management truce to allow the country to return to normalcy without being disturbed by waves of strikes and conflicts, and both sides had pledged to cooperate to this end in a spirit of patriotism and good will.

With respect to the leaders of MOSIT, the so-called national labor central organization that supported Pérez Jiménez and in many instances worked in collusion with the secret police, Pérez Salinas reported that its top leaders had disappeared or were arrested, while the local ones were in most cases expelled by a vote of the membership.

I was particularly pleased to read, at the conclusion of Pérez Salinas's report, assurances that the old CTV leaders remained alert and were determined to resist any attempt on the part of the Communists and their fellow travelers to take over the labor movement. He wrote:

Confidentially, we wish to report that the old CTV leadership is rapidly recovering all its influence. To this must be added that the metal workers, those employed in the electrification of the Caroni, the oil and chemical workers, the auto workers and those of other new industries in the ocuntry, when joining the local united union groups, looked first for our people, those who they knew belonged to the old CTV.

Within the framework of national unity we are not going to play the part of fools but rather to *guarantee and assure ourselves of a majority which will allow us to keep in our hands control of the central bodies of the national trade union movement.*

About a week after Pérez Salinas sent his report to ORIT, I got from Rómulo Betancourt a note in which he said briefly: "The reorganization of the trade union movement proceeds rapidly in every corner of the country. In most of the unions our democratic leaders are gaining the majority of the Executive Board. We do not rest a minute."

Aware of the loyalty of people like Pérez Salinas, Augusto Malavé, González Navarro, Luis Tovar, and others to the policies of AD and of their devotion to the AD chief, Rómulo Betancourt, I felt quite confident that the Communists would be thwarted in their scheme to manipulate the united front to their benefit. I sort of boasted, therefore, to whoever wanted to hear or read me, that our AD brothers (to use the standard trade union expression) were again in the saddle. In labor circles, as well as in government, in the Latin American embassies in Washington, and even in the New York business community interested in Venezuela, my opinion on the labor developments in that country was eagerly sought. With them I had acquired a reputation of knowing something about Venezuelan affairs—past, present, and future.

On July 2, 1958, after an absence of almost ten years, I was finally able to go back to Venezuela. I stayed there for only three days, spent in constant company with Rómulo Betancourt and the Venezuelan trade unionists with whom I had worked closely during their long years of exile.

The main topics of our discussions were how to secure the country from the insistently rumored coups by the military rightists [2] and how to preserve the democratic forces from the insidious infiltration from the left. I found determination among my friends in the labor movement; but I found also deep awareness of the perils facing them if they were to engage in battle without sufficient preparation and strength at their command that would give them assurance of victory. In the labor movement, the slogan of unity was in everybody's mouth. There were yet no visible, understandable causes to justify a break. Our AD labor friends had no other course, therefore, than to close ranks and wait for the opportune moment. Unity was also the password in the political arena. AD had by now convincingly demonstrated its strength in the countryside, but it was not too strong in Caracas and other large cities. Inside the AD party, too, the advocates of unity with all the other forces of the Revolution were being heard with a crescendo intensity. Rómulo Betancourt was being regarded and hailed as the leader from all sectors of the AD party, yet there were indications that certain elements, especially among those who had not gone abroad as exiles, might not be so easy to keep under control come the party's Convention next August.

The night of the Fourth of July the AD organization in Caracas held a mammoth concentration of popular forces at the Nuevo Circo. I was invited to attend. Leaders of the other parties participating in the political truce, including the Communists, were also invited to share the platform. There I met for the first and only time the Communist leader Gustavo Machado. There was much harmony and enthusiasm in the huge crowd, and when Betancourt was finally introduced as the main speaker of the evening, he was greeted with a demonstration that was quite impressive. But I noticed a certain nervousness in the sector where the Communists and other leftists, pointed out to me by my AD friends, were seated. There had been speculation that Betancourt might take advantage of that occasion to make public his aversion to any idea of a popular front with the Communists. And that was precisely what Betancourt did. In the midst of his address, in the guise of a forceful parenthesis which Rómulo delivered with a raised tone of voice giving emphasis to every word, he made it clear that he was, as he had been in the past, an irreconcilable foe of the Communists. Their allegiance to a foreign power and their belief in totalitarian methods—Rómulo proclaimed—were incompatible with the aspirations of a reborn democratic Venezuela.

Being scheduled to leave Caracas early the following morning, I rushed back to the hotel after the meeting was over, without the opportunity of talking again to Rómulo, who was engulfed in a crowd of well-wishers pressing around him to shake his hand, many for the first time since his return from exile. But I left for him a brief congratulatory note saying that his "masterly address" had made me very happy.

On August 8, 1959, I related to Betancourt how the political trends in Venezuela were viewed in democratic and labor circles abroad. I acquainted him, also, with the recurrence of attacks against him from pro-Jiménez and pro-Trujillo elements in the United States. I wrote in part:

As you can see from the enclosed clippings,[3] the "campaign" continues unabated. In spite of the overwhelming demonstration given by the Venezuelan people that they will not stand for any return to military dictatorship, a large number of true friends of Venezuelan democracy are sincerely worried about the possibility that sooner or later the military may again succeed in taking over the country. The alleged increasing influence of the Communists will, of course, be the excuse. However, if the democratic forces act in time with political sagacity and understanding, the "excuse" will then fool nobody.

I have never doubted—more so after my last conversation with you—the firm determination of AD to end, as soon as possible, the present status of "coexistence" with the Communist Party. Also, I never had any doubt as to your strong opposition to any form, explicit or implicit, of Popular Front. But I would not be true to our friendship if I were not to tell you that many, many friends of Venezuelan democracy in the United States as well as in Latin America, keep on asking: "Why must the Communists be represented in the leadership of the labor movement of Venezuela, even in those unions where the Communists are in insignificant minority?" If the Popular Front is to be rejected at the political and governmental level, why not reject it also in the labor field?

This issue came up at the last meeting of the ORIT Subcommittee, held last month in Mexico City, at the initiative of the Latin American members themselves, and not from those from the United States. I am happy to inform you, however, that the ORIT leaders reaffirmed their absolute confidence in their Venezuelan friends.

During the month of August, the AD forces consolidated their control over the vital National Federation of Petroleum Workers by winning overwhelmingly at its national Convention. Similar victories were scored in other national labor federations. At the AD Convention, the first one after the downfall of the dictatorship, Rómulo Betancourt and the so-called Old Guard scored an impressive victory over the left-wing. However, that Convention made it unmistakably clear that the AD dissidents were not an isolated voice. They were well organized, bound by an ideological cohesion, outspoken in their determination to eventually gain control of the Party and lead it along the path of Marxist revolutionary doctrine, if necessary in cooperation with—but in no event against—the Communists. They were a minority, but a militant one, with which it was obvious that the true democratic forces inside AD sooner or later would have to reckon. Meanwhile the Party needed unity in order to win the approaching presidential and congressional elections. This unity was needed by the old guard as well as by the dissidents themselves. So there were no purges, no immediate moves to remove the dissidents from the positions of power and influence they had already gained in the Party's press and internal organizational structure.

Another attempted military coup—stronger than the first one in July—took place early in September. Again the workers, with the Communists very active among them, rose in defense of the provisional regime. Bloody clashes ensued before the rebels surrendered.

To the friends of Venezuelan democracy abroad, the events of the first week of September 1958 appeared as another encouraging demonstration of the unbreakable will of the people to resist, even at the cost of lives, every attempt to restore the hated military regime; but they also showed how the leftist elements were taking advantage of these coups to extend their influence over the masses, especially the dwellers in the city slums. The military, in their lust for power, were playing into the hands of the Communists. Faced with a real threat from the military on the right, the Communists were able to regain the initiative in demanding stronger unity in the labor movement, closer coordination in the political field, a single list of congressional candidates and a single candidate for President whom "all revolutionary forces," including the Communists, could support.

Alarmed over the adverse consequences that these continued attempted military coups were having on the consolidation of Venezuelan democracy, on September 9, 1958, I wrote to Betancourt:

I firmly believe, if I can judge the situation correctly from such a far-away observatory, that the democratic forces should demand from the government the adoption of an iron-fisted policy to crush all those elements who attempt, by staging military coups, to stop the march of democratic reconstruction of the country. I am sure that public opinion in the Americas will understand and justify any required repressive measure, legitimized by the sacred duty of the overwhelming majority of the people to defend their rights to live in peace and freedom.

Negotiations toward the reaching of an electoral agreement between the various political groups for the selection of a single candidate had started as soon as the military-civilian junta announced its intention to call for elections. When it became obvious, after the various parties had proceeded to select their respective standard-bearers, that agreement on a single candidate would be too difficult, if not impossible, the idea was advanced of adopting a type of collegiate government, with each party represented, presided over by a neutral nonpolitical technician. For a while, the name of industrialist Eugenio Mendoza loomed as a possibility for chairman of the collegiate government.

Betancourt was not averse to the idea, provided the other prospective partners would recognize AD preeminence. However, it was becoming clear that the collegiate proposal could not prosper and AD finally resolved to go its own way with Betancourt as its presidential candidate and a separate slate of candidates for Congress. The three national parties agreed, however, in what became known as the *Pacto de Punto Fijo*— The Pact of Punto Fijo (from the name of Rafael Caldera's residence, where it was signed), to form a coalition Cabinet with representatives of the three groups, regardless of who should win the presidency. It had already been announced that Admiral Wolfgang Larrazabal would run for the URD and Rafael Caldera for the COPEI. Admiral Larrazabal, in order to run, resigned from the presidency of the junta, which was assumed by Professor Edgar Sanabria. But even after the respective candidates had been officially announced, efforts to revive the idea of the collegiate continued up to the very eve of the elections.

In a conversation Rómulo Betancourt had with me at the Tamanaco Hotel in Caracas the night of November 6, which lasted until 2 A.M., he argued that his AD party would risk committing virtual suicide were it to go before the electorate without its own separate flag. After having won overwhelmingly the elections of 1947, having been deposed by a military coup, having suffered by far the most during the years of the dictatorship, and after having led at the cost of so many victims the struggle in the underground and in exile, Rómulo stressed, "our decision to abdicate in favor of a vague, untried, and full-of-danger formula of the collegiate, would demoralize our followers and would be an historical mistake."

It was clear to me, too, that the collegiate form of government, in Venezuela of all places, would have broken down at the very first test that required decisiveness of action, since only unanimity—not always easy to obtain—could provide it.

The possibility of Rómulo Betancourt's return to the presidency alarmed those conservative elements, in the business community as well as the middle classes, who never liked the AD program of social and economic reforms. It was also opposed by most of the foreign companies and by certain strong elements inside the military-civilian junta itself. In their shortsightedness, they would rather have seen the military regain power than the reformers of AD, whom many of them considered "just as bad as the Communists"—an expression used indiscriminately against anyone who was against the economic and social *status quo*. As for the Communists, who had always violently opposed Betancourt and his AD party, and who correctly surmised that with Betancourt back in the presidential Miraflores Palace they would inevitably face rough going and leaner days, they concentrated on spreading the rumor that a vote for Rómulo would be a vote wasted because the military would, by all means, deny him the victory and would seize the government for themselves. The Communists were especially put out by Rómulo's repeated assertion that he did not want their help to win the presidency. They were for Admiral Larrazabal.

Other observers, impressed by the fact that AD was weak in Caracas and the big cities, and perhaps unaware of the overwhelming strength that AD was commanding in the countryside, thought that Betancourt would be defeated. Such sentiment prevailed, for instance, at the U.S. Embassy. A poll taken among twenty top Embassy officials showed sixteen to four predicting a Larrazabal victory.

All these pros and cons of the Betancourt candidacy were thoroughly gone over during that long night conversation at the Tamanaco. At the end, in parting, Rómulo told me: "I deeply feel inside me that I owe it to Venezuela, for her own sake, to run and win. But I also realize full well the harm that would ensue if I run and lose. Yet there is not the slightest possibility that this will happen. I have felt the pulse of my people, of my workers, of my *campesinos*. I know for sure that with them I am going to win."

The elections took place on December 7. Although it was a three-man race, Betancourt won with an absolute majority of the votes. The AD party also won a majority in Congress. When the count was approaching its end and his victory had been conceded, Rómulo penned in longhand, on the stationery of the AD party, this message to me:

The triumph has been assured. There is no danger, from any sector, of refusal to recognize the results. The armed forces are disciplined and I do not see any threat from that sector. I never thought that there would be any, as you remember from our conversation. I say no more now, only to assure you and our friends that I shall remain the same one of the exile, always!

Rómulo Betancourt was inaugurated President of Venezuela on February 13, 1959. The program of festivities connected with the event lasted a number of days. I was privileged to attend the ceremony, together with Mrs. Romualdi, as a member of the official United States delegation, appointed by President Eisenhower and headed by former New York Governor Thomas E. Dewey.[4] The Communist press protested my inclusion in the U.S. official delegation, claiming that my presence in Caracas "would bring a discordant note to the harmony prevailing in the labor movement of Venezuela."

The day after the swearing-in ceremony, the foreign delegations went to Miraflores Palace to pay their respects to the new President. Betancourt received us in the beautiful, large Ambassadors' Hall. One after another, in the order of precedence, the delegations were summoned before the President, who briefly chatted with the head of each successive delegation and then shook hands with its members. But when our Chairman Dewey called my name and I approached, Betancourt, with outstretched arms said: "With him there shall be no protocol." And he embraced and hugged me, in the full glare of the camera lights, and then whispered into my ear: "This is my answer to the Communists! . . ."

Also present at Betancourt's inauguration was my sister Lucy, whose husband Giuseppe Lupis, Italy's Undersecretary of State for Foreign Affairs, was chief of his country's special delegation. The night of the State Inaugural Ball, I spotted her, resplendent in evening gown, together with Governor Dewey, attired in formal white tie. They were seated, conversing in earnest, with Governor Dewey visibly pleased and making frequent gestures of accord.

"What were you talking about with Dewey?" I asked her when the conversation was over.

"I reminded him of his first political campaign, in 1936, when he ran for District Attorney in New York on the Labor Party ticket. Don't you remember? During the entire campaign, after working all day in the shop as dress finisher, I used to go down with my husband 'Peppino' to the Italian neighborhood of the East Side, around First Avenue, to harangue the crowd from a soapbox, urging them to vote for Dewey. The gangsters were then rampant, especially in the garment industry, and we all wanted Dewey to be elected so that he could start sending some of those crooks to jail. Which he promptly did, after he won."

Governor Dewey himself told me later how much he had enjoyed such a totally unexpected encounter with a former ILGWU dressmaker, and how pleased he was that my sister revived in him the memory of that first battle that launched him on his outstanding political career.

I do not know of any President, of the many I have met, who had to face so many problems, difficulties, military revolts, attempts on his life, sabotage, terrorism, arson, and political desertion as Betancourt did during his five-year term of office. Nor do I know of any President who in the midst of all those difficulties managed to accomplish so much in the fields of education, economic development, agrarian reform, and labor-management relations, as he did.

To begin with, the very first day in office he served notice that he intended to finish his term and to hand over the presidential sash to his legally elected successor.[5] This was then deemed almost impossible, because it had never happened in the long history of Venezuela—but Rómulo did it, in spite of the fact that the going was always rough. On one occasion, a segment of the armed forces, aided by Dominican dictator Trujillo, staged a serious revolt against his regime.[6] On another occasion, also at Trujillo's instigation, his body was maimed and he lay for days in bed fighting for his life.[7] The pressure from violence, disturbances, sabotage, and full-fledged guerrilla attacks became so intense toward the end of his term that foreign correspondents began to predict that Betancourt would fall either at the hands of the Communists or the military. But he did not fall. Instead, his determination and heroic resistance made it possible for the Venezuelans to defy the terrorists and to have free elections to choose Betancourt's successor. Rómulo's unique characteristic was a deep belief in his historic mission. With determined calm and supreme dedication, he never doubted his ultimate victory as statesman, as he had never doubted his ultimate victory as leader of the resistance.

To his people, his followers, the rank and file of his party, and above all to those whom he called the front line soldiers of the resistance, his word was law, his simple suggestion was a command. Enrique Tejera París, who is now Venezuelan Ambassador to the United States, told me of an episode in which he was involved, which is characteristic of the tremendous respect and obedience his "soldiers" had for Betancourt. In July 1957, when the struggle against Pérez Jiménez was approaching its end, Betancourt was working to bring about an alliance between AD, URD, and COPEI with the main immediate objective of unifying the forces of the resistance for the final push. He needed someone of high caliber and recognized ability to enter Venezuela clandestinely in order to discuss with Dr. Rafael Caldera, leader of COPEI, the details of the alliance. URD leader Jovito Villalba was in New York and contacts with him presented no difficulty. Tejera París was then employed at the UN Secretariat. He was invited by Rómulo to visit him in Puerto Rico. Once there, Rómulo asked him point-blank to undertake the mission to Venezuela, for which it would be necessary for him, of course, to resign from his post in order not to involve the UN in any way in the Venezuelan underground activity. "I accepted without batting an eyelash," Tejera París related to me years later, "happy and proud that the Chief had so much confidence in me as to ask me to undertake such an important and dangerous mission."

Months later, when Rómulo Betancourt had moved to New York and practically all the Venezuelan refugees living in the United States had also assembled in that city ready to fly back home as soon as the expected successful revolt inside Venezuela materialized, he was invited by a group of his countrymen to have dinner in a restaurant. Seats were not immediately available, so one of the group approached the headwaiter and in a tone of voice calculated to arouse respect and awe, said:

"Please, hurry up. The General has no time to wait."

"How do you like that, Rómulo?" interjected others—"being called a general, of all things! . . ."

"And why not?" replied Rómulo, not entirely joking. "After all, I *am* your General!"

General, Chief, or *Caudillo?* Which of these terms the Latin Americans reserve for their strong-willed leaders did Rómulo like best? Once he told me, after he had left the Presidency, that the *caudillo* has a place in the order of things in Venezuela and that people in his country did actually consider him a *caudillo*. Then, after a moment of pause he added: "A *caudillo,* unlike the tyrant or the dictator, commands following and respect through the exemplary performance of his whole life; through the ascendancy of his vision, probity, unselfishness, deeds, and courage."

Few outsiders shared Betancourt's innermost thinking and feelings, during his second presidency, as much as I did. On the occasion of my frequent visits to Venezuela he never failed to invite me to have breakfast or dinner with him. Knowing of my constant travels on behalf of the AFL-CIO, he listened carefully to whatever report or observation I had to make on the political or labor developments in this or that country. On his part, he never hesitated to confide in me his expectations, his plans and their chances of success, or his worries and difficulties, national and international. There were, of course, moments of anger, but never of despair. In one of these outbursts, he upbraided the United States foreign correspondents flocking in droves to Venezuela whenever there were spectacular acts of Communist violence to report. "They seem happy to create the impression that Venezuelan democracy is dying," he exploded. "But why do they never mention the tremendous support that my government is getting from the workers and peasants and the lack of any significant Communist penetration in the labor movement?"

Another frequent Betancourt explosion was directed against the necessary, yet incredibly annoying, security measures enforced to protect his life. Once he invited me to spend a day at the beach with him near Macuto. But at the last moment he cancelled the trip explaining: "How can I subject you to all this—surrounded by cars full of troops as we motor down; encircled by machine-gun-toting policemen as we enter the seashore establishment; flanked by armed personal guards as we venture into the water for a dip. This is worse than the walking jail I used to complain of during the exile." And then he would sigh: "I long for the day when I will be able to walk, alone, in the streets of some distance city, unrecognized by the people, stop in front of a bookstore, enter at will a movie theater, being free like so many millions of human beings . . . !" As a human being full of vitality, who knew how to indulge, when he could, in the *joie de vivre,* Romulo was, understandably, prone to occasional lapses into moods of annoyance and anger. But these were not his typical traits. His outstanding characteristics, which truly dominated him, especially when facing a political crisis or when handling affairs of state or of his Party, were calm and deliberate analysis, followed by a steely resolution to carry out, once his mind was made up, whatever he had decided to do. Then nothing would frighten him; nothing would stop him.

In the darkest years of his regime, 1962–1963, after the URD had left his government coalition and his own party had been reduced in strength by two splits,[8] Betancourt was governing with only the AD-COPEI partnership. It was then that the Communist violence reached an unprecedented peak. One Sunday afternoon bombs exploded in a suburban train going from Caracas to Los Teques. There were many killed, including children, all of the working class. Outraged public opinion demanded strong action from the government to suppress the terrorists. The Supreme Court had supported the outlawing of the Communist Party and the Revolutionary Left Movement (MIR), but the members of Congress belonging to these two parties continued to enjoy parliamentary immunity (or "impunity" as the people of the CTV used to say) which many good Venezuelan democrats, in COPEI as well as in AD, were determined to defend as they regarded it a bulwark of representative democracy. However, the Communist and MIR Congressmen brazenly abused their parliamentary immunity to direct the terroristic campaign against the government. Could this immunity apply to criminal acts of terrorism? No, resolved Betancourt; and when news of the train bombing, with so many men, women, and children killed, reached him in Punta de Hierro, state of Sucre, he radioed from a Navy frigate an order to proceed immediately to arrest the Communist and MIR members of Parliament.

"There was a possibility that the Cabinet would resign," Romulo told me a couple of years later.

"And what would you have done in such an eventuality," I ventured to ask. "Withdraw the order of arrest?"

"Oh, no," he replied. "I already had in my pocket a list of new Ministers, military and civilian technicians, to be sworn in. But it was not necessary. In such great emergency and supreme national peril, the Cabinet stood loyally by me."

The Cuban Castro revolution found in Venezuela a favorable echo. As a matter of fact it was being insistently rumored, in 1958, that arms and other forms of support were given to Castro by the civilian-military junta before Betancourt assumed power. The average Venezuelan, especially in the trade union field, regarded the Cuban revolution, at that time considered a democratic one, akin to their revolution against the Pérez Jiménez dictatorship. Rómulo Betancourt himself was never an admirer of Fidel Castro, and when the latter went to Venezuela in 1959, he received him properly but coolly. In the AD Party, however, as well as in the ranks of URD and even among the youth of COPEI, there were many who admired Castro and wanted close cooperation with his movement. When, therefore, the Castroites began to attack ORIT, and particularly my person among its leaders, as well as such spokesmen of the democratic anti-Communist left as President Figueres of Costa Rica and Governor Luis Múñoz Marín of Puerto Rico, the Youth Movement of AD, at their national plenum held in Caracas March 21–23, 1959, adopted a resolution offensive to ORIT and the above-mentioned democratic spokesmen. The National Executive Committee of AD, at a special meeting held April 1, under the chairmanship of Dr. Raul Leoni, adopted a statement disavowing the action taken by the Youth Section and reaffirmed its friendship and admiration for the persons and the organizations affected. The text of the AD statement was sent to me by President Betancourt himself, with a letter—a copy of which he sent to AFL-CIO President George Meany—in which he said:

I am attaching this document because I believe you will appreciate it, especially in this moment in which I presume you feel disturbed over the attacks against you launched by a group of Cuban trade unionists. On my part, I want to say to you that today more than ever I recognize your extremely effective contribution to the cause of civil liberties, among them freedom of trade union organization. We, the most responsible leaders who occupy positions of command in the popular democratic movements, see in you a true friend of Latin America.

I did not read Betancourt's letter until much later, in June, when I was able to return to my office in Washington after recovering from a coronary infarct which I suffered April 12 in Costa Rica while on a trade union mission there. While I was understandably pleased with the contents of the AD resolution—in which, as President Betancourt himself pointed out, AD and its trade union militants recognized the contribution of ORIT and ICFTU to the struggle against the dictatorship—I nevertheless realized that things in the democratic labor sector of Venezuela were not going as smoothly as we had anticipated. Of this we had a confirmation at the first national trade union Convention, held November 13–21,

1959, in the workers' seashore resort of Los Caracas, at which the Confederation of Labor of Venezuela (CTV) was reorganized. The AD delegates, although a majority,[9] gave in to the pressure of their strong left-wing minority faction, and for the sake of "unity" agreed to reduce their representation in the Executive Board to 7 out of 14, giving 3 to the Communists and 2 each to URD and COPEI—a representation out of proportion to their real strength at the Congress. The Executive Council, consisting of 57 members, was divided 29 AD, 14 Communists, 7 COPEI, and 7 URD. AD managed, however, to elect José González Navarro and Augusto Malavé Villalba to the key posts of President and General Secretary, respectively.

The weak performance of the AD members belonging to the CTV old guard at this CTV convention caused considerable apprehension and misgivings abroad. Their subsequent decision, in line with the unitarian policy of the CTV, to support a pact of alliance with the Castro-controlled CTC and to invite ORIT to participate in a round table conference in Caracas together with the Communists (an invitation which ORIT declined), and their reluctance to denounce the maneuvers of some of their colleagues in the CTV Executive Board in favor of the organization of a new Latin American trade union body rival to ORIT, prompted letters of warning on the part of friends, including myself. I was beginning to feel that our Venezuelan friends were perhaps sacrificing too much on the altar of unity.

On the other hand, I felt sure that a clash of ideologies, methods, and political tactics would soon erupt and force the AD leaders to split with the Communists and their supporters. It had also become quite obvious that this fight would be forced on the AD people, if for no other reason, as a measure of self-defense. The Communists became more and more aggressive in their opposition to the policy of the Betancourt government. The left wing of AD, which had seceded to form the MIR, began to cooperate with the Communists, and so did certain elements of URD. On the other hand, the members of COPEI—a loyal partner in the government coalition—were getting closer to the AD people. AD and COPEI members of both the Executive Board and the Executive Council had among themselves a clear majority which would enable them to strike . . . at the opportune moment.

Serious disturbances took place in Venezuela during the month of October 1960, provoked by extremist elements, with the complicity of the anti-Betancourt elements inside the CTV leadership itself. While these disturbances were still under way in Caracas, ORIT General Secretary Alfonso Sánchez Madariaga wired President Betancourt a message of solidarity and support and gave a statement to the press in which he described the disturbances set off by pro-Communist elements as "one more manifestation of the penetration campaign of extra-continental forces in the Americas which ORIT has been insistently denouncing."

Toward the end of October, in the course of a South American tour, I stopped for a few days in Venezuela in order to give Betancourt "the personal greetings of AFL-CIO President George Meany, and the assurances that the labor movement in the United States was in complete solidarity with his efforts to defend constitutional democracy in Venezuela from repeated mob rule attacks of Communist totalitarians and Fascist reactionaries." [10]

During my brief stay in Caracas, I conferred with the leaders of the democratic trade union movement belonging to the Democratic Action (AD) and Christian Democratic (COPEI) parties, assuring them of AFL-CIO support in their efforts to prevent the domination of the Venezuelan Confederation of Labor (CTV) by the Communist party and its allies.

On November 1, 1960, over 200,000 workers and peasants assembled in Caracas to demonstrate their solidarity with the democratic constitutional government. Among those who addressed this huge demonstration were José González Navarro, President of the CTV, and Dagoberto González, leader of the COPEI trade union forces.

Following a second wave of disturbances during the last week of November 1960, the CTV leadership again rallied in support of President Betancourt. José González Navarro joined with other national leaders, including the Archbishop of Caracas, Monsignor José Manuel Quintero, in repudiating the disorders caused by the Communists and their allies and in pledging continued support of the constitutional government.

Trade union leaders belonging to the AD met in a National Conference in Caracas, November 12 and 13, in order to examine the trade union situation and plan future action to consolidate democratic control of the labor movement. The best-known trade union leaders of Venezuela, those who had founded the labor movement and were in control of the most important organizations, attended the meeting, which was also addressed by the President of the Republic himself.

The AD trade union Conference recommended the immediate convocation of the Central Committee of the CTV for the purpose of reaffirming the resolution adopted at the III CTV Convention in November

1959, which pledged support of the constitutional government headed by President Rómulo Betancourt. The Conference also went on record favoring the calling, in the near future, of a special Convention of the CTV, "for the purpose of reorganizing its leadership." This move presaged elimination from any post of control in the CTV of Communist elements and their allies. The combined forces of the AD and COPEI parties had more than sufficient votes to bring about such needed reorganization.

The CTV Central Committee met in Caracas, December 16–20, 1960. After a four-day debate, in which the trade union forces comprising the democratic bloc took the offensive against the leftist coalition composed of Communist delegates and members of the MIR, five members of the Executive Board belonging to these two groups were condemned for their political revolutionary activity and were put on trial for violation of trade union discipline.[11]

These members were Martín Ramírez, Eloy Torres, and Rodolfo Quintero, Communists, and Américo Chacón and José Marcano, of the MIR. The five were specifically charged with having attempted to call general strikes during the months of October and November for the purpose of overthrowing the Betancourt administration. These subversive moves were made in violation of CTV policy.

The CTV Central Committee also approved a motion which abrogated the pact of solidarity and mutual assistance signed in 1959 between the CTV and the CTC of Cuba. The motion specified that fraternal relationships with the Cuban organization would be resumed only after civil rights and freedom of trade union organization were reestablished in that country.

The CTV Convention, called for November 1961, was preceded by elections in the unions and federations throughout the country. There were rival slates presented by AD and COPEI on the one hand, and the Communists, MIR and URD [12] on the other. As a result of these elections, the AD-COPEI combination came to control about 85 percent of the country's local unions and all but one of the national federations. They were thus able to control the overwhelming majority of the delegates to the CTV Convention—so much so that the Communists and the MIRistas decided at the last moment not to attend. The Convention removed all Communists and MIR members from the CTV leadership and extended the purge all the way down to the local unions. Since the Communists and the MIRistas did the same thing in the few unions they controlled, there took place a virtual split in the organized labor movement in Venezuela. For a while, the Communists, the MIRistas, the followers of URD, and the labor members of ARS—another small group that had split from AD—worked together and even set up a central labor organization of their own. But the CTV remained in firm control of the great majority of the country's unions and continued to be one of the bulwarks of President Betancourt's democratic regime.

In spite of the violence which kept Venezuela in constant turmoil, especially during the last two years of Betancourt's administration, and the political divisions inside the unions themselves, Venezuelan organized labor very seldom resorted to strikes to settle labor-management disputes.[13] Collective bargaining was the rule, with the result that Venezuela recorded an impressive rate of economic growth [14] and industrial expansion. Typical of the labor contracts that were negotiated in that period in Venezuela was the one in the sugar industry which I analyzed and reported on extensively in the November 1962 issue of the *Inter-American Labor Bulletin*.

The original collective agreement in the cane sugar industry of Venezuela, signed June 2, 1959, for a period of three years, had a provision which called for the establishment of a special Wage Commission which, one year before the expiration of the contract, would meet to decide whether in the collective agreement expected to go into effect on June 2, 1962, the wage scale should be altered. The Wage Commission recommended that in view of the fact that the price of sugar had remained the same, the wage scale should be extended without change for another three years.

However, the Commission also recommended the adoption of a social program which, when completed during the maximum period of three years, would involve the investment of about $10 million for the construction of low-cost housing for the workers, with expectations that the Alliance for Progress would extend credits for the supplementary financing of the project. The labor contract also provided for the establishment of fifteen consumers' cooperatives for which the employers were to furnish 90 percent of the capital. Other benefits gained in the agreement were life insurance for the workers and the establishment of an unemployment fund, financed exclusively by the employers, to subsidize the workers during the dead season which follows the sugar harvest.

Daniel Carías, President of the Venezuelan Federation of Sugar Workers, after the signing of the agreement declared: "We can now say that we have made a real Alliance for Progress." On behalf of the employers, Dr. Rafael Colmenares Peraza, President of the Association, added: "We are now engaged in a silent revolution."

On the occasion of my visit to Venezuela, during the last week of September 1962, I accepted an invitation extended to me jointly by the Federation of Cane Sugar Workers and the Association of Sugar Producers, to participate in ceremonies for the inauguration of a consumers' cooperative in the Central Tocuyo, in the state of Lara.

I was gratified to undertake the long journey, first by plane to Barquisimeto and then by car to Tocuyo, in the company of Daniel Carías and Dr. Colmenares Peraza. In addition to inspecting the consumers' cooperative in Tocuyo, before it was opened to the public, we visited another cooperative in a nearby center, already in operation, and two housing projects well under way. Everywhere I heard nothing but praise for the program, which had already substantially changed the economic outlook of the villages and towns benefited by it. I was astonished to hear, for example, that in each of the five communities where cooperatives were already operating (there were to be ten in all) the cost of the primary consumers' articles had gone down as much as 35 percent.

The two hosts explained to me that a survey conducted by the Sugar Employers' Association in the towns and villages where the bulk of the sugar workers live, brought to light the startling fact that 51 percent of the average wage was spent by its earner to provide food and other basic items for himself and his family. Thus arose the idea of establishing in each locality where the sugar mills operate, a consumers' cooperative, open to the public but owned by the sugar workers themselves.

A Sugar Industry Housing Foundation, financed exclusively by the employers of the ten sugar mills, but operating with the union's representation, provided all the necessary technical services and surveys leading to the construction of the housing projects.

The employer provided a down payment, not repayable, of from 40 percent of the value of the house (in the majority of cases) to 15 percent of the value for those in $350 monthly bracket. The balance was put up by the National Housing Development Bank on a mortgage repayable in twenty years at low interest. Those workers who already owned a house could either use the employer's down payment to wipe out their mortgage, or, if the house was substandard, to effectuate improvements or to build additions.

With this scheme, the agreement in the sugar industry brought nearer to realization President Betancourt's edict that "the *rancho* must go." [15] The scourge of the *rancho* was well illustrated by Daniel Carías, who, at the ceremony marking the signing of the agreement in Caracas, stated that the average Venezuelan sugar worker lived in a *rancho* that lacked the most elementary hygienic facilities and forced the family to live in promiscuity. "This deteriorates the concept of human dignity, breeds vice and alcoholism, and is also the direct cause of absenteeism and low productivity," said the sugar workers' leader.

When the terms of the Sugar Labor Contract were announced, criticism was voiced in Venezuelan leftist trade union circles because of its main feature of social-projects financing in lieu of wage increases. But by the time I joined Carías and Dr. Colmenares in the journey to Tocuyo, both told me that criticism had decreased and that in fact a number of other unions were making plans to advance similar proposals to their respective employers. Daniel Carías, a sugar worker himself [16] who knew the mores of his own people, disposed of the criticism with this frank remark:

If instead of all this (the housing and the cooperatives) we had simply asked the traditional triennial percentage of wage increase, the gain would soon have disappeared in the form of higher food prices and perhaps in more consumption of beer and rum. Furthermore, our homes would still be those *ranchos* [pointing to those still cluttering the land near the housing project we were visiting] and our children would still play in the mud instead of using the garden plots and lawns that go with the new homes.

Before leaving I obtained from the Sugar Workers' Federation and from the Sugar Employers' Group some interesting literature dealing with the operation of their joint efforts to raise the standard of living of the sugar workers. I learned, also, that as a logical result of the success of these efforts, Communist influence in the sugar unions had been reduced to almost zero.

Most interesting was a pamphlet entitled "Collective Bargaining in the Sugar Industry of Venezuela." It contained, as a sort of preface, the text of the address that Daniel Carías, as President of the Sugar Workers' Federation, delivered at the signing of the new collective agreement. I was particularly enthusiastic over the following passage, which, perhaps more than anything else, illustrates the new social thinking that, under Betancourt's government, was making headway among democratic trade union leaders:

I declare that we have every right to feel proud for having acted as pioneers in obtaining a new type of labor gain, adjusted to the degree of added cost that the industry can stand. We are not interested in destroying industrial enterprises nor in weakening the economic system. We want greater development which in turn will permit the industrialization of our country, its greater economic strength and independence, and the achievement of higher standards. . . .

By 1962 the struggle waged against the Betancourt administration by the wave of terrorism had assumed international ramifications. Cuban

Premier Fidel Castro, smarting under the rebukes suffered at the hands of the Organization of American States, intensified his efforts to topple, by internal subversion, Betancourt's government, which he and the Sino-Soviet Communist international conspiracy had proclaimed to be the No. 1 target of their Latin American offensive. On the other hand, all the democratic forces of the Western Hemisphere, including the Kennedy administration in Washington, and especially the free labor movement led by ORIT and the AFL-CIO, closed ranks in support of the besieged Venezuelan democratic president.

As if street fighting, bombings, and every form of sabotage and arson were not enough,[17] leftist opposition within the constitutional framework had deprived Betancourt of control of the House of Representatives, although the AD-COPEI coalition retained control of the Senate. The opposition's legislative objective was to block constructive efforts on the part of Betancourt's administration to rehabilitate Venezuela after the wasteful and corrupt Pérez Jiménez dictatorship, by withholding approval of loans from the United States and other countries for development programs.

However, as the violence increased and the legislative opposition became more obstructionist, a reaction developed inside the country. Adding their strength to the assured loyalty of the armed forces and organized labor, many middle-of-the-road and even conservative forces from the ranks of agriculture, industry, and commerce, which had in the past opposed Rómulo Betancourt's mixed-economy concepts as some form of dangerous socialism, came to his support, fully convinced that he was the only alternative to the leftist-sponsored chaos aimed at creating a popular front type of government which in no time would have gone the way of Castro's Cuba.

The technique of the opposition was to force Betancourt, both by acts of violence and by legislative obstructionism, to rule by decree so that he could then be accused of being a dictator. Had Rómulo fallen for the bait of the opposition, which at times adopted extremely provocative postures to force his hand, he would probably have incurred further loss of political support, which might have seriously impaired his continuation in office. Instead he waited. Realizing that public opinion was not yet ready for strong repressive measures promulgated by decree, which obviously were the only ones that could defeat the opposition, he temporized until he felt sure that the situation was mature and public opinion was ready for him to strike.

As a demonstration of the strength of his government and of his confidence in the loyal support of the armed forces and the people at large, in the month of February 1963 Rómulo Betancourt absented himself from Venezuela for a state visit to the United States and Mexico. The visit to the United States was a succession of triumphs. The interviews with President Kennedy, the receptions at the White House and State Department, the extensive press coverage and the laudatory editorial comments, the imposing dinner at the Waldorf-Astoria in New York tendered by the capitalist-studded Pan American Society, the breakfast in Miami given by the AFL-CIO Executive Council, the luncheon given by Governor Nelson A. Rockefeller at his Pocantico Hills estate, and finally the reception given by Betancourt himself at the Venezuelan Embassy in Washington were events that all contributed to dramatize the exalted status achieved by this statesman who, years before, in this very same country, had had to defend himself from continuous slanderous accusations of being a Communist and had had to endure the slights and humiliations inflicted on him by insensitive, shortsighted high government officials. Rómulo, of course, could not fail to register with satisfaction and pride the extraordinary change that had taken place, and to regard it as a sort of national manifestation of *desagravio* (moral reparation). But wherever he went and whenever he spoke, he made it a point to declare that his first and everlasting appreciation and gratitude would always go to organized labor.

For the Miami AFL-CIO Executive Council breakfast, Betancourt had a special government plane bring up from Venezuela José González Navarro, President of the CTV, and twenty other labor leaders so that they could mingle and fraternize with their colleagues from the AFL-CIO, thus signifying that their aspirations had merged, that they were engaged in the same international struggle for human dignity and freedom. Incidentally, that morning was also a fitting occasion to celebrate Betancourt's fifty-sixth birthday. But even more revealing of his sentiments of gratitude to United States labor was what he did and said at the reception he hosted at the Venezuelan Embassy in Washington. When my turn came at the receiving line to be introduced by him to President and Mrs. John F. Kennedy, Rómulo put an arm over my shoulder and punctuating his words with his left forefinger, said: "Here you have a countryman of yours, a naturalized American born in Italy, who in the decade of the fifties did more for inter-American understanding and the presentation of the democratic image of your country in Latin America than almost all of the Ambassadors sent by the State Department." President Kennedy assented, saying: "I know, I know! . . ." Later the same evening, when the time came to sit down for the buffet supper, Betancourt ignored

Cabinet Ministers and Ambassadors, Senators, Congressmen, and luminaries of the arts and sciences, world-famous columnists and kings of industry and finance. He looked instead for the AFL-CIO President and Mrs. Meany. When he spotted their table, he sat down by them saying: "I want to sit next to you, Mr. Meany, because I want to demonstrate the great debt of gratitude I owe you and your organization for the steadfast and loyal support given to me and democratic Venezuela during the long years of our exile!"

Presidential elections to choose the successor to President Betancourt were set for December 1, 1963. As the day approached, the Communists and their allies intensified their campaign of intimidation and terror with the aim of scaring the voters and inducing them to stay away from the polling places. By causing a large number of abstentions, they hoped to discredit the democratic process of the elections and its results. The government, however, stood firm, assured the citizens that all possible measures would be taken to protect them in the exercise of their civic rights, and organized a countercampaign to fight fear and terror. The forces of the CTV were again mobilized. They did such a magnificent job that the press was unanimous in giving them, and the disciplined armed forces, credit for the enthusiastic orderly way in which the elections were conducted. Ninety-one percent of the registered voters went to the polls. It was a tremendous demonstration of the will of the Venezuelan people to defend at all costs their freedom and their democratic way of life, and to repudiate with an avalanche of ballots the attempt of a group of fanatics at the service of foreign tyrants to impose their will through the use of violence and terror.

The free trade union movement everywhere noted with satisfaction and pride the contribution of the CTV to the democratic triumph in Venezuela. On December 3, 1963, President George Meany sent to Augusto Malavé Villalba, General Secretary of the CTV, the following radiogram:

Please accept the deep admiration of the AFL-CIO for the strong and courageous support given by the CTV and the people of Venezuela to the preservation of democratic institutions and ideals in the face of Communist harassment and criminal acts. I hope that you will also convey these sentiments to your government and civic leaders who have aided the responsible labor movement which you direct to maintain a free and democratic society not only in Venezuela but throughout the hemisphere.

The pledge by Rómulo Betancourt to hand over the presidential sash to his legally elected successor was fulfilled on March 11, 1964, when Raul

Leoni—Betancourt's lifetime comrade-in-arms in the days of struggle, exile, and victory—took the oath of office. After that, Betancourt enjoyed a long rest, traveled around the world, finally free again to walk at will, as he had longed for so many years, the streets of many cities, to stop in front of bookstores, to enter museums and movie theaters, to enjoy the freedom of the ordinary mortal.

In the late spring of 1965, Betancourt came back to the United States to renew friendships and acquaintances, and to attend a testimonial dinner tendered in his honor, the night of June 3, at the Roosevelt Hotel in New York, by the Inter-American Association for Democracy and Freedom, which he himself had done so much to bring into existence fifteen years before, in Havana, Cuba.

What a tremendous success that testimonial dinner was! Miss Frances Grant, the dedicated and remarkable Secretary-General of the Association, expected a large attendance all right, but not the avalanche of reservations that came in from the moment the dinner announcement was made. Twice she had to change the place for a bigger hall. Yet more people kept coming in until the very last moment, so that still more tables had to be added and a second dais had to be arranged. Ambassadors from all the democratic countries of Latin America, Congressmen, Senators, Governors, mixed with labor people, industrialists, writers, academicians, and political and trade union fighters still in exile. There were many representatives of government and political parties from Venezuela, and a host of personal friends, all there to pay respect to the man who by then had become, by vision, deeds, and achievements, the Statesman of the Americas. And there were also the personal representatives of Venezuelan President Raul Leoni, of Chilean President Eduardo Frei, and of the President and Vice-President of the United States.

While people were coming in, some going directly to the banquet hall, others to the parlor where a reception was in progress for Betancourt and the many VIPs present, Frances Grant, helped by volunteers, struggled valiantly to arrange and rearrange seats and place cards. Finally she gave up and threw the doors open for the honor guest to come in. Betancourt was greeted with a tremendous demonstration that went beyond the admiration and affection for the man; it was a reaffirmation of faith in the ideals of freedom and democratic inter-Americanism which Rómulo Betancourt had come to symbolize. By then, nobody really cared for protocol or where he or she was seated. "Happy" Rockefeller found herself an empty chair at a corner table; many standees were waiting . . . for the multiplication of floor space so that other tables could still be brought in. Latecomers were sent up to the balcony where they went without the dinner, glad nevertheless to be able to see and hear. They heard the warm messages of salutation and praise from the three Presidents and Vice-President Hubert Humphrey, as well as those of statesmen, writers, diplomats, and political leaders from all over Latin America.[18] The program of speakers started with a keynote address by historian Arthur Schlesinger, Jr., followed by speeches by Governor Nelson A. Rockefeller, former Puerto Rico Governor Luis Múñoz Marín, Senator Edward Kennedy, Norman Thomas, Roger Baldwin, Adolf A. Berle, and still others.[19]

Finally, Miss Frances Grant, whom the audience greeted with a standing ovation in recognition of her many years of dedication to the cause of human rights and freedom, introduced the guest of honor. It was a long time before Rómulo Betancourt could actually begin his address, so insistent was the tumultuous ovation the audience gave him. In his sharp, concise style, under the visible strain of profound emotion that at times almost choked his voice, he recalled many things that night, not forgetting the crisis in which Latin America then found itself as a result of the landing of U.S. troops in Santo Domingo. Betancourt ended with the plea that "the pacification of Latin America—the pacification of the spirit and the conscience—can come only through the establishment by the OAS of a democratic collective security mechanism, sponsored by the democratic governments of the Americas and with the determined support of the United States, that would guarantee the existence of democratic regimes elected by the people, at the service of the people."

During the long but exciting proceedings, I sat next to Aureliano Sánchez Arango, the courageous Cuban democratic leader, who fought in the underground against Batista, and then against Castro, and finally had to go into exile. Aureliano and I reminisced, way back to 1950, when we first joined hands and resources to organize and make possible the Havana Conference where the Inter-American Association for Democracy and Freedom was born. We recalled, also, some of the events that had happened before and since, in Venezuela, Argentina, Peru, his own unfortunate Cuba, Brazil, Colombia, Central America, all over the Western Hemisphere. As we looked around, that memorable night, surveying the bountiful harvest from the modest seeds planted fifteen years before, we kept repeating to each other: ". . . It has been a truly great, glorious, rewarding experience. . . . If you could, wouldn't you do it all over again?"

Notes

1. The CTV affiliated with the CIT in 1949, after the *coup d'état* that drove its leaders into the underground or exile, and also took part in the organization of ORIT in 1951. It also joined the ICFTU.

The National United Trade Union Committee adopted a position of neutrality with respect to the existing international trade union organizations, but the leaders of the old CTV maintained fraternal relations with ORIT-ICFTU and sent delegates to the 1958 and 1961 ORIT Conventions held in Bogotá and Rio de Janeiro, respectively. Formal affiliation to ORIT-ICFTU was voted at the CTV Convention of November 1961.

2. The first attempt actually came later in that same month of July with a revolt of a group of Army officers. This was suppressed by a contingent of loyal troops and by the quick mobilization of workers who took up arms in the defense of the government.

3. The August 4, 1958, issues of the *Washington Post & Times Herald* and *Time* magazine, both contained references to the growing strength of the Communists in Venezuela. Also, *The Congressional Record*, August 5, 1958, issue, p. 14969, contained an attack on Rómulo Betancourt by Congressman Gardner R. Withrow of Wisconsin, who charged that there was a conspiracy between Betancourt and the President of the civilian-military junta, Admiral Larrazabal, and others, to court the Communists. Said Congressman Withrow: "I charge that this conspiracy has promised Communists positions, including the important Ministry of Interior."

4. Other members of the official U.S. delegation were Edward J. Sparks, Ambassador to Venezuela; Roy R. Rubottom, Jr., Assistant Secretary of State for Inter-American Affairs; General Lyman Lemnitzer; Harry Darby, former Senator from Kansas; industrialists John Budinger and John R. Reitemeyer; and Carl Bartch and Charles Burrows from the State Department.

5. Three years later, in March 1962, during a press interview with thirteen United States editors and publishers attending a series of seminars in Venezuela, President Betancourt declared, in answer to a question from Arville Schalaben, managing editor of the Milwaukee *Journal*, what he considered the most important achievement of his administration. He stated:

I believe that three things may be considered very important. The first is the certainty that I am going to turn over my office to my successor after he has been chosen in free elections.

The second . . . is the great impulse that is now being given in Venezuela to education at all levels, from grade schools through the university. . . .

The third aspect which I consider fundamental is that we are carrying out a profound change in the systems of ownership and working of the land. . . . We have installed more than 40,000 families on more than half a million hectares (approximately 1,250,000 acres) and it is also a reasonably certain fact that at the end of the two years of office which remain to me there will have been installed 150,000 families, or half of the 300,000 families which do not have their own land.

The program of agrarian reform continued without interruption under the administration of Betancourt's successor, Dr. Raul Leoni. In an interview he granted to the author on December 3, 1966, President Leoni stated that at the end of his term he expects to have given land titles to 120,000 families, "with the prospect that when the new President takes over, there will be only a few hundred *campesinos* left without land of their own."

6. During the days of April 20–22, 1960, rebel forces led by General Castro León,

who slipped across the border from Colombia, seized control of the city of San Cristóbal, capital of the state of Tachira. The workers responded with a general strike. When other military units failed to join his forces, General Castro León attempted to flee but was captured by a group of armed peasants. A Commission of the Organization of American States, composed of the Ambassador of Panama, Erasmo de la Guardia, chairman; Ambassadors Emilio Donato del Carril, of Argentina; Vicente Sánchez Gavito, of Mexico; Carlos A. Clulow, of Uruguay, and the representative of the United States, Henry Clinton Reed, was appointed to investigate charges preferred by Venezuelan Ambassador Marcos Falcón Briceño that the attempted military coup had received aid from the government of the Dominican Republic. The report of the Commission, issued August 8, 1960, fully substantiated such charges.

7. The same OAS Commission referred to above found the government of the Dominican Republic directly involved in the preparation of the attempt against the life of President Betancourt perpetrated in Caracas, June 24 of the same year, while he was traveling in his limousine through the Avenida de los Próceres on his way to a military review. In the attempt, which consisted of an explosion set off by microwaves, the President was gravely burned on his hands and face, his military aide was killed, and other occupants of his car wounded. The Commission report specifically stated that:

(a) The attempt on the life of President Betancourt, perpetrated June 24, 1960, was part of a plot to overthrow the government of Venezuela;

(b) The people involved in the life attempt and plot received moral support and material aid from high officials of the government of the Dominican Republic;

(c) Such help consisted, primarily, in providing the conspirators with facilities to travel and enter the Dominican Republic in connection with their subversive plans; in having twice made possible the arrival and departure from the San Isidro Military Air Base in the Dominican Republic of an airplane of Venezuelan registry; in furnishing arms for the coup against the government of Venezuela and the electronic equipment and the bomb used on the attempt on the life of President Betancourt; and in having trained the actual perpetrators of the attempt in the use of the electronic equipment and the bomb, as well as in having demonstrated its destructive potential.

8. In 1960, the left segment of the Democratic Action Party, led by Domingo Alberto Rángel, seceded and formed its own group—the Revolutionary Left Movement (MIR). The following year, still another left group, led by Raul Ramos Giménez, formed its separate organization, which they called Acción Revolucionaria Socialista (ARS).

9. At this CTV Convention, 56 percent of the delegates belonged to AD; 24 percent to the Communists; 11 percent to the URD, and 9 percent to COPEI.

10. *Inter-American Labor Bulletin,* December 1960.

11. The Union Tribunal which examined the charges against the five suspended members of the Executive Board was headed by Humberto Hernández, leader of the Construction Workers Union and member of the Democratic Action Party. The Tribunal found the accused members guilty as charged and recommended their expulsion from the CTV.

12. Following the URD withdrawal from the government coalition, its trade union followers also went into opposition inside the CTV, and later left it altogether. However, in 1964, following their party's participation in the coalition government of President Raúl Leoni, URD trade unionists rejoined the CTV.

13. According to President Betancourt's final message to Congress in March 1964, there had been only 36 strikes, none of them industry-wide, during his five years in office, or approximately one for every 100 contracts signed.

14. According to the Central Bank of Venezuela, in the years 1962–1963 the Gross National Product increased 6.3 and 4.1 percent, respectively.

15. The typical Venezuelan "rancho" is a one-room hut, with bare ground for floor, and walls and ceiling covered with palm leaves.

16. Daniel Carías was a self-made colored worker who lacked formal education but who had developed into one of the most effective Venezuelan labor orators and thinkers. He died of a heart attack in 1963.

17. Bertram B. Johanson, the respected and most competent Latin American editor of *The Christian Science Monitor,* reported from Caracas, April 19, 1962 that "in the view of some observers here, a climax of this violence took place in the period between January 22–29 this year, when the country came as close to being toppled by Communist and MIR agitators as it has at any time during the Betancourt administration."

18. Among those who sent messages were: Rómulo Gallegos, former President of Venezuela; José Figueres, former President of Costa Rica; Ramón Villeda Morales, former President of Honduras; Gabriel del Mazo, former Minister of Defense of Argentina; Carlos Lleras Restrepo, President of the Liberal Party of Colombia; Rafael Caldera, General Secretary of the Social-Christian Party (COPEI) of Venezuela; Gonzalo Barrios, Minister of Interior of Venezuela; Jorge Font Saldaña, Minister of Economy, Commonwealth of Puerto Rico.

Also, Manuel Mantilla, General Secretary of the Presidency of the Republic of Venezuela; Ramiro Prialé, President of the Senate, Peru; Gonzalo Facio, Costa Rican Ambassador to the United States; Manuel Ordóñez, Christian Democratic leader, Argentina; Leopoldo Sucre Figarella, Minister of Public Works, Venezuela; Arturo Jáuregui, General Secretary, ORIT.

Also, U.S. Senator Jacob K. Javits; Peruvian Senator Carlos A. Izaguirre; Daniel Oduber, former Minister of Foreign Affairs, Costa Rica; and Fernando Volio Jiménez, Costa Rican Ambassador to the United Nations.

19. The list of speakers also included Luis Augusto Dubuc, official representative of the Democratic Action Party of Venezuela; Radomiro Tomic, Chilean Ambassador to the United States; Carlos Sosa Rodríguez, President of the Venezuelan Delegation to the United Nations; Germán Zea, Colombian Representative to the United Nations, who spoke on behalf of his other colleagues from Latin America; Gonzalo García Bustillos, representative of the Social-Christian Party (COPEI) of Venezuela; Enrique Tejera París, Venezuelan Ambassador to the United States, and Diogenes de la Rosa, Panamian Ambassador to the United States.

Index

ACWA, *see* Amalgamated Clothing Workers of America
AFL, *see* American Federation of Labor
AFSCME, *see* American Federation of State, County and Municipal Employees
AID, *see* Agency for International Development
AIFLD, *see* American Institute for Free Labor Development
APRA, *see* Alianza Popular Revolucionaria Americana
ATLAS, *see* Latin American Association of Trade Unions
Acción Demócrata, *see* Democratic Action Party
Acuña, Juan A., 39, 175
AD Party, *see* Democratic Action Party
Agency for International Development (AID), 259, 319, 420, 426–28
Aguirre, Francisco, 65, 75, 79, 94, 113, 119, 123, 126, 131, 180, 191, 213, 216, 388–91, 396, 441, 456–47, 459
Alessandri, Jorge, 334, 339
Alexander, Robert J., 158, 271, 330, 352, 470
Alianza Popular Revolucionaria Americana (American Revolutionary Popular Alliance; APRA), 34, 76, 81, 85, 87, 183, 292–95, 300, 304, 309, 311, 315–18, 320–21
Allende, Salvador, 331–32, 337–38
Alliance for Progress, 2, 138, 420, 423, 426, 504
Alonzo, José, 169–71
Amalgamated Clothing Workers of America (ACWA), 14
American Federation of Labor (AFL), *passim*
American Federation of State, County and Municipal Employees, 106, 108–109
American Institute for Free Labor Development (AIFLD), 169, 170, 260, 289, 319, 336, 340, 343, 345–46, 352, 415–31
Anaconda Copper Company, 327–30, 338–39, 430
Angarita, Isaias Medina, 438, 444
Antonini, Luigi, 18, 21, 22, 27, 28
Aprista Party (Peru), 39, 320, 437, 479
Aramburu, Pedro Eugenio, 156, 159, 160
Arango, Aureliano Sánchez, 184, 223, 441, 511
Arbenz, Guzmán, Jacobo, 128, 241, 243–44, 463, 473
Argentine Confederation of Labor, 61, 80
Argentine Federation of Commercial Employees, 51

515